Changing World of Business

Pearson

At Pearson, we have a simple mission: to help people make more of their lives through learning.

We combine innovative learning technology with trusted content and educational expertise to provide engaging and effective learning experience that serve people wherever and whenever they are learning.

We enable our customers to access a wide and expanding range of market-leading content from world-renowned authors and develop their own tailor-made book. From classroom to boardroom, our curriculum materials, digital learning tools and testing programmes help to educate millions of people worldwide — more than any other private enterprise.

Every day our work helps learning flourish, and wherever learning flourishes, so do people.

To learn more, please visit us at: www.pearson.com/uk

Changing World of Business

Selected chapters from:

The Business Environment
Seventh Edition
Ian Worthington and Chris Britton

Employability Skills
Second Edition
Frances Trought

The International Business Environment
Second Edition
Ian Brooks, Jamie Weatherston and Graham Wilkinson

Strategic Management
Seventh Edition
Richard Lynch

Understanding the Business Environment
Third Edition
Claire Capon

 Pearson

Harlow, England • London • New York • Boston • San Francisco • Toronto • Sydney • Dubai • Singapore • Hong Kong
Tokyo • Seoul • Taipei • New Dehli • Cape Town • São Paulo • Mexico City • Madrid • Amsterdam • Munich • Paris • Milan

Pearson
KAO Two
KAO Park
Harlow
Essex CM17 9NA

And associated companies throughout the world

Visit us on the World Wide Web at:
www.pearson.com/uk

Compiled from:

The Business Environment
Seventh Edition
Ian Worthington and Chris Britton
ISBN 978-0-273-75672-9
© Pearson Education Limited 2015 (print and electronic)

Employability Skills
Second Edition
Frances Trought
ISBN 978-1-292-15890-7
© Pearson Education Limited 2012, 2017 (print and electronic)

The International Business Environment
Second Edition
Ian Brooks, Jamie Weatherston and Graham Wilkinson
ISBN 978-0-273-72566-4
© Pearson Education Limited 2004, 2011

Strategic Management
Seventh Edition
Richard Lynch
ISBN 978-1-292-06466-6
© Richard Lynch 2015 (print and electronic)

Understanding the Business Environment
Third Edition
Claire Capon
ISBN 978-0-273-70814-8
© Pearson Education Limited 2009

ISBN 978-1-78726-**957-6**

Printed and bound in Great Britain by Bell and Bain Ltd, Glasgow

CONTENTS

1 Business organisations: the external environment

Ian Worthington

Business organisations differ in many ways, but they also have a common feature: the transformation of inputs into output. This transformation process takes place against a background of external influences which affect the firm and its activities. This external environment is complex, volatile and interactive, but it cannot be ignored in any meaningful analysis of business activity.

Learning outcomes

Having read this chapter you should be able to:

- indicate the basic features of business activity
- portray the business organisation as a system interacting with its environment
- demonstrate the range and complexity of the external influences on business activity
- identify the central themes inherent in the study of the business environment

Key terms

Environmental change
External environment
General (or contextual) environment

Immediate (or operational) environment
Inputs
Open system

Outputs
PESTLE analysis
Transformation system

Introduction

Business activity is a fundamental and universal feature of human existence and yet the concept of 'business' is difficult to define with any degree of precision. Dictionary definitions tend to describe it as being concerned with buying and selling, or with trade and commerce, or the concern of profit-making organisations, and clearly all of these would come within the accepted view of business. Such a restricted view, however, would exclude large parts of the work of government and its agencies and the activities of non-profit-making organisations – a perspective it would be hard to sustain in a climate in which business methods, skills, attitudes and objectives are being increasingly adopted by these organisations. It is this broader view of business and its activities that is adopted below and that forms the focus of an investigation into the business environment.

The business organisation and its environment

A model of business activity

Most business activity takes place within an organisational context and even a cursory investigation of the business world reveals the wide variety of organisations involved, ranging from the small local supplier of a single good or service to the multi-billion-dollar international or multinational corporation producing and trading on a global scale. Given this rich organisational diversity, most observers of the business scene tend to differentiate between organisations in terms of their size, type of product and/or market, methods of finance, scale of operations, legal status and so on. Nissan, for example, would be characterised as a major multinational car producer and distributor trading on world markets, while a local builder is likely to be seen as a small business operating at a local level with a limited market and relatively restricted turnover.

> **web link** Further information on Nissan is available at *www.nissan-global.com*
> The Nissan UK website address is *www.nissan.co.uk*

While such distinctions are both legitimate and informative, they can conceal the fact that all business organisations are ultimately involved in the same basic activity, namely, the transformation of **inputs** (resources) into **outputs** (goods or services). This process is illustrated in Figure 1.1.

In essence, all organisations acquire resources – including labour, premises, technology, finance, materials – and transform these resources into the goods or services required by their customers. While the type, amount and combination of resources will vary according to the needs of each organisation and may also vary over time, the simple process described above is common to all types of business organisation and provides a useful starting point for investigating business activity and the environment in which it takes place.

A more detailed analysis of business resources and those internal aspects of organisations which help to transform inputs into output can be found in Chapters 3 and 8 below. The need, here, is simply to appreciate the idea of the firm as a **transformation system** and to recognise that in producing and selling output, most organisations hope

Figure 1.1   The business organisation as a transformation system

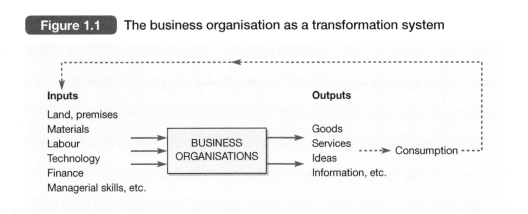

to earn sufficient revenue to allow them to maintain and replenish their resources, thus permitting them to produce further output which in turn produces further inputs. In short, inputs help to create output and output creates inputs. Moreover, the output of one organisation may represent an input for another, as in the case of the firm producing capital equipment or basic materials or information or ideas. This interrelationship between business organisations is just one example of the complex and integrated nature of business activity and it helps to highlight the fact that the fortunes of any single business organisation are invariably linked with those of another or others – a point clearly illustrated in many of the examples cited in the text.

The firm in its environment

The simple model of business activity described above is based on the systems approach to management. One of the benefits of this approach is that it stresses that organisatios are entities made up of interrelated parts which are intertwined with the outside world – the **external environment** in systems language. This environment comprises a wide range of influences – economic, demographic, social, political, legal, technological, etc. – which affects business activity in a variety of ways and which can impinge not only on the transformation process itself but also on the process of resource acquisition and on the creation and consumption of output. This idea of the firm in its environment is illustrated in Figure 1.2.

Figure 1.2   The firm in its environment

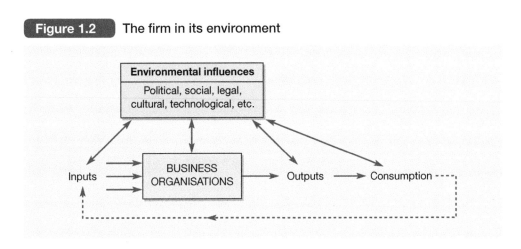

Figure 1.3   Two levels of environment

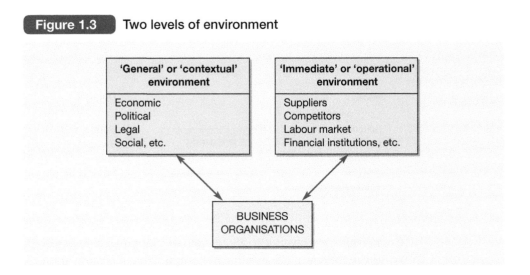

In examining the business environment, a useful distinction can be made between those external factors that tend to have a more immediate effect on the day-to-day operations of a firm and those that tend to have a more general influence. Figure 1.3 makes this distinction.

The **immediate** or **operational environment** for most firms includes suppliers, competitors, labour markets, financial institutions and customers, and may also include trade associations, trade unions and possibly a parent company. In contrast, the **general** or **contextual environment** comprises those macroenvironmental factors such as economic, political, socio-cultural, technological, legal and ethical influences on business which affect a wide variety of businesses and which can emanate not only from local and national sources but also from international and supranational developments.

This type of analysis can also be extended to the different functional areas of an organisation's activities such as marketing or personnel or production or finance, as illustrated in Figure 1.4. Such an analysis can be seen to be useful in at least two ways. First, it emphasises the influence of external factors on specific activities within the firm

Figure 1.4   Environmental influences on a firm's marketing system

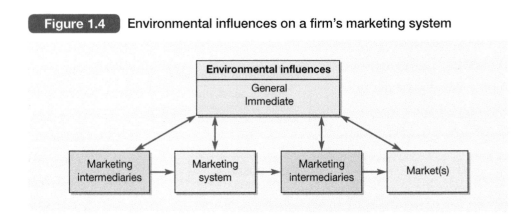

and in doing so underlines the importance of the interface between the internal and external environments. Second, by drawing attention to this interface, it highlights the fact that, while business organisations are often able to exercise some degree of control over their internal activities and processes, it is often very difficult, if not impossible, to control the external environment in which they operate.

The general or contextual environment

While the external factors referred to above form the subject matter of the rest of the book, it is useful at this point to gain an overview of the business environment by highlighting some of the key environmental influences on business activity. In keeping with the distinction made between general and more immediate influences, these are discussed separately below. In this section we examine what are frequently referred to as the 'PESTLE' factors (i.e. political, economic, socio-cultural, technological, legal and ethical influences). A **PESTLE** (or **PEST**) **analysis** can be used to analyse a firm's current and future environment as part of the strategic management process.

The political environment

A number of aspects of the political environment clearly impinge on business activity. These range from general questions concerning the nature of the political system and its institutions and processes to the more specific questions relating to government involvement in the working of the economy and its attempts to influence market structure and behaviour. Government activities, both directly and indirectly, influence business activity and government can be seen as the biggest business enterprise at national or local level. Given the trend towards the globalisation of markets and the existence of international trading organisations and blocs, international politico-economic influences on business activity represent one key feature of the business environment. Another is the influence of public, as well as political, opinion in areas such as environmental policy and corporate responsibility.

The economic environment

The distinction made between the political and economic environment – and, for that matter, the legal environment – is somewhat arbitrary. Government, as indicated above, plays a major role in the economy at both national and local level and its activities help to influence both the demand and supply side. Nevertheless there are a number of other economic aspects related to business activity which are worthy of consideration. These include various structural aspects of both firms and markets and a comparison of economic theory and practice.

mini case   The impact of regional economic conditions

For a company that trades in different markets across the world, macroeconomic conditions in a particular part of its overall market can play a key role in determining its corporate sales and profitability. French carmaker PSA Peugeot Citroën, for instance, experienced a significant decline in sales in 2012 as demand fell in southern Europe on the back of the recession in the Eurozone. In response to the problem, the company announced significant job cuts aimed at reducing costs and looked to the French government for a series of multi-billion-euro loans to keep it afloat until trading conditions improved.

Another company experiencing the impact of the recession in Europe was India's Tata Steel, which was affected by a downturn in the demand from the construction and carmaking industries, culminating in significant losses in the European

arm of its business in 2012–13. As with Peugeot Citroën, Tata announced steps to cut its costs and improve its efficiency via a programme of restructuring and redundancies, decisions which will clearly have an impact not only on employees but also on the communities in which they live and on other firms in Tata's supply chain.

Since market conditions can vary substantially in different locations, some businesses can experience significant variations in performance in different parts of their operations. US car giant Ford, for example, announced significant losses in Europe in 2012 alongside 'spectacular' results in its North American division. Like Chrysler and other competitors including GM, Ford was able to offset its European losses with stronger sales in the US. It also posted pre-tax profits in its South American and Asian markets.

web link   Further information on the organisations mentioned in this mini case is available at www.psa-peugeot-citroen.com; www.tatasteel.com; www.ford.com; www.chrysler.com; www.gm.com

The social, cultural and demographic environment

Both demand and supply are influenced by social, cultural and demographic factors. Cultural factors, for example, may affect the type of products being produced or sold, the markets they are sold in, the price at which they are sold and a range of other variables. People are a key organisational resource and a fundamental part of the market for goods and services. Accordingly, socio-cultural influences and developments have an important effect on business operations, as do demographic changes.

The technological environment

Technology is both an input and an output of business organisations as well as being an environmental influence on them. Investment in technology and innovation is frequently seen as a key to the success of an enterprise and has been used to explain differences in the relative competitiveness of different countries. It has also been responsible for significant developments in the internal organisation of businesses in the markets for economic resources.

The legal environment

Businesses operate within a framework of law, which has a significant impact on various aspects of their existence. Laws usually govern, among other things, the status of the organisation, its relationship with its customers and suppliers and certain internal procedures and activities. They may also influence market structures and behaviour. Since laws emanate from government (including supranational governments) and from the judgments of the courts, some understanding of the relevant institutions and processes is desirable.

The ethical and ecological environment

Ethical considerations have become an increasingly important influence on business behaviour, particularly among the larger, more high-profile companies. One area where this has been manifest is in the demand for firms to act in a more socially responsible way and to consider the impact they might have on people, their communities and the natural environment.

The immediate or operational environment

Resources and resource markets

An organisation's need for resources makes it dependent to a large degree on the suppliers of those resources, some of which operate in markets that are structured to a considerable extent. Some aspects of the operation of resource markets or indeed the activities of an individual supplier can have a fundamental impact on an organisation's success and on the way in which it structures its internal procedures and processes. By the same token, the success of suppliers is often intimately connected with the decisions and/or fortunes of their customers. While some organisations may seek to gain an advantage in price, quality or delivery by purchasing resources from overseas, such a decision can engender a degree of uncertainty, particularly where exchange rates are free rather than fixed. Equally, organisations may face uncertainty and change in the domestic markets for resources as a result of factors as varied as technological change, government intervention or public opinion (e.g. conservation issues).

Customers

Customers are vital to all organisations and the ability both to identify and to meet consumer needs is seen as one of the keys to organisational survival and prosperity – a point not overlooked by politicians, who are increasingly using business techniques to attract the support of the electorate. This idea of consumer sovereignty – where resources are allocated to produce output to satisfy customer demands – is a central tenet of the market economy and is part of an ideology whose influence has become allpervasive in recent years. Understanding the many factors affecting both individual and market demand, and the ways in which firms organise themselves to satisfy that demand, is a vital component of a business environment that is increasingly market led.

Competitors

Competition – both direct and indirect – is an important part of the context in which many firms operate and is a factor equally applicable to the input as well as the output side of business. The effects of competition, whether from domestic organisations or from overseas firms, are significant at the macro as well as the micro level and its influence can be seen in the changing structures of many advanced industrial economies. How firms respond to these competitive challenges (e.g Chapter 11) and the attitudes of governments to anti-competitive practices is a legitimate area of concern for students of business.

Analysing the business environment

In a subject as all-encompassing as the business environment it is possible to identify numerous approaches to the organisation of the material. One obvious solution would be to examine the various factors mentioned above, devoting separate chapters to each of the environmental influences and discussing their impact on business organisations. While this solution has much to recommend it – not least of which is its simplicity – the approach adopted below is based on the grouping of environmental influences into three main areas, in the belief that this helps to focus attention on key aspects of the business world, notably contexts, firms and their markets.

mini case   Fresh but not so easy

A recurring theme in this and previous editions of the book is the need for businesses to monitor and, where necessary, respond to changes in the business environment. Equally important is the requirement for a firm to understand the needs of the customers in the markets in which it currently operates or in which it wishes to expand its operations as a means of growing the organisation. Even some of the world's largest and most sophisticated companies can sometimes get this wrong.

Take the case of Tesco PLC's foray into the US grocery retailing market with the launch of its Fresh & Easy stores in 2007–8. Initially established in a number of states on the west coast of America, the experiment was aimed at providing a low-risk method of entry into a large and lucrative market, with the focus on providing fresh produce at low prices in competition with existing retailers such as Trader Joe's and Walmart. As a preliminary step, the company sent some of its senior executives to the US to live with American families for several months in order to understand their shopping habits and product preferences. It also ran a high-profile promotional campaign to support its plans to open up 1,000 stores in California and neighbouring states before launching the brand on the east coast.

Tesco's hope that it would be able to break even in two years quickly evaporated and the company was forced to pump hundreds of millions of pounds into the venture to keep it afloat. Apart from the rather unfortunate coincidence of the launch of its brand with the sub-prime crisis and subsequent recession in the US, retail analysts have pointed to some fundamental errors in understanding the preferences of US consumers. Mistakes are said to have included an unclear image; cold and antiseptic stores; the introduction of self-pay checkouts; using cling film on fresh products; an over-emphasis on ready meals; an unwillingness to embrace the 'coupon culture' that is an important part of the US shopping experience; and problems in ensuring high-quality produce. Some consumers also apparently complained that the name Fresh & Easy reminded them of a deodorant or a sanitary product.

By the time of its withdrawal from the market in 2013, Tesco had reputedly spent more than £1 billion on the venture and final losses are expected to be considerably higher. Efforts to break into a number of other overseas markets – particularly India and China – have also run into difficulty for a variety of reasons and underline the challenges that can face a business that embarks on a strategy of international expansion. On the positive side, the company learned in late December 2013 that India's foreign investment regulator had approved a multi-billion-pound investment plan which, if cleared by the Indian government, would allow Tesco to become the first foreign company to establish supermarkets in the country.

web link Tesco's website address is: *www.tesco.com*

Following a basic introduction to the idea of the 'business environment', in Part Two consideration is given to the political, economic, social, cultural, demographic, legal, ethical and ecological contexts within which businesses function. In addition to examining the influence of political and economic systems, institutions and processes on the conduct of business, this section focuses on the macroeconomic environment and on those broad social influences that affect both consumers and organisations alike. The legal system and the influence of law in a number of critical areas of business activity are also a primary concern and one which has links with Part Three.

In Part Three, attention is focused on three central structural aspects: legal structure, size structure and industrial structure. The chapter on legal structure examines the impact of different legal definitions on a firm's operations and considers possible variations in organisational goals based on legal and other influences. The focus then shifts to how differences in size can affect the organisation (e.g. access to capital, economies of scale) and to an examination of how changes in scale and/or direction can occur, including the role of government in assisting small business development and growth. One of the consequences of changes in the component elements of the economy is the effect on the overall structure of industry and commerce – a subject which helps to highlight the impact of international competition on the economic structure of many advanced industrial economies. Since government is a key actor in the economy, the section concludes with an analysis of government involvement in business and in particular its influence on the supply as well as the demand side of the economy at both national and local levels.

In Part Four, the aim is to compare theory with practice by examining issues such as pricing, market structure and foreign trade. The analysis of price theory illustrates the degree to which the theoretical models of economists shed light on the operation of business in the 'real' world. Similarly, by analysing basic models of market structure, it is possible to gain an understanding of the effects of competition on a firm's behaviour and to appreciate the significance of both price and non-price decisions in the operation of markets.

The analysis continues with an examination of external markets and the role of government in influencing both the structure and the operation of the marketplace. The chapter on international markets looks at the theoretical basis of trade and the development of overseas markets in practice, particularly in the context of recent institutional, economic and financial developments (e.g. the Single Market, globalisation, the euro). The section concludes with an investigation of the rationale for government intervention in markets and a review of government action in three areas, namely, privatisation and deregulation, competition policy and the operation of the labour market.

To emphasise the international dimension of the study of the business environment, each of the four main parts of the book concludes with a section entitled 'International business in action', which draws together some of the key themes discussed in the previous chapters. By examining specific issues and/or organisations, the aim is to highlight linkages between the material discussed in the text and to provide an appreciation of some of the ways in which business activity reaches well beyond national boundaries.

The concluding chapter in the book stresses the continuing need for organisations to monitor change in the business environment and examines a number of frameworks through which such an analysis can take place. In seeking to make sense of their environment, businesses need access to a wide range of information, much of which is available from published material, including government sources. Some of the major types of information available to students of business and to business organisations – including statistical and other forms of information – are considered in the final part of this chapter.

Central themes

A number of themes run through the text and it is useful to draw attention to these at this point.

Interaction with the environment

Viewed as an **open system**, the business organisation is in constant interaction with its environment. Changes in the environment can cause changes in inputs, in the transformation process and in outputs, and these in turn may engender further changes in the organisation's environment. The internal and external environments should be seen as interrelated and interdependent, not as separate entities.

Interaction between environmental variables

In addition to the interaction between the internal and external environments, the various external influences affecting business organisations are frequently interrelated. Changes in interest rates, for example, may affect consumer confidence and this can have an important bearing on business activity. Subsequent attempts by government to influence the level of demand could exacerbate the situation and this may lead to changes in general economic conditions, causing further problems for firms. The combined effect of these factors could be to create a turbulent environment which could result in uncertainty in the minds of managers. Failure to respond to the challenges (or opportunities) presented by such changes could signal the demise of the organisation or at best a significant decline in its potential performance.

The complexity of the environment

The environmental factors identified above are only some of the potential variables faced by all organisations. These external influences are almost infinite in number and variety and no study could hope to consider them all. For students of business and for managers alike, the requirement is to recognise the complexity of the external environment and to pay greater attention to those influences which appear to be the most pertinent and pressing for the organisation in question, rather than to attempt to consider all possible contingencies.

Environmental volatility and change

The organisation's external environment is further complicated by the tendency towards **environmental change**. This volatility may be particularly prevalent in some areas (e.g. technology) or in some markets or in some types of industry or organisation. As indicated above, a highly volatile environment causes uncertainty for the organisation (or for its sub-units) and this makes decision-making more difficult.

Environmental uniqueness

Implicit in the remarks above is the notion that each organisation has to some degree a unique environment in which it operates and which will affect it in a unique way. Thus, while it is possible to make generalisations about the impact of the external environment on the firm, it is necessary to recognise the existence of this uniqueness and where appropriate to take into account exceptions to the general rule.

Different spatial levels of analysis

External influences operate at different spatial levels – local, regional, national, supranational, international/global – exemplified by the concept of LoNGPEST/LoNGPESTLE. There are few businesses, if any, today that could justifiably claim to be unaffected by influences outside their immediate market(s).

Two-way flow of influence

As a final point, it is important to recognise that the flow of influence between the organisation and its environment operates in both directions. The external environment influences firms, but by the same token firms can influence their environment, and this is an acceptable feature of business in a democratic society which is operating through a market-based economic system.

Synopsis

In the process of transforming inputs into output, business organisations operate in a multifaceted environment which affects and is affected by their activities. This environment tends to be complex and volatile and comprises influences which are of both a general and an immediate kind and which operate at different spatial levels. Understanding this environment and its effects on business operations is vital to the study and practice of business.

Summary of key points

- Business activity is essentially concerned with transforming inputs into outputs for consumption purposes.

- All businesses operate within an external environment that shapes their operations and decisions.

- This environment comprises influences that are both operational and general.

- The operational environment of business is concerned with such factors as customers, suppliers, creditors and competitors.

- The general environment focuses on what are known as the PESTLE factors.

- In analysing a firm's external environment attention needs to be paid to the interaction between the different environmental variables, environmental complexity, volatility and change, and to the spatial influences.

- While all firms are affected by the environment in which they exist and operate, at times they help to shape that environment by their activities and behaviour.

<table>
<tr><td>**case study**</td><td>Facing the unexpected</td></tr>
</table>

In previous editions of the book we have stressed how the business environment can sometimes change dramatically and unexpectedly for the worse, using the September 11 2001 attack on the World Trade Center in the US as an example of what is known as an exogenous shock to the economic system. Mercifully, events of this kind tend to be relatively rare, but when they occur they present a considerable challenge to the businesses and industries affected.

The same is true when natural disasters occur, as the following recent examples illustrate.

2010 – the eruption of an Icelandic volcano sent a cloud of volcanic ash over large parts of Europe, resulting in the grounding of planes and weeks of disruption of air travel. Airlines in particular were badly affected and faced additional costs because of stranded passengers and cancelled flights. Beneficiaries included hoteliers who had to accommodate people unable to travel and alternative transport businesses (e.g. ferry operators).

2011 – an earthquake in Chile devastated the Chilean wine industry by destroying storage tanks and infrastructure. Another earthquake and a tsunami in Japan destroyed a major nuclear facility and led to damage and the temporary closure of major factories, including those of Nissan and Toyota. The negative impact on the Japanese economy resulted in a reduction in oil imports as industrial production declined and shortages of electricity occurred. To support the economy the Japanese government pumped billions of yen into the economic system.

2013 – sudden and devastating storms in the Burgundy and Bordeaux regions of France destroyed swathes of the French wine industry, resulting in a loss of jobs and income in the affected local communities, with a knock-on impact on local businesses. In China, a heatwave across the central and eastern parts of the country badly affected the farming industry and tempted the government to spend millions on artificial steps to trigger rain. In some areas power failures occurred as the demand for electricity soared as individuals and organisations turned on the air conditioning. Much warmer conditions were also experienced in parts of northern Europe, including the UK, resulting in increased sales of certain items (e.g. barbecues, sunscreen) and tempting many people to holiday at home. Other adverse natural events in 2013–14 included a super typhoon in the Philippines, extensive fires in parts of Australia, a major drought in California and severe storms and flooding in southern Britain, all of which had major effects on businesses and communities in the affected areas.

While there is little a business can do to protect itself totally against events of this kind, many larger firms, especially multinationals, tend to put in place contingency plans to manage unexpected crises, whether they are caused by human or natural events. A business continuity plan (BCP) can help an organisation to respond quickly and effectively to a negative situation and hopefully to survive the experience and learn from it. Smaller firms on the whole tend to lack the financial and human resources needed to adopt such resilience measures and some may not survive an adverse change in the external environment. For other organisations such a change may bring with it business opportunities, an unexpected though possibly welcome gain from an event that has a negative impact on other firms.

Case study questions

1 Can you think of any other examples of major unanticipated events in your own country (or areas of your own country) that have had a serious adverse effect on its firms and/or industries?

2 Can you think of any businesses that may have benefited commercially from this event or these events?

Review and discussion questions

1 In what senses could a college or university be described as a business organisation? How would you characterise its 'inputs' and 'outputs'?

2 Taking examples from a range of quality newspapers, illustrate ways in which business organisations are affected by their external environment.

3 Give examples of the ways in which business organisations can affect the external environment in which they operate.

Assignments

1 Assume you are a trainee in a firm of management consultants. As part of your induction process you have been asked to collect a file of information on an organisation of your choice. This file should contain information not only on the structure of the organisation and its products but also on the key external influences that have affected its operations in recent years.

2 For a firm or industry of your choice, undertake a PESTLE analysis indicating the likely major environmental influences to be faced by the firm/industry in the next five to ten years.

Further reading

Capon, C., *Understanding the Business Environment*, FT/Prentice Hall, 2009.

Daniels, J. D., Radebough, L. H. and Sullivan, D. P., *International Business: Environments and Operations*, 14th edition, Prentice Hall, 2012.

Fernando, A. C., *Business Environment*, Dorling Kindersley/Pearson Education India, 2011.

Steiner, G. A. and Steiner, J. F., *Business, Government and Society: A Managerial Perspective*, 13th edition, McGraw-Hill/Irwin, 2011.

Wetherly, P. and Otter, D. (eds) *The Business Environment: Themes and Issues*, Oxford University Press, 2011.

Worthington, I., Britton, C. and Rees, A., *Economics for Business: Blending Theory and Practice*, 2nd edition, Financial Times/Prentice Hall, 2005, Chapter 1.

CHAPTER 2

Employability skills valued by employers

The man (woman) who has no imagination has no wings

Mohammed Ali

When completing an application form or attending an interview, employers need evidence of your abilities: your competences. It is essential that on the application form you are able to demonstrate your skills through your experiences, and the more varied the situation the better. Judge for yourself: Is hearing about a group exercise where students fundraised and trekked to Kilimanjaro more interesting to read about than a group exercise where students completed a presentation?

Students need to consider how they build their skills and where. University presents the opportunity not only to develop your skills but to challenge yourself and develop a wide set of experiences which set you apart from other graduates. Those students who fail to engage with extracurricular activities run the risk of not only limiting their development but also the range of examples they can use when completing an application form.

The development of soft skills has become increasingly important in today's economy. It is argued that soft skills contribute £88 billion to the UK economy and it is forecast to rise to £109 billion. The importance of soft skills is reflected by employers: 97% of employers believe that soft skills (in particular teamwork and communication) are essential to business success and are becoming increasingly more important than academic results. (Development of Economics Ltd, 2015)

This chapter will help you not only identify the skills valued by employers, but will also provide examples of how you can build these skills.

Self-management

Are you good with meeting deadlines? Are you organised? Do you use your own initiative?

If you can answer yes to these questions that's great, but if you can't manage yourself how can employers expect you to manage at work? Employers will expect you to be organised, punctual, working to deadlines and a self-starter. How you manage yourself and your approach to your work is key to being employable. Your first management role is self-management.

So what do we mean when we talk about self-management?

The CBI (2011) defines self-management as the 'readiness to accept responsibility, flexibility, resilience, self-starting, appropriate assertiveness, time management, readiness to improve own performance based on feedback/reflective learning'.

So how can you demonstrate you are good at self-management to an employer? The best way to demonstrate self-management is to look for examples in your current roles.

Do you work part time? Do you have responsibilities at home? Are you a mentor? These are excellent examples to demonstrate your ability to be responsible.

Employers will expect you to manage your time effectively and use your own initiative. Think of examples of where you have had to balance several assignment deadlines. How did you achieve this? Preparation, planning and organisation are essential for effective time management.

You can always learn from your experiences, so it is important to use feedback and reflection to see how you could have performed a task better. There is always room for improvement.

 tip

Ask around and use feedback

You can gain valuable personal insight by gathering feedback from other students, your tutors or professors, mentors, friends and even family members. Ask them to think about both your strengths and areas you could improve on. For example:

- What should you do more of/keep doing?
- What should you do less of/stop doing?

Often others see you differently to how you see yourself and their answers will help you identify and build on your skills and areas of possible weaknesses.

Jo Blissett, Career Development Consultant, Career Quest

 example

Worried about juggling a new volunteer role alongside your existing study commitments?

First, do not fret, as flexible volunteering where you offer your services as a volunteer as and when it suits you is now increasingly common. Second, your commitment to a volunteer role demonstrates not only motivation and drive to a potential employer, but organisational skills including planning and time management.

Meeting and dealing with new people through voluntary work will not only develop your patience and empathy towards others, but will demonstrate your ability to negotiate new and sometimes stressful scenarios. Being able to remain calm under pressure and think positively will help you to stand out both during the recruitment process and in the workplace. To get involved with a cause you're passionate about that has you jumping out of bed on a rainy Sunday morning, take a look at Do-it.org (https://do-it.org/), a national volunteering database.

Jamie Ward-Smith, CEO, Do-it.org

Self-management is an excellent indicator for an employer of how you will cope in the workplace. You will have many tasks to manage and demonstrating that you can multi-task successfully is a great skill. The ability to balance a commitment alongside your academic studies is an excellent demonstration of your time management, organisational and self-management skills.

Teamworking

What do Barcelona FC, the United Nations and Great Ormond Street Hospital have in common? They all achieve success through teamwork. Each member of the team plays a vital role, and that ensures their success.

The CBI (2011) stated that at the heart of teamworking is 'respecting others, cooperating, negotiating/persuading, contributing to discussions, an awareness of interdependence with others'.

In today's workforce this has become even more prevalent, and as a result employers include teamworking exercises in their selection processes to assess how well new graduates work in teams. An assessment centre will often include a group exercise, centred around a team of potential candidates working together to find a solution to a problem. This provides the recruiters with a good indication of how candidates work with others, as often within the work environment, teams are formed across the organisation.

Why is teamworking important?

So why is teamworking important? In today's rapidly changing marketplace organisations are faced with challenges, which cannot be addressed by one department. The challenge affects the organisation as a whole, and so teams are drawn from both across functions, but also globally. When devising solutions an organisation will need to have the knowledge from within its organisation and possibly from an expert consultant drawn from within its particular sector.

Collaboration is key in developing competitive advantage within the marketplace. This can involve collaborating externally with suppliers to develop new processes or new products. Working in teams enables an organisation to harness the expertise which exists both internally and externally. A team is much better placed to respond to the challenges faced in the competitive marketplace, as it enables the organisation to consider the challenge from many perspectives at once, and develop a solution that incorporates the needs of all of the business.

Teams come in different shapes and sizes. One size does not fit all. Throughout your time at university students will experience many different types of teams. As a member of a student society or club, students may find themselves working as a team to organise events, recruit members and fundraise. Other opportunities to work within a team are through sports, volunteering or even a group assignment.

Developing teamworking skills

University is the perfect place to develop teamworking skills. Often students work part time, which presents the opportunity to develop teamworking skills in a live environment, and the experience will enhance many other employability skills such as communication.

Whether you work in retail, fast food or tourism you will be part of a team and begin to understand the dynamics of working collectively towards a common goal. This goal could be to meet sales targets, to fundraise a specific amount or to collectively work together to enhance the customer experience.

Within the work environment teams exist in varying formats. Project teams will be created to address a specific business challenge. Often a team can be created virtually in order to capture the knowledge and experience of co-workers located nationally or even globally. Technology, in particular Skype and Google Hangouts, facilitate the ability to speak with teams virtually.

When working virtually and internationally communication skills become even more important, especially if the team is drawn globally. Time zones, cultures and customs become important factors to ensure the team works effectively and respectfully together.

 example

Virtual teams

Virtual teams are now commonplace and I have run them for many years. In a global business coupled with cost pressures, virtual team-working is now a business necessity and doing this right can add a huge competitive advantage. Here are my top five tips for managing a successful team.

- **Manage cultural dynamics:** Many virtual teams will incorporate different cultures and there is a need to manage conscious and unconscious biases to ensure the right behaviours and expectations.
- **Communication:** Always have a clear agenda and appropriate lead time for pre-reading meeting documents. Allocate who will manage minutes, actions and general communications.

- **Time zones:** There is a need to be sensitive regarding time zones, if possible. Try to rotate times so that alternate time slots can be scheduled to limit individuals being subjected to regular early mornings or late night calls.

- **Respect:** Set out clear rules to ensure all team members can be heard and the team actually listens. The chair has to carefully manage engagement.

- **Technology platform:** The communication platform has to be stable and accessible. It can be very disruptive to have platforms that are unreliable. This will hamper the progress but also the overall morale in the team.

Virtual teams are invaluable in the workplace, but it must be set up for success. The above dynamics are just a handful of critical success factors to manage a virtual team.

Carol René, Enterprise Lead Information and
Data Architect, Shell International Petroleum Company

What role would you play in a team?

Teams are created to provide a collective response to challenges faced by the organisation. What role do you think you would play in a team? Review these team roles and see which role reflects your skills.

- The project manager manages the team and takes on the responsibility of ensuring the project is delivered on time.

- The expert, as the name suggests, is a specialist in their field and highlights the impact of any solutions to the organisation and end-users.

- The innovator challenges the status quo and adopts a creative approach to tasks.

- The analyst evaluates all of the proposed solutions and highlights possible risks.

- The finisher ensures that all of the documentation and other outputs from the team tasks are submitted.

To review your role within ask your careers service to conduct a Myers Briggs test, which will highlight your position of strength in a team.

Certain skills and attributes are needed for a team to perform effectively. Respect is essential as you will not always be working with people you know or even like. Teams are often required to present their results or write a progress report, which will require good communication skills. The ability to negotiate or persuade is central to sourcing resources or convincing the team of a particular course of action. The success of the team is dependent on members sharing their knowledge and skills. A 'critical friend' asking challenging questions ensures that solutions are debated in full.

 example

Conflict management and problem-solving

First, let me start by saying that when working in a team I believe conflict is inevitable and therefore unavoidable – even for those who really try their hardest to avoid it. Preparing yourselves in advance for any potential clashes by practising conflict management skills is a must if you wish to succeed in your chosen career.

One of the best ways to help you develop a constructive approach to conflict really begins long before you are even involved in one – by 'accepting' that conflict is inevitable and will occur at some point, as it will help you to positively prepare yourself. The ability to manage conflict in a constructive and positive manner is increasingly becoming a sought after 'soft skill' in the work environment.

How you manage the conflicts you face at work will play a huge part in your successes in life, as when carried out effectively, you will be able to create harmonious and respectful relationships which enhance the working environment around you. You will therefore increase your employability skills and begin to progress at work.

The top five qualities needed when managing conflict are the following:

- patience
- respect (for others)
- empathy
- (active) listening
- think win–win.

Lex A Showunmi, Company Director and
Conflict Management Trainer/Practitioner,
3S Partnerships Ltd

Teamworking is a vital part of any organisation. The structure and size of the team is dependent upon the nature of the task. Each member of the team plays a different role, which is equally important and contributes to the success of the project. In order for teams to work effectively team members must have a range of skills.

Business and customer awareness

Business and customer awareness is important to an employer as your opinions demonstrate how you can add value to their organisation. Employers will expect you to understand their markets, their customers and the challenges they face.

As stated by the CBI (2011) 'graduates should have a basic understanding of the key drivers for business success – including the importance of innovation and taking calculated risks – and the need to provide customer satisfaction and build customer loyalty'.

How do you develop specific sector knowledge?

An insight to your chosen industry sector can be gained by reading newspapers, journals and newsletters from professional bodies. This will not only help you with your employability skills, but you will find you have a better understanding of your lectures and assignments. Your industry knowledge will be more apparent in the conversations you have about your sector and the responses you give in interviews. Below are a few examples of how to stay abreast of your industry:

- Create a Google Alert to refer to a page.
- Company websites provide an insight into the industry and the challenges they face in the competitive market.
- Industry-specific events can help you meet people who work in the industry and give you an insight into the structure of the organisation and the various roles which exist.

Ultimately the best way to gain an insight into an industry is to gain work experience. Work shadowing, internships and placements all provide opportunities for you to not only understand the industry but to see if you want to work in it. As a result, you will gain an insight into how companies manage the users' experience and build brand loyalty. You can develop this knowledge by reflecting on your own experiences with companies. Customer retention is important for businesses as without customers there is no business. Review company websites and how they build loyalty with their customers.

Problem-solving

The CBI defines problem-solving as 'analysing facts and situations and applying creative thinking to develop appropriate solutions'.

Organisations continually face challenges from advancing technology, competitors and changing markets so they need employees who can develop innovative solutions that will keep them ahead of the competition. Graduates who are creative, innovative and use their own initiative are essential to developing solutions to the challenges of the future.

How do you develop problem-solving skills?

You already have problem-solving skills. You are faced with challenges every day in both your academic course and your personal life. The skills you use to address these problems are transferable to the workplace. Essentially all problem-solving revolves around 'gap analysis', the difference between a desired outcome and the actual outcome. Regardless of whether it is an academic problem or organising an event such as your brother's wedding you will need to follow a number of steps. These are defined by Bransford and Stein (1984) in their IDEAL problem-solving model, which can be used within a range of contexts.

Identify the problem. What are the essential elements of the problem?

Define the problem through thinking about it and sorting relevant information.

Explore solutions. What are the advantages and disadvantages of each solution?

Act on strategies.

Look back and evaluate the effects of your activity.

Finding a solution may need you to develop additional employability skills. For example, you may need to create a diverse team, use your communication and IT skills to present your ideas or use your numeracy skills to calculate the financial impact of your solutions. As a result, it is important that you recognise the employability skills that you are developing while completing your academic assignments and solving your daily life challenges.

 example

Do some problem-solving

Need to learn how to think on your feet? It's time to say hello to a voluntary role.

As a leader at your local youth club not only will you be entrusted with the safety of the children, but you may need to resolve misunderstandings between members.

As a charity shop supervisor you could be called upon to address customer concerns or negotiate weekly staff rotas. The beauty of volunteering? Things may not always go to plan but you're sure to be supported by a team of passionate people all working towards the same goal. While it may feel tough at the time, approaching a problem calmly is an important workplace skill that demonstrates your personal resilience and adaptability. Added bonus? Your volunteer experience will leave you ready and raring to go when faced with that old interview chestnut: 'Tell me about a situation where you had to overcome a difficult problem'. To find a voluntary role near you head to Do-it.org, a national volunteering database.

Jamie Ward-Smith, CEO, Do-it.org

Another tool to develop solutions to challenges is the '5 Whys' developed by the Toyota Motor Corporation in 1950. Toyota developed a method where, by repeating 'why' five times, the problem and the solution are revealed through the questioning process. The 5 Whys is used to unveil the root cause of a problem. Once the root has been identified, a solution is developed, which ensures that the problem doesn't reoccur.

It is important through the questioning phase that the key stakeholders are invited to participate in the process, i.e. all those affected by the problem or the situation. Once the team members have been identified, it is important to drill down at least five levels to identify the root cause of the problem, but initially the problem needs to be clearly defined for the process to work.

The five key stages in the 5 Whys process:

1 Identify the key stakeholders – those affected by the problem.

2 Assign a team leader to lead and document the process.

3 Ask 'why' five times.

4 Define the solution and assign responsibilities.

5 Communicate the outcomes with all stakeholders.

brilliant dos and don'ts

What to do and what not to do when problem-solving

✔ Be as specific as possible when thinking and investigating the problem – pinpoint the actual issues using factual information.

✔ Find the most important parts of the problem – what are the biggest issues or risks?

✗ Don't blame others, poor processes or systems for the problem – remain open-minded about the problem and its causes.

✗ Do not immediately assume you know what the problem is and the solutions are.

✗ Do not go straight to solve the problem before thinking, investigating and gathering information about it (facts, inference, speculation and opinion).

Mindmaps can give you an overview of a large subject while also holding large amounts of information. They can be an intuitive way to organise your thoughts, since they mimic the way our brains think – bouncing ideas off of each other, rather than thinking linearly.

Jo Blissett, Career Development Consultant, Career Quest

Communication

Communication in essence is the sending of a message by sender A to receiver B. The format of the message can take different forms and the language will vary dependent on the context. There are several different options available.

Face to face

Despite face to face appearing to be the easiest form of communication, messages can still be misinterpreted by the choice of words, body language, tone and the person delivering the message.

Telephone call

Without the aid of visual expression, the choice of words and tone become even more crucial to ensure the receiver interprets the message accurately. Telephone interviews are often used during the selection process, and students would be advised to practise beforehand, as diction, tone and clarity are paramount.

Written communication

Written communication can take various form, including CVs, reports and covering letters. The style of writing, presentation and choice of words can all affect the way the message is delivered and received.

Social media

Twitter, What'sApp, LinkedIn, Facebook and instant messaging can be misinterpreted due to the incorrect use of upper or lower case, the insertion of an emoticon or an abbreviation. Although an accepted means of communication, it is heavily criticised if not used in the right context.

Effective communication

So how can we communicate effectively? When delivering a message, you need to take into account the context. In what context is the message being delivered? Professional, academic or social. The mode of delivery should reflect the context along with the choice of words.

In addition, to avoid any confusion use the 7Cs of communication

1 **Clear:** Ensure the aim and purpose of your message is clear from the outset of your written or verbal communication.

2 **Concise:** Less is more when communicating so be brief and targeted.

3 **Concrete:** Be focused in your communication and ensure that you are specific, factual and provide the required level of detail.

4 **Correct:** Ensure that your spelling, facts and grammar are correct. Also ensure that the tone, language and choice of words fit the context.

5 **Coherent:** Reread your message to ensure that it is logical and your ideas flow smoothly.

6 **Complete:** Ensure your communication contains the necessary information required by the receiver to respond.

7 **Courteous:** Ensure that you address the recipient politely and appropriately.

(Modified from Cutlip and Center, 1952)

In summary, when communicating you need to understand the context within which the message is to be delivered, that you choose the right medium for delivery and you choose your words carefully. And then use the 7 Cs of communication to avoid any misinterpretation of your message.

Communication skills can be developed through your academic study or extracurricular activities. Academically your presentation skills and written assignments are all opportunities for you to be assessed on how well you communicate. In addition to the academic environment, opportunities will arise to develop communication skills in different contexts. For example, at networking meetings, engaging with student societies or participating in mock interviews. It is important that you are able to communicate in a wide range of contexts including professional, academic and social.

Application of IT

Technology is transforming, disrupting and reshaping all industries. No organisation is insulated from the rapid changes taking place within the technology sector, but it's the resounding ripples and waves that affect all industries as well. The dramatic advances in technology are causing industries to question their purpose in the future. An example of this is the retail banking sector.

'There are so many different ways that you can make payments these days; you can pay by email, by Paypal and you can pay by your mobile phone, but all of that relies on the same plumbing and predominately it's the banks that provide that plumbing. Right now it's of value to us but I think we are in danger of just becoming the plumbing.' (Mortimer, 2015)

Industries are not just facing change – they are facing disruption. As a graduate you will be expected to be IT savvy. Question how technology could improve your processes or add value to your role. Continually update your IT skills, undertake short courses to learn about new technologies and new ways of performing tasks.

The application of IT involves the ability to demonstrate basic IT skills, including the familiarity with word processing, spreadsheets, file management and email. These skills can be developed through completing the assessments on your courses: word processing your coursework, using visual aids for presentations. On campus there will be support classes to develop your IT skills. Extracurricular activities can also be used as a means to develop these skills.

IT skills are essential so don't leave university without them. And make sure you keep them up to date. Course providers, such as UDemy, Coursera or General Assembley, provide short courses to ensure your skills remain current.

Application of numeracy and data analysis

How's your mental maths? Can you analyse data and provide the best course of action? Are you financially literate? When was the last time you calculated an average, percentage or fraction? Well, all of these maths elements can and do feature in selection tests and assessment centres. Numeracy is like Marmite – you either love it or hate it. But either way employers love it.

 **definition**

Numeracy

'the manipulation of numbers, general mathematical awareness and its application in practical contexts'

CBI, 2011

Numbers are everywhere and underpin many decisions made in organisations, so as a future graduate you need to understand what numeracy means for your sector. Generally, employers will expect you to have an understanding of mental arithmetic tasks like addition, subtraction, multiplication and division. Graduates will also be expected to analyse quantitative and qualitative data, interpret them and present the data in a visual format. You will also need to understand the financial implications of changes in the marketplace on an organisation, their products and profit margins.

Whether you are an arts, law or tourism graduate you need to have basic numeracy skills. Selection processes can include timed mental maths tests, so it's important to refresh these skills before applying to internships or graduate roles.

Practice tests can be found at the following sites:

SHL Direct: www.cebglobal.com

Talentlens: www.talentlens.co.uk

Leadership

Are you a future leader? Are you a game changer? Or are you able to take ownership of a situation and bring it to resolution?

Leadership comes in many forms and varying personalities. There are some excellent examples of leadership in the public arena from Barack Obama to Steve Jobs, but on a daily basis many employees within organisations demonstrate leadership skills.

Organisations need leaders on many levels to drive and champion success throughout a business. Leaders are not only at the helm of an organisation, as in order to be sustainable an organisation needs talented individuals who contribute to its continued success. Graduate schemes develop the pipeline of future leaders within the organisation.

How do we define leadership? As stated by the Chartered Institute of Professional Development (CIPD): 'there is no single definition or concept of leadership that satisfies all'.

Leadership is expected from the CEO right down to the most junior employee. Everyone has their part to play in ensuring excellence is maintained. The CIPD defines leadership as:

'the capacity to influence people, by means of personal attributes and/or behaviours to achieve a common goal'.

This is applicable to the CEO, who has to devise the vision and strategy to the graduate, who joins the organisation and works together with the team to achieve a common goal.

 example

What to do and not do to be an effective leader

- Be yourself: There's no 'right' model for a leader, so don't feel you have to be someone else.
- Know your own strengths and weaknesses: As well as knowing where to improve, you can organise teams to complement your own skills.
- Resist the temptation to 'do it yourself': The best leaders encourage their teams to deliver.
- Define what success looks like: Help people to understand what they are aiming for – the more inspirational the better.
- Don't be afraid to admit when you are wrong: People will respect you more, not less.

What to do and not do when you are leading a task or group

- Be clear on the objective and keep reminding people of it to keep on track.
- Find out what the different strengths of your team members are, and make the most of them.
- Make sure everyone gets some recognition, especially afterwards.
- Don't allow those with the loudest voices to dominate the group. Make sure you involve everyone.
- Don't feel it's all down to you: your job is to get the best from the team not to have the best ideas yourself.
- Don't be afraid to make decisions. Consensus can't always be reached.

    John Garnett, Board Advisor, Consultant and former Managing Director

In your graduate application form or the interview you will undoubtedly be asked to provide examples of where you have demonstrated your leadership skills. While at university there are several opportunities for you to develop your skills such as student societies, part-time jobs, volunteering, etc.

Take ownership of a task by developing an action plan of how the goal will be achieved. Employers will be interested in how you approached the task and your learning points. The actual outcome (although a successful one is always good) is immaterial; the way you handle the challenge, plan your time and liaise with others is more important. These will show your ability to lead a team to resolution.

 example

The Duke of Edinburgh's Award and leadership skills

Strong leadership skills are developed while doing a DofE programme. As part of a small team, you will plan, practise and complete an expedition. You will have to do a volunteering activity, no doubt taking yourself out of your comfort zone. This will allow you to gain vital leadership skills, whether by encouraging the rest of your expedition group through a particularly tough time, or leading and guiding your local youth group or sports team. The skills developed will be something that you are able to take through life with you, and that will also become invaluable to future employers.

Peter Westgarth, Chief Executive, The Duke of Edinburgh's Award

Enterprise

In today's competitive market, regardless of the sector or role that you are recruited into, employers want graduates who are not afraid to disrupt the status quo. The ability to understand and interpret current processes, and how they are interconnected and interrelated, gives rise to opportunities to identify areas for improvement. Being entrepreneurial is not limited to starting your own business; organisations benefit from staff being intrapreneurs, developing new products and processes from within the organisation. This helps to maintain their competitive advantage.

The National Council for Graduate Entrepreneurship (NCGE) states that to add value an entrepreneurial graduate needs to: 'have the entrepreneurial skills that enable them to seize opportunities, solve issues and problems, generate and communicate ideas and make a difference in their communities'.

Students need to seize opportunities where they can be creative and innovative and develop their initiative skills. These can be achieved through involvement with either student societies or small businesses. Both provide opportunities for students to use their initiative to achieve specific goals. In particular, due to small businesses often operating with minimal staff, students can often find that they are exposed to more responsibility within a shorter timescale.

Being entrepreneurial is a must as students need to demonstrate how they will add value to the organisation.

Emotional intelligence

Businesses continually face challenging, demanding and transforming landscapes, and so workforces need to manage and respond accordingly. Companies increasingly realise that the emotional intelligence (EI) of their employees plays an important role in determining an individual's response to a situation or to other people.

As a result, emotional intelligence has become increasingly important when identifying new talent. The leaders of tomorrow need to develop their ability to remain objective and make decisions based on the facts and data related to the situation.

 **definition**

Emotional intelligence

'Emotional intelligence is the ability to perceive emotions, to access and generate emotions so as to assist thought, to understand emotions and emotional knowledge, and to reflectively regulate emotions so as to promote emotional and intellectual growth'

Mayer & Salovey, 1997, p. 87

Daniel Goleman (2014) identified four key components of an individual's emotional intelligence:

- **Self-awareness:** The ability to recognise how their feelings will affect their job performance

- **Self-management:** The ability to demonstrate self-control and remain calm and clear-headed even during highly pressured situations.

- **Social awareness:** The ability to listen to what is said and more importantly what is unsaid and allow this to guide both your interaction with others and your decision-making.

- **Relationship management:** Employees with high emotional intelligence have the ability to inspire, influence, develop others, challenge the status quo and manage conflict.

These four elements underpin the ability to perform effectively both within a team and when facing challenging situations within the workplace.

 example

Developing and improving your emotional intelligence

The ability to manage people and relationships is highly regarded by employers, so developing and using your EI can be a great way to show an employer why you stand out in the graduate recruitment market.

Carrying out your own self-evaluation is the first step to developing and improving your EI. You need to look at yourself honestly and identify your strengths and weakness. In addition, you can consider the points and advice in the table below.

Observe how you react to people	● Do you stereotype? ● Do you rush to judge individuals and their actions?	● Try to put yourself in their shoes ● Be more open and accepting of others' views and needs
Examine how you react to stressful situations	● Do you become upset if things don't happen the way you want? ● Do you blame others, even when it's not their fault? ● Do you allow your emotions to cloud your decisions and thoughts?	● Try to demonstrate the ability to stay calm and in control in stressful situations ● Ensure you keep your emotions in control when things go wrong
Consider how your actions will affect others – before you take action	● What will be the impact? ● How will others feel? ● Would you want that experience?	● Put yourself in their place ● Identify how you can help others deal with the effects

Jo Blissett, Career Development Consultant, Career Quest

When considering the importance of emotional intelligence, you must also consider resilience, the ability to bounce back following an adverse decision.

 **definition**

Resilience
'the process of adapting well in the face of adversity, trauma, tragedy, threats or even significant sources of stress'

The American Psychological Association

Having the resolve to continue, whether it be with applications or a challenging situation, is a testament to an individual's character. The graduate market is increasingly competitive in nature, forcing graduates to become more resilient in order to survive. One application is unlikely to result in a positive outcome, and so graduates will receive several rejection letters before securing a graduate position. As a result, resilience is becoming increasingly important to a graduate's success.

There are many opportunities to develop resilience throughout your time at university. For example, a willingness to strive for better grades and to act on feedback from your assignments. In extracurricular activities resilience can be demonstrated by completing challenging tasks such as charity fundraising sky dives, triathlons, marathons, etc.

 **example**

The Duke of Edinburgh's Award and resilience

Young people are stronger than they think, and the great thing about doing a DofE programme is that it shows them this. Resilience is a work-ready skill, demonstrating that the individual has the capacity to recover quickly from a difficult situation. Learning to put up a tent in all weathers and undertake an expedition in the pouring rain can really test a person. If you can achieve this, many employers will see that you have a trait in you that is gold dust within the workplace.

Peter Westgarth, Chief Executive, The Duke of Edinburgh's Award

 example

Resilience, opportunities and questions

I recognised my need for resilience upon graduation to avoid accepting my immediate reality. I asked myself what my purpose in life was and where I wanted to be. From there I bullet-pointed my answers and set myself deadlines. I looked for opportunities that would push me to my final destination, as opposed to going into a job that had better financial gain but less opportunity for growth.

I became proactive and sought successful people within my field and was not afraid to ask them questions about their routes to success and what barriers they faced. They said: 'Know your strengths and weaknesses, stand out from the crowd and get comfortable being uncomfortable, as when you're comfortable your success is limited'. I took these words and ran with it and each year from 2010 I have achieved something bigger and better.

After university, my full focus was to be the best version of myself within the sporting industry. I soon realised from assessing my strengths and weaknesses along with personal experiences that I had the drive and determination to start my own business. I set up SLR Fitness (personal training) and made many mistakes but learnt from them. I was also told you should not be fearful of failing in aid of wanting to do something you love or wanting to achieve something as it is all a learning curve.

Remember the most valuable stones (diamonds) come out of really dark places so when you feel all the walls are crashing in, do not stay in that dark place, step out and be that shining diamond.

Here are five tips to develop your resilience:

- Get comfortable being uncomfortable.
- Be persistent and do not take NO for an answer.
- Follow up on everything.
- Be opportunity-focused as opposed to money-focused.
- Be around positive, ambitious individuals in a better position than yourself and ask questions.

Stefan Lloyd, SLR Fitness

 recap

- Developing employability skills, competences and attributes underpin the success of today's graduate.
- In 2015 it is estimated that soft skills contribute £88 billion to the UK economy.
- 97% of UK employers believe that soft skills underpin the success of their business and their importance is valued more than academic results.
- 75% of employers have identified a soft skills gap in today's workforce.
- Self-management is your first trial at being a manager.
- The range of challenges faced by organisations require a multitude of skills and expertise to develop a comprehensive solution.
- Business and customer awareness are essential to understand the challenges and opportunities faced by the organisation.

- Organisations continually face challenges and it is important to identify the key stakeholders and collaborate to provide a solution.
- Communication is an essential skill and will underpin the ability to secure a role within an organisation, and to maintain that role.
- Graduates are the future leaders within an organisation.
- Emotional intelligence is just as important as the technical skills an individual brings to an organisation.

Global business needs global graduates

Today's graduates need to understand the challenges of the global market, but more importantly how to identify opportunities. Both private and public-sector organisations can no longer insulate themselves from the impact of the changing global landscape. Graduates need to understand how these changes will impact their discipline and their future industry.

What threats does the global market present? And what opportunities?

Employers need graduates who can navigate the changing global landscape and provide solutions which can guide organisations to continued success. An organisation's survival will be determined by its ability to be enterprising and harness the challenges of change and reinvent them into positive developments. The global graduate is at the heart of this success.

Why we need global graduates

In the twenty-first century graduates will work for organisations that operate in a landscape which has no boundaries and is continually changing, evolving and transforming. Friedman (2005) stated that 'the world is flat'.

Technology has transformed the way we communicate, the way we work and the way we do business. No industry has been able to insulate itself from the digital transformation that technology has brought to each and every industry; those that have tried are no longer with us. Many of the jobs which exist today did not exist ten years ago: from app developers, to cloud computing specialists and from sustainability experts to social media managers.

No aspect of the way we do business has remained the same. From the basics of how we select and pay for goods, to how those goods are transported and delivered. Technology has not only transformed industries, but also levelled the playing field (Friedman, 2007), so that competitors are now no longer the usual suspects.

The challenges posed by both BRIC (Brazil, Russia, China, India) countries and MINT (Mexico, Indonesia, Nigeria, Turkey) countries would be impossible without the transformations which have occurred in the marketplace.

So what does this mean for the twenty-first century graduate? With a backdrop of continual change, companies need graduates who can confidently work in diverse teams and often virtual teams located across the globe. As a result, companies need graduates who will not only help to defend their market but assist with both developing and operating in new markets. (Diamond et al., 2008)

Companies are therefore not limiting their graduate recruitment to national boundaries. Graduates face an increased level of competition, where companies seek to source the best talent with a global perspective.

 tip

Why you should have an international experience

1   Personal development and the opportunity to develop your employability skills.

2   Career opportunities – employers value the skills and attributes gained from students engaging with an international experience.

3   Hone your language skills.

4   Build an international network.

5   It's a life-changing experience.

Despite the importance of an international experience, the data from the Higher Education Statistical Agency (HESA) report on UK Student Mobility do not demonstrate a willingness among UK students to engage with international experiences.

In the academic year of 2014/15 only 1.3% of UK domiciled students undertook an international experience. The rate of adoption by UK students is very low, and not reflective of the level of international students taking advantage of global experiences within the UK Higher Education sector. In 2013 there were 'Nearly 4.3 million students. . .enrolled in University-level education outside their home country'. (OECD, 2013) The UK is one of the second highest destinations of international students globally, but ranks as one of the lowest for sending students abroad, as indicated by the HESA data.

The need for global graduates with a global outlook can be seen in the level of students seeking an international experience. The top five destinations for international students are: United States, United Kingdom, France, Australia and Germany.

Top 20 Destinations For International Students

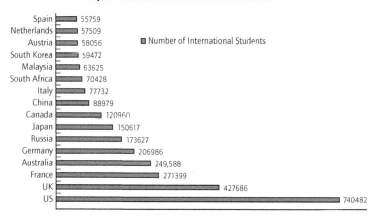

Source: UNESCO Institute for Statistics (UIS), http://www.uis.unesco.org, extracted July 2016

Global competences

Diamond et al. (2008) in a study of 12 graduate recruiters, who represent 3,500 graduate vacancies, identified a list of 'global competencies' which complement the generic employability skills. Regardless of a student's discipline, they would be expected to have generic employability skills as these serve as a baseline for graduates regardless of discipline.

The global competences identified in the study enable students to compete in the global arena. Students who develop these competences will be more able to work in a global capacity participating in global teams.

Employers were asked to rank 14 skills on a scale of 1 to 10, with 1 being the least important and 10 being the most important (and no number was to be used twice). This left four competences scoring zero. The findings of the ranking are listed below.

1   An ability to work collaboratively with teams of people from a range of backgrounds and countries.

2   Excellent communication skills: both speaking and listening.

3   A high degree of drive and resilience.

4   An ability to embrace multiple perspectives and challenge thinking.

5   A capacity to develop new skills and behaviours according to role requirements.

6   A high degree of self-awareness.

7   An ability to negotiate and influence clients across the globe from different cultures.

8   An ability to form professional, global networks.

9   An openness to and respect for a range of perspectives from around the world.

10 Multi-cultural learning agility.

11 Multi-lingualism.

12 Knowledge of foreign economies and own industry area overseas.

13 An understanding of one's position and role within a global context or economy.

14 A willingness to play an active role in society at a local, national and international level.

 example

Volunteering in Uganda

I spent the most amazing summer as an International Citizens Service (ICS) volunteer in Uganda. It was a heart-warming, eye-opening and life-changing time where I not only gained perspective on my work (and life) but also gained a new family for life by staying with a Ugandan host family.

The programme allowed me to work with seven entrepreneurs with businesses ranging from a sugar cane farm to selling cosmetics. I worked with them to launch their exciting and innovative businesses to create jobs and improve their lives. As part of my action at home, I currently have the responsibility of selecting the UK volunteers who wish to take part in ICS.

Hermon Amanuel, BA in Business and Enterprise

So how will students develop these skills and do you need to go overseas to develop them? 'Success is all in the global mindset'. (Govindarajan and Gupta 1998)

A global mindset instantly means that you are open to new ideas, willing to step out of your comfort zone, but ultimately curious about the world we live in and the people within it. Alongside the ability to develop a global mindset is the cultural agility and cultural dexterity to adapt your style of working to reflect that of the culture and customs within the country you are operating within.

'I think cultural dexterity is important: an ability not to impose one's own culture on another one, to be sensitive to other cultures and how to do business in different environments. There are certain ways of working with clients in the Middle East that you wouldn't adopt in Japan. (PwC) (Diamond et al., 2008, p. 9)

Central to the global mindset is the need for adaptability in every aspect of the way you work. If you are truly a global graduate, this will be reflected in the way you communicate in an international context.

Naturally you will be mindful of customs and demonstrate a level of understanding when operating in different countries. There is an acceptance that a diverse team is needed to secure an outcome which is globally acceptable and globally competitive. Operating in various countries around the world requires a certain level of flexibility, but an abundance of resilience. There is a definite willingness to go with the flow and accept a different way of doing things. As they say 'When in Rome, do as the Romans do'. In order to appreciate and fully develop solutions, which work on a global basis, it's important to fully immerse yourself into the culture to understand the challenges and the opportunities which exist.

To gauge the level of opportunity in any of the countries in which organisations operate requires a level of knowledge about global affairs. Reimers (2011) stated that commercial and business awareness for the global graduate is 'not just at one country level but at a global level'.

Global decisions are underpinned by a knowledge and awareness of the market which informs the decision-making process at every level. Graduates will be required to understand their industry on a local, national and international basis. Companies operating within this landscape with reduced boundaries need to understand where the next threat will come from or where opportunities are opening. Knowledge is at the heart of global success.

 example

Have an international experience

The benefits of an international experience – be it studying abroad or combining an international work placement with studying – are well documented. A number of recent studies have re-emphasised the benefits of international experience to students in terms of boosting employability prospects, starting salaries and academic achievement.

The latest Gone International report by the Higher Education International Unit (HEIU, 2016) found that unemployment rates for students six months after graduation were lower among internationally mobile students at 5%, compared with 7% for their non-mobile peers. Black and Asian students seemed to benefit the most from international experience, with their employment prospects showing the biggest improvement: 9.9% of non-mobile, black graduates were unemployed six months after graduation, compared to 5.4% of black, mobile graduates. The corresponding data for Asian students showed that unemployment fell to 4.4% for Asian, mobile students, compared with 9.5% for Asian, non-mobile graduates.

The report also found that employed graduates who had engaged in international experience were more likely (74.8%) than their non-mobile peers (67.1%) to gain employment within one of the top three socio-economic classifications.

Mobile students across almost all socio-economic backgrounds reported higher average salaries than their non-mobile peers. The average salary of a mobile student six months after graduation was £21,349 (compared to £20,519 for a non-mobile student).

The European Commission's Erasmus Impact Study (EIS, 2016) analyses the longer-term impact of mobility on career progression and revealed that former Erasmus students are half as likely to experience long-term unemployment compared to those without international experience.

Students in eastern Europe slashed their risk of long-term unemployment by 83% by taking part in Erasmus (European Commission, 2016). The positive employability impact existed even five to ten years after graduation, where the unemployment rate of mobile students was lower than that of non-mobile students. In particular, work placements were found to have a direct positive impact on employability, with one in three Erasmus students being offered employment by their host company.

Another interesting aspect of the study was the inclusion of personality trait tests for students before and after mobility. The approach looked at six 'memo© factors' that are seen as key employability traits. Ninety-three percent of employers surveyed confirmed that these six traits were key to the recruitment and professional development of employees. Erasmus students from all regions showed higher values for the six personality traits than non-mobile students, even prior to going abroad. Moreover, the mobility experience itself enhanced these traits, boosting the already existing advantage of Erasmus students over non-mobiles by a further 40%.

Here are some ways to overcome barriers to international experience:

- Research funding opportunities: Erasmus mobility grants are available to EU students (https://www.britishcouncil.org/study-work-create/opportunity/study-abroad/erasmus).

- Research scholarships at your university: You may find funding is available for flights or other expenditure linked to mobility.

- Consider a year abroad: This is typically heavily subsidised with students paying just 15 to 20% of annual fees.

- Consider a short international experience: This could be an international summer school. For example, the British Council website has information on short courses (https://www.britishcouncil.org/study-work-create/opportunity/study-abroad).

- Consider combining study abroad with an international work placement: You can seek assistance from companies such as InternshipGuru (www.internshipGuru.co.uk) that facilitate overseas work placements.

Karen St Jean-Kufuor, Principal Lecturer, Westminster Business School

Becoming a global graduate

So how do you become a global graduate? CIHE (2008) found that 29% of employers discovered that students were more employable once they had engaged with an opportunity to study overseas. As a result, the UK is challenged in that only 1.3% of the total UK domicile undergraduate students undertake international experiences, and so the opportunity to be fully immersed in an international culture is not sought after by UK students.

On the other hand, as the UK is the second highest destination for international learners, it enables UK students to develop their cultural sensitivity by learning side by side with international students. Despite this opportunity, it still does not outweigh the benefit of the experience of having to adapt to living in a different culture.

 **recap**

- Global businesses need global graduates.
- Technology has transformed the way we do business.
- No industry has been able to insulate itself from change.
- Competitors are no longer the usual suspects.
- Only 1.3% of UK domiciled students undertake student mobility.
- The top four global competences are collaboration, communication, drive and resilience and an ability to adopt multiple perspectives and challenge thinking.
- Employers value students who have had an international experience.
- Knowledge about international markets underpin global decision-making.
- A global mindset instantly states you are open to new ideas, willing to step out of your comfort zone, and are ultimately curious about the world we live in and the people within it.

References

AGCAS (2011), Employability: An AGCAS position statement http://agcas.org.uk/assets/download? file=2262&parent=725 (accessed June 2011)

Association of Graduate Recruiters (2016), Annual Survey 2015: Graduate Recruitment 2015

Bransford, J. and Stein, B. (1984), The IDEAL Problem Solver, New York: WH Freeman

CBI (2009), Future fit: Preparing graduates for the world of Work www.cbi.org.uk/pdf/20090326-CBI-FutureFit-Preparinggraduates-for-the-world-of-work.pdf (accessed June 2016)

CBI/EDI (2010), Ready to grow: Business priorities for education and skills: Education and Skills Survey 2010 www.cbi.org.uk/pdf/20100501-cbi-education-and-skills-survey-2010.pdf (accessed June 2016)

CBI (2011), Working Towards Your Future http://www.nus.co.uk/Global/CBI_NUS_Employability%20report_May%202011.pdf (accessed October 2016)

CBI (2015), Education and Skills Survey 2015: Inspiring Growth http://www.cbi.org.uk/news/cbi-pearsoneducation-and-skills-survey-2015/

CMI (2014), 21st Century Leaders: Building Practice into the Curriculum to Boost Employability http://www.managers.org.uk/~/media/Files/PDF/21st_Century_Leaders_June2014.ashx (accessed September 2016)

Cutlip, S. and Center, A. (1952), Effective Public Relations, New York, Prentice Hall

Dearing, Sir Ron (1997), 'The reports of the National Committee of Inquiry into Higher Education' (Dearing Report) www.leeds.ac.uk/educol/ncihe/nr_007.htm (accessed June 2011)

Department for Business Innovation and Skills (2016), The Graduate Labour Market Statistics: 2015 https://www.gov.uk/government/uploads/system/uploads/attachment_data/file/518654/bis-16-232-graduate-labour-market-statistics-2015.pdf

Development of Economics Ltd (2015), The Value of Soft Skills to the UK Economy: A Report Prepared on behalf of McDonalds UK http://www.backingsoftskills.co.uk/The%20Value%20of%20 Soft%20Skills%20to%20the%20UK%20Economy.pdf (accessed October 2016)

Diamond, A., et al. (2008), Global Graduates: Global Graduates into Global Leaders file:///C:/Users/Mauby/AppData/Local/Temp/ CIHE%20-%201111GlobalGradsFull.pdf (accessed October 2016)

European Commission (2016), The Erasmus Impact Study, Regional Analysis

Fisch, K. and McLeod, S. (2013), Preparing Students for What We Can't Prepare Them For, Teaching and Learning in Higher Education https://teachingandlearninginhighered.org/2013/07/15/preparing-students-for-what-we-cantprepare-them-for/ (accessed October 2016)

Friedman, T. (2005), The World is Flat: A Brief History of the 21st Century, New York, Farrar Straus Giroux

Goleman, D. (2014), Working with Emotional Intelligence, New York, St Martins Press

Govindarajan, V. and Gupta A. (1998), Success is All in the Mindset, Financial Times

Higher Education International Unit (2016), Gone International: The Value of Mobility http://www.go.international.ac.uk/sites/ default/files/GoneInternational2016_the%20value%20%of20mobi-lity.pdf (accessed 10 December 2016)

Higher Education Statistical Agency (2014/2015), Outward Mobility Data http://go.international.ac.uk/sites/default/files/HESA%20 2014%20to%202015%20printable%20analysis_2.pdf (accessed October 2016)

HESA (2015), Destination of Leavers in Higher Education https:// www.hesa.ac.uk/news/30-06-2016/sfr237-destinationsof-leavers (accessed October 2016)

High Fliers Research (2016), The graduate market in 2016 file:///C:/ Users/Mauby/AppData/Local/Microsoft/Windows/INetCache/IE/ 885FYRZU/GMReport16[1].pdf (accessed October 2016)

Institute of International Education, The Role of Study Abroad in Global Education file:///C:/Users/Mauby/AppData/Local/Temp/GSA-Teacher-Resource-1-An-Overview-of-Global-Education-and-the-Role-of-Study.pdf (accessed Ocstober 2016)

Karinthy, F. (1929), 'Chains' in Everything is Different (out of print)

Kotler, P., Armstrong, G., Wong, V. and Saunders, J. (2016), Principles of Marketing (electronic resource) 16th Edition, Harlow, Essex, Pearson Education

Mayer, J. D. and Salovey, P. (1997), What is emotional intelligence? In Salovey, P. and Sluyter, D. J., (Eds.), Emotional development and emotional intelligence: Educational implications (pp. 3–34), Harper Collins, New York

McNair, S. (2003), Employability in Higher Education, LTSN Generic Centre/University of Surrey

OECD (2013), *'How many students study abroad and where do they go?'* in Education at a Glance 2013: Highlights, OECD Publishing, Paris http://dx.doi.org/10.1787/eag_highlights-2013-12-en

Peters, T. (2004), In Search of Excellence: Lessons from America's Best Run Companies, London, Profile Books

Reimers, F. (2011), Introduction : Why Global Education? What is Global Competency? Harvard www.sd25.org/superintendent/GlobalEducation.pdf

René, C., The Students' Guide to Networking (unpublished work)

Robbins, L. (1963), Higher education report to the committee appointed by the Prime Minister under the chairmanship of Lord Robbins, 1961–63, HMSO. Chapter 2, para 25, p. 6

UK HE International Unit (2016), Gone International: the value of mobility, report on the 2013/14 graduating cohort

UNESCO, Institute for Statistics (July 2014), Top 20 Destinations for International Students https://www.theguardian.com/higher-education-network/blog/2014/jul/17/top-20-countriesinternational-students (accessed October 2016)

Willets, D. (2010), House of Commons debate, 8 July 2010, Column 511, Daily Hansard – Debate www.publications.parliament.uk/pa/cm201011/cmhansrd/cm100708/debtext/100708-0001.htm (accessed June 2011)

Yorke, M. (2006), Learning and Skills Series One: Employability: What it is and what it is not. Higher Education Academy, Enhancing Student Employability Co-ordination Team

Zhang, L., The Interview Technique You Should Be Using https://www.themuse.com/advice/the-interview-technique-youshould-be-using#! (accessed October 2016)

3 Business organisations: the internal environment

Ian Worthington

The systems approach to the study of business organisations stresses the interaction between a firm's internal and external environments. Key aspects of the internal context of business include the organisation's structure and functions and the way they are configured in pursuit of specified organisational objectives. If the enterprise is to remain successful, constant attention needs to be paid to balancing the different influences on the organisation and to the requirement to adapt to new external circumstances. This responsibility lies essentially with the organisation's management, which has the task of blending people, technologies, structures and environments.

Learning outcomes

Having read this chapter you should be able to:

- outline the broad approaches to organisation and management, paying particular attention to the systems approach
- identify alternative organisational structures used by business organisations
- discuss major aspects of the functional management of firms
- illustrate the interaction between a firm's internal and external environments

Key terms

Bureaucracy	Human relations approach	Profit centre
Classical theories of organisation	Human resource management	Project team
Contingency approach	Management	Public sector
Divisional structure	Marketing	Re-engineering
Downsizing	Marketing concept	Scientific management
Formal structures	Marketing mix	Sub-systems
Functional organisation	Matrix structure	Systems approach
Functional specialisation	Organisation by product	Theory X and Theory Y
Hierarchy of needs	Organisation chart	Theory Z
Holding company	Private sector	Virtual organisation
		Voluntary (or third) sector

Introduction

Under the systems approach to understanding business activity presented in Chapter 1, the organisation lies at the heart of the transformation process and tends to be seen as a kind of 'black box' which contains a multitude of elements – including structures, processes, people, resources and technologies – that brings about the transformation of inputs into outputs (see below). While the study of the business environment rightly focuses on the external context of business organisations, it is important to recognise that firms also have an internal environment that both shapes and is shaped by the external context in which they operate and make decisions. This notion of the interplay between an organisation's internal and external environments is a theme that runs through many of the chapters in this book.

As students of business and management will be aware, the internal features of business organisations have received considerable attention from scholars research- ing these fields, and a large number of texts have been devoted to this aspect of busi- ness studies.[1] In the discussion below, the aim is to focus on three areas of the internal organisation that relate directly to a study of the business environment: approaches to understanding organisations, organisational structures, and key functions within the enterprise. Further insight into these aspects and into management and organisational behaviour generally can be gained by consulting the many specialist books in this field, a number of which are mentioned at the end of this chapter.

A central theme running through any analysis of the internal environment is the idea of **management**, which has been subjected to a wide variety of definitions. As used in this context, management is seen both as a system of roles fulfilled by individuals who man- age the organisation (e.g. entrepreneur, resource manager, coordinator, leader, motiva- tor, organiser) and as a process that enables an organisation to achieve its objectives. The essential point is that management should be seen as a function of organisations, rather than as a controlling element, and its task is to enable the organisation to identify and achieve its objectives and to adapt to change. Managers need to integrate the vari- ous influences on the organisation – including people, technology, systems and the envi- ronment – in a manner best designed to meet the needs of the enterprise at the time in question and be prepared to institute change as and when circumstances dictate.

The concept of the organisation: an initial comment

According to Stoner and Freeman (1992: 4), an organisation can be defined as two or more people who work together in a structured way to achieve a specific goal or set of goals. Defined in this way, the term covers a vast array of structures in the:

- **private sector** – that part of the economy where ownership and control of the organisation is in the hands of private individuals or groups and where profit- seeking is a central goal;
- **public sector** – that part of the economy under the control of government and its agencies and where the state establishes and runs the different types of organisa- tion on behalf of its citizens and for their general well-being;

- **voluntary (or third) sector** – comprising those organisations, including charities, voluntary bodies and community businesses, that are not-for-profit enterprises and non-governmental.

Leaving aside the blurring of definitions of these three generic sectors that has occurred over recent years (e.g. where third-sector organisations deliver public services), the concept of the 'business organisation' as used in this text covers enterprises of all types and in all sectors. It also encapsulates those organisations where the objectives are set by one individual who both owns and controls the business and has no other employees (i.e. sole traders with zero staff).

Despite coming in a wide variety of shapes, forms and sizes, business organisations share a number of common features. Mullins (2010) identifies four such features:

- people (i.e. employees);
- objectives (i.e. what the organisation is set up to achieve);
- structure (i.e. the organisational framework through which the objectives are pursued and efforts are coordinated);
- management (i.e. the directing and controlling aspect of the enterprise).

To these we could add the idea of resources (including finance) and technologies. We also need to recognise the existence of an external environment that faces all types of enterprise. This is, after all, a fundamental feature of the systems approach to understanding business organisations and how they operate.

Understanding the nature of organisations: theories of organisation and management

To gain an insight into the principles that are felt to underlie the process of management, it is useful to undertake a brief examination of organisational theories. These theories or approaches – some of which date back to the late nineteenth century – represent the views of both practising managers and academics as to the factors that determine organisational effectiveness and the influences on individuals and groups within the work environment. Broadly speaking, these approaches can be broken down into three main categories: the classical approach, the human relations approach and the systems approach.[2] Since the last of these encompasses the model presented in Chapter 1, particular attention is paid to this perspective.

The classical approach

Classical theories of organisation and management mostly date from the first half of the twentieth century and are associated with the work of writers such as Taylor, Fayol, Urwick and Brech. In essence, the classicists viewed organisations as **formal structures** established to achieve a particular number of objectives under the direction of management, the emphasis being on purpose, structure, hierarchy and common principles. By identifying a set of guidelines to assist managers in the design of the organisational structure, the proponents of the classical view believed that organisations would be able to achieve their objectives more effectively. Fayol, for example, identified fourteen principles which included the division of work, the scalar chain, centralisation and the unity of command – features which also found expression in Weber's notion of 'bureaucracy'. Urwick's rules or principles similarly emphasised aspects of organisation structure and operations – such as specialisation, coordination, authority, responsibility and the span of control – and were presented essentially as a code of good management practice.

Within the classical approach special attention is often given to two important sub-groupings, known as **scientific management** and **bureaucracy**. The former is associated with the pioneering work of F. W. Taylor (1856–1915), who believed that scientific methods could be attached to the design of work so that productivity could be increased. For Taylor, the systematic analysis of jobs (e.g. using some form of work study technique) was seen as the key to finding the best way to perform a particular task and thereby achieving significant productivity gains from individuals, which would earn them increased financial rewards. In Taylor's view, the responsibility for the institution of a scientific approach lay with management, under whose control and direction the workers would operate to the mutual benefit of all concerned.

The second sub-group, bureaucracy, draws heavily on the work of Max Weber (1864–1920), whose studies of authority structures highlighted the importance of 'office' and 'rules' in the operation of organisations. According to Weber, bureaucracy – with its system of rules and procedures, specified spheres of competence, hierarchical organisation of offices, appointment based on merit, high level of specialisation and impersonality – possessed a degree of technical superiority over other forms of organisation, and this explained why an increasing number of enterprises were becoming bureaucratic in structure. Despite Weber's analysis appearing somewhat dated nowadays, bureaucratic organisation remains a key feature of many enterprises throughout the world and is clearly linked to increasing organisational size and complexity. Notwithstanding the many valid criticisms of Weber's work, it is difficult to imagine how it could be otherwise.

The human relations approach

Whereas the classical approach focuses largely on structure and on the formal organisation, the **human relations approach** to management emphasises the importance of people in the work situation and the influence of social and psychological factors in shaping organisational behaviour. Human relations theorists have primarily been concerned with issues such as individual motivation, leadership, communications and group dynamics, and have stressed the significance of the informal pattern of relationships that exists within the formal structure. The factors influencing human behaviour have accordingly been portrayed as a key to achieving greater organisational effectiveness, thus elevating the 'management of people' to a prime position in the determination of managerial strategies.

The early work in this field is associated with Elton Mayo (1880–1949) and with the famous Hawthorne Experiments, conducted at the Western Electric Company (USA) between 1924 and 1932. What these experiments basically showed was that individuals at work were members of informal (i.e. unofficial) as well as formal groups and that group influences were fundamental to explaining individual behaviour. Later

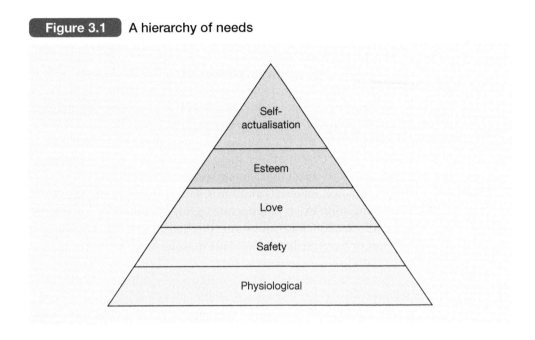

Figure 3.1 A hierarchy of needs

work by writers such as Maslow, McGregor, Argyris, Likert and Herzberg continued to stress the importance of the human factor in determining organisational effectiveness, but tended to adopt a more psychological orientation, as exemplified by Maslow's **'hierarchy of needs'** and McGregor's **'Theory X and Theory Y'**. Maslow's central proposition was that individuals seek to satisfy specific groups of needs, ranging from basic physiological requirements (e.g. food, sleep, sex), through safety, love and esteem, to self-actualisation (i.e. self-fulfilment), progressing systematically up the hierarchy as each lower-level need is satisfied (see Figure 3.1). To McGregor, individuals at work were seen by management as either inherently lazy (Theory X) or committed to the organisation's objectives and often actively seeking responsibility (Theory Y). These perceptions consequently provided the basis for different styles of management, which ranged from the coercive to the supportive.

McGregor's concern with management styles is reflected in later studies, including Ouichi's notion of **Theory Z.**[3] According to Ouichi, one of the key factors in the success of Japanese manufacturing industries was their approach to the management of people. Theory Z organisations were those that offered workers long-term (often lifetime) employment, a share in decision-making, opportunities for training, development and promotion, and a number of other advantages which gave them a positive orientation towards the organisation. For Ouichi, the key to organisational effectiveness lay in the development of a Japanese-style Theory Z environment, adapted to western requirements.

The systems approach

More recent approaches to organisation and management have helped to integrate previous work on structures, people and technology, by portraying organisations as socio-technical systems interacting with their environment. Under this approach – which became popular in the 1960s – organisations were seen as complex systems of people, tasks and technologies that were part of and interacted with a larger environment, comprising a wide range of influences (see Chapter 1). This environment was frequently subject to fluctuations, which on occasions could become turbulent (i.e. involving rapid and often unpredictable change). For organisations to survive and prosper, adaptation to environmental demands was seen as a necessary requirement and one that was central to the process of management.

The essence of the **systems approach** has been described in Chapter 1 but is worth repeating here. Organisations, including those involved in business, are open systems, interacting with their environment as they convert inputs into output. Inputs include people, finance, materials and information, provided by the environment in which the organisation exists and operates. Output comprises such items as goods and services, information, ideas and waste, discharged into the environment for consumption by 'end' or 'intermediate' users and in some cases representing inputs used by other organisations.

Systems invariably comprise a number of **sub-systems** through which the process of conversion or transformation occurs. Business organisations, for example, usually have sub-systems that deal with activities such as production, marketing, accounting and human resource management, and each of these in turn may involve smaller sub-systems (e.g. sales, quality control, training) which collectively constitute the whole. Just as the organisation as a system interacts with its environment, so do the sub-systems and their component elements, which also interact with each other. In the case of the latter, the boundary between sub-systems is usually known as an 'interface'.

While the obvious complexities of the systems approach need not be discussed, it is important to emphasise that most modern views of organisations draw heavily on the work in this area, paying particular attention to the interactions between people, technology, structure and environment and to the key role of management in directing the organisation's activities towards the achievement of its goals. Broadly speaking, management is seen as a critical sub-system within the total organisation, responsible for the coordination of the other sub-systems and for ensuring that internal and external relationships are managed effectively. As changes occur in one part of the system, these will induce changes elsewhere and this will require a management response that will have implications for the organisation and for its sub-systems. Such changes may be either the cause or effect of changes in the relationship between the organisation and its environment, and the requirement for managers is to adapt to the new conditions without reducing the organisation's effectiveness.

Given the complex nature of organisations and the environments in which they operate, a number of writers have suggested a **contingency approach** to organisational design and management (e.g. Lawrence and Lorsch, Woodward, Perrow, Burns and Stalker).[4] In essence, this approach argues that there is no single form of organisation best suited to all situations and that the most appropriate organisational structure and system of management is dependent upon the contingencies of the situation (e.g. size, technology, environment) for each organisation. In some cases a bureaucratic structure might be the best way to operate, while in others much looser and more organic methods of organisation might be more effective. In short, issues of organisational design and management depend on choosing the best combination in the light of the relevant situational variables; this might mean different structures and styles coexisting within an organisation.

Other theoretical approaches

To complement these traditional approaches to understanding the nature of organisations, Mullins (2010) highlights the contribution of theories of decision-making and social action. Decision-making theory, he suggests, can be seen as a sub-division of the systems approach in which the focus of attention is on the process of managerial decision-making and how information is gathered, processed and used in deciding how to act. The organisation in effect is seen as an information-processing network and successful management is concerned with making choices and resolving conflicts, often against a background of a changing internal and external environment.

Social action approaches emphasise the need to view the organisation from the standpoint of the individual employees or actors, each of whom has their own goals and interpretation of their work situation and whose behaviour is guided by their view of what work means to them and the satisfaction they are seeking. Organisations are portrayed as arenas in which individuals with different views and expectations interact. Conflicts of interest are regarded as a normal feature of human behaviour and an inevitable part of organisational life.

Organisational structures

Apart from the very simplest form of enterprise in which one individual carries out all tasks and responsibilities, business organisations are characterised by a division of labour which allows employees to specialise in particular roles and to occupy designated positions in pursuit of the organisation's objectives. The resulting pattern of relationships between individuals and roles constitutes what is known as the organisation's structure and represents the means by which the purpose and work of the enterprise are carried out. It also provides a framework through which communications can occur and within which the processes of management can be applied.

Responsibility for establishing the formal structure of the organisation lies with management and a variety of options is available. Whatever form is chosen, the basic need is to identify a structure that will best sustain the success of the enterprise and will permit the achievement of a number of important objectives. Through its structure an organisation should be able to:

- achieve efficiency in the utilisation of resources;
- provide opportunities for monitoring organisational performance;
- ensure the accountability of individuals;
- guarantee coordination between the different parts of the enterprise;
- provide an efficient and effective means of organisational communication;
- create job satisfaction, including opportunities for progression;
- adapt to changing circumstances brought about by internal or external developments.

In short, structure is not an end in itself but a means to an end and should ideally reflect the needs of the organisation within its existing context and taking into account its future requirements.

mini case **'Into the Dragon's Den'**

As the chapter illustrates, the structure of an organisation is a means by which an enterprise can achieve its objectives. As the environment in which a business operates changes, a firm should be willing to adapt the structure to meet the new circumstances. This might mean moving beyond the traditional models discussed below, in an effort to improve performance.

The global pharmaceutical giant GlaxoSmithKline (GSK) illustrates this idea of an evolving organisational structure. In July 2008, GSK announced that in future its scientists would have to pitch their ideas for new drugs to a development board, based essentially on the lines of *Dragons' Den*, a popular UK television programme where would-be entrepreneurs seek to gain backing for their ideas from a group of financiers. The board would include two venture capitalists and would be a mixture of executives from inside the company and GSK outsiders, the plan being to stimulate innovation by requiring smaller teams of scientists to pitch three-year business plans to the new drug discovery investment board in an effort to secure funding for new drug treatments.

 web link You can access the website for GSK at *www.gsk.com*

The essence of structure is the division of work between individuals and the formal organisational relationships that are created between them. These relationships will be reflected not only in individual job descriptions but also in the overall **organisation chart**, which designates the formal pattern of role relationships, and the interactions between roles and the individuals occupying those roles. Individual authority relationships can be classified as line, staff, functional and lateral and arise from the defined pattern of responsibilities, as follows:

- *Line relationships* occur when authority flows vertically downwards through the structure from superior to subordinate (e.g. managers–section leader–staff).
- *Staff relationships* are created when senior personnel appoint assistants who normally have no authority over other staff but act as an extension of their superior.
- *Functional relationships* are those between specialists (or advisers) and line managers and their subordinates (e.g. when a specialist provides a common service throughout the organisation but has no authority over the users of the service). The personnel or computing function may be one such service that creates a functional relationship. (Note that specialists have line relationships with their own subordinates.)
- *Lateral relationships* exist across the organisation, particularly between individuals occupying equivalent positions within different departments or sections (e.g. committees, heads of departments, section leaders).

With regard to the division of work and the grouping of organisational activities, this can occur in a variety of ways. These include:

- *by function or major purpose*, associated particularly with departmental structures;
- *by product or service*, where individuals responsible for a particular product or service are grouped together;

- *by location*, based on geographical criteria;
- *by common processes* (e.g. particular skills or methods of operation);
- *by client group* (e.g. children, the disabled, the elderly).

In some organisations a particular method of grouping will predominate, in others there will tend to be a variety of types, and each has its own particular advantages and disadvantages. In the next section, we examine five popular methods of grouping activities in business organisations. Students should attempt to discover what types of structure exist within their own educational institution and the logic (if any) that underlies the choices made.

Functional organisation

The functional approach to organisation is depicted in Figure 3.2. As its name indicates, in this type of structure activities are clustered together by common purpose or function. All marketing activities, for example, are grouped together as a common function, typically within a marketing department. Similarly, other areas of activity, such as production, finance, personnel and research and development, have their own specialised sections or departments, responsible for all the tasks required of that function.

Apart from its obvious simplicity, the **functional organisation** structure allows individuals to be grouped together on the basis of their specialisms and technical expertise, and this can facilitate the development of the function they offer as well as providing a recognised path for promotion and career development. On the downside, functional specialisation, particularly through departments, is likely to create sectional interests which may operate to the disadvantage of the organisation as a whole, particularly where inequalities in resource allocation between functions become a cause for inter-function rivalry. It could also be argued that this form of structure is most suited to single-product firms and that it becomes less appropriate as organisations diversify their products and/or markets. In such circumstances, the tendency will be for businesses to look for the benefits that can arise from specialisation by product or from the divisionalisation of the enterprise.

Figure 3.2 A functional organisation structure

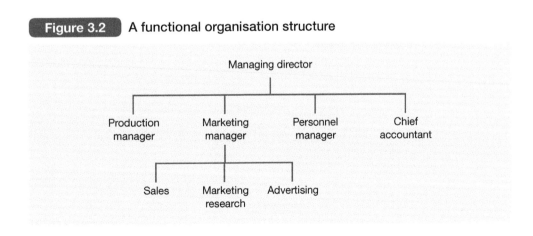

Organisation by product or service

In this case the division of work and the grouping of activities are dictated by the product or service provided (see Figure 3.3), such that each group responsible for a particular part of the output of the organisation may have its own specialist in the different functional areas (e.g. marketing, finance, personnel). One advantage of this type of structure is that it allows an organisation to offer a diversified range of products, as exemplified by the different services available in National Health Service hospitals (e.g. maternity, orthopaedic, geriatric and so forth). Its main disadvantage is the danger that the separate units or divisions within the enterprise may attempt to become too autonomous, even at the expense of other parts of the organisation, and this can present management with problems of coordination and control.

The divisional structure

As firms diversify their products and/or markets – often as a result of merger or takeover – a structure is needed to coordinate and control the different parts of the organisation. This structure is likely to be the divisional (or multi-divisional) company.

A **divisional structure** is formed when an organisation is split up into a number of self-contained business units, each of which operates as a profit centre. This may occur on the basis of product or market or a combination of the two, with each unit tending to operate along functional or product lines, but with certain key functions (e.g. finance, personnel, corporate planning) provided centrally, usually at company headquarters (see Figure 3.4).

The main benefit of the multi-divisional company is that it allows each part of what can be a very diverse organisation to operate semi-independently in producing and marketing its products, thus permitting each division to design its offering to suit local market conditions – a factor of prime importance where the firm operates on a multinational basis. The dual existence of divisional **profit centres** and a central unit responsible for establishing strategy at a global level can, however, be a source of considerable tension, particularly where the needs and aims of the centre appear to conflict with operations at the local level or to impose burdens seen to be unreasonable by divisional managers (e.g. the allocation of central overhead costs).

Much the same kind of arguments apply to the **holding company**, though this tends to be a much looser structure for managing diverse organisations, favoured by both UK

Figure 3.3 A product-based structure

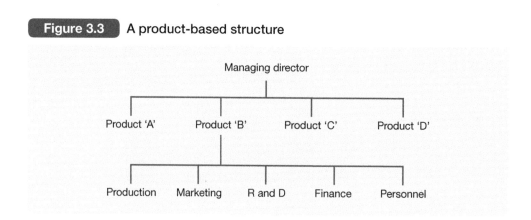

Figure 3.4   A divisional structure

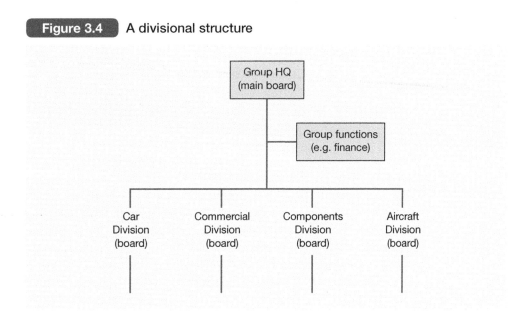

and Japanese companies. Under this arrangement, the different elements of the organisation (usually companies) are coordinated and controlled by a parent body, which may be just a financial entity established to maintain or gain control of other trading companies. Holding companies are associated with the growth of firms by acquisition, which gives rise to a high degree of product or market diversification. They are also a popular means of operating a multinational organisation.

---

mini case   A merger of equals?

Announced in July 2013, the planned merger between the French company Publicis and America's Omnicom will create the world's largest marketing and advertising business, assuming it receives regulatory approval, which, at the time of writing (October 2013), seems likely.

Publicis Omnicom Group – as the holding company will be known – plans to have dual headquarters in Paris and New York and will be led by the chief executive officers (CEOs) of the two organisations for the first two and a half years of its life. Thereafter the plan is to make one of the CEOs a non-executive chairman and the other the lead

CEO for the whole group. In the spirit of what has been dubbed a 'merger of equals', the combined business will operate through a 16-person single-tier board, comprising the two CEOs and seven non-executive directors drawn from each part of the merged enterprise.

Observers have suggested that the newly formed organisation might experience some teething problems because of differences in culture and management style and because the two companies currently represent clients drawn from competing brands (e.g. Omnicom's clients include Volkswagen and Nissan; Publicis represents BMW and Renault).

web link   For information on the proposed merger see, for example, *www.reuters.com*

Matrix structures

A **matrix structure** is an arrangement for combining functional specialisation (e.g. through departments) with structures built around products, projects or programmes (see Figure 3.5). The resulting grid (or matrix) has a two-way flow of authority and responsibility. Within the functional elements, the flow is vertically down the line from superior to subordinate and this creates a degree of stability and certainty for the individuals located within the department or unit. Simultaneously, as a member of a project group or product team, an individual is normally answerable horizontally to the project manager whose responsibility is to oversee the successful completion of the project, which in some cases may be of very limited duration.

Matrix structures offer various advantages, most notably flexibility, opportunities for staff development, an enhanced sense of ownership of a project or programme, customer orientation and the coordination of information and expertise. On the negative side, difficulties can include problems of coordination and control, conflicting loyalties for staff and uncertain lines of authority. It is not uncommon in an organisation designed on matrix lines for project or programme leaders to be unsure of their authority over the staff from the contributing departments. Nor is it unknown for functional managers to withdraw their cooperation and/or support for projects located outside their immediate sphere of influence.

Project teams

Despite its flexibility, the matrix often has a degree of permanence; in contrast, the **project team** is essentially a temporary structure established as a means of carrying out a particular task, often in a highly unstable environment. Once the task is complete, the

Figure 3.5   A matrix structure in a business school

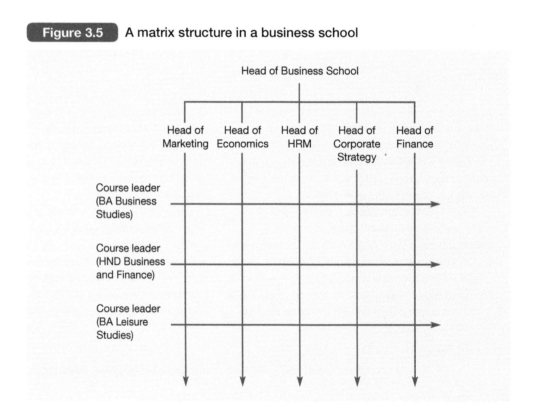

team is disbanded and individuals return to their usual departments or are assigned to a new project.

Fashioned around technical expertise rather than managerial rank, and often operating closely with clients, project teams are increasingly common in high-technology firms, construction companies and some types of service industry, especially management consultancies and advertising. Rather than being a replacement for the existing structure, they operate alongside it and utilise in-house staff (and, in some cases, outside specialists) on a project-by-project basis. While this can present logistical and scheduling problems and may involve some duplication of resources, it can assist an organisation in adapting to change and uncertainty and in providing products to the customer's specifications. Project teams tend to be at their most effective when objectives and tasks are well defined, when the client is clear as to the desired outcome and when the team is chosen with care.

The virtual organisation

As indicated above, traditional organisations have structures that are designed to facilitate the transformation of inputs into output. Increasingly, as the business environment changes, relationships both within and between organisations have needed to become more flexible and this has given rise to such developments as the growth in teleworking and the establishment of dynamic broker/agent networks involving considerable outsourcing of sub-tasks to 'agents' (e.g. manufacturing, distribution) by the core organisation (the 'broker'). It is fair to say that this demand for greater flexibility has been driven partly by the market and partly by cost considerations, and the process of change has been facilitated by relatively rapid developments in information technology. One area currently exciting the interest of writers on management and organisation is the concept of the **virtual organisation**, arguably the ultimate form of organisational flexibility.

The term virtual organisation or firm signifies an extremely loose web of essentially freelance businesses or individuals who organise themselves to produce a specific customer product (e.g. an individual holiday package with particular features unique to the customer). Without any permanent structure or hierarchy this so-called firm can constantly change its shape and, despite existing across space and time, tends to appear edgeless, with its inputs, outputs and employees increasingly dispersed across the linked world of information systems. Given modern forms of communication, opportunities exist for the creation of totally electronic-based organisations trading in expertise and information with no real-world physical identity. This stands in stark contrast to the traditional view of the firm as an arrangement which adds value by transforming basic economic inputs (e.g. land, labour, capital) into physical outputs or services.

Structural change

Internal change is an important feature of the modern business organisation. In order to remain competitive and meet stakeholder needs, a firm may have to find ways to restructure its organisation as the environment in which it operates changes.

Solutions can range from a partial or wholesale shift in the organisation's structural form to strategies for reducing the overall size and shape of the company (e.g. **downsizing**) or a radical redesign of business processes (e.g. **re-engineering**).

Whereas business re-engineering normally connotes a root-and-branch reform of the way in which the business operates, downsizing essentially involves shrinking the organisation to make it leaner and fitter and hopefully more flexible in its response to the marketplace. For some companies this means little more than reducing the size of the workforce through natural wastage and/or redundancies, as and when opportunities arise; for others it involves delayering the organisation by removing a tier, or tiers, of management, thus effectively flattening the organisation's hierarchy and helping it to reduce its unit costs of production.

In its most systematic and long-term form, downsizing can be used as a vehicle for cultural change through which an organisation's employees are encouraged to embrace notions of continuous improvement and innovation, and to accept that structural reform is a permanent and natural state of affairs. Under this approach, retraining and reskilling become vital tools in implementing the chosen strategy and in shaping the organisation to meet the demands of its changing environment. The danger is, however, that a firm may become too concerned with restructuring as a cure for all its problems, when the real cause of its difficulties lies in its marketplace. Cutting the number of employees, in such a situation, is unlikely to make unattractive products attractive, nor is it likely to boost morale within the organisation.

Aspects of functional management

Most organisation structures reflect a degree of **functional specialisation**, with individuals occupying roles in departments, units or sections which have titles such as Production, Finance, Marketing, Personnel, and Research and Development. These functional areas of the internal organisation, and the individuals who are allocated to them, are central to the process of transforming organisational inputs into output. The management of these functions and of the relationships between them will be a key factor in the success of the enterprise and in its ability to respond to external demands for change.

The interdependence of the internal functions can be demonstrated by a simple example. Providing goods and services to meet the market's needs often involves research and development, which necessitates a financial input, usually from the capital market or the organisation's own resources. It also requires, as do all the other functions, the recruitment of staff of the right quality, a task which is more often than not the responsibility of the Personnel or Human Resources department. If research and development activities lead to a good idea which the Marketing department is able to sell, then the Production department is required to produce it in the right quantities, to the right specifications and at the time the market needs it. This depends not only on internal scheduling procedures within the Production department but also on having the right kinds of materials supplied on time by the Purchasing department, an appropriate system of quality control and work monitoring, machinery that is working and regularly serviced, the finished items packed, despatched and delivered, and a multitude of other activities, all operating towards the same end.

The extent to which all of these requirements can be met simultaneously depends on internal factors, many of which are controllable, and also on a host of external influences, the majority of which tend to be beyond the organisation's control. To demonstrate this interface between the internal and external environments, two key areas of functional management are discussed briefly below – marketing and human resource management. An examination of the other functions within the organisation would yield similar findings.

Human resource management (HRM)

People are the key organisational resource; without them organisations would not exist or function. All businesses need to plan for and manage the people they employ if they are to use this resource effectively and efficiently in pursuit of their objectives. In modern and forward-looking organisations this implies a proactive approach to the management of people that goes beyond the bounds of traditional personnel management and involves the establishment of systems for planning, monitoring, appraisal and evaluation, training and development, and integrating the internal needs of the organisation with the external demands of the marketplace. Such an approach is associated with the idea of **human resource management**.

As in other areas of management, HRM involves a wide variety of activities related to the formulation and implementation of appropriate organisational policies, the provision of opportunities for monitoring, evaluation and change, and the application of resources to the fulfilment of organisational ends. Key aspects of 'people management' include:

- recruitment and selection;
- working conditions;
- training and career development;
- job evaluation;
- employee relations;
- manpower planning;
- legal aspects of employment.

In most, if not all, cases these will be affected by both internal and external influences (e.g. size of the firm, management style, competition, economic and political developments), some of which will vary over time as well as between organisations.

The provision of these activities within an organisation can occur in a variety of ways and to different degrees of sophistication. Some very small firms may have little in the way of a recognisable HRM function, being concerned primarily with questions of hiring and firing, pay and other working conditions, but not with notions of career development, staff appraisal or job enrichment. In contrast, very large companies may have a specialist HRM or personnel department, often organised on functional lines and responsible for the formulation and implementation of personnel policies throughout the organisation. Such centralisation provides not only some economies of scale but also a degree of standardisation and consistency across departments. To allow for flexibility, centralised systems are often combined with an element of decentralisation which permits individual departments or sections to exercise some influence in matters such as the recruitment and selection of staff, working conditions, training and career development.

To illustrate how the different aspects of HRM are influenced by external factors, one part of this function – recruitment and selection of staff – has been chosen. This is the activity within the organisation that seeks to ensure that it has the right quantity and quality of labour in the right place and at the right time to meet its requirements at all levels. To achieve this aim, the organisation initially needs to consider a large number of factors, including possible changes in the demand for labour, the need for new skills and likely labour turnover, before the processes of recruitment and selection can begin. These aspects in turn will be conditioned by a variety of factors such as changes in the demand for the product, the introduction of new technology, and social, economic and demographic changes, some of which may not be anticipated or expected by strategic planners.

Once recruitment and selection are ready to begin, a further raft of influences will impinge upon the process, some of which emanate from external sources. In drawing up a job specification, for example, attention will normally need to be paid to the state of the local labour market, including skill availability, competition from other employers, wage rates in comparable jobs and/or organisations, and socio-demographic trends. If the quality of labour required is in short supply, an organisation may find itself having to offer improved pay and working conditions simply to attract a sufficient number of applicants to fill the vacancies on offer. Equally, in fashioning its job advertisements and drawing up the material it sends out to potential applicants, a firm will need to pay due attention to the needs of current legislation in areas such as equal opportunities, race discrimination and employment protection, if it is not to infringe the law.

Among the other external factors the enterprise may need to take into consideration in recruiting and selecting staff will be:

- the relative cost and effectiveness of the different advertising media;
- existing relationships with external sources of recruitment (e.g. job centres, schools, colleges, universities);
- commitments to the local community;
- relationships with employee organisations (e.g. trade unions, staff associations);
- opportunities for staff training and development in local training and educational institutions.

Ideally, it should also pay some attention to possible future changes in the technology of the workplace, in order to recruit individuals either with appropriate skills or who can be retrained relatively easily with a minimum amount of disruption and expense to the organisation.

The marketing function

The processes of human resource management are a good illustration of the interactions between a firm's internal and external environments. An even better example is provided by an examination of its marketing activities, which are directed primarily, though not exclusively, towards what is happening outside the organisation.

Like 'management', the term **marketing** has been defined in a wide variety of ways, ranging from Kotler's essentially economic notion of an activity directed at satisfying human needs and wants through exchange processes, to the more managerial definitions associated with bodies such as the Chartered Institute of Marketing.[5] A common thread running through many of these definitions is the idea that marketing is concerned with meeting the needs of the consumer in a way that is profitable to the enterprise. Hence, strategic marketing management is normally characterised as the process of ensuring a good fit between the opportunities afforded by the marketplace and the abilities and resources of an organisation operating in it.

> **web link** Information about the Chartered Institute of Marketing is available at *www.cim.co.uk*

This notion of marketing as an integrative function within the organisation – linking the needs of the consumer with the various functional areas of the firm – is central to modern definitions of the term and lies at the heart of what is known as the **marketing concept**. This is the idea that the customer is of prime importance to the organisation and that the most significant managerial task in any enterprise is first to identify the needs and wants of the consumer and then to ensure that its operations are geared to meeting those requirements profitably. Though it would be true to say that not all organisations subscribe to this view, it is generally accepted that the successful businesses are predominantly those with a customer rather than a production or sales orientation. Equally, the evidence suggests that the need to adopt such a customer-centred approach applies not only to private sector trading organisations but also increasingly to public sector enterprises and to bodies not established for the pursuit of profits but for other purposes (e.g. charities, political parties, trade unions).

When viewed from a customer perspective, marketing can be seen to comprise a range of activities that goes beyond the simple production of an item for sale. These activities include:

- identifying the needs of consumers (e.g. through marketing research);
- designing different 'offerings' to meet the needs of different types of customers (e.g. through market segmentation);
- choosing products, prices, promotional techniques and distribution channels that are appropriate to a particular market (i.e. designing a 'marketing mix' strategy);
- undertaking market and product planning;
- deciding on brand names, types of packages and methods of communicating with the customer;
- creating a marketing information system.

As already indicated, in carrying out these activities the firm is brought into contact with a range of external influences of both an immediate and an indirect kind. This external marketing environment can have a fundamental impact on the degree to which the firm is able to develop and maintain successful transactions with its customers and hence on its profitability and chances of survival.

To illustrate how a firm's marketing effort can be influenced by external factors, the following brief discussion focuses on 'pricing', which is one of the key elements of the **marketing mix**, that is, the set of controllable variables that a business can use to influence the buyer's response, namely, product, price, promotion and place – the 4Ps. Of all the mix elements, price is the only one that generates revenue, while the others result in expenditure. It is therefore a prime determinant of a firm's turnover and profitability and can have a considerable influence on the demand for its products and frequently for those of its competitors.

Web link There are lots of useful websites discussing the idea of the 'marketing mix'. Try typing the term into Google.

Leaving aside the broader question of a firm's pricing goals and the fact that prices will tend to vary according to the stage a product has reached in its life cycle, price determination can be said to be influenced by a number of factors. Of these, the costs of production, the prices charged by one's competitors and the price sensitivity of consumers tend to be the most significant.

In the case of cost-based pricing, this occurs when a firm relates its price to the cost of buying or producing the product, adding a profit margin or 'mark-up' to arrive at the final selling price. Such an approach tends to be common among smaller enterprises (e.g. builders, corner shops) where costs are often easier to estimate and where likely consumer reactions are given less attention than the need to make an adequate return on the effort involved. The essential point about this form of price determination is that many of the firm's costs are influenced by external organisations – including the suppliers of materials, components and energy – and hence pricing will often vary according to changes in the prices of inputs. Only larger organisations, or a group of small businesses operating together, will generally be able to exercise some influence over input prices and even then not all costs will be controllable by the enterprise.

Organisations that take an essentially cost-based approach to pricing will sometimes be influenced by the prices charged by competitors – particularly in markets where considerable competition exists and where the products are largely homogeneous and a buyer's market is evident (e.g. builders during a recession). The competitive approach to pricing, however, is also found in markets where only a few large firms operate and where the need to increase or maintain market share can give rise to virtually identical prices and to fierce non-price competition between the market leaders. In Britain, for instance, a big cross-Channel ferry operator will normally provide the service to customers at the same price as its rivals, differentiating its offering in terms of additional benefits (e.g. on-board entertainment) rather than price. Where this is the case, the external demands of the market rather than costs constitute the primary influence on a firm's decisions, and changes in market conditions (e.g. the actual or potential entry of new firms; changes in a competitor's prices; economic recession) will tend to be reflected in price changes.

This idea of market factors influencing pricing decisions also applies to situations where firms fix their prices according to the actual or anticipated reactions of consumers to the price charged for a product – known in economics as the price elasticity of demand. In this case, the customer rather than a firm's competitors is the chief influence on price determination, although the two are often interrelated in that consumers are usually more price sensitive in markets where some choice exists. Differential levels of price sensitivity between consumers of a product normally arise when a market has distinct segments based on factors such as differences in income or age or location. In such cases a firm will often fix its prices according to the segment of the market it is serving, a process known as 'price discrimination' and one that is familiar to students claiming concessionary fares on public transport.

While the above discussion has been oversimplified and does not take into account factors such as the price of other products in an organisation's product portfolio (e.g. different models of car), it illustrates quite clearly how even one of the so-called controllable variables in a firm's marketing mix is subject to a range of external influences that is often beyond its ability to control. The same argument applies to the other elements of the marketing function and students could usefully add to their understanding of the internal/external interface by examining how the external environment impinges upon such marketing activities as promotion, distribution or market research.

Synopsis

The internal dimension of business organisations constitutes an extensive field of study and one to which students of business devote a considerable amount of time. In seeking to illustrate how a firm's internal organisation is influenced by its external environment, emphasis has been placed on a selected number of aspects of a firm's internal operations. Of these, its structure and functions were seen to provide a good illustration of the interface between the internal and external environments. Appreciating the existence of this interface is facilitated by adopting a systems approach to organisational analysis.

Summary of key points

- Management is a key aspect of the internal environment of the business organisation.

- Theories of organisation and management fall broadly into three categories: classical theories, human relations approaches, systems approaches.

- The systems view of organisations depicts businesses as open systems interacting with their external environment as they convert inputs into outputs.

- The external environment of the organisation affects all aspects of the business, including its structures, functions and processes.

- To carry out their tasks, businesses can structure themselves in a variety of ways, including functionally, by product/service, by divisions, in a matrix format or via project teams. Each has its advantages and disadvantages.

- Structural change tends to be a feature of large modern organisations.

- Within the organisation the different business functions such as marketing, production, HRM, purchasing and so on are influenced by external factors of both a general and operational kind.

- An examination of the marketing and HRM functions reveals the importance of the wide range of external influences that can impinge upon these day-to-day areas of organisational work.

- Investigations of other functional areas within the organisation would produce a similar picture.

case study   Reshuffle at Microsoft

When an organisation's fortunes appear to change for the worse, there is always a temptation to seek a remedy through a change in senior personnel and/or in the overall structure of the enterprise (e.g. leading professional football teams in Europe seem to change managers fairly regularly when results go badly). Whether this is invariably a good idea is open to question. Supporters see it as a way of revitalising the business by bringing in new faces with new ideas, of challenging existing ways of thinking and working; critics frequently portray it as 'reorganising the deckchairs on the Titanic', a failure to address the fundamental problem(s) facing the organisation. Time will tell which of these two viewpoints applies to the global business examined in this case study.

Faced with a demonstrable shift in consumer demand away from PCs and towards tablets, smartphones and touch devices – where it was struggling to compete with companies such as Apple and Google – Microsoft Chief Executive Steve Ballmer announced a major reorganisation of the business in July 2013. Aimed at promoting faster innovation and a much sharper focus on meeting consumer needs, Ballmer heralded the demise of the divisional approach favoured by his predecessor (Bill Gates), which was evidently seen as creating a hierarchical structure of competing businesses, each with its own strategy and with separate finance and marketing teams. Under the new arrangements, emphasis appears to be on how devices function rather than centred on particular products, the hope being that this will help to encourage greater cooperation across the organisation in place of internal rivalry.

The centrepiece of the new arrangements is the organisation of the business on the basis of function. Instead of divisions, Microsoft will operate via a number of functional groupings, including engineering, marketing, finance, advanced strategy and research, and business development and evangelism. In what is likely to prove an important change, the engineering division will be split into four major areas or groupings: operating systems, devices and studios, applications and services, cloud and enterprise. Responsibility for running the main functions within the new organisation will be vested in a reshuffled senior executive team.

Commenting on the new arrangements, *The Guardian* (12 July 2013: 24) suggested that they were reminiscent of the reorganisation undertaken by its rival Apple the previous October. This, it suggested, had been designed to encourage even greater collaboration between various aspects of the business: the world-class hardware, its software and its services teams. Put another way, structure can sometimes be an aid and sometimes an obstacle to a firm achieving its strategic objectives. Where the latter is the case, a partial or even radical restructuring of the organisation may be a necessary condition for putting the business on the right track. On its own, though, it is unlikely to prove sufficient in most cases.

Case study questions

1 What are thought to be the main advantages of restructuring an organisation that is facing problems?

2 Why is a decision to restructure an organisation unlikely to prove a 'sufficient condition' for its future success?

Review and discussion questions

1 In the systems approach to organisations, reference is made to 'feedback'. What is meant by this term and how can feedback influence the process of transforming 'inputs' into 'output'?

2 Should a firm's internal structure be influenced by considerations of management or by the market it serves? Are the two incompatible?

3 Examine ways in which a firm's external environment can influence one of the following functional areas: finance or production or research and development.

4 Describe the structure of an organisation with which you are familiar (e.g. through employment or work experience), indicating why the organisation is structured in the way it is. Are there any alternative forms of structure the organisation could adopt?

Assignments

1 As a student on a business studies course, you have decided to get some practical experience of the business world by running a small venture with a number of colleagues which you hope will also earn you enough income to support you during your time at college or university. Your idea involves printing and selling customised T-shirts throughout the institution and possibly to a wider market. Design an appropriate organisational structure which you feel will help you achieve your objectives, indicating your rationale for choosing such a structure and the formal pattern of relationships between individuals.

2 In self-selecting groups of three or four, identify an organisation you feel has a bureaucratic structure. Produce a report indicating:

(a) those features of the organisation's structure, management and operations that best fit the idea of bureaucracy;
(b) the practical consequences of these features for the working of the organisation.

Give examples to support your comments.

Notes and references

1 See, for example, Mullins, L. J., *Management and Organisational Behaviour*, 9th edition, Financial Times/Prentice Hall, 2010; Cole, G. A. and Kelly, P., *Management: Theory and Practice*, 7th edition, International Thomson Business Press, 2011.

2 For a more detailed account of the three approaches see, *inter alia*, the texts referred to in note 1.

3 Ouichi, W. G., *Theory Z: How American Business Can Meet the Japanese Challenge*, Addison-Wesley, 1981.

4 The contingency approach is discussed in Cole, *op. cit.*

5 See, for example, Kotler, P. and Armstrong, G., *Principles of Marketing*, 15th edition, Prentice Hall, 2013.

Further reading

Campbell, D. J. and Craig, T., *Organizations and the Business Environment*, 2nd edition, Butterworth-Heinemann, 2005.

Cole, G. A. and Kelly, P., *Management: Theory and Practice*, 7th edition, International Thomson Business Press, 2011.

Daft, R. L., *Organizational Theory and Design*, 11th edition, South-Western Cengage Learning, 2012.

Handy, C., *The Age of Unreason*, 2nd edition, Arrow Books, 1995.

Morrison, J., *The International Business Environment: Global and Local Marketplaces in a Changing World*, 2nd revised edition, Palgrave Macmillan, 2006.

Mullins, L. J., *Management and Organisational Behaviour*, 9th edition, Financial Times/Prentice Hall, 2010. A tenth edition is scheduled for publication in 2014.

Mullins, L. J., *Essentials of Organisational Behaviour*, 3rd edition, FT/Prentice Hall, 2011.

Pugh, D. S. and Hickson, D. J., *Great Writers on Organizations*, 2nd omnibus edition, Ashgate, 2007.

Stoner, J. and Freeman, R., *Management*, 5th edition, Prentice Hall, 1992.

Web links and further questions are available on the website at:
www.pearsoned.co.uk/worthington

4 Formative Essay

No Additional Readings

5 The political environment

Ian Worthington

Politics is a universal activity which affects the business world in a variety of ways. Understanding political systems, institutions and processes provides a greater insight into business decisions and into the complexities of the business environment. Given the increasing globalisation of markets, this environment has an international as well as a domestic element and the two are closely interrelated. Appreciating some of the key aspects of this environment and its impact on business organisations is vital for students of business and managers alike.

Learning outcomes

Having read this chapter you should be able to:

- explain the political context within which business operates
- demonstrate the relevance of political values to the organisation of business activity
- identify and discuss key political institutions and processes at a variety of spatial levels
- illustrate how business organisations can influence, as well as be influenced by, the political environment

Key terms

Authoritarianism	First-past-the-post system	Politics
Backbench MPs	Government	Presidential system of
Bureaucrats	Government departments	government
Cabinet	House of Commons	Pressure groups
Checks and balances	House of Lords	Prime Minister
Civil servants	Judiciary	Professional lobbyist
Coalition government	Legislature	Proportional representation
Constitution	Lobbies	Qualified majority vote (qmv)
Council of Ministers	Manifesto	Recommendations and
Decisions	MEPs	opinions
Democracy	Ministers	Referendums
Direct (or pure) democracy	MPs	Regulations
Directives	Parliament	Representative government
Directorates-General	Parliamentary system	Secretary of State
Electoral system	of government	Separation of powers
European Commission	Plebiscites	Sovereignty
European Council	Political accountability	Supreme Court
European Court of Justice	Political executive	The Council of the European
European Parliament	Political parties	Union
Federal system of government	Political sovereignty	Unitary system of government

Introduction

In February 2013, the US and European Union announced a plan to open up negotiations on establishing a transatlantic free trade pact aimed at eliminating or minimising barriers to trade across all key industries from agriculture and pharmaceuticals to vehicles, services and investment. Faced with the growing influence of China in the global trading environment and the impact of the global recession in many of the world's leading economies, the proposed trade agreement was seen as a way of boosting economic performance in the participant countries and of circumventing the long-running stalemate in the Doha round of the world trade talks. Despite widespread support from political and business leaders on both sides of the Atlantic, it is accepted that establishing such a comprehensive trade pact will not be easy and will be affected by a variety of economic and political factors, including national interests and the electoral cycle (e.g. European elections in 2014). The expectation is that any agreement will take at least two years to negotiate and will require some concessions by both parties if the anticipated economic and commercial benefits are to be achieved.

What this simple example reminds us is that business activity takes place not only within but also across state boundaries and frequently involves governments, whether directly or indirectly, in shaping the business environment. Consequently the political and economic arrangements within the state in which a business is located and/or with which it is trading can have a fundamental impact on its operations – even to the extent of determining whether it is willing, or in some cases able, to trade at all. It is this politico-economic context within which businesses function and the philosophical foundations on which it is based that are the focus of this and the following chapter.

As a prelude to a detailed analysis of the political environment, it is necessary to make a number of general observations regarding political change and uncertainty and the impact on business activity. First, the nature of a country's political system – including its governmental institutions – tends to reflect certain underlying social values and philosophies which help to determine how decisions are made, including decisions about the allocation of resources. Thus, while governments may come and go, the values on which their decisions are based tend to be more enduring and as a result disputes normally centre around 'means' (e.g. sources of revenue) rather than 'ends' (e.g. controlling inflation). While this gives a certain degree of stability to the business environment, this stability cannot be taken for granted, as events in eastern Europe and the Middle East have readily demonstrated. In short, the political environment of business is a dynamic environment, containing elements of both continuity and change, and students and practitioners of business alike need to be constantly aware of developments in this area if they are to gain a greater insight into the background of business decision-making.

Second, changes in the political environment also emanate from a country's institutional arrangements. The tendency in democratic states, for example, to have regular elections, competing political parties offering alternative policies and a system of pressure groups helps to generate a degree of discontinuity, which renders predictions about the future more uncertain. For a business, such uncertainty can create not only opportunities but also a degree of risk which will often be an important influence on its decisions. Moreover, given that perceptions of such risks (or opportunities) are also normally reflected in the attitudes and behaviour of a country's financial and other markets, this represents a further variable that at times can be critical for an organisation's future prospects. For many businesses, taking steps to maximise opportunities (or to minimise risk) may ultimately make the difference between short-term failure and long-term survival.

Third, it is important to emphasise that political influences are not restricted to national boundaries – a point emphasised by the opening paragraph to this chapter and by the increasing importance of international and supranational groupings such as the G8 nations, the European Union and the World Trade Organisation, all of which are discussed below. These external politico-economic influences form part of the environment in which a country's governmental institutions take decisions, and their impact on domestic policy and on business activity can often be fundamental. No discussion of the business environment would be complete without an analysis of their role and impact, particularly in shaping international political and economic relationships.

Fourth, the precise impact of political factors on a business tends to vary to some degree according to the type of organisation involved. Multinational corporations – operating on a global scale – will be more concerned with questions such as the stability of overseas political regimes than will the small local firm operating in a localised market, where the primary concern will be with local market conditions. That said, there will undoubtedly be occasions when even locally based enterprises will be affected either directly or indirectly by political developments in other parts of the globe – as in the case of an interruption in supplies or the cancellation of a foreign order in which a small business is involved as a subcontractor. In short, while some broad generalisations can be made about the impact of global (or domestic) political developments on an individual organisation, each case is to some extent unique in both space and time, and observers of the business scene need to be cautious and open-minded in their analysis if they are to avoid the twin dangers of oversimplification and empiricism.

Finally, it needs to be recognised that businesses are not merely reactive to changes in the political environment, they can also help to shape the political context in which they operate and can influence government decision-makers, often in a way that is beneficial to their own perceived needs. One of the hallmarks of **democracy** is the right of individuals and groups to seek to influence government, and businesses – both individually and collectively – have been active in this sphere for centuries. It would be a mistake to underestimate their impact on government policy or on the shaping of values in the established capitalist nations of western Europe and elsewhere.

Political systems

The nature of political activity

All social situations at certain times require decisions to be made between alternative courses of action. Parents may disagree with their offspring about the kind of clothes they wear or how late they stay out at night or how long they grow their hair. Students may challenge lecturers about a particular perspective on an issue or when they should submit a piece of work. The members of the board of directors of a company may have different views about future investment or diversification or the location of a new factory. In all these cases, some solution needs to be found, even if the eventual decision is to do nothing. It is the processes involved in arriving at a solution to a problem, where a conflict of opinion occurs, that are the very essence of political activity.

Politics, in short, is concerned with those processes that help to determine how conflicts are contained, modified, postponed or settled, and as such can be seen as a universal social activity. Hence, individuals often talk of 'office politics' or the 'politics of the board room' or the 'mediating role' played by a parent in the event of a family dispute. For most individuals, however, the term 'politics' tends to be associated with activities at state level, where the resolution of conflict often involves large numbers of people and may even involve individuals in other states. Political activity at this level is clearly qualitatively different from the other social situations mentioned, and given the scale and complexity of the modern state, the problems requiring solutions can often be acute and chronic. Solving those problems tends to be seen, at least in part, as the function of government.

Government as a process is concerned with the pursuit and exercise of power – the power to make decisions which affect the lives of substantial numbers of people, be it at local, regional, national or even international level. Government may also refer to the institutions through which power tends to be formally and legitimately exercised, whether they be cabinets, parliaments, councils, committees or congresses. Whereas the pursuit and exercise of power tends to be an enduring feature of any society, governments are normally transitory, comprising those individuals and/or groups who, at a particular time, have the responsibility for controlling the state, including making laws for 'the good of society'. How governments exercise their power and the ideological foundations on which this is based helps to indicate the nature of the political system and its likely approaches to the resolution of conflicts.

Authoritarian political systems

Broadly speaking, political systems can be seen to range across two extremes, on the one hand authoritarian and on the other democratic. In an **authoritarian** political system the disposition is to settle conflicts through the enforcement of rules, regulations and orders by an established authority. This authority may be an individual (e.g. a monarch or other powerful individual) or a group of individuals (e.g. a political party or military junta) which may have assumed political power in a variety of ways (e.g. by birth, election or coup). Once in power, the individual or group will tend to act so as to limit the degree of participation by others in the process of decision-making, even to the extent of monopolising the process altogether and permitting no opposition to occur. Where this is the case, a society is often described as being 'totalitarian' and is perhaps best exemplified by Nazi Germany and Stalinist Russia.

Democratic political systems

In contrast, in a democratic political system, the assumption is that as far as possible conflicts should be resolved by rational discussions between the various parties concerned, with the final solution being accepted voluntarily by all participants, even if they disagree. At one extreme, such consultation may involve all individuals, who have – in theory at least – equal influence over the final outcome (e.g. as in **referendums** or **plebiscites**).

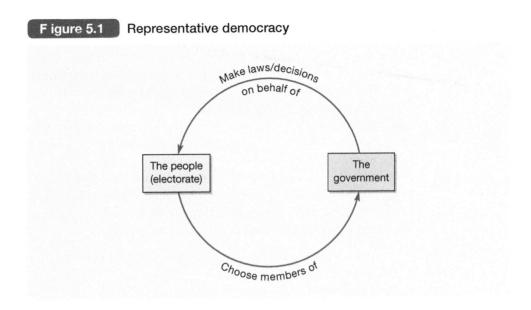

F igure 5.1   Representative democracy

Given the scale and complexity of modern states, however, such examples of **direct (or pure) democracy** tend to be rare and it is invariably the case that the democratic solution to conflict resolution is achieved 'indirectly' through a system of political representation and responsibility. Under such a system, the wishes and views of individuals are said to be represented in an established authority (e.g. a government) that has normally been chosen by the people and is accountable (responsible) to them at regular intervals through a variety of mechanisms, including regular and free elections (see Figure 5.1). Implicit in this, of course, is the requirement that individuals are able to change this authority and select another individual or group to represent them. Monopolisation of political power by any one individual or group can only occur, therefore, with the expressed consent of the people.

Government in democratic states

Democratic institutions and processes

Democracy means far more than just popular government or a system of regular elections; the democratic approach to government implies the existence of a complex array of institutions and processes through which the wishes of the people are articulated and carried out. While the specific institutional arrangements tend to vary between states, countries that are held to be democratic invariably have a political system which comprises four common and interlocking elements: an electoral system, a party system, a representative assembly and a system for the articulation of sectional interests. The generic roles of these major building blocks of democratic government are discussed below. Location-specific information on how the system operates in a national (i.e. United Kingdom) and a supranational (i.e. European Union) context can be found in the appendices to this chapter. Non-UK readers are encouraged to substitute their own political arrangements for those described in the appendices.

The electoral system

As indicated above, in a representative democracy the **electoral system** links the people (the electorate) with government; it is through elections that a country's citizens periodically get to choose who will exercise the power to make decisions which will ultimately shape the lives of individuals. Elections, in short, are a vital ingredient of a **representative system of government**. That said, the fact that elections exist in a particular country is not a sufficient guarantee that it is democratic in the accepted sense of the word.

In order to operate in a way that is normally regarded as democratic, a country's electoral system would need to exhibit a number of features which suggest that the wishes of individual citizens – as expressed through the ballot box – are reasonably reflected in the choice of government. Such features would include:

- a system of regular elections (e.g. every four to five years) based on universal adult suffrage;
- basic freedoms of speech, movement, assembly, etc.;
- freedom from coercion and the absence of illegal electoral practices;
- a secret ballot;
- free media.

Where conditions such as these are absent or are not fully operational, there will always be a suspicion that the electoral outcome may not be a true reflection of the wishes of the people. The act of voting, in other words, needs to be accompanied by a set of legal prescriptions that provides some kind of guarantee that an election to choose part, if not all, of the government is both free and fair.

To be democratic the electoral system must not only be transparent, it must also ensure that the wishes of the majority – as expressed through the number of votes cast – are reflected in the final result. In a **first-past-the-post system** (e.g. in most current UK elections) a simple majority is sufficient to ensure victory; as a consequence some winning candidates may be elected with fewer than half of the votes cast. Where a system of **proportional representation** operates (e.g. in many other European countries) a redistribution of votes occurs when there is no outright winner, resulting in a final decision that can be said to more closely represent the wishes of the whole electorate. While the intricacies of different electoral systems are beyond the scope of this book, it is worth observing that the voting system a country uses can have important ramifications for the government elected to office. On the whole, a plurality or first-past-the-post system of voting usually – though not inevitably (e.g. the 2010 election in the UK) – results in majority government, with a single party dominating the organs of decision-making and able to pursue its legislative programme relatively free from constraint by the losing side(s). In contrast, where a proportional representation system is used, the result is often a **coalition government** made up of different parties, some of which may hold significantly or even radically different views from the largest party within the coalition. In effect, coalition government is predominantly a matter of negotiation, accommodation and compromise, an exercise in consensus building and persuasion, as commonly found in most types of organisational setting, including the business world.

The party system

While it is possible to have democratic government in a one-party state, democracy is normally taken to imply that citizens get to choose between alternative candidates when casting their vote at an election. Invariably such candidates tend to represent different **political parties** and to this extent a vote for a specific candidate can be said to equate to a vote for the party that he or she represents and which is ultimately hoping to form the government.

The existence of political parties, which compete for office at election time, is clearly a convenient – if sometimes questionable – means of organising a system of representative democracy; hence the universality of party systems in democratic states and the relative lack of candidates standing with no party tag at governmental elections at all spatial levels. Parties not only help to choose most of the candidates who compete in these elections, they usually also support and sustain them (e.g. financially) before, during and after the election campaign and help to organise a system of (largely unpaid) volunteers to work to get them elected, as well as providing candidates with a platform of policies on which to stand for office. Whereas some of these activities tend to be the responsibility of the party at national level, others are undertaken at a regional and/or local level, often in the constituency (i.e. geographical area) that a candidate represents. Since questions of organisation, policy-making and finance are central to the operation and success of a political party in modern democratic states, party structures have tended to become complex, bureaucratic, multi-layered and increasingly professionalised. As in other types of organisational framework, they also provide an arena in which a substantial degree of in-fighting occurs between individuals of different temperaments, views and ambitions who are seeking to push the party in a particular direction.

From the electors' point of view, one of the primary benefits of the party system is that it provides a means of selecting political leaders and the kind of policies they are likely to pursue if the party achieves political office. Describing candidates by a party label (e.g. Democratic, Republican, Socialist, Conservative, Liberal, etc.) allows voters to choose those candidates whose views most closely represent their own, given that parties normally have an identifiable policy stance and produce some form of statement (or **manifesto**) outlining their policy preferences during an election campaign. Thus, while an individual elector is unlikely to agree with every single policy or proposed piece of legislation that a party puts forward in its attempts to gain office, he/she is at least able to express a preference between alternative approaches to government at the ballot box. To that extent it can be argued that there is likely to be a degree of congruence between the legislative programme of the party democratically elected to form the government and the wishes of the people who elected it, albeit that in some cases the government may have received less than 50 per cent of the popular vote.

It is worth remembering that party labels are not always a good guide to the policy or legislative preferences of individual candidates, since someone described as a 'Democrat' or 'Liberal' in one part of a country may hold radically different views on a range of issues from others of the same title elected to constituencies in other areas. If anything, identifying election candidates in party political terms gives voters a broad indication of the underlying values and beliefs to which an individual subscribes:

parties in practice are always destined to be (sometimes fragile) coalitions of groups and individuals representing a range of opinions and preferences under a party banner.

A representative assembly

As previously indicated, one of the key features of democratic government is the existence of a representative decision-making body, a group of individuals chosen by a country's citizens to help make important decisions on their behalf. In the same way that shareholders in a public company elect directors to guide the organisation and to represent their interest, voters at election time choose individuals they wish to represent them in government in the various organs of decision-making and policy implementation (see below). While not everyone chosen by the electorate becomes part of the small group of key decision-makers (the government or **political executive**), all normally have some kind of role to play in the decision-making process and usually get an opportunity to scrutinise policy and legislative proposals put forward by the governing element and to vote upon them. The fact that the electorate periodically has the opportunity to express its opinion on the performance of the incumbent decision-makers – and where necessary to replace them – provides for a degree of **political accountability**, a central tenet of a democratic system of government.

As more than two centuries of political theory have demonstrated, the concept of representation can have at least two meanings: decision-makers may represent the views of their constituents in the literal sense that they articulate them in or to government, or they may simply represent them in so far as they have been elected by a majority (simple or otherwise) of voters to be the representative of a geographical area. In practice, both these interpretations of representation can be seen to operate at different times, according to the predispositions of individual decision-makers and the influences emanating from the prevailing political culture in a country, region or area. For example, in a system of government where national political parties are relatively weak and where an individual's success in elections depends very much on supporting policies that are consistent with those of significant elements in one's electorate (e.g. in the United States), representation tends to be seen in the more literal sense of supporting local views and preferences. In contrast, where there is a strong party system and where individuals are held to be elected on the basis of party affiliation (e.g. the United Kingdom), elected representatives are generally expected to be loyal to the party in a policy sense, even if on occasion this results in a conflict with the views of the majority of one's constituents.

In modern democratic states the model of representative decision-making usually operates at all spatial levels. In Europe, for example, voters not only elect their own national governments but also choose decision-makers at a local and/or regional level and many European citizens are also able to vote in elections for pan-European institutions. One of the consequences of this arrangement is that sometimes the party (or parties) elected to office at national level may be different from that (or those) in power locally, regionally and/or supranationally. Where this occurs, clashes between decision-makers representing different geographical areas tend to be inevitable and can give rise to problems of decision-making and policy implementation, thus potentially disrupting the programme on which a government has been elected to office.

In this context a useful distinction can be drawn between a **federal** and a **unitary system of government**. In the former, **sovereignty** (i.e. the legitimate power to make decisions) is divided between two levels of government (e.g. national and local/regional), each with independent powers that are usually laid down in a written constitution which is interpreted by the courts. Thus, in the United States, education is in the hands of the elected government at state (i.e. subnational) level, while defence and foreign affairs are federal (i.e. national) governmental responsibilities. In Germany, the federal government similarly has exclusive jurisdiction over foreign and defence policy and environmental protection, while the Länder (states) control such areas as education and the police.

In contrast, under a unitary system ultimate authority rests with the national government and any powers granted to subnational levels by the central sovereign authority can ultimately be rescinded, including the right of government at subnational level to exist. Under such an arrangement – particularly where it is written down in the form of a **constitution** – government at national level clearly holds the whip hand and would normally expect its view to prevail where a dispute over an issue or policy occurs between it and a subnational authority. That said, decision-makers in democratic states at all levels and under different governmental systems have, on the whole, a tendency to settle such conflicts through negotiation, bargaining and compromise rather than by exerting their power and authority, although this might be used on occasions. This predisposition goes some way to explaining why in democratic systems of government, the policies and legislative programmes of elected governments are much more likely to be incremental than they are to be radical.

mini case   Brought to book

Politicians can have a significant impact on business activity at both the macro and micro levels. In addition to making decisions on how the economy should be managed overall, elected representatives can make or propose changes to regulations and legislation which affect how businesses operate, what they can and cannot do, and how they treat their employees, customers, suppliers and so on.

An illustration of how the political environment can potentially shape a firm's operations can be seen in the decision made by French MPs in October 2013 to support a bill to curb the discounting power of the globally influential company Amazon. Concerned that small, independent bookstores were facing unfair competition from the US giant, MPs from across all parties voted for a measure aimed at preventing Amazon from combining free delivery with 5 per cent discounts on books. Since 1981, France has had a law that establishes fixed book prices so that customers effectively pay the same for a book however or from wherever it is purchased, with extensive discounting banned. French legislators believe that small bookstores should be treated as a 'cultural exception' and should, if necessary, be protected from the kind of experiences suffered by UK independent book retailers when fixed prices were abandoned back in the 1990s.

A system for articulating sectional interests

Elections and a party system provide one way in which the views of an individual can be represented in government; an alternative is via **pressure group** activity. Like competing political parties, the existence of pressure groups is usually regarded as an important indicator of a democratic system of government. For many citizens in democratic countries, joining such a group is seen as a much more effective way of influencing government than through the party system.

Whereas political parties seek influence by formally contesting political office, pressure groups seek to influence government in other ways, although this distinction is increasingly becoming blurred. In essence, pressure groups (or **lobbies**) are collections of like-minded people who have voluntarily joined together to try to influence government thinking and behaviour and to represent the interests of their members. Nowadays, many of these groups are highly organised and are powerful bodies, supported by substantial funding and formidable research facilities. Such groups (frequently referred to as non-governmental or civic society organisations) provide a vehicle through which a collective and non-party political view can be articulated in decision-making circles; as such they can be said to operate as a kind of safety valve within a democratic system of government.

Traditionally in pressure group literature, a distinction tends to be drawn between groups which represent 'somebody' and those that represent 'something'. The former are usually referred to as 'interest groups' or 'protective groups' and would include groups representing a particular section of the community, such as trade unions or professional associations. The latter tend to be known as 'cause groups' or 'issue groups', as exemplified by Greenpeace, Amnesty International and the various animal rights groups. In practice, of course, it is often difficult to make such a clear-cut distinction, given that some interest groups such as trade unions often associate themselves with particular causes and may campaign vigorously alongside other groups in support of or against the issue concerned.

> **web link**
>
> Most large pressure groups have websites offering useful information. Greenpeace, for example, can be accessed at *www.greenpeace.org*

From a governmental point of view the existence of structures for articulating sectional interests is seen as an aid to efficient and representative decision-making. Pressure groups not only provide government with detailed information on specific areas of everyday activity without which rational decision-making would be difficult, they also fulfil a number of other important functions in a democratic system. These would include:

- helping to defend minority interests;
- assisting in the implementation of government policy and legislation;
- providing for continuity in communication and consultation between the governors and the governed between elections.

The successful introduction of reforms in a country's health service, for example, is dependent upon support from the various arms of the medical profession and from organisations representing the different interests of health service workers. Similarly, the effectiveness of government economic policies, and their subsequent impact on the business community, will be conditioned at least in part by the reactions of groups representing large employers, small and medium enterprises, workers, financial interests, etc., as well as by individual entrepreneurs and consumers.

This relative interdependence between government and pressure groups under a democratic system is exemplified by the practice of prior consultation; this is the arrangement whereby the elected government actively seeks the views of interested parties during the policy and/or legislative process. Such consultation may be 'formal' (e.g. where a group has representation on an advisory or executive body or where it is invited to offer its views on a proposal) or 'informal' (e.g. off-the-record meetings between representatives of the group and the government) or a mixture of the two; it may also involve a group in hiring the services of a **professional lobbyist** – often a former politician or bureaucrat familiar with the structure of decision-making in government and with access to key decision-makers (see the case study at the end of this chapter). Groups that are regularly consulted and whose opinion is readily sought by government may acquire 'insider status' and may even be incorporated into the formal decision-making process – prizes that are highly valued since they imply that the group has a legitimate right to be consulted by government prior to deciding on a particular course of action or inaction. In comparison, 'outsider groups' often find it difficult to make their voice heard in decision-making circles and for this reason may be forced to resort to different forms of direct action in order to publicise their views in the wider community in the hope of gaining influence through public sympathy and support.

As this discussion of 'insider' and 'outsider' groups illustrates, pressure groups can use a variety of methods to attract support for their cause or to protect and promote the interests of their members. These range from direct lobbying of government to marches, strikes, disruption and other forms of demonstrative action designed to attract media and hence public attention – although frequently such action can have an adverse effect. In addition, some of the larger and better-resourced groups may employ experts to advise on policy issues and/or establish their own research facilities to provide information to strengthen their case (e.g. Greenpeace).

What method(s) a group employs and where it seeks to bring its influence to bear tends to vary from issue to issue and group to group, and generally reflects not only differences in group status and resources but also the structure of decision-making within the policy community concerned. In the United States, for instance, direct lobbying of Congressmen/women is a common tactic used by pressure groups, given the relative weakness of the party system and the tendency for an individual's electoral fortunes to be tied up with the views of key groups in the constituency. In the United Kingdom, the pressures of party discipline, the domination of the executive branch of government and the influence of senior civil servants tend to make direct appeals to key actors in government a more effective method of achieving political influence than operating at constituency level.

As a final comment it is worth recalling that decisions in a democracy may be made locally, nationally, supranationally or internationally and often require cooperation between different levels of government and/or between different agencies and arms of government at both the formulation and the implementation stages. Accordingly, pressure groups are increasingly to be found operating at the interface between the institutions of government and across the whole range of spatial levels from the local to the global. Given the large number of pressure points where vested interests can bring their influence to bear, it tends to be easier for a group to prevent or limit government action than to persuade decision-makers to change the direction of policy. To this extent policy formulation and implementation in democratic states is perhaps best portrayed as the 'art of the possible' rather than the 'science of the desirable'.

The three branches or functions of government

In a broad sense the process of governing involves three major activities: making decisions, putting them into effect and adjudicating over them in the event of dispute or non-compliance. Each of these functions or branches of government, as they operate at a national level, is discussed in turn below. A similar form of analysis could, if necessary, be applied at other spatial levels.

The legislative function

Governing, as we have seen, is about making decisions which affect the lives of large numbers of people. Some of these decisions require new laws or changes to existing laws to bring them into effect so that the individuals and/or groups to whom they apply become aware of the government's wishes and requirements. In a democratic system of government this formal power to make the law (i.e. to legislate) is vested in a legislative body (the **legislature**) which is elected either wholly or partly by the people. As indicated above, this process of choosing a representative decision-making body by popular election is a central feature of the democratic approach to government.

Leaving aside for one moment the relative power of the legislative and executive branches of government, it is possible to identify a number of common features that apply to legislatures and the legislative function in most, if not all, democratic states. These include the following:

A *bicameral legislature,* that is, a legislature with two chambers: an upper house and a lower house, each with specific powers and roles in the legislative process. In most countries each chamber comprises representatives chosen by a separate electoral process and hence may be dominated by the same party or different parties or by no single party, depending on the electoral outcome. For a legislative proposal to be accepted, the consent of both chambers is normally required. This is one of the many **checks and balances** normally found in democratic systems of government (see below).

A *multi-stage legislative process,* involving the drafting of a legislative proposal, its discussion and consideration, and where necessary amendment, further debate and consideration and ultimate acceptance or rejection by either or both legislative chambers. Debates on the general principles of a proposed piece of legislation would normally involve all members of each chamber, whereas detailed discussion tends to take place in smaller groups or committees.

An *executive-led process,* that is, one in which most major legislative proposals emanate from the executive branch of government. In a **presidential system of government** (e.g. the USA), the chief executive (the president) is normally elected separately by the people and is not part of the legislature (in other words, there is a **separation of powers**). In a **parliamentary system of government** (e.g. the UK), members of the executive may also be members of the legislative body and hence may be in a position to control the legislative process.

Opportunities for legislative initiatives by ordinary representatives, that is, arangements that permit ordinary members of the legislative assembly to propose new laws or changes to existing laws. In practice such opportunities tend to be limited and dependent to a large degree for their success on a positive response from the political executive.

Opportunities to criticise and censure the government and, in some cases, remove it from office (e.g. through impeachment) – this is a vital function within a democratic system of government in that it forces decision-makers to defend their proposals, explain the logic of their actions and account for any mistakes they may have made. Opposition parties play an important role in this context within the legislative body and through media coverage can attack the government and articulate alternative views to the wider public. Specialist and standing committees for scrutinising legislation and the day-to-day work of the executive branch of government also usually exist in democratic regimes.

Control of the purse strings, that is, the power to grant or deny government the money required to carry out its policies and legislative programme. In theory this is a formidable power, given that no government can operate without funds. In practice the power of the legislature to deny funding to a democratically elected government may be more apparent than real and, where necessary, compromise tends to occur between the executive and legislative branches of government.

mini case   The power of the purse

In 2013 the Republican-led US House of Representatives used its constitutional power to impose an annual borrowing limit on the US Treasury aimed at reducing the size of the country's budget deficit. In what was widely seen as an attempt to derail President Obama's healthcare reforms, the House set a debt ceiling limit that would be insufficient to cover the President's budgetary requirements, including the interest on public borrowings that were becoming due for repayment. The threat that the USA would become technically bankrupt during October of that year – with potentially serious consequences for the recovery of the global economy – set alarm bells ringing in financial markets and led to calls from international bodies including the IMF for urgent action to find a way around the impasse that had developed between the White House and Congress.

Pending a solution to the crisis, the US government laid off hundreds of thousands of federal employees, a decision which affected not only the provision of public services but also many of the businesses dependent on the spending of the state and its employees. In Washington, for example, a wide range of smaller businesses – including hairdressers, taxi firms, cafes and restaurants – experienced a sudden loss of trade as their pool of regular customers declined substantially. For these business owners, the threat of a prolonged period of declining revenues was far more important than esoteric discussions about the appropriate level at which to set the country's debt ceiling.

Since a great deal of media coverage of the issue at the time understandably focused on the partisan roots of the problem and on possible compromises, it is easy to forget that both action and inaction by political decision-makers almost invariably has consequences for a country's citizens and its businesses. As the next chapter demonstrates, decisions on taxing and spending by government have a major impact on the economy at both the macro and micro levels; spending and income are after all opposite sides of the same coin.

As will be evident from the comments above, legislating is a complex and time-consuming process, offering numerous opportunities for individuals and groups both within and outside the legislative body (e.g. pressure groups) to delay and disrupt the passage of legislation. While no government can guarantee to achieve all its legislative aims, there is a cultural expectation in a democracy that, as far as possible, promises made before an election will be put into effect at the earliest opportunity by the democratically elected government. Such an expectation usually provides the incumbent administration with a powerful argument for legislative support on the occasions when it is confronted with intransigence within the legislative assembly or with hostility from outside sectional interests.

The executive function

Governing is not only about making decisions, it is also about ensuring that these decisions are put into effect in order to achieve the government's objectives. Implementing governmental decisions is the responsibility of the executive branch of government.

In modern states the term 'the executive' refers to that relatively small group of individuals chosen to decide on policy and to oversee its implementation; some of these individuals will hold political office, others will be career administrators and advisers, although some of the latter may also be political appointees. Together they are part of a complex political and administrative structure designed to carry out the essential work of government and to ensure that those responsible for policy-making and implementation are ultimately accountable for their actions.

The policy-making aspect of the executive function is normally the responsibility of a small political executive chosen (wholly or in part) by popular election. Under a presidential system of government, the chief executive or president is usually chosen by separate election for a given period of office and becomes both the nominal and political head of state. He/she subsequently appoints individuals to head the various government departments/ministries/bureaux which are responsible for shaping and implementing government policy. Neither the president nor the heads of departments normally sit in the legislative assembly, although there are sometimes exceptions to this rule (e.g. the Vice-President in the United States).

In contrast, in a parliamentary system the roles of head of state and head of government are separated, with the former usually largely ceremonial and carried out by either a president (e.g. Germany, India) or a monarch (e.g. UK, Japan). The head of government (e.g. prime minister), while officially appointed by the head of state, is an elected politician, invariably the head of the party victorious in a general election or at least seen to be capable of forming a government, possibly in coalition with other parties. Once appointed, the head of government chooses other individuals to head the different government departments/ministries and to be part of a collective decision-making body (e.g. a **Cabinet**) which meets to sanction policy proposals put forward through a system of executive committees and subcommittees (e.g. Cabinet committees). These individuals, along with the head of government, are not only part of the executive machinery of the state but also usually members of the legislative assembly and both 'individually' and 'collectively' responsible to the legislature for the work of government.

The day-to-day administration of government policy is largely carried out by non-elected government officials (sometimes referred to as **civil servants** or **bureaucrats**), who work for the most part in complex, bureaucratic organisations within the state bureaucracy. Apart from their role in implementing public policy, government officials help to advise **ministers** on the different policy options and on the political and administrative aspects of particular courses of action. Needless to say, this gives them a potentially critical role in shaping government policy, a role which has been substantially enhanced over the years by the practice of granting officials a significant degree of discretion in deciding on the details of particular policies and/or on how they should be administered.

Whereas politicians in the executive branch of government tend to be transitory figures – who come and go at the whim of the head of government or of the electorate – most, if not all, officials are permanent, professional appointees who may serve a variety of governments of different political complexions and preferences during a long career in public administration. Whatever government is in power, officials are generally expected to operate in a non-partisan (i.e. neutral) way when advising their political masters and when overseeing the implementation of government policy. Their loyalty in short is to the current administration in office, a principle which helps to ensure a smooth transition of government and to guarantee that the upheaval caused by a general election does not prevent the business of the state from being carried out as usual.

The judicial function

Governing is not just about making and implementing laws, it is also about ensuring that they are applied and enforced. The latter is essentially the role of the third arm of government, namely the **judiciary** and the system of courts. Like political institutions, legal structures and processes tend to a degree to be country specific and vary according to a number of influences, including history, culture and politics. For example, while some states have a relatively unified legal system, others organised on a federal basis usually have a system of parallel courts adjudicating on federal and state/provincial law, with a **Supreme Court** arbitrating in the event of a dispute. In some countries a proportion of the judges may be directly or indirectly elected by the public, in others they may be appointed by government and/or co-opted by fellow judges. Business students should make themselves familiar with the legal arrangements within their own country. In this section we look briefly at the judicial function as related to the concept of democracy.

Whereas in totalitarian systems of government the judiciary is essentially the servant of the ruling élite (e.g. the 'party'), in a democracy it is an accepted principle that there should be a separation between the judicial function and the other two branches of government in order to protect the citizen from a too-powerful state. This notion of an impartial and independent judiciary, free to challenge the government and to review its decisions, is regarded as one of the hallmarks of a democratic system of government, a further manifestation of the doctrine of the separation of powers.

In practice, of course, notions of judicial independence and role within the democratic political process tend to be the subject of a certain amount of debate, particularly in countries where senior appointments to the judiciary appear to be in the gift of politicians (e.g. Supreme Court judges in the United States are nominated by the President with the consent of the Senate) or where individuals with judicial powers also have an executive and/or legislative role (e.g. the Home Secretary in Britain). Equally there are questions over the degree to which the courts should have the power to review the constitutionality of decisions made by a democratically elected government. In the United States, for example, the Supreme Court has a long-established right to declare a law void if it conflicts with its own interpretation of the American constitution. In Britain, the legal sovereignty of Parliament and the absence of a codified written constitution push the judiciary towards trying to interpret the intentions of the framers of government legislation and any legal decision unwelcomed by the government can be reversed by further legislation. That said, it is interesting to note that in recent years there has been an increased willingness on the part of the British judiciary to review administrative decisions, particularly those made by ministers.

Other aspects, too, call into question how far in modern democratic states there is a total separation between the different arms of government (e.g. increasing use of administrative courts/tribunals) and whether it makes sense to rigidly distinguish between rule making and rule adjudication. Certainly some of the past judgments by the United States Supreme Court (e.g. in the area of civil rights) demonstrate that the courts can be influential in shaping decisions on major issues of policy and suggest that the judiciary are susceptible to influences from their own values or to general societal pressures. In short, it seems fair to suggest that under current legal arrangements, legal adjudication is not far removed from the world of politics; arguably we may like to perpetuate the myth of an entirely separate and independent judiciary since this is a necessary aspect of the stability of many existing political systems.

Checks and balances in democracies

As will be evident from the analysis above, democracy implies the existence of a system of checks and balances, arrangements which serve to curb government action and restrict its influence on the day-to-day lives of its citizens. These restraints on the actions of the state at national level can be divided into two main types: political and social/economic.

Political checks and balances emanate primarily from three main sources:

- the separation of powers – particularly the notion that the three arms of government are in separate hands and that decisions require the concurrence of all branches of government;
- a bicameral legislature – with legislation having to be accepted by both houses and subject to scrutiny and amendment by opposition parties;
- the territorial division of powers – whether under a federal arrangement or through the devolution of power to regional bodies and/or local authorities. Supranationalism is a further development.

The point is not that these arrangements necessarily exist in their most complete form in democratic states but that – however imperfect in practice – their existence helps to provide time for reflection and delay in the decision-making process and to encourage consultation, negotiation and consensus building, the essence of the democratic approach to conflict resolution.

The notion of social and economic checks and balances refers to those countervailing pressures on the activities of the state and its agencies that derive from the existence of non-state structures and processes which affect the lives of individuals and which ultimately restrict the scope of government influence. These include private business organisations, professional associations, promotional bodies, churches and other groups which help to shape our economic, social and moral environment. As subsequent chapters will demonstrate, the bulk of economic decisions in democratic states are not taken by the government but by private individuals and organisations (i.e. firms) interacting through a market system. This acts as a kind of check and balance on the free activity of the public sector and is a fundamental characteristic of democratic government.

A model of the policy process

It is appropriate to conclude this examination of the political environment with a brief discussion of the process of governmental decision-making in democratic systems. Here, the basic model of the organisation in its environment introduced in Chapter 1 serves as a useful analytical tool (see Figure 5.2). Governments, like firms, are organisations which transform inputs into output and they do so in an environment largely the same as that which confronts other types of enterprise. Like other organisations, government is a user of resources, especially land, labour, capital, finance and expertise, but in addition all governments face political demands and supports when considering their policy options.

As indicated above, political demands – including those directly or indirectly impinging on business activity – become translated into action through a variety of mechanisms, including the electoral system, party activity, pressure group influence and political communication; hence a government is always keen to point out that electoral victory implies that it has a mandate for its policies. The supports of the political system are those customs, conventions, rules, assumptions and sentiments that provide a basis for the existence of the political community and its constituent parts and thus give legitimacy to the actions and existence of the incumbent government. In democratic systems, the belief in democratic principles, and the doctrines and practices emanating from that belief, are seen as central to the activities of government and its agencies.

The outputs of the political system vary considerably and range from public goods and services (e.g. healthcare) – provided predominantly from money raised through taxation – to rules and regulations (e.g. legislation, administrative procedures, directives) and transfer payments (i.e. where the government acts as a reallocator of resources, as in the case of the provision of state benefits). Taken together, the nature, range and extent of government output not only tend to make government the single biggest business in a state, they also influence the environment in which other businesses operate and increasingly in which other governments make decisions.

F igure 5.2   Government and its environment

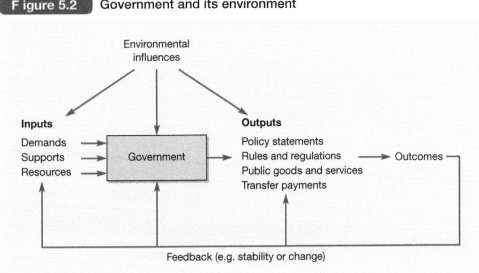

As far as governmental decision-making is concerned, this is clearly a highly complex process which in practice does not replicate the simple sequence of events suggested by the model. Certainly governments require 'means' (inputs) to achieve 'ends' (outputs), but the outputs of the political system normally emerge only after a complex, varied and ongoing process involving a wide range of individuals, groups and agencies. To add further confusion, those involved in the process tend to vary according to the decision under discussion as well as over time, making analysis fraught with difficulties. One possible solution may be to distinguish between the early development of a policy proposal ('initiation') and its subsequent 'formulation' and 'implementation', in the hope that a discernible 'policy community' can be identified at each stage. But even this approach involves a degree of guesswork and arbitrary decision-making, not least because of the difficulty of distinguishing precisely between the different stages of policy-making and of discerning the influence of individuals and groups at each phase of the process.

Notwithstanding these difficulties, it is important for students of business and for businesses themselves to have some understanding of the structure of decision-making, and of the underlying values and beliefs that tend to shape governmental action, if they are to appreciate (and possibly influence) the political environment in which they exist. Studies of political systems, institutions and processes help to provide insight into how and why government decisions are made, who is important in shaping those decisions and how influence can be brought to bear on the decision-making process. As an increasing number of individuals and groups recognise, knowledge of this kind can prove a valuable organisational resource that on occasions is of no less significance than the other inputs into the productive process.

Synopsis

Laws and policies that influence business activity are made by politicians and bureaucrats, operating at a variety of spatial levels. In democracies, decisions by governmental policy-makers emanate from a complex process of discussion and negotiation involving a range of formal and informal institutions, including political parties and pressure groups, and frequently involving international and supranational bodies. This process is part of the democratic approach to decision-making and provides opportunities for individuals and groups to influence government thinking on both the formulation and implementation of policy and legislation. Students of business and managers need to have a broad understanding of this political environment in order to appreciate one of the key influences on a firm's operations.

Summary of key points

- Politics is a universal activity that affects businesses of all types and sizes.

- It occurs at a variety of spatial levels from the local to the global.

- Political systems, structures and processes reflect underlying social values and philosophies and these influence the ways in which major decisions are taken.

- In any democratic system of government the key political institutions are likely to include an electoral system, a party system, a representative decision-making assembly and a system for articulating sectional interests.

- The three key functions of government are legislative, executive and judicial.

- While political institutions, practices and processes tend to vary between countries, democratic government is typified by a system of representative democracy and by political, social and economic checks and balances which act as a constraint on the actions of government.

- Such checks and balances in the system include the activities of pressure groups, which seek to influence government through a variety of means, and which often play a key role in policy formulation and implementation.

- Business organisations and the bodies that represent them are key pressure groups in democratic societies and an important part of the external environment in which government and its agencies operate.

Appendix 5.1   A democratic political system in action: UK national government

As far as the United Kingdom is concerned, the four interrelated elements of a democratic system of government are illustrated in Figure 5.3.

Through a system of regular elections, British citizens (the electorate) vote for candidates of competing political parties who are seeking to form the national government (or to be members of the devolved assemblies in Northern Ireland, Scotland or Wales). (Note that a referendum on Scottish independence to be held in September 2014 may result in an independent Scottish Parliament.) Successful candidates at the national elections become Members of Parliament (MPs) and the party with the largest

Figure 5.3   The elected government at Westminster

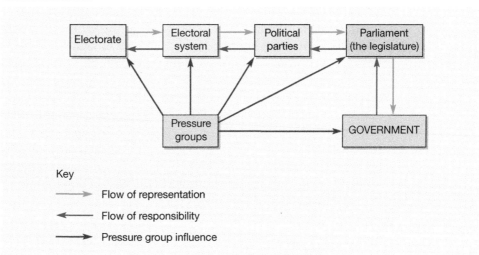

number of MPs is invited by the monarch to form a government, with individuals within the government being allocated specific responsibilities for particular areas of work. The work of government is scrutinised by Parliament (see below), which acts as the people's representative between elections, thereby providing for a measure of public accountability. Equally, between (or during) elections individuals are free to seek to influence government by joining pressure groups or other types of organisation (e.g. political parties) and by making their views known to their elected representatives. The media is free and therefore able to scrutinise the government's performance and to inform the public about political developments.

 web link For information on the political arrangements in Northern Ireland, Scotland and Wales, see, for example, *www.nidirect.gov.uk*; *www.niassembly.gov.uk*; *www.scottish. parliament.uk*; *www.scotland.gov.uk*; *www.assemblywales.org*; *wales.gov.uk*

The legislative branch of government at national level

As indicated above, a directly elected legislature – representative of the people and responsible for making laws – is an important component of a democratic system of government. In the United Kingdom as a whole this function is carried out by **Parliament**, which comprises a non-elected upper chamber (the **House of Lords**) and an elected lower chamber (the **House of Commons**) whose members (currently 650 **MPs**) are elected by universal suffrage by the majority of citizens aged 18 and over. While it is true to say that the Lords retains some important powers, including the power to delay and scrutinise government legislation, the House of Commons remains the most important part of the UK legislature, particularly since it contains key members of the political executive, including the Prime Minister and most of the Cabinet. For this reason the discussion below focuses on the role of the House of Commons.

web link Website addresses for the UK Parliament include *www.publications.parliament.uk* and *www.parliament.uk*

Political representation and responsibility are achieved in a number of ways. For a start, Members of Parliament are directly elected by their constituents and one of the MP's main roles is to represent the constituency for the period between general elections. Apart from holding regular surgeries at which individuals (including businessmen and women) can discuss their problems and views with their representative, MPs also speak on constituency matters in Parliament, frequently raise questions which require answers from government ministers, and generally scrutinise government proposals for any potential effects they may have on the constituency, including key groups within the local electorate (e.g. local businesses). As alluded to previously, there will be occasions when the views of the elected member may differ from those of his or her constituents, particularly those who voted for candidates of an opposing political party, but this does not negate the idea of representation under the British system of parliamentary democracy. MPs represent their constituents first and foremost by having been elected *by them* and hence they provide a direct link between the electorate and the government of the day, which is essentially drawn from the senior members of the majority party in Parliament. In the event of a coalition government (e.g. the UK after the 2010 election), the government will contain representatives of those parties making up the coalition.

Parliament also provides opportunities for the people's representatives to scrutinise and, where necessary, to criticise and challenge the decisions of government. In addition to such parliamentary mechanisms as question time and the adjournment debate, Parliament provides for a system of select committees of **backbench MPs** whose primary role is to scrutinise the work of government departments and other state agencies. Such committees – chaired by both government and opposition backbenchers – are able to question ministers and civil servants, call for departmental papers, cross-examine experts from outside government, and generally investigate the work of the executive, prior to reporting to Parliament on their findings. In bringing their views before Parliament and the public generally (especially through the media), select committees provide a check on government activity and hence form one of the strands by which governments remain answerable to the electorate in the period between elections.

Another significant strand is provided by the opposition, which represents not only an alternative choice of government but also a means of scrutinising and criticising the work of the incumbent administration. Fundamental to this role is the ability of opposition MPs to publicise the decisions of government and to present alternative views to the public via party political broadcasts or promotional literature or debates in parliament, or by general media coverage. Such free and open discussion of issues and policies is a necessary condition for democracy and is an important element in the political education of the nation. Even where governments have large majorities, the role of opposition parties remains a vital component of democracy and helps to provide a curb on unlimited government action.

Turning to its role as a legislative body, there is little doubt that the UK Parliament is largely a legitimising institution, giving formal authority to the wishes of the majority party or coalition. Through its control of the process of legislation, the parliamentary timetable, the flow of information and the votes of its members, the government is able to ensure that its legislative proposals not only come before Parliament but also are almost invariably accepted, even if some delay occurs from time to time in enacting the government's programme, particularly in the event of coalition government where a degree of compromise is often necessary. Opportunities for individual MPs to sponsor legislation (e.g. through private members' bills) are few and far between and the outcome of such proposals depends ultimately on government support (or reluctant acquiescence) if the legislation is to get through its various stages in Parliament. Not surprisingly, this effective stranglehold by the government on the legislative process has led some commentators to talk of an 'elective dictatorship' and to question the true extent of democratic decision-making, particularly when modern governments are invariably elected by less than 50 per cent of the electorate.

The executive branch of government

Putting laws and policies into effect is formally the work of the executive. In the UK this role is carried out by a wide variety of institutions and agencies that is part of the machinery of government. These include the Cabinet, government departments, local authorities, nationalised industries and a large number of other non-departmental public bodies or quasi-autonomous national government agencies, often referred to as 'quangos'.[1] In the discussion below we focus initially on the key institutions at central level since these are fundamental to the process of decision-making in Britain. Discussion of some of the other agencies can be found in subsequent sections of this chapter.

> **web link** Information on non-departmental public bodies (NDPBs) is available via the Cabinet Office website at *www.gov.uk/government/organisations/cabinet-office*

Under the British system of government, the core of the executive is the Cabinet, headed by the **Prime Minister**, an office of crucial importance given the absence of an elected head of state with effective political powers. British Prime Ministers not only have a number of significant political roles – including leader of the governing party, head of the government and head of the Cabinet – but also have traditionally held a formidable array of political powers, including the power to:

- choose members of the Cabinet;
- choose other non-Cabinet ministers;
- promote, demote or dismiss ministers;
- appoint individuals to chair Cabinet committees;
- appoint top civil servants and oversee the operation of the civil service;
- confer certain appointments and titles; and
- determine the date of the general election within the five-year term of office.

This latter power no longer exists following the decision (in 2011) to institute a system of five-year fixed-term parliaments.

While the existence of such rights and responsibilities does not infer that Prime Ministers will inevitably be all-powerful, it is clear that holders of the office have a key role to play in the decision-making process and much will depend upon how an individual interprets that role, upon their personality and upon the constraints they face (both 'real' and 'imagined') in carrying it out. As the Conservative Prime Minister Mrs Thatcher (1979–90) found to her cost, retaining the office of Prime Minister is dependent not only on the electorate but also on maintaining the support and confidence of parliamentary colleagues in the period between elections. In the event of a coalition government, a Prime Minister also has to take account of the wishes of the other party leaders in the coalition and may involve them in some of the decisions outlined below.

As head of the Cabinet the Prime Minister chairs the committee of senior ministers that is the overall directing force – or board of management – within British central government. Comprising about 20 to 25 ministers who have been appointed by the Prime Minister to head the various government departments (or to fulfil some other important functions), the Cabinet is responsible for directing and coordinating the work of the whole executive machine. Its functions include:

- making decisions on the nature and direction of government policy, including public expenditure, economic policy, defence, foreign relations, industrial policy, and so on;
- overseeing and coordinating the administration of government;

- arbitrating in the event of disputes between ministers or departments;
- discussing, deciding and generally directing the government's legislative programme, including laws relating to business.

A large part of this work, of course, is carried out using a system of committees and subcommittees, comprised of individuals chosen by the Prime Minister (including the chairperson) and supported by a small but powerful secretariat, headed by the Cabinet secretary (a civil servant). Apart from providing an opportunity for more detailed discussions of issues and policies prior to full consideration by the Cabinet, the committee system has the advantage of allowing non-members of the Cabinet (including non-Cabinet ministers and civil servants) to participate in discussions in which they may have an interest. In this way, the system helps to provide a mechanism for communication and coordination between government departments and serves as a training ground for junior ministers, many of whom will subsequently achieve full Cabinet responsibilities. An illustrative list of selected Cabinet committees in July 2013 is shown in Table 5.1.

Table 5.1 Selected Cabinet committees, 2013

Committee name
Coalition Committee
Home Affairs Committee
Economic Affairs Committee
Public Expenditure Committee
Parliamentary Business and Legislation Committee
Banking Reform Committee

Source: Cabinet Office.

Much of the day-to-day work of central government is carried out in vast and complex administrative structures called government departments – a selected list of which is shown in Table 5.2. Working together with a substantial number of executive agencies and other public bodies, **government departments** are usually headed by a Cabinet minister (normally called a **Secretary of State**) and include other ministers outside the Cabinet (e.g. Ministers of State, Parliamentary Under Secretaries of State) who have been appointed by the Prime Minister and who may include individuals drawn from the world of business. Together these ministers constitute the political executive. As the head of a department, the Secretary of State has ultimate responsibility for its work and is answerable to Parliament through the various mechanisms referred to above.[2] In addition, he or she is expected to give overall direction to the work of the department – within the policy of the government as a whole – and to represent its interest in the Cabinet (e.g. over the size and use of its budget), in Parliament (e.g. in steering through legislation) and in the outside world (e.g. in the media). Large areas of this work are delegated to the Ministers of State who assume responsibility for specific areas of departmental work and they in turn will tend to delegate some duties to the department's junior ministers. Such an arrangement not only ensures coverage of the different aspects of a department's responsibilities, it also provides invaluable experience and training for ambitious young MPs appointed to a ministerial post.

Table 5.2 Key government departments, September 2013

Cabinet Office
HM Treasury
Foreign and Commonwealth Office
Business, Innovation and Skills
Communities and Local Government
Energy and Climate Change
Home Office
Environment, Food and Rural Affairs
Defence
Health
Work and Pensions
Culture, Media and Sport

> **web link**
>
> Each government department has its own website with lots of useful material. Examples of current addresses include:
> *www.gov.uk/government/organisations/department-for-business-innovation-skills,*
> *www.defra.gov.uk, www.gov.uk/government/organisations/hm-treasury*

Ministers are assisted in their work by permanent officials, known as **civil servants**, many of whom have spent a large part of their working lives in the government machine and hence are familiar with how it works and how to manipulate it in order to achieve particular objectives. Whereas ministers are politicians, civil servants are administrators vested formally with the task of carrying out the policies of the incumbent government, irrespective of their own political views and preferences. Perhaps not surprisingly, as key advisers to ministers on policy formulation and implementation, senior civil servants can exercise considerable influence over the nature and shape of government policy and legislation.[3] For this reason, individuals or groups seeking to shape government thinking on an issue or piece of legislation frequently 'target' senior departmental officials in the hope of gaining influence in the policy process.

This potential for influence by senior civil servants is, of course, enhanced by the scope and complexities of modern government and by the fact that government ministers have a wide range of non-departmental as well as departmental responsibilities (e.g. as constituency MPs). Ministers consequently rely heavily on their officials for information and advice and civil servants are normally entrusted, under ministers, with the conduct of the whole gamut of government activities, including filling in the details of some legislation. Added to this, the need for policy coordination between departments requires regular meetings between senior officials, in groups that mirror the meetings of Cabinet subcommittees. Since these meetings of officials help to provide the groundwork and briefing papers for future discussions by ministers, they permit civil servants to influence the course of events, especially when a particular line or policy option is agreed by the senior officials in a number of departments.

It is perhaps worth noting at this point that, however pervasive its influence, the civil service is not the only source of policy advice for governments. Apart from traditional bureaucratic channels, ministers often turn to specially appointed bodies for help and guidance in making policy choices. Some of these sources are permanent (or relatively permanent) and include the various executive and advisory bodies set up by past and present governments to assist in the policy process in specific functional areas (e.g. Natural Environment Research Council). Others are temporary, having been specially constituted by government to consider a particular problem and to report on their findings prior to going out of existence (e.g. public inquiries, Royal Commissions). While the appointment of these advisory sources does not oblige the government to follow their advice, they can be regarded as useful sources of information, ideas and advice from outside the formal bureaucratic machine. Moreover, the fact that they tend to have a membership representing a wide cross-section of interests (including representatives of particular pressure groups, industrialists, trade unionists, MPs, academics and others drawn from the list of 'the great and the good') helps to widen the scope of consultation and thus to enhance the democratic process.

The last generation has also seen governments turning increasingly to special advisers and policy planning units for help with policy development. Whereas advisers are individuals appointed by ministers (including the Prime Minister), usually from outside the civil service, policy planning units and/or research units are groups of individuals generally recruited from and located within the government machine, with the aim of providing a range of policy and programme advice to both policy-makers and administrators. Often comprised of young and highly qualified individuals seconded to a unit from a wide range of occupational categories and disciplines (including statisticians, social scientists, economists and general administrators), policy units are a valuable source of information and advice, and their operation at both central and local government level provides policy-makers with detailed research and analysis with which to support their policy judgements.

A further important development has been the increased use of 'focus groups', collections of individual citizens consulted by government on policy proposals prior to legislation and/or implementation. In canvassing the views of individuals affected by government policy, government hopes to improve the policy process in a wide range of areas, including the delivery of public services where there has been a programme to provide round-the-clock availability and (ultimately) complete electronic access. While some see citizens' panels or focus groups as nothing more than a gimmick, others regard their use as a move towards a more modern and democratic form of government with increased levels of public accountability and access to information.

The judicial branch of government

The third arm of government, the judiciary – comprising the judges and the courts – is formally separate from and independent of Parliament and the government, despite the fact that until recently the head of the judiciary, the Lord Chancellor, was both a member of the government and a member of the House of Lords, where he or she presided as Speaker. In essence the role of the judiciary is to put into effect the laws enacted by Parliament and to keep the government within the limits of its powers as laid down in statutes and in common law, as interpreted by the judiciary. Since 1973, it has also been responsible for interpreting European Union law. Given the complexities of the legal system and its relevance to the world of business, it is important to examine this aspect of government in more detail.

Appendix 5.2

Subnational government: UK local authorities

Democratic government occurs at subnational as well as national level and takes a wide variety of forms. In addition to the local branches of central government departments and public utilities, many states have local agencies for the administration of justice, local special-purpose authorities (e.g. in the health service) and a system of regional and/or local government, whether under a federal or a unitary arrangement. Such decentralisation and deconcentration of political authority is generally seen as beneficial, since it brings the formulation and administration of policy 'nearer to the people' and is said to provide for decisions that are more sensitive to local needs and aspirations. It can, however, raise the question as to the degree of autonomy of local agencies within a centralised system of government, a controversial and perennial source of debate and dispute in many parts of the world, as recent history has demonstrated.

Within the United Kingdom as a whole, political power is devolved at two main levels: regionally and locally. Scotland, Wales and Northern Ireland have their own directly elected regional assemblies (the Scottish Parliament; the National Assembly for Wales; the Northern Ireland Assembly) and systems of executive government (the Scottish Executive; the Welsh Assembly Government; the Northern Ireland Executive), each with differing levels of devolved authority. The future referendum on independence in Scotland may result in a change in the current system. In England (outside of London), regional government does not currently exist, although voluntary regional chambers or assemblies were set up in the English regions to perform a number of core functions relating to regional issues such as housing development, planning, transport and strategic development. These have now been abolished.

Local government – the focus of this section – has a considerable historical pedigree and remains a key element of the country's system of institutionalised democracy and a major actor in the national as well as the local economy. Given its impact in the business environment, it deserves special attention.

As one form of local administration, local government has a number of distinctive features. For a start it involves self-government by the people of the locality as well as for them, with local authorities exercising considerable discretion in the ways they apply national laws within their areas. In addition, local decision-makers (councillors) are elected to oversee multi-purpose authorities, financed by revenue raised predominantly from local sources – although the proportion from central government has risen in recent years. In short, each local authority constitutes a miniature political and administrative system: each has the institutions and processes of government – including an electoral system, a legislative body (the council), appointed officials (local government officers), party activity, and conflict between individuals and groups within the local community over the allocation of resources and the enforcement of values.

Figure 5.4 illustrates this parallel between the basic operation of government at central and local level. The electorate in each local constituency (district, county, unitary, metropolitan district) periodically choose between candidates who are mostly representing the same parties as those found at national level and the successful candidates

Figure 5.4   The local government system

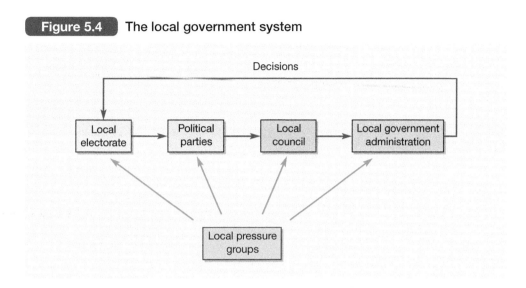

in the election are elected to represent their constituency in the deliberating body (the council). Senior members of this body are chosen to serve on the various committees and subcommittees, with the leading party on the council having an in-built majority in the committee system, where most decisions have traditionally been made prior to being sanctioned (or not) by the full council. Since the passage of the Local Government Act (2000), councils have been allowed to adopt one of three broad categories of constitution which provide for a separate executive. These three categories are (1) a directly elected mayor with a Cabinet selected by the mayor, (2) a Cabinet either elected by the council or appointed by its leader, and (3) a directly elected mayor and council manager.

For the most part, senior councillors are the political heads of the various local authority departments and agencies (e.g. housing, social services, education and so on) that are responsible for providing those services within the local community which national laws require or, in some cases (e.g. sports centres), do not forbid. Much of this work is carried out by local officials who are appointed by the local authority to administer local services and to advise councillors on policy matters. As the local equivalent of civil servants, local government officers exercise considerable influence over the formulation as well as the implementation of local decisions. For this reason, they too tend to be targeted by local pressure groups which operate at all levels and stages of the political process in their attempts to influence local decision-making.

The current structure of local government in the United Kingdom is illustrated in Table 5.3. In England, outside the metropolitan areas, most 'shire' counties have a two-tier structure of county councils and district, borough or city councils, with the former providing the larger services (e.g. education and social services) while the latter have responsibility for a range of other services (such as housing, leisure, refuse collection and local planning). Elsewhere (e.g. Avon, Cleveland, Humberside, Isle of Wight) 'unitary authorities' have either taken over the functions of the former county and district councils or operate alongside them as all-purpose authorities (e.g. Leicester, York). In the metropolitan areas (including London) the single tier of district councils (or London borough councils) remains unchanged from previous years.

Table 5.3 The structure of UK local government, 2013

Types of local authority		
England	**Wales and Scotland**	**N. Ireland**
Non-metropolitan areas County councils District councils Unitary councils (plus joint arrangements)	*All mainland areas* Unitary councils (plus three island councils in Orkney, Shetland and the Western Isles)	For the purpose of local government Northern Ireland has 26 district councils with limited powers (e.g. collecting rubbish and providing leisure facilities)
Metropolitan areas Metropolitan district councils (plus joint boards)		
London London Borough Councils (plus Corporation of the City of London and joint boards)		

Following legislation in 1994, the two-tier structure in Wales and Scotland was abolished and was replaced (on 1 April 1996) with single-tier, all-purpose, unitary authorities, which have inherited the majority of the functions of the previous councils. In Northern Ireland the system of single-tier district councils remains, although these authorities still have limited responsibility for service provision.

Appendix 5.3   Supranational government: the European Union

Decisions and law affecting business activity are increasingly being made at supranational as well as national and subnational levels. Nowhere is this more evident than in western Europe, where the influence of the European Union is profound. As a significant part of the political environment of the major world economies, the EU deserves special consideration, particularly since its decisions often have global as well as regional consequences – affecting not only firms within its member states but also businesses and governments trading with these states, both directly and indirectly. The following analysis concentrates on the political institutions of the European Union and their relative importance in the process of decision-making.[4]

The EU's official website, called 'Europa', can be accessed at *europa.eu*
This provides links to lots of other useful sites.

The European Parliament

The **European Parliament** is a directly elected body, at the time of writing constituting 766 members (**MEPs**), with each member state's representation being roughly equivalent to the size of its population. The United Kingdom, for example, has

73 MEPs, elected at five-yearly intervals by UK citizens using a regional list system of proportional representation introduced for the June 1999 European elections.[5] Since voting under a proportional system enhances the prospects of representation by smaller political parties, the European Parliament contains members representing a diversity of political parties who sit in political groups with similar affiliations. Table 5.4 shows, for example, the number of MEPs by broad affiliation as they stood following the 2014 elections. The next elections are due to be held in 2014.

Table 5.4 MEPs by broad affiliation, 2014 election

Political group	Seats
EPP	273
S&D	196
ALDE	83
GREENS/EFA	57
ECR	57
GUE/NGL	35
EFD	31
NI	33
Total	765

Key
EPP: Group of the European People's Party (Christian Democrats)
S&D: Group of the Progressive Alliance of Socialists and Democrats in the European Parliament
ALDE: Group of the Alliance of Liberals and Democrats for Europe
GREENS/EFA: Group of the Greens/European Free Alliance
ECR: European Conservatives and Reformists Group
GUE/NGL: Confederal Group of the European United Left/Nordic Green Left
EFD: Europe of Freedom and Democracy group
NI: Non-attached Members
Source: *www.europarl.europa.eu*

 For information on the European Parliament see *www.europarl.europa.eu*

The importance of party affiliation is emphasised by the fact that Parliament's organisation is deliberately biased in favour of multinational groupings, with recognition of a political grouping entitling the group to offices, funding, representation on committees and influence in debates and legislation. In order to decide its attitude to an issue or policy proposal coming before the Parliament or one of its committees, a group would normally meet for several days in the week before each session and the issue would be discussed and an agreed line would be decided. As in the case of national parliaments, the attitudes of the political groups have a significant impact on the discussions and decisions within the European Parliament, both in committee and when the House is in full session. Given the number of party groups, however, and the fact that no single group tends to have an absolute majority – unlike in some national parliaments – there is often a need for a group to try to build a coalition of support if it is to achieve its objectives in Parliament. Understandably – and perhaps inevitably – decisions by the European Parliament thus tend to involve compromise between individuals and groups, with the final outcome frequently being a course of action that is acceptable to a majority.

In terms of its role and methods of operation, the European Parliament essentially mirrors national parliaments. Under an elected president who is responsible for directing Parliament's activities and representing it externally and with other EU institutions, much of its detailed work is handled by specialist committees, meeting mostly in Brussels, which report on and offer recommendations to full sessions of the House, which take place in Strasbourg. Membership of each committee is broadly representative of the strengths of the party groupings and the chairmen and women of the permanent committees tend to be influential figures in their own right. In addition to drawing up legislative proposals and carrying out detailed examination and amendment of draft laws, the committees discuss issues (e.g. women's rights, consumer protection, employment), question officials, hold public hearings at which experts and representatives of specialist organisations give evidence, and generally offer their opinion and advice on issues of concern to the EU. As in the case of national parliaments, detailed discussion in committee prior to debate and decision by the full house provides Parliament with an effective means of carrying out its duties and serves as a mechanism for scrutinising the work of both the Council and the Commission.

With regard to its functions, these predominantly fall into five main areas:

Legislation. The Parliament's formal approval is required on most proposals before they can be adopted by the Council of Ministers (see below), i.e. the vast majority of European laws are adopted jointly by the European Parliament and the Council. Under the Lisbon Treaty (2009), the range of issues covered by the co-decision procedure has increased.

The budget. Along with the Council of Ministers, the Parliament acts as the Community's 'budgetary authority' and can reject the Council's draft budget and may modify expenditure proposals on 'non-compulsory' items. It can question the Commission's management of the budget and call in the Court of Auditors.

Supervision. The Parliament supervises the Commission, which it has the power to dismiss by a vote of censure and whose work it scrutinises using a variety of mechanisms. Under the Maastricht Treaty (1992) it has the right to be consulted on the appointment of a new Commission and can veto its appointment. The power of democratic supervision has been extended to other EU institutions, including the Council of Ministers.

Initiative. This includes debates on important regional and international issues and demands for changes to existing policies and/or legislation. Parliament must also approve applications from countries wishing to join the EU.

Relations with national parliaments. The European Parliament holds regular meetings with member states' national parliaments.

In the legislative field, authority traditionally rested with the Council of Ministers and the Commission, and Parliament's role was largely to sanction proposals put before it. Changes under the Single European Act (1986), the Maastricht Treaty (1992), the Amsterdam Treaty (1997), the Nice Treaty (2001) and the Lisbon Treaty (2009) have, however, helped to strengthen Parliament's position by establishing and subsequently extending new procedures for 'assent', 'cooperating' and 'co-decision', now known as the 'Ordinary legislative procedure'. Thus:

- In certain fields an absolute majority of the European Parliament must vote to approve laws before they are passed (e.g. foreign treaties, accession treaties, the Common Agricultural Policy).
- In specified areas Parliament now has a second reading of proposals and its rejection of such proposals can be overturned only by a unanimous decision of the Council of Ministers (e.g. Single Market laws, trans-European networks).

- Parliament can also reject certain legislation by an absolute majority vote if, after the second reading of a proposal and subsequent conciliation, the Council and Parliament are unable to agree (e.g. education and training, health, consumer protection).

The Lisbon Treaty also gave Parliament the power to appoint the President of the European Commission.

The Council of the European Union (the Council of Ministers)

The Council of the European Union (the **Council of Ministers**) – the Union's ultimate decision-making body – comprises one minister from each of the member states, with participants on the Council varying according to the issue under discussion (e.g. agricultural issues are discussed by Ministers of Agriculture from each state). Meetings of the Council, which are mainly held in Brussels, are chaired predominantly by the minister from the country holding the presidency, which currently rotates on a six-monthly basis (e.g. Greece and Italy held the presidency in 2014). Along with the meetings of ministers are regular meetings of officials (Council Working Groups), together with the work of the Committee of Permanent Representatives of the Member States (COREPER), whose task is to coordinate the groundwork for Union decisions undertaken by the numerous meetings of senior officials. In addition, the Council is serviced by a general secretariat, also based in Brussels.

web link

> The Council of Ministers' website is at *www.consilium.europa.eu*
> Information is also available through the EU's main website at *europa.eu*

The role of the Council of Ministers is to make major policy decisions and to respond to legislative proposals put forward mainly by the Commission. Its key roles are to pass EU laws, coordinate EU economic policy, approve the EU budget, sign international agreements and develop EU foreign and defence policies. Major EU decisions require unanimity in the Council, but increasingly, many decisions (especially after the Amsterdam and Nice Treaties) are now being taken by a **qualified majority vote (qmv)**. Member states have weighted votes in the Council that are roughly proportional to their relative population sizes, with the total number of votes being 352 at the time of writing. A qualified majority is reached if two conditions are met: 1) a majority of member states approve (in some cases a two-thirds majority is needed); 2) a minimum of 260 votes is cast in favour of the proposal. In addition, a member state can ask for confirmation that the votes in favour represent at least 62 per cent of the total population of the EU. If not, the decision will not be adopted. From 2014 the system is to be changed so that a proposal will require support by both a majority of countries and a majority (at least 65 per cent) of the total EU population.

While the 'right of initiative' under the Treaties rests with the Commission, the power of decision essentially lies with the Council, which may adopt Commission proposals as drafted, amend them, reject them, or simply take no decision, having consulted the European Parliament and normally a number of other bodies.

If adopted, Council of Ministers' decisions have the force of law and are described as regulations, directives, decisions, or recommendations and opinions. **Regulations** apply directly to all member states and do not have to be confirmed by national parliaments to have binding legal effect. **Directives** lay down compulsory objectives, but leave it to member states to translate them into national legislation. **Decisions** are binding on those states, companies or individuals to which they are addressed, while **recommendations and opinions** have no binding force but merely state the view of the institution that issues them.

The Council's power to pass a law – even if the European Parliament disagrees with it – was reduced under the Maastricht Treaty. In specified policy areas, joint approval is now necessary and MEPs have an effective veto if the two sides cannot reach agreement following conciliation. Moreover, following Maastricht a Committee of the Regions has been established to advise the Commission and the Council on issues concerning the European regions – a development which should help to ensure a stronger regional voice at European level. That said, it is still the case that the Council remains responsible for setting general policy within the EU and relies on the Commission to take decisions on the detailed application of legislation or to adapt legislative details to meet changing circumstances. To this extent – and given the Commission's other responsibilities – the ultimate influence over EU decisions is, to say the very least, open to question, as is often the case at national level.

The European Council

The work of the 'specialist' councils within the Council of Ministers (e.g. Agriculture, Economics and Finance, Employment and Social Affairs) is coordinated by the General Affairs Council, comprising the Foreign Ministers of the member states. This Council is also responsible for preparing for the meetings of the **European Council**, which occur around four times each year. The European Council is attended by the heads of government/state of each member state, the EU's representative for foreign affairs, the President of the Commission and the European Council President, and its work invariably attracts substantial media coverage. Under the chairmanship of its permanent President, the European Council's role is to discuss important policy issues affecting the EU and to set the EU's general political direction and priorities. These so-called 'summits' of heads of governments can have a profound effect on the development of the Union and its institutions.

> **web link** Information on the European Council is available via the Council of Ministers' website. See above.

The European Commission

The **European Commission**, which has its headquarters in Brussels and Luxembourg, is the EU's bureaucratic arm, currently comprising 28 Commissioners (one from each member state), nominated by their respective governments, and a staff of about 23,000 permanent civil servants drawn from all member states. Headed by a President, and organised into **Directorates-General**, each with a Commissioner responsible for its work, the European Commission's role is essentially that of initiator, supervisor and executive. More specifically its tasks are:

- to act as guardian of the Treaties so as to ensure that EU rules and principles are respected and implemented;
- to propose policies and legislation for the European Parliament and Council of Ministers to discuss and, if appropriate, adopt or amend;
- to implement EU policies and supervise the day-to-day running of these policies, including managing the funds that account for most of the EU budget (e.g. EAGGF, ERDF, ECSC);[6]
- to represent the EU internationally (e.g. in the World Trade Organisation).

 You can find further information on the Commission at *ec.europa.eu*

In carrying out these duties, the Commissioners are required to act in the interests of the EU as a whole and may not receive instructions from any national government or from any other body (Article 157 of the Treaty of Rome). Moreover, while each Commissioner is responsible for formulating proposals within his or her area of responsibility, the final decision is taken on a collegiate basis and the work is subject to the supervision of the European Parliament. As mentioned above, Parliament is the only body that can force the Commission to resign collectively; interestingly, it has no authority over individual Commissioners, although its endorsement is needed when the President of the Commission and the other Commissioners are appointed.

Much of the undoubted power and influence of the Commission stems from its central involvement in the legislative process. Proposals for consideration by the Council and the Parliament are initially drafted by the Commission, usually following consultation with the Economic and Social Committee (representing the interests of employers, trade unions, farmers, consumers, etc.) and other advisory bodies as appropriate. Moreover, EU Treaties specifically give the Commission the power to make regulations, issue directives, take decisions, make recommendations and deliver opinions, as well as to implement policies based on either Council decisions or Treaty provisions. Thus, while legislative power in the EU in general rests with the Council of Ministers and the EU Parliament, the Commission is also able to legislate in order to implement earlier Council regulations, particularly where technical or routine matters are concerned – a situation that has parallels in the operation of government at national level.

Further powers with regard to specific sectors (e.g. coal and steel) or particular aspects of EU work (e.g. the budget, international agreements) serve to enhance the Commission's influence and to confirm its position as the 'driving force' of the Union. Perhaps understandably, pressure groups seeking to influence the policy process within the European Union regard the Commission as an important institution to target, together with Parliament and the Council of Ministers. Future changes in the relationship between these three institutions will undoubtedly have an effect not only on the legislative process but also on the practice of lobbying within the EU context.

The European Court of Justice

The **European Court of Justice**, which sits in Luxembourg, comprises twenty-eight judges, who are appointed for a six-year period by consent of the member states, and eight advocates-general. The Court's role is:

- to pass judgment, at the request of a national court, on the interpretation or validity of points of EU law;
- to quash, at the request of an EU institution, government or individual, any measures adopted by the Commission, the Council or national governments which are judged to be incompatible with the existing treaties;
- to consider actions brought by individuals, companies or organisations against EU decisions or actions.

The Court can also be invited to offer an opinion, which then becomes binding, on agreements the EU proposes to undertake with third countries.

Three aspects of its work are particularly worthy of note:

- Individuals as well as member states can bring cases to the Court, and its judgments and interpretations apply to all (i.e. EU institutions, member states, national courts and private citizens) and are backed by a system of penalties for non-compliance.
- Its rulings on matters of European law, which has primacy over national law, are final and its decisions are binding on member countries.
- The Court has tended to follow the principle that EU Treaties should be interpreted with a degree of flexibility so as to take account of changing conditions and circumstances. This has permitted the Community to legislate in areas where there are no specific Treaty provisions, such as the fight against pollution.

 The Court of Justice website can be accessed at *curia.europa.eu*. See also *europa.eu* for general information.

The business of lobbying

A key characteristic of a democratic political system is the right of individuals, groups and organisations to seek to influence government thinking and behaviour. For a business wishing to have its voice heard in official circles, a variety of approaches is possible, ranging from direct appeals to decision-makers to joint action with other firms via an industry body, trade association or a business representative organisation. A firm may even consider hiring the services of a professional lobby organisation to act on its behalf.

Professional lobby organisations are essentially businesses that have been specifically set up to influence others on behalf of their clients. Where government decisions are concerned, the complexities of modern political and administrative structures provide numerous opportunities and points of access for professional lobbyists, who often have extensive knowledge of the decision-making process and of the individuals to approach on a given issue. In order to bring influence to bear in the places and institutions where important decisions are made, many lobbying firms have established a presence in major centres of power, including Washington, Brussels and London, often employing hundreds of permanent staff whose job is to lobby for or against a particular policy or piece of legislation according to the needs of their client.

A recent example of how businesses can use the services of professional lobbyists is the case of the EU's Tobacco Products Directive. Concerned over the health implications of smoking for EU citizens, EU member state governments agreed in June 2012 to a proposal that would require mandatory text and picture health warnings covering 75 per cent of the front and back of cigarette packets and to ban the sale of flavoured cigarettes that particularly appeal to younger smokers. A draft directive setting out these requirements was then sent to the European Parliament for a decision on whether to move forward on the issue or to allow time for further amendments.

To protect their interests, the major tobacco companies responded by launching an intense lobbying campaign aimed at potentially sympathetic MEPs whom they hoped would help to persuade others to oppose the suggested measures. Some estimates suggest that Philip Morris International – the makers of the brand Marlboro – alone spent more than €1 million wooing elected representatives to water down the proposals, reputedly employing over 150 staff and consultants during the process prior to the vote in the European Parliament. According to the Corporate Europe Observatory, which monitors the use of corporate lobbying in the EU, the tobacco industry has about 100 full-time lobbyists based in Brussels, with an annual budget of more than

€5 million. Given this resource, it is not surprising to learn that a report in *Reuters* on 4 October 2013 claimed that EU officials were concerned that lobbying activity by the industry was threatening to derail the proposed anti-smoking legislation.

When the issue was finally discussed in the Parliament after some delay, the original proposals regarding both the sale and promotion of cigarettes within the EU were considerably scaled back. MEPs rejected the plan to ban 'slim' cigarettes and opted for menthol-flavoured products to be phased out over eight rather than three years as had been proposed. They also agreed to reduce health warnings from 75 per cent to 65 per cent of the packet, the latter evidently having been put forward as a compromise by the industry. Following subsequent negotiations between the Council of the EU and the EP, a revised directive was put forward which included the provision that member states retain the right to introduce more stringent measures, including plain packaging. Differences between the original scheme agreed by EU governments and the new revised plans would need to be resolved ahead of the May 2014 elections for the European Parliament before the directive could come into effect. No doubt the battle is still far from over.

Case study questions

1 Why do governments frequently express concern over the activities of professional lobby organisations?

2 Why do some businesses and industries choose to use such organisations?

Review and discussion questions

1 To what extent do you think a change of government in your country would affect the business community?

2 Many top civil servants take directorships in large companies on retirement from government. Why should companies be keen to recruit retired bureaucrats?

3 How far is the enlargement of the European Union likely to benefit UK businesses?

4 In what ways could a business organisation seek to influence central government decision-makers on issues in which it has an interest (e.g. taxes on company profits or the level of interest rates)?

Assignments

1 You are employed as a research assistant by a group representing the interests of small and medium-sized enterprises (e.g. a Chamber of Commerce). Using contemporary source material (e.g. the internet, manifestos, etc.), produce a draft report highlighting current government policy for the SME sector.

2 Imagine you are employed as a political lobbyist, with a special interest in conservation issues. You have been approached by a local conservation group, which is concerned about government plans to build a bypass round a village in its area. The government's proposals for the road would cause significant damage to a Site of Special Scientific Interest (SSSI) and the group is determined to oppose the plans. Your brief is to draft an 'action plan' for the group, indicating what forms of pressure group activity you would recommend, in what sequence and using which channels of potential influence.

Notes and references

1 See, for example, Barker, A., *Quangos in Rritain,* Macmillan, 1982; Ridley, F. F. and Wilson, D. (eds), *The Quango Debate,* Oxford University Press/Hansard Society, 1995; Pollitt, C. and Talbot, C., *Unbundled Government,* Routledge, 2004.

2 Individual ministerial responsibility should not be confused with collective Cabinet responsibility, both of which apply to Ministers of the Crown.

3 Senior civil servants who are in a position to influence policy are sometimes called 'mandarins', a term that applies to a very small percentage of the civil service. Most civil servants are engaged in more routine administrative work, including providing services directly to the public (e.g. paying benefits and pensions).

4 There are numerous books on the EU. Students can also gain information by contacting EU institutions directly, particularly through their national offices, or by accessing the numerous websites.

5 The UK's continued membership of the EU is somewhat uncertain following the proposal – by the majority party in the current government – to hold an in/out referendum in 2017, assuming it is returned to office in the 2015 general election. The result of the Scottish referendum on independence could also complicate the picture further.

6 European Agriculture Guarantee and Guidance Fund (EAGGF); European Regional Development Fund (ERDF); European Coal and Steel Community (ECSC).

Further reading

Cocker, P. and Jones, A., *Contemporary British Politics and Government,* 4th edition, Liverpool Academic Press/Cambridge Media Group, 2014 (forthcoming).

Coen, D. and Richardson, J., *Lobbying the European Union: Institutions, Actors and Issues,* Oxford University Press, 2009.

Hix, S., *The Political System of the European Union,* 2nd edition, Palgrave Macmillan, 2005.

Kavanagh, D. and Moran, M., *Politics UK,* Pearson Education, 2007.

Leach, R., Coxall, W. and Robins, L., *British Politics,* Palgrave Macmillan, 2011.

Massey, A. and Pyper, R., *Public Management and Modernisation in Britain,* Palgrave Macmillan, 2005.

Moran, M., *Politics and Governance in the UK,* 2nd edition, Palgrave Macmillan, 2011.

Peterson, J. and Shackleton, M. (eds), *The Institutions of the European Union,* 3rd edition, Oxford University Press, 2012.

Wilson, D. and Game, C., *Local Government in the United Kingdom,* Palgrave Macmillan, 2011.

6 The macroeconomic environment

Ian Worthington

Business organisations operate in an economic environment which shapes, and is shaped by, their activities. In market-based economies this environment comprises variables that are dynamic, interactive and mobile and which, in part, are affected by government in pursuit of its various roles in the economy. As a vital component in the macroeconomy, government exercises a significant degree of influence over the flow of income and hence over the level and pattern of output by the public and private sectors. Other key influences include a country's financial institutions and the international economic organisations and groupings to which it belongs or subscribes.

Learning outcomes

Having read this chapter you should be able to:

- compare alternative economic systems and their underlying principles and discuss the problems of transition from a centrally planned to a market-based economy
- illustrate flows of income, output and expenditure in a market economy and account for changes in the level and pattern of economic activity
- analyse the role of government in the macroeconomy, including government macroeconomic policies and the objectives on which they are based
- explain the role of financial institutions
- identify the key international economic institutions and organisations that influence the business environment in open, market economies

Key terms

Accelerator effect
Aggregate monetary demand
Balance of payments
Capital market
Capitalist economy
Central bank
Centrally planned economy
Circular flow of income model
Consumer Price Index (CPI)
Consumer sovereignty
Credit rating agency
Crowding out
Cyclical unemployment
Deindustrialisation
Direct controls
Direct taxation
Economic growth
Economic scarcity
Economics
European Central Bank (ECB)

Exchange rate
Factory gate prices
Financial intermediaries
Fiscal policy
Free-market economy
Full employment
Government spending
Gross domestic product
Headline inflation
Income flows
Indirect taxation
Inflation
Injections
Interest rates
Leakages
Macroeconomic analysis
Macroeconomic environment
Microeconomic analysis
Monetary aggregates
Monetary policies

Money market
Money stock
Multiplier effect
National debt
Opportunity cost
Public sector net borrowing
Quantitative easing (QE)
Real cost
Real flows
Real interest rates
Real national income
Recession
Retail Price Index (RPI)
State bank
Stock exchange
Structural unemployment
Technological unemployment
Underlying rate of inflation
Wages/prices inflationary spiral
Withdrawals

Introduction

In April 2013, Japan's central bank announced its intention to embark on a huge programme of quantitative easing (see the case study at the end of this chapter) aimed at boosting the Japanese economy and ridding it of the deflation that had haunted the country for more than a decade. The plan was for the Bank of Japan to create new money and use it to buy trillions of yen worth of government bonds each month in the hope of increasing the overall level of demand, thereby pushing up both prices and wages. Part of a set of new macroeconomic policies known as 'Abenomics' – after Japan's new Prime Minister, Shinzo Abe – the scheme to effectively double the country's money supply had the support of the Bank of Japan, the Ministry of Finance and the private sector, which saw it as a means of persuading individuals to spend rather than hoard cash. Similar schemes in other countries, including the USA and the UK, represent one form of interventionary approach by governmental policy-makers aimed at steering the economy along a particular path thought to be beneficial for consumers and businesses alike.

What this simple example is designed to demonstrate is the intimate relationship between business activity and the wider economic context in which it takes place, and a glance at any quality newspaper will provide a range of similar illustrations of this interface between business and **economics**. What is important at this point is not to understand the complexities of global economic forces or their effect on businesses but to appreciate in broad terms the importance of the **macroeconomic environment** for business organisations and, in particular, the degree of compatibility between the preoccupations of the entrepreneur and those of the economist. To the economist, for example, a recession is generally marked by falling demand, rising unemployment, a slowing down in economic growth and a fall in investment. To the firm, it usually implies a loss of orders, a likely reduction in the workforce, a decline in output (or a growth in stocks) and a general reluctance to invest in capital equipment and/or new projects.

Much of the detailed discussion of the economic aspects of business can be found in Parts Three and Four. In this chapter we concentrate on the broader question of the economic structure and processes of a market-based economy and on the macroeconomic influences affecting and being affected by business activity in this type of economic system. As suggested in the previous chapter, an understanding of the overall economic context within which businesses operate – including its core values and principles – is central to any meaningful analysis of the business environment.

Three further points are worth highlighting at this juncture. First, business activity not only is shaped by the economic context in which it takes place but helps to shape that context; consequently the success or otherwise of government economic policy depends to some degree on the reactions of both the firms and the markets (e.g. the stock market) that are affected by government decisions. Second, economic influences operate at a variety of spatial levels, as illustrated by the opening paragraph, and governments can sometimes find that circumstances largely or totally beyond their control can affect businesses, either favourably or adversely. Third, the economic (and for that matter, political) influence of industry and commerce can be considerable and this ensures that business organisations – both individually and collectively – usually constitute one of the chief pressure groups in democratic states.

Economic systems

The concept of economic scarcity

Like politics, the term 'economic' tends to be used in a variety of ways and contexts to describe certain aspects of human behaviour, ranging from activities such as producing, distributing and consuming, to the idea of frugality in the use of a resource (e.g. being 'economical' with the truth). Modern definitions stress how such behaviour, and the institutions in which it takes place (e.g. households, firms, governments, banks), are concerned with the satisfaction of human needs and wants through the transformation of resources into goods and services which are consumed by society. These processes are said to take place under conditions of **economic scarcity**.

The economist's idea of 'scarcity' centres on the relationship between a society's needs and wants and the resources available to satisfy them, the argument being that whereas needs and wants tend to be unlimited, the resources that can be used to meet those needs and wants are finite such that no society at any time has the capacity to provide for all its actual or potential requirements. The assumption here is that both individual and collective needs and wants consistently outstrip the means available to satisfy them, as exemplified, for instance, by the inability of governments to provide instant health care, the best roads, education, defence, railways and so on at a time and place and of a quality convenient to the user. This being the case, 'choices' have to be made by both individuals and society concerning priorities in the use of resources, and every choice inevitably involves a 'sacrifice' (i.e. forgoing an alternative). Economists describe this sacrifice as the **opportunity cost** or **real cost** of the decision that is taken (e.g. every pound spent on the health service is a pound not spent on some other public service) and it is one faced by individuals, organisations (including firms), governments and society alike.

From a societal point of view the existence of economic scarcity poses three serious problems concerning the use of resources:

1 What to use the available resources for. That is, what goods and services should be produced (or not produced) with the resources (sometimes described as the 'guns v. butter' argument)?
2 How best to use those resources. For example, in what combinations, using what techniques and what methods?
3 How best to distribute the goods and services produced with them. That is, who gets what, how much and on what basis?

In practice, of course, these problems tend to be solved in a variety of ways, including barter (voluntary, bilateral exchange), price signals and the market, queuing and rationing, government instruction and corruption (e.g. resources allocated in exchange for personal favours), and examples of each of these solutions can be found in most, if not all, societies, at all times. Normally, however, one or other main approach to resource allocation tends to predominate and this allows analytical distinctions to be made between different types of economic system, one important distinction being between those economies that are centrally planned and those that operate predominantly through market forces where prices form the integrating mechanism. Understanding this distinction is fundamental to an examination of the way in which business is conducted and represents the foundation on which much of the subsequent analysis is built.

The centrally planned economy

In this type of economic system – associated with the post-Second World War socialist economies of eastern Europe, China, Cuba and elsewhere – most of the key decisions on production are taken by a central planning authority, normally the state and its agencies. Under this arrangement, the state typically:

- owns and/or controls the main economic resources;
- establishes priorities in the use of those resources;
- sets output targets for businesses which are largely under state ownership and/or control;
- directs resources in an effort to achieve these predetermined targets; and
- seeks to coordinate production in such a way as to ensure consistency between output and input demands.

The fact that an economy is centrally planned does not necessarily imply that all economic decisions are taken at central level; in many cases decision-making may be devolved to subordinate agencies, including local committees and enterprises. Ultimately, however, these agencies are responsible to the centre and it is the latter which retains overall control of the economy and directs the use of scarce productive resources.

The problem of coordinating inputs and output in a modern planned economy is, of course, a daunting task and one which invariably involves an array of state planners and a central plan or blueprint normally covering a number of years (e.g. a five-year plan). Under such a plan, the state planners establish annual output targets for each sector of the economy and for each enterprise within the sector, identify the inputs of materials, labour and capital needed to achieve the set targets and allocate resources accordingly. Given that the outputs of some industries (e.g. agricultural machinery) are the inputs of others (e.g. collective farms), it is not difficult to see how the over-all effectiveness of the plan would depend in part on a high degree of cooperation and coordination between sectors and enterprises, as well as on good judgement, good decisions and a considerable element of good luck. The available evidence from planned economies suggests that none of these can be taken for granted and each is often in short supply.

Even in the most centralised of economies, state planning does not normally extend to telling individuals what they must buy in shops or how to use their labour, although an element of state direction at times may exist (e.g. conscription of the armed forces). Instead, it tends to condition *what* is available for purchase and the *prices* at which exchange takes place, and both of these are essentially the outcome of political choices, rather than a reflection of consumer demands. All too often consumers tend to be faced by queues and 'black markets' for some consumer products and overproduction of others, as state enterprises strive to meet targets frequently unrelated to the needs and wants of consumers. By the same token, businesses that make losses do not have to close down, as the state would normally make additional funds available to cover any difference between sales revenue and costs. This being the case, the emphasis at firm level tends to be more on meeting targets than on achieving efficiency in the use of resources and hence a considerable degree of duplication and wastage tends to occur.

Given such an environment, the traditional entrepreneurial skills of efficient resource management, price setting and risk taking have little, if any, scope for development and managers behave essentially as technicians and bureaucrats, administering decisions largely made elsewhere. Firms, in effect, are mainly servants of the state and their activities are conditioned by social and political considerations, rather than by the needs of the market – although some market activity normally occurs in planned economies (especially in agriculture and a number of private services). Accordingly, businesses and their employees are not fully sensitised to the needs of the consumer and as a result quality and choice (where they exist) may suffer, particularly where incentives to improved efficiency and performance are negligible. Equally, the system tends to encourage bribery and corruption and the development of a substantial black market, with differences in income, status and political influence being important determinants of individual consumption and of living standards.

The free-market economy

The **free-market economy** (or **capitalist economy**) stands in direct contrast to the centrally planned system. Whereas in the latter the state controls most economic decisions, in the former the key economic agencies are private individuals (sometimes called 'households') and firms, and these interact in free markets, through a system of prices, to determine the allocation of resources.

The key features of this type of economic system are as follows:

- Resources are in private ownership and the individuals owning them are free to use them as they wish.
- Firms, also in private ownership, are equally able to make decisions on production, free from state interference.
- No blueprint (or master plan) exists to direct production and consumption.
- Decisions on resource allocation are the result of a decentralised system of markets and prices, in which the decisions of millions of consumers and hundreds of thousands of firms are automatically coordinated.
- The consumer is deemed to be sovereign, i.e. dictates the pattern of supply and hence the pattern of resource allocation.

In short, the three problems of what to produce, how to produce and how to distribute are solved by market forces.

Figure 6.1 illustrates the basic operation of a market economy. Individuals are owners of resources (e.g. labour) and consumers of products; firms are users of resources and producers of products. What products are produced – and hence how resources are used – depends on consumers, who indicate their demands by purchasing (i.e. paying the price) or not purchasing, and this acts as a signal to producers to acquire the resources necessary (i.e. pay the price) to meet the preferences of consumers. If consumer demands change, for whatever reason, this will cause an automatic reallocation of resources, as firms respond to the new market conditions. Equally, competition between producers seeking to gain or retain customers is said to guarantee that resources are used efficiently and to ensure that the most appropriate production methods (i.e. how to produce) are employed in the pursuit of profits.

Figure 6.1   The market economy

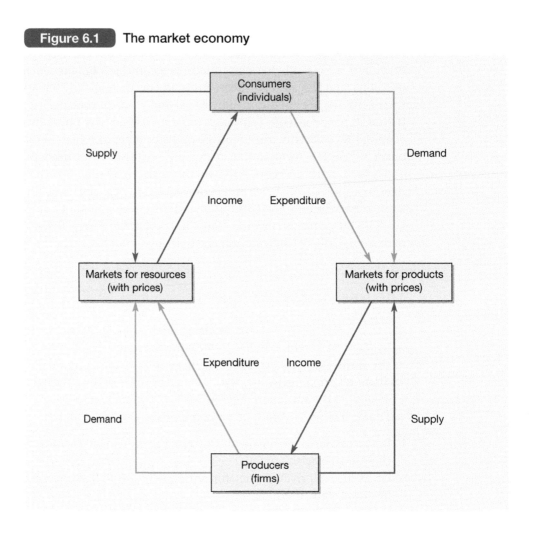

The distribution of output is also determined by market forces, in this case operating in the markets for productive services. Individuals supplying a resource (e.g. labour) receive an income (i.e. a price) from the firms using that resource and this allows them to purchase goods and services in the markets for products, which in turn provides an income for firms that can be spent on the purchase of further resources (see below). Should the demand for a particular type of productive resource increase – say, as a result of an increase in the demand for the product produced by that resource – the price paid to the provider of the resource will tend to rise and hence, other things being equal, allow more output to be purchased. Concomitantly, it is also likely to result in a shift of resources from uses which are relatively less lucrative to those which are relatively more rewarding.

In practice, of course, no economy operates entirely in the manner suggested above; after all, firms are influenced by costs and supply decisions as well as by demand and generally seek to shape that demand, as well as simply responding to it. Nor for that matter is a market-based economy devoid of government involvement in the process of resource allocation, as evidenced by the existence of a public sector responsible for substantial levels of consumption and output and for helping to shape the conditions under which the private sector operates. In short, any study of the market economy needs to incorporate the role of government and to examine, in particular, its influence on the activities of both firms and households. Such an analysis can be found in the later sections of this chapter.

Economies in transition

Most of the world's economies operate under a predominantly market-based system and the **centrally planned economy** in its original form is now largely a rare phenomenon. Three decades of reform have seen the old planned systems in eastern Europe and elsewhere gradually giving way to the march of free enterprise, with some former communist states (e.g. Czech Republic) now members of the European Union, while others – including Russia, China and Cuba – have gradually been experimenting with schemes aimed at developing an entrepreneurial culture and introducing capitalist market principles. Allowing business start-ups and expansion, deregulating some markets, partial privatisation of industries and sectors and encouraging foreign investment are just some of the ways in which this economic transition has been taking place.

For states anxious to move from an entrenched system of state planning to a market-based economic system, the obstacles can be formidable and can help to slow down the progress of economic (and political) reform. For example, among the problems faced by eastern European countries in the transitionary phase were:

- the need to create a legal and commercial framework to support the change to a market economy (e.g. company laws, laws on property rights, competition, external trade, the development of an appropriate accounting system);
- the need to establish different forms of free enterprise and to develop financial institutions capable of providing risk and venture capital, at commercial rates of return;
- the need to develop truly competitive markets, free from state control and protection;
- the need to liberalise labour markets and to develop entrepreneurial skills in a workforce traditionally demotivated by the old bureaucratic system;
- the need to allow prices to move to levels determined by market forces, rather than by political decision;
- the need to achieve macroeconomic stability as markets become more open, both internally and externally;
- the need to reduce the burden of international debt;
- the need to attract substantial overseas investment to assist in the rebuilding of the collapsed old socialist economies.

Meeting these requirements was not made any easier by economic collapse and the perceived need on the part of some reformers to bring about rapid economic change whatever the consequences. In Russia, in particular, widespread bribery, corruption and criminal activity have continued to undermine an economy struggling with economic and political instability that appears endemic and on occasions this has had a negative impact on foreign investment. We should not be surprised if the moves to restructure state economies prove a long and painful process for some countries in the coming years.

Politico-economic synthesis

The economic problem of resource allocation, described above, clearly has a political dimension, given its focus on the ownership, control and use of wealth-producing assets within society. This allows links to be made between a country's chosen economic system and its political regime. A useful way of representing possible relationships is illustrated in Figure 6.2. As suggested in Chapter 5, political systems can be characterised as ranging from democratic to authoritarian, depending on the degree of public involvement in decision-making processes. Similarly, economic systems can be seen to range from free market to planned, according to the level of state intervention in the process of resource allocation. This two-dimensional model thus provides for four major combinations of politico-economic systems, ranging from democratic–free-market on the one hand (quadrant 1) to authoritarian–planned on the other (quadrant 3).

In applying this model to specific cases, it is clear that free-market approaches to resource allocation have predominantly been associated with democratic states. Such a link is not surprising. Democracy, after all, includes the notion of individuals being able to express their preferences through the ballot box and having the opportunity to replace one government with another at periodic intervals. In free markets, similar processes are at work, with individuals effectively 'voting' for goods and services through the price system and their expressed preferences being reflected in the pattern of resource allocation.

A link between authoritarian regimes and planned economic systems can equally be rationalised, in that government control over the political system is considerably facilitated if it also directs the economy through the ownership and/or control of the means of production, distribution and exchange. In effect, the relative absence of democratic mechanisms, such as free elections and choice between alternative forms of

Figure 6.2   Politico-economic systems

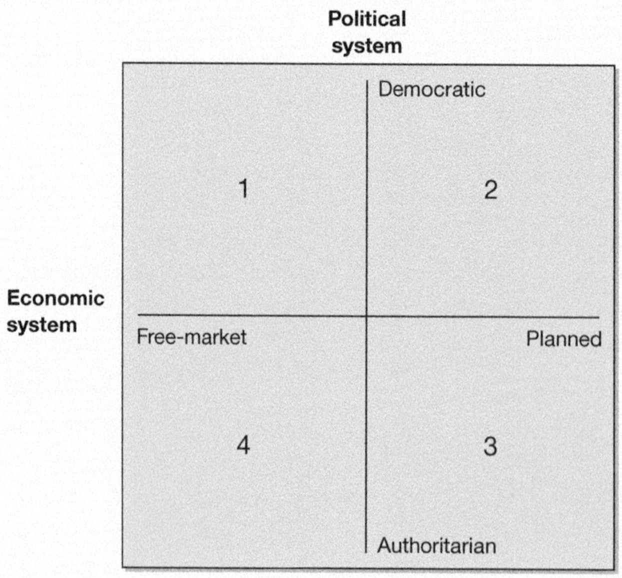

government, is echoed in the economic sphere by the inability of individuals to exercise any real influence over resource allocation. At the extreme, this could involve a government ban on any forms of free enterprise and total government control of the pattern of output and consumption in an economy which is devoid of effective **consumer sovereignty**.

Naturally the true picture is much more complicated than suggested by this simple dichotomy. Some authoritarian states, for instance, have predominantly capitalist economic systems (quadrant 4), while some democratic countries have a substantial degree of government intervention (i.e. moving them towards quadrant 2), either by choice or from necessity (e.g. wartime). Added to this, even in states where the political or economic system appears to be the same, considerable differences can occur at an operational and/or institutional level and this gives each country a degree of uniqueness not adequately portrayed by the model. That said, it is still the case that the basic congruity between democracy and free-market systems represents a powerful and pervasive influence in the business environment of the world's principal democratic states. The process of economic reform – as in eastern Europe – accordingly tends to be accompanied by corresponding pressures for political change and these are often resisted by regimes not prepared to give up their political and economic powers and their élite status.

The macroeconomy

Levels of analysis

As indicated above, economics is concerned with the study of how society deals with the problem of scarcity and the resultant problems of what to produce, how to produce and how to distribute. Within this broad framework the economist typically distinguishes between two types of analysis:

1 **Microeconomic analysis**, which is concerned with the study of economic decision-taking by both individuals and firms.
2 **Macroeconomic analysis**, which is concerned with interactions in the economy as a whole (i.e. with economic aggregates).

The microeconomic approach is exemplified by the analysis of markets and prices, which shows how individual consumers in a market might be affected by a price change. This analysis could be extended to an investigation of how the total market might respond to a movement in the price, or how a firm's (or market's) decisions on supply are affected by changes in wage rates or production techniques or some other factor. Note that in these examples, the focus of attention is on decision-taking by individuals and firms in a single industry, while interactions between this industry and the rest of the economy are ignored; this is what economists call a 'partial analysis'.

In the real world all sectors of the economy are interrelated to some degree. A pay award, for example, in a particular industry (or in a single firm) may set a new pay norm that workers in other industries take up and these pay increases may subsequently influence employment, production and consumer demand in the economy as a whole, which could also have repercussions on the demand for a given product. Sometimes such repercussions may be relatively minor and so effectively can be ignored. In such situations the basic microeconomic approach remains valid.

The macroeconomics perspective recognises the interdependent nature of markets and therefore studies interactions in the economy as a whole, dealing with such questions as the overall level of employment, the rate of inflation, the percentage growth of output in the economy and many other economy-wide aggregates – exemplified by the analysis of international trade and by the macroeconomic model discussed below. It is worth noting that while the distinction between the micro and macro approaches remains useful for analytical purposes, in many instances the two become intertwined. For example, the reference at the start of this chapter to Japan's manipulation of the monetary base to overcome deflation in the economy is clearly a macroeconomic proposition. The idea that this approach will encourage households to spend rather than hoard cash leans heavily on microeconomic analysis, including notions of consumer preferences and anticipated price rises. Given that macroeconomic phenomena are the result of aggregating the behaviour of individual firms and consumers, this is obviously a common situation and one that is useful to bear in mind in any study of either the firm or the economy as a whole.

The 'flows' of economic activity

Economic activity can be portrayed as a flow of economic resources into firms (i.e. productive organisations) which are used to produce output for consumption, and a corresponding flow of payments from firms to the providers of those resources who use them primarily to purchase the goods and services produced. These flows of resources, production, income and expenditure accordingly represent the fundamental activities of an economy at work. Figure 6.3 illustrates the flow of resources and of goods and services in the economy – what economists describe as **real flows**.

In effect, firms use economic resources to produce goods and services, which are consumed by private individuals (private domestic consumption) or government (government

Figure 6.3   'Real flows' in the economy

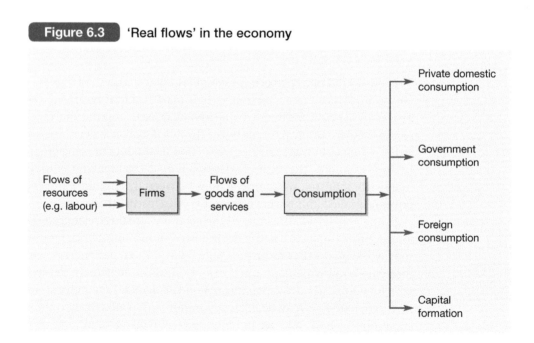

consumption) or by overseas purchasers (foreign consumption) or by other firms (capital formation). This consumption gives rise to a flow of expenditures that represents an income for firms, which they use to purchase further resources in order to produce further output for consumption. This flow of income and expenditures is shown in Figure 6.4.

The interrelationship between **income flows** and real flows can be seen by combining the two figures into one, which for the sake of simplification assumes only two groups operate in the economy: firms as producers and users of resources, and private individuals as consumers and providers of those resources (see Figure 6.5). Real flows are shown by the arrows moving in an anti-clockwise direction, income flows by the arrows flowing in a clockwise direction.

Despite a degree of oversimplification, the model of the economy illustrated in Figure 6.5 is a useful analytical tool, which highlights some vital aspects of economic activity of direct relevance to the study of business. The model shows that:

1 Income flows around the economy, passing from households to firms and back to households and on to firms and so on, with these income flows having corresponding real flows of resources, goods and services.
2 What constitutes an income to one group (e.g. firms) represents an expenditure to another (e.g. households), indicating that income generation in the economy is related to spending on consumption of goods and services and on resources (e.g. the use of labour).
3 The output of firms must be related to expenditure by households on goods and services, which in turn is related to the income the latter receive from supplying resources.
4 The use of resources (including the number of jobs created in the economy) must also be related to expenditure by households on consumption, given that resources are used to produce output for sale to households.
5 Levels of income, output, expenditure and employment in the economy are, in effect, interrelated.

Figure 6.4   Income flows in the economy

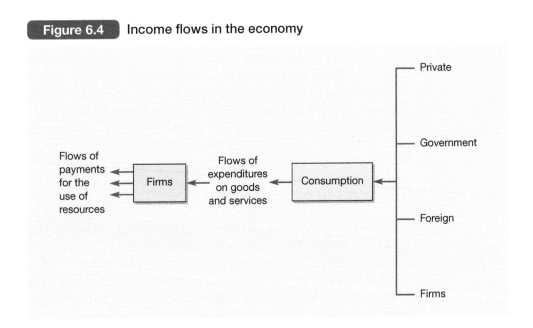

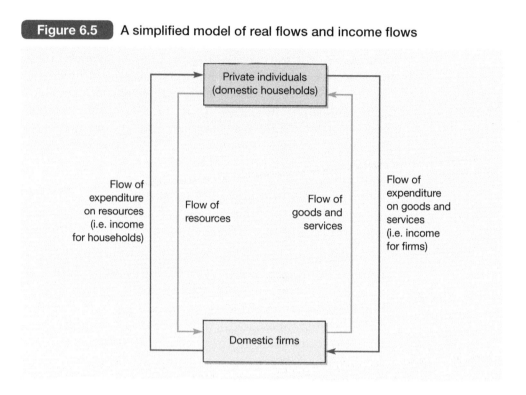

Figure 6.5 A simplified model of real flows and income flows

From the point of view of firms, it is clear from the model that their fortunes are intimately connected with the spending decisions of households and any changes in the level of spending can have repercussions for business activity at the micro as well as at the macro level. In a recession, an overall fall in demand can cause some businesses to close down while others experience a reduction in turnover and may be forced to make some staff redundant and/or delay investment decisions. As unemployment grows and investment is postponed or cancelled, demand may fall further and this will have a negative impact on many businesses. Once the economy gradually recovers and business confidence returns, many firms generally find the order book improves and this can have a positive effect on investment and employment as well as on turnover and profits.

The question then is, what can cause such variations in the overall level of spending in the economy? In order to gain a clearer view of how the economy works and why changes occur over time, it is necessary to refine the basic model by incorporating a number of other key variables – including other forms of consumption – that influence economic activity. These variables – notably savings, investment, government spending and taxation, overseas trade – are discussed below.

Changes in economic activity

The level of spending by consumers on goods and services produced by indigenous firms is influenced by a variety of factors. For a start, most households pay tax on income earned, which has the effect of reducing the level of income available for consumption. Added to this, some consumers prefer to save (i.e. not spend) a proportion of their income or to spend it on imported products, both of which mean that the income of domestic firms is less than it would have been had the income been spent with them.

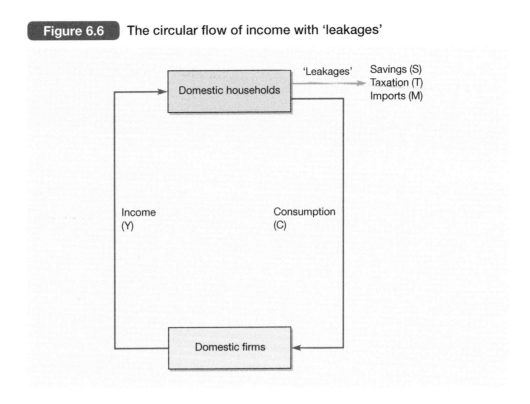

Figure 6.6   The circular flow of income with 'leakages'

Circumstances such as these represent what economists call a **leakage** (or **withdrawal**) from the **circular flow of income** and help to explain why the revenue of businesses can fluctuate over time (see Figure 6.6).

At the same time as such 'leakages' are occurring, additional forms of spending in the economy are helping to boost the potential income of domestic firms. Savings by some consumers may be borrowed by firms to spend on investment in capital equipment or plant or premises (known as investment spending) and this generates income for firms producing capital goods. Similarly, governments use taxation to spend on the provision of public goods and services (public or government expenditure) and overseas buyers purchase products produced by indigenous firms (export spending). Together, these additional forms of spending represent an **injection** of income into the circular flow (see Figure 6.7).

While the revised model of the economy illustrated in Figure 6.7 is still highly simplified (e.g. consumers also borrow savings to spend on consumption or imports; firms also save and buy imports; governments also invest in capital projects), it demonstrates quite clearly that fluctuations in the level of economic activity are the result of changes in a number of variables, many of which are outside the control of firms or governments. Some of these changes are autonomous (i.e. spontaneous), as in the case of an increased demand for imports, while others may be deliberate or overt, as when the government decides to increase its own spending or to reduce taxation in order to stimulate demand. Equally, from time to time an economy may be subject to 'external shocks', such as the onset of recession among its principal trading partners or a significant price rise in a key commodity (e.g. oil price rises in 2007–8), which can have an important effect on internal income flows. Taken together, these and other changes help to explain why demand for goods and services constantly fluctuates and why changes occur not only

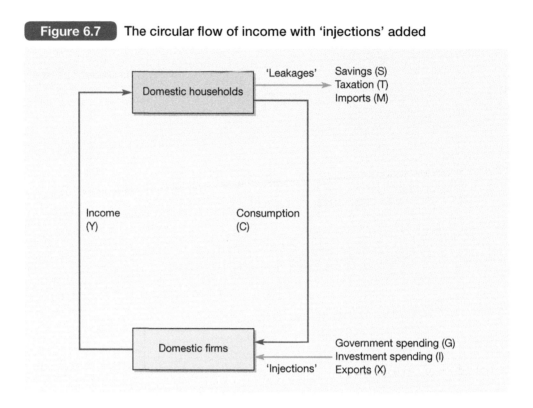

Figure 6.7   The circular flow of income with 'injections' added

in an economy's capacity to produce output but also in its structure and performance over time.

It is important to recognise that where changes in spending do occur, these invariably have consequences for the economy that go beyond the initial 'injection' or 'withdrawal' of income. For example, a decision by government to increase spending on infrastructure would benefit the firms involved in the various projects and some of the additional income they receive would undoubtedly be spent on hiring labour. The additional workers employed would have more income to spend on consumption and this would boost the income for firms producing consumer goods, which in turn might hire more staff, generating further consumption and so on. In short, the initial increase in spending by government will have additional effects on income and spending in the economy, as the extra spending circulates from households to firms and back again. Economists refer to this as the **multiplier effect** to emphasise the reverberative consequences of any increase or decrease in spending by consumers, firms, governments or overseas buyers.

Multiple increases in income and consumption can also give rise to an **accelerator effect**, which is the term used to describe a change in investment spending by firms as a result of a change in consumer spending. In the example above it is possible that the increase in consumption caused by the increase in government spending might persuade some firms to invest in more stock and capital equipment to meet increased consumer demands. Demand for capital goods would therefore rise, and this could cause further increases in the demand for industrial products (e.g. components, machinery) and also for consumer goods, as firms seek to increase their output to meet the changing market conditions. Should consumer spending fall, a reverse accelerator may occur and the same would apply to the multiplier as the reduction in consumption reverberates through the economy and causes further cuts in both consumption and investment. As the late Peter Donaldson has suggested, everything in the economy affects everything else; the economy is dynamic, interactive and mobile and is far more complex than implied by the model used in the analysis above.[1]

Government and the macroeconomy: objectives

Notwithstanding the complexities of the real economy, the link between business activity and spending is clear to see. This spending, as indicated above, comes from consumers, firms, governments and external sources and collectively can be said to represent total demand in the economy for goods and services. Economists frequently indicate this with the following notation:

Aggregate monetary demand = Consumer spending + Investment spending
+ Government spending + Export spending
– Import spending

or $$AMD = C + I + G + X - M$$

Within this equation, consumer spending (C) is regarded as by far the most important factor in determining the level of total demand.

While economists might disagree about what are the most significant influences on the component elements of AMD, it is widely accepted that governments have a crucial role to play in shaping demand, not only in their own sector but also on the market side of the economy. Government policies on spending and taxation, or on interest rates, clearly have both a direct and indirect influence on the behaviour of individuals and firms, which can affect both the demand and supply sides of the economy in a variety of ways. Underlying these policies is a number of key objectives pursued by government as a prerequisite to a healthy economy and which help to guide the choice of policy options. Understanding the broad choice of policies available to government, and the objectives associated with them, is of prime importance to students of the business environment.

Most governments appear to have a number of key economic objectives, the most important of which are normally the control of inflation, the pursuit of economic growth, a reduction in unemployment, the achievement of an acceptable balance of payments situation, controlling public (i.e. government) borrowing, and a relatively stable exchange rate.

Controlling inflation

Inflation is usually defined as an upward and persistent movement in the general level of prices over a given period of time; it can also be characterised as a fall in the value of money. For governments of all political complexions, reducing such movements to a minimum is seen as a primary economic objective (e.g. under the **Consumer Price Index** the UK government's declared inflation target is 2 per cent).

Monitoring trends in periodic price movements tends to take a number of forms. In the UK these have included:

1 The use of a **Retail Price Index (RPI)**, which measures how an average family's spending on goods and services is affected by price changes. The RPI has traditionally been the measure used for **headline inflation** in the UK and includes mortgage interest payments.
2 An examination of the **underlying rate of inflation**, which excludes the effects of mortgage payments (known as RPIX in the UK).
3 Measuring **factory gate prices**, to indicate likely future changes in consumer prices.
4 Comparing domestic inflation rates with those of the United Kingdom's chief overseas competitors, as an indication of the international competitiveness of UK firms.

With regard to the latter, the UK now uses a new measure of inflation known as the Consumer Price Index (CPI) to allow for a more direct comparison of the inflation rate in the UK with that of the rest of Europe. The CPI excludes a number of items that have historically been part of the RPIX, especially items relating to housing costs (e.g. mortgage interest payments and council tax).

In addition, changes in **monetary aggregates**, which measure the amount of money (and therefore potential spending power) in circulation in the economy, and movements of exchange rates (especially a depreciating currency) are also seen as a guide to possible future price increases, as their effects work through the economy.

Explanations as to why prices tend to rise over time vary considerably, but broadly speaking fall into two main categories. Supply-siders tend to focus on rising production costs – particularly wages, energy and imported materials – as a major reason for inflation, with firms passing on increased costs to the consumer in the form of higher wholesale and/or retail prices. Demand-siders, in contrast, tend to emphasise the importance of excessive demand in the economy, brought about, for example, by tax cuts, cheaper borrowing or excessive government spending, which encourages firms to take advantage of the consumer's willingness to spend money by increasing their prices. Where indigenous firms are unable to satisfy all the additional demand, the tendency is for imports to increase. This may not only cause further price rises, particularly if imported goods are more expensive or if exchange rate movements become unfavourable, but also can herald a deteriorating balance of payments situation and difficult trading conditions for domestic businesses.

Government concern with inflation – which crosses both party and state boundaries – reflects the fact that rising price levels can have serious consequences for the economy in general and for businesses in particular, especially if a country's domestic inflation rates are significantly higher than those of its main competitors. In markets where price is an important determinant of demand, rising prices may result in some businesses losing sales, and this can affect turnover and may ultimately affect employment if firms reduce their labour force in order to reduce their costs. Added to this, the uncertainty caused by a difficult trading environment may make some businesses unwilling to invest in new plant and equipment, particularly if interest rates are high and if inflation looks unlikely to fall for some time. Such a response, while understandable, is unlikely to improve a firm's future competitiveness or its ability to exploit any possible increases in demand as market conditions change.

Rising prices may also affect businesses by encouraging employees to seek higher wages in order to maintain or increase their living standards. Where firms agree to such wage increases, the temptation, of course, is to pass this on to the consumer in the form of a price rise, especially if demand looks unlikely to be affected to any great extent. Should this process occur generally in the economy, the result may be a **wages/prices inflationary spiral**, in which wage increases push up prices which push up wage increases which further push up prices and so on. From an international competitive point of view, such an occurrence, if allowed to continue unchecked, could be disastrous for both firms and the economy. Thankfully, such a situation tends to be relatively uncommon in most economies, but, as recent problems in Zimbabwe have illustrated, hyperinflation can have disastrous consequences for a country's economy and its population (in mid-2008, for example, annual inflation in Zimbabwe was estimated at around 40 million per cent!).

Economic growth

Growth is an objective shared by governments and organisations alike. For governments, the aim is usually to achieve steady and sustained levels of non-inflationary growth, preferably led by exports (i.e. export-led growth), with growth being indicated by annual increases in **real national income** or **gross domestic product** (where 'real' = allowing for inflation and 'gross domestic product (GDP)' = the economy's annual output of goods and services measured in monetary terms).[2] To compensate for changes in the size of the population, growth rates tend to be expressed in terms of real national income per capita (i.e. real GDP divided by population).

Exactly what constitutes desirable levels of growth is difficult to say, except in very broad terms. If given a choice, governments would basically prefer:

- steady levels of real growth (e.g. 3–4 per cent p.a.), rather than annual increases in output which vary widely over the business cycle;
- growth rates higher than those of one's chief competitors; and
- growth based on investment in technology and on increased export sales, rather than on excessive government spending or current consumption.

It is worth remembering that, when measured on a monthly or quarterly basis, increases in output can occur at a declining rate and GDP growth can become negative. In the United Kingdom, a **recession** is said to exist following two consecutive quarters of negative GDP.

From a business point of view, the fact that increases in output are related to increases in consumption suggests that **economic growth** is good for business prospects and hence for investment and employment, and by and large this is the case. The rising living standards normally associated with such growth may, however, encourage increased consumption of imported goods and services at the expense of indigenous producers, to a point where some domestic firms are forced out of business and the economy's manufacturing base becomes significantly reduced (often called **deindustrialisation**). Equally, if increased consumption is based largely on excessive state spending, the potential gains for businesses may be offset by the need to increase interest rates to fund that spending (where government borrowing is involved) and by the tendency of government demands for funding to **crowd out** the private sector's search for investment capital. In such cases, the short-term benefits from government-induced consumption may be more than offset by the medium- and long-term problems for the economy that are likely to arise.

Where growth prospects for the economy look good, business confidence tends to increase and, as indicated above, this is often reflected in increased levels of investment and stock holding and ultimately in levels of employment. In Britain, for example, the monthly and quarterly surveys by the Confederation of British Industry (CBI) provide evidence of how output, investment and stock levels change at different points of the business cycle and these are generally seen as a good indication of future business trends, as interpreted by entrepreneurs. Other indicators – including the state of the housing market and construction generally – help to provide a guide to the current and future state of the economy, including its prospects for growth in the short and medium term.

> **web link**   The CBI's website address is *www.cbi.org.uk*

Reducing unemployment

In most democratic states the goal of **full employment** is no longer part of the political agenda; instead government pronouncements on employment tend to focus on job creation and maintenance and on developing the skills appropriate to future demands. The consensus seems to be that in technologically advanced market-based economies, some unemployment is inevitable and that the basic aim should be to reduce unemployment to a level that is both politically and socially acceptable.

As with growth and inflation, unemployment levels tend to be measured at regular intervals (e.g. monthly, quarterly, annually), with the figures being adjusted to take into account seasonal influences (e.g. school-leavers entering the job market). Official statistics usually provide information on trends in long-term unemployment, areas of skill shortage and international comparisons, as well as sectoral changes within the economy. All of these indicators provide clues to the current state of the economy and to the prospects for businesses in the coming months and years, but need to be used with care. Unemployment, for example, tends to continue rising for a time even when a recession is over; equally, it is not uncommon for government definitions of unemployment to change or for international unemployment data to be based on different criteria.

The broader social and economic consequences of high levels of unemployment are well documented: it is a waste of resources; it puts pressure on the public services and on the Exchequer (e.g. by reducing tax yields and increasing public expenditure on welfare provision); it is frequently linked with growing social and health problems. Its implication for businesses, however, tends to be less clear-cut. On the one hand, a high level of unemployment implies a pool of labour available for firms seeking workers (though not necessarily with the right skills), generally at wage levels lower than when a shortage of labour occurs. On the other hand, it can also give rise to a fall in overall demand for goods and services, which could exacerbate any existing deflationary forces in the economy, causing further unemployment and with it further reductions in demand. Where this occurs, economists tend to describe it as **cyclical unemployment** (i.e. caused by a general deficiency in demand) in order to differentiate it from unemployment caused by a deficiency in demand for the goods produced by a particular industry (**structural unemployment**) or by the introduction of new technology which replaces labour (**technological unemployment**).

A favourable balance of payments

A country's **balance of payments** is essentially the net balance of credits (earnings) and debits (payments) arising from its international trade over a given period of time. Where credits exceed debits, a balance of payments surplus exists, the opposite being described as a deficit. Understandably, governments tend to prefer either equilibrium in the balance of payments, or surpluses rather than deficits. For a government facing persistent balance of payments deficits, a sustained reduction in the size of the deficit may also be regarded as signifying a 'favourable' balance of payments situation.

Like other economic indicators, the balance of payments statistics come in a variety of forms and at different levels of disaggregation, allowing useful comparisons to be made not only on a country's comparative trading performance but also on the international competitiveness of particular industries and commodity groups or on the development or decline of specific external markets. Particular emphasis tends to be given to the balance of payments on current account, which measures imports and exports of goods and services and is thus seen as an indicator of the competitiveness of an economy's firms and industries. Sustained current account surpluses tend to suggest favourable trading conditions, which can help to boost growth, increase employment and investment and create a general feeling of confidence among the business community. They may also give rise to surpluses which domestic firms can use to finance overseas lending and investment, thus helping to generate higher levels of corporate foreign earnings in future years.

While it does not follow that a sustained current account deficit is inevitably bad for the country concerned, it often implies structural problems in particular sectors of its economy or possibly an exchange rate which favours importers rather than exporters. Many observers believe that the progressive decline of Britain's visible trading position after 1983 was an indication of the growing uncompetitiveness of its firms, particularly those producing finished manufactured goods for consumer markets at home and abroad. By the same token, Japan's current account trade surplus of around $120 billion in late 1995 was portrayed as a sign of the cut-throat competition of Japanese firms, particularly those involved in producing cars, electrical and electronic products, and photographic equipment.

Controlling public borrowing

Governments raise large amounts of revenue annually, mainly through taxation, and use this income to spend on a wide variety of public goods and services (see below). Where annual revenue exceeds government spending, a budget surplus occurs and the excess is often used to repay past debt (formerly known in the United Kingdom as the 'public sector debt repayment' or PSDR). The accumulated debt of past and present governments represents a country's **national debt**. In the UK this stood at around £1.16 trillion in 2013, which was more than 70 per cent of GDP.

Where governments face annual budget deficits rather than budget surpluses, they are said to have a 'public sector borrowing requirement' or PSBR (now known in the UK as **public sector net borrowing** or PSNB). While such deficits are not inevitably a problem, in the same way that a small personal overdraft is not necessarily critical for an individual, large-scale and persistent deficits are generally seen as a sign of an economy facing current and future difficulties which require urgent government action. The overriding concern over high levels of public borrowing tends to be focused on:

1 Its impact on interest rates, given that higher interest rates tend to be needed to attract funds from private sector uses to public sector uses.
2 The impact of high interest rates on consumption and investment and hence on the prospects of businesses.
3 The danger of the public sector 'crowding out' the private sector's search for funds for investment.
4 The opportunity cost of debt interest, especially in terms of other forms of public spending.
5 The general lack of confidence in the markets about the government's ability to control the economy and the likely effect this might have on inflation, growth and the balance of payments.
6 The need to meet the 'convergence criteria' laid down at Maastricht for entry to the single currency (e.g. central government debt no higher than 3 per cent of GDP).

The consensus seems to be that controlling public borrowing is best tackled by restraining the rate of growth of public spending rather than by increasing revenue through changes in taxation, since the latter could depress demand.

A stable exchange rate

A country's currency has two values: an internal value and an external value. Internally, its value is expressed in terms of the goods and services it can buy and hence it is affected by changes in domestic prices. Externally, its value is expressed as an **exchange rate**, which governs how much of another country's currency it can purchase (e.g. £1 = $2 or £1 = €1.20). Since foreign trade normally involves an exchange of currencies, fluctuations in the external value of a currency will influence the price of imports and exports and hence can affect the trading prospects for business, as well as a country's balance of payments and its rate of inflation.

On the whole, governments and businesses involved in international trade tend to prefer exchange rates to remain relatively stable, because of the greater degree of certainty this brings to the trading environment; it also tends to make overseas investors more confident that their funds are likely to hold their value. To this extent, schemes that seek to fix exchange rates within predetermined levels (e.g. the European Exchange Rate Mechanism (ERM)), or that encourage the use of a common currency (e.g. the euro), tend to have the support of the business community, which prefers predictability to uncertainty where trading conditions are concerned.

mini case   Digging in for the long term

For firms engaged in international trade, the strength of the currency (i.e. the exchange rate) is an important consideration. As the value of one currency changes against other currencies, this usually alters the price of imported/exported products and this can make them more/less attractive to potential customers. To mitigate the impact of exchange rate changes, some firms engage in a process known as hedging, which basically involves trying to reduce or eliminate exchange rate risks, for example by buying a proportion of a currency forward (i.e. before it is needed) at an agreed price. An alternative strategy is to consider producing the product in different locations (e.g. setting up manufacturing facilities in other countries), which can offset some of the impact of currency fluctuations, as well as providing other potential benefits to a business.

A good example of the latter approach is provided by JCB, the UK-owned private company famous for its yellow construction equipment (e.g. diggers). In the 1990s, the company's business was mainly based in the UK and parts of western Europe, but faced with a limited market and a strengthening pound, which made exporting difficult, the firm decided to seek a global presence by investing in manufacturing abroad. Focusing first on the USA, JCB built a plant in Georgia in the late 1990s to exploit the US market; this was followed by further plants in Sao Paulo in Brazil and new plants in India near Mumbai. It also acquired a German construction firm in 2005 and opened a further factory near Shanghai in 2006, thereby adding to its global reach.

Despite having to shed some jobs in the global recession, by 2013 the company's global workforce numbered around 10,000 based on four continents and it was selling its product in 150 countries via a network of dealerships. In September of that year the firm opened the world's biggest JCB dealer depot in Ekaterinberg, Russia, following a multi-million-pound investment.

In addition to the potential currency benefits of operating in different countries, JCB has gained a number of other advantages, including establishing a global brand name, access to low-cost suppliers and to developing markets, and reducing freight costs and tariff barriers. Globalisation, in short, can offer businesses many 'opportunities', but we must not forget that it can also give rise to substantial 'threats' at the corporate level, not least the danger of low-cost competitors invading one's own markets.

Government and the macroeconomy: policies

Governments throughout Europe and beyond play various key roles in their respective economies. These include the following functions:

- consumer of resources (e.g. employer, landowner);
- supplier of resources (e.g. infrastructure, information);
- consumer of goods and services (e.g. government spending);
- supplier of goods and services (e.g. nationalised industries);
- regulator of business activity (e.g. employment laws, consumer laws);
- regulator of the economy (e.g. fiscal and monetary policies); and
- redistributor of income and wealth (e.g. taxation system).

The extent of these roles, and their impact on the economy in general and on business in particular, varies from country to country as well as over time.

Despite the economic significance of these roles, in most market-based economies democratically elected governments prefer levels and patterns of production and consumption to be determined largely by market forces, with a minimum of government interference. At the same time, the recognition that market forces alone are unable to guarantee that an economy will automatically achieve the objectives established by governments has meant that state intervention – to curb inflation, encourage growth, reduce unemployment, correct a balance of payments or budgetary problem or restore currency stability – invariably occurs to some degree in all countries. In broad terms, this intervention usually takes three main forms, described as fiscal policy, monetary policy and direct controls. These policy instruments – or 'instrumental variables' – and their effects on the business community are discussed below.

Fiscal policy

As indicated above, each year governments raise and spend huge amounts of money. The UK government's estimates for 2013, for example, suggested that **government spending** would be about £720 billion and was to be allocated in the manner illustrated in Figure 6.8. This spending was to be funded mainly from **taxation (direct and indirect)** and national insurance contributions (see Figure 6.9). The PSNB was estimated at £108 billion.

Fiscal policy involves the use of changes in government spending and taxation to influence the level and composition of aggregate demand in the economy and, given the amounts involved, this clearly has important implications for business. Elementary circular flow analysis suggests, for instance, that reductions in taxation and/or increases in government spending will inject additional income into the economy and will, via the multiplier effect, increase the demand for goods and services, with favourable consequences for business. Reductions in government spending and/or increases in taxation will have the opposite effect, depressing business prospects and probably discouraging investment and causing a rise in unemployment.

Apart from their overall impact on aggregate demand, fiscal changes can be used to achieve specific objectives, some of which will be of direct or indirect benefit to the business community. Reductions in taxes on company profits and/or increases in tax allowances for investment in capital equipment can be used to encourage business to increase investment spending, hence boosting the income of firms producing industrial products and causing some additional spending on consumption. Similarly, increased government spending targeted at firms involved in exporting, or at the creation of new business, will encourage increased business activity and additionally may lead to more output and employment in the economy.

In considering the use of fiscal policy to achieve their objectives, governments tend to be faced with a large number of practical problems that generally limit their room for manoeuvre. Boosting the economy through increases in spending or reductions in taxation could cause inflationary pressures, as well as encouraging an inflow of imports and increasing the public sector deficit, none of which would be particularly welcomed by entrepreneurs or by the financial markets. By the same token, fiscal attempts to restrain demand in order to reduce inflation will generally depress the economy, causing a fall in output and employment and encouraging firms to abandon or defer investment projects until business prospects improve.

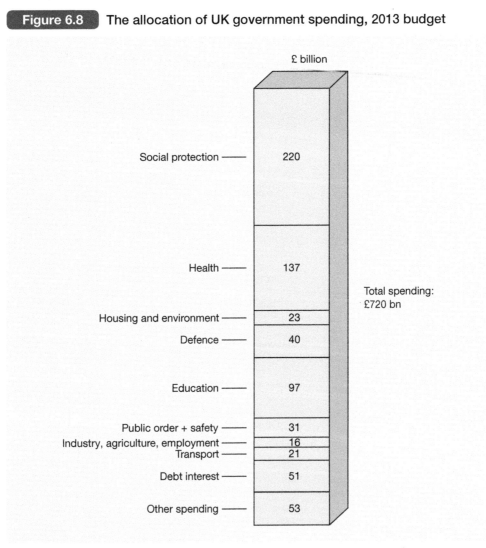

Figure 6.8   The allocation of UK government spending, 2013 budget

£ billion

Social protection —— 220

Health —— 137

Housing and environment —— 23

Defence —— 40

Education —— 97

Public order + safety —— 31

Industry, agriculture, employment —— 16

Transport —— 21

Debt interest —— 51

Other spending —— 53

Total spending:
£720 bn

Source: Adapted from Budget Statement, 2013.

Added to this, it should not be forgotten that government decision-makers are politicians who need to consider the political as well as the economic implications of their chosen courses of action. Thus, while cuts in taxation may receive public approval, increases may not, and, if implemented, the latter may encourage higher wage demands. Similarly, the redistribution of government spending from one programme area to another is likely to give rise to widespread protests from those on the receiving end of any cuts, so much so that governments tend to be restricted for the most part to changes at the margin, rather than undertaking a radical reallocation of resources and they may be tempted to fix budgetary allocations for a number of years ahead (e.g. the introduction of the Comprehensive Spending Review in the UK).

Other factors too – including changes in economic thinking, self-imposed fiscal rules, external constraints on borrowing and international agreements – can play their part in restraining the use of fiscal policy as an instrument of demand management, whatever a government's preferred course of action may be. Simple prescriptions to boost the economy through large-scale cuts in taxation or increases in government spending

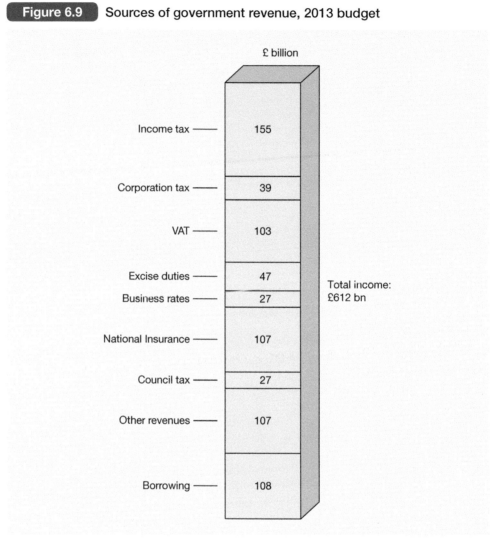

Figure 6.9   Sources of government revenue, 2013 budget

Source: Adapted from Budget Statement, 2013.

often fail to take into account the political and economic realities of the situation faced by most governments.

Monetary policy

Monetary policy seeks to influence monetary variables such as the money supply or rates of interest in order to regulate the economy. While the supply of money and interest rates (i.e. the cost of borrowing) are interrelated, it is convenient to consider them separately.

As far as changes in **interest rates** are concerned, these clearly have implications for business activity, as circular flow analysis demonstrates. Lower interest rates not only encourage firms to invest as the cost of borrowing falls, they also encourage consumption as disposable incomes rise (predominantly through the mortgage effect) and as the cost of loans and overdrafts decreases. Such increased consumption tends to be an added spur to investment, particularly if inflation rates (and therefore **'real' interest rates**) are low, and this can help to boost the economy in the short term, as well as improving the supply side in the longer term.[3]

Raising interest rates tends to have the opposite effect – causing a fall in consumption as mortgages and other prices rise, and deferring investment because of the additional cost of borrowing and the decline in business confidence as consumer spending falls. If interest rates remain persistently high, the encouragement given to savers and the discouragement given to borrowers and spenders may help to generate a recession, characterised by falling output, income, spending and employment and by increasing business failure.

Changes in the **money stock** (especially credit) affect the capacity of individuals and firms to borrow and, therefore, to spend. Increases in money supply are generally related to increases in spending and this tends to be good for business prospects, particularly if interest rates are falling as the money supply rises (see the case study at this end of this chapter). Restrictions on monetary growth normally work in the opposite direction, especially if such restrictions help to generate increases in interest rates which feed through to both consumption and investment, both of which will tend to decline.

As in the case of fiscal policy, government is usually able to manipulate monetary variables in a variety of ways, including taking action in the money markets to influence interest rates and controlling its own spending to influence monetary growth. Once again, however, circumstances tend to dictate how far and in what way government is free to operate. Attempting to boost the economy by allowing the money supply to grow substantially, for instance, threatens to cause inflationary pressures and to increase spending on imports, both of which run counter to government objectives and do little to assist domestic firms. Similarly, policies to boost consumption and investment through lower interest rates, while welcomed generally by industry, offer no guarantee that any additional spending will be on domestically produced goods and services, and also tend to make the financial markets nervous about government commitments to control inflation in the longer term (see below, 'The role of the central bank').

This nervousness among market dealers reflects the fact that in modern market economies a government's policies on interest rates and monetary growth cannot be taken in isolation from those of its major trading partners and this operates as an important constraint on government action. The fact is that a reduction in interest rates to boost output and growth in an economy also tends to be reflected in the exchange rate; this usually falls as foreign exchange dealers move funds into those currencies that yield a better return and that also appear a safer investment if the market believes a government is abandoning its counter-inflationary policy. As the UK government found in the early 1990s, persistently high rates of interest in Germany severely restricted its room for manoeuvre on interest rates for fear of the consequences for sterling if relative interest rates got too far out of line.

Direct controls

Fiscal and monetary policies currently represent the chief policy instruments used in modern market economies and hence they have been discussed in some detail. Governments, however, also use a number of other weapons from time to time in their attempts to achieve their macroeconomic objectives. Such weapons, which are designed essentially to achieve a specific objective – such as limiting imports or controlling wage increases – tend to be known as **direct controls**. Examples of such policies include:

- *incomes policies*, which seek to control inflationary pressures by influencing the rate at which wages and salaries rise;
- *import controls*, which attempt to improve a country's balance of payments situation, by reducing either the supply of, or the demand for, imported goods and services;
- *regional and urban policies*, which are aimed at alleviating urban and regional problems, particularly differences in income, output, employment, and local and regional decline.

A brief discussion of some of these policy instruments is found at various points in the text below. Students wishing to study these in more detail are recommended to consult the books referred to at the end of this chapter.

The role of financial institutions

Interactions in the macroeconomy between governments, businesses and consumers take place within an institutional environment that includes a large number of financial intermediaries. These range from banks and building societies to pension funds, insurance companies, investment trusts and issuing houses, all of which provide a number of services of both direct and indirect benefit to businesses. As part of the financial system within a market-based economy, these institutions fulfil a vital role in channelling funds from those able and willing to lend, to those individuals and organisations wishing to borrow in order to consume or invest. It is appropriate to consider briefly this role of financial intermediation and the supervision exercised over the financial system by the central bank, before concluding the chapter with a review of important international economic institutions.

Elements of the financial system

A financial system basically comprises three main elements:

1 *Lenders and borrowers* – these may be individuals, organisations or governments.
2 *Financial institutions*, of various kinds, which act as intermediaries between lenders and borrowers and which manage their own asset portfolios in the interest of their shareholders and/or depositors.
3 *Financial markets*, in which lending and borrowing take place through the transfer of money and/or other types of asset, including paper assets such as shares and stock.

Financial institutions, as indicated above, comprise a wide variety of organisations, many of which are public companies with shareholders. Markets include the markets for short-term funds of various types (usually termed **money markets**) and those for long-term finance for both the private and public sectors (usually called the **capital market**). **Stock exchanges** normally lie at the centre of the latter and constitute an important market for existing securities issued by both companies and government.

The vital role played by **financial intermediaries** in the operation of the financial system is illustrated in Figure 6.10 and reflects the various benefits that derive from using an intermediary rather than lending direct to a borrower (e.g. creating a large pool of savings, spreading risk, transferring short-term lending into longer-term borrowing, providing various types of funds transfer services). Lenders on the whole prefer low risk, high returns, flexibility and liquidity, while borrowers prefer to minimise the cost of borrowing and to use the funds in a way that is best suited to their needs. Companies, for example, may borrow to finance stock or work-in-progress or to meet short-term debts and such borrowing may need to be as flexible as possible. Alternatively, they may wish to borrow in order to replace plant and equipment or to buy new premises – borrowing which needs to be over a much longer term and which hopefully will yield a rate of return that makes the use of the funds and the cost of borrowing worthwhile.

The process of channelling funds from lenders to borrowers often gives rise to paper claims, which are generated either by the financial intermediary issuing a claim to the lender (e.g. when a bank borrows by issuing a certificate of deposit) or by the borrower issuing a claim to the financial intermediary (e.g. when government sells stock to a financial institution). These paper claims represent a liability to the issuer and an asset to the holder and can be traded on a secondary market (i.e. a market for existing securities), according to the needs of the individual or organisation holding the paper claim. At any point, financial intermediaries tend to hold a wide range of such assets (claims on borrowers), which they buy or sell ('manage') in order to yield a profit and/or improve their liquidity position. Decisions of this kind, taken on a daily basis, invariably affect

Figure 6.10 The role of financial intermediaries

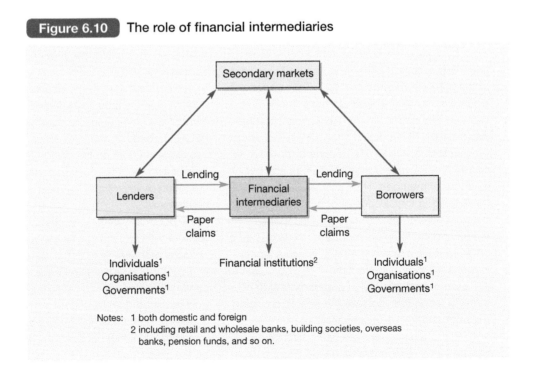

Notes: 1 both domestic and foreign
2 including retail and wholesale banks, building societies, overseas banks, pension funds, and so on.

the position of investors (e.g. shareholders) and customers (e.g. depositors) and can, under certain circumstances, have serious consequences for the financial intermediary and its stakeholders (e.g. the bad debts faced by financial institutions in the wake of the sub-prime mortgage crisis in the USA from 2007–8 onwards).

Given the element of risk, it is perhaps not surprising that some financial institutions have historically been conservative in their attitude towards lending on funds deposited with them, especially in view of their responsibilities to their various stakeholders. In general, UK retail banks have a long-standing preference for financing industry's working capital rather than investment spending, and hence the latter has tended to be financed largely by internally generated funds (e.g. retained profits) or by share issues. In comparison, banks in Germany, France, the United States and Japan tend to be more ready to meet industry's medium- and longer-term needs and are often directly involved in regular discussions with their clients concerning corporate strategy, in contrast to the arm's length approach favoured by many of their UK counterparts.[4] As the global financial crisis has illustrated, however, the increasing complexity of financial instruments and the willingness of some traders to take risks in pursuit of higher corporate (and personal) rewards suggests that the past deregulation of the financial system may have come at a significant price.

mini case   A new kid on the block: the rise of the credit rating agency

Credit rating agencies have become powerful and influential organisations in world finance, rating the 'credit worthiness' of both companies and countries and thereby often helping to influence lending and investment decisions.

Of more than 150 agencies worldwide, the three best known are Standard & Poor's, Moody's and Fitch, which together rate about 95 per cent of the market for corporate debt. These agencies, which date back to the early 20th century, first came to prominence in the 1980s following the deregulation of the global financial system and the increasing willingness of large businesses to borrow from a wider range of sources and by a variety of methods. Their assessments of the likelihood that a country or a company will default on its debts are widely trailed in the media and can play an important role in deciding on the price (i.e. interest rate) at which a lender is prepared to provide funding to the borrower. In the case of both sovereign and corporate debt, a falling rating can increase the cost of servicing the debt and hence is something borrowers are keen to avoid. Once the rating falls below a certain level – where AAA is the gold standard –

this is known as 'junk status', indicating that a default is more likely and invariably pushing up interest rates significantly.

It is interesting to note that credit rating agencies are funded by the companies they rate, with organisations wishing to acquire a rating having to pay a fee for the privilege, which varies according to the size of the business. Some observers believe that this creates a potential conflict of interest by encouraging an agency to award the company the rating it would like. Others have criticised the agencies for regularly inaccurate assessments both on the upside and the downside or for being too influential, particularly where the rating of sovereign (i.e. government) debt is concerned.

By potentially helping to push up interest rates for countries struggling with serious economic and financial problems (e.g. certain Eurozone countries in recent years), adverse rating agency judgements can make it more difficult and more costly for a government to turn its situation round. In the real economy, both firms and households may be forced to pay a higher price than might otherwise be the case.

The role of the central bank

A critical element in a country's financial system is its **central** or **state bank**; in the United Kingdom this is the Bank of England. Like most of its overseas counterparts, the Bank of England exercises overall supervision over the banking sector, with the aim of maintaining a stable and efficient financial framework as part of its contribution to a healthy economy. Its activities have a significant influence in the financial markets (especially the foreign exchange market, the gilts market and the sterling money market). These activities include the following roles:

- banker to the government;
- banker to the clearing banks;
- manager of the country's foreign reserves;
- manager of the national debt;
- manager of the issue of notes and coins;
- supervisor of the monetary sector; and
- implementer of the government's monetary policy.

Since 1997 the Bank has also been granted 'operational independence' to set interest rates and to conduct other aspects of monetary policy free from Treasury interference as part of its core purpose of ensuring monetary stability (e.g. controlling inflation and protecting the currency). Interest rates are set at the monthly meetings of the Bank's Monetary Policy Committee (MPC), which is chaired by the Bank governor. In order to facilitate forward planning by businesses and financial institutions and to promote market stability, the MPC also now provides forward guidance on aspects of monetary policy, particularly interest rates.

In response to the problems resulting from the global financial crisis, the Bank has recently acquired an enhanced role in promoting and developing greater financial stability. Under the Financial Services Act 2012, a Financial Policy Committee has been established with responsibility for taking action to remove or reduce systemic risks in the financial system and generally supporting government economic policy (i.e. a macro-level role). Alongside this new body is a Prudential Regulation Authority that has been set up to supervise the key financial institutions (e.g. banks, building societies, insurers) so as to protect policy-holders and investors and promote sound practices within the financial system (i.e. a micro-level role).

 web link   For further information on the Bank of England you should consult *www.bankofengland.co.uk*

While central banks are nationally-based institutions, the EU also has its own central bank, the **European Central Bank (ECB)**, which is based in Frankfurt. The main task of the ECB is to maintain the purchasing power of the euro and hence to promote price stability within the Eurozone. Among its key roles are defining and implementing monetary policy for the Eurozone, including foreign exchange operations and issuing euro banknotes. It has also been heavily involved in bond purchasing in struggling EU economies to support the value of the euro.

web link   The ECB's website is *www.ecb.europa.eu*

International economic institutions and organisations

Given that external factors constrain the ability of governments to regulate their economy, it is appropriate to conclude this analysis of the macroeconomic context of business with a brief review of a number of important international economic institutions and organisations that affect the trading environment. Foremost among these is the European Union. In the discussions below we look at the International Monetary Fund (IMF), the Organisation for Economic Co-operation and Development (OECD), the European Bank for Reconstruction and Development (EBRD), the World Trade Organisation (WTO) and the World Bank (IBRD).

The International Monetary Fund (IMF)

The IMF is an international organisation currently of 184 member countries. It came into being in 1946 following discussions at Bretton Woods in the USA which sought to agree a world financial order for the post-Second World War period that would avoid the problems associated with the worldwide depression in the inter-war years. Its original role was to provide a pool of foreign currencies from its member states that would be used to smooth out trade imbalances between countries, thereby promoting a structured growth in world trade and encouraging exchange rate stability. In this way, the architects of the Fund believed that the danger of international protectionism would be reduced and that all countries would consequently benefit from the boost given to world trade and the greater stability of the international trading environment.

 The IMF's website is *www.imf.org*

While this role as international 'lender of last resort' still exists, the IMF's focus in recent years has tended to switch towards international surveillance and to helping the developing economies with their mounting debt problems and assisting eastern Europe with reconstruction, following the break-up of the Soviet empire.[5] More recently it has played a major role in lending to countries caught up in the global financial crisis in order to boost the global economy. To some extent its position as an international decision-making body has been diminished by the tendency of the world's leading economic countries to deal with global economic problems outside the IMF's institutional framework. The United States, Japan, Germany, France, Italy, Canada, Britain and Russia now meet regularly as the Group of Eight (G8) leading industrial economies to discuss issues of mutual interest (e.g. the environment, eastern Europe). These world economic summits, as they are frequently called, have tended to supersede discussions in the IMF and as a result normally attract greater media attention. Key global and economic issues are also discussed at meetings of the **G20**, which includes the G8 countries and a number of other key players, including China, India and Brazil.

The Organisation for Economic Co-operation and Development (OECD)

The OECD came into being in 1961, but its roots go back to 1948 when the Organisation for European Economic Co-operation (OEEC) was established to coordinate the distribution of Marshall Aid to the war-torn economies of western Europe. Today it comprises 34 members, drawn from the rich industrial countries and including the G7 nations, Australia, New Zealand and most other European states. Collectively, these countries account for less than 20 per cent of the world's population but produce around two-thirds of its output – hence the tendency of commentators to refer to the OECD as the 'rich man's club'.

You can access the OECD's website at *www.oecd.org*

The OECD is the main forum in which the governments of the world's leading industrial economies meet to discuss economic matters, particularly questions concerned with promoting stable growth and freer trade and with supporting development in poorer non-member countries. Through its council and committees, and backed by an independent secretariat, the organisation is able to take decisions which set out an agreed view and/or course of action on important social and economic issues of common concern. While it does not have the authority to impose ideas, its influence lies in its capacity for intellectual persuasion, particularly its ability through discussion to promote convergent thinking on international economic problems. To assist in the task, the OECD provides a wide variety of economic data on member countries, using standardised measures for national accounting, unemployment and purchasing-power parities. It is for these data – and especially its economic forecasts and surveys – that the organisation is perhaps best known.

The European Bank for Reconstruction and Development (EBRD)

The aims of the EBRD, which was inaugurated in April 1991, are to facilitate the transformation of the states of central and eastern Europe and beyond from centrally planned to free-market economies and to promote political and economic democracy, respect for human rights and respect for the environment. It is particularly involved with the privatisation process, project financing, technical assistance, training and investment in upgrading of the infrastructure and in facilitating economic, legal and financial restructuring. It works in cooperation with its members, private companies and organisations such as the IMF, OECD, the World Bank and the United Nations.

Information on the EBRD can be obtained at *www.ebrd.com*

The World Trade Organisation (WTO)

The World Trade Organisation, which came into being on 1 January 1995, superseded the General Agreement on Tariffs and Trade (the GATT), which dated back to 1947. Like the IMF and the International Bank for Reconstruction and Development (see below), which were established at the same time, the GATT was part of an attempt to reconstruct the international politico-economic environment in the period after the end of the Second World War. Its replacement by the WTO can be said to mark an attempt to put the question of liberalising world trade higher up on the international political agenda.

 The WTO can be accessed at *www.wto.org*

With a membership of more than 150 states (plus other observers), the WTO is a permanent international organisation charged with the task of liberalising world trade within an agreed legal and institutional framework. In addition it administers and implements a number of multilateral agreements in fields such as agriculture, textiles and services and is responsible for dealing with disputes arising from the Uruguay Round Final Act. It also provides a forum for the debate, negotiation and adjudication of trade problems and in the latter context is said to have a much stronger and quicker trade compliance and enforcement mechanism than existed under the GATT.

The World Bank (IBRD)

Established in 1945, the World Bank (more formally known as the International Bank for Reconstruction and Development, or IBRD) is a specialised agency of the United Nations, set up to encourage economic growth in developing countries through the provision of loans and technical assistance. The IBRD currently has over 180 members.

 The IBRD can be accessed at *www.worldbank.org*

The European Investment Bank (EIB)

The European Investment Bank was created in 1958 under the Treaty of Rome and is the financing institution of the European Union. Its main task is to contribute to the integration, balanced development and the economic and social cohesion of EU member states. Using funds raised on the markets, it finances capital projects which support EU objectives within the European Union and elsewhere. Its interests include environmental schemes, projects relating to transport and energy, and support for small and medium-sized enterprises.

For further information on the EIB see *www.eib.org*

Synopsis

Business and economics are inextricably linked. Economics is concerned with the problem of allocating scarce productive resources to alternative uses – a fundamental aspect of business activity. In market-based economies, this problem of resource allocation is largely solved through the operation of free markets, in which price is a vital ingredient. The existence of such markets tends to be associated primarily, though not exclusively, with democratic political regimes.

In all democratic states, government is a key component of the market economy and exercises considerable influence over the level and pattern of business activity – a point illustrated by the use of elementary circular flow analysis. A government's aims for the economy help to shape the policies it uses and these policies have both direct and indirect consequences for business organisations of all kinds.

In examining the economic context in which firms exist, due attention needs to be paid to the influence of a wide range of institutions and organisations, some of which operate at the international level. Equally, as markets become more open and business becomes more global, the fortunes of firms in trading economies become increasingly connected and hence subject to fluctuations that go beyond the boundaries of any individual state.

Summary of key points

- Business activity exists in and is affected by the broader macroeconomic environment; it also helps to shape that environment.

- Economics is concerned with how societies allocate scarce economic resources to alternative uses and the 'real costs' of the choices that are made.

- Broadly speaking, two main approaches to the problem of resource allocation exist: state planning and the market.

- Most economies in the world are market-based economies which operate through a price mechanism. Within such economies the state also plays a key role in some allocative decisions.

- In market economies, economic activity essentially involves 'real flows' and corresponding flows of income and expenditure between producers and consumers.

- Combining these flows into a simple model of the macroeconomy illustrates that income basically flows round the economy in a circular motion.

- Levels of income in the economy are related to levels of output, expenditure and employment.

- Changes in the level of economic activity can be explained by examining changes in one or more of the key economic variables such as consumer spending, saving, government decisions on state spending/taxation and external trade.

- Within the macroeconomy, governments often play a key role in influencing both the levels and patterns of demand in pursuit of their macroeconomic objectives.

- Key government objectives usually include controlling inflation, promoting economic growth, reducing unemployment, and creating a stable macroeconomic environment.

- To pursue these objectives governments use a range of policies, most notably fiscal and monetary policies.

- Government policy decisions take place within a broader economic and financial framework, which includes the influence of financial institutions and markets and the requirements that accrue from membership of different supranational and international organisations.

case study

Quantitative easing (QE)

As indicated by the analysis presented in this chapter, governments have a variety of options available when tackling a problem such as recession in the economy. Where monetary policy is concerned, a traditional approach has been to lower interest rates in the hope of boosting demand. This option has become increasingly difficult in recent years as interest rates in many countries have fallen to historically low levels in the wake of the global financial crisis that occurred after 2008.

An alternative approach that has become widely used in recent years (e.g. in Japan, the UK, the USA) is the policy known as quantitative (or credit) easing. In simple terms this involves a country's central bank 'creating' money electronically by crediting the accounts of financial institutions (e.g. banks, pension funds, insurance companies) in return for the purchase of assets, particularly government bonds held by these investors. By buying bonds, the central bank reduces their supply in the market, resulting in an increase in the price of these assets. Since bond prices move inversely to the yield they generate (i.e. the rate of interest on the asset), an increase in prices reduces long-term interest rates, thus making borrowing cheaper for businesses and mortgage holders. This, it is hoped, will help to stimulate demand, boost the housing and stock markets, and generally increase confidence among both firms and consumers.

The additional cash held by the financial institutions as a result of QE can also be used to purchase other assets, including equities and corporate bonds, and this could encourage firms to issue new stock to fund investment. In the case of the banks, this additional money can be lent on directly to consumers and businesses, thereby cascading through the economy and generally increasing economic activity. Coupled with low interest rates and a rising stock market, the conditions for a return to growth appear to be an inevitable consequence of this form of monetary stimulus to the economy.

Critics of QE tend to be less sanguine about its ability to achieve its objectives of boosting economic growth and reducing unemployment associated with a recession. One criticism is that there is no guarantee that the banks will pass on the additional cash to consumers and businesses. Instead, they may use it to speculate in, say, commodities (e.g. oil), thus pushing up commodity prices and making conditions even tougher for consumers, some of whom (e.g. pensioners about to invest in an annuity and savers generally) are already being adversely affected by low interest rates. Others have suggested that QE might be being used by a country surreptitiously to depress the value of its currency in the hope of making its exports more attractive on international markets. Given the tough global trading conditions that are affecting many countries at the moment, this development could prove highly controversial and could spark off an exchange rate and trading war.

A further concern has been that some of the global tidal wave of cheap money has found its way into emerging markets, such as India, and has helped to mask some underlying economic problems. With the Federal Reserve's announcement that it intends to taper off QE in the future – thereby reversing the huge investment flows – currencies such as the rupee have come under severe pressure in the currency markets as traders are beginning to question whether inflationary pressures can be contained and whether the country will be able to fund its trade deficit in the future. There are also fears that any phasing out of QE, if handled badly, could have adverse consequences for global bond markets and interest rates (see, for example, the IMF's Global Financial Stability Report, October 2013).

While it is probably too early to judge whether QE will work as intended, its adoption by central banks in different countries does at least underline the belief among policy-makers that it is sometimes necessary to intervene in the economy in order to tackle or fend off economic problems. As with most things in economics, what the best approach is tends to be a matter of opinion; matching ends and means is rarely free of controversy.

Case study questions

1 QE is seen as one way in which a government can stimulate the economy. What other approaches could it use?

2 Could QE lead to inflationary pressures in an economy, and if so, how?

Review and discussion questions

1 To what extent do you agree with the proposition that the market economy is the 'best' form of economic system? Do you have any reservations?

2 Explain how interest rates could be used to boost the economy. Why, then, do governments frequently hesitate to take such steps?

3 Using circular flow analysis, suggest why a large programme of capital expenditure by government (e.g. on new motorways, roads, railways) will benefit businesses. How could such a programme be financed?

4 Which businesses are likely to benefit from a recovery in a country's housing market?

Assignments

1 Imagine you work in the economic development unit of a local authority. Produce a draft report outlining the benefits to the local economy of encouraging direct inward investment. Indicate any disadvantages.

2 You are a trainee journalist on a regional or national newspaper. As part of your first big assignment, you have been asked to provide information on the 'privatisation' of eastern European economies. Using journals and newspapers, provide a scrapbook of information indicating the different ways in which western companies have sought to exploit business opportunities in eastern Europe.

Notes and references

1 Donaldson, P. and Farquhar, J., *Understanding the British Economy*, Penguin, 1988, p. 84.

2 See also the concept of gross value added (GVA), which is an important measure in the estimation of GDP. National Statistics Online has a good explanation of GVA.

3 Real interest rates allow for inflation.

4 See, for example, Neale, A. and Haslam, C., *Economics in a Business Context*, Chapman & Hall, 1991, p. 141.

5 The role of assisting reconstruction in eastern Europe is also undertaken by the European Bank for Reconstruction and Development (EBRD). See text below.

Further reading

Begg, D. and Ward, D., *Economics for Business*, 3rd edition, McGraw-Hill, 2009.

Donaldson, P. and Farquhar, J., *Understanding the British Economy*, Penguin, 1991.

Griffiths, A. and Wall, S. (eds), *Applied Economics*, 12th edition, Financial Times/Prentice Hall, 2011.

Griffiths, A. and Wall, S., *Economics for Business and Management*, 3rd edition, Financial Times/Prentice Hall, 2011.

Mulhearn, C., Vane, H. R. and Eden, J., *Economics for Business*, 2nd edition, Palgrave Macmillan, 2011.

Neale, A., Haslam, C. and Johal, S., *Economics in a Business Context*, Thomson Learning, 3rd edition, 2010.

Worthington, I., Britton, C. and Rees, A., *Economics for Business: Blending Theory and Practice*, 2nd edition, Financial Times/Prentice Hall, 2005.

7

The international cultural, demographic and social environment

Jon Stephens and Tony Purdie

Learning outcomes

On completion of this chapter you should be able to:

- understand the concept of national culture and its link with globalisation;
- have increased awareness of differences in national cultures and the reasons for this;
- identify differences in business cultures through the work of Hofstede and Trompenaars;
- appreciate the key factors that determine changes in a country's population;
- understand how demographic changes can be significant for both businesses and governments;
- have a clearer understanding of some of the key social trends in terms of family, lifestyle and crime;
- appreciate how the nature of organised labour has changed.

Key concepts

- national culture
- the convergence/divergence debate
- Hofstede's five dimensions of national culture
- Trompenaars' dimensions of national culture
- culture shock and culture shift
- national culture and business practices
- the rate of natural population change
- birth rate and death rate
- replacement fertility rate
- population pyramids
- dependency ratios
- international migration
- patterns of family development
- lifestyle trends
- organised labour
- changing work trends.

| Minicase 7.1 | The new Ford Fiesta |

In 1993 Ford Europe launched a new car, the Ford Mondeo. As the name implies, this was intended to be Ford's 'world car' that, with minor changes, would be sold by all Ford's regional businesses. The aim of this ambitious global strategy was primarily to reduce the cost of new product development by removing duplication of activities throughout the company. Why design a new car four or five times, when a single design could be sold everywhere?

Sadly, while the Mondeo sold well in Europe, it was not successful anywhere else. It was too small for the North American market and too large for the Far Eastern market. Furthermore, the design was deliberately bland so that it would be reasonably acceptable in all cultures – and ended up being considered unattractive compared with more stylish competitors.

After this relative failure, it might have been surprising to many when in 2008 Ford launched a new version of the smaller-sized Fiesta as part of its 'One Ford' strategy – in other words, another attempt to build a 'world car'. The new model, with small changes, was to go on sale in China in 2009 and America in 2010. Why should this venture prove more successful than the last one? An article in the *Economist* (2008) magazine gave an insight into the company's thinking.

The company believed that this smaller car (classed as a 'supermini') would be suitable for Far Eastern markets. In America, higher fuel prices and the approaching recession were encouraging buyers to trade down from the traditional 'gas guzzlers' to more fuel efficient cars, especially in urban areas. But the greatest change in thinking was the styling of the new car which was described as 'kinetic' and quite different in nature to the dull, staid look for which Ford had been known. The aim was to make the car into a 'fashion item' – to be 'drop-dead gorgeous' both inside and outside. The target market was to be young, prosperous, style-conscious adults – what the *Economist* calls the 'iPod' generation. As the global success of the iPod shows, this demographic group exists in most regions of the world.

If Ford has got its market research right, the new Fiesta will be the car that drags the company away from the threshold of bankruptcy.

Questions

1 Find out the latest sales figures for the new Fiesta in Europe and other regions of the world. Has the car been successful?

2 Can you identify other products which have been designed to appeal to this demographic group? What risks does a company face when it targets this group?

7.1 Introduction

This chapter covers some of the wider factors present in the increasingly complex business environment facing firms in the twenty-first century. It will start by examining the national cultural environment which is becoming more and more important as the process of globalisation continues and companies have to deal with and operate in different countries. This may be through direct investment or through joint ventures or strategic alliances but it will mean that management styles and practices that are used in the home country may or may not function efficiently in a different cultural environment. If these issues are not addressed by companies it could even lead to a 'culture shock' which can have a damaging impact on their overseas performance.

The first section of this chapter will identify some of the issues that determine cultural differences, making use of some key theoretical studies such as those by Hofstede and Trompenaars, and then will show how cultural differences can create problems within the business environment, before seeking to show how some of these cultural differences can be overcome and even turned into competitive advantage for companies that handle cultural differences effectively.

The second part of the chapter will look at the demographic environment and many of the issues arising from the demographic structures faced by organisations when they are operating internationally. Demographic changes are some of the most predictable changes in the business environment and the first section will look at some of the key components of natural population growth and the factors that influence these with examples drawn from many countries. The issue of international migration has also become more significant in determining population size and both legal and illegal migration will be looked at in this context. While the absolute size and the change in size of population will be very significant, it is also important for organisations to examine the changing structures of populations as this may have important implications for market attractiveness. One way of looking at changing populations is by using population pyramids and these will also be examined in this chapter. The structure of the population may have very important implications for governments as well as business organisations. One of the major issues facing governments in Western Europe is the impact of ageing populations and particularly the implications of this trend for public pension provision in the future.

The final part of the chapter will explore the social environment and again look at some of the implications of these changes for the business environment. There are more and more studies of changing social trends and there is such a wealth of data (see *'Further reading'*) that one can analyse information at local and regional level as well as at national and inter-country levels. One of the factors that links with the previous section on ageing population is the issue of the changing nature of the modern family both in terms of family size and the changing relationships and lifestyles within families. Within the context of lifestyle changes we will look at changes in trends of consumer behaviour, in smoking and drinking, and also in crime trends. The changing nature of work is also explored, especially in terms of the impact of new technologies and the resultant trend to more flexible working practices and some of the implications of these changes for organised labour. Wider social trends such as education and crime trends are also explored as both of these may be of significance for companies and managers who may be operating outside their home country.

7.2 The national cultural environment

The examination of the national cultural environment presents us with an opportunity of understanding differences and similarities between different cultures. We start this analysis by looking at what we understand national culture to be.

7.2.1 Definitions of national culture

One of the immediate problems faced when looking at national culture is to find an acceptable definition of what it is. Kroeber and Kluckhohn (1985) found over 160 definitions when they were researching this issue. The culture of countries was originally examined from an anthropological or sociological one as opposed to a business one, although the development of globalisation has thrown the national cultural issue much higher up the agenda for businesspeople who are working in countries other than their own. One of the most commonly used definitions is that of Hofstede and Hofstede (2005) who defines national culture as:

The collective programming of the mind which distinguishes the members of one group or category of people from others.

Hofstede and Hofstede go on to point out that values form the core of culture.

This definition highlights the significance of values and the fundamental taken-for-granted assumptions that are held by a large group of people in the country and which in turn will influence their behaviour. It is often differences in these sets of values that will drive differences in national culture and perceptions of what is acceptable and not acceptable behaviour in the culture. This can obviously be of great significance for business operations in countries other than your own, an issue that will be explored later in the chapter. Development psychologists believe that by the age of ten most children have their basic value system firmly in place and that after this age changes are more difficult to obtain.

Figure 7.1 shows that national cultural values will be influenced by a range of factors and the degree of difference between these factors may well determine the degree of difference between national cultures.

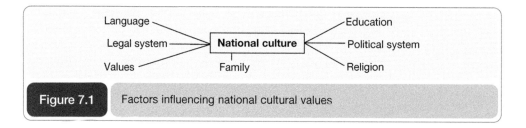

Figure 7.1 Factors influencing national cultural values

One of the most significant factors is that of language and thus countries that speak the same language tend to be closer culturally than where there are strong linguistic differences. It could also explain why there can often be significant sub-cultures in a country built around different languages. An example in Europe would be Switzerland where citizens might speak either French, German, Italian or Romansch. Sometimes there might be a shift in languages taught in countries, which might have some impact on cultural attitudes; an example here would be the shift towards Mandarin Chinese from Cantonese Chinese in Hong Kong since Hong Kong was returned to China in 1997. Sometimes these language changes can be fiercely resisted as has been seen in France where there has been some resistance from the *Academie Française* to the new 'pop culture' words which are mainly English in origin.

One should not discount the impact of religion upon culture, especially where the political systems and religious systems are closely intertwined, as in many countries in the Middle East where the impact of Islam and Judaism has been very strong and has conditioned cultural attitudes strongly as it directly affects the value systems of individuals which we have seen is a central factor influencing culture. One of the main reasons why Eastern cultures are significantly different from Western ones is the impact of Confucianism on the region.

It should be stressed that whereas country analysis does suggest certain national behavioural patterns, there do still remain significant sub-cultures in many countries where the national pattern may be modified. These sub-cultures can be because of historical factors and may be enhanced by different religious or linguistic patterns.

7.2.2 National culture and globalisation

The role of national culture and potential national cultural differences has become an increasingly important part of the business environment as a result of the increase in globalisation, with more and more countries looking to operate outside their home base and thus finding that they are coming into increasing contact with different cultures. One of the key questions companies have to ask themselves when they internationalise is the extent to which they need to adapt to the new culture they are operating in. This could mean adaptation of things such as:

- marketing;
- human resource management;

- the product itself;
- management styles used in the company.

This reflects a wider debate called the convergence/divergence debate which has been a key feature of understanding the globalisation process.

The convergence perspective (Kerr *et al.*, 1960; Levitt, 1983) suggests that globalisation is inevitably leading to more and more standardisation as consumers become aware of global brands, and companies realise the advantages of having standardised products or practices that can be used throughout the company, no matter which country they are operating in. Brands such as Coca-Cola, Nike and Nokia are recognised globally, which means the potential global market is enormous and opens up opportunities for economies of scale through global advertising campaigns and standardised manufacturing. Even football clubs are seeking global identities; Manchester United developed links with the New York Yankees for the North American market in 2001 and devotes considerable resources to building the Manchester United brand name in China and South East Asia. This is a good example of how technology has driven globalisation – with fans all over the world able to watch the club every week on television.

The divergence perspective suggests that in reality it is not always that easy to transfer brands across countries and that companies may face difficulties when transferring management practices because of national cultural differences. This may be especially so where the company has an ethnocentric perspective in which it assumes that the practices used in its home country will work in any other country (the opposite is a polycentric perspective, where different strategies may be adopted if significant local differences occur). As can be seen, the degree of national cultural differences may well determine whether practices can be easily transferred from the home company to its overseas business units. A close cultural fit (for example the USA and UK) would probably suggest that little adaptation is needed and therefore the convergence perspective might be a valid one to follow, whereas if there were significant cultural differences, then adopting an ethnocentric approach might be a high risk strategy.

One of the most famous examples of this was the early stages of the operation of the EuroDisney theme park in France in 1992. The early stages of the project were fraught with problems both in terms of customer retention (the French were not happy about wine being unavailable in the Park) and in keeping staff (in the early days there was a very high rate of staff turnover) with the result that the project nearly failed. It has been argued that one of the main problems here was misunderstanding between managers (mainly American and Canadian) and staff (predominantly French). It was only with the appointment of a French CEO that things began to turn around to the point that the park (now renamed Disneyland Paris) is now well established. Having learned from this experience, the company took great care to work in partnership with local government during the planning and construction of Hong Kong Disneyland which opened in 2005. *Chapter 13* discusses a number of other issues around globalisation.

7.2.3 Identifying differences in national culture

As can be seen from the convergence/divergence debate, the cultural fit (or difference) between two countries is an important factor in the international business environment. While we can make various generalisations arising out of historical, linguistic, religious and other factors, we need some more precise criteria to evaluate the differences in national culture from a business perspective. Here we shall turn to two of the most significant writers about national culture who both provided frameworks against which we could test a country's national culture in order to see how closely it fits with other countries' patterns.

One of the most significant writers on national culture is Geert Hofstede who wrote *Culture's Consequences* in 1984 and updated in Hofstede and Hofstede (2005). This provided a useful framework by which we can measure national cultures. A significant limitation in

Hofstede's work is that it was based solely on the responses of staff from a single company (IBM). This meant that it might have been influenced by the corporate culture of IBM and also that it was limited in its scope, because in 1984 IBM did not have offices in certain countries such as China and Russia. However, the research is still important because it identified certain dimensions around which one can examine cultures and these remain valid.

Hofstede and Hofstede (2005) identify, four variables or dimensions around which one could begin to evaluate differences in national culture and some of these are identified in *Table 7.1*.

The first of these dimensions is power distance which represents the social distance between people of different rank. If we look at a country with a high power-distance score (Malaysia for example), this would suggest that there is a clear gap between superiors and subordinates in this country. This would be reflected in the way that superiors are addressed (formal or informal) and the willingness or unwillingness to question any decision made by a superior, i.e. in a high power-distance country superiors' decisions are more likely to be accepted without discussion and superiors would carry great respect. This is very common in Asian cultures where this is underpinned by the Confucian philosophy, which encourages respect for superiors and elders. Low power-distance countries would suggest cultures where managers may be challenged more openly and where respect may draw more from ability than seniority.

The second dimension identified by Hofstede is individualism which reflects the extent to which an individual relies on a group or collectivist approach to issues (a low individualism score) or the extent to which the individual takes individual initiatives to solve problems or make decisions (a high individualism score). *Table 7.1* shows the high score for the USA, one of the most individualistic cultures in the world, whereas Singapore reflects a much more

Table 7.1	Selected examples of cultural dimensions taken from Hofstede and Hofstede

Country	Power distance (PDI)	Individualism (IDV)	Masculinity (MAS)	Uncertainty avoidance (UA)	Long-term orientation (LTO)
Denmark	18	74	16	23	46*
Sweden	31	71	5	29	33
Japan	54	46	95	92	80
Singapore	74	20	48	8	48
UK	35	89	66	35	25
France	68	71	43	86	39*
Germany	35	67	66	65	31
Italy	50	76	70	75	34*
Spain	57	51	42	86	19*
Brazil	69	38	49	76	65
Australia	36	90	61	51	31
USA	40	91	62	46	29

Note: 1. The figures show the relative positions of each country – the closer the values, the closer is the cultural fit for that dimension.
2. The LTO scores are taken from the Chinese Culture Connection (1987) article, except for those marked (*) which were based on replications.
Source: Hofstede and Hofstede (2005)

collectivist approach (hence a low individualism score), which again is quite common in Asian cultures.

The third dimension identified by Hofstede is uncertainty avoidance, which essentially reflects people's attitudes towards ambiguity in a society or country. When there is a high score for uncertainty avoidance it suggests a culture where people are unhappy with ambiguous situations and prefer more direction. It also suggests that in these countries it will be hard to undertake rapid changes in the organisation because this would probably cause anxiety and stress, as the nature of rapid change is that it does lead to uncertainty. According to the Hofstede data, Greece has a high level of uncertainty avoidance whereas in a country such as Sweden uncertainty would be much more tolerated and thus change programmes might be likely to receive less resistance.

The final dimension identified by Hofstede was that of masculinity, which is probably one of the more complex of his variables. It reflects values that are widely considered to be more 'masculine', such as assertiveness, competitiveness and the need to achieve results. A low masculinity figure suggests a higher degree of co-operation and more caring approaches to dealing with people in the organisation. This value can also reflect the level of discrimination against women in the organisation, i.e. it might be hard for a female manager to progress in a high-masculinity culture or to have the same degree of respect as a male manager. A good example in this context is Japan, which has the highest masculinity index in Hofstede's survey and where it is seen as very difficult for female managers to progress up the corporate ladder.

Although there were only four dimensions of culture in his original work, Hofstede identified a fifth dimension through work carried out with Bond and the Chinese Culture Connection Group (1988) which was evaluating the Asian context of national culture. The main outcome of Bond and Hofstede's later work was evidence that most Asian cultures seemed to have a long-term perspective about work and relationships as opposed to a much shorter-term perspective found primarily in Western cultures. This might explain why Asian companies prefer to build relationships with Western companies through joint ventures and strategic alliances rather than attempting mergers.

A further development from Hofstede's work is the idea that you can place countries in clusters of those showing similar patterns of the dimensions just described. If, for example, we look at the two variables of power distance and uncertainty avoidance we could end up with a pattern as suggested in *Figure 7.2*.

It is interesting to note here that although countries may be geographically close (e.g. France and the UK) they may have very different cultural characteristics which might be significant when managers of these two countries are working together. *Figure 7.2* suggests that

Denmark	UA:23 PD:18		
Sweden	UA:29 PD:31		
UK	UA:35 PD:35		
USA	UA:46 PD:40		
		Italy	UA:75 PD:50
		France	UA:86 PD:68
		Greece	UA:112 PD:60
		Japan	UA:92 PD:54
		Spain	UA:86 PD:57

Figure 7.2 Cultural clusters

Spanish managers would be much more at ease with their French counterparts than with, say, Swedish managers, because of the different perceptions about how to deal with subordinates and how much direction to give to other managers.

The second key writer on cultural differences is Fons Trompenaars, who drew on the work of Hofstede and others such as Kluckhohn and Strodtbeck (1961). Following a questionnaire survey of 15,000 respondents, he identified seven areas where cultural differences could occur. The seven areas identified were:

- universalism vs. particularism;
- affective vs. neutral;
- collectivism vs. individualism;
- specific vs. diffuse relationships;
- achieving vs. ascribing status;
- time as sequence vs. time as synchronisation;
- inner directed vs. outer directed.

The first of these, universalism vs. particularism, is where a universalist approach suggests that culture should be driven by rules and that there are universal rules that should be respected, whereas a particularist culture tends to have a more flexible interpretation of rules and draws more on people relationships. Universalist cultures tend to be found more in the UK and USA, whereas particularist cultures are more common in Asia. This may cause problems in negotiating between these countries as managers may have different conceptions as to what rules of business behaviour will apply.

Affective vs. neutral cultures relates to the extent to which emotion is used and is acceptable in a culture. In some countries people keep emotions under check (the 'stiff upper lip' approach), whereas in others emotional behaviour would be expected and condoned within a working environment. The implications for the successful operation of international teams are self-evident.

Collectivism vs. individualism reproduces the dimension previously identified by Hofstede, whereas specific vs. diffuse relationships relate to the extent to which managers separate their work relationships from other relationships. In a specific culture the manager–subordinate relationship may be observed at work but is not necessarily replicated in their relationship outside work, whereas in a diffuse culture (as is often found in Asia) the relationship at work influences all other relationships.

The issue of status is also identified in terms of achieving vs. ascribing status. In a culture with an achieving status, status is seen very much as something that is achieved by individuals through their own actions. In an ascribing culture, status might be ascribed to an individual through factors such as age or gender. You would find achievement status cultures in Scandinavia; ascribing status cultures are found in Asian countries as well as Argentina and Egypt.

Another dimension identified by Trompenaars was how time is perceived in a culture and he identified time as sequence vs. time as synchronisation. Time as sequence suggests a rational linear approach to issues where one issue is dealt with before another begins (one step at a time approach). Time as synchronisation suggests that time is seen as circular in the sense that a number of parallel activities can continue at the same time. A sequential time approach is found in Germany. The French tend to have a more synchronic approach which again may have implications for joint projects or team working between these two cultures.

The final dimension is inner directed vs. outer directed. This contrasts those countries such as the USA and Switzerland where there is a belief that the individual can determine events and control situations (inner directed) with those countries where the belief is that the individual's actions are determined by other forces such as the need for harmony with nature. This belief is central to both Confucianism and Buddhism and thus colours attitudes in Asian cultures (outer directed).

Through looking at the frameworks provided by Hofstede and Trompenaars it can be seen that there are a number of dimensions against which differences of national culture can be measured. We have also seen how some cultures have a relatively close fit with each other, whereas others have significant cultural differences where the divergence theory becomes more significant. Sometimes the differences in culture can lead to the phenomenon of culture shock where businesspeople operating in a different culture may suddenly find themselves disoriented as they realise they are having problems adapting to the local culture. Torbiorn (1982) suggests that businesspeople working overseas usually have an initial 'honeymoon period' where the excitement of working in a different country outweighs any initial problems encountered. It is only later, as cultural misunderstandings and confusion occur, that this initial positive dimension fades. There might also be the problem of language, which means that communications do not run smoothly, which again leads to confusion and stress. This is where the culture shock begins as the manager realises that cultural misunderstandings are undermining their effectiveness and their confidence.

Much will depend upon the ability of the individual manager to overcome this and the support given by the manager's organisation through cross-cultural training and support. Without this there is the danger that the manager will reject the culture they are operating in and turn very negative against it. Sometimes they may seek other expatriates and create an expatriate 'bubble' in terms of seeking to surround themselves with other people from their own culture and thus restrict contact with the local culture. The other extreme is that they will completely adapt to the local culture and 'go native', which has advantages but might affect their loyalties when difficult decisions have to be made on a corporate basis. In the twenty-first century the demand is for managers who are culturally aware and who can operate in a range of cultures, as opposed to the traditional expatriate who might work for many years in one base overseas.

7.2.4 The impact of national culture on business practices

If one accepts that national cultural differences can be significant in terms of affecting the international business environment, then the question arises as to identifying some of the key areas of business practice where some cultural adaptation may be necessary (especially when there is a significant gap in the cultures of the countries concerned). This idea can be explored further in *Minicase 7.2*.

With increased globalisation there has been a significant increase in international mergers, alliances and joint ventures, where the successful adaptation to national cultural differences

---

| Minicase 7.2 | American investment in China: some cultural dimensions |

By 2001 the People's Republic of China (PRC) had become the primary location for global foreign direct investment with over US$47 billion being invested, with a large amount of that figure coming from corporate investors in the USA, which remains the base for a majority of the world's largest multinational corporations. Although there is some direct investment in China, the preferred method of market entry is by forming a joint venture with a Chinese company. This has the advantages for the investing firm that the Chinese company will have useful contacts and an existing distribution system, while the Chinese company can benefit from using improved management techniques and technology transfer. Given the significant increase of Chinese–US joint ventures, there will be increased pressure on managers from the two countries to work together in order to make the joint ventures or direct investment work effectively.

This is where the issue of national culture comes increasingly important as it will be necessary for managers to identify and adapt to national cultural differences if they are to work together effectively. We can use the data from Hofstede and Hofstede (2005) and Trompenaars (1997) to have a look at cultural characteristics of China, Hong Kong and the USA.

	PRC	Hong Kong	USA
Table 1 Cultural characteristics			
Hofstede and Hofstede (2005) ranking			
Power distance	20	15	38
Uncertainty avoidance	1	49	43
Individualism	23	37	1
Masculinity	54	18	15
Trompenaars (1993) ranking			
Achievement	32	20	2
Universalism	39	38	7
Internal control	19	8	7
Specificity	34	16	17
Affectivity	41	38	20

From the table we can immediately see that there are significant cultural differences between the PRC and USA. It is interesting to note the position of Hong Kong. It is close to the PRC in some respects and close to the USA in others. This reflects the phenomenon of culture shift in that Hong Kong has been exposed to both Eastern and Western business cultures over many years, and so its cultural behaviour may have changed in some respects. Thus an American company would probably find less of a culture clash if setting up in Hong Kong than in mainland PRC. However, since its handover from the UK back to the PRC in 1997 it is possible that Hong Kong's culture may be changing again.

There remain, however, significant differences in management styles, reflecting some of the cultural differences and so the ability of managers to adapt to each other's cultures will appear to be a significant factor in the potential success of American–Chinese joint ventures.

Questions

1 Imagine an initial meeting taking place between Chinese and American managers concerning a new joint venture. Using material from the case and above, try and imagine potential problems that might arise in this meeting through cultural misunderstanding – look at it from the perspective of both the American and Chinese manager.

2 You have been asked to lead the American delegation in the negotiations above. How would you brief them in terms of the management style to be adopted with the Chinese? Should you adapt or not?

may be an important factor in determining their effectiveness. Any such venture would require a number of meetings where negotiations would take place. This is where issues such as effective communication between the prospective partners would be significant and where cultural factors could come into play, e.g. in a German business culture humour is not usually used in business discussion whereas it is much more common in British business culture and therefore the use of jokes by the British managers may be misunderstood by German managers. Humour is also acceptable in Chinese business cultures, although Chinese humour may differ from British humour. The issue of power distance would also come into communications in terms of how people are addressed, i.e. formally or informally, and certain forms of non-verbal communication might be frowned upon in different cultures. In China this rather formal approach can be observed in unlikely situations. Part of the ritual at meals invariably requires toasts to be made to each other – often downing *Moutai*, a highly potent liquor. Visitors must be on their guard if they are to get through the evening! In recent years, the *Moutai* has been replaced by beer or even a soft drink – this may be a sign of greater acceptance being shown by hosts. It is also evident that the culture of younger Chinese managers, especially those who have been educated at universities in America, Europe and Australia, is slowly changing. In Malaysia the smile can mean many things. A smile and a nod may suggest that your opinion is respected but it does not mean that the person agrees with you; or a smile may be a cover for extreme embarrassment when the person wants to avoid losing face.

One consequence of international mergers, joint ventures and alliances is the increased use of international teams and, again, issues of how the team works together might be significant, e.g. when there are different perspectives on time (sequential vs. synchronic), attitudes to hierarchy in the group (power distance) and the way the group handles ambiguity (uncertainty avoidance).

We can look at these cultural differences in more depth by comparing American and Chinese management styles. We have already seen that the American management style is very individualistic in nature and there is relatively low uncertainty avoidance – individuals will be expected to make decisions and to react to change effectively. It is certainly a hard-working culture where excessive working will be encouraged and where the practice of the business breakfast is well established. Americans like decisive leaders and new ideas are generally welcomed. Communication is generally informal in nature with the use of first names between senior managers and their subordinates. The American manager will tend to be short-termist in nature and will be looking for instant results from a meeting, and status in the organisation is more likely to be based on salary size than age.

If we contrast this with the Chinese management style we might notice a few differences. The Chinese manager will be influenced by the Confucian influence that pervades many aspects of Chinese life. Thus there will be great respect for more senior people in the organisation (linked to high power distance), respect for elder people, and especially the need for politeness and harmony in their working life. The Chinese manager will also be a hard worker and a lot of time will be spent on developing relationships (*guanxi*) with people both inside and outside the organisation. Communication will usually be very formal and often top-down and great effort will be made that no one loses 'face' in discussions or negotiations, although the Chinese manager may not be expecting an instant decision from the meeting – it may be more about building up the *guanxi* with new partners. The Chinese manager might also be more comfortable about working in groups rather than on an individual level, although less happy about close physical contact with other people and they would not be happy about any personal disclosures, preferring to talk solely about the business in hand. Meals will be an important part of negotiations and humour is very acceptable in these situations. *Minicase 7.2* poses some further questions.

There will also be functional areas of business that will be affected by cultural differences, most notably in marketing and human resource management (HRM). From the marketing perspective there will be the discussion of whether to go with global marketing campaigns (the convergence perspective) or whether there is a need to adapt the product for the particular cultural needs of the country concerned. The attractions of following the convergence approach would be in terms of economies of scale in that the same advert could be used on a global basis, thus reducing costs and also developing a global brand image. The divergence approach might be needed if the product needs adapting for particular markets. For example, the British tend to use a lot of humour in their advertising, but this humour might not be seen as humour in other countries and thus there is a need to adapt the campaign according to local demands. Although McDonald's in many respects follows a convergence perspective in terms of common approaches to layout, design and a common brand, it still adapts its product range in different countries, especially in countries where certain foods may be banned for religious reasons, for example cows are sacred to Hindus in India and elsewhere, so lamb is served as an alternative.

From the HRM perspective, national culture may be very significant when looking at areas such as training, appraisal and recruitment. In terms of training, it may be dangerous to use direct training approaches such as direct discussion/questions or role-play situations when you are working in an environment where there is a high power distance and people prefer to be told what to do rather than discussing it with the trainer. It may also be difficult to get responses in Eastern cultures where there is the fear of loss of face. Performance appraisal might also have to be adapted as it suggests an appraisal of a subordinate by a superior, whereas modern styles of appraisal such as 360-degree appraisal would also include assessment by fellow workers and subordinates as well as their line manager. This might be difficult to translate into a culture where there is traditionally a high power distance. The issue of recruitment might also be significant in terms of whether you employ expatriate managers (from your home country) or local managers (who will know local conditions but may be less familiar with the corporate culture of the company). Daniels *et al.* (2009) suggest that it is getting harder to find managers willing to spend long periods abroad. The trend is clearly towards managers spending shorter periods abroad but in a variety of countries, and many of these managers will become more culturally sensitive through training and experience.

7.3 The demographic environment

Demography concerns the study of population and population change and can be seen as another important factor that will affect the business environment. Whereas many of the environmental indicators such as social and technology trends are hard to forecast, the impact of demographic changes can be more confidently predicted, i.e. if we know the number of 5-year-olds in a country in 2010 we will have a pretty clear idea of the number of 15-year-olds there will be in 2020 and 25-year-olds in 2030 and this may be useful when predicting potential markets.

This section will examine some of the key drivers of population change and explain some of the main trends that are affecting population change worldwide and then look at some of the implications of population change for individuals, businesses and government.

7.3.1 Key drivers of population change

The two main indicators of natural population change are birth rate and death rate. Birth rate can be defined as:

> the number of live births per thousand of the population.

The death rate can be defined as:

> the number of deaths per thousand of the population.

When these two figures are put together you will get the natural increase or decrease of the population, again measured per thousand of the population.

However, there is another factor that has to be taken into account when looking at population change. This is the net migration per thousand of the population, which reflects the difference between immigration (into a country) and emigration (out of a country). If we add this figure to the natural change in population we will see the overall increase or decrease in the population. Information on population change in selected European countries between 2010 and 2015 is shown in *Table 7.2*

From the information in *Table 7.2* we can see that there are some significant differences in population patterns in Europe. Ireland has a birth rate which is far in excess of its death rate, and also has a lot of inward migration which means that its population is increasing

| Table 7.2 | Estimated population change in selected European countries 2010–2015 |

	BR	DR	NC	NM	TC
Bulgaria	9.6	14.6	−5.0	−1.4	−6.4
France	11.4	9.0	2.4	1.6	4.0
Germany	7.9	11.0	−3.1	1.3	−1.8
Greece	9.1	10.4	−1.3	2.7	1.4
Ireland	14.8	6.5	8.3	4.2	12.5
Italy	8.6	10.5	−1.9	3.6	1.7
Poland	9.8	10.5	−0.7	−0.6	−1.3
Portugal	9.2	10.5	−1.3	2.3	1.0
Sweden	11.5	9.8	1.7	2.7	4.4
UK	12.0	9.8	2.2	3.0	5.2

Key: BR = birth rate/thousand; *DR = death rate/thousand; NC = natural population change (BR − DR)/ thousand; NM = net migration (immigrants − emigrants)/thousand; TC = total rate of population change/ thousand.*
Source: adapted from United Nations Population Information Network website, http:www.un.org/popin/data.html

relatively quickly. This could be contrasted with the figures from Germany where the death rate exceeds the birth rate, meaning that the natural population is declining. This is only partially offset by inward migration, meaning that the total population in Germany is forecast to decline in the future. A further example can be seen with the case of Bulgaria where not only does the death rate exceed the birth rate but there is also a net outflow in migration, all leading to a rapid decline in the population. The EU has carried out forecasts of population change by 2050 based on current trends and, whereas strong population growth is expected in Ireland (increasing 31 percent), the UK (increasing 13 percent) and France (increasing 10 percent), population decline is anticipated in other countries such as Germany (declining 4 percent), Spain (declining 8 percent), Italy (declining 22 percent) and Russia (declining 30 percent). These trends obviously have significance for businesses which will be exploring potentially high-growth markets against those where demand is likely to fall as a result of population decline.

To understand why these changes are taking place we need to understand why birth rates, death rates and migration rates are changing.

7.3.2 Birth rate factors

Birth rates tend to be more volatile than the death rates and thus may have more short-run impact on population changes. Birth rate may be affected by many factors such as attitudes towards family size. The trend seen in most of Europe is a decline in family size. The usual quick test in this respect is to look at your family size and then compare it with your parents' family size and grandparents' family size and so on. One undoubted factor here is the fact that more women wish to follow their own careers before having children and so delay the age at which they have children. The cost of having children might also be taken into account as well as the degree of flexibility in the labour market which determines the extent to which women (or men) can follow more flexible work patterns in order to look after children while continuing in work. Other determinant factors could be the values of the country or the impact of religion on attitudes towards children or the availability and use of

Table 7.3	Forecast total fertility rates, 2010–2015
India	2.52
Sri Lanka	2.22
USA	2.02
UK	1.85
France	1.85
Sweden	1.85
China	1.79
Spain	1.56
Bulgaria	1.50
Russian Federation	1.46
Italy	1.41
Greece	1.41
Germany	1.34

Source: adapted from United Nations Population Information Network website, http:www.un.popin/functional/population.html

contraception in a country. These factors may come together to account for the remarkably high birth rate in Ireland, for example.

A critical indicator which will reflect all these factors is the total fertility rate which reflects the average number of children per female. Even more significant is the replacement fertility rate, the fertility rate needed if a population is to replace itself. The recognised replacement rate needed for this is 2.1 children.

If we look at *Table 7.3* we can see some of the current predicted figures for total fertility rates as suggested by the UN.

From *Table 7.3* we can see that Sri Lanka has a figure which just exceeds the desired replacement rate, while the USA is almost exactly at the desired rate. France and the UK have relatively good rates, which are reflected in their higher birth rates and their predicted population growth. The lowest figures seem to come from either Eastern European countries, where generally weaker economic performance may be a factor in smaller family size, or the Mediterranean countries (such as Italy, Spain and Greece) where the cause is less easy to define but may be linked to inflexible labour markets and changing attitudes among women. The notable exception is Germany; comparison with data from previous years suggest that its fertility rate is almost exactly the same as ten years ago, while that of the other countries in *Table 7.3* has increased. Certainly this decline in the number of children in these areas may be having a significant impact not only on the future population size of these countries but also on the future age structure, as this trend will (other factors remaining equal) lead to a rapid ageing of the population with all the implications that has for businesses and government (see section 7.4 *'Patterns of population change'* and *Minicase 7.4*).

7.3.3 Death rate factors

As has been previously suggested, the death rate tends to be more stable than the birth rate and it usually reflects the changing age structure of the population. A higher concentration of older people will tend to lead to a gradual increase in the death rate. Death rates have come down in many parts of the world as a result of better medicines and improved sanitation and healthcare, although there are still significant discrepancies between the developed and the developing world. In many parts of the developing world people generally have very basic diets which might make them more vulnerable to epidemics or illnesses, such as those illnesses linked to poor drinking water. These factors help explain the higher death rates and lower life expectancies in these countries.

There is also the impact of armed conflict which may have an impact on the death rate if there is a prolonged civil war, as has been seen in several countries in Central Africa. With globalisation and improvements in transport, diseases can travel much more quickly as can be seen with a number of health scares in the last ten years. In 2003 the SARS outbreak spread very quickly from Guandong province in China to Hong Kong and thence to several places, most notably Toronto in Canada. In 2005 a variant of the H5N1 influenza virus known as Bird Flu spread rapidly in the Far East (although with relatively little impact on other regions). Most recently, an H1N1 variant known as Swine Flu was declared to be a worldwide pandemic by the WHO but, at the time of writing, was not expected to cause a significantly high number of deaths, thanks to better living conditions and improved healthcare.

A much more significant epidemic in terms of its impact has been the spread of the HIV/AIDS virus. While this virus has spread throughout the world, its most serious effects are being felt in sub-Saharan Africa as *Minicase 7.3* illustrates.

Minicase 7.3	Life chances in the UK and Malawi

When looking at population change it is usually considered that birth rate is more volatile than death rates and that change in population is primarily driven by changes in birth rates and replacement fertility rates. Sometimes, however, the key driver affecting a country's rate of population change can be a dramatic change in the death rate. A region that has been devastated by an epidemic is sub-Saharan Africa where the HIV/AIDS virus has spread alarmingly in some countries and has led to severe changes in mortality rates.

We can highlight these changes by contrasting life chances between Malawi and the UK using data published by the United Nations in 2007 (http://esa.un.org/unpd/wpp2008/index.htm). Malawi is a much smaller country in population terms than the UK (13.9 million in Malawi compared with 60.7 million in the UK) and is also a much poorer one; the healthcare spend per capita in Malawi was $19 compared with $2,900 in the UK.

This has meant that Malawi was poorly positioned to deal with the HIV/AIDS virus. If we look at the UK we can see that HIV prevalence was about 0.2 percent of the population which meant that in 2005 there were about 68,000 people with HIV. AIDS deaths in that year were less than 1,000. While these figures are significant, they have not had a major impact on mortality rates in the UK; in fact life expectancy in the UK is gradually rising and was estimated in 2007 as being 79 years.

The impact of HIV/AIDS has been much more devastating in Malawi with over 14 percent of the population being affected by the illness and with AIDS deaths in 2005 being estimated at 78,000. The effect of the epidemic has been to leave many children orphaned (550,000 in 2005) and many of those, in turn, may carry the virus. This is having a significant effect on life expectancy; the UN estimated that if HIV/AIDS did not exist, the typical life expectancy of a Malawi child would be 64; this has been reduced to 48 by the virus. One in five children in Malawi does not make it past their fifth year.

Even much more advanced countries such as South Africa have been seriously affected. With a population of 48.5 million, there were 320,000 deaths from HIV/AIDS in 2005 and life expectancy for those with HIV/AIDS was only 50 years compared with 67 years for those without HIV/AIDS. There has been severe criticism of the South African government for its inappropriate and ineffective policies towards the epidemic.

Questions

1 What can Malawi do to control and eradicate the HIV/AIDS epidemic in the country? What resources are needed for this to happen?
2 Do you feel that the ease with which viruses spread (e.g. H1N1 and HIV/AIDS) is linked to increased globalisation or can they be controlled locally?

7.3.4 Migration factors

Migration of people across borders has long been a feature of history and in the modern globalised economy it seems that migration is seen as a global issue rather than a regional one. An economic migrant from Afghanistan would now look as much at migrating to Western Europe as to moving to the countries adjacent to Afghanistan. Historically there have been many great shifts of population. In the nineteenth century there was great movement from Western Europe to the USA, Canada, Australia and Argentina where there were new prospects for economic development and there were more opportunities. People migrating in search of new opportunities for work are seen as economic migrants, whereas those migrating to escape oppression and persecution in their home country could be seen as political migrants. Many of the people who migrate are younger and more ambitious. They can enrich the economy into which they move in terms of providing new skills and filling gaps in the labour market.

The Republic of Ireland has for a long time experienced significant outward migration, predominantly to the USA, UK and Australia. It is said that there are more people of Irish descent in New York than there are in Ireland – it is believed that there are 44 million Americans of Irish descent. The horrific potato famine in 1845/46 was a significant spur to migration, primarily to the 'New World', and continual waves of outward migration occurred as younger people looked for new opportunities away from the depressed economy. This is obviously a loss for the country as the younger people are the most flexible in terms of taking up new job opportunities and in learning new skills. Irish migrants were seen as an asset to the UK where many worked in the construction industry. What is interesting now is that the economic resurgence of Ireland in the 1990s, (the 'tiger economy' of Europe), has led to greater opportunities for young Irish people within Ireland and this has considerably reduced the flow of young Irish people abroad. Indeed, we can see from *Table 7.2* that a strong inflow of migrants to Ireland is forecast for 2010 to 2015, suggesting that the traditional outward flow has reversed itself. Unfortunately the Irish economy has been hit relatively hard by the recession in 2008/9 with companies such as Dell Computers shifting European production to low-wage rate countries such as Poland. It is quite possible that the migration trend will reverse if the Irish economy fails to recover quickly.

If we look at the same table we can see the case of Germany where the inward migration is partially offsetting the decline in natural population growth. Germany has traditionally been a magnet to economic migrants because of its successful economic growth record, which has encouraged inflows of migrants, predominantly from Turkey and Eastern Europe. However, the result has often been political and social tensions manifested by racial attacks and have encouraged the growth of far-right political parties, a feature found across Europe. Migrants also face other problems with some of them finding themselves in areas characterised by low-quality and poorly maintained housing with all the resulting social problems that follow from that. In 2005 riots broke out in a *banlieu* (suburb) in north-eastern Paris which had a high concentration of immigrants and high unemployment. Unrest rapidly spread to other parts of Paris and other cities throughout France, and has recurred occasionally. So, whereas the influx of migrants can be a boost for a country's labour supply and can improve mobility of labour, it can result in some of the tensions identified above.

One of the biggest challenges faced by the EU in the twenty-first century is that of illegal migration, which constitutes mainly economic migrants looking for new opportunities and deriving mainly from developing countries. An example of this is the influx of Albanians coming illegally into Italy with some moving on to other countries and some staying in the 'hidden economy' of Italy where they don't have to declare their earnings. It often poses a quandary for governments as to how tight their restrictions should be. One could look at Italy with its predicted 22 percent fall in natural population by 2050 and question whether, in fact, inward migration might be necessary for the country to maintain its current economic structure.

Another migration issue that can be seen throughout Europe and many developing economies is the shift from rural locations to urban locations, leaving many villages in the more remote regions populated mainly by older people. However, this in turn causes problems in cities with uncontrolled urban sprawl and increased congestion. Some major urban areas continue to suffer from poor housing and education, overstretched services, increasing crime and general social and economic hardship. The better-off tend to move to the affluent suburbs leaving the very old, the unskilled and certain ethnic minority groups concentrated in inner-city areas. This leads to a range of social problems allied to high crime rates which pose additional problems for governments.

A similar challenge has faced the Chinese government with migration from impoverished rural areas to the many huge and growing cities. The trend is unlikely to be reversed without great investment in rural economies and in early 2009 Xinhua, the official Chinese news agency, reported a statement by President Hu Jintao that the promotion of stable agricultural and rural development would be a priority for the government.

7.4 Patterns of population change

At this stage it will be useful to look at some of the issues surrounding population change.

7.4.1 The impact of population growth

Table 7.4 shows how the world's population has changed together with the predicted population figure for 2050.

It took 123 years for the world's population to increase from 1 billion to 2 billion but only another 33 years to increase from 2 billion to 3 billion, with the last landmark of 6 billion being passed in October 1999, a mere 12 years after reaching 5 billion. This does reflect a

Table 7.4	World population growth 1950–2000 and forecast for 2010–2050
1950	2.5 billion
1960	3.0 billion
1970	3.7 billion
1980	4.4 billion
1990	5.3 billion
2000	6.1 billion
2010	6.9 billion
2020	7.7 billion
2030	8.3 billion
2040	8.8 billion
2050	9.1 billion

Source: adapted from United Nations Population Information Network website, http:www.un.popin/functional/population.html

quickening of population growth, driven primarily by population growth in developing countries where high birth rates have been accompanied by falling death rates (through improved medicine and sanitation), thus creating population growth. This high rate of growth, if unchecked, will continue to put extreme pressures on the world's resources unless they could be developed at a commensurate rate (e.g. increasing agricultural production through more use of genetically modified crops).

In some countries high population growth could be seen as a real inhibitor to economic growth and development. In Bangladesh, for example, the population was 123 million in 1998, is now 160 million and is predicted to grow to 210 million by 2020. It is characterised by a high birth rate and low death rate and 45 percent of the population are currently under 15 (compared to only 13 percent of the EU's population being under 15 in 1998). Bangladesh has some fertile countryside but is prone to flooding and there is limited room for further agricultural expansion, with the result that the increasing population is putting tremendous pressure on existing resources. The country needs to double agricultural output by 2020 to stand still and already 50 percent of the population are below the poverty line, so the need for more control on population growth is very clear in order to reduce the existing pressure on resources. One country that has managed this very well is China with its 'one-child policy' where significant social pressure is brought on couples to have just one child, with the result that the recent surge in economic growth in China is not being held back by too rapid a population growth.

However, *Table 7.4* shows that world population, although still increasing, is forecast to grow at a slower rate (the increase from 2040 to 2050 is around 4 percent compared with a 20 percent rise from 1950 to 1960). This is because of the effect noticed earlier (in *Table 7.2*) of many countries (especially European ones) where population growth is practically static or is even declining through the very low fertility rates identified in *Table 7.3*. This does suggest in the future something of a redistribution of world population away from areas such as Europe towards areas such as East and South East Asia and this may have implications for businesses' long-term investment plans and development strategies.

7.4.2 The distribution of population

While it is interesting to look at actual population changes, it is also important to look at the structure of the population in terms of the relevant age structures as this will also give us clues as to how the population is evolving and some of the implications of this for both businesses and governments. The distribution of population can be looked at both within a country and between countries.

The age structure of a country or region can best be illustrated by a population pyramid and an example of such a pyramid is shown in *Figure 5.3*, which shows how the age structure of the EU will change between 1990 and 2020.

If the birth and death rates for men and women are similar and remain constant, then one would expect to see the widest bars of the pyramid at the bottom and a smooth reduction in width all the way to the highest age groups. But short-term and long-term trends will distort this picture. For example, World War II (1939–1945) caused the deaths of many people, especially young men born between 1915 and 1930, which probably accounts for the asymmetry of the pyramid at the highest ages.

What is most interesting for us are the effects of longer-term changes in birth and death rates. This population pyramid clearly shows that the population of the EU is ageing. At all ages greater than 45 the numbers (as a percentage of the population) will increase by 2020, whereas at all ages below that they will decrease. This is because of the 'baby boom' in the 1980s followed by a forecast reduction in births. We shall see more and more older people and relatively fewer younger people than at present. We have already seen the very low replacement fertility rates in many European countries and this is a prime causal factor for this change, allied to the fact that older people are living longer. If we look at the global picture we see that in 1950, 27 percent of the world's population

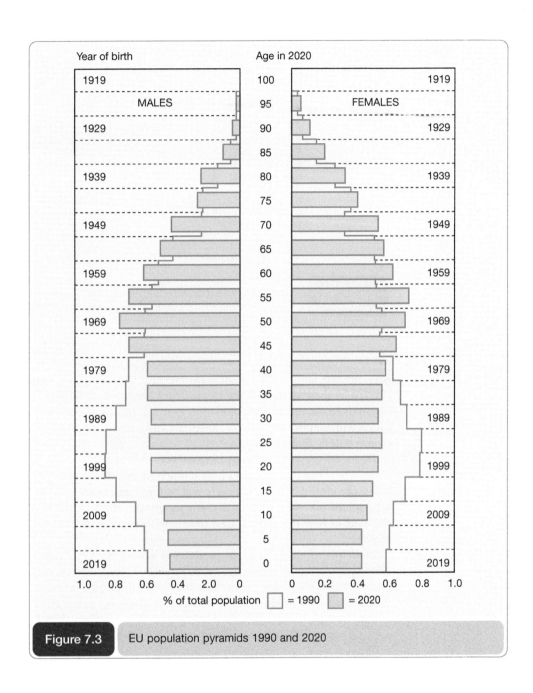

| Figure 7.3 | EU population pyramids 1990 and 2020 |

was under 15 and only 12 percent above 60. By 1998 the figures were nearly level with 19.1 percent of the world's population under 15 and 18.8 percent over 60, and by 2050 the predicted figures are much more dramatic with 15 percent of the world's population predicted to be under 15 and 33 percent over 60. It is perhaps these figures that are more significant than the figures for overall population growth as they show a relatively rapid ageing of the world's population. The predicted figures for Europe in 2050 are even more extreme with only 13 percent of the population predicted to be 15 or less compared with 39 percent being over 60. This will also be reflected in changes in the average age of the population. The average age in the UK in 1950 was 35, which had risen to 38 in 2000 and is predicted to rise to 44 by 2050. In rapidly ageing countries such as Italy it will rise even higher to 52 in 2050.

These rapidly ageing populations (unless they are changed by significant influxes of young migrants) may pose problems for companies who operate in these markets and for

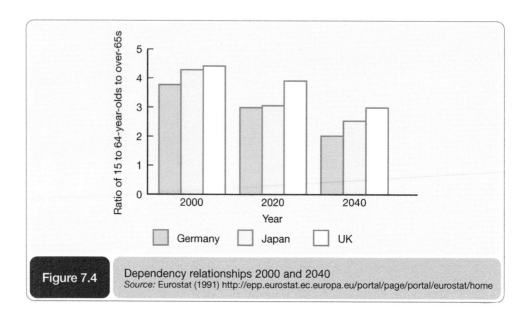

Figure 7.4	Dependency relationships 2000 and 2040 *Source:* Eurostat (1991) http://epp.eurostat.ec.europa.eu/portal/page/portal/eurostat/home

governments faced with a significant increase in older people. One critical ratio that is affected by these changes is the Dependency Ratio, which reflects the number of 15 to 64-year-olds to the rest of the population as it is from this group that the taxes will be raised which will support the schools, hospitals and other support services that are needed for groups outside that age range.

Figure 7.4 shows the ratio of 15 to 64-year-olds to the over-65s in the UK, Germany and Japan. These last two countries have a much more rapidly ageing population than the UK, and it can clearly be seen that there will be fewer and fewer numbers of people available to support the over-65s, which has many significant implications for governments, not least the issue of how to support these people with pensions without resorting to massive tax increases.

In sectors where demand for products is based around younger age groups, the rapidly ageing population may have important strategic considerations. A company, such as Mothercare, started out in 1961 by serving the needs of mothers-to-be and very young children, then extended its product ranges to older children, up to age eight, partly as a result of a decline in the number of children being born. The brewing industry depends for a significant part of its sales on the male age group from 18 to 30, with a male in this group on average consuming 70 percent more beer than males in the over-40s group. With a prospective fall in this age group across Europe, brewing companies have to think up longer-term strategies which can accommodate this. Hence, there has been a shift towards speciality beers and drinks which might be attractive as alternatives to traditional beer and also the shift by companies into catering in pubs which would appeal to more mature adults and families. The brewing companies have also sought to diversify into other sectors such as hotel ownership and recreation facilities.

On the other hand, the growth in the proportion of older people throws up opportunities for businesses which seek to target this group (see *Minicase 7.4*). Examples of this would be travel firms which seek to cater to the needs of the older consumer or the potential for pharmaceutical companies producing drugs which are much more likely to be used by this age group. Numerous financial services groups target this sector offering products at those who are retired or are about to retire. There has also been a significant increase in the number of registered nursing and retirement homes which cater for the older citizen and which provide more sheltered housing for older people. Older people tend to prefer wine to beer and there is evidence of a gradual increase in wine drinking in the UK.

Minicase 7.4	Saga Group

In the mid-1950s, entrepreneur Sidney De Haan decided to offer cheap holidays to retired people at off-peak times. He took advantage of the low prices offered by hoteliers who were only too willing to see their poor occupancy rates rise. Fifty years on, Saga (now a subsidiary of Acromas Holdings) had a turnover in excess of £700 million in 2007, offers holidays, financial services and magazines to the over-50s. Saga recognised that the special needs of older customers represented a market opportunity. It has even started an online messaging service for older people.

Retired people have grown progressively wealthier and Saga now offers holidays trekking in the Himalayas and round-the-world cruises costing up to £30,000 per head. It has expanded in the lucrative US market. It has also developed its 'product' portfolio to include financial services such as insurance brokering. It can negotiate many preferential rates for its low-risk customers, since, for example, older people tend not to drive great distances hence reducing the probability of being involved in a car accident. They also spend more of their time in their houses, so reducing the opportunity for burglars to strike.

Saga employs around 2,000 staff in its travel business with approximately the same number in the financial services side of the business. What is more, it has found its business is virtually recession-proof, as a decline in a national economic cycle has little influence on the income of retired people. What is damaging, however, is a decline in interest rates which does adversely influence the incomes of its clients.

An unexpected threat to the business was posed by the UK Government's Equality Bill which went through Parliament in 2009. As written, this would have forced Saga to make its services available to all age groups. In a written submission to Parliament in June 2009 Saga stated '. . . the Bill as it stands risks negatively affecting our customers' ability to buy the holidays they want and the financial and other services they need at a competitive price.' The reason for this is that the company would lose some of the financial advantages mentioned earlier if it had to offer its products to people of all ages.

Questions

1 Saga has been one of the most successful companies in terms of catering to the needs of the older population. What other companies and industries have responded to the increased demand from this group?
2 Which types of companies have suffered from the ageing of the population and what strategies can they follow to counteract these problems?

7.4.3 Wider implications of population change

As has been previously suggested, population change is relatively slow and is the most predictable aspect about the business environment. At the same time it will have important wider implications, which can be seen at individual, corporate and governmental levels.

At the individual level the changes we have looked at will be reflected in the sort of life people can expect to live in the twenty-first century. One of the key indicators will be that of life expectancy as that reflects the changes of lifestyle and medical improvements, which means that people can generally expect longer lives than in previous times. *Table 7.5* shows some examples of life expectancy for people born in the period 2010–2015.

From this it can be seen that women usually outlive men by some years, which explains the relatively high number of women found in the older age ranges of the population pyramid (see *Figure 7.3*). However, the trends of life expectancy have seen a gradual increase to the extent that more people are living to 100 years of age. Against this generally positive picture one should not forget that average life expectancies can also decrease as in sub-Saharan Africa (see *Minicase 7.3*). Another indicator of improvements in living standards is the decline of the infant mortality rate, which shows that children have a much stronger chance of survival in their first year as a result of medical and sanitary improvements, particularly

Table 7.5	Selected examples of life expectancies, 2010–2015		
Country	**Men**	**Women**	**Both**
France	78.6	85.1	81.9
Germany	77.8	83.1	80.5
Greece	77.7	82.5	80.1
Italy	78.6	84.6	81.6
Switzerland	80.2	84.7	82.5
Bulgaria	74.3	70.9	74.3
China	72.3	75.9	74.0
Poland	72.3	80.4	76.4
Russian Federation	61.9	74.1	67.9
UK	77.8	82.3	80.1
India	63.7	66.9	65.2
Singapore	78.5	83.4	81.0
South Africa	51.8	53.8	52.9
USA	77.7	82.1	79.9
Brazil	69.9	77.2	70.5
Zimbabwe	50.4	49.8	50.4

Source: adapted from United Nations Population Information Network website, http:www.un.popin/functional/population.html

in developing countries. However, one should not forget that there are still serious global discrepancies in this respect as in 2009 approximately one-sixth of the world's population does not have access to safe water and approximately three-fifths of the world's population do not have adequate sanitation.

At the corporate level we have already seen how businesses in markets with ageing populations may have to refocus their selling strategies. This is particularly relevant when the older age groups have more spending than previously, which has led to the concept of 'grey power'. In developing countries, where there is still a high birth rate and a significantly higher proportion of younger people, companies may find substantial markets for products which are wanted by this age range – this could apply to certain global products with strong brand images that are associated with younger people and may sometimes be seen as essential fashion accessories. An example here would be the effect that satellite television has had on the merchandising of football clothing linked to well-known global clubs such as Manchester United and Real Madrid, especially in South East Asia.

Another factor that might be significant for companies when considering overseas investment decisions is the geographical mobility of labour, which reflects the ease with which labour can move around the country in search of employment, and also the occupational mobility of labour, which reflects the ease with which labour can move between jobs and how quickly they can be retrained. It is usually the case that younger people are more mobile both in terms of geographical and occupational mobility and so a younger age-profile might be attractive to some companies, especially those who invest in labour-intensive industries. It has been noticeable that many large organisations have been moving their labour-intensive call centres to developing countries where there is an established pool of young, educated people who are available for work.

Perhaps the most challenging dimension of demographic change is that faced by governments. When there is high population growth (as we saw in the case of Bangladesh), there are enormous pressures on governments to provide adequate resources for the growing population. While the prime requirement is for food and water, there will also be requirements for educational and medical facilities which will be very difficult to fulfil without help from other sources. In the situation of Europe and Japan, where the trend is essentially that of an ageing population, the governments will face other issues. One factor will be a gradual decline in the number of younger people. This might mean that in some cases schools have to be closed down, especially in areas where natural population decline has been exacerbated by migration. On the other hand, with a significant increase in the number of older people there will be a significant increase in the demand for medical services, especially as older people generally require significantly more medical support than younger people. Thus the demand for hospitals and medical support provided by the government will grow and governments will have to become increasingly aware of the needs of older people when determining their political programmes.

7.5 Social dynamics

The final part of this chapter will examine some of the social trends that have occurred over the last years and assess some of the implications of these for the way we live and how they might be significant for the business environment.

Social dynamics will be looked at from three perspectives, with current trends identified in each case. The first dynamic of social change relates to changes in the changing family. The family is the basic building block of society and yet it has been influenced by many factors over the last 20 years. We have already seen how the falling birth rates might be significant for family size, although we will also examine changes in family structure and changes in the patterns of relationships. A very good source to identify such trends is the National Census in the UK which first took place in 1801 and has taken place every ten years since that date with the next census due in 2011. An additional source is the General Household Survey which began in 1971 and which is carried out each year based on a sample of 9,000 households. The second social dynamic we will examine will be the change in lifestyles. This will reflect some different aspects of how we live and how we spend our leisure time and what we spend our money on. It will also reflect how healthy our lifestyle is and our educational needs as well as looking at trends in crime in our society. The third social dynamic to be examined will be the change in work and the extent to which the nature of work is changing in the twenty-first century and will also cover other work-related issues such as the minimum wage and changes in organised labour.

7.5.1 The changing family

Statistics from various UK sources have been widely used in this section. However, it must be recognised that in this section we are describing a trend that is evident in many more countries than the UK.

Using information published by the UK Office of National Statistics, we can learn about many social changes in the past 40 years. We have already identified that falling birth rates have tended to lead to a reduction in family size. In the UK, household size has declined in a fairly consistent pattern from a figure of 2.91 persons in 1971 to a figure of 2.48 in 1991 and then again to 2.4 in 2003/4. Many of the reasons for this have been discussed above; also more people are living alone than at any previous time. One-person households have increased from 17 percent of all households in 1971 to 30 percent in the census of 2003/4 (a total of 6.5 million households). There are always a number of older people who live alone, but the figure for this group has remained stable, with the big increase in single households occurring in the 25–44 age group. This may be significant for companies who might target this age group and might be one of the factors behind the significant increase in demand for satellite television in the UK. The 'traditional' family pattern, where there exists a married or cohabiting couple with dependent children, has changed; the number of dependent children living in such a family declined by 1 million between 1998 and 2008 (70 to 63 percent). The proportion of children living with one-parent families increased 22 to 23 percent over the same period. Companies might have to start thinking about non-traditional targets when they target their markets.

Another area of change in the family is that of changing family relationships. One key issue here is that of marital status. In 2006, the majority of people were married (52 percent of men and 50 percent of women). However, the proportion of unmarried people cohabiting rather than marrying has increased significantly (24 percent of men aged 16 to 59 in 2006 compared with 11 percent in 1986 and 25 percent of women compared with 11 percent in 1986) and this trend appeared to be stronger in the younger age ranges. This is reflected by the fact that people seem to be marrying at a later age as they seek to develop their careers or move through the cohabiting phase previously identified.

A factor influencing this is the changing role of women in society and the increased career expectations of women. More women want to develop their own careers before having children and the increased availability of flexible working allows them to return to work on a full- or part-time basis much more easily than in the past. One consequence of this is the massive increase in demand for child-caring facilities, such as nurseries, where the demand has mushroomed, despite there being a gradual decline in the birth rate.

There are also some changes in traditional family roles, where the roles may be shared more between the household members. There are increasing cases where the female partner or wife may earn a higher income than her husband/partner and so we see the development of the 'househusband'.

Another factor that has contributed to the increase in single households (especially in the 25–44 age group) is the increase in divorce in the UK. Over the period 1973 to 1993 the number of divorces rose by nearly 60 percent although many divorced people re-marry. The latest figures suggest that the number of divorces has fallen to the lowest number since 1977– but this probably reflects the greater number of couple cohabiting rather than marrying.

There are significant differences in divorce rates across Europe which reflect different religious, social, legal and cultural factors, with the countries in Northern and Western Europe typically having higher divorce rates than Southern Europe. In 2005 the EU average for divorce was 2 per thousand people and the highest rate in 2007 was in Belgium (2.8 per 1,000) with the UK also above the EU average (2.4 per 1,000). Not surprisingly, the lowest rates in 2007 were found in Ireland and Italy where the rate was 0.8 per 1,000.

The role of the family in society also varies across Europe. Vogel (1998) suggests that there are three clusters of European Society:

- the Nordic countries, comprising Denmark, Sweden, Norway and Finland;
- the Southern European countries of Greece, Italy, Spain and Portugal (although Ireland could also be included in many respects);
- most of the continental countries in between, which show characteristics of the first two clusters but not as strongly – this group would include France, Germany and the Netherlands.

The differences between these clusters would be determined by religious, social, political and cultural factors but might also be linked to the labour market and the role of the state. The Nordic cluster operates in a climate of large government spending on social programmes and high rates of labour market participation (through full-time and part-time work). There is less financial dependence on the traditional family unit and more opportunities for people to follow their own course and live independently (another factor contributing to the increase in single households).

The Southern European countries tend to have less comprehensive social programmes and more rigid labour markets with less opportunity for flexible working. There tends to be a higher financial dependence on the traditional extended family that is familiar in Italy, for example. While the traditional extended family undoubtedly has many benefits, such as emotional security and personal identity, it might also account for fewer younger people leaving home until a much later age and having some degree of social control and psychological constraints being placed upon them. It might be particularly difficult for women in these cultures to enter the labour market and reduce their financial reliance on the family. This will certainly create different lifestyle experiences within these countries and might also be significant for companies planning European marketing campaigns. In Southern Europe, advertisements would be much more likely to revolve around the 'traditional family' than in Northern Europe.

7.5.2 Changing lifestyles

Whereas the earlier population censuses focused on demographic factors, more recent ones have begun to explore much more about lifestyle in order to measure how lifestyle may have changed over time. One aspect of this might be to look at how our use of consumer durables has changed over time. In the 1950s, televisions were extremely rare and seen as a luxury item, whereas a television is now seen as almost as a necessity by many people and there is practically 100 percent saturation in the UK. In the UK in 1972 only 37 percent of households had central heating and 42 percent a telephone. In 2007, according to the UK Expenditure and Food Survey, the corresponding figures were 95 percent for central heating and 89 percent for telephones. While the figure for telephones might seem surprisingly small (and has actually fallen in the last few years), it should be remembered that between 2001 and 2007 ownership of mobile phones rose from 26 percent to 78 percent so almost all homes have one way or another of communicating via telephone. Companies operating in such saturated markets may find it difficult to achieve high rates of growth unless they can convince consumers to upgrade their products (possibly as a result of new technological breakthroughs). An example here would be in the saturated television market where there is a move to flat-screen and digital technology – this switch has been so marked that Dixons, a major high street retailer, announced in 2008 that it would no longer sell traditional cathode ray tube televisions.

What the surveys do show is that there was still considerable market growth potential in new products, particularly in new technology and home entertainment. The percentage of UK homes with computers has risen from 49 percent of households in 2001 to 67 percent in 2007 and 61 percent of households had internet access. For higher income homes, the percentages are approaching 100 percent, suggesting that there may still be opportunities for lower priced computers for lower income households. The increase in home entertainment had been equally rapid with sharp increases in the number of satellite, cable and digital television receivers (up from 29 percent of households in 1998 to 77 percent of households in 2007) and 88 per cent of households had a video recorder or DVD player (18 percent in 1983).

We also appear to be much more mobile than 30 years ago. In 1972, 48 percent of households had no car whereas the figure in 2007 is 25 percent, which may reflect improved income levels stimulating the demand for cars. Interestingly, the number of one-car households has hardly changed (43 percent in 1972 to 44 percent in 2007) but the most significant change is in households with two or more cars, which has increased from 7 percent in 1971 to 26 percent in 2007. This might be a reflection of more dual-income households where two cars are needed for work purposes or it might reflect greater affluence. What it certainly shows is a greater concentration of cars which has boosted the car market but it also implies that there is a likelihood of increased pollution and overcrowding on the road system as a result of this trend.

These changes in spending are obviously of great significance for companies operating in these sectors but they also can suggest a picture of how lifestyle has changed in the twenty-first century from previous decades with the wider implications of that.

7.5.3 Health

Another aspect of lifestyle is the issue of health and how healthy our lifestyle has become. One way of looking at this is to look at healthcare systems. The amount spent on healthcare systems varies considerably with high rates of spending in the USA and Germany contrasting with much lower rates of spending in countries such as Ireland, the UK and Turkey. There are also some contradictory trends occurring which reflect differing attitudes towards having a healthy lifestyle and some of these issues are covered in *Minicase 7.5*, which contrasts the increasing evidence of obesity in Europe with the massive explosion of health and fitness clubs.

Minicase 7.5	Calorie wars: couch potatoes or fitness fanatics?

An article in *The Observer* in June 2003 (Revill, 2003) identified the potential problems of increased obesity in the UK population and the potential health risks that the population faced as a result of this. The UK health and fitness industry grew very quickly in the early 2000s; about 12 percent of the UK's population belonged to a fitness club in 2007. So it appears that one part of the population is getting increasingly unhealthy in terms of their eating and fitness habits and adding on the calories, whereas another part is rushing off to the gym to burn some calories. These 'calorie wars' seem to reflect changing social trends in our society.

If we look at the obesity issue first, according to the WHO *Atlas of Health in Europe* (2008), the proportion of overweight adult males in the period 2000–2006 varied from 67 percent in Greece to 45 percent in Switzerland. During the same period the proportion of obese male adults varied from 26 percent in Greece to 7.4 percent in Italy. Surveys suggest that the differences between regions in Europe are reducing – that is, even in the countries where the prevalence of obesity is historically low, the trend is upwards.

Curiously, the UK is not included in the WHO publication, but other studies suggest that it is near the top of the scale with one in five adults classified as obese and also one in nine children. The reasons usually quoted are to do with changing lifestyles in terms of increased consumption of 'junk' foods and a lack of physical exercise for many people, with people staying at home more for their entertainment (the couch-potato lifestyle). The main concern is with children, with 9 percent of boys and 13 percent of girls classified as obese, a figure that quadrupled between 1984 and 1994. When children become overweight it vastly increases the risk of them developing diabetes – and the rate of diabetes has increased considerably. There have been government initiatives to try and counter this trend, such as encouraging families to eat five portions of fruit and vegetables a day and to make it easier for people to walk to work, although one could question how effective this will be when addressed to the socio-economic groups which are most obese.

At the same time we see more and more people joining health clubs with a significant expansion in this area. The drivers for this are obviously health-linked but it has also become a lifestyle trend, even to the extent of individuals having personal trainers. When surveyed on why they had joined health clubs, the majority had joined to get fit, although 30 percent had also joined to lose weight and 31 percent had joined to relax and relieve stress, with 10 percent joining for social purposes. Fitness chain operators such as Fitness First and David Lloyd Leisure grew at a rate of up to 10 percent per annum in 2004, despite the relatively high cost of some of these clubs. However, growth has slowed in recent years with a lot of consolidation in the industry.

Questions

1 How can you explain the fact that we have a trend towards increasing obesity and a trend towards increased use of health clubs at the same time?

2 Many developed countries face a similar situation. Should all governments do more to tackle the problem? How could they do this?

7.5.4 Smoking and alcohol

Two key areas which link both health and consumer spending are the trends in drinking and smoking. Both of these areas reflect lifestyle decisions made by people and they are also both multi-million pound industries and yet at the same time there is a health dimension involved because of the specific diseases linked with these two products.

In the UK, the trend in the 1990s was for a slight increase in overall alcohol consumption for men, but a much more marked increase for women, especially younger women. UK consumption is still relatively low by European comparisons (see *Table 7.6*). The reason for this is that many Central and Southern European countries are wine producers and it is much more normal to drink with a meal than is the case in Northern Europe. There are signs of changing drinking habits, however, with a decline of beer drinking in Northern European countries as many people have switched to wine and other beverages. In the traditional wine-growing countries the reverse effect has been noticed with less consumption of wine, especially among younger people. This has implications for beer and wine producers who may diversify into new areas.

There are also significant differences in the pattern of alcohol consumption across Europe. In Southern Europe daily drinking will be most common and yet the quantity consumed per drinking occasion is much higher in Northern Europe. This has been linked to the concept of 'binge drinking' (Institute of Alcohol Studies, 2002), which is defined as 'the consumption of five or more standard drinks in a single drinking occasion'. This has been found to be particularly prevalent in Northern Europe, especially Finland, Sweden and the UK and even more prevalent in teenagers and young adults where British, Irish and Danish teenagers have been identified as the heaviest drinkers in Europe and are more likely to get drunk and report problems associated with drinking compared with their counterparts in other European countries. This raises ethical questions about drinks companies who target this age group in these countries.

Table 7.6	Alcohol consumption by country (1997–2006)			
Country	**1997**	**1999**	**2000**	**2006***
Luxembourg	11.4	12.2	12.3	15.6
Romania	9.8	12.2	12.1	9.7
Portugal	11.3	10.3	11.7	11.5
Republic of Ireland	9.7	11.0	10.8	13.7
Czech Republic	10.5	10.5	10.6	13.0
France	10.9	10.7	10.5	11.4
Germany	10.8	10.6	10.5	12.0
Spain	10.2	9.9	10.0	11.7
Denmark	9.9	9.5	9.5	11.7
UK	8.2	8.4	8.4	11.8
Greece	8.3	8.2	8.0	9.0
Latvia	6.9	7.7	7.4	9.6
USA	6.6	6.7	6.7	8.6
Japan	6.4	6.6	6.5	7.6

Note: Measured in litres of pure alcohol per capita consumption.
Source: IAS (2001) www.ias.org.uk *Data in this column from the WHO and may not be strictly comparable with the IAS data (www.who.int/)

When looking at the trends in smoking it can be seen through the General Household Survey results that the prevalence of cigarette smoking fell substantially in the UK in the 1970s and 1980s and, to a lesser extent, in the 1990s and 2000s. The decline has been strongest in men, from 51 percent of men smoking in 1974 to 22 percent in 2007, although it has also declined among women with 20 percent of women smoking in 2007. The highest rates of smoking are found in the 20–24 age group.

When looking at the European picture on smoking the decline observed in the UK is not so common and there is increasing debate about the effectiveness of tobacco control systems in Europe. Ashraf (2003) comments on the disappointing results from the WHO for its third action plan, which covered the period 1997 to 2001 and was aimed at reducing the level of smoking within Europe through stronger anti-smoking measures. The WHO report identified that 30 percent of adult Europeans are smokers (38 percent of men and 24 percent of women), although it noticed an increasing gap between Western and Eastern Europe with regards to cigarette consumption in that 34 percent of men in western Europe smoked compared with 47 percent of men in Eastern Europe. More recent data suggest that the gap remains very wide: the WHO *Atlas of Health in Europe* (2008) shows that around 60 percent of males smoke in the Ukraine and the Russian Federation compared with around 14 percent in Sweden. This might reflect response of the tobacco companies who, faced with stronger anti-smoking legislation in Western Europe, are targeting the new high-growth markets of Eastern Europe. The prevalence of smoking among young people was 30 percent and the report noted that there had been no decrease in cigarette consumption for this age group over the period of the report. The health dimension linked to smoking is the occurrence of lung cancer and here the death rate for men in Western Europe has stabilised at a rate of 73 per 100,000. Another trend identified by the report was the massive increase in cigarette smuggling in order to avoid paying government duty on cigarettes. It is now estimated that one-third of cigarettes traded worldwide are smuggled, although the figures are slightly lower in Europe, where the UK government has estimated that about 20 percent of the cigarettes consumed in the country are smuggled. There is undoubtedly a move towards more tobacco controls through taxation, advertising bans and protection of the rights of non-smokers but this is only leading to different strategies from the big tobacco companies.

7.5.5 Crime

Another area of changing lifestyle is the issue of crime: see also *Chapter 9*. Heidensohn (1991) suggests that the quite dramatic change that continues to affect family life and gender roles may have an impact on crime. She points out that a growing number of children are being raised in one-parent households, often poorly housed in the worst areas. It seems that these children may be more likely to be 'pushed' into criminal activity.

On the other hand, UK government statistics from the British Crime Survey (BCS), which is an annual survey based on a sample of 40,000 people and which began in 1995, have shown a gradual decrease in crime in the UK and they suggest that there has been a 36 percent fall in crime for the period 1997 to 2008/9. Studies, such as that by Barclay *et al.* (2001), who carried out an international comparison of criminal justice statistics for the Home Office, show that during the period 1995–1999 recorded crime fell by 10 percent in the UK compared with the EU average of a 1 percent decline.

More recent international comparisons suggest that, where data are available, in 2007 the highest levels of homicide in Western and Central Europe during this period were found in Switzerland with a rate of 2.26 per 100,000 followed by Finland on 2.17. The figure for England and Wales was 1.37, well down the list – yet Scotland's most recent figure of 2.13 points to remarkably wide variations even within fairly small geographical areas. Some of the highest figures came from Honduras (48), South Africa (37.3), Russia (16.5), while the USA (5.8), though well down the list, seems to be still a more violent country than most of Western Europe. These figures might be significant as high levels of violence and homicide may be a factor influencing the willingness of executives to live in these cities, and could be a deterrent to inward investment. South Africa, in particular, has a serious image problem with crime which the government has failed to tackle effectively.

Computer crime is a new area of crime that seems to be on the increase and which is becoming a major concern to governments and business corporations. A 1995 study of 1,200 American companies by the management consultants Ernst and Young showed that over half the companies in their survey had suffered financial losses related to computer security. The theft of computers and computer parts, rather than the theft of information, seems to be one of the major problems facing small businesses. No one is exempt from the risks associated with computer crime. However, as Wall (2007) points out, it is very difficult to find accurate statistics about what he calls 'cybercrime'. This is because different groups use different terminology, many firms and individuals do not report cybercrime for various reasons and finally because computer security firms have been known to publicise dubious statistics, that are designed to frighten businesses into buying their products or services. But the potential for serious crime is shown by the well-publicised theft, in 2008, of credit card details of over 38,000 online customers of Cotton Traders, a UK-based clothing firm, by a hacker. With the rapid growth in electronic commerce, the potential for such crime is growing, which contributes to concerns about the security of e-commerce transactions and thus inhibits growth in the sector.

7.5.6 Terrorism

The last aspect of crime that we shall briefly consider is that of terrorism. This is not a new form of crime, but before 2001 it was generally regarded as 'local' in that terrorist acts took place mostly in regions with political, social, religious or ethnic problems – for example, the 'troubles' in Northern Ireland during the latter part of the twentieth century. The 9/11 attack on New York in 2001 marked a new trend – the threat of terrorist acts in places that do not have the problems referred to above, but are somehow associated with conflicts taking place in other countries. Terrorists are now aiming at economies and businesses – for example, by choosing targets associated with travel and tourism. After tourism. After 9/11 transatlantic air travel in particular declined sharply and this brought to an end the mergers and acquisition boom in the first years of the twenty-first century. A number of airlines collapsed due to the global reduction in air travel.

Although air travel recovered after a few months, the much more intensive security measures introduced at most airports have made international travel much more time-consuming. In addition, companies may be less inclined to do business in areas affected by unrest in case they become targets of local terrorist and kidnappers, and where insurance costs may be prohibitive. For a recent review of the challenges posed by these threats see the chapter by Andrew Lee in Ibeh and Davies (2009). *Minicase 7.6* shows how criminal and terrorist activity is impacting more and more on the daily life of ordinary citizens.

7.5.7 Education

We shall now consider briefly the worldwide trends in education. This is an important part of the international business environment because of the close relationship between education levels and economic prosperity. As Porter (1990) pointed out, a nation's knowledge and skills resources are a key factor affecting national competitive advantage. A well-educated workforce leads to growing levels of economic prosperity which in turn leads to greater availability and demand for education in that country – a virtuous circle. Conversely, a weak economy means that a nation cannot afford to invest in education – and so the nation is unable to develop its economy – a vicious circle. From the perspective of international business, growing economies offer new markets; and an educated workforce means that companies can set up subsidiaries in these growing markets making use of the local workforce rather than expatriates. But how can the vicious circle be broken?

| Minicase 7.6 | The surveillance society |

Criminal and terrorist activity means that citizens are now under closer scrutiny than ever before. Listed below are some of the actual and potential mechanisms for monitoring your movements and activities:

- Credit card details show exactly what you purchased, where and when. Supermarket loyalty cards do the same.
- Mobile phones act as tracking device that pinpoint where they are. Your location when you make a call is known and mobile calls and text messages can easily be recorded.
- Email traffic is probably being intercepted and read, for security reasons, on a sampling basis. Past connection, albeit innocent, to a person or organisation deemed by security services to be of interest could put your email traffic under scrutiny – just in case. Your employer can monitor your email and web usage.
- Computer records show all the websites that you have visited.
- On your shopping trips, you are filmed in most shops that you enter and some CCTV cameras in public places can compare faces with facial recognition software against databases of people of 'interest' to the authorities. Facial recognition software needs to be more accurate than it is now if it is to be more widely used – but these times will come.
- On your drive to work, cameras can record registration numbers fixing a vehicle in place and time and, potentially, run the number against databases such as motor insurers.

Questions

1 To what extent should routine surveillance of normal, law-abiding activities be tolerated in a free society?
2 How will society benefit from routine surveillance and database checking of people going about their everyday life?

In 2000, a meeting sponsored by UNESCO and attended by governments from 164 nations, established a 'collective commitment to dramatically expand educational opportunities for children, youth and adults by 2015'. A mid-term report on the Education for All programme was published by UNESCO in 2008. Progress has been made, but there is still a long way to go – but there is no doubt that, if reasonably successful, this initiative will be one of the main drivers behind the global shift in economic power from the developed nations to the less-developed world, with new threats and opportunities for businesses everywhere.

7.5.8 Work trends

Finally we need to look at changing work trends which will affect people in society, although many of these themes are developed in more depth in *Chapter 13*. One of the trends we have already identified is the increased possibility of part-time working in countries with more flexible working practices where there are opportunities for part-time working, teleworking, job-sharing and outsourcing of labour to specialist agencies. This throws up new opportunities for part-time work, especially for women. It is interesting here to compare data for part-time and full-time working for women with the society clusters suggested earlier by Vogel (1998). In the Northern European cluster of countries such as Scandinavia and the UK, the most recent figures show that female employment has increased dramatically since 1997 and is gradually approaching the level of male employment as more opportunities through flexible working, better childcare facilities and greater independence have seen more opportunities for working women. Much of the growth, however, has been in part-time jobs. At the lower end of the scale we see again the cluster of Southern European countries and Ireland, all of which have large proportions of traditional families with full-time housewives. In Italy, for example, 47.2 percent of females were in employment compared with 70.3 percent of males in 2008 and the proportion is fairly static. This may be a problem when companies try to introduce more flexible working patterns in certain countries and can lead to rigidities in the labour market.

Another aspect of labour is the extent of organised labour in countries, usually reflected by membership of trade unions. The general trend in trade union membership has been for a steady decline in numbers. Metcalfe (1990) argues that the decline in union membership is the result of an interaction of five factors:

- the macroeconomic environment;
- the composition of jobs and the workforce including the relative decline in manufacturing industry;
- the policy of the state;
- the attitudes and conduct of employers;
- the stance taken by employers.

For example, in the UK one of the main factors was the big increase in legislation during the 1980s' Thatcher government which significantly changed the behaviour and practices of trade unions. The trend can clearly be seen in the UK where trade union membership fell from 13.3 million in 1979 to 7.6 million in 2006. It is very interesting to look more closely at these figures. If we look at the union membership density (i.e. the proportion of employees belonging to a recognised trade union) then we can see that for men, the density fell from around 35.4 percent in 1995 to 27.3 percent in 2006. Over the same period, the density for women has reduced from just under 30 percent in 1995 to 28.5 percent in 2001 and has since risen back to 28.8 percent in 2006. This marked difference probably reflects the decline of UK manufacturing industries (which tended to employ males) and the growth in service industries.

In Germany and Belgium there are works councils, which have the right to be consulted over closures or prospective merger activities, and European legislation has also seen the introduction of minimum wage levels to protect the lowest-paid sectors of the community. The minimum wage was finally introduced in the UK in April 1999 when it was set at a basic level of £3.60 an hour. In 2009 the UK minimum wage was £5.80 compared with Portugal's £2.59 an hour and Belgium's £8.32 an hour. This may be a factor that would need to be taken on board in industries which depend on low-paid and largely unskilled labour.

Hillman (1996) has examined the wider trends in the working environment and how we will work in the twenty-first century and he suggests that there will be a transformation in social life and the way we work. He suggests that the key trends in the twenty-first century will be:

- increasingly footloose economic activity;
- fierce global competition, fuelled by advances in information and communication technologies;
- shifts in occupational patterns in favour of managerial, professional and technical jobs in the service sector and a shift to knowledge workers;
- a growth in the importance of small and medium-sized enterprises, reflecting changes in the nature and organisation of work as many large organisations are forced to restructure;
- more flexible labour markets in many countries, with part-time and temporary work, weaker relationships between employers and employees and the threat of recurrent unemployment and underemployment;
- fractured career patterns and work/leisure boundaries, with training increasingly the responsibility of individuals themselves;
- increasing dangers of exclusion for socially and economically disadvantaged groups.

Many of these trends are already becoming clearer in the years since Hillman (1996) wrote about these issues and make the way we will work in the future much more complex than in the past. The likelihood of staying with one employer for the bulk of your working life is becoming increasingly remote, with more emphasis being placed on the individual to develop their skill base to cope with more flexible working environments of the future. One could argue that this is making the working environment much more stressful than in the past but also more challenging and potentially rewarding.

7.6 Conclusion

This chapter has covered a number of cultural, demographic and social aspects of the business environment which may have significance for companies. We have seen that when companies have an international dimension then they are much more likely to be influenced by exposure to other cultures and it may well be the success with which the company handles these differences that will determine its success in any overseas activities, although the extent of the problem may be determined by the closeness or otherwise of the cultural fit between countries.

We have also seen that companies and governments have to pay increasing attention to changes in the demographic structure within the business environment. Population changes may be gradual, compared with other areas such as technological change, but their significance is becoming increasingly recognised and nowhere more than in those countries that are facing rapidly ageing populations, as we have seen in Europe and Japan.

Finally we have examined a number of social changes in terms of family changes, changing lifestyles and the changing nature of work, all of which may be very significant for businesses in certain sectors in terms of identifying developing or declining markets and developing strategies to deal with these.

Summary of main points

- When businesses operate internationally, they will need a clearer understanding of national cultural differences.
- Hofstede and Trompenaars give us frameworks for understanding differences in national business cultures.
- The extent of cultural adaptation will depend upon the closeness of the cultural fit between countries.
- Businesses may have to alter their management styles, their marketing policies and their HRM policies to take cultural differences into account.
- Demographic changes can be easily identified and easily predicted.
- The pattern of falling fertility rates is leading to a rapid ageing of the population in Europe and Japan.
- The increased pressure on the working population to support the retired population will put severe pressures on governments.
- The nature of the family and family relationships is changing rapidly in the UK.
- The role of the family varies across Europe.
- Changing lifestyles are leading to changing consumption of tobacco and alcohol, although there is clear evidence of increased obesity – especially among younger people.
- The level of criminal activity may influence international investment decisions.
- Trade union membership has continued to decline against a background of more flexible working patterns in the country.
- There is a close relationship between education levels and economic prosperity.

Discussion questions

1 By using data from Hofstede in the text, compare the national culture of France and the USA. How might the differences you identify have affected the relationship between American managers and French workers in the early days of Disneyland Paris?

2 Imagine that there is a proposed merger between your Italian company and a British company and you have been appointed to lead a team made up of managers from both countries to examine any cultural problems linked to the proposed merger. How close would the cultural fit be and how might you seek to improve cultural understanding between the two groups of managers?

3 Critically assess the extent to which some companies would benefit and some face a crisis through the ageing of the population. Look for examples in your own country of companies who will be affected by this trend and suggest strategies they could follow in response to this.

4 To what extent do you agree with Vogel's (1998) views about the three clusters of European society? To what extent does your own country fit into the family behaviour suggested in this analysis?

5 To what extent do you feel that the level of crime (or perception about crime) is becoming a bigger factor in the social environment? To what extent will it influence investment decisions by companies?

6 Assess the extent to which the overall decline in trade union membership is likely to continue into the twenty-first century. Are there any factors that might reverse the current trends?

Further reading/sources of information

The web links are some that have been found useful when researching this chapter.

Census (www.ons.gov.uk/census/index.html) The next UK national census will take place in 2011. This site gives access to data from the last national census of 2001 as well as summary data from previous censuses.

EU (http://epp.eurostat.ec.europa.eu/portal/page/portal/eurostat/home) This is the home page of the EU's statistics services through which you can find a wide range of materials on the EU.

Executive Planet (www.executiveplanet.com/index.php?title=Main_Page) This website will give you a fascinating range of information on business culture in many countries – including how to greet people and how to behave in business situations.

UK Natural Statistics (www.statistics.gov.uk/hub/index.html) This site is the gateway to UK national statistics covering a very wide range of social and demographic areas. You can even get information down to the level of your local neighbourhood and compare this with UK averages.

UN (www.un.org/popin/) This is the home page of the United Nations Population Information Network from which you can find any material you need on population as well as special reports.

Up my street (http://upmystreet.com) This website will give you lots of socio-economic information down to the level of individual postcodes.

Halsey, A.H. and Webb, J. (2000) *Twentieth Century British Social Trends,* 3rd edn. Basingstoke: Macmillan. Covers all the main social changes that occurred in the twentieth century, although it is a lengthy book.

McFarlin, D.B. and Sweeney, P.D. (2006) *International Management: Strategic Opportunities and Cultural Challenges*, 3rd edn. Boston, MA: Houghton Mifflin Company. A useful book which examines cross-cultural communication and the management of intercultural groups.

Stephens, J. (2009) National Culture, in Brooks, I. *Organisational Behaviour: Individuals, Groups and Organisations*, 4th edn. Harlow: FT/Prentice Hall, pp. 283–320. The chapter gives a good general overview of the main theories and issues concerned with national culture.

Tayeb, M. (2003) *International Management: Theories and Practice*. Harlow: FT/Prentice Hall. Another book which is very good on the management implications of national cultures.

United Nations Department of Economic and Social Affairs (2006) *Demographic Yearbook*, New York: United Nations Publications. Lots of fascinating data from around the world – in English *and* French.

References

Ashraf, H. (2003) European Tobacco Control Reaches a Critical Phase. *The Lancet*, 359, 585–586.

Barclay, G., Tavares, C. and Siddique, A. (2001) *International Comparisons of Criminal Justice Statistics 1999*, Home Office Statistical Bulletin, Issue 6/01.

Chinese Culture Connection (1987) 'Chinese values and the search for culture-free dimensions of culture', *Journal of Cross-Cultural Psychology* 18 (2), pp. 143–64.

Daniels, J.D., Radebaugh, L.H. and Sullivan, D.P. (2009) *International Business: Environments and Operations*, 12th edn. Upper Saddle River, NJ: Prentice Hall.

Economist (2008) Ford's European Arm Lends a Hand. March.

Heidensohn, M. (1991) *Crime and Society: Sociology for a Changing World*. Basingstoke: Macmillan.

Hillman, J. (1996) *University for Industry: Creating a National Learning Framework*. London: Institute for Public Policy Research.

Hofstede, G. (1984) *Cultures Consequences: International Differences in Work-related Values*, abridged edn. Beverley Hills, CA: Sage.

Hofstede, G. and Bond, M.H. (1988) Confucius and Economic Growth: New Trends in Culture's Consequences. *Organisational Dynamics*, 16, 4–21.

Hofstede, G. and Hofstede, G.J. (2005) *Cultures and Organisations: Software of the Mind*, 2nd edn. New York: Mcgraw-Hill.

Ibeh, K. and Davies, S. (eds) (2009) *Contemporary Challenges to International Business*. Basingstoke: Palgrave Macmillan Institute of Alcohol Studies (2002) **www.ias.org.uk/**

Kerr, C., Dunlop, J.T., Harbison, F. and Myers C.A. (1960) *Industrialism and Industrial Man: The Problems of Labour and the Management of Economic Growth*. Cambridge, MA: Harvard University Press.

Kluckhohn, F. and Strodtbeck, F. (1961) *Variations in Value Orientations*. New York: Peterson.

Kroeber, A. and Kluckhohn, C. (1985) *Culture: A Critical Review of Concepts and Definitions*. New York: Random House.

Levitt, T. (1983) The Globalisation of Markets. *Harvard Business* Review, May–June, 92–102.

Metcalfe, D. (1990) Union Presence and Labour Productivity in British Manufacturing Industry: A Reply to Nolan and Marginson. *British Journal of Industrial Relations*, 28, 249–266.

Porter, M.E. (1990) *The Competitive Advantage of Nations*. New York: Free Press.

Revill, J. (2003) Fat Chance. *The Observer*, 8 June.

Torbiorn (1982) *Living Abroad: Personal Adjustment and Personnel Policy in an Overseas Setting*. New York: Wiley.

Trompenaars, F. (1993) *Riding the Waves of Culture*. London: Nicholas Brealey.

Vogel, J. (1998) *Three Types of European Society*, available at **www.nnn.se/n-model/europe3/europe3.htm**

Wall, D.S. (2007) *Cybercrime*. Cambridge: Polity Press.

World Health Organisation *Atlas of Health in Europe*, available at **www.euro.who.int/Document/E91713.pdf**

8 The resource context: people, technology and natural resources

Chris Britton

Businesses carry out a variety of activities, but their main activity is to produce goods and services to be sold on the market. In the production process, inputs are turned into outputs. Key inputs into the production process are people, technology and natural resources.

Learning outcomes

Having read this chapter you should be able to:

- illustrate the importance of people, technology and natural resources to business
- explain what determines the quality of labour in the economy
- demonstrate the effect of technological change on business
- outline the main issues affecting natural resources

Key terms

Capital	Land	Research and
Computer-aided design	Minimum wage	development
(CAD)	Natural resources	Resources
Derived demand	Negademand	Social capital
Educated workforce	Net investment	Stock
Factor of production	Non-renewable resources	Technological change
Fixed capital	NVQs	Technological
Fracking	Occupational immobility	unemployment
Geographical immobility	Occupational structure	Technology
Gross investment	Participation rate	Trade union
Immobility of labour	People	Wage rate
Information technology	Process innovation	Wages
Infrastructure	Product innovation	Workforce
Innovation	Renewable resources	Working capital
Investment	Replacement investment	Working week

Introduction

The main aim of business is to produce goods and services that people want. This production cannot take place without people, technology and natural resources. In economics, these three are called the factors of production and are categorised under the headings of labour, capital and land. This chapter will consider each of these in turn. **Resources** can be renewable or non-renewable. **Renewable resources** would include labour, water, fishing stocks, soil, air and solar power, even though many of these might not be renewable for a long period of time. **Non-renewable resources** would be most minerals, including oil, iron ore and coal, agricultural land, forests and electricity (in so far as most electricity is derived from minerals).

People

People are important in the economy as both producers and consumers of goods and services. For most products that are produced, people are the most important input the production process. Therefore the quantity and quality of the people available in an economy will have a considerable impact upon the economy's ability to produce.

The quantity of people available for work depends upon a variety of factors:

- the size of the total population;
- the age structure of the population;
- the working population;
- the length of the working week;
- the wage level.

As well as the quantity of labour, productivity will be affected by its quality. This in turn depends upon:

- education and training;
- working conditions;
- welfare services (e.g. national insurance schemes, which cover sickness pay, the NHS, which maintains the health of workers; also many firms provide their own welfare services such as private pension plans, and so on);
- motivation;
- the quality of the other factors of production.

In this section we concentrate on the idea of the 'workforce' and associated issues, before considering the question of labour quality.

The workforce

The **workforce** is the number of people who are eligible and available to work and offer themselves up as such. The size of the workforce will be determined by the age at which people can enter employment, which in the United Kingdom is 18 years, and the age at which they leave employment. In the United Kingdom the retirement age for men is 65 years and for women will be 65 by 2020. Those included in the definition of the workforce are:

- those working in paid employment, even if they are over retirement age;
- part-time workers;
- the claimant unemployed;
- members of the armed forces;
- the self-employed.

The workforce in 2013 was 32.3 million, which is about 51 per cent of the total population. The importance of the workforce is two-fold: it produces the goods and services needed in the economy, and through the payment of taxes it supports the dependent population (i.e. the very old and the very young).

An important determinant of the size of the workforce is the **participation rate** (i.e. the proportion of the population who actually work). Table 8.1 shows that the participation rate for women in the UK was 75.3 per cent in the summer of 2013, somewhat lower than the male figure of 83.5 per cent. The figures have, however, been converging over the years. There has been a rise in participation rates for women at the same time as a fall in participation rates for men.

Table 8.1 Economic activity by gender (% men 16–64 and women 16–59), July 2013

	Men	Women
Economically active	83.5	75.3
In employment	76.4	69.7
Unemployed	8.5	7.4
Economically inactive	16.5	24.7

Source: Adapted from Table A03 Summary of National LFS Data, *www.ons.gov.uk*

The trend has been for increased participation rates for women over time as families have become smaller and because of the changing role of women in society as a whole, labour-saving devices in the home, government legislation to promote equal pay and treatment, and the increase in the pension age of women. Also important in this process are the changes in industrial structure which have led to more part-time service jobs.

There has been an increase in participation rates of married or cohabiting women with dependent children, from 67 per cent in 1996 to 70 per cent by 2013. There has been a similar increase in participation rates of lone mothers – from 43 per cent to 60 per cent over the same time period.

Table 8.2 gives some comparisons with other EU countries. The United Kingdom has the third-highest activity rates for men and women after Denmark and Germany. There are marked differences in the activity rates for women across the EU, but in every country they are lower than the male activity rate.

web link

For more information on labour markets:
in the UK see *www.statistics.gov.uk/hub/labour-market/*
in Europe see *http://epp.eurostat.ec.europa.eu*
and in the world *www.oecd.org*

Table 8.2 Economic activity rates* by sex for selected EU countries (%), 2010

	Males	Females	All
UK	74.5	64.8	69.5
France	68.3	59.9	64.0
Germany	76.0	66.1	71.1
Belgium	67.4	56.5	62.0
Italy	67.7	46.2	56.9
Denmark	75.8	71.1	73.4
EU-27 average	70.1	58.6	64.2

Note: *As a percentage of the working-age population.
Source: Adapted from Table 2.2, *http://epp.eurostat.ec.europa.eu/cache/ITY_OFFPUB/1*, © *European Union, 1995–2014.*

The length of the working week

The average length of time for which people work is also a significant determinant of the quantity of labour that is available in an economy. Generally, the shorter the **working week**, the less labour there is available. There has been, over the last 100 years, a gradual reduction in the length of the working week; 40 hours is now roughly the norm, with a gradual increase in the number of holidays that people take. More recently, this trend has been reversed: the average working week in the UK was 42.8 hours in 2010. Table 8.3 shows the length of the average working week in selected EU countries.

Table 8.3 Average hours worked per week* for selected EU countries, 2010

	All
UK	42.8
France	41.1
Germany	41.8
Belgium	41.2
Italy	40.7
Denmark	41.8
Netherlands	41.0
EU 15 average	41.5
EU 25 average	41.6

Note: *Full-time employees.
Source: Table 2.8, *http://epp.eurostat.ec.europa.eu/cache/ITY_OFFPUB/1*, © *European Union, 1995–2014.*

Both men and women in the UK work a longer week than men and women in all other EU countries. A relatively new phenomenon in the UK is the use of zero-hours contracts – see mini case study.

mini case   Zero-hours contracts

A growing trend in the UK is the use of the zero-hours contract (ZHC), where employees are not guaranteed any hours' work per week but are expected to be 'on call'. They can be called in as and when they are required. They often typically work much more than zero hours, but nothing is

Figure 8.1 Numbers employed on zero-hours contracts, Oct–Dec, UK, thousands

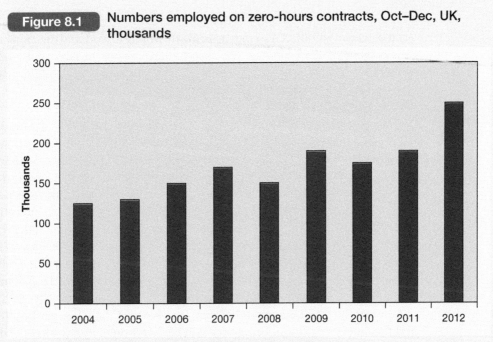

Source: Adapted from 'Working Zero Hours, 2005–2012', *www.ons.gov.uk*

guaranteed. They are only paid for the work they do and often have to ask their employer's permission to take other employment. These sorts of contracts are not new – there are some jobs which by their very nature require ZHCs, examination invigilation for example. Schools, colleges and universities have a big demand for invigilators at certain times of the year. It would be uneconomic for them to use permanent full- or even part-time employees for this job. In this case ZHCs benefit the employees as well, many invigilators being retired teachers who are happy with this working arrangement.

The Labour Force Survey (LFS) estimated that in quarter 4 of 2012, 0.8 per cent of the UK workforce (250,000) were on ZHCs. This number is disputed by the Chartered Institute of Personnel and Development (CIPD) and the Unite trade union as being a gross underestimate of the total (the Labour Force Survey data is based on a survey and there could be misunderstandings of the questions). The CIPD estimates that in 2013 3–4 per cent of the workforce was employed on ZHCs, approximately 1 million people. Even using the LFS data, there is a definite upward trend in the use of ZHCs, as Figure 8.1 shows.

ZHCs are more commonly used in large companies (23 per cent of companies with more than 100 employees compared with 11 per cent of those companies with 50–99 employees). There are differences between sectors: they are most common in hotels and restaurants (19 per cent in 2011), health (13 per cent in 2011) and education (10 per cent in 2011).[1] It is estimated that some retailers and hospitality companies have more than 80 per cent of their workers on ZHCs.

There are arguments for and against ZHCs:

1 ZHCs give flexibility to both employer and employee.
2 There is less security for employees.
3 Employees are open to possible exploitation by employers.
4 There are problems with arranging child care at short notice.

Although there is much bad press about ZHCs, it is not all negative. The CIPD found that the levels of job satisfaction of those on ZHCs were just as high as those of other employees. More than half of the employees surveyed by the CIPD said that they would not want to work longer hours (but they may be working more hours anyway). The debate continues in the press and has reached the level of government debate, with possible legislation on ZHCs in 2014.

Wages

It is clear that **wages** will affect how much people are willing to work and therefore the overall supply of labour in the economy. The analysis here will use the basic tools of demand and supply. It is advisable to review that chapter before proceeding.

The market for labour can be likened to the market for any other commodity, in that there will be a demand for and a supply of labour. The demand for labour will come from the firm that wishes to produce goods and services that can be sold in the market. The demand for labour is a '**derived demand**' as its demand is derived from the demand that exists for what it produces. The demand curve can be assumed to be a normal downward-sloping demand curve which indicates that – everything else being equal – as the wage rate goes up, the demand for labour goes down.[2] The supply of labour comes from people. It is equally likely that the total supply curve has the normal upward slope, indicating that as the wage rate increases the supply of labour increases. It is argued that as the wage rate increases past a certain level, people would prefer to substitute leisure for wages. The individual supply curve will therefore bend backwards at that wage rate. The total supply curve, however, will be upward sloping, indicating that those not working will be encouraged to offer their services and that those already working might be encouraged to work overtime.

Assuming for the time being that the labour market is a totally free market, the **wage rate** and the amount of labour being used will be determined by the forces of demand and supply, as in Figure 8.2. The equilibrium wage rate is £W and the equilibrium quantity of labour is L. If there is a change in the level of demand or supply, there will be a corresponding change in the wages and quantity of labour.

Trade unions and wages

In the UK there are four different types of **trade union**:

1 *Craft unions*. They represent one particular craft or skill, like the Boilermakers Union, which was formed in 1834 and was the longest-lived craft union in the TUC when it merged with the GMB in 1982. These were the earliest type of union.

Figure 8.2   The market for labour

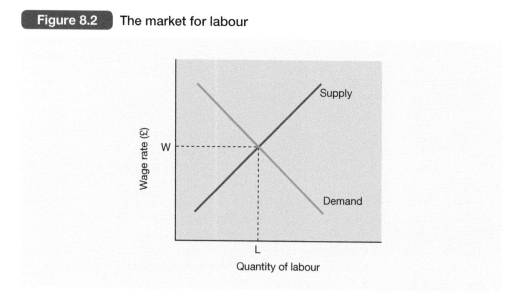

Quantity of labour

2 *Industrial unions.* They have members doing different jobs but in the same industry. Industrial unions are more common in other countries, but some UK unions come close to this type; for example, the National Union of Miners.

3 *General unions.* They contain members doing different jobs in different industries, such as the Transport and General Workers Union.

4 *White collar unions.* They represent the non-manual workers like teachers, social workers and so forth. An example is UNISON.

 web link   For information on trade unions in the UK see *www.tuc.org.uk*

One of the main aims for all types of union has been to counteract and protect their members from the power of the employer. As far as wages are concerned, this has been achieved through collective bargaining. Over the years a situation has been reached where hardly any wage contracts are negotiated individually. Rather, they are collectively negotiated by trade unions and employers. Although there does seem to be a trend away from collective bargaining, coinciding with the anti-trade union legislation of the 1980s and decline in the membership and power of the trade unions, the majority of wage increases are still negotiated by trade unions.

It is argued that the activities of trade unions through collective bargaining have served to increase the wage rate above its equilibrium level and thus cause unemployment. Figure 8.3 demonstrates this effect. Assume that the market clearing wage rate is £W and the quantity of labour being used is L. Assume now that a trade union enters the market that has the power to enforce a wage increase to £W_1. At this wage rate the market does not clear, the demand for labour is L_1 while the supply of labour is L_2. There is therefore excess supply of labour, or unemployment. In this way trade unions are blamed for keeping wages at too high a level so that the market cannot clear.

Figure 8.3 can be used to illustrate the argument of those who oppose the setting of a minimum wage. Although this argument seems plausible enough, it is not quite as simple

Figure 8.3   The effect of trade unions on the labour market

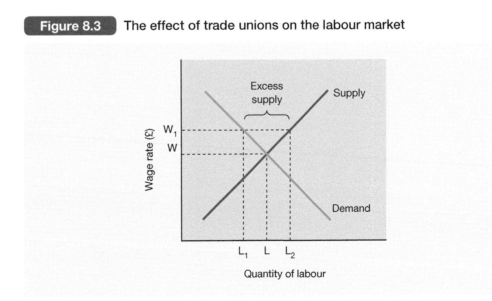

as it seems. There are other market imperfections which prevent the market from operating as smoothly as suggested and which contribute towards creating unemployment. There are some industries that have only one or two employers who can exercise a great deal of power over the market. The arguments over the **minimum wage** are also more complicated and centre on much wider economic and social issues. There are additional factors that may prevent people moving easily and smoothly between jobs. For example, people may not easily be able to change jobs if they are geographically or occupationally immobile.

Immobility of labour

People are **geographically immobile (immobility of labour)** for a variety of reasons:

- The cost of moving – it is an expensive business to move to another part of the country, particularly to areas where housing costs are high, such as London.
- There may be shortages of housing in certain areas, or it may be difficult or even impossible to sell a house in other areas.
- There will be many social ties in the form of family and friends that people may be reluctant to leave.
- For people with children, schooling will be important. For example, parents are reluctant to relocate when their children are working for important examinations.

People may also experience **occupational immobility** for the following reasons:

- Some jobs require some natural ability that an individual may not possess (e.g. entertainers, footballers and so on).
- Training is required by many occupations (e.g. doctors, engineers). Without this training an individual could not do the job and the length of training might be a deterrent.
- To enter some occupations (like starting up your own business), a certain amount of capital is required. In some cases the amount of capital needed will be very high (dry cleaning, for example, where the machines are expensive to purchase), and for many this might prove to be a barrier to mobility.

In order to help people to be more mobile so that the labour market works more smoothly, the government over the years has evolved a variety of policies. Job centres and similar places attempt to overcome the lack of knowledge of available jobs. Training schemes are offered so that people can retrain, and relocation allowances can be paid to alleviate the cost of moving.

These are some of the factors that determine the number of people who are available in an economy for producing goods and services. However, it is not just the quantity of labour but also its quality that is important. The quality of the workforce is determined by many factors already mentioned, but most importantly by the level of education and training of the workforce.

The level of education and training of the workforce

An **educated workforce** is necessary for an advanced industrial nation, in terms of both general qualifications and specific job-related training. The UK does not fare well in either of these areas compared with other countries, being ranked 23rd for reading, 26th for mathematics and 20th for science out of 65 countries in the Programme for International Student Assessment (PISA) produced by the OECD.[3]

In the UK, a stated aim of the government is to increase the proportion of young people staying on at school after the statutory minimum leaving age. In September 2013 the school leaving age was raised to 17 years and in 2015 it will rise again to 18 years old. The UK government also has put in place policies aimed towards vocational courses for the over-16s. Table 8.4 gives some examples of these over the last three decades.

Table 8.4 Examples of vocational courses for over-16s

Year	Scheme	Description
1983	Youth Training Scheme	Provided work-related training for 16- and 17-year-olds, both on and off the job. Largely introduced to fill the gap left by the demise of the traditional apprenticeships.
1985	Certificate of Pre-vocational Education	Full-time vocational courses for over-16s containing an element of work experience.
1992	National Vocational Qualifications (NVQs), General National Vocational Qualifications (GNVQs)	A comprehensive system of vocational qualifications at four levels of achievement.
1998	Work-based Training for Young People	This replaced the Youth Training Scheme with the aim of ensuring that young people have access to post-compulsory education or training.
2004	National Qualifications Framework	This brings together general and vocational qualifications into one framework.
2010	Qualifications and Credit Framework	National credit transfer system.

National Vocational Qualifications (**NVQs**) are qualifications that cover a specific skill, such as plumbing or carpentry, while General National Vocational Qualifications (GNVQs) are more general and indicate a broad knowledge of an area, such as the built environment. NVQ level 2 equates to GNVQ intermediate level and is equivalent to five GCSE grades A* to C. NVQ level 3 equates to GNVQ advanced level and is equivalent to two GCE A-levels, and level 4 equates to a degree or higher vocational qualification.

The Qualifications and Credit Framework (QCF) replaced the National Qualifications Framework in 2010. Under the QCF each qualification carries a credit value. There are three sizes of qualification: award, which equals 1–12 credits; certificate, which equals 13–36 credits; and diploma, which equals 37+ credits. The new system corresponds with the EU system so that the credits are internationally comparable. Part of the framework is shown in Table 8.5.

Table 8.5 National Qualifications Framework, up to level 3

Level	General	Vocational	Occupational
3 National Diploma, National Certificate	A level	BTEC national award	NVQ level 3
2 First Diploma	GCSE (grade A*–C)	BTEC first diploma	NVQ level 2
1 Foundation	GCSE (grade D–G)	BTEC introductory certificate	NVQ level 1

Source: Qualifications and Credit Framework, qca.org.uk, 2005.

The UK government has used a variety of policies in an attempt to increase educational attainment and training. These include:

- the National Literacy and Numeracy Strategy, launched in 1998, which provides for a dedicated literacy hour and one mathematics lesson every day for primary school children;
- the use of Education Action Zones in areas of educational disadvantage;
- the introduction of the Education Maintenance Allowance, which offers financial incentives to young people from low-income homes to remain in education;
- an increased number of Modern Advanced Apprenticeships;
- e2e (entry to employment), which is an entry to a level 1 programme that uses work-based learning;
- in 2001 43 Learning and Skills Councils were set up with responsibility for all post-16 education up to university level;
- in 2002 Sector Skills Councils were set up;
- in 2010 the Learning and Skills Council was replaced by the Skills Funding Agency.

As well as school and higher education, job-related training is important in improving the quality of the workforce. Training at work can be of two types: on-the-job training and off-the-job training. There has been the development of a competence-based approach to training, which partly stems from the introduction of NVQs. The system is designed to be easily understood and to provide workers with the skills that are needed by industry. It is designed to unify what is a very diverse system of qualifications existing in the United Kingdom at present. Recent developments include:

- the Commission for Employment and Skills was set up in 2008 to bring industry into the heart of decision-making;
- in 2011 the Work Programme was set up to help long-term unemployed people back into work through work experience and training;
- in 2013 the Help to Work scheme was introduced to offer training for those who had been unemployed for more than three years.

The government also sponsors training for young people. This includes Apprenticeships and Advanced Apprenticeships. These schemes are designed for the 16–25-year age group and aim to provide training leading to recognised vocational qualifications – Apprenticeships at NVQ level 2 and Advanced Apprenticeships at NVQ level 3.

The Investors in People initiative has had an impact on training as it is based on four principles:

- top-level commitment to develop all employees;
- regular reviews of training and development of all employees;
- action to train and develop employees throughout their employment; and
- evaluation of the outcome of training as a basis for continuous improvement.

By October 2013, more than 37,000 UK organisations had achieved recognition under the standard, representing 38 per cent of the UK workforce.

The number of women receiving job-related training has increased over the last 20 years relative to men, and there has been a gradual increase for both sexes over the time period. There are significant differences between industries, with, for example, the service sector having a much higher level of training than agriculture, forestry and fishing, and between occupations.

Training is an important issue not just for school leavers and the unemployed but for all employees. The *UK Employers' Skills Survey*, carried out in the UK in 2013, found that 31 per cent of vacancies were skill shortage vacancies. In 2013, only 38 per cent of establishments had a training plan, down from 48 per cent in 2007, although 60 per cent of establishments do provide training.

web link

> For information on training schemes see
> *www.gov.uk* (Department for Business, Innovation & Skills)
> *www2.warwick.ac.uk/fac/soc/ier* (Institute for Employment Research)
> *www.nfer.ac.uk* (National Foundation for Educational Research)
> *www.ukes.org.uk*
> *http://skillsfundingagency.bis.gov.uk/*
> *www.ssda.org.uk*

Occupational structure of the population

There will be changes in the **occupational structure** of the population over time. These will be caused by changes in industrial structure and technological change. There has been an increase in the number of non-manufacturing jobs at the same time as a fall in the number of manufacturing jobs. There are more women in the workforce now because there has been an increase in demand for the types of goods that have been produced by women. There has also been an increase in the availability and quality of labour-saving devices in the home, which has released women into the workforce. There has been a decrease in the average family size so that if women leave the workforce to look after their children, they now do so for a shorter period of time. There has also been a change in attitude towards women working.

Figure 8.4 shows the structure of occupations in the UK by gender. There is a higher percentage of men than women in the professional/managerial occupations and there are more men working in skilled trades than women. Women are clearly concentrated in clerical/selling-type occupations.

Figure 8.4 The structure of occupations in the UK by gender

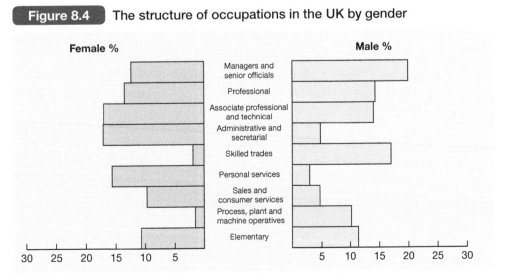

Source: Adapted from EMP08: All in employment by occupation, *www.ons.gov.uk*

There was a fundamental change in the nature of working life throughout the 1980s and on into the 1990s, and this has to do with the notion of 'flexibility'. There has been an increase in the incidence of part-time working, for both men and women, and an increased use of temporary contract and flexible working patterns. In 2013, 8 million people worked part time in the UK; this represents about a fifth of the workforce. Approximately 3 million people were self-employed (see mini case study on zero-hours contracts).

Technology

Technology is defined as 'the sum of knowledge of the means and methods of producing goods and services' (*Penguin Dictionary of Economics*). It is increasingly science based, encompassing subjects such as chemistry, physics and electronics, and refers to the organisation of production as well as the actual techniques of production itself. **Technological change** leads to the introduction of new products, changes in the methods and organisation of production, changes in the quality of resources and products, new ways of distributing the product and new ways of storing and disseminating information. Technology has a very big impact upon the world of business in all of these areas and has an important effect on the level and type of investment that takes place in an economy and therefore the rate of economic growth.

Technological change

There have been massive changes in technology in the past ten years. This section will consider a few of these and assess their impact upon business and the economy.

Information technology

Developments in **information technology** have had the effect of transforming existing business activities as well as creating entirely new ones, involving the collection, handling, analysis and transmission of information. There has been a huge increase in the demand for information and, on the supply side, continued advances in the miniaturisation of components. These will continue even when the capabilities of the silicon chip have been exhausted, with the development of superconductors and optronics. There are also advances in the computing area such as the development of new languages and artificial intelligence.

Advances in information technology have many impacts upon business. They are creating new products and making old products more profitable to produce through things such as **computer-aided design (CAD)**. The effects they are having on the different functions carried out by businesses can easily be seen:

- *Administration*. The administration of businesses has been revolutionised by the introduction of information technology. Most businesses have computer systems, records have been computerised and filing has become unnecessary.
- *Communication*. This has been eased by the introduction of fax machines and e-mail. Video conferencing has contributed to the change in working practices by making it possible for people to work anywhere. Telecommunications companies,

such as BT, are working on desktop video conferencing systems, where the video camera is attached to the desktop PC.

- *Production.* The use of CAD will shorten the design and planning phase of the product and shorten the life cycle of the product. Japan applied this very early on in the field of consumer electronics and many of the products are withdrawn from sale and redesigned within a very short period of time.
- *Storage and distribution.* The computerisation of stock control has had implications for the storage requirements of firms. It has made implementation of the just-in-time method of stock control possible. This is easily seen in the case of supermarkets where the use of bar-codes on products makes it possible to carry out a stock check of a whole supermarket in a matter of hours. The shelves can then be loaded up as the stock check continues. Similarly, the use of bar-codes with Electronic Point of Sale (EPOS) makes stock control simpler.
- *Electronic Funds Transfer at Point of Sale (EFTPOS).* This system has also had a revolutionary effect in the area of retailing. Most shops now accept credit cards or Switch cards where funds are immediately transferred from bank accounts to the supermarkets.
- *The internet.* The potential for the internet is enormous, although it is still, relatively speaking, in its infancy. In quarter 2 of 2012, there were an estimated 1.5 billion people wired to the internet. The highest percentage population penetration was in the US (78.6 per cent), the lowest in Africa (15.6 per cent). There are three projects operating that will provide a cable system under the Indian Ocean linking African countries.
- *Artificial intelligence.* As the mini case study shows, the developments in this area have been huge and the growth is exponential. The use of robotisation and artificial intelligence has implications for many areas of business and law.

One aspect of business where information technology has become particularly important is in providing opportunities for firms to interact immediately with their customers and suppliers, whoever and wherever they might be. Concepts such as e-commerce, e-business and e-markets are now part of the business lexicon and are an important area of study for undergraduate and postgraduate students alike.

mini case The robots are coming

The pace of technological change over the past 50 years has been incredible and there is no sign of a slowdown. A few of these technological developments are discussed in this mini case study, together with their implications for the business world.

Robotisation

The increased use of robotisation can be seen in many areas of life: self-service checkouts at the supermarket; online education courses;

hotels without reception staff; driverless cars. All of these replace people with machines so they have implications for the labour force: will the main occupation be designing and maintaining machines? What many argue will happen is the loss of jobs in the middle of the market (admin and logistics, for example) but an increase in jobs that are IT related at the top of the market and a continuing demand at the bottom end of the market for jobs that cannot be carried out by machines: care for the elderly and children, for example.

Some of these developments will have legal implications and often the law is slow to keep pace with technological change. A good example is the case of driverless cars – who will hold the insurance? The CEO of Amazon announced in November 2012 that within 5 years Amazon would be delivering parcels to customers using GPS-operated 'octocopters' – parcels could be delivered within 30 minutes of placing the order. This is another example that has huge implications for the labour force (loss of jobs) and the law – there are no rules in place for the use of commercial drones in the USA and there is much resistance from the general public. Several US states have banned the police from using drones.

Virtual wallets

In 2011 Google launched Google Wallet in the USA. It is a mobile payment system that allows consumers to pay for goods, use loyalty cards or gift cards, and receive special offers, all on their mobile phones. Its adoption has been very slow because of technical difficulties and consumer resistance, and it has not made it across to Europe.

But now the three biggest mobile networks in the UK (EE, Vodafone and O2) have come together to form a company called Weve, which is developing the concept for the UK. The plan is that by using GPS, your mobile phone will know when you are outside a particular shop and will alert you of any special offers in that shop. This concept has clear implications for marketing and most commentators see this as the big development for 2014. The US market, which was estimated at £12.8 billion in 2012, is predicted to grow to $90 billion by 2017.

There are many other examples of technological developments, such as the 3D printer and all of them will have a dramatic impact on business. It is clear that these developments will continue apace. Apple has been investing millions in developing supply chain robotisation and acquired Prime Sense, the company that developed 3D sensing technology. Amazon acquired Kiva Systems in 2012 – a company that developed warehouse automation. And in December 2013 Google bought Dynamics, a military robot company, only the latest in a succession of similar purchases. Watch this space!

Other technological developments

- *New materials*. The new material being heralded as the 'miracle material' of the 21st century is graphene. It consists of a single layer of carbon atoms bonded together in hexagons and is the strongest material ever measured. It is a replacement for silicon and will revolutionise computers.
- *Biotechnology*. This is expected to have wide-ranging effects on many fields. The development of new products like computers that can imitate the activity of the brain can shorten the development process for certain products by speeding up existing processes.
- *Energy*. The kind of developments that can take place in this field are the use of superconductors to transport electricity and research that might make solar energy a viable source of energy.

Technology and investment

The second input into the production process after people is **capital**. In economics, capital has a special meaning: it refers to all man-made resources that are used in production. Capital is usually divided into **working capital** and **fixed capital**. Working capital consists of the stocks of raw materials and components used in producing things. Fixed capital consists of buildings, plant and machinery. The main difference between the two is that fixed capital gives a flow of services over a long period of time, while working capital needs to be replaced on a regular basis. Because of its nature, working capital is much more mobile than fixed capital (i.e. it can be used for other purposes much more easily). Capital is a '**stock**' of goods used in the production process, a stock which is continually being used and therefore needing to be replaced. This stock provides a flow of services for the production process.

Capital includes a wide diversity of items, including factory premises, machinery, raw materials in stock, transport vehicles and partly finished goods. As well as these, there is what is often called '**social capital**', which refers to capital that is owned by the community, such as schools and hospitals. There is also spending on the **infrastructure**, which is important to all businesses rather than being linked to one particular business. The main components of this are transport, energy, water and information. The transportation system is obviously very important to a developed economy. Road, rail, air and water are used to transport goods, services and raw materials. The capital stock in transport and communications in the UK was £345 billion in 2009. The same is true for energy and water; both are used by industry in great quantities, and a good infrastructure in these is essential. The information distribution system is also part of the infrastructure and would include telephone systems and the post.

Table 8.6 shows the capital stock of the United Kingdom in 2001 and 2009 by industry. The level of capital stock increased over the period by 21.7 per cent, but there are marked differences between industries, ranging from a growth of 75 per cent in other services to a fall of –11 per cent in mining and quarrying.

Table 8.6 Gross capital stock in 2001 and 2009 by industry at 2006 replacement costs in UK (£ billion)

Industry	2001	2009	% change
Agriculture, forestry and fishing	46.5	44.2	– 5.0
Mining and quarrying	133.6	118.9	– 11.0
Manufacturing	374.2	346.1	– 7.5
Electricity, gas and water supply	164.9	180.1	+ 9.2
Construction	27.4	44.2	+ 61.3
Distribution	17.3	284.8	+ 52.0
Hotels and restaurants	58.5	93.7	+ 60.0
Transport and communications	236.9	345.0	+ 45.1
Financial intermediation	101.6	130.8	+ 28.7
Dwellings	1786.1	2053.3	+ 15.0
Real estate, renting and business activities	210.5	311.8	+ 48.0
Public administration	339.7	407.5	+ 20.0
Education	138.7	186.9	+ 34.8
Health and social welfare	891.0	121.1	+ 35.9
Other services	137.3	240.2	+ 75.0
Total	**4032.3**	**4908.6**	**+ 21.7**

Source: Adapted from *www.ons.gov.uk*

The increase in the stock of capital over time is called **investment**. Investment will serve to increase the productive potential of the firm and the economy. Investment usually refers to the purchase of new assets, as the purchase of second-hand assets merely represents a change in ownership and therefore does not represent a change in productive potential. Investment is important for the firm as it is a mechanism for growth; it is an integral part of the **innovation** process and can have disastrous results for a firm if an

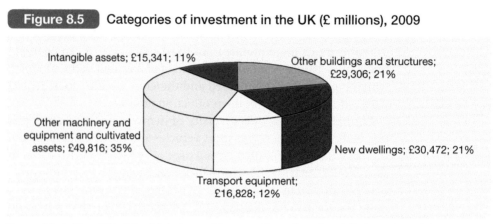

Figure 8.5 Categories of investment in the UK (£ millions), 2009

Source: Adapted from Table 4, Capital stocks, capital consumption and non-financial balance sheets, 2010, *www.ons.gov.uk*

investment goes wrong. Generally, the higher the level of investment in a country, the higher will be the level of economic growth.[4]

Total or **gross investment** can be broken down into **replacement investment**, which is investment to replace obsolete or worn-out machines, and new investment, which is any investment over and above this. This includes investment by firms, individuals (in dwellings mainly) and governments (see Figure 8.5). As might be expected, the level of investment is affected by the state of the economy. There was a fall in the level of investment in the early 1980s, again in the early 1990s, and a gradual fall in investment levels since 2005, all of these as a result of the recession in the economy (see Figure 8.6). The level of investment in 2009 represented 23 per cent of GDP.

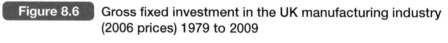

Figure 8.6 Gross fixed investment in the UK manufacturing industry (2006 prices) 1979 to 2009

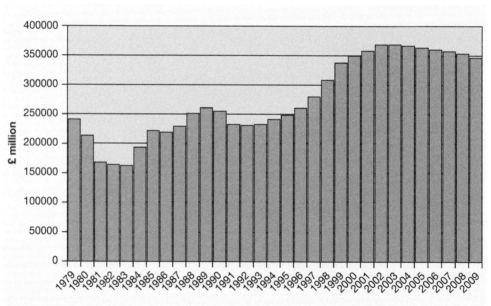

Source: Adapted from Table 2.2.2 Capital Stocks, capital consumption and non-financial balance sheets, 2010, *www.ons.gov.uk*

There is an important relationship between investment and technological change which runs in both directions. Investment can form the basis for improvements in technology, while improved technology, which brings about new ways of producing goods, will lead to greater investment. For private firms, the main determinants of the level of investment will be the rate of technological change and the scope for extra profit as a result of these changes.

Innovation and technology

There are two types of innovation that can occur as a result of technological change: **product innovation** and **process innovation**. Product innovation is the development of new products, such as the microprocessor, which will have far-reaching effects on business. New products impact upon the industrial structure of a country, as new industries grow and old industries disappear. This in turn will lead to changes in the occupational structure of the workforce, as we have seen. It has even had the effect of reducing the benefits large firms derive from economies of scale in cases where the technological change can be exploited by small firms as well as it can by large firms. Another example of product innovation which has affected the level of competition in the market is the development of quartz watches, which allowed Japan to enter the market and compete with Switzerland.

Process innovation, meanwhile, refers to changes that take place in the production process, such as the introduction of assembly-line production in the manufacture of cars. The two types of innovation are related, as the above examples show. The microprocessor (product innovation), which is a new product, has led to massive changes in the way that production and offices operate (process innovation).

Not all innovation is technological in nature; for example, changes in fashion in clothing are not technological. Innovative activity is important for all industry, whether manufacturing or non-manufacturing. In some industries (e.g. pharmaceuticals, computers), innovation is essential if firms wish to remain competitive.

 For information on innovation see the Department for Business, Innovation & Skills website at *www.gov.uk*

Research and development

Most, but not all, technological changes have occurred through the process of **research and development (R&D)**. 'Research' can be theoretical or applied, and 'development' refers to the using of the research in the production process. Most research and development carried out by private companies is directed towards applied research and development. It is designed to develop new products and production processes that will render production more profitable. It is also aimed at improving existing products and processes. Most basic theoretical research carried out in the United Kingdom is financed from public sources and is undertaken in places like the universities.

Table 8.7 shows that the level of research and development expenditure in manufacturing industries in the UK in 2011 was £17,408 million, which represents around 1.2 per cent of GDP. Although total spending in real terms has risen over the past 20 years, the percentage share of R&D in GDP fell from 1.4 per cent in 1995 to 1.2 per cent in 2011. This is a long way short of the UK government target of 1.7 per cent by the end of 2014.

Table 8.7 Spending on R&D (£ million) in 2011 (2011 prices)

Product group	£ million	% of total
All product groups	17 408	100
All products of manufacturing industry	12 552	72
Chemical industries	5539	32
Mechanical engineering	1089	6
Electrical machinery	1199	7
Aerospace	1417	8
Transport	1833	10
Other manufactured products	1475	8
Non-manufactured products	4856	28

Source: Adapted from Table 15, Business Enterprise and Development, 2011, *www.ons.gov.uk*

It can be seen that there are wide differences in expenditure between industries, with manufacturing involved in a great deal more research and development spending than non-manufacturing. Even within the broad category of manufacturing there are wide differences, with chemicals accounting for more than a quarter of the expenditure. Table 8.8 shows the sources from which R&D is financed. As we can see, the majority of R&D is financed by companies themselves. If R&D is split into civil and defence spending, the government finances the majority of defence R&D, as would be expected.

Table 8.8 Sources of funds for R&D within industry in the UK for selected years

	1985	1990	1996	2000	2005	2006	2007	2008	2009	2010	2011
Total (£ million)	5 122	8 082	9 362	10 417	13 310	14 306	15 676	15 814	15 532	16 053	17 408
Government funds (%)	23	17	10	9	8	7.5	6.8	7.2	8.5	8.7	9.3
Overseas funds (%)	11	16	22	21	26	23	23	24	22	24	21
Mainly own funds (%)	66	68	69	70	66	66	70	70	70	68	69

Source: Adapted from Table 15, Business Enterprise and Development, 2012, *www.ons.gov.uk*

 For information on R&D see *www.oecd.org* **or** *http://epp.europa.eu.int/eurostat.eu*

Figure 8.7 shows that the UK tends to fare badly in international comparisons of research and development spending.

Limits to technological change

Technological change has many effects on the economy and the environment and if uncontrolled can lead to problems, including high levels of unemployment or the exhaustion of natural resources. One area of concern is energy. The world's stock of energy is finite and we are still heavily dependent upon fuel that was formed millions of years ago. The development of nuclear power again represents a finite source of energy, and also carries with it other problems, such as the disposal of nuclear waste and the possibility of accidents. For these and other reasons the scale of technological change needs to be controlled.

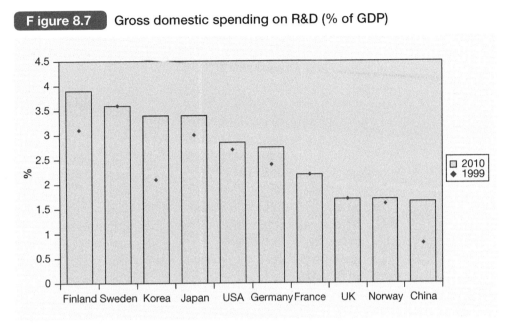

Figure 8.7   Gross domestic spending on R&D (% of GDP)

Source: Adapted from Figure 14, 'The UK R&D Landscape', CIHE and UK-irc

It is also the case that technological change can lead to high levels of unemployment in industries that are in decline. This type of unemployment often takes on a regional bias as the older traditional industries tend to be located in particular parts of the country. **Technological unemployment** is in some respects inevitable as in a changing world it would be expected that new industries would emerge and old industries die. The problem can be tackled by the government and industry through retraining, but what is also needed is a new and more flexible view of work where less time is spent working and more on leisure. Technological change can also give rise to the opposite problem of skill shortage in new industries, where particular skills are required. Technological change has not led to the massive increase in unemployment predicted by many in the 1970s and 1980s, but what might happen in the future is unknown.

Natural resources

In economics, **natural resources** are put under the heading of **land** as a **factor of production**. It would include all natural resources like the soil, minerals, oil, forests, fish, water, the sun and so on. The uneven distribution of natural resources throughout the world means that they can be used as economic and political weapons.

Although the area of land in a country is fixed, land as a factor of production is not completely fixed in supply as more land can be made available through land reclamation schemes and better irrigation. The productivity of agricultural land can be increased by the use of fertilisers. It is true, however, that our natural resources are in finite supply. And often their true extent is not known with certainty.

It is in the area of natural resources that the distinction between renewable and non-renewable resources is most important. Natural resources can be either. Land can often be used for more than one purpose – for example, agricultural land can be used to grow one crop one year and another the next – but oil, once it is used up, cannot be used again. Technological developments such as **fracking** (see case study at the end of the chapter) will impact upon the level of natural resources. Fracking has enabled the extraction of natural gas and oil that was bound up in the shale rock, therefore increasing the quantities of these resources. However, they remain non-renewable. And even though land can sometimes be used for more than one purpose, it is immobile geographically and frequently occupationally. For example, land can be used for agriculture or industry, but using it for one of these makes it more difficult to use it for the other. If a factory is built on a piece of land, it would be both expensive and time consuming to clear the land for farming.

Table 8.9 shows the changing usage of agricultural land in the UK between 1971 and 2011. There are slight differences between the years, most notably the inclusion of 'set aside' land in the 1993–2007 columns. This was part of EU Common Agricultural Policy where farmers were paid not to use land in an attempt to reduce the overproduction of agricultural goods.

Table 8.9 The use of agricultural land in selected years in the UK (thousand hectares)

	1971	1993	1997	2000	2003	2007	2011
Crops	4838	4519	4990	4709	4478	4350	4694
Bare fallow	74	47	29	33	29	165	–
Grasses	7240	6770	6687	6767	6884	7141	7343
Rough grazing*	6678	5840	5878	5803	5565	5552	5402
Set aside	–	677	306	572	689	440	–
Woodland and other land on agricultural holdings	285	678	763	789	792	954	1297
Total	19 115	18 531	18 653	18 579	18 438	18 602	18 736

Note: *Includes sole-right rough grazing and common rough grazing.
Source: Adapted from Table 21.3, *Annual Abstract of Statistics 2011, www.ons.gov.uk*

Protection of the environment

Increased knowledge of the effects of depletion of natural resources has led to increased environmental awareness among the population. There has been an increased interest in conservation and recycling and the search for alternative forms of energy. A survey by the Department of the Environment found that 90 per cent of the adult population in the UK was either 'fairly concerned' or 'very concerned' about the environment. The issues that have caused this concern include traffic congestion, global warming, air and water pollution and depletion of the ozone layer. This change in public opinion has already had a major impact on the way in which business operates and is likely to have even bigger effects.

Governments in the UK and elsewhere have a variety of targets for environmental protection relating to issues such as greenhouse gas emissions, biodiversity, renewable energy, recycling, packaging and so on. Some of these targets are set through negotiations with other countries at both international (e.g. Kyoto Protocol) and supranational (e.g. EU) levels and hence are influenced by political, economic, social and technological considerations and by a variety of state and non-state actors (see Chapter 5). Given the growing importance of environmental issues in business, a separate chapter on ethics and the natural environment has been added.

One important resource in business whose exploitation and use have a significant impact on the natural environment is energy. The UK is not well endowed with high-grade minerals; the main natural resource is energy. There is a good deposit of coal and the discovery of North Sea oil and gas made the UK self-sufficient in energy supplies, and now fracking might do the same again. The usage of energy has doubled since 1970, but as Table 8.10 shows, there has been a change in the relative importance of the different sources of energy.

Table 8.10 Final energy consumption by source in the UK (%)

	1950	1970	1980	1990	2000	2010	2012
Solid fuel	79	47	36	31	16	15	20
Gas	6	5	22	24	41	43	36
Oil	12	44	37	36	33	32	32
Electricity	3	4	5	8	9	7	9
Renewable energy	–	–	–	0.3	1	3.2	3.8

Source: Adapted from Table 1.02, Energy consumption in UK, 2013 updates, *www.ons.gov.uk*

Coal has lost its place to oil and gas as the most important sources of energy. The increase in the usage of both oil and gas is due to the discovery of North Sea oil and gas. The biggest single user of energy in the UK is the domestic sector (32 per cent of energy produced), followed by transport (28 per cent) and industry (22 per cent). A small but growing source of energy in the UK is renewables, with the government's target by 2020 being 15 per cent.

There is great variation in the fuels used for the generation of electricity across Europe, as Table 8.11 shows.

Table 8.11 Fuel used for electricity generation, selected EU countries (%), 2009

	Nuclear	Coal and ignite	Oil	Gas	Renewable energy	Other
France	74.9	4.7	1.1	4.4	14.0	1.0
Belgium	50.9	5.6	0.6	32.6	8.5	1.8
Sweden	38.1	0.9	0.5	1.4	58.9	0.2
Spain	17.4	11.9	5.5	35.8	26.2	3.0
Germany	22.3	41.5	1.6	14.0	17.4	3.1
UK	18.1	27.6	1.2	44.0	8.1	1.0
The Netherlands	3.7	21.4	1.3	62.6	10.9	0.2
EU-27	27.5	25.3	2.9	23.1	19.6	1.7

Source: Adapted from Figure 3, *Electricity Production by Fuel*, European Environment Agency, 2012.

There has been a fall in the amount of electricity generated by nuclear power since 2004, although some EU countries use it as their primary generator of electricity. While its use produces lower emissions of greenhouse gases, there is an increased risk of accidental leakage of radioactivity as well as the problem of the disposal of radioactive waste. Electricity generation from oil and gas has tended to fall and an EU Directive now requires 20 per cent of electricity (for the EU-27 countries) to come from renewable sources by 2020. The figure for 2009 is close to the target, but as Table 8.11 shows, there are huge differences between countries. There is clearly a growing demand for alternative sources of energy. The alternatives of hydro, wind and solar energy sources will also grow in importance. In the UK, the government has tried to promote the search for renewable energy sources through projects like the Renewables Obligation, which requires licensed electricity producers to obtain an increasing percentage of their electricity from clean sources (11 per cent in 2012). It also funds experimental work in the search for new sources of energy. One such source is 'biogas', which generates gas from household waste. The Committee on Climate Change claims that 1 in 20 of UK homes could be supplied with gas from this source. Biogas could also lead to fewer carbon emissions.

As well as recycling and searching for new sources of energy there is the concept of **'negademand'**, where the use of less produces negative demand for those commodities. This concept can be applied to energy and water saving, driving and shopping. It is possible that technological change (like the 3D printer) could reduce the demand for energy.

For information on the natural environment in the UK see *www.environment-agency.gov.uk* or *www.theccc.org.uk* (the Committee on Climate Change)
In the EU see *www.eea.europa.eu* (the European Environment Agency)
In the world see *www.oecd.org*

Synopsis

This chapter looked at the three main inputs into the production process: people, technology and natural resources. It considered each in turn and examined their importance to business and the main factors that determine both the quality and the quantity of these factors of production.

People are important in two ways: they are the producers of goods and services, and also the consumers of goods and services. The quantity of human resources available in an economy depends upon things like total population size, participation rates, length of working week and wages. The quality depends upon such things as the level of health care, education and training. There have been significant changes in the labour market over recent years.

One of the main features of the last 50 years has been the immense changes in technology that have had an enormous impact upon business, resulting in new products and markets and new methods of production and distribution.

As far as natural resources are concerned, the traditional view was that they were fixed in supply and therefore did not receive much consideration. However, with increased environmental awareness there is growing concern that this is not the case and that many of our natural resources are non-renewable and therefore need to be conserved.

Each of the three inputs into the production process has been considered separately, but they are interlinked and difficult to separate in reality. It has already been said that the productivity of people will be affected by the technology at their disposal, and this is also true of natural resources. All of the three inputs are 'stocks', from which streams of resources flow to firms. These flows are crucial to business, as without them production could not take place. Both the quantities and qualities of our stocks of these resources are important, as too is the replacement of the stocks that are being used.

Summary of key points

- Three main resources are used in the production of goods and services – labour, capital and land.

- The quantity of labour available depends upon population size, regulations in the labour market, the length of the working week and wage levels.

- The level of education and training determines the quality of available labour.

- The quantity and quality of capital depends on the level and type of investment taking place, the extent of research and development and the level of innovation.

- The quantity and quality of land are important elements in the production process and will depend on many things, including environmental controls.

case study   Fracking

The world's stock of natural resources is finite and in the 1970s there was much talk of energy crises that might occur when the world's stock of fossil fuels ran out. Hubbert (1956) put forward the theory that there was a point (he called the 'peak') where maximum oil production is reached, after which it would decline and eventually run out. This is a supply-side factor, in addition to which there are demand factors in play – there have been massive increases in the demand for oil because of economic growth (in countries like China) and population growth. Both the demand and supply factors can lead to energy crises.

Hubbert predicted that peak oil would occur in the USA between 1965 and 1971. Modern-day peak oil theory suggests that peak oil production will be reached after 2020, and that reductions in the demand for oil and the search for alternative sources of energy continue to be essential.

The demand for and the supply of natural gas in the USA was in balance in 1986, after which demand exceeded supply, the excess being met by imported natural gas from Canada. This all changed in 2006 when new drilling techniques were used, which dramatically increased the output of natural gas. This technique is called hydraulic fracturing, or fracking. Natural gas extracted through fracking made up 10 per cent of all gas production in 2007 and this rose to 30 per cent by 2010.

Fracking involves the release of oil and gas which are bound up in shale rock through the use of high-powered water sprays mixed with sand being pumped into the rocks. The oil and gas are then pushed up into the wells. Fracking has been used extensively in the USA and has been credited with powering the economic recovery and driving down energy prices.

1 USA

Fracking is taking place across America from Ohio to Dakota and Texas. The production of oil in the country has increased by 30 per cent since 2008 and the production of natural gas has increased by 33 per ▶

cent. It is estimated that the USA will overtake Russia and Saudi Arabia in 2014 in becoming the world's largest oil producer. Since 2008 the price of gas has fallen by two-thirds; in 2013 it stood at $4 per million British Thermal Units. It is estimated that between now and 2020 shale gas and oil will add $380–690 billion to annual GDP (2–4 per cent) and will create 1.7 million permanent jobs. This will happen through growth in the energy industries – direct spending on fracking and pipelines and also indirect spending on infrastructure to support and distribute the fuels. Coal-fired electricity generation will be changed for the use of gas. Since gas is cleaner than coal in terms of CO_2 emissions, there was a 10 per cent fall in the emission of greenhouse gases in the USA between 2010 and 2012. It is estimated that by 2020 gas-generated electricity will constitute 33 per cent of total electricity production; it was 21 per cent in 2008.

Much of this is good news for the US economy. It is on its way to being energy independent and it can now be an exporter of coal. The falling cost of gas has a positive effect on manufacturing as its costs will be lower, and it is argued that this gives the USA a competitive advantage over other countries.

2 Europe

A recent report (Poyry Management Consulting and Cambridge Econometrics) estimated that the widespread use of fracking in the EU could produce 1 million new jobs and add £3 trillion to EU economies. It would also reduce the dependence of the EU on gas imports.

The attitude to fracking varies across the EU. The UK and Poland are very receptive to the idea, while France, Germany, Spain and Bulgaria are less keen. At present in the EU fracking is covered by the same environmental legislation that applies to full-scale oil drilling. This makes it an expensive process. The European Commission is considering the issue of fracking at the time of writing and aims to produce guidelines soon.

In the EU there is much more public opposition to fracking than in the USA. In the UK, exploratory drilling by Cuadrilla in Balcombe was halted in August 2013 because of local protests. Without exploratory investigation, it is impossible to determine how much oil and gas is contained in the shale rocks. In Poland, exploratory drilling was abandoned largely because of legislative uncertainties.

3 Pros and cons of fracking

The arguments against fracking include the following:

(a) Fracking requires huge amounts of water which needs to be transported to the site. This has environmental implications and for some countries (the UK, for example) many argue that water shortages would preclude fracking.
(b) It is argued that fracking could contaminate the water table through use of and generation of harmful chemicals and that it could lead to carcinogenic chemicals in the soil.
(c) Fracking can lead to earth tremors. In Blackpool in the UK, there were two small earthquakes in 2011 following fracking in the vicinity. Supporters of fracking argue that the possibility of earth tremors has more to do with the construction of the wells rather than the fracking itself.
(d) Opponents argue that the race towards fracking is stopping the energy companies looking at other renewable sources of energy. One such source that environmentalists argue is being ignored is biogas, where waste is used to generate gas.

The arguments in favour include:

(a) Fracking will increase the supply of oil and gas and provide for the world's growing energy needs.
(b) In the USA fracking has led to a fall in the price of gas and this is good for industry and consumers alike. Whether this would be true in the EU is unclear as not enough is known about the extent of the reserves or the cost of extraction. In the UK the cost of extraction under the North Sea will be very high.
(c) If prices did fall, the corresponding fall in costs to firms would increase international competitiveness.
(d) There will be energy security which could extend as far as the next 100 years. The facts are not known – the International Energy agency predicts that the USA will be the biggest oil producer from 2015 to 2030 and that its reserves will start to decline in the 2020s.
(e) The burning of gas produces half of the CO_2 emissions of burning coal, so the use of a natural gas is good for the environment. CO_2 emissions in the USA have fallen faster than in the EU.

The debate over fracking is a heated one, with strong proponents on both sides, and the debate is ongoing. Even the strong arguments used in favour in the USA can be qualified. For example, the one about the lower cost of gas – the price of gas in 2013 ($4 per million BTU) is lower than the cost of extraction ($6 per million BTU), which means that it is not sustainable unless natural gas is seen as a by-product of the extraction of oil. This makes the production of natural gas dependent upon the price of oil; if this were to fall, then what might happen to the production of natural gas? In Europe, the future of fracking depends upon public opinion; without exploratory studies it is impossible to know what reserves are present or what the cost of extraction might be. The guidelines being produced by the European Commission should prove interesting.

Case study questions

1 The debate on fracking was in its infancy at the time of writing. How has development continued? Has the general public accepted fracking? Have the predictions of quantities of oil and gas proved correct?

2 What impact will increased fracking have on OPEC and the price of oil?

Review and discussion questions

1 Why are industries such as electricity 'natural monopolies'? What other examples are there of natural monopolies?

2 Think of one technological advance that has been made recently. What have been the effects of that change on the economy, business and the consumer?

3 In what ways can the general and specific skills of the British workforce be improved?

4 What impact will increased use of the internet, both for customer information and purchasing, have on call centres?

Assignments

1 You work in the economic development unit of your local council. The unit is compiling a bid to central government in order to win some resources to improve the basic infrastructure in the locality. Your job is to identify the economic problems that exist in your local town and explain why an increase in resources would overcome the problems. Write a briefing paper to the management committee of the unit on your results.

2 You are a member of your local Chartered Institute of Personnel and Development branch and have been asked to give a talk on 'Flexibility in working practices' to a group of trainee managers from a variety of functional and industrial backgrounds. They are particularly interested in three questions:

- What is meant by flexibility?
- Why is flexibility needed?
- What are the implications of greater flexibility?

(Sources for this would include the second edition of this text and *People Management*, CIPD.)

Notes and references

1 See *Workplace Employment Relations Study*, BIS, July 2013, available at *www.ons.gov.uk*

2 For further reading on this area see Begg, D., Fischer, S. and Dornbusch, R., *Economics*, McGraw-Hill, 2011.

3 See PISA *www.oecd.org/PISA*

4 The relationship between investment and the rate of growth is difficult to prove, but there does seem to be high correlation between the level of investment in a country and its associated level of economic growth. It should be remembered, however, that high correlation does not prove that one thing causes another.

Further reading

Blowfield, M., *Business and Sustainability*, Oxford University Press, 2012.

Christensen, C. M., *The Innovator's Dilemma: When New Technologies Cause Great Firms to Fail*, Harvard Business Review Press, 2013.

Razin, A. and Sadka, E., *Population Economics*, MIT Press, 2013.

Worthington, I., Britton, C. and Rees, A., *Economics for Business: Blending Theory and Practice*, Financial Times/Prentice Hall, 2nd edition, 2005.

9

The legal environment

Chris Jeffs

Learning outcomes

On completion of this chapter you should be able to:

- understand the purpose of laws and how they are modified over time;
- be familiar with the sources of difference between legal systems in different countries;
- recognise how EU law is incorporated into national law;
- describe how to form a new business entity;
- be able to recognise the impact of personal liability;
- recognise the importance and relevance of different laws and how they may affect business;
- understand the importance of contracts in defining the terms and conditions of a business transaction;
- be familiar with the range and purpose of consumer protection laws;
- understand the purpose of competition law and its role in regulating cartels and monopolies;
- recognise the importance of protecting intellectual property rights in business and the mechanisms to achieve this;
- outline the key legislation behind employer–employee relationships, and how these are stipulated in contracts of employment;
- appreciate the business implications of health and safety legislation;
- outline the difference between laws that are generated by nations in order to control foreign trade and ownership, and international laws and treaties;
- recognise the importance of international treaties, the organisations that create them and how they are governed;
- outline several key international treaties, the purpose of them and the mechanisms of enforcement;
- outline the risks that businesses undertake when they do businesses internationally;
- describe the forms of international dispute resolution and the purpose and mechanisms of international arbitration.

Key concepts

- law and morality
- public and private law
- court hierarchy
- liability
- national law systems

- supranationality and the influence of European law on member states
- business liability
- contracts
- negligence and the law of tort in relation to business
- criminal law and business
- consumer protection
- competition law, cartels and monopoly regulation
- forms and laws relating to intellectual property rights
- employment law
- health and safety
- sanctions and embargoes
- nationalisation, expropriation and confiscation
- constraints on FDI
- role of international organisations and treaties
- role of international courts
- inadequacies of treaties and conventions
- international business risks
- importance of international contractual terms and conditions
- international dispute resolution
- mechanisms of international arbitration.

| Minicase 9.1 | The Danone–Wahaha feud |

The longest lawsuit in Chinese history, which become known as the 'Danone–Wahaha feud', may be close to being resolved. The dispute has been running for three years and involves the Paris-based global dairy foods group Danone and Wahaha, the largest beverage company in China. Danone–Wahaha formed a partnership in 1996 and for ten years it was considered to be a highly profitable, rapidly growing alliance. In 2006 a disagreement escalated into a complex legal dispute which was to be played out in many countries. The main issues behind the legal dispute are the 'status' of Wahaha's other business ventures and the ownership of the Wahaha trademark.

There are actually five joint ventures (JVs) between Danone and Wahaha, all of which use the Wahaha brand. Danone has investments in each and Wahaha is responsible for the operation and management of them. Under their JV contract, Wahaha promised not to undertake any production or operations which competed with the JV companies, and Danone agreed not to damage the status of the JV. In April 2006, Danone alleged that Wahaha had infringed the contract by setting up other ventures in competition with the Danone–Wahaha JVs. As compensation for these actions, Danone demanded that Wahaha give them a 51 percent ownership in the new ventures, valued at 4 billion yuan (approx. 400 million euros). Wahaha rejected the request considering that it amounted to a hostile takeover.

In addition, Danone claims that the Wahaha trademark belongs to the Danone–Wahaha joint venture, and that Wahaha's use of the trademark in other ventures constituted an infringement of the JV contract. However, the Wahaha Group disagrees, claiming that it is the true holder of the trademark and the use of the trademark by other Wahaha ventures was legal.

Danone has since filed more than 37 lawsuits against Wahaha for violating the JV contract and the illegal use of the Wahaha trademark in countries such as France, Italy, the USA and China. Danone has even taken the wife and daughter of the Chairman of Wahaha to a US court, accusing them of co-plotting the actions that led to 'damaging Danone's interests'. This was despite the daughter being at a US school at the time of the alleged action. So far, all the indictments and court cases both in China and abroad have ruled against Danone.

Mediation has been tried on a number of occasions; the French president Nicolas Sarkozy has also been involved, but on each occasion no agreement could be found. The Danone–Wahaha JV contract stated that any disputes that might arise should be submitted to the Stockholm Chamber of Commerce (SCC) for arbitration. In May 2007, Danone filed a number of arbitration applications to the SCC accusing Wahaha of unlawful competition and fraud, claiming compensation of up to 890 million euros, which is the expected loss of profit during the remaining 39 years of the contract term. In response, Wahaha claimed that the ventures had no production or operations business and were therefore not in direct competition; they also stated that these companies were known to Danone from the start. In retaliation, Wahaha also claims that Danone has breached the JV contract by acquiring the Chinese beverage company Robust, which in 2000 was the largest competitor of Wahaha.

In its indictments Danone has tried to avoid Chinese law; contractually, however, their dispute is to be governed under Chinese law and, in accordance with international laws, the SCC will also consider the outcomes of the previous rulings. At the time of writing the companies are still waiting for a final judgment.

Questions

1 Why was the Stockholm Chamber of Commerce (SCC) cited in the original contract for dispute resolution?
2 Why do you think that Danone wanted to avoid legal action in China?

9.1 Introduction

The opening case describes the legal complexities of trading across borders with local disputes ending in global litigation. This chapter will discuss the purpose of laws and their influence on the operation of national and international business.

Increasingly, laws governing supply, transportation, investment, human rights, environmental protection and e-commerce are becoming internationally regulated. It is therefore vital that multinational companies are aware of all the international and national legislation in the regions that they manufacture, transport through and trade with. For example, a US company conducting business in Poland will have to comply not just with Polish law, but also regional EU as well as US federal and state law. Fortunately much of this legislation overlaps and so long as there is an awareness of unusual legal issues, and steps are made to abide by the most stringent laws, most organisations will manage.

9.2 The law

Laws consist of a set of rules imposed upon members of society. In a democracy these laws are defined, modified and enforced through an elected assembly with a separation of powers between the political body and the judiciary. Laws can be viewed as a form of contract; we obey the laws and in return the government (aided by the police, courts and penal system) agrees to protect us from those who break the law. Anyone that disobeys the law in effect breaks that contract and can be penalised under the rule of law.

National law can be subdivided into that which is public and that which is private:

- Public law regulates the relationship between the public and the state.
- Private law regulates the relationship between members of the public.

A car crash involving two members of the public is an example of where private law might be used. The collision may result in action being taken against one of the parties for negligent driving.

International law can also be subdivided into public and private categories:

- Public international law is concerned with establishing the rules to be followed by nation states, particularly in relation with each other.
- Private international law is concerned with establishing which national law is to be used in the case of an international dispute.

Private international law may be used if, for instance, a dispute arises between a Chinese company and an American company.

9.2.1 The law and morality

Issues of morality are of great importance to law making, society and business. Morality is a form of informal rules and codes of conduct that are embedded in and generally accepted by the majority of people in society.

Morals are formed from the culture, upbringing, religious beliefs, education and behaviour of the population. Indeed, over time morality has formed the basis of laws in most countries. However, due to the fact that each individual has a different set of moral codes, some people will be more likely to infringe laws. For instance, many people have broken the law by driving at speed in a restricted area or have illegally downloaded music or video files, but do not consider themselves as acting illegally; whereas they would never break the law by stealing from or harming another human being.

As morals change, laws also have to change to reflect the expectations of the citizens. Examples of laws which have been decriminalised include those banning homosexuality, abortion and the distribution of hard-core pornography, all of which were illegal in the UK less than 50 years ago. The smoking of cannabis and the use of brothels have been legalised in the Netherlands, and the personal use of hard drugs is no longer illegal in Portugal. In June 2009, the 148-year-old law prohibiting homosexual activity, which dated back to British colonial rule in India, was overturned under human rights legislation in a Delhi court. In business the word 'morality' is not commonly used; however, you will find the terms *'business ethics'* and *'corporate social responsibility'* which broadly equate to the same thing.

9.2.2 The law and national boundaries

Within the EU there is increasing trade, and political and legal integration. This has a direct impact on national law-making bodies, because, as national laws become inadequate, transnational laws are created to bridge the gap. Legislation has therefore become highly complex; however, for clarity, we will subdivide the types of law into the following categories: national, regional (e.g. EU), business and international laws, although you will see as the chapter progresses that these classifications are somewhat arbitrary.

9.2.3 National law

On a national level a transparent and well-regulated legal system is important to ensure that businesses can thrive. Any systems of government which offer fully separate powers between the political leaders and the legal system will provide a set of checks and balances which reduce the likelihood of bribery, coercion and corruption.

National legal systems are often very different from one another due to historical, cultural, religious and political reasons. However, all of the world's legislative systems share two components:

- that of legislation or law-making; and
- adjudication or dispute settlement.

International businesses have to be aware of not only the major differences between national legal systems but also the subtle differences between them; hence lawyers are always required for their specialist and local knowledge.

It is useful to categorise the different types of national legal systems that are found around the world by their historical foundations. The following types of national legal system are commonly recognised:

- common law;
- civil law;
- theocratic (religious) law;
- bureaucratic law;
- mixed law (combination of civil and common laws).

Common law

The common law process is the basis of the legal systems in the UK and many of its formal colonies including the USA, Canada, Australia, India, Barbados and Malaysia. The common law tradition dates back to 1189 which is prior to that of the establishment of the English parliament. The distinguishing feature of common law is that it is based on the cumulative judgments of individual court decisions. On occasion, judgments can create new legal precedents which must be followed by other judges hearing similar cases. As the common law system is continually evolving, it creates different legal precedents in different common law countries: for instance, there are many important differences in areas of patent law between the USA and UK.

Civil law

Civil law is an older form of law than common law and is based on the documentation (or codification) of what is legal and what is not. The Romans first implemented this form of law-making and spread it throughout their empire into the Western world. Subsequently, Napoleon Bonaparte implemented his civil law codes (French Civil Code, 1804) in countries conquered by France in the late eighteenth and early nineteenth centuries, thus embedding this method of law-making in Western Europe. It is for this reason that civil law is also sometimes called Napoleonic law. Countries that use civil law include: France, Germany, Greece and Italy; the South American countries of Argentina, Brazil and Chile, and other countries such as Japan and Sweden.

Historically the civil code was focused on private law, but in modern times it has been supplemented by commercial and civil codes. There are some important differences in civil law over common law. For example, the fact that there is only one single source of pre-coded law means that it is anticipatory in nature, rather than being reactive, as in the common law system. Another important difference between civil and common law is that of the role of the judge. In civil law cases the judge decides on the breadth and depth of the evidence to be submitted to the court, whereas in common law courts this is for the lawyers to decide. Civil laws can also be rushed through quickly and may often be done so in the name of political expediency. For example, in February 2009, the Italian government of Silvio Berlusconi decreed a new law allowing the authorities to detain immigrants for six months while their requests for asylum were being processed (BBC, 2009a). This was in response to public pressure following a spate of rapes which had been blamed on immigrants.

Theocratic law

Theocratic law is similar to that of common law in that it is not a written law. A theocracy is a country that applies religious law to both civil and criminal cases. Iran, Afghanistan (under the rule of the Taliban) and the Vatican City are well-known examples of theocracies where religious leaders pass judgment through their interpretation of the Koran or Bible. In each case the religious leaders have the power of veto in all legal matters. This was demonstrated in 2009 when Iran's Supreme Leader Ayatollah Ali Khamenei vetoed calls for an annulment of the June election (Fathi, 2009). Islamic law is based on the Sharia law (God's rules or path) and provides guidance on many aspects of day-to-day life, including economics, banking, contracts, hygiene and sexuality.

Islamic practice can be aligned largely to the dominant Sunni or Shi'ite schools. The Sunni school itself comprises a number of schools of thought, ranging from the most orthodox Hanbali school (practised in Saudi Arabia and by the Taliban) to the more liberal Hanafi school (dominant in Central Asia, Egypt, Pakistan, India and Turkey). Shia Muslims follow the Ja'fari school, which is dominant in Iran. These differences have more impact on the legal systems in each country rather than how individual Muslims live their lives. For example, Sharia law prohibits the paying or charging of interest on loans and deposits which could be restrictive for business enterprises. In order to conform to the law, Muslim banks offer alternative leasing arrangements with fees payable up front, while depositors receive shares in lieu of interest payments.

Bureaucratic law

The legal system in countries ruled by dictatorships is often called bureaucratic law. Examples of bureaucratic countries include North Korea, under the dictatorship of Kim Jong-il, and Myanmar, ruled by the dictator Than Shwe. Under bureaucratic law dictators and their bureaucrats may change the rules of the law, or previous contractual agreements, with little notice, regardless of what is stated in the constitution. This provides numerous problems for companies dealing in such countries where there is a lack of consistency and often poorly defined appeals procedures. Increasingly the political situation in Zimbabwe is that of a dictatorship that is ruling under bureaucratic law. In May 2009 President Robert Mugabe enacted a law which forces foreign companies, including mines and banks, to sell a 51 percent ownership to members of the Zimbabwean black community; alternately the government can seize 25 percent of shares without paying (Dzirutwe, 2009). In response to these laws and the unpredictable political situation, international mining companies have reduced investment and wound down operations in the country.

Mixed law

Mixed law systems are usually combinations of common law and civil law systems, where there is an element of codified legislation and new precedents set by judges. The EU is gradually moving towards a mixed system, with the combination of civil and common law across its member states. Other examples of mixed systems include Quebec, South Africa, Botswana, Sri Lanka and Scotland. Despite the fact that the Scots and English have close geographic proximity and shared political systems, there are some significant differences between Scottish and English laws particularly in the areas of criminal, property, inheritance and family law. One obvious difference is in the legal 'age of majority' or adulthood, which is 16 years in Scotland but 18 in England. However, the two countries are broadly similar in areas of taxation, business and consumer law.

It has been demonstrated that there are significant differences between legal systems in different countries. However, national laws of member states of the EU are also influenced by European legislature. To illustrate this, this chapter will look at how the English and the EU legislatures work together in partnership.

9.3 The English system of law

Despite the law in England being historically based on common law principles, in reality most new laws are set by parliament via statute law, which are otherwise known as 'Acts of Parliament'. However, many criminal laws in England and Wales, such as that of murder, are still legislated through common law and are not actually illegal under statute law. One of the earliest statutes was that of the Magna Carta (1215), with the revised version of 1297 still on the statute books of England and Wales. Nowadays statutes are created in a long process involving readings, debate and amendment, the bill passing through both the House of Commons and the House of Lords. Once finalised and approved, the bill passes to the Queen for Royal Assent. Increasingly, however, statutes originate from EU directives which demonstrate a convergence with civil law.

English law can be classified into public and private (civil) law. Civil law in this context should not be confused with the civil (Napoleonic) form of law, as it is only concerned with civil procedure and not, for example, criminal law. *Figure 9.1,* provides examples of the areas jurisdiction (cover) for England and Wales.

Civil law (private law) provides legal rights to individuals or corporate bodies and exists primarily to govern their relationships. If a case goes to court it is typically heard in a county or high court and the claimant must prove that the defendant is liable on the balance of probability. However, most civil law claims never get to court as they are more often settled by agreement before the trial begins. If a party is found guilty, the penalties are usually in the form of damages which may be covered by the defendant's insurance policy. Disputes between private citizens and the state are usually heard by tribunals. The tribunal service in England and Wales hears approximately 1 million cases per year and deals with a wide range of disputes including social security, income tax, mental health, special needs education, care standards, asylum support and specialist military and employment tribunals (Tribunals Service, 2009).

Criminal law is a form of public law. The enforcement of these laws is usually by the police rather than an individual. If the police charge someone with a criminal offence the

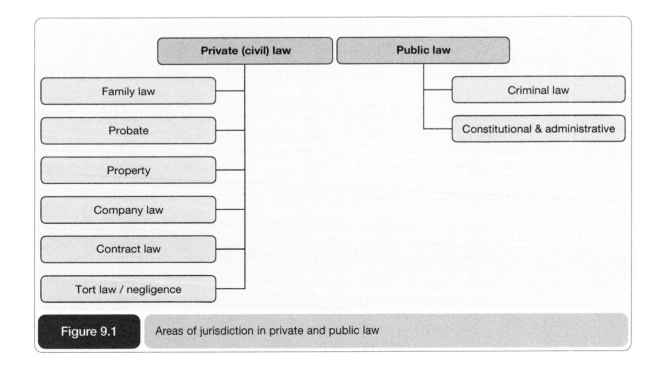

Figure 9.1   Areas of jurisdiction in private and public law

Crown Prosecution Service (CPS) in England and Wales has to decide whether there is enough evidence to proceed with the case. Depending upon the severity of the crime, it is either heard in a magistrates' or a crown court. In a crown court the prosecution must prove that the subject is guilty and, if so, the penalties may include fines, rehabilitation or prison sentences. It is worth remembering that businesses are also capable of committing criminal acts, for instance by not complying with health and safety legislation. Since April 2008, the law of Corporate Manslaughter (killing through negligence) has been enacted in England and Wales, and can now be used to hold senior management personally liable for corporate negligence. In June 2009, a director of Cotswold Geotechnical Holdings was the first to be charged under the new gross negligence legislation following a mud landslide that killed a 27-year-old company employee (Morris, 2009).

9.3.1 Courts in England and Wales

The criminal court structure in England and Wales is based on a pyramid of hierarchy with:

- the magistrates' court at the bottom (accounting for 95 percent of all criminal offences);
- the crown court;
- the court of appeal (criminal division); and
- the Supreme Court at the top.

Cases that start in a low court such as the magistrates' court can if necessary be passed up to a higher court. Decisions of superior courts are binding on the lower courts.

Magistrates' courts handle routine and petty cases such as environmental health, shoplifting and acts of criminal damage. They also have the power to grant alcohol licenses and enforce payment of council bills. The Justice of the Peace (JP), who presides over the court, can sentence with penalties of a maximum of 6 months imprisonment or £5,000 fine. Crown courts are adversarial in nature with the judge presiding over the case to ensure that the rules of evidence are obeyed and to decide, usually with the aid of a jury, who the winning party is. Under this system the burden of proof is on the accuser and it is they that have to produce the most convincing evidence. Unlike many European countries, under English law the judge cannot be involved with the drawing out of the evidence.

9.4 European Union law

The mechanism of law-making within the EU starts with the EC which sets legal guidelines for the commission to follow. The Commission then defines the laws and regulations across a broad range of issues, including economic and monetary union, the single market, social and asylum policy, and common agricultural and fisheries policy. Other policies such as foreign and security policy and home affairs policies are controlled directly by the European council.

The Commission can propose two types of laws:

- Regulations: which relate to existing laws and therefore do not need new legislation at a national level.
- Directives: which need new legislation and which require approval at a national level.

Member countries of the EU implement directives from the EU into their national law-making structures. While EU directives provide strict guidelines for member states, some flexibility is available in the way that member states can 'translate' the directive into national law. In the UK this is typically achieved by passing an Act of Parliament. Once passed, the citizens of the member state may then use the new law through the appropriate channels

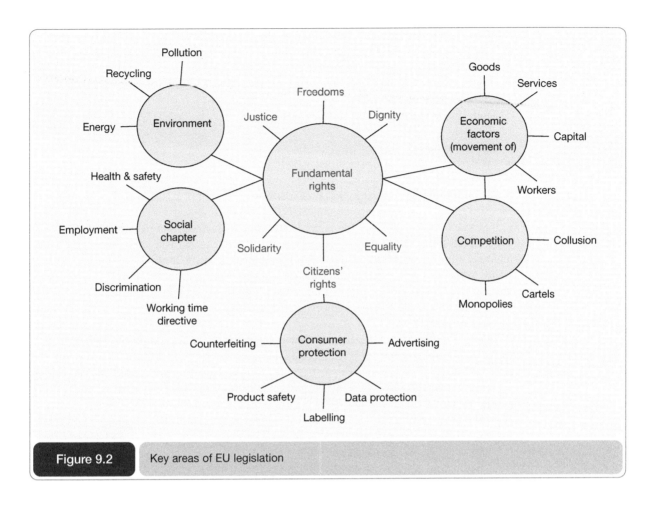

| Figure 9.2 | Key areas of EU legislation |

through their own national legislature. In many areas of law the EU has brought harmonisation to what was otherwise a somewhat diverse collection of national laws.

The most significant EU legislation is bound into treaties and charters; some of the key areas are highlighted in *Figure 9.2*, and are discussed later in this chapter.

The European Court of Justice (ECJ) is the legal authority responsible for ensuring that EU laws are implemented. It has the power to take legal action against a member state if it is not fully complying with EU legislation. As the EU has a higher authority in these areas of law, these are often called *supranational laws*.

The legal relationship between the EU and its member states is a complex one. For example, in Britain in 1972, Parliament recognised the *European Communities Act* through which European Community law was incorporated into UK law. Under this and subsequent legislation the Supreme Court has ultimate authority over domestic matters, and the ECJ has overall authority on EU laws. However, it is still disputed, in some areas of law at least, which law-making authority should be supreme.

9.5 Business law

9.5.1 Forming a business entity

Business law may be characterised as those laws that are related to the formation and running of a company (the business entity) and those that have to be followed when conducting business. The laws that relate to different businesses entities will depend on the focus, size and type of company, and these are determined at a national level. For example, the type of private company will dictate the cost of establishing the business, how the accounts are to be disclosed, access to capital, taxation and personal liability. Liability is the obligation to repay a debt or to settle a wrongful act.

There are four main types of business entity:

- the sole trader;
- the partnership;
- the private limited company;
- the public limited company and other specialised types of organisation.

The *sole trader* who might, for example, be a plumber, electrician or hairdresser is one of the simplest forms of business to set up and run. The sole trader will often own all the assets and take all the profits but are also liable for any losses, which could mean the sole trader's house might have to be sold in order to meet large debts. To set yourself up as a sole trader you just need to register a unique name (if the proprietor's name in not used).

Partnerships may be formed in one of three ways, the characteristics of each are summarised in *Table 9.1*.

In an *unlimited partnership* two or more people share the risks and profits each partner is in fact self-employed and must register as such. Debts can be reclaimed by acquiring the personal assets of either or both partners, even those debts that are caused by only one of the partners. In this respect unlimited partnerships have the same personal liability as that of sole traders. Partnership arrangements are typically detailed in a partnership contract of deed and are common, for example, in professional partnerships such as doctor's and solicitor's practices.

A *limited partnership* is possible if one partner takes full liability for any accrued debts, the remaining partners are protected by limited liability. However, these partnerships are not commonly used in business but they are found in finance management schemes such as unit trusts.

A *limited liability partnership* (LLP) is a relatively new form of partnership in the UK (Limited Liability Partnership Act, 2000): it occurs where each of the partners (or members) contribute to the business but are not personally liable beyond what they have invested.

Table 9.1	Characteristics of partnerships		
Partnerships	**Liability/risk**	**Legal requirements**	**Examples**
Unlimited	Share risks and profits Both equally liable for debts	Register as self-employed. Partnership contract	Doctors Dentists Architects
Limited	Share risks and profits One partner takes full debt liability	Register as self-employed. Partnership contract	Financial management schemes
Limited liability (LLP)	No liability beyond what is invested	Register as self-employed. Partnership contract or deed Register & submit annual accounts to Companies House	Solicitors Accountants

The LLP has proven to be particularly popular with solicitors and accountants, where personal negligence claims against the company may be high (see the football league *Minicase 9.2* as an example). Like other forms of partnership, each member has to register as being self-employed; however, the LLP must also register and submit annual accounts to Companies House.

In law a company has its own legal identity, separate from that of its owners (shareholders). This means that the shareholders do not have any liability for debts beyond what they have invested, i.e. the company's finances are separate from its personal finances. A registered limited liability company requires shares to be distributed to the owners in proportion to the amount contributed. In the case of *private limited companies,* such as the Virgin Group Ltd, shares are not offered to the public but are sold or gifted to private individuals. With the example of the Virgin Group the majority of shares are owned by Richard Branson. *Public limited companies (plcs)* such as British Airways plc are freely traded through the stock exchange and require a minimum of £50,000 of shares to be available. Both types of limited company must register a memorandum and articles of association with Companies House and submit annual reports for external audit. Profits are distributed to the shareholders in the form of dividends and of course shareholders are keen to see their share value increase. In order to maintain appropriate procedures (governance), it is usual for companies to have a secondary or non-executive board, whose purpose is to ensure transparency and accountability to the shareholders.

In order to encourage a healthy investment in stocks and inflate the value of the company, plc executives will often do their best to 'talk up' the future prospects of the company. This was demonstrated in 2004 when the oil company Royal Dutch Shell was maintaining a healthy share price with a 20 percent exaggeration of its oil reserves. Once it was known that the company had deliberately misled the shareholders and an indictment of fraud was being considered, the stock value plummeted by £3 billion (BBC, 2004).

The principle of limited corporations is common around the world but there are different systems in use. *Table 9.2* provides a list of company limited liability suffixes and their approximate equivalents; different countries apply different prerequisites to these business entities.

In addition to the laws that govern the setting-up and running of the business, there is a whole range of additional laws that relate specifically to the act of doing business. These may be categorised as to whether the legislation is predominantly national, regional or of international origin. Historically these laws have been designed and enforced at a national level, but increasingly there is an international dimension with legislation occurring at a regional level or through conventions and treaties at an international level. This has left many areas

Table 9.2	Company liability suffix in different countries

Country	Limited liability suffix	Translation
UK, USA, S. Korea	Ltd or Plc	Private limited company or public limited company
Brazil	Ltd or SA	Limitada or Sociedade Anônima
Denmark	Ap/S or A/S	Anpartsselskab or Aktieselskap
France	Sàrl or SA	Société à responsabilité limitée or Société Anonym
Germany	GmbH or AG	Gesellschaft mit beschrankter Haftung or Aktiengesellschaft
India	Pvt. Ltd or Ltd	Private limited company or Public limited company
Netherlands	BV or NV	Besloten Vennootschap or Naamloze Vennootschap
Spain	SL or SA	Sociedad Limitada or Sociedad Anónima

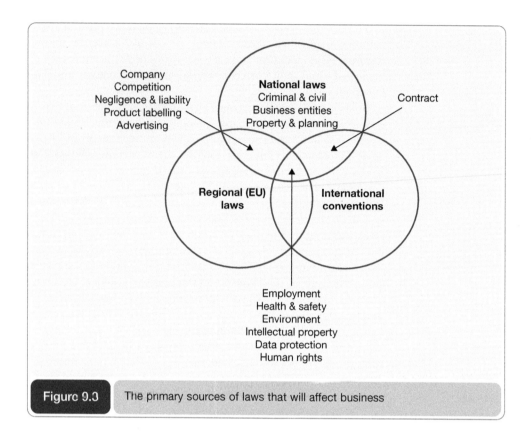

Company
Competition
Negligence & liability
Product labelling
Advertising

National laws
Criminal & civil
Business entities
Property & planning

Contract

**Regional (EU)
laws**

**International
conventions**

Employment
Health & safety
Environment
Intellectual property
Data protection
Human rights

Figure 9.3   The primary sources of laws that will affect business

of law with overlapping jurisdictions. Examples of laws that might affect businesses and the primary sources of these laws are illustrated in *Figure 9.3*.

9.5.2 Contract law

Businesses that enter into negotiations will usually formalise the deal in a mutually acceptable, legally binding contract. These contracts can be in written or verbal form, depending on the historical precedent in the country concerned; however, a written contract is easier to contest in a court of law. Contracts come in different forms but are mainly used to govern relationships between buyers and sellers or between organisations and their employees. Regardless of the purpose, all contracts detail the terms and conditions of the agreement such as price or salary, timescales, warranty, delivery, etc. If the contract conditions are not met over a specified timescale, one party will be in breach of contract and can be legally challenged. For example, in 2008 the clothing store Primark cancelled orders with three of its Indian suppliers after being informed that they were sub-contracting work to other suppliers that used child labour. Primark claimed that unapproved sub-contracting was in breach of their contract (Arnott, 2008).

9.5.3 Tort – Negligence and liability

Business tort law is concerned with damage to a reputation or damage as a result of deliberate action or negligence. It covers areas such as patents and counterfeit goods, defective goods, data protection and poor advice or duty of care, such as in medical, accounting or legal cases (see Football League *Minicase 9.2*). The international law firm Fulbright and Jaworski found, in their fifth annual survey, that the type of litigation which is of the greatest concern to UK

| Minicase 9.2 | The English Football League sues its legal advisers for professional negligence |

Following the collapse of ITV Digital in 2002, the English Football League made one of the largest claims for professional negligence in British legal history (Harris, 2006).

Without the broadcasting deal the Football League was significantly out of pocket and initially sued Carlton and Granada, the owners of ITV Digital, in an attempt to recover the £132 million in broadcasting fees it was owed. However, the High Court ruled that the owners were under no legal obligation to repay the debts of their subsidiary.

Following this ruling, the Football League sued their solicitors for professional negligence for failing to stipulate payment guarantees when negotiating the broadcasting deal with ITV Digital.

In the High Court in June 2006, Mr Justice Rimmer ruled in favour of the legal advisers finding them liable in only two minor counts of breach of duty, for which they were fined a token £4. Summing up, Mr Rimmer said, 'Is the solicitor supposed to review the whole range of commercial considerations that underlie a particular deal, work out which ones he is concerned the client may not have given sufficient thought to and remind him about them? … in my opinion the answer is no.' The High Court decided that the Football League already knew about the risks when they signed the contract and were ordered to pay the defendants legal costs in the case. Not surprisingly the defendants agreed, saying, 'This decision confirms that solicitors cannot be expected to underwrite the success of their clients' commercial transactions nor to advise them of things they know already' (Harris, 2006).

Questions

1 Why do you think the Football League decided to sue the solicitors that acted for them?
2 How would liability insurance have helped the defending solicitors in this case?

---

and US companies is contracts litigation, followed by labour and employment. Personal injury and product liability are concerns to only one in five of the companies surveyed (Fulbright, 2008).

Negligence indictments are usually for relatively minor claims, for example customers suing businesses for accidents such as slipping on wet floors or claiming for damage to cars in a car wash. A number of small cases may also build into a much larger case that may reveal persistent negligence. This occurred in the famous case of *Liebeck* v. *McDonald's* in 1994. The McDonald's restaurant chain stipulated that beverages should be served at between 83 and 88 degrees, more than 20 degrees hotter than most other coffee providers and hot enough to cause third-degree burns. After 700 previous complaints to McDonald's had been demonstrated and a particularly severe case of burning was proven, significant damages amounting to hundreds of thousands of dollars were awarded to the plaintive (Public Citizen, 1999).

Class actions are lawsuits against particular companies on the behalf of many, possibly hundreds, of individuals or companies. In the USA, liability through group or class actions is common in the pharmaceutical, oil and chemical industries, and includes claims for environmental damage, side-effects of drugs and disease resulting from exposure to asbestos and tobacco. Specialist legal companies advertise potential class actions and promise to act on the individual's behalf on the basis that it will be easier and cheaper to settle claims in one large court case rather than hundreds of individual ones. A recent class action in a case of tort was settled in New York in 2008 in the favour of 153 water companies based across 17 states, after it was found that drinking water was contaminated with a the potential carcinogen MTBE. The settling defendants included the oil companies BP Amoco, Chevron and ConocoPhillips (US Legal 500, 2008).

Class actions are less common in the UK or the EU, but tort cases are on the increase. In 2007, GMTV, which is part-owned by ITV and the Disney Corporation, were accused of gross negligence in television phone voting over a period of four years. It was found that the tele-phone lines were often held open in order to raise additional revenue, despite the fact that the competition had closed. The UK media watchdog Ofcom fined the broadcaster GMTV a record £2 million for gross negligence (Sabbagh, 2007).

Fortunately, insurance companies offer various types of liability insurance, such as employer, public and product liability insurance, which are designed to protect businesses against these costs. In many parts of the world it is compulsory for businesses to have employer liability insurance; however this can be very expensive, so many large companies prefer to 'manage the risk' rather than pay high premiums. Companies that are aware of their stakeholders and their impact on the environment are thought to be less likely to be indicted in tort claims.

9.5.4 International business law

Recognising the significant differences between business laws in nation states, the UN Commis-sion on International Trade Law (UNICITRAL) adopted a Convention of Contracts for the International Sale of Goods (CISG) which came into force in 1988. These regulations have resulted in significant moves towards harmonising the terminology, rules and obligations docu-mented in contracts. At the time of writing, the CISG has been ratified by 76 countries, including all the major trading nations with the notable exception of the UK (UNICITRAL, 2009). The CISG exists in six different languages (Arabic, Chinese, English, French, Russian and Spanish) and aims to reduce the confusion over translation and wording disputes in contracts.

9.6 Criminal law

Obviously businesses can protect themselves from criminal legal action by conducting their activities according to national and international laws. However, it is still surprising to note the high number of indictments against companies or their executives for criminal acts. These indictments are typically the result of not complying with national laws on health and safety, financial reporting, bribery, money laundering, fraud, mis-selling of goods, unsafe products, environmental damage, counterfeiting, unlawful importations, corporate manslaughter, etc. The 2001 case of Enron is a well-known example of where the criminal laws of money laundering, fraud, insider trading and making false statements, were found to be broken (BBC, 2003). The scandal not only led to Enron's senior executives being jailed, but it also brought down Enron, at that time America's seventh largest company. Arthur Andersen, which at the time was one of the largest accounting and consultancy companies in the world, was also broken up after they were found to have destroyed evidence relating to the case. Cases such as this highlight the need for transparent practices, efficient governance and an awareness of business ethics and corporate social responsibility.

9.7 Consumer protection

Laws protecting the consumer have been used since the Middle Ages; however, additional legislation has been drafted in more recent times and now covers issues such as:

- defective products;
- misleading advertisements;
- doorstep and distance (also internet) selling;
- cancellation of contracts;

- returns and warranties;
- safety of food and medicines;
- weights and volumes;
- advice and labelling of products;
- as well as specific regulation on, for example, package tour holidays, data protection and safety standards.

The UK Trade Description Act (1968) was drawn up to protect consumers from goods or services that have been given a false description or a wrong price. Local authorities may enforce this Act under criminal legislation and following a conviction a magistrate can fine or imprison the culprit. In addition to this Act, stricter consumer protection laws are to be introduced into the UK as a result of changes in EU legislation. For example, since May 2009, EU legislation includes previously excluded trades, such as fortune tellers, spiritualists and astrologists. These service providers now have to clearly state in writing that what they offer is for entertainment only and that they cannot guarantee the accuracy of their predictions. Those that break the new law will be liable to fines up to £5,000 or two years in jail (Gibb, 2008).

Safety and quality standards are often created by government bodies in order that companies can show that their product or service meets the required standard and they can then advertise this fact in their product information. This is particularly useful to those organisations that act in a socially responsible manner. Examples of safety standards certificates include the British Standards Institute (BSI) KiteMark and the European CE mark which cover products as diverse as electrical appliances, fire safety extinguishers, soft toys, crash helmets and concrete. China has also made great strides in this area of law and has now amalgamated its previous schemes into a single China Compulsory Certificate (CCC) which applies in particular to electrical, mechanical and safety products.

Safety and quality marks may be a useful differentiator in a market and essential if you wish to export to other markets but in some sectors legislation regarding packaging and labelling is also important. Food, medicines and potentially hazardous products have to conform to each nation's requirements, which is why on international products consumers are now used to seeing multiple languages and different international symbols on the packaging.

In the USA, the Food and Drug Administration (FDA) regulates and enforces laws that protect consumers in the areas of food, medicines, medical devices and cosmetics. The EU also legislates in this area with the aim to standardise practice across the region. In the UK the Food Standards Agency is the government department which protects public health and consumer interests. As part of its role it checks the correct labelling of food products according to the appropriate legislation. The Food Safety Act (1990) also lays down compositional rules for products such as bread and flour, chocolate, fruit juice, infant formula, jams, sausages, mineral waters, spreadable fats, etc. *Figure 9.4* provides a list of details that must be clearly shown on food products in the UK (Food Standards Agency, 2009).

While food labelling regulations are in place in most parts of the world, regulations for food labelling are less stringent in some regions, for example China requires only a small number of the above items to be displayed. However, as in most countries, if a product arrives without the appropriate information it will be refused entry or confiscated. Inappropriate labelling can also cause confusion. For example, it was alleged that a Chinese supermarket placed the German children's cereal Brugel among the pet foods. The store and customers were clearly unable to determine what the product was. This was perhaps understandable as the cereal package had no Chinese writing on the label and was printed with cartoon animals such as dogs, cats, birds and monkeys.

Advertising laws also differ widely from country to country, especially with regards to the content and placement of advertisements. For example, tobacco advertising is banned on radio and television in the USA but the EU also bans tobacco advertising in print and on the internet. The advertising of alcohol is also a contentious issue and has wide variations in how legislation is applied. The laws range from weak 'industry regulated' advertising in Australia,

1 The name of the food.
2 A list of the ingredients.
3 The amount of an ingredient which is named or associated with the food.
4 An appropriate durability indication (sell by/use by dates).
5 Special storage conditions.
6 The name of business and manufacturer.
7 The place of origin (depending on the product).
8 The process used in manufacture (depending on the product).
9 Instructions for use (depending on the product).

Figure 9.4   UK requirements for food labelling

to strict bans on all forms of alcohol advertising and consumption in Saudi Arabia and Libya as Sharia law dictates. In order to produce some harmonisation across the EU, in 2005 a framework of guidelines was implemented for member states. To comply with these regulations advertisements should not be directed to minors or be linked with higher performance, or indicate that a higher alcohol content is preferable to a lower one. Implementation of these laws has ironically meant that Sweden, who previously had a total advertising ban on high alcohol drinks, has now relaxed its laws and applies health warnings instead.

With increasing ease and reducing costs, organisations routinely store and share information about individuals, whether they are employees, suppliers or customers. There is hardly a business, bank, credit card company, telephone provider, utility supplier, medical or educational institution or other government body that does not hold data on most individuals. This does not even start to consider the freely available information and photos that you provide for the world to see through your favourite social networking site! Consider, as an example, the grocery retailer Tesco. Via your store card they not only hold your personal details, but from your buying patterns they could also determine:

- how much alcohol you drink;
- if you are a heath food fanatic;
- if you have any children;
- if you are trying to lose weight;
- if you have a medical condition;
- if you have a pet.

It is likely that, as customers, we would want to keep this information confidential, and in this case, because it provides Tesco with a distinct competitive advantage, it is unlikely that it would be shared. However, in different circumstances the selling of databases to other organisations is a common, lucrative and legal source of income. Companies are prepared to purchase this information as it can be used to help to target marketing campaigns or, for instance, be used to filter appropriate candidates for interview.

Legislation to protect personal information has been slow to develop, especially when set against the rapid changes in information technology. There has, however, been some progress, for example under EU legislation all personal data should be protected in a number of ways (ICO, 2009). With regard to stored data it should be possible for an individual to stop the data being used for the purposes of direct marketing. Furthermore stored data should:

- be processed in an appropriate manner that is relevant to a specific purpose;
- only contain information that is selected for a specific purpose;
- be accurate, secure and regularly updated;

- be kept for no longer than is necessary and then destroyed;
- be available so that individuals can ask what information is held on them;

Data protection legislation has numerous implications for business as it impacts what information can be stored and shared across organisations, between organisations and between countries. It also requires significant resources to manage the database and comply with requests for information. Businesses are also struggling to clarify the legal perspective in 'grey areas' such as their right to covertly monitor employees' telephone calls and web activities while at work. Also banks, call centres and government departments have found themselves open to charges of providing poor data security when their systems have been open to hacking and poor practice has allowed data to fall into the wrong hands.

9.7.1 Competition law

In most parts of the world businesses are governed by anti-competitive laws which aim to protect consumers, encourage entrepreneurial development and help to ensure a fair and open competitive market. In the UK this is the job of the Competition Commission and the Office of Fair Trading. In the USA it is the Antitrust Division of the Department of Justice that regulates the competitiveness of industry. In August 2008 China established its own anti-trust laws; however, outside China there are initial concerns that these might not be thoroughly or equally enforced. In the EU competition law relates to three main areas:

- cartels;
- monopolies and mergers;
- government assistance.

Forming a cartel is highly tempting to some business sectors as it can reduce competition and optimise profits. In order to protect consumers from this abuse of power, cartels have been made illegal in many parts of the world, including the USA, Europe and more recently in India (2008) and China (2008). In order to combat cartels, the EC encourages whistle-blowing, or the exchange of information in return for leniency, and can impose fines of up to 10 percent of the company's worldwide revenue. Indeed in many parts of the world, including the USA, France, Japan and Brazil, criminal sanctions can be applied, resulting in the imprisonment of company executives. During 2008, the Antitrust Division of the Department of Justice in the USA imposed more than US$1 billion in criminal fines, typically averaging at more than $100 million per company (*Global Competition Review*, 2009). In 2008, the UK's Office of Fair Trading brought criminal charges against three former and one current BA executives under the Enterprise Act (2002) for allegedly fixing prices with respect to air passenger fuel surcharges (Prosser, 2008). *Table 9.3* lists the ten highest cartel fines in Europe since 2000.

Table 9.3	Ten highest cartel fines per undertaking		
Year	**Undertaking**	**Case**	**Amount in €**
2008	Saint Gobain	Car glass	896,000,000
2009	E.ON	Gas	553,000,000
2009	GDF Suez	Gas	553,000,000
2007	ThyssenKrupp	Elevators and escalators	479,669,850
2001	F. Hoffmann-La Roche AG	Vitamins	462,000,000
2007	Siemens AG	Gas insulated switchgear	396,562,500
2008	Pilkington	Car glass	370,000,000
2008	Sasol Ltd	Candle waxes	318,200,000
2006	Eni SpA	Synthetic rubber	272,250,000
2002	Lafarge SA	Plasterboard	249,600,000

Source: Europa (2009a)

Monopoly legislation is another means to prevent a company from getting into a dominant market position. If there is only one or a small number of competitors they are more likely to either abuse their position by charging high prices or alternatively put their rivals out of business by undercutting their competitors' prices. Either way, in the long term it is not good for the customer. A high profile case was that of Microsoft and Netscape and their competitive internet browsers. See *Minicase 9 .3* which discusses *AOL Time Warner* vs. *Microsoft*.

The European Competition Commission also regulates proposed mergers to ensure that they will not significantly reduce the level of competition and will also investigate a proposed merger if it is referred to them by the national regulatory body of a member state. For example, in May 2009 the Commission approved Lufthansa's proposed takeover of BMI. This was on the basis that it would not significantly affect competition across the EU as the two companies had already co-operated with each other through the Star Alliance (Europa, 2009b). However, if the EC decides that competition could be distorted, then mergers might be refused or only given conditional approval. Conditional approval might, for instance, be granted if parts of the new business are sold off or specialised technologies are made available to other companies, possibly though licensing deals. For example, when My Travel and Thomas Cook merged in the summer of 2007, the Commission found that the merger would cause a monopoly situation in Ireland, as it

---

Minicase 9.3   *AOL Time Warner vs. Microsoft*

In the early 1990s, AOL Time Warner's Netscape was the most used internet browser, commanding an 80–90 percent worldwide market share (Market Share, 2009). However, by the mid-1990s it was losing ground and under severe competitive pressure from Microsoft's Internet Explorer. In 1996, AOL Time Warner accused Microsoft of abusing its near monopoly market position by bundling its Internet Explorer software with the Windows operating system, which meant that the majority of the world's PC users had a copy of Internet Explorer. In its defence, Microsoft claimed that the Internet Explorer product was a result of innovation of the Windows operating system and the two products should be considered as one: the product was a feature of Windows and was provided for free. These claims were refuted by AOL Time Warner, who stated that the internet browser was not integral to the operating system, as the operating systems could run without it.

In parallel to this dispute, Microsoft was also in the courts having been indicted by the Department of Justice and 20 USA states for unfair competitive practices and abuse of its dominant market position in operating systems and internet browsers. In April 2000, the judge pronounced that Microsoft was guilty of the charges and suggested that Microsoft was split into two companies: one selling the operating system the other selling applications. Following an appeal by Microsoft, the verdict was overturned and in September 2001 the Department of Justice claimed to no longer be looking to split up Microsoft and was instead seeking an alternative resolution. In November 2001, the Department of Justice settled, with Microsoft having agreed that it would share its application programming interfaces with other third-party developers. This ruling at the time was widely condemned as being weak and ineffective as it did not tackle the key anti-competitive issues in the case.

In 2003, the legal dispute between AOL Time Warner and Microsoft was finally resolved. AOL Time Warner was awarded $750 million in compensation and a seven-year free licensing option for Internet Explorer (HU, 2003). While this deal provided useful finance to AOL Time Warner, it was widely perceived in the industry as a win–win resolution for Microsoft, who could easily afford to pay compensation at this level. Since the deal there has been a significant decline in sales of the Netscape browser, which resulted in the withdrawal of the Netscape product in 2007.

In 2009 the global consumer still has a limited choice of internet browsers. In the world market, 65.5 percent use the bundled Internet Explorer which comes with Microsoft Windows, and 22.5 percent of the world market uses Mozilla's Firefox as an internet browser. Between them the companies command a monopoly position with an 88 percent share of the web browser market (Market Share, 2009).

Questions

1 Why do you think that these court cases have taken so long to come to a resolution?
2 Do you think that the Netscape–Microsoft deal has benefited consumers in the long run?

would control more than 50 percent of the travel market in this region. To counter these concerns, Thomas Cook offered to divest its Irish business, Budget Travel. The conditional merger was approved and the combined group is now the largest travel company in Europe (Europa, 2009c).

Increasingly, global organisations such as the WTO, the UNCTAD and the OECD have been investigating the implementation of anti-trust legislation. However, it is doubtful that, even if it happens, the LDCs will not have the necessary legislative and enforcement procedures to effectively implement the new legislation.

Free competition can also be compromised by governments that provide unfair inducements in the forms of state aid, low taxation or 'free loans'. However, regulations that protect the principle of fair play are somewhat unique to the EU and do not apply within other regional trade agreements. During the 2008 financial crisis these rules were severely tested, as more than 50 banks across Europe and the airline Alitalia were spared bankruptcy through support of their respective governments. It was argued by some that, during the global economic slowdown, rules sometimes have to be adapted as the consequences of denying state aid might be disastrous. For example, in May 2009 General Motors in Europe was looking for 3.3 billion euros in financial assistance to avoid bankruptcy (Massey, 2009). It was estimated that a total of 300,000 jobs were at risk across the EU, in Germany, Belgium, Great Britain, Poland, Spain and Sweden. Under EU rules, state aid might be permitted if the company is in danger of going out of business. However, other European automobile manufacturers might consider that if aid were provided then it would amount to unfair practice and a distortion of free competition.

9.8 Intellectual property rights (IPR)

Another area of law that concerns businesses is that of the protection of *intellectual property* (IP). The benefit of IP protection is that it encourages innovation and entrepreneurship which are both important features of a growing economy. If an invention is protected, the owner has the right to sue the infringer under civil law. It is for this reason that companies prefer to trade in regions that provide stringent enforcement of IPR. Intellectual property rights oversee a number of different areas of the business, including trademarks, copyrights, design registration, licensing, patents, etc.

The purpose of a trademark is that it provides instant recognition of the origin, design and quality of the product. Trademarks are typically a word, phrase, company logo or brand, and, like patents, they should ideally be registered in order to be protected. One of the oldest trademarks is Stella Artois which has reportedly been in use since 1366. This example demonstrates a characteristic of trademarks in that they do not expire so long as they remain in use. Trademarks can be recognised by the suffix ™ when they are unregistered, or ® when they have been formally registered. Many large organisations such as Microsoft have registered many hundreds of trademarks, such as the original MS-DOS® (operating system), Calibri® (font name), Brute Force® (video game), Excel® (spreadsheet) and the Xbox® (gaming system). Trademarks are often rigorously defended, as was the case in June 2009 when Psion successfully defended its trademark rights over Intel's use of the word 'NetBook®' (Meyer, 2009).

Legislation in this area has had to be adapted in order to protect trademark use and regulation on the internet. This was partly in response to 'cyber-squatting', 'land grabbing' or 'domain name parking'. This practice occurred in the 1990s when familiar web names were purchased with the intention of either selling them on at profit, or alternatively making financial gains from misdirected pay-per-click advertising. Recent legislation has meant that large companies have been able to sue over infringements of trademarks in order to protect the continuity of their web content. Previous 'cyber-squatted' domain names such as www.kodak.ru and www.bbcnews.com have been successfully defended by the parent corporations (Lynn, 2009). Following this ruling you might like to see what happens when you attempt to connect to these sites.

Copyrights differ from trademarks as they automatically apply to most forms of literary, artistic and musical works across all forms of media, and can be recognised by the symbol ©. One of the oldest copyrights might be the tune 'happy birthday to you' which was composed in 1859 and copyrighted in 1935. The copyright was due to expire in 2010, 75 years after registration, but it has now been extended until 2035 by the owners AOL Time Warner. Music copyright is currently in the news as the music industry is struggling to keep up with the rapidly changing world of file sharing, through both illegal and legal means. Napster was one of the first, and certainly the most high profile, internet sites which offered free peer–peer copying of music. However, in 2007 they lost a seven-year battle for copyright infringement brought by the large record labels (Kravets, 2007). European sound recordings are currently protected by copyright for 50 years, which means many of the original recordings by, for example, Elvis Presley, the Rolling Stones and the early Beatles albums are due to expire. In order to combat the loss of income the record companies are pushing for an extension of the copyright term, beyond the current 50 years. The music and lyrics, rather than the recording, is protected for 70 years after the songwriter's death. Many industry watchers feel that it is time for the songwriters and composers to make some direct financial returns. The BBC provides some useful information on how to ensure that you can prove copyright ownership which, among other things, involves posting the new material to yourself by recorded delivery. (BBC, 2009b).

In the UK, businesses can also protect a new product design by registering the design for a maximum of 25 years. This is a simple and inexpensive process but one that is not much more robust than that of the automatic copyright of design drawings. However, should the company wish to license its design to other companies it may make the licensing process easier.

Unlike trademarks and copyrights, patents must be formally registered and are thereafter typically protected from copying for a period of 20 years. Patents may then be renewed for shorter periods of time but this tends to be a very expensive process and may require a modification to the invention. Copying a product is, of course, made easier once the patent design is registered and published. Despite the legal protection of a patent it is quite often only a matter of time before a competitor either finds a legal way around the patent, or sells counterfeit products in parts of the world that are not covered by the patent or where patent enforcement is weak. To get around this problem some organisations license the IP to other companies in order to maximise their returns in as short a time as possible. *Minicase 9.4* provides more detail on the mechanism and issues behind the patenting of pharmaceuticals. Examples of patent infringement are also described in the *Minicase 9.5*.

Traditionally, patents have been the preserve of national legislation; however, the registration of international patents across many countries has been made simpler since 1980 when the European Patent Office started granting patents which can now cover as many as 38 countries. Nevertheless, there are still significant differences between the European Patent

---

Minicase 9.4   Patenting pharmaceutical products

The pharmaceutical industry is particularly keen to optimise patent life, as the cost of drug development can run to hundreds of millions of dollars and take 8–10 years. As the patent is applied for early on in the drug development process, often 5–8 years of the patent life has already expired before the drug is marketed. In order to overcome this limitation, pharmaceutical companies are keen to quickly license the manufacture and marketing of the drug around the world, to maximise their returns in as short a time as possible. At the same time the pharmaceutical industry spends vast amounts of money defending its patents from counterfeit products and illegal generic substitutes which are commonly sold through the internet.

Generic drugs are licensed drugs that are marketed without their original brand name. They are generally less expensive than brand-name drugs, they are chemically identical and meet the same regulatory standards demanded by the FDA (US Food and Drug Administration) and other regulatory bodies for safety, purity and effectiveness. Generic drugs can be authorised and licensed by the original patent holder or unauthorised and manufactured by a competitive company.

Pharmaceutical companies spend significant resources in changing the purpose (use), chemical structure or formulation of the drug with the aim of being granted a patent extension, a process that is called ever-greening. The expiration of a patent removes the monopoly of the patent holder on drug sales and it is particularly at this time that generic manufacturers enter the market. For example, Valium is the brand name of a tranquiliser or sedative that was first patented by Roche in 1981. Since the expiry of its patent in 2002, it has been marketed by many other companies, often at significantly reduced prices, under its generic name Diazepam. Roche has since ceased to manufacture and market the product as it sees little profit in the generic market.

Questions

1   Why do you think that generic pharmaceutical manufacturers watch to see when patents are due to expire?
2   Is it possible for generic companies to apply for a patent on their generic drugs? If not, why not?

Office and, for example, the USA Patent and Trademark Office in the way patents are applied for and what is considered patentable. Some of these differences are highlighted in *Table 9.4*.

Table 9.4   Major differences between US and EU patent laws

US patents	EU patents
Protection in the whole territory of the USA	Protection across 38 European countries
Patent office will investigate logbooks, publications, prototypes and other evidence before making a decision as to who invented it first	The first to file and be awarded a successful patent is considered the inventor
The inventor has a one-year grace period after making the invention known before a patent must be applied for	Patents will not be granted if the information was first made public or disclosed to another person without a non-disclosure agreement
Requires the inventor to include details on the best way to use the invention	A means of use must be stated but this may not be the best way to use the invention
Computer software and business processes can be patented	These are only patentable if they have a 'technical effect' (i.e. a company can patent an operating system but not a game – this will be protected by copyright)

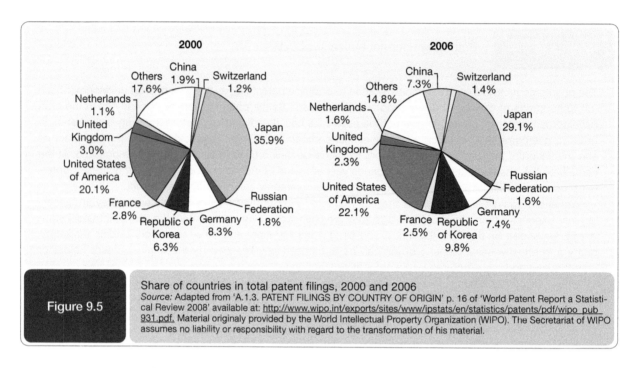

Figure 9.5

Share of countries in total patent filings, 2000 and 2006
Source: Adapted from 'A.1.3. PATENT FILINGS BY COUNTRY OF ORIGIN' p. 16 of 'World Patent Report a Statistical Review 2008' available at: http://www.wipo.int/exports/sites/www/ipstats/en/statistics/patents/pdf/wipo_pub_931.pdf. Material originaly provided by the World Intellectual Property Organization (WIPO). The Secretariat of WIPO assumes no liability or responsibility with regard to the transformation of his material.

To try to overcome these differences there have been encouraging attempts to standardise patent protection and simplify the patent application process across a broader range of countries. Following on from the 1970 Patent Co-operation Treaty (PCT), the World Intellectual Property Organisation (WIPO) has worked as a specialised agency of the UN and, in 1996, entered into a co-operation agreement with the WTO. WIPO is now able to grant international patents in 141 countries from Afghanistan, Brazil and China to Zimbabwe. The applicants do not have to register in all member countries; they can stipulate which countries they wish for their patents to apply. In 2007 WIPO handled 158,400 international PCT patents, of which 33.6 percent were filed from the USA, with Japan filing the next largest number of patents accounting for 17.5 percent of the total (WIPO, 2008). *Figure 9.5* displays the patents filed through WIPO plus the patent filings in the country of residence. Note the decrease in total patent findings from Japan and the increase over the same six-year period of total patent filings from China and the Republic of Korea.

It is worth noting that a comparison of the number a patent submissions is often used as a crude mechanism to evaluate how innovative a country is. However, a comparison of this sort does not take into consideration the size or the litigious nature of the country, or the quality of the submitted patents. Also, when a patent is granted it does not always represent a technological or commercial breakthrough, so this form of comparison should be treated with some caution.

9.9 Employer relationships

There are many laws that govern the relationship between an employee and an employer and these include the following:

- contract law including termination of contract;
- health and safety and liability;
- anti-discrimination (gender, sexual orientation, race, disability, age);
- wrongful dismissal and redundancy;
- minimum wage;
- working time regulations (including holiday entitlement);

- sick pay entitlement;
- maternity/paternity leave;
- recognition of trade unions;
- employment of minors.

In Western democracies many of these laws are taken for granted, almost as a citizen's right. Indeed, in some social democracies, like Sweden, employment benefits such as those of paternal leave are more generous than those that are detailed in European legislation. Many organisations will also routinely exceed the legal minimal requirements in an effort to demonstrate their credentials as a socially responsible company. With the aim of ensuring that EU member states enforce European legislation, the EU will on occasion take nations to court. In 2006, the EC brought a case against the UK government in the European Court of Justice, after the UK had failed to enforce the EU daily and weekly rest rules (Eironline, 2006).

Not surprisingly, the employee and employer relationship is based on the contract of employment. In the UK changes in the law have enhanced the rights of employees. Employers can no longer selectively recruit and fire staff at will. Recruitment and dismissal must be demonstrated to be non-discriminatory by race, age, gender, disability, religion and sexual orientation. In the USA in 2005 there was widespread media coverage of a dispute at Dell Computers in Tennessee, when Somali Muslim shift workers were sacked after they sought to perform the Maghreb prayer each day after sunset. It was concluded that this case breached the US Civil Rights Act of 1964 which requires an employer to accommodate religious practices, unless it causes 'undue hardship'. The employees were reinstated and the mangers at the plant were given extra training on religious practices and employment law (Spooner, 2005).

Like the contract of sale, the contract of employment also states terms and conditions of the contractual arrangement. In the UK these conditions must fall within the national legislation guidelines found in the Working Time Regulations Act (1998). In the contract of service an employee should expect to see details of pay, sick pay, holiday, pension rights, length of notice to be given on termination (by both parties), a job description, a place of work, etc.

As with all contracts there must also be a level of goodwill between both the parties and so, while they may not be explicitly stated, under common law the employees are expected to undertake their work with reasonable care and obey reasonable orders. The emphasis here is on the word 'reasonable'. For instance, if a manager told an employee to falsify records and the employee refused, the employee will not be breaching his or her contract of employment. From the employer's perspective it must pay the employee on time (at a rate of the minimum wage or above), provide safe working conditions and implicitly must not undermine the employees' trust and confidence.

Despite having the appropriate legislation and being a signatory to the United Nations Convention on Child Rights, the laws are not always enforced. Of the many employment laws in India there is one specifically dealing with child labour, the Child Labour (Prohibition & Regulation) Act 1986. This states that children under the age of 14 are not permitted to work in mines, factories or other hazardous environments. According to Indian government statistics, India has 17 million child labourers, the highest number of child labourers in the world (Khattar, 2009). Some children are even forced to live at their workplace, in 'bonded labour', which is also illegal in India. The law is there but the resources to enforce it are not, a situation that the Indian government is very keen to rectify. Whether Western businesses choose to work with companies that are breaking national and international law may be down to their ethical stance.

9.9.1 Health and safety

The health and safety of all employees should be paramount to all employers regardless of the local criminal law legislation. However, this legislation is not solely the remit of the employer, the employee also takes some responsibility to ensure legislation is being followed.

In the UK, the Health and Safety at Work Act 1974 has been regularly updated and influenced by EU legislation. Although not a comprehensive list, health and safety legislation in the EU broadly applies to the following occupational issues and facilities:

- mechanical, electrical, construction, dangerous substance, noise pollution, gas and fire safety hazards;
- product safety, including food and drink;
- the lifting and moving of heavy goods;
- working at height and in confined spaces;
- stress in the workplace;
- the correct use of computer screens;
- appropriate and well-maintained tools and equipment;
- provision of first-aid facilities and documented emergency procedures;
- provision of protective clothing, hazard warning signs and appropriate training.

In the UK preventable accidents which lead to stress, physical injury or death are referred to the Health and Safety Executive (HSE). The HSE will investigate to ensure that the correct procedures have been followed, for example, by checking that work has undergone an appropriate risk assessment and that the subsequent health and safety plan has been implemented. If the guidelines have not been followed and a preventable accident occurs, the company may be fined, or, in the circumstances of corporate manslaughter, the directors could be imprisoned. In June 2009 PFG Plant Hire in Omagh was charged with not completing an adequate risk assessment and was fined £30,000. This related to a fatal accident in January 2008 when an employee died after a wall he was demolishing collapsed upon him. After the verdict a spokesperson for the Health and Safety Executive in Northern Ireland said, 'It is vital that all companies properly identify and address hazards within the workplace and implement systems to minimise and control risks' (BBC, 2009c).

Health and safety legislation can also be applied to cases where poor internal practices endanger the public. In 2007, Cadbury Schweppes was taken to court over a salmonella outbreak, during which it had to recall 1 million chocolate bars. A leaking pipe was the cause of the incident. After pleading guilty, the company was fined £1 million under health and safety legislation (Herman and Jordan, 2007). Cadbury Schweppes was found liable for placing unsafe goods on the market, inadequate testing during the manufacturing process and for the delay in notifying the authorities of the outbreak. Counterfeit medicines and toys can also lead to a breach of health and safety legislation, as is described in *Minicase 9.5*.

9.10 International law

International law can be sub-divided into two areas:

- nationally legislated laws affecting international business;
- international laws which are agreed by nation states through international organisations.

9.10.1 Nationally legislated laws affecting international business

Laws are sometimes implemented in order to limit trade and put pressure on rogue states, oppressive regimes or those with nuclear ambitions. These laws are usually politically motivated and may also be driven by foreign policy and military objectives. They include:

- sanctions and embargoes;
- extraterritoriality;
- constraints on foreign ownership;
- nationalisation, expropriation and confiscation.

Minicase 9.5	The dangers of counterfeiting

While globalisation and the lowering of trade barriers are generally considered to be good things, these have also created new opportunities for illegal trade. According to the EC (European Commission, 2008) the sale of some counterfeit goods is now more profitable than that of drug trafficking. The bogus product is produced on an industrial scale, with false papers and changed origins implying that the pirated goods are authentic.

The counterfeiting of goods is a multifaceted issue. Not only does it create a black market where consumer protection and taxation do not apply, it also undermines the intellectual property rights and the profitability of legitimate businesses. A recent EC report (European Commission, 2008) claims that counterfeiting is an increasing problem for Europe, with the majority (60 percent) of all the counterfeit products coming from China.

Counterfeit seizures of medicines in the EU increased by 50 percent in one year (2006–2007) with fake drugs coming in from Switzerland (40 percent), India (35 percent) and the UAE (15 percent). In one case customs officials in the EU seized counterfeit 'heart medication' which consisted of a mixture of brick dust and yellow paint coated in varnish (European Commission, 2008). The risks of counterfeiting drugs are not just financial, the counterfeiters may also put lives at risk. The WHO claims that in some countries fake medicine may account for 30 to 50 percent of pharmaceutical sales. This has led to a number of disasters, for instance in Niger fake meningitis vaccines killed 2,500 people, fake cough syrup killed 89 people in Haiti and fake anti-malarial tablets killed 30 in Cambodia (WHO, 2006).

Counterfeit toys are also a major health and safety issue due to inflammability, mechanical and electrical safety, toxicity, sharp edges and small parts which can be swallowed by children. In 2007 millions of Chinese-made toys were recalled by the EU and the USA following health and safety concerns. Most notably 1.5 million wooden toy trains were recalled as they had been decorated with paint containing lead (Lipton and Barboza, 2007).

There is, however, evidence that China is trying to stop the production of counterfeit products. In 2006 China held up several high-profile examples where it had successfully prosecuted Chinese companies that had been infringing intellectual property (IP) laws. One case was that of the *Sony Corporation* vs. *Guangzhou Top Power Electronics*. Guangzhou Top Power Electronics was found to be manufacturing counterfeit Sony camcorder batteries. The Guangzhou Intermediate People's Court ordered Top Power Electronics to cease infringement of the Sony trademark and patents rights and ordered stocks and moulds to be destroyed. Sony was awarded 600,000 yuan (approx. 62,000 euros) in compensation (Lawfuel, 2007).

Questions

1 Why is counterfeiting so harmful to:
   a) other legal business?
   b) the consumer?
   c) the economy?
2 What additional measures can be taken to protect against counterfeit goods?

9.10.2 Sanctions

Sanctions are restrictions in trade with a specific country. They may include the restriction of or the withdrawal of trade deals. This can be achieved:

- by increasing tariffs;
- by boycotting goods from the country;
- by banning imports;
- through the cancellation of technology transfer arrangements.

A sanction may be unilateral, with just a single country participating, or multilateral, with several participating countries. The UN and other regional bodies, such as the EU, have the power to stipulate multilateral sanctions against trade with specified countries. The Ivory Coast (officially Republic of Côte d'Ivoire), currently has UN sanctions applied against all forms of diamond trade. This follows decades of violence and human rights violations, funded in part from the illegal sale of 'conflict diamonds'. The UN has made it clear that these sanctions will be reviewed once the country holds a free presidential election.

The EU also applies sanctions 'on behalf' of its members: Myanmar (Burma) has had EU trade sanctions applied against it since 2006. These will be in place until democratic progress has been made, which includes the freeing of the political prisoners, such as the opposition leader Aung Suu Kyi, who has spent 13 of the last 19 years under house arrest (CNN, 2009). EU sanctions against Burma include a travel ban on the country's top officials, a trade ban on timber, metals and precious stones, an arms embargo and a freeze of Burmese assets in Europe.

9.10.3 Embargos

An embargo is a complete ban against all trade with a specified country. Since February 1962, following the 1959 revolution when Fidel Castro seized power in Cuba, the USA has had a unilateral trade embargo against Cuba. It was originally imposed in response to Castro's forced nationalisation of American-owned companies. The intention was to deprive Cuba of foreign currency and bring down the Communist regime. The embargo was further strengthened in 1996 by new laws which punished US companies that traded with Cuba. However, in March 2009, USA President Barack Obama eased some sanctions by allowing Cuban-Americans to travel to the island once a year and to send money, food and medicines to relatives there (Carroll, 2009). However, it has been made clear by President Obama that the remaining trade embargo will stay in place until democratic elections are held in Cuba.

Sanctions and embargoes are often ignored by countries and businesses that are looking to show solidarity with the country concerned, or by those wishing to make the most of a business opportunity. Countries such as China, South Africa and Russia are often accused of breaking embargoes, for instance the arms embargo against the Democratic Republic of Congo (BBC, 2006). Embargoes come with a predefined list of what is and is not permitted. However, some items for export may have a dual purpose, one legal and the other illegal, and it is this loophole that is often used to circumvent the embargo. In June 2009 three men were jailed in the UK after buying military parts on eBay for fighter jets in Iran. They denied that they were breaking the UK arms trading embargo, claiming that the equipment was to be used in the Iranian health sector as ambulance breathing apparatus (BBC, 2009d).

9.10.4 Extraterritoriality

Countries also attempt to control legal activities outside their own national border. This practice is called *extraterritoriality* – the exemption from national legal jurisdiction. It provides a mechanism where the state is exempt from local law and is commonly applied to foreign diplomats and civil ships in foreign waters. In the reverse situation, extraterritoriality can also be applied to citizens when they have committed a crime overseas. In 2005 an Afghan warlord was convicted in the UK and jailed for 20 years after being found guilty of kidnap and torture in his own country (BBC, 2005). Faryadi Zardad had been found working in a pizza restaurant in London.

Extraterritoriality can sometimes be used as a means to abdicate responsibility for the rule of law, as is the case for the US naval base of Guantanamo Bay in eastern Cuba. From 2002 the base was used to house suspected terrorists from Afghanistan and Iraq. The US government initially claimed that the detainees had no legal rights as the base was not subject to US law as it was outside its jurisdiction. Additionally, as 'unlawful combatants', the USA stated that the prisoners were not entitled to protection under the Geneva Convention.

However, in 2004, a US Supreme Court ruled that, despite the base being in Cuba, it was entirely controlled by the USA and therefore the detainees were subject to a defence under the Fifth Amendment. In January 2009, President Obama signalled his intent to close the camp and release or transfer the prisoners elsewhere (Goldenberg, 2009).

Businesses are also obliged to fulfil local contractual obligations even when their customers are overseas. In October 2007 the British House of Lords ruled that credit card companies were still required to insure and refund their customers should they purchase goods or services that are undelivered, damaged or otherwise misrepresented. Tesco Personal Finance and Lloyd's TSB had been appealing against the decision of a previous appeals court that the insurance-backed guarantee should only apply to UK purchases. However, the Law Lords said that under the 1974 Consumer Credit Act, there was no territorial limitation that excluded foreign purchases and that the standard insurance protection should also be offered on foreign transactions (BBC, 2007).

Extraterritoriality is increasingly common in international trade, as countries often lack confidence in other nations to regulate business with appropriate law, especially in areas such as taxation, competition laws (e.g. cartels), security, organised crime, corporate governance and data protection. Extraterritoriality causes additional complications for international businesses that already have to negotiate complex and often conflicting legal systems in different countries. For this reason organisations such as the International Chamber of Commerce (ICC) are encouraging nation states to harmonise national laws and to recognise equivalent standards.

Concerns around the world are frequently raised over foreign companies controlling key domestic industries. In order to counter this, many governments have placed constraints on the levels of foreign ownership, or *foreign direct investment* (FDI) as it is also known. This is achieved in one of four ways, as illustrated in *Figure 9.6*.

Limits to foreign ownership can be found in most countries and industries: for instance most European and North American airlines, newspaper ownership in Canada and the telecommunications industry in Japan restrict FDI. Total bans of foreign ownership in

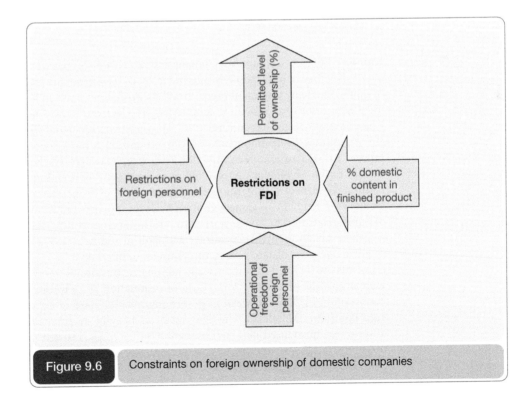

Figure 9.6 Constraints on foreign ownership of domestic companies

domestic industries are effectively state monopolies and these include critical industries such as the fishing and energy sectors in Iceland and the oil industry in Mexico. The UK is one of the least restricted countries in the world with significant foreign ownership in power generation, utilities, media and telecommunications. Multinational companies have to consider the consequences of limited foreign investment. Even if major ownership is not part of their long-term strategy, circumstances might change which could frustrate their ownership ambitions in the future.

Nation states have the right to decide on their own macro economic policy agenda. The degree of public ownership (whether foreign or domestic) is often the result of the political leanings of the government. Major industries are more likely to be state or publicly owned under socialist or communist governments, whereas capitalist governments will be more in favour of free market trading. Under free market systems even key utilities, such as electricity generation are privately owned perhaps even by foreign companies. The process of taking a business from private to public ownership is called *nationalisation*. Expropriation and confiscation are types of compulsory nationalisation.

9.10.5 Nationalisation

Nationalisation is the transfer of ownership from the private to the public sector. Large industries such as mining, energy, water, steel, chemicals, oil production, etc. are often targets for nationalisation on the basis that the industries are key to the economy, and that they are a useful source of income. However, nationalisation is not just the preserve of socialist states, it also occurs in more free market economies. Recent nationalised companies include the financial institutions AIG, Northern Rock and Hypo Real Estate by the US, UK and German governments respectively. All these companies are now majority owned by their governments and in these instances it is not because of political ideology, but in order to save a wider financial collapse and national panic following the economic crisis of 2008.

9.10.6 Expropriation

Expropriation is the compulsory purchase of a private company by a government. Foreign companies may be compulsorily purchased by governments for political or financial ends. In 2005 H.J. Heinz was encouraged to sell its processing plant in Venezuela to the government after troops had seized the disused factory (*Business Week*, 2005). Since then President Chávez's government has continued to expropriate national and foreign industries such as energy, utilities, telecommunications, cement and oil companies. This trend towards compulsory nationalisation, in conjunction with steep tax increases, has persuaded companies such as Exxon Mobil and ConocoPhillips to leave Venezuela and to seek international arbitration. Venezuela is not the only country that expropriates private companies; the Democratic Republic of Congo, Guinea, Ecuador, Mexico and Zimbabwe all have a history of expropriation. The concern of many multinational companies is that the worldwide recession is likely to further encourage nationalism and nationalisation.

Fortunately the blatant seizure or confiscation of companies is uncommon. Even if governments are inclined to compulsorily nationalise businesses, most tend to take ownership with at least the pretence of some form of negotiation and expropriation rather than direct confiscation. In 2000 the Mexican government was accused of expropriation against a foreign company: Metalclad who had invested heavily in a Mexican waste facility. The government introduced new environmental buffer zones, insisted that the company had to fund local social and medical welfare systems, declared the area a protected environmental zone and finally refused permission for its use as a landfill (DePalma, 2000). In summary, it made what was once a promising business financially unviable.

9.11 International laws and treaties

The chapter now turns its attention to international laws which are agreed by nation states through international organisations such as the UN. It is important to recognise that, unlike nation states, in the international arena there is no legislature, written constitution or international court to which countries are legally bound to submit.

National disputes can, however, be voluntarily submitted to the International Court of Justice (ICJ), which is based in The Hague under the jurisdiction of the UN. Countries are encouraged to take this route in order for international disputes to be resolved in a non-confrontational and peaceful manner. The ICJ is composed of 15 judges who have been elected by the UN General Assembly and the Security Council each for a maximum period of nine years. The ICJ has been asked to arbitrate on a wide variety of national disagreements, ranging from navigational rights between Nicaragua and Costa Rica, to passing judgment over Georgian charges of racial discrimination against the Russian Federation following the attacks and ethnic expulsion of Georgians in the region of South Ossetia (ICJ, 2009).

As there are no predefined forms of international law, the ICJ derives its legislation from the sources listed in *Table 9.5*.

9.11.1 International conventions

An international convention is the signed agreement between several and often many nation states that establishes a relationship governed by international law. Many conventions are subsequently registered with the UN in order that they can be regarded as a binding treaty. The principle of treaties was developed by the International Law Commission over a 20-year period. In 1980 it resulted in the Vienna Convention on the Law of Treaties (VCLT) which details the essential elements of international treaty law and has since been ratified by 109 states. Treaties come in two forms, either bi-partite as between two nations or multi-partite between several nations. *Table 9.6* lists some of the important administrative areas for international treaties. They have been categorised as having either external or internal jurisdictions and are reviewed in this chapter. A full list of UN treaties can be found on the UN Treaty Collection web page (UNTC, 2009).

Territory is definable as the area that a nation state regards as its own and exercises sovereignty over. This includes all water, subsoil, the airspace, the territorial sea and land under the territorial sea. Conquest is the taking of territory by military force; however, the use of force is

Table 9.5	Sources of legislation for the ICJ
Legal sources	**Examples of other influences**
International Conventions and Treaties	Equity and fairness
International Custom (generally accepted legal practice)	Other international organisations such as:
The decisions of highly qualified layers of different nations, e.g. the International Law Commission	The Council of Europe The European Union The African Union The Organisation of American states

Source: ICJ (2009)

Table 9.6	Key areas of international legislation

External responsibilities	Internal responsibilities
Territory, conquest and the use of force	Treatment of foreign nationals
The law and the sea	Environmental protection
	Human rights
	Terrorism and security
	Data protection

no longer legal under international law as stipulated in a series of UN charters, such as the 1970 Declaration of Principles of International Law. The UN has ruled that the Israeli invasion of Palestine in 1967 and the Iraqi invasion of Kuwait in 1990 have both involved the forceful taking of territory and were condemned as illegal by the UN Security Council at the time.

Disputes over territory in the Polar Regions have been common for many years, with Denmark, Norway, the Russian Federation and Canada making claims on the Artic and the USA, Argentina, Chile, France, Australia, Norway, the UK and New Zealand, claiming territorial rights in Antarctica. However, two main treaties, the Antarctic Treaty of 1961 and the 1991 Madrid Protocol on Environmental Protection, have designated the region for peaceful and scientific purposes, and prohibit all military incursions and activities relating to mineral resources until the year 2041. Dispute settlements in this area must be referred to the ICJ.

These conventions were primarily defined in 1982 with the Convention on the Law of the Sea which details the responsibilities of the nation state to:

- a territorial sea limit of 12 nautical miles;
- a delineation of territorial sea between adjacent states (for example, the Anglo-French division of the Straits of Dover);
- a peaceful passage through territorial waters;
- 'freedoms of' high seas (non-territorial);
- deep sea mining;
- nuclear testing
- confirmed nationality of ships; and
- the protection of the marine environment.

During 2008 the Laws of the Sea were a regular feature in news articles, highlighting acts of piracy in the Gulf of Aden and the Indian Ocean. Somali pirates held ships and crews for ransom until they were paid by the ship owners. It is estimated that in 2008 the owners of the hijacked ships handed over about $80 million in ransom payments (BBC, 2009e). Piracy is specifically covered in the Laws of the Sea and dictates that nation states may seize pirate ships and arrest the persons on board. This has lead to several nations sending their warships to patrol the area and capture pirate ships in the region.

State responsibility is the requirement of one state to another to observe international law. Hence if one nation state or one of its officials breaks an international law, the state may be liable. These laws also cover the treatment of foreign citizens in that they should be treated in a civilised manner and their human rights should be respected. For instance, the Organization of American States, the EU and the Organisation of African Unity have agreed on common criteria to be applied to refugees and asylum seekers.

Nation states have a responsibility for the environment both in their own territory and that affecting the neighbouring territory, and in recent years regulation in this area has increased dramatically. The Rio Declaration on the Environment (1992) declares that nation states must implement policies which protect and enhance the natural environment. One of the most notable agreements in this area is the Kyoto Protocol which came into force in 2005. Under this agreement, developed nation states are required to reduce their greenhouse gas emissions according to individual targets (UNFCC, 2009).

Since the advent of global sourcing, living and working conditions, health and education have become international issues. Together they can be categorised under the title of human rights. A number of international human rights treaties have been adopted since the signing of the United Nations Universal Declaration of Human Rights in1948. Unfortunately the UN Declaration of Human Rights was only a resolution, so while the content was well-meaning it was not legally binding. However all the declarations, principles, guidelines, rules and recommendations produced by the UN do at least provide moral guidance to nation states. They also serve as a blueprint for regional (e.g. EU) and national legislation, and provide a comprehensive body of legislation to protect individual and group human rights. The human rights covenants, statutes, protocols and conventions are, however, legally binding for those nations that ratify them. Nevertheless, putting the principles into practice is not always easy; developing countries, for instance, often have other pressing priorities such as sustaining food supplies and encouraging economic growth. Some of the key human rights UN treaties are listed in *Table 9.7*.

Another important legacy of the Declaration of Human Rights (1948) was the creation in Strasbourg of the European Court of Human Rights. Over the past 50 years this court has heard over 10,000 cases. Its rulings have been binding on the member states and have

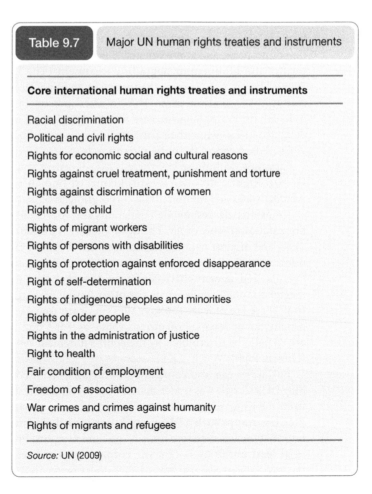

Table 9.7	Major UN human rights treaties and instruments

Core international human rights treaties and instruments

Racial discrimination

Political and civil rights

Rights for economic social and cultural reasons

Rights against cruel treatment, punishment and torture

Rights against discrimination of women

Rights of the child

Rights of migrant workers

Rights of persons with disabilities

Rights of protection against enforced disappearance

Right of self-determination

Rights of indigenous peoples and minorities

Rights of older people

Rights in the administration of justice

Right to health

Fair condition of employment

Freedom of association

War crimes and crimes against humanity

Rights of migrants and refugees

Source: UN (2009)

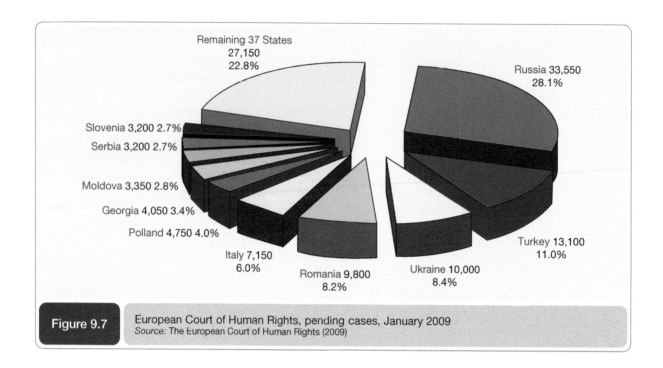

Figure 9.7	European Court of Human Rights, pending cases, January 2009
	Source: The European Court of Human Rights (2009)

resulted in many changes in legislation. In January 2009, there were more than 97,000 cases pending, more than half of these cited Russia, Turkey and Romania: see *Figure 9.7*. Most of the violations related to complaints on the fairness or the length of legal proceedings in the host country; 64 per cent of violations were concerning a right to a fair trial and the protection of property, and approximately 8 per cent concern the right to life or the prohibition of torture and inhuman or degrading treatment (The European Court of Human Rights, 2009). The cases range from the torture of an opposition leader in Azerbaijan (2007), to the compulsory isolation of an HIV-infected person in Sweden (2005). The UK is often indicted, for example in the case of a prohibition on marriage between father-in-law and daughter-in-law while their former spouses were still alive (2005). All these instances have violated the terms of the human rights Acts.

Currently, within the UN there is no equivalent court to that of the European Court of Human Rights, although a 'world court of human rights' that would try cases against member states and multinational corporations is often called for.

Unfortunately, despite the regulations and courts judgments, serious human rights violations still commonly occur. The death penalty is prohibited for juveniles under international treaty and in most national legislatures; the USA for example banned the execution of juveniles in 2005. However, since January 2005, five countries–Iran, Saudi Arabia, Sudan, Pakistan and Yemen – have confirmed that they have executed juvenile offenders. Iran has executed more juveniles than any other nation and, according to human rights lawyers in Iran, there are at least 130 juveniles on death row. For some offences, in Iran, the death penalty can be imposed on girls as young as 9 and boys from the age of 15, but the minimal age can also be determined by the court's judgment on when the child has reached puberty (Human Rights Watch, 2009).

Businesses can also come under scrutiny when it comes to human rights legislation. In May 2008 Google was under shareholder pressure to justify why it had submitted to pressure from the Chinese government to censor areas of the search engine in China (Google.cn). Pressure groups such as Amnesty International claim that censorship restricts freedom of information and therefore impacts on human rights. Pressure groups have called on Google to at least notify users that the content has been restricted due to legal pressure from the government. Google argued that it was better to comply with the Chinese government legislation and provide a somewhat restricted service to the Chinese population than to provide no form of service at all. It is unclear if this form of censorship is illegal under the terms of human rights legislation or if it is more of an ethical issue. However, Google became increasingly concerned by events in China and, in early 2010, was considering revising its position and withdrawing from the Chinese market.

9.12 Terrorism and security

Increasing cross-border terrorism has resulted in a rush of new national and international legislation in the areas such as intelligence sharing, illicit weapons trading, nuclear proliferation, money laundering, etc. As an example see *Minicase 9.6* on money laundering. Global security is also controlled through arms treaties and the Nuclear Non-Proliferation Treaty (1970). Since it came into force it has been ratified by 189 nations, including those that possess nuclear weapons, the USA, UK, France, China and Russia. All the signatory nations support disarmament, non-proliferation and the use of nuclear energy for peaceful means only. However, despite international pressure from non-nuclear nations, the nuclear countries still have substantial nuclear arsenals. It is estimated that Russia and the USA still own 23,000 active

Minicase 9.6	Money laundering

Money laundering is the means by which criminals conceal from investigators the source and original ownership of funds that are generated from illegal activities. The criminal intent is to convert income whether it is from embezzlement, fraud, bank robbery, smuggling or the drug trade into 'legitimate funds'.

Money can often be made to 'disappear' through, for example, the Caribbean and Pacific islands which have strict privacy laws and less than transparent banking systems. The Pacific island of Nauru, for instance, has 400 registered banks, despite only having a population of a few thousand citizens, and is widely considered to be the money laundering route of choice for the Russian mafia (BBC, 2001).

Tracking illegal funds can be a likened to looking for a 'needle in a haystack'. With millions of electronic transactions every day the investigators rely on 'tip-offs' from financial institutions whenever there is a suspicious transaction. Investigating only major transactions encourages the criminals to move money around in smaller amounts. The funding of terrorist activities is particularly difficult to trace: the sums used are often very small, e.g. $50,000, and are relatively easy to hide within legitimate business transactions. There are also suspicions that some charities might be used as fronts for money laundering. For example, in May 2009 the two founders of a Dallas-based Islamic 'charity' were given 65-year prison sentences after they were found guilty of illegally funneling $12.4 million to the Palestinian militant group Hamas. The 'charity' was claiming to be providing legitimate disaster relief aid to Palestinian refugees (Reuters, 2009).

If it is difficult to trace illegal funds through Western financial systems, it is harder still to trace laundered money through informal money transfer networks, such as those in the Middle East, India, Pakistan, Afghanistan and China. Many of these systems are hundreds of years old and are also used for legitimate purposes. Fortunately for the criminals, records are often not held and money is transferred by the use of tokens or passwords, with financial transactions being made predominantly based on trust.

Questions

1 Why is it so important that money laundering is stopped?
2 What actions can governments implement in order to make it easier to trace illegal funds?

warheads, sufficient to destroy the world many times over (BBC, 2009f). Nevertheless these same countries put pressure on nations such as India, Pakistan and North Korea who openly test their nuclear weapons and who are not signatories to the treaty.

9.12.1 Legal risks

Multinational companies are exposed to a wide range of potentially damaging risks as they trade in many different countries. The main risks can be categorised as legal, cultural or political and economic. The main legal risks are listed below:

- a general respect for the rule of law;
- level of enforcement, e.g. of intellectual property;
- contract enforceability;
- degree of corruption;
- impartial legal systems;
- efficiency of legal systems;
- transparency and governance;
- liability for sub-contractors.

Legal risks may be based on the differences in legislature, the way that the legal system works, the relative lack of legal enforcement, corruption and the lengthy delays and bureaucracy of the legal system. India is renowned for its corrupt officials and the backlog of untried cases which, according to the Chief Justice, at the current rate could take 466 years to clear. The UN development programme estimates that there are 20 million cases waiting to be heard in India, 646 of these are over 20 years old (Associated Press, 2009). The legal system in Japan does not have these problems and the legislature is broadly similar to European countries as it is based on the civil code of Germany and France. However, unlike these countries, Japan, prior to May 2009, did not even conduct severe crimes by jury (*Taipei Times*, 2009). Also in Japan, negligence cases are also more likely to be tried under the criminal system, even though a Western company might consider the circumstances to be relatively minor. Japanese contracts also tend to be light on detail, relying instead on the honesty of their business partners. However, when contracts are used, most of the terms and conditions should be familiar to European companies.

Corruption is a serious issue, particularly in many less developed countries. It causes problems to business by circumventing the legal processes and tends to protect the wealthy and powerful rather than the deserving. It may also slow down or subvert legal cases, making them too time-consuming and costly to administer. From a competitive perspective it may produce an unbalanced competitive market with bribes being paid for the award of contracts or the preferential distribution of goods.

Some risks, such as those connected with politics and currency, are outside the control of the company. Civil unrest, curfews, currency crises, terrorism, expropriation or confiscation of assets can also lead to unmanageable risk and significant financial loss. For those that require it, businesses can insure against specific political risks. For example, Western oil companies based in Nigeria may request insurance cover against acts of terrorism on their pipelines. As with all forms of insurance, the bigger the risk the larger the premium will be.

9.12.2 International dispute resolution

Disputes between transnational businesses cannot always be resolved in a national court. So when an international business dispute occurs, the complexity of the different jurisdictions and types of law make the legal process a difficult one to manage. As a starting point towards a resolution, the answers to the following five questions have to be agreed, some possible alternatives have also been listed:

1 Which countries' law should be used?
   a. The domestic law of one of the companies
   b. A country neutral to both parties
2 In which country (forum) should the hearing be resolved?
   a. The home country of one of the companies
   b. A country neutral to both parties
3 Which system should be used to resolve the dispute?
   a. Negotiation
   b. Mediation
   c. Arbitration
   d. Litigation
4 Will both parties be bound by the resolution?
5 How shall it be enforced?

Fortunately, in anticipation of possible disputes, most of these details are already agreed and stipulated in the terms and conditions of the contract. However if a company has not specified a choice of law to resolve disputes, then under the 1980 Rome Convention on the law applicable to contracts, the contract is governed by the law of the nation that is most closely connected to the company that is implementing the contract. In this chapter's opening *Minicase 13.1* (The Danone–Wahaha feud), the JVs were all based and managed in China, therefore Chinese laws mainly applied to the dispute resolution. The outcomes of this decision are important to international businesses, as different national jurisdictions will apply a more or less favourable history of litigation with larger or smaller compensation rulings. For instance, US law typically awards higher settlements in product defect cases than courts in European countries.

Expensive, time-consuming and potentially embarrassing litigation through the courts is only one mechanism to achieve a resolution to a business dispute. Many international business disputes are actually settled without litigation and outside of a court of law. Mediation or arbitration are the alternative means to achieve a resolution. Mediation is a simple and relatively informal process where a neutral mediator supervises the process, provides advice and works with both parties to find agreement. It is important to note that the mediator is a facilitator in this process rather than a judge. Under arbitration, however, the process is more akin to an informal court case where an arbiter acts as a judge, or 'neutral' as they are known. The lawyers for each side present their arguments and the neutral proposes a solution to resolve the dispute. This judgment can be legally binding if the parties have agreed this in advance, but even non-binding arbitration can often provide a means towards constructive negotiation.

There are a numerous organisations that are willing to act as arbiters in order to resolve business disputes. These include the International Center for the Settlement of Investment Disputes (ICSID), which is a part of the World Bank in Washington, and the Paris-based International Chamber of Commerce (ICC), which provides international dispute resolution services to over 500 businesses a year. Dispute resolution may be managed through the ICC's Amicable Dispute Resolution (ADR) service, dispute boards or the International Court of Arbitration.

In the Danone–Wahaha opening case, the Stockholm Chamber of Commerce arbitration service was stipulated in the contract and is being used to resolve the long-running dispute.

9.13 Conclusion

Businesses are increasingly interconnected by international trade which is regulated by national, regional and international laws and treaties. International businesses need to be aware of the differences between legislatures and other risks of conducting businesses overseas. When international disputes occur between companies, it is prudent to stipulate in a contract the arbitration services and the forms of law which are going to be used, so that a resolution may be achieved as soon as possible. Most disputes are the result of poor initial communication or unrealistic expectations. Businesses that are based on long-term partnerships are built upon trust and are the least likely to require legal intervention.

Summary of main points

In this chapter we have identified some of the issues in the legal environment that are important to countries, companies and individuals. The main points are:

- Laws are created and enforced at national, regional and international levels.
- National laws are based on historical precedents and culture and are used to regulate society.
- Different countries have different legal systems.
- The English legal system is based on a hierarchy of courts and is increasingly influenced by EU law.
- Significant EU legislation is bound into treaties and charters, covering fundamental rights, trade, consumer protection, social welfare and the environment.
- Business ownership is highly regulated and is based on differing liabilities.
- National, regional and international laws often have overlapping jurisdictions.
- Contract law governs both internal and external relationships.
- Contracts stipulate the terms and conditions of the agreement.
- Negligence and liability indictments range from small claims to large class actions and are pursued particularly vigorously in the USA.
- Criminal law can also be applied to businesses and the owners of businesses.
- Consumer protection is an old concept and aims to protect the consumer from poor quality goods and services and forms of mis-selling.
- Quality may be assured by the use of quality standards, accurate labelling and government enforcement.
- Proper use of personal data is unlikely to breach data protection laws, but organisations must manage the data appropriately.
- Governments and the EU protect the consumer by ensuring that businesses are not acting in collusion or are in a position to abuse monopoly power.
- Protecting intellectual property is vital in encouraging innovation and entrepreneurship.
- There are a number of organisations, such as the World Intellectual Property Organisation (WIPO) that provide multiple country patent protection services.
- Counterfeit goods create black markets which undermine product investment and reduce tax revenues.
- Employers have the legal responsibility to look after their employees in terms of their welfare and health and safety.
- Nation states can legislate to nationalise and control foreign ownership of domestic companies, and through sanctions and embargoes they can apply international pressure on other countries.
- International laws are agreed by nation states though international organisations such as the UN.

- The role of the International Court of Justice is to resolve disagreements between nations in a non-confrontational manner.
- The Declaration of Human Rights was the forerunner of a broad series of international treaties which have been incorporated into the legislature of many nations.
- The European Court of Human Rights pronounces on violations of human rights in its member states.
- State-sponsored violations of human rights occur in many nations regardless of international legislation or the nation's constitution.
- All international business involves some risk as there are many different and unknown variables, such as those in law.
- There are a number of international mediation services, such as the International Chamber of Commerce (ICC), to which companies can apply to in order to resolve international disputes.
- Negotiation, mediation, arbitration and litigation may all be used to solve disputes.

Discussion questions

1. With the use of examples, describe the main differences between common law and civil law.
2. Illustrating with examples, describe the different forms of tort law and demonstrate how liability might effect businesses.
3. List, with examples, six different areas of law concerned with consumer protection.
4. Which regulators govern competition law in the USA, EU and the UK?
5. Discuss three types of national laws which will impact international business ownership and trade.
6. In the case of international disputes, which questions do the companies have to answer before the dispute resolution process starts and which organisation(s) might they turn to for assistance?

Further reading/sources of information

The web links below provide the most up-to-date sources. Access to any topic should be possible through the links.

Data Protection (**www.guardianedge.com/resources/data-protection.php**) Worldwide interactive data protection laws map, podcasts and datasheets.

EU Commission (**http://ec.europa.eu/competition/index_en.html**) EU Commission, competition rulings and past cases by industry.

Human Rights Watch (**www.hrw.org/en/home**) Human rights watch, news, podcasts and videos from around the world.

International Centre for the Settlement for International Disputes (**http://icsid.worldbank.org/ICSID/Index.jsp**) World Bank, International Centre for the Settlement for International Disputes (ICSID), details of current and past disputes.

International Chamber of Commerce (**www.iccwbo.org/id96/index.html**) How the International Chamber of Commerce (ICC) works.

International Court of Justice (**www.icj-cij.org/homepage/index.php?p1=0**) The International Court of Justice (ICJ) home page, cases and rulings.

International Law (**www.law.cornell.edu/world/** and **http://www.jus.uio.no/lm/index.html**) For two excellent sources of material on international law and trade law by country.

Statute Law (**www.statutelaw.gov.uk/**) The UK statute law database enables you to view UK laws and trace how they have changed over time.

Strange Court Cases (**www.paralegaltraining.net/blog/strange-court-cases**) A fun website with examples of strange court cases from around the world.

United Nation (**www.un.org/en/rights/** and **http://www2.ohchr.org/english/law/index.htm#core**) The United Nations (UN) human rights home page, news, cases, humanitarian affairs and international law.

UN treaties (**http://treaties.un.org/Pages/UNTSOnline.aspx?id=1**) Listing of current UN treaties and who has ratified them.

World Intellectual Property Organisation (**www.wipo.int/pct/en/distance_learning/**) World Intellectual Property Organisation (WIPO) free internet course on the patent co-operation treaty (PCT).

World Intellectual Property Organisation (**www.wipo.int/portal/index.html.en**) How the World Intellectual Property Organisation (WIPO) works and the services it provides.

Adams, A. (2006) *Law for Business Students,* 4th edn. Harlow: Pearson Education.

Keenan, D. and Riches, S. (2005) *Business Law,* 7th edn. Harlow: Pearson Education.

Wallace, R.M.M. (2005) *International Law,* 5th edn. London: Thompson.

References

Arnott, S. (2008) Primark Drops Three Indian Suppliers for Using Child Workers. *The Independent,* 17 June [online], available from **www.independent.co.uk/news/business/news/primark-drops-three-indian-suppliers-for-using-child-workers-848564.html**

Associated Press (2009) It Would Take Delhi HC 466 Year to Clear the Backlog: CJ (sic), *Express India,* 13 February [online], available from **www.expressindia.com/latest-news/It-would-take-Delhi-HC-466-yrs-to-clear-backlog-CJ/423127/**

BBC (2001) Tiny Island Talks Tough on Tax Havens, available from **http://news.bbc.co.uk/1/hi/business/1496492.stm**

BBC (2003) The Enron Affair, available from **http://news.bbc.co.uk/1/hi/in_depth/business/2002/enron/default.stm**

BBC (2004). Oil Giant Shell's Investors Shocked, available from **http://news.bbc.co.uk/1/hi/business/3890045.stm**

BBC (2005) Afghan Warlord Guilty of Torture, available from **http://news.bbc.co.uk/1/hi/uk/4693239.stm**

BBC (2006) DR Congo Arms Embargo Failing, available from **http://news.bbc.co.uk/1/hi/world/africa/6055864.stm**

BBC (2007) Card Companies Lose Refund Case, available from **http://news.bbc.co.uk/1/hi/business/7070720.stm**

BBC (2009a) Italy Passes Emergency Rape Law, available from **http://news.bbc.co.uk/1/hi/world/europe/7902107.stm**

BBC (2009b) One Music – How to Copyright, available from **http://www.bbc.co.uk/radio1/onemusic/legal/copyrightp03.shtml**

BBC (2009c) £30k Fine After Employee Death, available from **http://news.bbc.co.uk/1/hi/northern_ireland/8097373.stm**

BBC (2009d) Iran Air Part Sales Trio Jailed, available from http://news.bbc.co.uk/1/hi/england/berkshire/8083791.stm

BBC (2009e) Somali Pirates Seize Another Boat, available from http://news.bbc.co.uk/1/hi/world/africa/7994980.stm

BBC (2009f) Obama Seeks Thaw in US–Russia Ties, available from http://news.bbc.co.uk/1/hi/programmes/from_our_own_correspondent/8133457.stm

Business Week (2005) Chávez' Oil-fueled Revolution. *Business Week* 10 October [online], available from www.businessweek.com/magazine/content/05_41/b3954088.htm

Carroll, R. (2009) Obama Will Use Spring Summit to Bring Cuba in From the Cold *The Guardian*, 8 March [online], available from www.guardian.co.uk/world/2009/mar/08/cuba-obama-administration

CNN (2009) Court Grants Appeal in Suu Kyi Case. *CNN.com*, 17 June [online], available from http://edition.cnn.com/2009/WORLD/asiapcf/06/17/myanmar.suu.kyi/index.html

DePalma A. (2000) Mexico Is Ordered to Pay a US Company $16.7 Million. *The New York Times*, 31 August [online], available from www.nytimes.com/2000/08/31/business/international-business-mexico-is-ordered-to-pay-a-us-company-16.7-million.html?scp=1&sq=metalclad%20mexico&st=cse&pagewanted=2

Dzirutwe, M. (2009) Mining Firms in Zimbabwe Challenge Ownership Law. *Reuters*, 8 May [online], available from http://uk.reuters.com/article/idUKL7100933320090508

Eironline (2006) European Court Finds UK in Breach of Working Time Directive, available from www.eurofound.europa.eu/eiro/2006/10/articles/UK0610029I.htm

Europa (2009a) Latest Figures on Fines, Statistics, available from http://ec.europa.eu/competition/cartels/overview/index_en.html

Europa (2009b) Mergers: Commission Clears Proposed Takeover of SN Brussels Airlines by Lufthansa, available from http://europa.eu/rapid/pressReleasesAction.do?reference=IP/09/974&format=HTML&aged=0&language=EN&guiLanguage=en

Europa (2009c) Mergers: Commission Approves Proposed Acquisition of MyTravel Group by KarstadtQuelle, available from http://europa.eu/rapid/pressReleasesAction. do?reference=IP/07/614

European Commission (2008) Customs: Commission Publishes 2007 Customs Seizures of Counterfeit Goods at the EU's External Border, available from http://europa.eu/rapid/pressReleasesAction.do?reference=IP/08/757

Fathi, N. (2009) Iran's Top Leader Dashes Hopes for a Compromise. *The New York Times*, 19 June [online], available from www.nytimes.com/2009/06/20/world/middleeast/20iran.html

Food Standards Agency (2009) Understanding Labeling Rules, available from www.food.gov.uk/foodlabelling/ull/

Fulbright (2008) Fifth Annual Litigation Survey Findings, available from www.fulbright.com/index.cfm?fuseaction=news.detail&article_id=7637&site_id=286

Gibb, F. (2008) Fortune Tellers Targeted in New Consumer Protection Regulations. *Timesonline*, 23 May [online], available from http://business.timesonline.co.uk/tol/business/law/article3987725.ece

Global Competition Review (2009) Getting the Deal Through, Cartel Regulation, available from www.gettingthedealthrough.com/narrative_pdf.php?id=126

Goldenberg, S. (2009) With One Draft Order, Obama Signals the End of Guantanamo. *The Guardian*, 22 January [online], available from www.guardian.co.uk/world/2009/jan/22/obama-ends-guantanamo

Harris, J. (2006) Hammonds Wins Football League Claims, but Pays £4 Damages. *The Lawyer*, 23 June [online], available from www.thelawyer.com/hammonds-wins-football-league-claim-but-pays-%C2%A34-damages/120618.article

Harris, N. (2006) Football League Sues its Solicitors Over ITV Digital Collapse. *The Independent*, 9 February [online], available from www.independent.co.uk/sport/football/football-league/football-league-sues-its-solicitors-over-itv-digital-collapse-465976.html

Herman, M. and Jordan, D. (2007) Cadbury Fined £1 Million Over Salmonella Outbreak. *Timesonline,* 16 July [online], available from **http://business.timesonline.co.uk/tol/ business/industry_sectors/consumer_goods/article2083030.ece**

Hu, J. (2003) AOL, Microsoft's Peace a Sign of Times (sic). *Cnet news,* 23 May [online], available from **http://news.cnet.com/AOL,**-Microsofts-peace-a-sign-of-times/2100-1026_ 3-1011700.html

Human Rights Watch (2009). Secret Execution of Juvenile Offender, available from **www.hrw.org/en/news/2009/05/01/iran-secret-execution-juvenile-offender**

ICJ (2009) List of Cases Referred to the Court Since 1946 by Date of Introduction, available from **www.icj-cij.org/docket/index.php?p1=3&p2=2**

ICO (2009) Data Protection Act: The Basics, available from **www.ico.gov.uk/what_we_ cover/data_protection/the_basics.aspx**

Khattar, S. (2009) Education is Key to Abolish Child Labour (sic). *The Times of India,* 15 June [online], available from **http://timesofindia.indiatimes.com/Education-is-key-to- abolish-child-labour/articleshow/4656555.cms**

Kravets, D. (2007) Napster Trial Ends Seven Years Later, Defining Online Sharing Along the Way. *wired,* 31 August [online], available from **www.wired.com/threatlevel/2007/08/ napster-trial-e/**

Lawfuel (2007) Hong Kong, June 11, 2007, available from **www.lawfuel.com/show-release. asp?ID=12984**

Lipton, E. and Barboza, D. (2007) As More Toys are Recalled, Trail Ends in China. *The New York Times,* 19 June [online], available from **www.nytimes.com/2007/06/19/business/ worldbusiness/ 19toys.html**

Lynn, J, (2009) Cybersquatting Cases Hit Record in 2008. *Reuters,* 15 March [online], available from **www.reuters.com/article/technologyNews/idUSTRE52E22G20090315**

Market Share (2009) Browser Market Share, available from **http://marketshare.hitslink. com/browser-market-share.aspx?qprid=0**

Morris, S. (2009) Company Director Faces First Corporate Manslaughter Charge. *Guardian,* 17 June [online], available from **www.guardian.co.uk/uk/2009/jun/17/mudslide-corpo- rate-manslaughter-charge**

Massey, R. (2009) Mandelson Mulls Vauxhall Rescue After GM Warning. *This Is Money,* 6 March [online], available from **http://www.thisismoney.co.uk/markets/article.html? in_article_id=480172&in_page_id=3**

Meyer, D. (2009) Psion Settle Netbook® Trademark Dispute. *Cnet news,* 1 June [online], available from **http://news.cnet.com/8301-1001_3-10253210-92.html**

Prosser, D. (2008) BA Chiefs Charged in Price Fixing Case. *The Independent,* 8 August [online], available from **www.independent.co.uk/news/business/news/ba-chiefs- chargedin-price-fixing-case-888370.html**

Public Citizen (1999) Legal Myths: The McDonald's 'Hot Coffee' Case, available from **http://www.citizen.org/print_article.cfm?ID=785**

Reuters (2009) Islamic Charity Leaders Get 65 Year Jail Terms, available from **www.reuters .com/article/domesticNews/idUSTRE54Q6AP20090527**

Sabbagh, D. (2007) GMTV Fined Record £2 Million by Watchdog Over Phone-in Scandal. *Timesonline,* 26 September [online], available from **http://business.timesonline.co.uk/tol/ business/industry_sectors/media/article2536674.ece**

Spooner, J.G. (2005) Dell: Dispute Over Muslim Prayers Resolved. *Cnet News,* 21 March, available at **http://news.cnet.com/Dell-Dispute-over-Muslim-prayers-resolved/2110- 1047_3-5628889.html**

Taipei Times (2009) Launch of Japanese Jury System Arouses Concern, available from **www.taipeitimes.com/News/world/archives/2009/05/22/2003444186**

The European Court of Human Rights (2009) Some Facts and Figures: 1959–2009, available from **www.echr.coe.int/NR/rdonlyres/65172EB7-DE1C-4BB8-93B1-B28676C2C844/0/ FactsAndFiguresEN.pdf**

Transparency International (2009) 2008 Corruption Perceptions Index, available from **www.transparency.org/news_room/in_focus/2008/cpi2008/cpi_2008_table**

Tribunals Service (2009) Home page, available from **www.tribunals.gov.uk/**

UN (2009) The Universal Declaration of Human Rights, available from **www.un.org/en/documents/udhr/**

UNCITRAL (2009) Status: 1980 – United Nations Convention on Contracts for the International Sale of Goods, available from **www.uncitral.org/uncitral/en/uncitral_texts/sale_goods/1980CISG_status.html**

UNFCC (2009) Kyoto Protocol, available from **unfccc.int/kyoto_protocol/items/2830.php**

UNTC (2009) United National Treaty Series, available from **http://treaties.un.org/Pages/UNTSOnline.aspx?id=1**

US Legal 500 (2008) Mass Tort and Class Action: Toxic Tort, available from **www.legal500.com/c/us/litigation/mass-tort-and-class-action-plaintiff-representation-toxic-tort**

WHO (2006) Counterfeit Medicines: Fact Sheet, available from **www.who.int/medicines/services/counterfeit/impact/ImpactF_S/en/**

CHAPTER 10
Analysing the strategic environment

LEARNING OUTCOMES

When you have worked through this chapter, you will be able to:

- explain why it is important to study the environment of the organisation;
- outline the main environmental influences on the organisation and relate the degree of change to prescriptive and emergent strategic approaches;
- undertake a PESTEL analysis of the general influences on the organisation;
- understand the implications of market growth and market cyclicality for strategic management;
- identify the key factors for success in an industry;
- carry out a Five Forces Analysis of the specific influences on the organisation;
- develop a Four Links Analysis of the organisation's co-operators;
- undertake a competitor profile and identify the competitor's advantages;
- explore the relationship between the organisation and its customers.

INTRODUCTION

In recent years, the term 'environment' has taken on a rather specialised meaning: it involves 'green' issues and the poisoning of our planet by human activity. These concerns are certainly part of our considerations in this book, but we use the term 'environment' in a much broader sense to describe everything and everyone outside the organisation. This includes customers, competitors, suppliers, distributors, government and social institutions.

As the starting point in the development of both prescriptive and emergent strategy, it is useful to begin by exploring the nine basic analytical tools of the environment that will influence the organisation's strategy (see Figure 10.1). Elements of the environment can change so the organisation needs to adjust its strategy accordingly. Prescriptive strategies will want to anticipate how the environment will change in the future in order to meet future needs ahead of competing organisations. Emergent strategies will be content with an understanding of the environment.

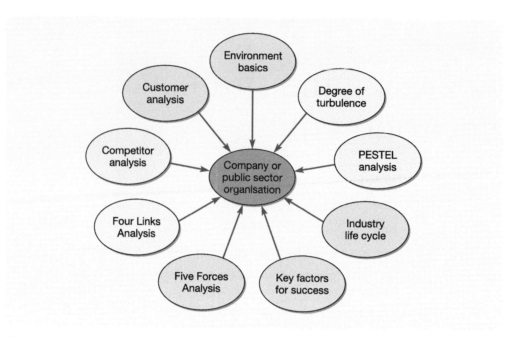

Figure 10.1 Analysing the strategic environment – the nine basic analytical tools

The Blockbuster video store chain was the subject of an $8.4 billion takeover in 1994. Twenty years later, the business was just a memory. Why? What are the implications for analysing the strategic environment?

By 2014, Blockbuster stores were just empty shells, the victim of technology change and questionable strategy
Photo courtesy of Steve Corbett

Background

Back in 1994, the Blockbuster video store chain was a fast-growing group of retail stores that hired out video films. It had begun in the USA and was beginning to expand into Europe. Each store had a wide range of the latest Hollywood films that were rented over night by customers to play on their home video recorders and then return the following day. The company had special contracts with the major film companies to ensure that it was able to stock the latest films soon after showing in cinemas. It kept 60 per cent of the rental income and passed the other 40 per cent back to the film studios: a viable business model at that time.

Blockbuster takeover

In 1994, the US media conglomerate Viacom acquired Blockbuster for $8.4 billion. Viacom was partially interested in Blockbuster's $1.5 billion cash which it needed for another acquisition, Paramount Pictures. It was also possible that it over-valued Blockbuster even at that time because the Blockbuster profits were much lower in the year after its sale. But Viacom continued to invest in the store chain over the next ten years. In addition, there were reported to be synergies from the purchase that would benefit both companies. They would come from cross-marketing Viacom's MTV television channels with Blockbuster and from selling add-on merchandise like *Star Trek* watches – part of the Viacom franchise – through Blockbuster stores. None of this happened. According to one insider at Viacom, 'The MTV folks were very protective of their domain.'

Nevertheless by 2004, Blockbuster group was reported to employ 60,000 people and have 9,000 stores. It had moved to sell DVDs alongside its VHS tapes as the technology changed. It also expanded into DVD delivery by mail for those customers unable or unwilling to visit its stores. But it was facing major competition from other retail outlets. Blockbuster's suppliers, the film studios, had begun selling film videos directly to its competitors. These retail outlets included supermarkets who were able to sell rather than rent video tapes and discs. Moreover, they were able to compete at very low prices. Initially, Blockbuster had rejected the concept of selling low profit margin DVDs because it would cannibalise its more profitable rental income. But the competitive pressures were too great.

Perhaps to the surprise of some commentators, Viacom then sold the Blockbuster chain in 2004 for just under $900 million. Part of the reason for the sale was that Viacom had other media priorities such as further investment in its BET (Black Entertainment Television) and MTV (Music Television) networks. But Viacom could also see the future and Blockbuster was making losses by this time.

Technology change

Over the years to 2004, there was a substantial change in technology. Not only were DVDs replacing video tapes, but also broadband was beginning to deliver fast and large computer files to some customers. New companies were springing up to exploit this change. For example, a small company called Netflix was expanding: it was already selling DVDs by mail but it was also beginning to deliver the same content by broadband in the USA. It is reported that Blockbuster turned down the opportunity to acquire Netflix in year 2000 for $50 million.

The outcome

In 2004, Viacom sold its subsidiary at the right time. Blockbuster's brand name and range of film and television contracts were its chief assets. But the company's chain of retail stores was a liability when customers could obtain the same product without leaving their homes. The internet revolution was about to claim one of its early victims.

In 2010, Blockbuster still had 4,000 stores in the USA and 2,500 stores in other countries. The company could still see a future for its business up to that time. However, broadband speeds were increasing. More customers were learning how to download media. Companies like Netflix, LoveFilm in Europe and Hulu in the USA were expanding fast. Blockbuster filed for bankruptcy in late 2010. Some 1,700 stores were acquired by Dish TV for $300 million (including debts) with the rest being closed over the next three years.

By 2014, the Blockbuster company had completely disappeared. However, the name was still present in a chain of video rental kiosks called 'Blockbuster Express,' but this company had no connection with the original company and was still a viable business.

Case questions

1 What elements of strategic analysis are relevant here? Would scenario building have helped Blockbuster strategy around year 2000?

2 Are other industries threatened by the internet in the same way as Blockbuster? What strategy would you recommend for these industries?

10.1 EXPLORING THE COMPETITIVE ENVIRONMENT

10.1.1 Why studying the competitive environment is important

Definition ▶ **In strategy, the environment means everything and everyone outside the organisation: competitors, customers, suppliers plus other influential institutions such as local and national governments.** Strategists are agreed that an understanding of the competitive environment is an essential element of the development of strategic management. It is important to study the environment surrounding the organisation for three main reasons. First, most organisations compete against others – for example, films like *Lord of the Rings* compete against other films for finance from the film studios – see Case 10.4. Hence a study of the environment will provide information on the nature of competition as a step to developing *sustainable competitive advantage.*[2] Sustainable competitive advantage is an advantage over competitors that cannot easily be imitated. Second, most organisations will perceive *opportunities* that might be explored and *threats* that need to be contained.[3] For example, the *Lord of the Rings* trilogy was seen by some film backers to have more threats than opportunities. Such opportunities and threats may come not just from competitors but also from government decisions, changes in technology and social developments and many other factors. Third, there are opportunities for networks and other linkages, which lead to sustainable co-operation. For example, Peter Jackson met his old friend

Mark Ordesky when needing some help in the final negotiations to finance *Lord of the Rings*. Such linkages with others may strengthen an organisation in its environment by providing mutual support. By contrast, Blockbuster – see Case 10.1 – shows what can happen when companies fail to exploit such linkages.

However, there are three difficulties in determining the connection between the organisation's strategic management and its environment.

1 *The prescriptive versus emergent debate.* The first problem arises from the fundamental disagreement about the strategic management processes that were explored in Part 1 of this book. Some prescriptive strategists take the view that, in spite of the various uncertainties, the environment can usefully be predicted for many markets. Some (but not all) emergent strategists believe that the environment is so turbulent and chaotic that prediction is likely to be inaccurate and serve no useful purpose. Each of these interpretations implies a quite different status for the same basic topic. This difficulty is explored further in Section 10.2.

2 *The uncertainty.* Whatever view is taken about prediction, all strategists regard the environment as uncertain. New strategies have to be undertaken against a backdrop that cannot be guaranteed and this difficulty must be addressed as strategies are developed. For example, Case 10.4 shows that the risks were so high in financing the film *Lord of the Rings* that nearly every studio declined to finance it. Uncertainty was initially lower at Blockbuster, but new technology changed all that.

3 *The range of influences.* It is conceivable, at least in theory, that every element of an organisation's environment may influence strategic management. One solution to the problem posed by such a wide range of factors might be to produce a list of every element. This would be a strategic mistake, however, because organisations and individuals would find it difficult to develop and manage every item. In strategic management, the production of comprehensive lists that include every major eventuality and have no priorities has no value. A better solution is to identify the key factors for success in the industry and then to direct the environmental analysis towards these factors. This is considered later in this chapter in Section 10.6.

10.1.2 The main elements of environmental analysis

To analyse an organisation's environment, while at the same time addressing the three difficulties outlined in Section 10.1.1, certain basic analytical procedures can be undertaken (see Table 10.1).

10.1.3 The distinction between proactive and reactive outcomes

When analysing the environment, it is useful to draw a distinction between two types of results from the analysis:

1 *Proactive outcomes.* The environmental analysis will identify positive opportunities or negative threats. The organisation will then develop proactive strategies to exploit or cope with the situation. For example, film producers might develop cross-financing co-operation as a result of identifying new market opportunities.

2 *Reactive outcomes.* The environmental analysis will highlight important strategic changes over which the organisation has no control but to which, if they happen, it will need to be able to react. For example, new EU legislation on cultural content and investment might influence strategic activity in the European film industry.

Table 10.1 Nine basic stages in environmental analysis

Stage	Techniques	Outcome of stage
1 Environment basics – an opening evaluation to define and explore basic characteristics of the environment (*see* Section 10.2)	Estimates of some basic factors surrounding the environment: • Market definition and size • Market growth • Market share	Basic strategic analysis: • Scope the strategic opportunity • Establish future growth prospects • Begin to structure market competition
2 Consideration of the degree of turbulence in the environment (*see* Section 10.3)	General considerations: • Change: fast or slow? • Repetitive or surprising future? • Forecastable or unpredictable? • Complex or simple influences on the organisation?	Guidance on initial questions: • Is the environment too turbulent to undertake useful predictions? • What are the opportunities and threats for the organisation?
3 Background factors that influence the competitive environment (*see* Section 10.4)	PESTEL analysis and scenarios	• Identify key influences • Predict, if possible • Understand interconnections between events
4 Analysis of stages of market growth (*see* Section 10.5)	Industry life cycle	• Identify growth stage • Consider implications for strategy • Identify maturity, over-production and cyclicality issues
5 Factors specific to the industry: what delivers success? (*see* Section 10.6)	Key factors for success analysis	• Identify factors relevant to strategy • Focus strategic analysis and development
6 Factors specific to the competitive balance of power in the industry (*see* Section 10.7)	Five Forces Analysis	• Static and descriptive analysis of competitive forces
7 Factors specific to co-operation in the industry (*see* Section 10.8)	Four Links Analysis	• Analysis of current and future organisations with whom co-operation is possible • Network analysis
8 Factors specific to immediate competitors (*see* Section 10.9)	Competitor analysis and product portfolio analysis	• Competitor profile • Analysis of relative market strengths
9 Customer analysis (*see* Section 10.10)	Market and segmentation studies	• Strategy targeted at existing and potential customers • Market segmentation and positioning within segment

In both cases, the environment will need to be analysed but the strategic implications are very different.

> ## KEY STRATEGIC PRINCIPLES
>
> - Environmental analysis is important because it helps in developing sustainable competitive advantage, identifies opportunities and threats and may provide opportunities for productive co-operation with other organisations.
> - There are three difficulties in studying the environment: the use to which the analysis will be put; uncertainty in the topic; coping with the wide range of environmental influences.
> - Environmental analysis can be used to provide a *proactive* strategy outcome or highlight a *reactive* strategic situation that will need to be monitored.

10.2   STRATEGIC ENVIRONMENT – THE BASICS

In order to begin the environmental analysis, it is useful to start with some basic factors that are sometimes forgotten in the academic concepts but contribute to the strategic analysis of the environment.[4] We can divide the basics into three areas:

1 Market definition and size

2 Market growth

3 Market share

10.2.1   Market definition and size[5]

In analysing the strategic environment, most organisations will want an answer to the basic question – 'What is the size of the market?' This is important because it will assist in defining the strategic task. Markets are usually described in terms of annual sales. From a strategy perspective, a 'large' market may be more attractive than a 'small' market. The words 'large' and 'small' need to be defined carefully – for example, a 'large' opportunity to Peter Jackson who directed the major film trilogy *Lord of the Rings* might be $200 million – see Case 10.4 later in this chapter. However, a 'large' opportunity to Warner Brothers who ultimately funded the film and have much broader film interests might be $1 billion. Despite such problems, it is a useful starting point to attempt to assess the strategic opportunity (or the lack of it).

Measuring market size raises a related problem – how to define the 'market'. For example, is the annual market for the film trilogy *Lord of the Rings* (LOTR) defined as *fantasy films* only – worth, say, $500 million? Or is the annual LOTR market *all adventure films*, including *Lord of the Rings* but also covering others from James Bond films to those starring Clint Eastwood – worth, say, $10 billion? The answer will depend on the customers and the extent to which other products are a real substitute. Although some market definitions may seem obvious – for example, 'the ice cream market' would seem to be clearly defined – they need to be treated with care: perhaps another snack will substitute for ice cream and should be included within the definition?

10.2.2   Market growth

In establishing the size of the market, it is also common practice to estimate how much the market has grown over the previous period – usually the previous year. From a strategy perspective, the importance of growth relates to the organisation's objectives. An organisation wishing to grow rapidly might be more attracted to a market growing rapidly. Clearly any such estimate also needs to take into account the argument about market definition made above.

10.2.3 Market share

Although some strategists disagree, a large share of a market is usually regarded as being strategically beneficial.[6] The reason is that a large share may make it possible to influence prices and may also reduce costs through scope for economics of scale, thereby increasing profitability.[7] Clearly, there are definitional problems here – see Section 10.2.1 above – but some estimate of market share is desirable from a strategy perspective. In practice, it may be difficult to establish a precise market share – for example, the share of the film market taken by *Lord of the Rings* in 2002 will depend on the fact that it had a high share during the few weeks after its general release and greatest popularity – but this may not matter. From a strategy perspective, the important point is that *Lord of the Rings* took a significant share of the *fragmented* film market during that year. Equally, there will be other strategic circumstances where a *dominant* share may be identified – for example, the market share held by companies supplying domestic water to households – without necessarily being able to measure the precise share.

KEY STRATEGIC PRINCIPLES

- Environmental analysis can usefully begin with a basic assessment of the market definition and size, the market growth and the market share.
- Market definition is important because it will determine the size and scope of the strategic opportunity. Market definition will be defined by a consideration of customers and the availability of substitute products.
- Market growth is commonly estimated early in any strategic analysis because of its importance with regard to the growth objectives of an organisation.
- A basic estimate of market share can be used to estimate whether an organisation has a significant share of a market as a starting point in exploring the strategic implications.

10.3 DEGREE OF TURBULENCE IN THE ENVIRONMENT[8]

At the general level of environmental analysis, it is important to consider the basic conditions surrounding the organisation. Special attention needs to be directed to the nature and strength of the forces driving strategic change – the *dynamics* of the environment. One reason for this consideration is that, if the forces are exceptionally turbulent, they may make it difficult to use some of the analytical techniques – like Porter's 'Five Forces', discussed later in this chapter. Another reason is that the nature of the environment may influence the way that the organisation is structured to cope with such changes.

The environmental forces surrounding the organisation can be assessed according to two main measures:

Definition ▶ 1 **Changeability – the degree to which the environment is likely to change.** For example, there is low changeability in the liquid milk market and high changeability in the various internet markets.

Definition ▶ 2 **Predictability – the degree to which such changes can be predicted.** For example, changes can be predicted with some certainty in the mobile telephone market but remain largely unknown in biogenetics.

These measures can each be subdivided further. Changeability comprises:

- *Complexity* – the degree to which the organisation's environment is affected by factors such as internationalisation and technological, social and political complications.
- *Novelty* – the degree to which the environment presents the organisation with new situations.

Table 10.2 Assessing the dynamics of the environment

	Environmental turbulence	Repetitive	Expanding	Changing	Discontinuous	Surprising
Changeability	*Complexity*	National	National	Regional Technological	Regional Socio-political	Global Economic
	Familiarity of events	Familiar	Extrapolable		Discontinuous Familiar	Discontinuous Novel
Predictability	*Rapidity of change*	Slower than response		Comparable to response		Faster than response
	Visibility of future	Recurring	Forecastable	Predictable	Partially predictable	Unpredictable surprises
	Turbulence level	Low 1	2	3	4	5 High

Source: Ansoff, I and McDonnell, E (1990) *Implanting Strategic Management*, FT Prentice-Hall. With permission.

Predictability can be further subdivided into:

- *rate of change* of the environment (from slow to fast);
- *visibility of the future* in terms of the availability and usefulness of the information used to predict the future.

Using these factors as a basis, it is then possible to build a spectrum that categorises the environment and provides a rating for its *degree of turbulence* (see Table 10.2).

When turbulence is low, it may be possible to predict the future with confidence. For example, film companies like Warner Brothers might be able to use data on their film customers around the world, along with international economic data, to predict future demand for different types of films.

When turbulence is higher, such predictions may have little meaning. The changeability elements influencing the organisation may contain *many* and *complex* items and the *novelty* being introduced into the market place may be high. For example, new services, new suppliers, new ideas, new software and new payment systems were all being launched for the internet at the same time. Turbulence was high. Predicting the specific outcome of such developments was virtually impossible.

If the level of turbulence is high – called *hypercompetition*[9] by some strategists – and as a result the environment is difficult to study, the analysis recommended in some of the sections that follow may need to be treated with some caution. However, for most fast-growing situations, including the internet, there is merit in at least attempting to understand the main areas of the environment influencing the organisation. It may not be possible to undertake formal predictions, but it will certainly be possible to identify the most important elements.

KEY STRATEGIC PRINCIPLES

- It is important to begin an analysis of the environment with a general consideration of the degree of turbulence in that environment. If it is high, then this will make prediction difficult and impact on prescriptive approaches to strategy development.
- There are two measures of turbulence: changeability, i.e. the degree to which the environment is likely to change; and predictability, i.e. the degree to which such change can be predicted.
- Each of the two measures can then be further subdivided: changeability can be split into complexity and novelty; predictability can be divided into rate of change and visibility of the future. All these elements can then be used to explore turbulence.

10.4 ANALYSING THE GENERAL ENVIRONMENT

In any consideration of the factors surrounding the organisation, two techniques can be used to explore the general environment: these are the PESTEL checklist and scenarios.

10.4.1 PESTEL checklist

Definition ▶

It is already clear that there are no simple rules governing an analysis of the organisation. Each analysis needs to be guided by what is relevant for that particular organisation. However, it may be useful to begin the process with **the PESTEL checklist, which consists of the Political, Economic, Socio-cultural, Technological, Environmental and Legal aspects of the environment.**

Exhibit 10.1 presents some of the main items that might be considered when undertaking a PESTEL analysis.

EXHIBIT 10.1

Checklist for a PESTEL analysis

Political future

- Political parties and alignments at local, national and European or regional trading-block level
- Legislation, e.g. on taxation and employment law
- Relations between government and the organisation (possibly influencing the preceding items in a major way and forming a part of future strategic management)
- Government ownership of industry and attitude to monopolies and competition

Socio-cultural future

- Shifts in values and culture
- Change in lifestyle
- Attitudes to work and leisure
- 'Green' environmental issues
- Education and health
- Demographic changes
- Distribution of income

Economic future

- Total GDP and GDP per head
- Inflation
- Consumer expenditure and disposable income
- Interest rates
- Currency fluctuations and exchange rates

- Investment - by the state, private enterprise and foreign companies
- Cyclicality
- Unemployment
- Energy costs, transport costs, communications costs, raw materials costs

Technological future

- Government and EU investment policy
- Identified new research initiatives
- New patents and products
- Speed of change and adoption of new technology
- Level of expenditure on R&D by organisation's rivals
- Developments in nominally unrelated industries that might be applicable

Environmental future

- 'Green' issues that affect the environment and impact on the company
- Level and type of energy consumed - renewable energy?
- Rubbish, waste and its disposal

Legal future

- Competition law and government policy
- Employment and safety law
- Product safety issues

Comment

Importantly, there is no underpinning logic to a PESTEL checklist, unlike many other strategy environmental concepts, such as the degree of turbulence or the market share and growth analysis explored above. PESTEL is purely a reminder checklist and should be used selectively.

Like all checklists, a PESTEL analysis is really only as good as the individual or group preparing it. Listing every conceivable item has little value and betrays a lack of serious consideration and logic in the strategic management process. Better to have three or four well-thought-out items that are explored and justified with evidence than a lengthy 'laundry list' of items. This is why this book does not recommend simple + and − signs and accompanying short bullet points, although these might provide a useful summary.

To the prescriptive strategists, although the items in a PESTEL analysis rely on *past* events and experience, the analysis can be used as a *forecast of the future*. The past is history and strategic management is concerned with future action, but the best evidence about the future *may* derive from what happened in the past. Prescriptive strategists would suggest that it is worth attempting the task because major new investments make this hidden assumption anyway. For example, when Warner Brothers invested several hundred million dollars in the first *Harry Potter* film, it was making an assumption that the fantasy film market would remain attractive; it might as well *formalise* this through a structured PESTEL analysis, even if the outcome is difficult to predict.

The emergent corporate strategists may well comment that the future is so uncertain that prediction is useless. If this view is held, a PESTEL analysis will fulfil a different role in *interpreting* past events and their interrelationships. In practice, some emergent strategists may give words of caution but still be tempted to predict the future. For example, one prominent strategist, Herbert Simon, wrote a rather rash article in 1960 predicting that, 'We will have the technical ability, by 1985, to run corporations by machine.'[10] The emergent strategists are correct in suggesting that prediction in some fast-moving markets may have little value. Overall, when used wisely, the PESTEL checklist has a role in strategic management.

10.4.2 Analysing the role of government

Although 'politics' appears as a checklist item in the PESTEL analysis above, this does not do justice to the importance of government in some areas of strategy development. At government policy level, politics and economics are inextricably linked. Strategic management is not concerned with forming such policies but does need to understand the implications of the decisions taken. Governments can stimulate national economies, encourage new research projects, impose new taxes and introduce many other initiatives that affect the organisation and its ability to develop corporate strategy. To analyse these influences, it is useful to identify three areas: the environment of the nation, its system of government and its policies. All these are summarised in the E–S–P paradigm – see Figure 10.2.

More generally, political decisions have been an important driver of industrial growth. Strategic management therefore needs to consider the opportunities and difficulties that derive from such policies. Other areas of government interest, such as public expenditure, competition policy and taxation issues, also need to be analysed. Influencing government policy in these areas may actually form an important part of an organisation's strategy: perhaps because the organisation is a government customer or perhaps because it is heavily dependent on some aspect of favourable government treatment such as tax. Finally, macroeconomic conditions – that is, economic activity at the general level of the national economy – can have a significant impact on strategic management. It therefore needs to be explored and assessed.

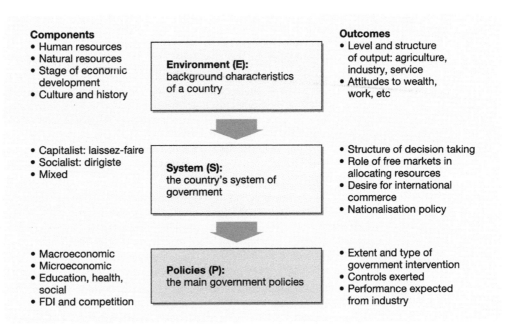

Figure 10.2 E–S–P paradigm: analysing the role of government

Source: adapted from Koopman, K and Montias, J M (1971) 'On the description and comparison of economic systems', in Eckstein, A (ed) *Comparison of Economic Systems: Theoretical and Methodological Approaches*, University of California Press, Berkeley, CA. Copyright © The Regents of the University of California. With permission.

10.4.3 Scenario-based analysis

In the context of a scenario-based analysis, a scenario is a model of a possible future environment for the organisation, whose strategic implications can then be investigated. For example, a scenario might be developed to explore the question: 'What would happen if broadband allowed every film to be delivered in-home by the year 2020 and demand for multi-screen cinema showings collapsed as a result? What impact would this have on film producers and cinema chains?'

Scenarios are concerned with peering into the future, not predicting the future. Prediction takes the *current* situation and extrapolates it forward. Scenarios take *different* situations with *alternative* starting points. The aim is not to predict but to explore a set of possibilities; a combination of events is usually gathered together into a scenario and then this combination is explored for its strategic significance. The organisation then explores its ability to handle this scenario – not because it necessarily expects it to happen but because it is a useful exercise in understanding the dynamics of the strategic environment. Exhibit 10.2 provides some guidance on the development of scenarios.

EXHIBIT 10.2

Some guidance on building scenarios . . . with an example from Case 10.4 on Hollywood blockbuster films

- Start from an *unusual viewpoint*. Examples might include the stance of a major competitor, a substantial change in technology, a radical change of government or the outbreak of war.
  Example: What are the consequences if one of the leading male actors dies half way through filming?

- Develop a *qualitative description* of a group of possible events or a *narrative* that shows how events will unfold. It is unlikely that this will involve a quantitative projection.

Example: The actor dies on day 45 (out of a 90-day shoot). The press are informed the same day. The producers then need to find another actor but also face problems over what they do about existing film footage: Do they re-shoot? Do they change the story? Do they invent another character?

- Explore the *outcomes* of this description or narrative of events by building two or three scenarios of what might happen. It is usually difficult to handle more than three scenarios. Two scenarios often lend themselves to a 'most optimistic outcome' and a 'worst possible outcome'.

  Example: Scenario 1 – the worst possible outcome is a total re-shoot including the withdrawal of other stars because they have other film commitments. Scenario 2 – change the storyline to fit the new situation with costs in terms of reworking the script, hiring another actor, perhaps re-shooting some scenes. The financial consequences of each of these scenarios (and more) can be calculated – what does it cost to hire script writers? Etc.

- Include the inevitable *uncertainty* in each scenario and explore the *consequences* of this uncertainty for the organisation concerned – for example, 'What would happen if the most optimistic outcome was achieved?' The PESTEL factors may provide some clues here.

  *Example: Scenario 1 – When **precisely** will other actors need to leave – after all, we still have another 45 days of contractual shooting? What does this really mean for the shoot? Surely we can do some rewrite that will help? Perhaps scenario 1 is actually too pessimistic?*

- Test the usefulness of the scenario by the extent to which it leads to *new strategic thinking* rather than merely the continuance of existing strategy.

  *Example: Importantly in terms of radical thinking: if the actor was so important in the first place, why didn't we **take out special insurance against his life** on the possibility of such an event before filming began?*

- Recall that the objective of scenario building is to develop strategies to cope with uncertainty, *not* to predict the future.

  Example: No-one wants a leading actor to die but imaginative scenarios help protect against uncertainties and unusual consequences.

KEY STRATEGIC PRINCIPLES

- The PESTEL checklist – the study of Political, Economic, Socio-cultural, Technological, Environmental and Legal factors – provides a useful starting point to any analysis of the general environment surrounding an organisation. It is vital to select among the items from such a generalised list and explore the chosen areas in depth; long lists of items are usually of no use.

- Prescriptive and emergent strategists take different views on the merits of projecting forward the main elements of the PESTEL checklist. The prescriptive approach favours the development of projections because they are often implied in major strategic decisions in any event. Emergent strategists believe the turbulence of the environment makes projections of limited value.

- In analysing the role and influence of government on strategy, the ESP Paradigm – Environment, System, Policies – can form a useful structure for this purpose. Influencing government policy may form an important element of strategy.

- A scenario is a picture of a possible future environment for the organisation, whose strategic implications can then be investigated. It is less concerned with prediction and more involved with developing different perspectives on the future. The aim is to stimulate new strategic thought about the possible consequences of events, rather than make an accurate prediction of the future.

CASE STUDY 10.2
Life cycle impact on strategy in the European ice cream market

During the period up to year 2004, the European ice cream market underwent significant change: some segments were relatively mature while some were experiencing strong growth. The North American market was more mature and fragmented with stronger regional brands. This case shows how the positions of the main European segments can be plotted in terms of the industry evolution (see Figure 10.3) and how strategies vary from one segment to another.

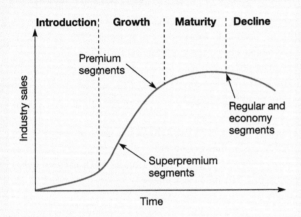

Figure 10.3 Industry evolution in the European ice cream market

Some ice cream products – like traditional tubs – need little strategic investment. Others – like premium ice creams from Haagen-Dazs and Ben & Jerry's – need investment to support their high price/strong market position.

The market can be divided into four distinct segments:

1 The *superpremium segment*, typified by Häagen-Dazs, was still in the early stages of its growth at this time. New companies were still entering the segment, for example Ben and Jerry's from the USA had been acquired by Unilever, but it had yet to be launched in some parts of continental Europe. New products were being tried using new methods of carton presentation and new high prices.

2 The *premium segment* had developed significantly in 1989 with the introduction of premium-priced Mars ice cream. By the year 2000, there were few new companies entering the market. The basic product ranges had become established among the leading players; the strategic battle was for distribution and branding.

3 The *regular* and 4 *economy segments* were typified by Unilever's bulk packs, sold under the name Carte d'Or across much of Europe. These had existed for many years but were still growing at around 5–6 per cent per annum (still regarded as a growth market according to some

definitions). The segment also had a large number of other suppliers, not all of whom were national, let alone European. There was keen competition on price and with own-label products from grocery retailers. There was relatively little product innovation.

Case questions

1 What strategies are suggested for each segment of the market from the conventional view of the industry life cycle? (Refer to Table 10.3.)

2 Thinking of strategy as doing the unconventional, how might you modify the strategies identified in Question 1?

10.5 ANALYSING THE STAGES OF MARKET GROWTH

The well-known strategy writer, Professor Michael Porter from Harvard University Business School, has described the *industry life cycle* as 'the grandfather of concepts for predicting industry evolution'. The basic hypothesis is that an industry – or a market segment within an industry – goes through four basic phases of development, each of which has implications for strategy – see Case 10.2 for

Definition ▶ an example. **The four main phases of the industry life cycle are usually identified as introduction, growth, maturity and decline** and are shown in Figure 10.4.

10.5.1 Industry life cycle

The nature of strategic management will change as industries move along the life cycle. In the *introductory* phase, organisations attempt to develop interest in the product. As the industry moves towards *growth*, competitors are attracted by its potential and enter the market: from a strategic perspective, competition increases. As all the available customers are satisfied by the product, growth slows down and the market becomes *mature*. Although growth has slowed, new competitors may still be attracted into the market: each company then has to compete harder for its market share, which becomes more fragmented – that is, the market share is broken down into smaller parts. Sales enter a period of *decline*.

To explore the strategic implications, it is useful to start by identifying what stage an industry has reached in terms of its development. For each stage in the cycle there are a number of commonly accepted strategies (see Table 10.3). In the case of ice cream customers in Case 10.2, the *introduction* phase will be used to present the product or service to new customers – perhaps a premium ice cream flavour to those who have never tasted it. By contrast, the *maturity* phase assumes that most customers are aware of the product and little new trial is required – perhaps a small tub of traditional chocolate ice cream.

As in other areas of strategic management, there are differing views regarding the choice of appropriate strategies for each phase of the industry life cycle. Table 10.3 represents the *conventional* view of the appropriate strategy for a particular stage in the industry's evolution. In strategic management, however, there are often good arguments for doing the *unconventional*, so this list would be seen as a starting point for analysing the dynamics of an industry. The most innovative strategy might well come by doing something different and breaking the mould.

As an example of the conventional view of such an analysis, the industry life cycle suggests that in the *early stages* of an industry's development there may be more opportunities for new and radical R&D. When an industry is more *mature*, rather less investment is needed in R&D.[11] However, the unconventional view argues that it is the mature industry that requires new growth and therefore

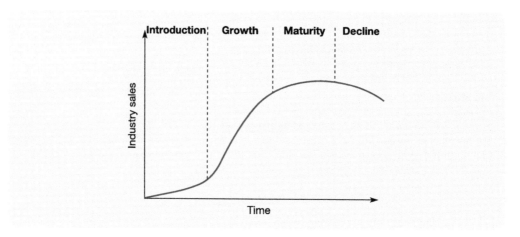

Figure 10.4 Stages of the industry life cycle

Table 10.3 The industry life cycle and its strategy implications – a conventional view

	Introduction phase	Growth phase	Maturity phase	Decline phase
Customer strategy	• Early customers may experiment with product and will accept some unreliability • Need to explain nature of innovation	• Growing group of customers • Quality and reliability important for growth	• Mass market • Little new trial of product or service • Brand switching	• Know the product well • Select on basis of price rather than innovation
R&D strategy	• High	• Seek extensions before competition	• Low	
Company strategy	• Seek to dominate market • R&D and production particularly important to ensure product quality	• React to competition with marketing expenditure and initiatives	• Expensive to increase market share if not already market leader • Seek cost reductions	• Cost control particularly important
Impact on profitability	• High price, but probably making a loss due to investment in new category	• Profits should emerge here, but prices may well decline as competitors enter market	• Profits under pressure from need for continuing investment coupled with continued distributor and competitive pressure	• Price competition and low growth may lead to losses or need to cut costs drastically to maintain profitability
Competitor strategy	• Keen interest in new category • Attempt to replicate new product	• Market entry (if not before) • Attempt to innovate and invest in category	• Competition largely on advertising and quality • Lower product differentiation • Lower product change	• Competition based primarily on price • Some companies may seek to exit the industry

R&D or some other strategic initiative. In the ice cream case, a market leader in traditional ice cream might benefit from investment in more modern facilities to reduce costs further. This suggests that, even in the mature phase of a market, heavy investment is often necessary to remain competitive in the market. It is for this reason that the life cycle concept can best be seen as a starting point for growth analysis.

It is important to note in the development of strategy the two consequences of the industry life cycle that can have a significant impact on industries:

1 *Advantages of early entry.* There is substantial empirical evidence that the first company into a new market has the most substantial strategic advantage. For example, Aaker[12] quotes a study of 500 mature industrial businesses showing that pioneer firms average a market share of 29 per cent, early followers 21 per cent and the late entrants 15 per cent. Although there are clearly risks in early market entry, there may also be long-term advantages that deserve careful consideration in strategic development.

2 *Industry market share fragmentation.* In the early years, markets that are growing fast attract new entrants. This is both natural and inevitable. The consequence as markets reach maturity is that each new company is fighting for market share and the market becomes more fragmented. Again, this has important implications for strategy because it suggests that mature markets need revised strategies – perhaps associated with a segment of the market.

For strategic purposes, it may be better to examine different *segments* of an industry, rather than the market *as a whole*, as different segments may be at different stages of the industry life cycle and may require different strategies (see the European ice cream industry example in Case 10.2). For example, it is possible to take a totally different industry such as the global travel industry and apply the same thinking: in recent years, some special-interest holidays, such as wildlife and photography, were still growing strongly whereas standard beach-and-sun holidays were in the mature stage of the life cycle.

10.5.2 Critical comment on the industry life cycle

The concept of the industry life cycle has both supporters and critics. Smallwood[13] and Baker[14] defend its usefulness and offer empirical support for the basic concept. Dhalla and Yuspeh[15] have led the criticisms, some of which certainly have a degree of validity (see Exhibit 10.3).

There are certainly some difficulties with the industry life cycle approach, but the reason for such an analysis is to identify the *dynamic factors that are shaping the industry's evolution*. The industry life cycle helps us to do this; it will then be possible to compare the organisation's own strategy with this analysis.

EXHIBIT 10.3

Criticisms of the industry life cycle

1 It is *difficult to determine the duration* of some life cycles and to identify the precise stage an industry has reached. For example, the Mars Bar was launched in the 1930s and is certainly not in decline – but is it in the growth or mature phase?

2 Some industries miss stages or *cannot be clearly identified* in their stages, particularly as a result of technological change. For example, has the bicycle reached the mature phase or has it reached a new lease of life as the petrol-driven car pollutes city atmospheres?

3 Companies themselves can instigate change in their products and can, as a result, *alter the shape of the curve*. For example, new life has been brought into the camera industry by the introduction of miniaturisation and, more recently, by the use of electronic storage in place of film.

KEY STRATEGIC PRINCIPLES

- The industry life cycle – charting the development of a market from introduction, through growth and maturity to decline – is useful to identify the dynamic factors shaping the industry's evolution, although there are criticisms of its use.

- It also helps to specify the conventional view of the strategies that are appropriate to each stage of the cycle, even if these are then changed for logical reasons.

- Aspects of life cycle analysis that are worthy of special consideration include: the advantages of early entry, the fragmentation of market share as markets mature, the incidence of cyclicality and its effect on demand in mature markets.

CASE STUDY 10.3

Bajaj Motorcycles: should the company move into cars?

One of India's largest motorcycle manufacturers, Bajaj Motorcycles, faces a major strategic decision over the next few years – whether to move into the Indian car market and, if so, with what model. This case explores the issues.

Background

Unlike Western countries, where motorcycles are a minority form of transport, the Indian transport market is dominated by motorcycles, scooters and three-wheelers. Over 7 million such vehicles were sold in 2010, rising to 16 million in 2013. Indian markets were growing at 5 per cent per year in 2010 but were virtually static by 2013 mainly because of national government economic policies. Their engine sizes are quite small by inter-national standards – typically 120cc machines in India versus 400cc ones in the West – and relatively cheap in India with prices around $2,000 compared with $8,000 in more wealthy Western countries. In addition, motorcycles are family transport in India – two children on the handlebars and mother side-saddle on the back behind the father – whereas motorcycles are largely for individuals in Western countries. All this reflects the fact that family incomes are substantially lower on average in India than in the West – typically, $5,000 per year versus anything up to $25–30,000 in the West. But typical Indian customers are becoming more wealthy and there is a growing middle class with significantly higher incomes – hence the possible scope for a small family car.

Strategy at Bajaj for motorcycles and three-wheelers

In 1998, Bajaj sold 1.4 million vehicles. By 2013, the company's annual sales had grown to almost 3.8 million of which nearly 1 million were exported. Its major product area was motorcycles which accounted for around 90 per cent of the above sales.

In addition, the company had another important line of vehicles: Bajaj was the leading company in the Indian three-wheeler market and had a profitable revenue stream from this market segment. Three-wheelers are unusual in Western markets but form a major part of many Asian markets, including Indonesia and the Philippines. They are open at the sides and often have no doors. They can be used as passenger carriers and also as goods carriers. Bajaj was the market leader in this market with 480,000 unit sales in 2013 and a dominant 57 per cent market share of the Indian domestic market.

In order to develop its early motorcycle business, Bajaj signed an agreement with the Japanese motorcycle company Kawasaki back in the early 1990s to employ Kawasaki's technology. In the early years, Bajaj was motorcycle market leader in India. However, Bajaj Auto lost its market leadership in motorcycles to a rival company, Hero Honda, over the years. The Bajaj market share was a steady 31 per cent in 2014. It had declined slightly in 2009 and 2010 because the company had limited success in launching successful models into the fast-growing executive segment of the Indian motorcycle market, where its major rival, Hero Honda, had established market leadership. Table 10.4 gives examples of models and prices.

Bajaj Auto was well established in 2013 as a major motorcycle and three-wheeler manufacturer in India. It had created three major manufacturing facilities for motorcycles and three-wheelers. It had also developed a strong distribution and service

network and an important R&D facility, which had led to the introduction of new Digital Twin Spark Ignition Technology. The company had also become a major exporter of motorcycles in the Asian region and had set up a manufacturing facility in Indonesia.

To refresh its market position in motorcycles, Bajaj developed three major strategies:

1. *New 'executive' top of the range machines.* This was the fastest-growing market segment in India. The company had set up a new R&D facility at its main manufacturing plant in Pune to deliver new technology. Importantly, it was the executive segment that had the highest profit margins as a result of a premium pricing strategy associated with the top of the range.

2. *Cost reduction.* Bajaj had in its early years some 900 suppliers of parts for its motorcycles. This large number meant that its suppliers were fragmented and unable to gain true economies of scale in production. Bajaj therefore spent considerable effort over the 10 years 1998 to 2007 reducing the numbers of suppliers back to around 80 and, at the same time, locating them closer to its assembly lines – similar to Toyota's 'just-in-time' delivery systems described in the free web-based case (Toyota: does it rely too heavily on production for world leadership?) linked to Part 6 of this book. Low costs were particularly important in the smaller motorcycle segment where price competition was particularly fierce and profit margins low.

3. *Exports and overseas production.* Bajaj promoted overseas sales from its three factories. By 2010, the company was selling over 800,000 motorcycles and three-wheelers annually to countries such as Sri Lanka, Nepal, Columbia, Bangladesh, Mexico, Peru and Egypt.

The one lakh car – a new threat or an opportunity for Bajaj?

Up to 2008, the annual market for cars in India was substantially smaller than motorcycles – nearly 2 million cars versus around 7 million motorcycles. The main reason was that typical car prices were $5,000 and upwards – affordable only to the more wealthy middle-class Indian family and substantially higher than motorcycle prices. (The detailed figures are given in Case 7 on Tata Motors in Part 6 of this book.)

Then along came one of India's most famous companies, the Tata Group, with a sensational new car launch in January 2008. Its brand name was the *Nano* and it was marketed as the 'One Lakh Car' being priced at 100,000 Indian rupees – 100,000 being called 'one lakh' in the Indian numbering system. Tata had produced the cheapest car in the world – one lakh was equivalent to around $2,500. The company had spent years working on a clever new car design that combined space, economy and simplicity. The on-road price would be somewhat higher – probably around 1.3 million lakh or $3,250 – but it would still be competitive with the top-of-the-range motorcycles. And this was the new threat and opportunity for Bajaj.

Initially, Tata Motors was planning to introduce the first prototypes from their new production line in June 2008 with

Table 10.4 Indian motorcycle market 2007

Company	Examples of models	Pricing
Hero Honda	CDDeLuxe (97cc), Splendor (125cc), Passion (125cc), Hunk, CBZ Xtreme	CD DeLuxe – $3,000 Hunk – $3,800
Bajaj	Platina (100cc), XCD, Pulsar (150 and 220cc), Discover	Pulsar 150 – $2,800 Pulsar 200 – $3,200
TVS	TVS Victor, Flame	
Yamaha	Gladiator (125cc)	Gladiator $2,000

Other manufacturers include Honda Japan and Suzuki Japan

Source: author direct visits to Indian and Nepali motorcycle stores November 2007 with some updating thereafter.

Bajaj Motorcycles is one of India's leading companies. It faces a major strategic decision – whether or not to move into the fast-growing Indian car market.

full production in October 2008. The company planned to manufacture 250,000 Nano cars in the first year but expected this to rise towards 1 million cars after several years. The response to the new car was highly favourable. 'Nano is expected to change the automobile market in India. It would cater to a typical middle-income Indian family of four who want to avoid rain, wind and dust. It's freedom for four,' commented Dilip Chenoy of the Society of Indian Motor Manufacturers.

Even motorcycle manufacturers were impressed: 'It's a nice car and, as an Indian, I am proud of the product. I really liked it but I don't feel that it will impact two-wheelers very much. There is a huge market for two-wheelers and we are not worried about any market erosion.' That was the view of Pawan Munjal, the Managing Director of Hero Honda. But Tata was taking a different line: it argued that the Nano was far safer than a motorcycle and, if only 10 per cent of the motorcycle market switched to the Nano, then this would give Tata annual sales of 700,000 vehicles. It would bring down the cost of car ownership in India by at least 30 per cent and make cars affordable to many more people.

As Case 7 in Part 6 of this book explains in more detail, the Nano did not sell in the numbers originally predicted. By 2013, Tata was selling only around 50–60,000 Nanos per year – far short of the initial projections.

Implications for Bajaj strategy

Up to 2013, the sales of the Nano had no impact on the Indian motorcycle market. But companies like Bajaj were aware that the car's competitive price was much the same as its profitable executive model, the 'Pulsar'. They would have read the comment in the Indian press of one Bajaj Pulsar user: 'I would definitely consider buying the Nano as the cost of the car

fits my pocket and above all it has good mileage.' However, the company was also aware of the widely publicised weaker sales of the Nano up to 2013.

Tata acknowledged that its own ideas for the Nano would help other manufacturers. 'It is not our god-given domain,' explained Rajan Tata, the Chairman of the Tata Group, when introducing the Nano. 'It will be an easier task for them than it was for us.' However, even allowing for this, it would be no easy task for Bajaj Group or any other company.

Back in 2008, Bajaj had discussions with the French car company Renault about the possibility of a joint venture in the Indian car market. This led to an outline joint agreement to produce an ultra low-cost car (code-named the ULC) for the Indian market similar to the Nano.

Subsequently, there were two changes in strategic thinking. First, Renault decided that it would like to enter the Indian domestic market with its own range and therefore began planning this for launch around 2013–2014. This meant that it was less interested in the ULC – possibly supported by the relatively poor sales of the Nano. Second, Bajaj itself became increasingly doubtful about the market demand for the ULC. As an alternative, it was actively examining the possibility of dropping the ULC and developing an extended version of its three-wheeler vehicles – one with four wheels – but with the open design body work of the three-wheeler with no doors, rather than the closed design of a car body.

At the time of writing this case, Bajaj clearly had some major strategic decisions to take: should it make a ULC car like the Nano? Should it make a four-wheeler to complement its existing three-wheel range? Or should it just stay with motorcycles?

According to its 2013 annual report, the company has clearly designed policies, including an extensive contribution in the related areas of education and health activities.

Case questions

1 Why did Bajaj lose market share and how did it respond?

2 What are the most profitable segments of the Indian motorcycle market? Why were they threatened initially by the Nano?

3 Should Bajaj move into car manufacture? What are the arguments in favour and what against? What would you recommend?

10.6 KEY FACTORS FOR SUCCESS IN AN INDUSTRY

In a strategic analysis of the environment, there is an immense range of issues that can potentially be explored, creating a problem for most organisations, which have neither the time nor the resources to cope with such an open-ended task. The Japanese strategist Kenichi Ohmae,[17] the former head of the management consultants McKinsey, in Japan, has suggested a way of tackling this matter by identifying *the key factors for success (KFS)* that are *likely* to deliver the company's objectives. These can then be used to focus the analysis on particularly important industry matters.

Definition ▶   **Key factors for success in an industry are those resources, skills and attributes of the organisations in an industry that are essential to deliver success in the market place.** Ohmae argued that, when resources of capital, labour and time are scarce, it is important that they should be *concentrated* on the key activities of the business – that is, those most important to the delivery of whatever the organisation regards as success.

This concept of key factors for success is also consistent with Porter's view[18] that there are factors that determine the relative competitive positions of companies within an industry. Moreover, the foundation of Kay's approach[19] is that it is important to concentrate resources on the specific areas of the business that are most likely to prove successful. Amit and Schoemaker[20] provide a more extended theoretical framework for the same topic, but call their treatment 'Strategic Industry Factors'. All the above have said that identifying the key factors is not an easy task.

KFS are common to all the major organisations in the industry and do not differentiate one company from another. For example, in Case 10.3, the factors mentioned – low labour costs, servicing centres, parts suppliers of motorbikes, etc. – are common to other similar companies to Bajaj. Such factors will vary from one industry to another. For example, by contrast, in the perfume and cosmetics industry the factors will include branding, product distribution and product performance, but they are unlikely to include labour costs.

When undertaking a strategic analysis of the environment, the identification of the KFS for an industry may provide a useful starting point. For example, the motorbike KFS item of 'low labour costs' would suggest an environmental analysis of the following areas:

- general wage levels in the country;

- government regulations and attitudes to worker redundancy, because high wage costs could be reduced by sacking employees;

- trade union strength to fight labour force redundancies.

In the Indian motorbike industry, these elements of the environment would benefit from careful study, whereas, in the cosmetics and perfume industry, they might have some relevance but would be far less important than other areas.

10.6.1 Identifying the key factors for success in the industry

Key factors concern not only the resources of organisations in the industry but also the *competitive environment* in which organisations operate. There are three principal areas that need to be analysed – Ohmae's *three Cs.*[21]

1 *Customers.* What do customers really want? What are the segments in the market place? Can we direct our strategy towards a group?

2 *Competition.* How can the organisation beat or at least survive against competition? What resources and customers does it have that make it particularly successful? How does the organisation compare on price, quality, etc.? Does the organisation have a stronger distributive network than its competitors?

3 *Corporation.* What special resources does the company itself possess and how do they compare with those of competitors? How does the company compare on costs with its rivals? And on technologies? Skills? Organisational ability? Marketing?

Exhibit 3.4 sets out some key questions in more detail. No single area is more important than another. The *corporate* factors relate to the *resource* issues.

10.6.2   Critical comment on the concept

Criticism of the key factors for success has concentrated on four issues:[22]

1 *Identification.* It is difficult to pick out the important factors.

2 *Causality of relationships.* Even though they have been identified, it may not be clear *how* they operate or interact.

3 *Dangers of generalising.* The competitive advantage of a single organisation, by definition, cannot be obtained by seeking what is commonly accepted as bringing success to all organisations in an industry.

4 *Disregard of emergent perspectives.* Success may come from change in an industry, rather than the identification of the current key factors for success.

Beyond these specific criticisms, some strategists have a more general concern about industry analysis (this is explored in the next section). Some of the criticisms can be countered if key factors for success are regarded as *guidelines* for directing strategy development, rather than rigid rules. But the criticisms suggest that key factors for success should be explored with caution. They are only a starting point in strategy analysis – the 'best' strategy may be to reject the key factors and do something completely different!

EXHIBIT 10.4

Identifying key factors for success in an industry

Note that key factors for success are directed at *all companies in an industry*, not just the target company for strategy development.

1 Customers

Who are the customers? Who are the potential customers? Are there any special segments? Why do customers buy from us? And from our competitors?

- *Price.* Is the market segmented by high, medium and economy pricing? For example, the market for European ice cream.
- *Service.* Do some customers value service while others simply want to buy the product? For example, top-class fashion retailers versus standard clothing shops.
- *Product or service reliability.* Is product performance crucial to the customer or is reliability useful but not really important? For example, heart pacemakers and pharmaceuticals.
- *Quality.* Some customers will pay higher prices for actual or perceived quality differences. Does this provide a route to success? For example, organic vegetables.
- *Technical specifications.* In some industrial and financial services, technical details will provide major attractions for some customers. Is this relevant in this industry? For example, specialist financial bond dealers.
- *Branding.* How important is branding for the customer? For example, Coca-Cola and Pepsi Cola.

2 Competition

Who are the main competitors? What are the main factors in the market that influence competition? How intense is competition? What is necessary to achieve market superiority? What resources do competitors possess that we lack and vice versa?

- *Cost comparisons.* Which companies have the lowest costs? Why? For example, Toyota until the mid-1990s.
- *Price comparisons.* Which companies have high prices? For example, Daimler-Benz does not make cheap cars.
- *Quality issues.* Which companies have the highest quality? Why? How? For example, Xerox (USA) in the light of fierce competition from Japanese companies such as Canon.
- *Market dominance.* Which companies dominate the market? For example, Nestlé, with the strongest coffee product range in the world and the largest market share.
- *Service.* Are there companies in the industry that offer superior service levels? For example, industrial markets, such as those served by Asea Brown Boveri, which need high levels of service to operate and maintain sophisticated equipment.
- *Distributors.* Which companies have the best distributive network? Lowest costs? Fastest delivery? Competent distributors that really know the product or service? For example, major glass companies such as St Gobain (France) and Pilkington (UK).

3 Corporation

What are our key resources and those of our competitors? What do they deliver to customers? Where are the majority of the industry costs concentrated? A small percentage reduction to a large part of the total costs will deliver more than a large percentage reduction in an area of lower total costs.

- *Low-cost operations.* Are low-cost operations important for ourselves or our competitors? For example, Aldi (Germany) and Tesco (UK) are both low-cost supermarket operators.
- *Economies of scale.* Do these exist in the industry? How important are they? For example, large-scale petroleum chemical refinery operations such as those operated by Royal Dutch/Shell.
- *Labour costs.* Does our industry rely heavily on low labour costs for competitive operations? For example, Philips (Netherlands) has moved its production to Singapore and Malaysia to lower labour costs.
- *Production output levels.* Does our industry need full utilisation of plant capacity? For example, European paper and packaging companies.
- *Quality operations.* Do customers need consistent and reliable quality? How do we compare with others in the industry? For example, McDonald's has applied the same standards around the world in its restaurants.
- *Innovative ability.* Does our industry place a high reliance on our ability to produce a constant stream of new innovations? For example, computer hardware and software companies such as Apple, Epson and Microsoft.
- *Labour/management relations.* Is our industry heavily reliant on good relations? Are there real problems if disputes arise? For example, European large-scale steel production, at companies such as Usinor/Arbed.
- *Technologies and copyright.* Does the industry rely on specialist technologies, especially those that are patented and provide a real competitive advantage? For example, News International (Australia), which has exclusive global control over some forms of decoder cards for satellite television.
- *Skills.* Do organisations in the industry possess exceptional human skills and people? What are such skills? For example, advertising agencies and leading consultancy companies.

KEY STRATEGIC PRINCIPLES

- Identifying the key factors for success shapes the key areas of strategic analysis.

- Such factors can conveniently be considered under three headings: customers, competition and corporation. By 'corporation' is meant the resources of the organisation.

- Key factors can be found in any area of the organisation and relate to skills, competitive advantage, competitive resources of an organisation in the industry, special technologies or customer contacts.

- Four criticisms of key factors have been made: identification, causality of relationships, dangers of generalising, and disregard of emergent perspectives. Caution is therefore needed in their application.

CASE STUDY 10.4
Strategic bargaining to film *Lord of the Rings*

FT

In the highly competitive and risky environment of Hollywood film-making, it is essential to analyse those who have the power to make things happen. This case explores the strategic environment surrounding one of the most profitable films ever made – and how the deal and the movie almost failed.

Background

It was one of the biggest gambles in movie history – handing $300 million to shoot an epic trilogy in one take to a virtually unknown director with no record of big-budget Hollywood pictures. And letting him do it 7,000 miles away, so that studio executives had little control over what actually happened on the set.

There were plenty of recent examples of how a huge investment in what seemed a sure-fire blockbuster had backfired, leaving massive dents in the studio's finances – *Waterworld, Heaven's Gate* and so on. Somehow, though, *Lord of the Rings* did get made and took over $500 million in its first year as well as winning four Oscars. It is easy to forget the scale of the risk involved and the convoluted strategic bargaining that was necessary before a single scene was shot.

For Peter Jackson, the film's New Zealand-born director, and his agent, Ken Kamins from ICM, the story behind *Lord of the Rings* is one of a project that very nearly failed to see the light of day.

Competitive environment

When Jackson and Kamins set out to make the film in 1995, they first had to secure the rights to JRR Tolkien's novels,

The Fellowship of the Ring, The Two Towers and *The Return of the King*. Producer Saul Zaentz had bought the rights from Professor Tolkien for a rumoured $15,000 30 years earlier and he had no intention of selling them. Up to that point, Jackson was known only for low-budget horror movies such as *Braindead*. However, an Oscar nomination in 1995 for the screenplay of his $3.5 million arthouse drama *Heavenly Creatures* had earned him a first-look deal with Harvey Goldstein, head of Miramax, the independent studio allied to Disney. So Jackson and Kamins approached Weinstein that year with the idea for a *Lord of the Rings* adaptation.

'When we told Harvey that Saul held the rights, he was immediately enthusiastic,' says Kamins, 'as he had just helped Saul on *The English Patient* [Miramax had stepped in to pick up the film after Fox, part of News Corporation, dropped it on the eve of production]. That created the moral window by which Harvey could ask. But this wasn't charity either. Saul had Harvey pay a pretty penny – I've been told somewhere in the $3 million range.'

New bargaining problems

Having secured the film rights, the Miramax boss sent Jackson and his partner, Fran Walsh, off to write the scripts for a two-

Outdoor advertising in Hollywood, USA. Even after the strategy was negotiated and implemented, it was important to promote the film.

part adaptation, with both parts being filmed one after the other. Production research was also to begin in New Zealand. Just when things seemed to be going smoothly, the next wave of problems emerged. 'It soon became clear to Miramax that it was going to be a very expensive proposition,' says Kamins, 'maybe more expensive than their brief as defined by Disney allowed them to get involved in. Harvey then went to Disney and asked whether they would want a partner in the project. When Disney said no, Miramax got concerned about the cost. And of course [started] asking obvious questions: what happens if the first movie doesn't work?'

Faced with such a risky and expensive project, Weinstein asked Jackson to make the trilogy as one film of no more than three hours. Jackson declined, and, instead, he and Kamins asked to take the project to another studio. Weinstein agreed, although he imposed very tough conditions. Says Kamins: 'We had three weeks to set it up somewhere else. Harvey also demanded that the $12 million that Miramax had already spent in development had to be repaid within 72 hours of the agreement being signed. Now this is highly unusual in the movie business. Normally, a studio would simply pay the former studio a 10 per cent option or they would work out a deal in the budget of the film once the

movie got made. Most importantly, he and a partner insisted on 5 per cent of the gross, whether there was one movie, two movies or eight.'

The deal hangs on a knife-edge

With three weeks to find another studio, Jackson and Kamins decided to do two things. While Kamins started submitting the screenplays for the two-part adaptation to every studio in Hollywood, Jackson flew to New Zealand to produce a 35-minute documentary with $50,000 of his own money. The idea was that, if any of the studios was interested, the documentary would show them where Miramax's $12 million had gone, and, most importantly, why Jackson was the right director. But Kamins had little success – every studio said no, except two, Polygram and New Line, which was owned by Warner Brothers. Then Polygram pulled out at the last minute: 'So we went to New Line realising that they were the last Popsicle stand in the desert, and them not knowing that,' said Kamins.

But at New Line, they had some luck. Jackson's old friend, Mark Ordesky, turned out to be one of those making the decision. New Line then asked: 'Why are you making two movies? It's three books, so it's three movies.' Negotiations started the next day. Many in the business doubted the sanity of the decision, especially making three rather than two films. 'But Peter's presentation made it clear that he had an absolutely commanding vision for the film . . . You would be surprised how, in the movie business, some of these commitments are made on far less sturdy ground.'

By 2002, AOL Time Warner was estimated to have one of the biggest money-spinners in entertainment history on its hands. New Line and its distribution partners had turned *Lord of the Rings* into a worldwide franchise in the *Star Wars* mould, and were exploiting the brand name across a huge range of platforms – DVD, video games, the internet, merchandise of every sort. The gamble was starting to pay.

Case questions

1 Who has the bargaining power in this strategic environment? And who has the co-operating power? Identify and analyse the players – use the concepts from Sections 10.6 and 10.7 to help you.

2 What useful strategic concepts, if any, from this chapter can be used in analysing the strategic environment? And what cannot be used? Why?

3 If risk and judgement are important in business decisions, can prescriptive strategic analysis be usefully employed?

10.7 ANALYSING THE COMPETITIVE INDUSTRY ENVIRONMENT – THE CONTRIBUTION OF PORTER

An industry analysis usually begins with a general examination of the forces influencing the organisation. The objective of such a study is to use this to develop the *competitive advantage* of the organisation to enable it to defeat its rival companies. Much of this analysis was structured and presented by Professor Michael Porter of Harvard University Business School.[23] His contribution to our understanding of the competitive environment of the firm has wide implications for many organisations in both the private and public sectors.

This type of analysis is often undertaken using the structure proposed by Porter; his basic model is illustrated in Figure 10.5. This is often called *Porter's Five Forces Model* because he identifies five basic forces that can act on the organisation:

1 the bargaining power of suppliers;

2 the bargaining power of buyers;

3 the threat of potential new entrants;

4 the threat of substitutes;

5 the extent of competitive rivalry.

The objective of such an analysis is to investigate how the organisation needs to form its strategy in order to develop opportunities in its environment and protect itself against competition and other threats. Porter himself cautiously described[24] his analysis as being concerned with the 'forces driving industry competition'. However, the general principles can perhaps be applied to public service and not-for-profit organisations where they compete for resources, such as government funding or charitable donations.

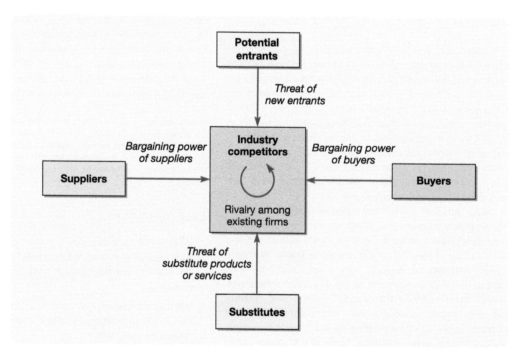

Figure 10.5 Porter's Five Forces Model

10.7.1 The bargaining power of suppliers

Virtually every organisation has suppliers of raw materials or services which are used to produce the final goods or services. Porter suggested that suppliers are more powerful under the following conditions:

- *If there are only a few suppliers.* This means that it is difficult to switch from one to another if a supplier starts to exert its power.
- *If there are no substitutes for the supplies they offer.* This is especially the case if the supplies are important for technical reasons – perhaps they form a crucial ingredient in a production process or the service they offer is vital to smooth production.
- *If suppliers' prices form a large part of the total costs of the organisation.* Any increase in price would hit value added unless the organisation was able to raise its own prices in compensation.
- *If a supplier can potentially undertake the value-added process of the organisation.* Occasionally a supplier will have power if it is able to integrate forward and undertake the value-added process undertaken by the organisation; this could pose a real threat to the survival of the organisation.

In the case of motorcycle companies like Bajaj, suppliers' bargaining powers are in some respects low. There are many sources of supply for some motorcycle parts. However, in terms of more sophisticated electronic parts that make a substantial difference to the performance of the machines, suppliers may have higher bargaining power.

10.7.2 The bargaining power of buyers

In his model, Porter used the term *buyers* to describe what might also be called the *customers* of the organisation. Buyers have more bargaining power under the following conditions:

- *If buyers are concentrated and there are few of them.* When the organisation has little option but to negotiate with a buyer because there are few alternative buyers around, the organisation is clearly in a weak position: national government contracts in defence, health and education are obvious examples where the government can, in theory at least, drive a hard bargain with organisations.
- *If the product from the organisation is undifferentiated.* If an organisation's product is much the same as that from other organisations, the buyer can easily switch from one to another without problems. The buyer is even more likely to make such a shift if the quality of the buyer's product is unaffected by such a change.
- *If backward integration is possible.* As with suppliers above, the buyer's bargaining power is increased if the buyer is able to backward-integrate and take over the role of the organisation.
- *If the selling price from the organisation is unimportant to the total costs of the buyer.*

In the case of Indian motorcycle customers, private buyers are unlikely to have much bargaining power with companies of the size of Bajaj; a letter from an individual customer, threatening to switch from its motorcycle purchase to Hero Honda, is unlikely to have much impact – the threat is low. For the sake of clarity, this reasoning does not imply that Bajaj would ignore a letter from an individual customer – just that the bargaining power of that individual is not high according to Porter's theory. However, if a large purchaser of motorcycles like a police authority were to make such a threat, then it would clearly have to be taken more seriously because of the potential impact on sales. In this latter case, the threat is high.

10.7.3 The threat of potential new entrants

New entrants come into a market place when the profit margins are attractive and the barriers to entry are low. The allure of high profitability is clear and so the major strategic issue is that of barriers to entry into a market.

Porter argued that there were seven[25] major sources of barriers to entry:

1 *Economies of scale.* Unit costs of production may be reduced as the absolute volume per period is increased. Such cost reductions occur in many industries and present barriers because they mean that any new entrant has to come in on a large scale in order to achieve the low cost levels of those already present: such a scale is risky. We have already examined the computer and motorcycle industries where such cost reductions are vital.

2 *Product differentiation.* Branding, customer knowledge, special levels of service and many other aspects may create barriers by forcing new entrants to spend extra funds or simply take longer to become established in the market. Real barriers to entry can be created in strategic terms by long-established companies with such strengths in a market. Retailers such as IKEA with strong branding and specialist product lines and expertise are examples of companies with differentiated products.

3 *Capital requirements.* Entry into some markets may involve major investment in technology, plant, distribution, service outlets and other areas. The ability to raise such finance and the risks associated with such outlays of capital will deter some companies – for example, the high capital cost of investing in new motorcycle production capacity in Case 10.3 earlier in this chapter.

4 *Switching costs.* When a buyer is satisfied with the existing product or service, it is naturally difficult to switch that buyer to a new entrant. The cost of making the switch would naturally fall to the new entrant and will represent a barrier to entry. Persuading buyers to switch their purchases of computer software from Microsoft Windows to Apple has an obvious cost and inconvenience to many companies that would need to be overcome. In addition to the costs of persuading customers to switch, organisations should expect that existing companies will retaliate with further actions designed to drive out new entrants. For example, Microsoft has not hesitated to upgrade its products and reduce its prices to retain customers that might otherwise switch.

5 *Access to distribution channels.* It is not enough to produce a quality product; it must be distributed to the customer through channels that may be controlled by companies already in the market. For many years, the leading petrol companies have owned their own retail petrol sites to ensure that they have access to retail customers.

6 *Cost disadvantages independent of scale.* Where an established company knows the market well, has the confidence of major buyers, has invested heavily in infrastructure to service the market and has specialist expertise, it becomes a daunting task for new entrants to gain a foothold in the market. Korean and Malaysian car companies are attempting to enter the European and American car markets and face these barriers created by well-entrenched companies such as Ford, Volkswagen and Renault.

7 *Government policy.* For many years, governments have enacted legislation to protect companies and industries: monopolies in telecommunications, health authorities, utilities such as gas and electricity are examples where entry has been difficult if not impossible. The European Commission has been working alongside European governments to remove some but not all such barriers over the past few years. The Chinese government will not allow foreign steel companies to take a controlling interest in Chinese steel companies.

10.7.4 The threat of substitutes

Occasionally, substitutes render a product in an industry redundant. For example, SmithKline Beecham lost sales from its product Tagamet for the treatment of ulcers, due to the introduction of more effective products – first the introduction of Zantac from Glaxo in the 1980s and then, in the 1990s, Losec from the Swedish company Astra. Tagamet is still on sale as an over-the-counter remedy, but its major public health sales have largely ceased. More recently, Losec sales have also suffered as the drug patents protecting prices have come to an end and cheaper low-price substitutes have been launched by rival companies – the so-called 'generic' drugs, sourced from countries like India.

More often, substitutes do not entirely replace existing products but introduce new technology or reduce the costs of producing the same product. Effectively, substitutes may limit the profits in an industry by keeping prices down.

From a strategy viewpoint, the key issues to be analysed are:

- the possible threat of obsolescence;
- the ability of customers to switch to the substitute;
- the costs of providing some extra aspect of the service that will prevent switching;
- the likely reduction in profit margin if prices come down or are held.

In the motorcycle market, there is the possibility of substituting cars and three-wheelers depending on the price and usage. The threat of substitution may therefore be high, but this depends on the technology and end-use.

10.7.5 The extent of competitive rivalry

Some markets are more competitive than others. Higher competitive rivalry may occur in the following circumstances:

- *When competitors are roughly of equal size and one competitor decides to gain share over the others*, then rivalry increases significantly and profits fall. In a market with a dominant company, there may be less rivalry because the larger company is often able to stop quickly any move by its smaller competitors. In the UK market for electricity supply, there are only six major suppliers each with roughly equal market shares. If one was to bid for a major increase in share, then the others would have to follow.
- *If a market is growing slowly and a company wishes to gain dominance*, then by definition it must take its sales from its competitors – increasing rivalry.
- *Where fixed costs or the costs of storing finished products in an industry are high*, then companies may attempt to gain market share in order to achieve break-even or higher levels of profitability. Paper making, steel manufacture and car production are all examples of industries where there is a real case for cutting prices to achieve basic sales volumes – thus increasing rivalry.
- *If extra production capacity in an industry comes in large increments*, then companies may be tempted to fill that capacity by reducing prices, at least temporarily. For example, the bulk chemicals industry usually has to build major new plants and cannot simply add small increments of capacity. In the steel and oil industries, it is not possible to half-build a new processing plant: either it is built or not.
- *If it is difficult to differentiate products or services*, then competition is essentially price-based and it is difficult to ensure customer loyalty. Markets in basic pharmaceutical products such as aspirin have become increasingly subject to such pressures. In the steel market, flat-rolled steel from one manufacturer is much the same as that of another, so competition is price-based. However, where specialist steels are made with unique performance characteristics, the products are differentiated on performance and price rivalry is lower.
- *When it is difficult or expensive to exit from an industry* (perhaps due to legislation on redundancy costs or the cost of closing dirty plant), there is likely to be excess production capacity in the industry and increased rivalry. The steel industry has suffered from problems in this area during the past few years.
- *If entrants have expressed a determination to achieve a strategic stake in that market*, the costs of such an entry would be relatively unimportant when related to the total costs of the company concerned and the long-term advantages of a presence in the market. Japanese car manufacturing in the EU has advantages for Toyota and Nissan beyond the short-term costs of building plant, as EU car markets were opened to full Japanese competition around the year 2000.

10.7.6 Strategy implications from the general industry and competitive analysis

In strategic management, it is not enough just to produce an analysis; it is important to consider the implications for the organisation's future strategy. Some issues that might arise from the above include:

- *Is there a case for changing the strategic relationships with suppliers?* Could more be gained by moving into close partnership with selected suppliers rather than regarding them as rivals? The Japanese car industry has sought to obtain much closer co-operation with suppliers and mutual cost reduction as a result.[26] (See Case 4 on global cars in Part 6.)

- *Is there a case for forming a new relationship with large buyers?* Manufacture of own-label products for large customers in the retail industry may be undertaken at lower margins than branded business but has proved a highly successful strategy for some leading European companies.[27] Even Cereal Partners is now engaged in this strategy in order to build volume through its plants.

- *What are the key factors for success that drive an industry and influence its strategic development?* What are the lessons for the future that need to be built into the organisation's strategic management? We looked at these questions in Section 10.6.

- *Are there any major technical developments that rivals are working on that could fundamentally alter the nature of the environment?* What is the timespan and level of investment for such activity? What action should we take, if any?

10.7.7 Critical comment on the Five Forces Model

Porter's Five Forces Model is a useful early step in analysing the environment, but it has been the subject of some critical comment:

- The analytical framework is essentially *static*, whereas the competitive environment in practice is constantly changing. Forces may move from high to low, or vice versa, rather more rapidly than the model can show.

- It assumes that the organisation's own interests come first; for some charitable institutions and government bodies, this assumption may be incorrect.

- It assumes that buyers (called customers elsewhere in this book) have no greater importance than any other aspect of the micro-environment. Other commentators such as Aaker,[28] Baker[29] and Harvey-Jones[30] would fundamentally disagree on this point: they argue that the customer is more important than other aspects of strategy development and is not to be treated as an equal aspect of such an analysis.

- In general, its starting point is that the environment poses a threat to the organisation – leading to the consideration of suppliers and buyers as threats that need to be tackled. As pointed out above, some companies have found it useful to engage in closer *co-operation* with suppliers; such a strategy may be excluded if they are regarded purely as threats. This is explained more fully in Section 10.8.

- Porter's strategic analysis largely ignores the human resource aspects of strategy: it makes little attempt to recognise, let alone resolve, aspects of the micro-environment that might connect people to their own and other organisations. For example, it considers neither the country cultures, nor the management skills aspects of strategic management.

- Porter's analysis proceeds on the basis that, once such an analysis has been undertaken, then the organisation can formulate a strategy to handle the results: *prescriptive* rather than *emergent*. Some commentators would challenge this basic assessment.

In spite of these critical comments, the approach taken in this book is that Porter's model provides a very useful starting point in the analysis of the environment. It has real merit because of the issues it raises in a logical and structured framework. It is therefore recommended as a useful first step in strategy development.

Professor Porter presented his Five Forces Model as an early stage in strategic analysis and development. He followed it with two further analyses: an analysis of *industry evolution* – the extent to which the micro-environment is still growing or has reached maturity[31] – and the study of *strategic groups* within a market.

KEY STRATEGIC PRINCIPLES

- The purpose of industry and competitive strategic analysis is to enable the organisation to develop competitive advantage.
- Porter's Five Forces Model provides a useful starting point for such an analysis.
- Suppliers are particularly strong when they can command a price premium for their products and when their delivery schedules or quality can affect the final product.
- Buyers (or customers) are strong when they have substantial negotiating power or other leverage points associated with price, quality and service.
- New entrants pose a substantial threat when they are easily able to enter a market and when they are able to compete strongly through lower costs or other means.
- Substitutes usually pose a threat as a result of a technological or low-cost breakthrough.
- Competitive rivalry is the essence of such an analysis. It is necessary to build defences against competitive threat.
- The model has been the subject of some critical comment, but it remains a useful starting point for competitive strategic analysis.

10.8 ANALYSING THE CO-OPERATIVE ENVIRONMENT

10.8.1 The four links model

As well as competing with rivals, most organisations also co-operate with others, for example through informal supply relationships or through formal and legally binding joint ventures. Until recently, such links were rarely analysed in strategy development – the analysis stopped at Porter's Five Forces and some in-depth studies of one or two competitors (see Section 10.9). However, it is now becoming increasingly clear that *co-operation* between the organisation and others in its environment is also important as:

- it may help in the achievement of sustainable competitive advantage;
- it may open up new markets and increase business opportunities;
- it may produce lower costs;
- it may deliver more sustainable relationships with those outside the organisation.

It should be noted that an extreme form of co-operation – collusion between competitors to rig markets – is illegal in most countries and is not explored further here. But there are many other forms of co-operation that are highly beneficial and should form part of any analysis of the environment. For example, European steel companies have formed joint ventures with Brazilian steel companies for the benefit of both parties, and Krupp Thyssen Stahl is co-operating with its energy suppliers to reduce costs. Moreover, all the main European steel companies are co-operating with the government of the EU on policy matters affecting the industry. Equally, North American steel companies are co-operating with Federal and state governments for the benefit of the industry. Joint ventures, alliances and other formal methods of co-operation.

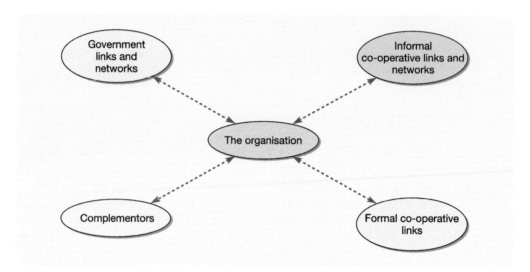

Figure 10.6 Analysing co-operation: the Four Links Model

The basic co-operative linkages between the organisation and its environment can usefully be explored under four headings:

1 informal co-operative links and networks
2 formal co-operative links
3 complementors
4 government links and networks.

The objective of such an analysis is to establish the strength and nature of the co-operation that exists between the organisation and its environment. It can be conducted through the *Four Links Model* – see Figure 10.6.

10.8.2 Opportunities and threats from informal co-operative links and networks

Informal co-operative links and networks are the occasions when organisations link together for a mutual or common purpose *without* a legally binding contractual relationship. They have long been recognised as providing an important means of understanding the strategy of the firm.[32] By their nature, they may well occur by accident as well as by design. They will include many forms of contact, ranging from formal industry bodies that represent industry matters with other interested parties – for example, the European Confederation of Iron and Steel Industries – to informal contacts that take place when like-minded individuals from a variety of industries meet at a social function – for example, a local Chamber of Commerce meeting.

The analysis will need to assess the opportunities that such links and networks present. Occasionally, there may also be threats from arrangements. In analysing them, it is the *strength or weakness* of the relationship that matters. For example, in some parts of the world such as Japan and Korea, the networks are called *keiretsu* and *chaebol*, respectively, and have provided strong mutual support to those companies that belong to them. In some services, such as international banking, it is the strength of the network that provides the competitive advantage for those involved in it and excludes those that are not.[33]

10.8.3 Opportunities and threats from formal co-operative linkages

Formal co-operative linkages can take many business forms but are usually bound together by some form of legal contract. They differ from the networks described above in the higher degree of formality and permanence of the link with the organisation. They are shown in alliances, joint ventures, joint shareholdings and many other deals that exist to provide competitive advantage and mutual support over many years. Some companies like the UK retailer Marks & Spencer, the Japanese car manufacturer Toyota and the Italian clothing company Benetton have developed such linkages into vital contributors to the uniqueness of their strategies. Suppliers, distributors and other formal co-operators with such companies provide essential products and services at lower prices and higher service levels than those offered to others in the industry. Essentially, formal co-operative linkages develop out of many years of discussion and understanding. They are very difficult for other companies to copy.[34] The *strengths and weaknesses* of such linkages should therefore be measured in terms of their depth, longevity and degree of mutual trust. Although the main interest may come from opportunities offered by such formal linkages, threats may arise from those developed by competitors.

10.8.4 The opportunities and threats presented by complementors

Definition ▶ **Complementors are those companies whose products add more value to the products of the base organisation than they would derive from their own products by themselves.**[35] For example, computer hardware companies are worth little without the software that goes with them – one product *complements* the other. In strategic terms, there may be real benefits from developing new complementor opportunities that enhance both parties and contribute further to the links that exist between them. Typically, complementors come from different industries with different resources and skills that work together to present new and sustainable *joint offerings* to customers. Again, it is the *strengths and weaknesses* of the relationship that need to be analysed. Although the main interest may come from opportunities offered by complementors, threats may arise from the complementor linkages developed by competitors.

10.8.5 Opportunities and threats from government links and networks

Government links and networks concern the relationships that many organisations have with a country's national parliament, regional assemblies and the associated government administrations. In the case of the EU and other international treaties, these clearly extend beyond national boundaries. Such contact may be formal, through business negotiations on investment, legal issues and tax matters. It may also be informal, through representation on government/industry organisations in connection with investment and trade.

Government links and networks can be vital in tax and legal matters, such as the interpretation of competition law. Equally, governments can be important customers of organisations, for example in defence equipment and pharmaceuticals. Many organisations have come to devote significant time and effort to developing and cultivating such relationships through lobbying and other related activities. Because of the nature and role of government, it may need to remain relatively remote in its legislative and regulatory dealings with outside organisations. However, it is appropriate to evaluate the degree of co-operation or hostility between government and outside bodies. Thus outside organisations will wish to consider the *opportunities and threats* posed by government activities. These may form a significant part of their corporate strategic development, especially at very senior levels within an organisation.

10.8.6 Critical comment on Four Links Model

At least in part, such a model may not have the precision and clarity of the Five Forces Model and other competitor analyses: networks come and go, complementors may come to disagree, alliances may fall apart and democratic governments fail to be re-elected. All linkage relationships lack the simplicity of the bargaining power and competitive threat analyses of the Five Forces Model. However, the Four Links Model is essentially concerned with co-operation between organisations (see Figure 10.6). This will have many facets that go beyond simple bargaining relationships.

Developing such links is likely to involve, at least in part, an emergent approach to strategy development. Linkages may provide opportunities to experiment and develop new and original strategies. They may allow an unusual move in strategy development that will deliver sustainable competitive advantage. Hence, even though they may be imprecise and lacking in the simplicities of economic logic, such linkages deserve careful analysis.

Beyond the analysis of co-operation, companies have now come to recognise that co-operation provides new strategic opportunities. Strategic alliances, joint ventures and other forms of co-operation have been identified as possibilities for strategy development.

KEY STRATEGIC PRINCIPLES

- In addition to competing against rivals, most organisations also co-operate with other organisations. Such co-operation can deliver sustainable competitive advantage.

- The main elements that need to be analysed for co-operation are captured in the *Four Links Model*: informal co-operative links and networks, formal co-operative links, complementors and government links and networks.

- *Informal co-operative links and networks* are the range of contacts that arise from organisations joining together informally for a common purpose. *Formal co-operative linkages* are usually bound by some form of legal contract – examples include alliances and joint ventures. *Complementors* are those companies whose products add more value to the products of the base organisation than they would derive from their own products by themselves. *Government links and networks* concern the relationships that exist between national and international governments and organisations, including those concerning tax, legislation and formal government purchasing.

- Such relationships can be measured by the strength of the linkage in the case of the first three. In the case of government, they may be better measured by considering the opportunities and threats posed by the relationship. All such links are often less structured and formalised than those involving competitor analysis but may represent significant areas of long-term competitive advantage.

10.9 ANALYSING ONE OR MORE IMMEDIATE COMPETITORS IN DEPTH

In any analysis of competitors and their relationship to the organisation, it is useful to analyse some immediate and close competitors: this is often called competitor profiling. The purpose is to identify the competitive advantages (and disadvantages) of the organisation against its competitors.

10.9.1 What are the sustainable competitive advantages of our competitors?

Definition ▶ **Sustainable competitive advantage is an advantage over competitors that cannot easily be imitated.** Broad surveys of competitive forces are useful in strategy analysis. But it is normal to select one or two companies for more detailed examination to identify the competitive advantage of our company against one or two rivals. The reason is that sustainable competitive advantage becomes more precise and meaningful when we make a specific analysis of our competitors. Some rival companies will have competitive advantages that make them formidable opponents; for example, well-respected brand names like Coca-Cola and Volkswagen, specialist technologies such as laser printer production at the Japanese company Canon, and unique locations of hotels and restaurants, such as those owned by McDonald's. We focus in this section on analysing the competitive advantages of our competitors in the strategic environment.

10.9.2 Competitor profiling

As a starting point, it is useful to undertake competitor profiling – that is, the basic analysis of a leading competitor, covering its objectives, resources, market strength and current strategies.

In many markets, there will be more than one competitor and it will not be possible to analyse them all. It will be necessary to make a choice – usually the one or two that represent the most direct threat. In public service organisations where the competition may be for *resources* rather than for *customers*, the same principle can be adopted, with the choice being made among the agencies competing for funds. In small businesses, the need to understand competitors is just as great, although here it may be more difficult to identify which company will pose the most direct threat; a *typical* competitor may be selected in these circumstances. Once the choice has been made, the following aspects of the competitor's organisation need to be explored:

- *Objectives.* If the competitor is seeking sales growth or market share growth, this may involve an aggressive stance in the market place. If the company is seeking profit growth, it may choose to achieve this by investing in new plant or by some other means that might take time to implement. If this is the case, there will be less of an immediate impact on others in the market place, but new plant may mean lower costs and a longer-term impact on prices. Company annual reports and press statements may be helpful here in defining what the competitor says it wants to do. These need to be treated with some caution, however, since the company may be bluffing or using some other competitive technique.

- *Resources.* The scale and size of the company's resources are an important indicator of its competitive threat – perhaps it has superior or inferior technology, perhaps over-manning at its plants, perhaps financial problems.

- *Past record of performance.* Although this may be a poor guide to the future, it is direct evidence that is publicly available through financial statements and stockbrokers' reports.

- *Current products and services.* Many companies buy competing products or services for the sole purpose of tearing them apart. They analyse customers, quality, performance, after-sales service, promotional material and some will even interview former employees – unethical perhaps, but it does happen.

- *Links with other organisations.* Joint members, alliances and other forms of co-operation may deliver significant competitive advantage.

- *Present strategies.* Attitudes to subjects such as innovation, leading customers, finance and investment, human resource management, market share, cost reduction, product range, pricing and branding all deserve investigation.

Competitor profiling is time-consuming but vital to the development of strategic management. Some larger companies employ whole departments whose sole task is to monitor leading competitors. Small businesses also often have an acute awareness of their competitors, although this may be derived more informally at trade meetings, social occasions, exhibitions and so on. In strategic management, it is vital to gain a 'feel' for competitors.

10.9.3 Emergent perspectives on competition

One of the main dangers of competitive profiling is that it will be seen as essentially static. In practice, all organisations are changing all the time. Moreover, the competitive profiling process should be regarded as one of discovery and one that never finishes. Emergent perspectives on competitor analysis, which emphasise this changing nature, will deliver useful insights, especially where the environment is changing rapidly. For example, emergent perspectives are *essential* when analysing internet competitors in the recorded music industry – see, for example, Case 13 in Part 6.

10.9.4 Outcome of competitor profiling

However imprecisely, it is important to draw up a clear statement of the competitive advantages held by a rival organisation compared to ourselves. A useful means of summarising this is the SWOT analysis.

KEY STRATEGIC PRINCIPLES

- An environmental analysis needs to identify the competitive advantages of rival companies. This is undertaken using competitor profiling. It will seek to identify the competitive advantages by focusing on one or two rival companies in depth.

- More generally, it will explore the objectives, resources, past performance, current products and services, and present strategies of one or two competitors.

- Competitor profiling should be regarded as an ongoing task. Its emergent nature is particularly important in fast-moving markets.

10.10 ANALYSING THE CUSTOMER AND MARKET SEGMENTATION

Since customers generate the revenues that keep the organisation in existence and deliver its profits, customers are crucial in strategic management. In this context it is perhaps surprising that much greater emphasis has been given in some aspects of strategic development to *competition* rather than to the customer.[36] The reason is that the focus of the purchase decision for the customer is a competitive selection between the different products or services on offer. While this is undoubtedly true, it is easy to lose sight of the direct strategic importance of the customer.

There are three useful dimensions to an analysis of the customer:

1 identification of the customer and the market;

2 market segmentation and its strategic implications;

3 market positioning usually within a segment.

10.10.1 Identification of the customer and the market

Back in the 1960s, Levitt[37] wrote a famous article that argued that the main reason some organisations were in decline was because they had become too heavily product-oriented, and were not sufficiently customer-oriented. As a result, they defined their customer base too narrowly. To help this process, a useful distinction can be made between:[38]

- *immediate customer base* – for example, those travelling on railways; and

- *wider customer franchise* – for example, those travelling by public transport, including railways, aircraft and buses.

In order to define accurately this aspect of the environment it is important to develop strategies that identify customers and competitors. Ultimately, if the market environment is incorrectly defined, then competitors may creep up and steal customers without the company realising it until it is too late. Furthermore, it is vital to analyse *future* customers as well as the *current* customer profile.

10.10.2 Market segmentation

For many markets, customer analysis needs to move beyond the consideration of basic markets to an analysis of specific parts of a market – *market segmentation* – and to the competitive stance of organisations within the segment – their *market positioning*, which is explored in the next section.

Definition ▶ **Market segmentation is the identification of specific groups (or segments) of customers who respond to competitive strategies differently from other groups.**

The basic sequence for exploring the approach is shown in Figure 10.7. It employs a *prescriptive* approach as a first step in order to explore the elements. In practice, the sequence is likely to be more experimental and, in this sense, *emergent*, because it is often necessary to explore a number of positioning areas: this is also outlined in Figure 10.7.

The three prescriptive stages are:

1 *Identify market segment(s).* Identification of specialist needs of segments will lead to customer profiles of those in the segments.

2 *Evaluate segment(s).* Some segments are likely to be more attractive than others. They need to be identified and targeted.

3 *Position within market segment.* Within the segment, companies will then need to develop a differential advantage over competitors. See the example in Figure 10.8.

In the development of customer strategy, customer analysis will often move rapidly to an examination of market segmentation.[39] Market segmentation may be defined as the identification of specific groups (or segments) of customers who respond differently from other groups to competitive strategies. The advantages of identifying a market segment include:

- Strength in (and possibly dominance of) a group, even though the overall market is large. It may be more profitable to have a large share of a group than a small share of the main market. Thus competitive advantage may be stronger in a segment than in the broader market.

- Closer matching of customer needs and the organisation's resources through targeting the segment. This will enhance sustainable competitive advantage.

- Concentration of effort on a smaller area, so that the company's resources can be employed more effectively.

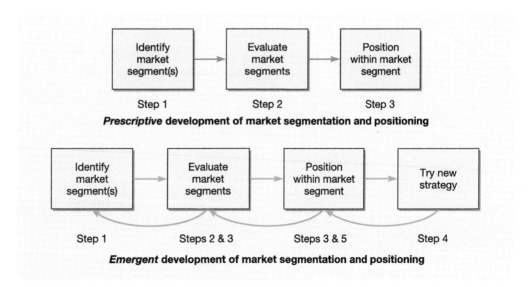

Figure 10.7 Market segmentation and position

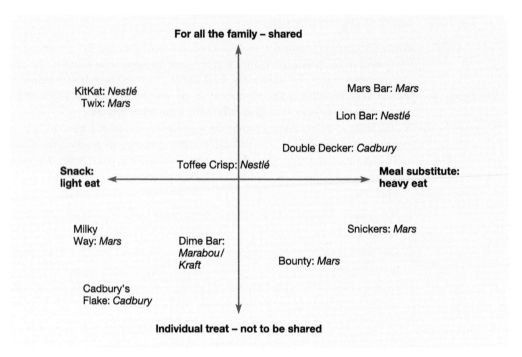

Figure 10.8 An example of market positioning – chocolate countlines

Hence, from a strategic viewpoint, the key advantage of market segmentation is probably the ability to dominate a sector of a market and then target benefits that will sustain this position, as in the case of Dyson's domination of the premium-priced vacuum cleaner segment.

Typical bases for segmentation in consumer and industrial markets are listed in Table 10.5. However, markets can be segmented by any criteria that prove helpful and do not necessarily need to conform to this list.

Having established the segments, strategic customer analysis then proceeds to evaluate the *usefulness* of each segment: Step 2 in Figure 10.7. It is not enough for a segment to be different. There are four important characteristics of any segment if it is to be useful in strategic customer analysis. It must be:

1 *Distinguishable.* Customers must be distinguishable so that they can be isolated in some way.

2 *Relevant to purchasing.* The distinguishing criteria must relate to differences in market demand. For example, they may pay higher prices for higher quality.

3 *Sufficiently large.* If the segment is too small, then it will not justify the resources needed to reach it.

4 *Reachable.* It must be possible to direct the strategy to that segment.

It is also important to assess the future growth prospects of the segment.

Table 10.5 Typical bases for market segmentation

Consumer products	Industrial products
• Geographic	• Area or region of country
• Demographic (age, sex, education, etc.)	• End-use
• Socio-economic and income	• Customer business
• Ethnic group	• Buying situation
• Benefits sought	• Market served
• Usage rate and brand loyalty	• Value added by customer
• Attitudes	• Source of competitive advantage (price, service, etc.)
• Lifestyle	• Emphasis on R&D and innovation
• Situation (where the consumption takes place)	• Professional membership

KEY STRATEGIC PRINCIPLES

- There are three prescriptive stages in developing market segmentation and positioning: identify potential segments, evaluate and select segment(s), and position within segment(s).
- Market segmentation is the identification of specific groups of customers who respond differently from other groups to competitive strategies. They can be important in strategy development because they provide the opportunity to dominate part of the market.
- Identification of gaps in segment provision may provide the basis of new strategic opportunities.

10.10.3 Competitive positioning[40]

Although a useful segment has been identified, this does not in itself resolve the organisation's strategy. The competitive position within the segment then needs to be explored, because only this will show how the organisation will compete within the segment. **Competitive positioning is the choice of differential advantage possessed by an organisation that allows it to compete and survive in a market place or in a segment of a market place.** A typical example of positioning is shown in Figure 10.8.

Definition ▶

For example, both the Mars Company (USA) and Nestlé (Switzerland) compete in the market for chocolate products. However, the Mars' product Snickers is positioned as a 'meal substitute' – it can be eaten in place of a meal, whereas the Nestlé product KitKat is positioned as a 'snack' – it can be eaten as a break but is not substantial enough to be a substitute for a meal. Competitive positioning is thus the choice of differential advantage that the product or service will possess against its competitors. To develop positioning, it is useful to follow a two-stage process – first identify the segment gaps, second identify positioning within segments.

Identification of segmentation gaps and their competitive positioning implications

From a strategy viewpoint, the most useful strategic analysis often emerges by exploring where there are *gaps* in the segments of an industry: amongst others, Porter[41] and Ohmae[42] recommend this route. The starting point for such work is to map out the current segmentation position and then place companies and their products into the segments: it should then become clear where segments exist that are not served or are poorly served by current products. This is shown in Exhibit 10.5 using the European ice cream case as an example.

EXHIBIT 10.5

New or under-utilised segment gaps: Unilever's presence in the European ice cream market, early 2000s

Market basis for possible segmentation

	Buyer type 1	Buyer type 2	Buyer type 3, etc.
Product variety 1			
Product variety 2			
Product variety 3, etc.			

Step 1: Existing segments with Unilever's European presence shown

	Grocery supermarkets	Small grocery stores	Restaurants and takeaways	Newsagents and leisure facilities
Superpremium	✔ market test only			✔ few
Premium	✔	✔		✔ most
Regular	✔			
Economy	✔	✔ some		

Step 2: Some possible new segments in addition to the above

	Garages	Temporary facilities at sporting and cultural events	Factory canteens and restaurants: contract catering
Superpremium		✔	
Premium	✔		
Regular			✔
Economy			✔

Note: For the sake of clarity, only Unilever's presence is shown in the above. Moreover, the example is *illustrative only* and may not represent the actual practice of the Unilever subsidiaries in each country. Further segmentation analyses based on criteria such as the geographical country might also produce some useful additional information.

Comment: It will be evident that there are some gaps in the existing coverage of the market. The segmentation criteria outlined in the text above could be used to assess whether it would be worthwhile filling the gaps. One obvious area where Unilever could take action was in the superpremium sector.

Identifying the positioning within the segment[43]

From a strategy perspective, some gaps may be more attractive than others. For example, they may have limited competition or poorly supported products. In addition, some gaps may possess a clear advantage in terms of competitive positioning. Others may not. To explore the development of positioning, we can return to our earlier example of two chocolate countlines from Nestlé and Mars. The full positioning map for the range of such products was shown earlier in the chapter in Figure 10.8.

The process of developing positioning of chocolate countlines runs as follows:

1 *Perceptual mapping* – in-depth qualitative research on actual and prospective customers on the way that they make their decisions in the market place, for example, strong versus weak, cheap versus expensive, modern versus traditional. In the case of chocolate the dimensions of meal/snack and family/individual were established.

2 *Positioning.* Brands or products are then placed on the map using the research dimensions. Figure 10.8 presents the existing configuration.

3 *Options development.* Take existing and new products and use their existing strengths and weaknesses to devise possible new positions on the map. Figure 10.8 shows some gaps for some companies and some products that have an unclear position – Toffee Crisp at the time of the research.

4 *Testing* – first with simple statements with customers, then at a later stage in the market place.

It will be evident that this is essentially an emergent rather than a prescriptive process, involving experimentation with actual and potential customers.

KEY STRATEGIC PRINCIPLES

- Competitive positioning is the choice of differential advantage that the product or service will possess against its competitors.

- The sequence for developing competitive positioning has four main steps: perceptual mapping, positioning, options development and testing. The process is essentially emergent rather than prescriptive.

CASE STUDY 10.5
Arçelik aims for Europe

When Arçelik's home market demand declined in 2000, Turkey's leading domestic appliance company aimed its export strategy at Europe. This case explains its four main strategies and how they made the company the third largest in Europe.

Background: domestic strength in the 1990s

Arçelik has been making domestic appliances – washing machines, refrigerators, freezers and ovens – since the 1950s. It is controlled by one of Turkey's leading and most respected industrial groups, Koç Holdings. The holding company had sales of $43 billion in 2010 and, within this, Arçelik had sales of $3.5 billion – by any standards, an important company.

Back in the 1990s, Arçelik's domestic appliance business had been steadily expanded to dominate its Turkish home market. The country itself had a population of over 70 million with rapidly rising wealth. Arçelik's nearest competitor was another Turkish company called Vestel. But Arçelik's strategies were so successful that it had almost four times the sales of its rival. There were four key strategies:

1 branding under the Arçelik and Beko brand names;

2 quality-driven products;

3 efficient low-cost production;

4 extensive and dominant distribution outlets in all the main Turkish towns.

Arçelik's strategy in Turkey relies on distribution through its own retail stores. But this retail strategy would take too long and be too expensive to set up across Europe.

Change in the strategic environment: Turkey's economy takes a downturn

Around year 2000, Turkey's economy took a severe downturn. Arçelik was already exporting its domestic appliances outside Turkey in small quantities, but this only amounted to 15 per cent of its business. Suddenly, the company was faced with a serious profit problem. Economies of scale are a key factor for success in the domestic appliance business, but the local Turkish market was in decline. The company decided to export more of its products. But which countries and with what strategies?

Arçelik's export strategies in year 2000

Western European markets for domestic appliances – like Germany, the UK and France – were large but relatively mature. The lack of growth made it more difficult for new companies to enter, especially those from outside the European Union (EU). However, the EU had agreed to reduce its trade barriers with Turkey back in 1996, so EU markets were at least open to Arçelik in 2000. The problem was rather different in Eastern Europe. Markets were just beginning to open up after the fall of communism. Wealth and demand for consumer products was rising, but there were few good manufacturers.

As a result of these differences, Arçelik decided on a two-pronged strategy. In Western Europe, it would export domestic appliances from its Turkish factories and acquire some European brand names. In the east, it would also export but would also set up factories that would serve regional markets. The outcome was a significant increase in international sales – see Figure 10.9. Much of this increase was founded on the four home strategies outlined above. However, there was one difference. Arçelik judged that it would take too long and be too expensive to copy the home market competitive advantage of its own shops and distribution outlets. It would simply sell Arçelik products through existing stores.

Arçelik's strategies in Western Europe

In order to gain a rapid foothold, Arçelik bought a series of small companies in France, Germany and the UK. These acquisitions were not wholly successful because the company needed to manufacture its products from its efficient plants in Turkey so it was really only buying brand names and reputations such as its purchases of the Flavel brand in the UK and the Grundig name in Germany. There were also reported to be other brand and company acquisitions, for example Arctic in Romania, Blomberg in Germany and Elektra Bregenz in Austria with most of these becoming sales and service companies for the Arçelik/Beko range. In addition to its acquisitions, Arçelik

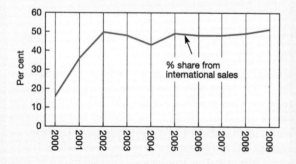

Figure 10.9 The outcome of Arçelik's export strategy

Source: author from Koç holding company report and accounts and research by Dr Tanses Gulsoy of Beykent University.

had to make another strategic decision: whether to make OEM goods or sell branded products.

Original equipment manufacture (OEM) refers to products that are made by one manufacturer and then sold to a second company who will re-brand them with the name of the second company. For example, Arçelik had the opportunity to make washing machines which were then sold in the UK under the brand name of a well-known retailer such as Tesco. The problem with OEM is that such contracts depend largely on price. Customers can switch over time to rivals offering lower prices. Competitive advantage is therefore low. By contrast, branding is initially more expensive in terms with, for example, the costs of advertising and sponsorship. However, it has several advantages. It allows companies like Arçelik to develop innovative and patented products and to develop a widely respected brand name over time. Importantly, branding and quality products were closer to Arçelik's core competencies back in its home country and thus familiar strategies for this company to develop and manage.

Initially, Arçelik undertook some OEM contracts. But its main strategy in Western Europe was brand building with the *Beko* brand name: the Turkish name Arçelik had some problems in terms of spelling the specialist Turkish letter ç and pronunciation in Western markets. Its acquisitions were supported but the main strategic effort was put behind the brand name Beko. Arguably, the acquisitions were expensive and unnecessary in the long term. Moreover, Arçelik had registered over 130 patents across Europe in a range of domestic appliance applications, thus delivering potential competitive advantages for its Beko branded product range.

Over the years from 2001, Beko slowly built its branded sales in some Western European countries. By 2010, it had become the second largest brand in the UK using advertising and sponsorship, strong retail distribution, good design and relatively low prices. It was less successful in Europe's biggest market, Germany, where the international and local brand competition was particularly strong. International brands included Electrolux and domestic brands included the German companies Bosch and Miele.

Arçelik in Eastern Europe and beyond

Given the low labour costs and potential for higher growth in Eastern Europe, Arçelik's strategy in this area was different. There were no acquisitions because there were no attractive companies. However, there were some opportunities, to set up new factories and build brands. As a result, by 2010, Arçelik had set up new plant in Romania and Russia and its brands held 35 per cent of the Romanian market and nearly 10 per cent of the Polish market.

Back in 2000, Arçelik opened up a sales office in China. Market demand was such that the company decided to expand its operations in 2007 by opening up its first factory in that country. It then followed this with a small number of Chinese domestic appliance stores – similar to those back in Turkey.

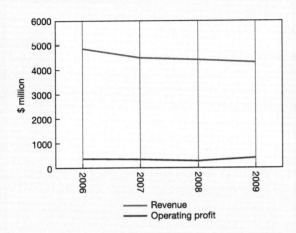

— Revenue
— Operating profit

Figure 10.10 Arçelik's profit downturn with declining national economies

Source: author from Koç holding company report and accounts.

Arçelik's profit record

Although the company made major advances in Europe in the period to 2010, it also suffered a dip in profits over this time – see Figure 10.10. In 2008, its profits were still based largely on its Turkish production plants and had declined by 25 per cent compared with two years earlier. This was primarily due to a drop in sales as European market demand declined as a result of international economic pressures: economies of scale can be affected disproportionately by declines in sales. Arçelik reacted by new cost cutting and efficiency strategies inside the company: better inventory management and improved stock turnover resulting in lower working capital. By 2011, Arçelik had become the third largest domestic appliance brand in Western Europe behind Electrolux from Sweden and Indesit from Italy.

Arçelik has been using its R&D facilities to develop new, greener domestic appliances. The Koç group has a strong record of sustainability projects.

Case questions

1 What strategic environmental factors have influenced Arçelik's strategic decisions? And with what outcomes?

2 What were Arçelik's competitive advantages? Why was OEM inconsistent with these? Given its profit problems in 2008, would you have advised Arçelik to change strategy and pursue some OEM contracts?

3 Thinking about the various possible growth markets around the world, would you advise Arçelik to open up more country markets as part of its growth strategy? Or should the company concentrate primarily on its existing countries? You can assume that Arçelik is typical of many companies with only a limited amount of resources – both financial and human – to undertake further expansion.

CRITICAL REFLECTION

What purpose is served by analysing the strategic environment?

There are two fundamental assumptions that underpin this chapter. First, strategic analysis assumes that it is possible to learn from past events. This assumption is important because strategy is essentially about future actions. Second, such a study implicitly assumes that the future is predictable in some way – otherwise, there would be little point in drawing any lessons from the analysis. Both these assumptions may rest on shaky foundations.

'Learning from the past' may examine a strategic environment with strategic perceptions and definitions that no longer apply: for example, the traditional market for air travel has been revolutionised by redefining it as being just like getting on a bus where aircraft seats are readily available without lengthy booking procedures. In the same way, 'Predicting the future' always runs the risk of making an incorrect prediction: for example, who would have predicted 15 years ago how the internet would develop?

Perhaps, in developing new strategies, we cannot learn much from the past. Perhaps we cannot usefully predict the future. In which case, what purpose is served by PESTEL Analysis, Porter's Five Forces, etc.?

SUMMARY

In analysing the environment surrounding the organisation, ten main factors were identified.

- *Environmental analysis can usefully begin with a basic assessment of the market definition and size, the market growth and the market share.* Market definition is important because it will determine the size and scope of the strategic opportunity. Market growth is commonly estimated early in any strategic analysis because of its importance with regard to the growth objectives of an organisation. A basic estimate of market share can be used to estimate whether an organisation has a significant share of a market as a starting point in exploring the strategic implications.

- *A general consideration of the nature of the environment and, in particular, the degree of turbulence.* When events are particularly uncertain and prone to sudden and significant change, strategic management needs to become more flexible and organise its procedures to cope with the situation.

- *A general analysis of the factors that will affect many industries.* This can be undertaken by two procedures: the PESTEL analysis and scenarios. The PESTEL analysis explores political, economic, socio-cultural, technological, environmental and legal influences on the organisation. It is important when undertaking such an analysis to develop a shortlist of only the most important items, not a long list under every heading. In analysing the role and influence of government on strategy, the E–S–P Paradigm – Environment, System, Policies – can form a useful structure for this purpose. Influencing government policy may form an important element of strategy. In developing scenarios, it should be recognised that they provide a different view of conceivable future events, rather than predict the future.

- *Growth characteristics* can be explored using the industry life cycle concept. Markets are divided into a series of development stages: introduction, growth, maturity and decline. In addition, the maturity stage may be subject to the cyclical variations associated with general economic or other factors over which the company has little control.

- Different stages of the life cycle demand different corporate strategies. The early stages probably require greater investment in R&D and marketing to develop and explain the product. The later stages should be more profitable on a conventional view of the life cycle. However, there is an argument that takes a more unconventional stance: it suggests that it is during the mature phase that investment should increase in order to restore growth.

- *Key factors for success in an industry:* identifying these can help focus strategy development on those areas that really matter. They can conveniently be considered under three headings: customers, competition and corporation. By 'corporation' is meant the resources of the organisation. Key factors can be found in any area of the organisation and relate to skills, competitive advantage, competitive resources of an organisation in the industry, special technologies or customer contacts. Four criticisms of key factors have been made: identification, causality of relationships, dangers of generalising, and disregard of emergent perspectives. Caution is therefore needed in their application.

- *A Five Forces Analysis.* This will involve an examination of buyers, suppliers, new entrants, substitutes and the competition in the industry. The aim is to analyse the balance of power between each force and the organisation in the industry.

- *A Four Links Analysis* of those outside bodies cooperating with the organisation. This will include a study of the complementors, networks and legal links that the organisation has with its environment. The purpose is to analyse the relative strengths of such links and their ability to enhance the competitive advantages of the organisation.

- *A study of selected direct competitors.* An environmental analysis needs to identify the competitive advantages of rival companies. This is undertaken using competitor profiling. It will seek to identify the competitive advantages by focusing on one or two rival companies in depth. More generally, it will explore the objectives, resources, past performance, current products and services, and present strategies of one or two competitors. Such a study needs to recognise the fluid and changing nature of competitors and their resources.

- *A study of customers, market segmentation and positioning.* The final area of analysis is concerned with actual and potential customers and their importance to the organisation. Segmentation of markets derives from customer analysis and plays an important role in strategic management development. Positioning then determines how products will compete to attract customers in a particular part of the market.

QUESTIONS

1 Using Case 10.4 and your judgement, determine the degree of turbulence in the Hollywood film industry. Give reasons for your views.

2 Undertake a general environmental analysis of an industry of your choice, using both the PESTEL format and scenarios to draw out the major strategic issues.

3 Develop and compare the key factors for success in the following three industries: the computer industry (see companies like Acer and Hewlett-Packard in Case 11 in Part 6), the ice cream industry and the Indian motorcycle industry (Chapter 10).

4 For the Indian motorcycle industry, analyse the competitive forces within the industry using the Five Forces Model. Identify also any forms of co-operation in the industry using a Four Links Analysis.

5 Based on your answers to the previous questions, what strategic advice would you offer Bajaj? Use Section 10.7.6 to assist you.

6 Undertake a life cycle analysis of an industry of your choice. What strategic conclusions would you draw for

organisations in the industry, if any? Comment specifically on the difficulties of this approach.

7 Prepare a full environmental analysis for an industry of your choice and make recommendations on its future strategic management.

8 Undertake a customer analysis for your own organisation. What segments can you identify? What role is played by customer service and quality? What strategic conclusions can you draw?

9 Do you agree with the statement that stable environments favour prescriptive approaches to strategy whereas turbulent environments demand emergent strategies? Consider carefully the impact technology may have on a stable environment and the problem of long-term investment, even in turbulent industries – remember Blockbuster at the beginning of this chapter.

10 To what extent can competitive analytical techniques be applied to the public sector and charitable institutions?

FURTHER READING

M E Porter's *Competitive Strategy: Techniques for Analysing Industries and Competitors* (The Free Press, Harvard, MA, 1980) has careful and detailed studies for analysis of the immediate competitive environment. Mona Makhija's paper (2003) 'Comparing the resource-based and market-based views of the firm: empirical evidence from Czech privatisation', *Strategic Management Journal*, Vol 24, pp 433–451.

Professor Porter's article, 'How competitive forces shape strategy' (1979) *Harvard Business Review*, March–April, pp 136–145,

is probably the classic short analysis here, but note that it says little or nothing about the importance of co-operation.

Finally, for a comprehensive review of the underpinning economic theory, read Séan Rickard's Chapter 5 entitled 'Industrial Organisation Economics Perspective' in the edited text: Mark Jenkins and Veronique Ambrosini with Nardine Collier (2007) *Advanced Strategic Management*, 2nd edn, Palgrave Macmillan, Basingstoke, pp 61–82.

NOTES AND REFERENCES

1 Sources for the Blockbuster case: *Financial Times*: 8 November 2011, p 23; 11 October 2011, p 17; 10 January 2012, p 18; 6 December 2012, p 28; Blockbuster website: http://web. archive.org/web/19961224035012/http://blockbuster.com/; *Blockbuster press releases*: 31 December 2003; 3 January 2007; 23 September 2010; *CNN Money*, 1 July 2003, 'He Began Blockbuster. So What? David Cook created a household name,

but he refuses to become one', Joshua Hyatt; *New York Times*, 8 April 2011, 'Other Retailers Find Ex-Blockbuster Stores Just Right', Stephanie Clifford; *Los Angeles Times*, 7 April 2011, Dish network wins bidding for assets of bankrupt Blockbuster; *Digital Trends*: http://www.digitaltrends.com/ home-theater/dish-network-shutting-down-a-third-of-all-remaining-blockbuster-stores/#!bh97ek.

2 Porter, M E (1980) *Competitive Strategy*, The Free Press, New York.

3 Andrews, K (1987) *The Concept of Corporate Strategy*, Irwin, Homewood, IL.

4 Many strategy texts (including previous editions of this one!) set out in great depth various environmental concepts and forget that it is useful to begin with some basic data.

5 Levitt, T (1960) 'Marketing myopia', *Harvard Business Review*, July–August, pp 45–56. Levitt's paper challenged the traditional definitions of the market.

6 There may be tautological problems here, but it is not appropriate to explore these at this early stage in strategy analysis. Suffice to say that it is possible to pursue this academic debate by starting with the well-known text by Buzzell, R D and Gale, B T (1987) *The PIMS Principles*, The Free Press, London. Follow this up with Baker, M (1993) *Marketing Strategy and Management*, 2nd edn, Macmillan, London.

7 Porter, M E (1980) Op. cit., Ch 2.

8 The early part of this section is based on Ansoff, I and MacDonnell, E (1990) *Implanting Strategic Management*, 2nd edn, Prentice Hall, Englewood Cliffs, NJ.

9 D'Aveni, R (1994) *Hypercompetitive Rivalries*, Free Press, New York.

10 Simon, H 'The corporation: will it be managed by machine?', in Leavitt, H and Pondy, L (eds) (1964) *Readings in Managerial Psychology*, University of Chicago Press, Chicago, IL, pp 592–617.

11 Baden-Fuller, C and Stopford, J (1992) *Rejuvenating the Mature Business*, Routledge, Ch 2.

12 Aaker, D R (1992) *Strategic Marketing Management*, 3rd edn, Wiley, New York, p 236.

13 Smallwood, J E (1973) 'The product life cycle: a key to strategic marketing planning', *MSU Business Topics*, Winter, pp 29–35.

14 Baker, M (1993) *Marketing Strategy and Management*, 2nd edn, Macmillan, London, p 100 *et seq.* presents a short defence and interesting discussion of the main areas.

15 Dallah, N Y and Yuspeh, S (1976) 'Forget the product life cycle concept', *Harvard Business Review*, January–February, p 101 *et seq.*

16 Sources for the Bajaj case: *Financial Times*: 12 May 1999, p 31; 4 September 2007, p 14; 9 January 2008, p 30. *DNA Money Mumbai*: 24 November 2007, p 27; 26 November 2007, p 25. *The Economist*, 10 January 2008. *Economic Times*, 11 January 2008 – extracted from the *Times of India* website. Websites: www.bajaj.com and www.herohonda.com. Bajaj Auto annual report and accounts 2010: all the market data is sourced from this well-presented and clearly written document.

17 Ohmae, K (1983) *The Mind of the Strategist*, Penguin, Harmondsworth, Ch 3.

18 Porter, M E (1985) *Competitive Advantage*, The Free Press, New York, Ch 7.

19 Kay, J (1993) *Foundations of Corporate Success*, Oxford University Press, Oxford, Chs 5 to 8.

20 Amit, R and Schoemaker, P (1993) 'Strategic assets and organizational rent', *Strategic Management Journal*, Vol 14, pp 33–46.

21 Ohmae, K (1983) Op. cit., p 96.

22 Ghemawat, P (1991) *Commitment*, The Free Press, New York.

23 Porter, M E (1980) Op. cit. Note that Porter's work owes much to the writings of Professor Joel Bain and others in the 1950s on industrial economies. However, it was Porter who gave this earlier material its strategic focus. See also Porter's article, 'How competitive forces shape strategy' (1979) *Harvard Business Review*, March–April, pp 136–145, which is a useful summary of the main points from the early part of his book.

24 Op. cit., p 4.

25 Porter (1980) actually refers in his book to 'six' areas and then goes on to list seven!

26 Cusumano, M and Takeishi, A (1991) 'Supplier relations and management: a survey of Japanese, Japanese transplant and US auto plants', *Strategic Management Journal*, Vol 12, pp 563–588.

27 Nielsen, A C (1988) *International Food and Drug Store Trends*, Nielsen, Oxford.

28 Aaker, D (1992) Op. cit.

29 Baker, M (1993) Op. cit

30 Harvey-Jones, J (1991) *Getting it Together*, Heinemann, London, Ch 14.

31 Porter (1980) Op. cit., Chs 7 and 8.

32 Reve, T (1990) 'The firm as a nexus of internal and external contracts', *The Firm as a Nexus of Treaties*, Aoki, M, Gustafson, M and Williamson, O E (eds), Sage, London. See also Kay, J (1993) *The Foundations of Corporate Success*, Oxford University Press, Oxford, Ch 5.

33 Kay, J (1993) Op. cit., p 80.

34 Kay, J (1993) Op. cit.: Ch 5 on architecture explores this topic in depth.

35 Nalebuff, B J and Brandenburger, A M (1997) *Coopetition*, HarperCollins Business, London.

36 For example, Porter, M E (1980) Op. cit.

37 Levitt, T (1960) 'Marketing myopia', *Harvard Business Review*, July–August, p 45.

38 Davidson, H (1987) *Offensive Marketing*, Penguin, Harmondsworth.

39 Aaker, D (1992) Op. cit., p 48.

40 It should be noted that, in theory at least, it is not necessary to segment a market before exploring its competitive positioning. However, it is usual and much easier to select part of a market before undertaking positioning. Many marketing strategy texts do not make this clear.

41 Porter, M E (1985) *Competitive Advantage*, The Free Press, New York, p 233.

42 Ohmae, K (1983) *The Mind of the Strategist*, Penguin, Harmondsworth, p 103.

43 Probably the best-known text exploring positioning issues in depth is: Hooley, G J and Saunders, J (1999) *Competitive Positioning*, Prentice Hall, Hemel Hempstead.

11 Size structure of firms

Chris Britton

Businesses range in size from the single proprietor at one extreme to the large multinational at the other which employs thousands of people over several countries. The structures of these businesses will be very different and the problems they face will vary as a result of the differences in size. The size structure of business will depend on many factors, which range from choice (the sole proprietor may choose to remain small) to external factors that are beyond the control of the firm.

Learning outcomes

Having read this chapter you should be able to:

- outline the size structure of UK industry
- provide reasons for why organisations grow in size
- demonstrate the way in which organisations grow and the methods of finance
- explain the limitations to growth
- survey the level of merger activity in the United Kingdom and the European Union
- demonstrate the role and importance of the small-firm sector
- discuss the idea of networking between firms

Key terms

Capital market	External growth	Networking
Concentration	Flexible firm	Profit
Conglomerate merger	Gearing	Small firm
Debentures	Horizontal merger	Stock Exchange
Diseconomies of scale	Industrial concentration	Subcontracting
Diversification	Internal growth	Takeover
Dividends	Joint venture	Vertical integration
Enterprise	Merger	Virtual organisation
Equity	Money market	
Establishment	Multinational corporation	

Introduction

Evidence suggests that national concentration levels have increased over time due to mergers and takeovers but that global concentration levels are lower than national ones.[1] Such an increase in the size of business organisations gives rise to worries about the concentration of power in the hands of a few producers and potential abuses of this power. If the companies are multinationals, they may be beyond the control even of national governments. More recently the trend towards greater **concentration** has been reversed and there seems to be a movement towards employment in smaller units. This chapter will look at the size structure of British industry and the reasons for such a structure, with some international comparisons. It will consider the role of small and large firms in the economy. It will also examine the reasons for growth, the ways in which organisations grow, the financing of growth and the limits to growth. Consideration will be given to the relatively more recent trend towards cooperation in production, rather than competition, through activities such as joint ventures and networking.

The size structure of UK industry

When looking at the size of firms it is important to define the terms used in official data. The firm, or '**enterprise**', is the organisation as a whole, and it might be comprised of several units or '**establishments**'. Small firms like the corner shop will mostly be enterprises with only one establishment. Large firms like Sainsbury's will have many establishments as they have branches in most towns.

There are many different ways to measure the size of firms. Common measures used are turnover, the value of output, the capital employed or the level of employment. Such measurement is beset by problems, not least the difficulty of defining the small firm, as we will see later in this chapter. The three measures mentioned above might give conflicting pictures, as an industry that is becoming increasingly mechanised will probably have rising levels of average capital employed and output but falling average levels of employment. Table 11.1 shows the 'top ten' companies in the United Kingdom in 2012 using two of these measures and it illustrates the point

Table 11.1 The ten largest companies in the UK, 2012

Ranking by turnover	Ranking by employment
1 EDF Trading Ltd	1 G4S plc
2 Tesco plc	2 Tesco plc
3 Vodafone Group plc	3 Compass Group plc
4 Unilever plc	4 HSBC Holdings plc
5 ConocoPhillips Holdings Ltd	5 Royal Mail Holdings plc
6 SSE Energy Supply Ltd	6 Asda Group Ltd
7 SSE plc	7 Wal-Mart Stores (UK) Ltd
8 Imperial Tobacco Group plc	8 Asda Stores Ltd
9 Aviva plc	9 Unilever plc
10 Phillips 66 Ltd	10 Royal Mail Group plc

Source: Key British Enterprises, 2013.

Table 11.2 Size structure of UK industry by employment, 2013

Employment size group	Number of units	% of total	Employment (000s)	% of total
1–9	2 170 080	82.7	3 848	19.2
10–49	367 055	14.0	3 471	17.4
50–249	76 635	2.9	2 909	14.6
250 +	11 720	0.4	9 763	48.8

Source: Adapted from Table A1.2 UK Business: Activity, size and location, 2013, *www.ons.gov.uk*

that different measures of the size of a firm will give different rankings. Some of these names will be familiar to the reader while others will be less so. Compass Group plc, for example, is a food service organisation that provides catering and support services to its clients, and ConocoPhillips Holdings Ltd is a multinational petrochemical company.

The most common measure of size used is the level of employment. Table 11.2 shows the size structure of units in all industries by the number of employees in the UK in 2013. The table shows that smaller firms predominate in terms of numbers, with 96.7 per cent of firms employing fewer than 50 employees. In terms of employment, however, these firms account for only 36.6 per cent of the total level of employment in manufacturing. At the other end of the scale, establishments with more than 250 employees account for only 0.4 per cent of the total number but 48.8 per cent of total employment. The pattern of size structure varies across industries and over time. In the last 30 years there seems to have been an increase in the importance of small firms and a decline in the importance of large firms in their contribution to employment. In 1980, establishments with fewer than 200 employees accounted for 31.9 per cent of total employment and establishments with more than 500 employees accounted for 49.8 per cent. The comparable figures for 2013 were 41.0 per cent and 48.9 per cent.

Many of the large companies listed in Table 11.1 operate in more than one country and are therefore multinationals. **Multinational corporations** strictly defined are enterprises operating in a number of countries and having production or service facilities outside the country of their origin.[2] Multinationals pose particular problems for governments and economies because of their size.

Organisational growth

The reasons for organisational growth

Firms grow in size for many reasons. Growth could be an explicit objective of management or could be necessary for the successful operation of the firm:

- Growth could be a managerial objective if it brings benefits to management such as greater security and higher remuneration.
- It could be that the market in which the business operates is expanding and growth is necessary to maintain market share. This is especially the case as markets become more international.
- Growth enables the organisation to reap the benefits of economies of scale.

- Growth enables firms to diversify into other markets, which means that risk can be spread further.
- Industries that are capital intensive will of necessity be comprised of large firms.
- In the area of product development it is possible that the necessary research and development could be carried out by large companies only.
- Growth could be pursued as a defensive strategy, as a reaction to the activities of competitors.

The European Commission puts forward the following motives for merger and acquisition activities: a search for efficiency gains through new combinations of material and immaterial assets; a drive to increase market shares and market power; a desire to safeguard access to important inputs; a search for access to new technologies and know-how; a drive to gain access to new customer groups or new geographic markets; and a desire for **diversification**.[3] The OECD[4] recognises that there are efficiencies involved in growth and it classifies these into 'static' and 'dynamic' efficiencies. Static efficiencies are one-off improvements such as economies of scale in production. Dynamic efficiencies are those that enable improvements in cost, quality, service or new product development on an ongoing basis. In considering the benefits of a takeover or merger, for example, it may be that the dynamic efficiencies will eventually overtake the initially bigger static efficiencies. Examples of dynamic efficiencies include:

- economies of scale and scope in R&D;
- better risk-spreading, especially for R&D;
- increased financial resources for R&D;
- better intellectual property rights protection.

In industrial economics, firm size is seen as a function of growth. It is suggested that although there is no limit on the size of a firm, there are limits on the rate of expansion. Growth rates are seen by different theorists to depend on different things, including the availability of finance, the level of consumer demand and the limitations of management. These theories, however, are primarily concerned with large firms and their development. Small firms are seen as potentially large firms that failed to grow for some reason or other. One interesting theory of growth is the stages model, where the firm is seen as passing through various stages in its development from small sole proprietor/partnership through the decision to expand into a large organisation. This again is a 'grow or fail' theory, which does not apply well to industries that are dominated by successful small firms, as we will see later in the chapter.

Methods of growth

Firms grow in size internally as part of normal business operation or externally through takeover and merger.

Internal growth

Growth is a natural process for many firms that start small, capture a segment of the market and then continue to expand either by producing more of the same goods or by extending their product lines. The advantage of **internal growth** over external growth is that the company grows within the existing structure of management; there are none of the problems of bringing together two different management systems. There might also be economies of scale from building a bigger plant that might not be available when companies merge and plant size does not change. Set against these, internal growth has certain disadvantages and this is why most of the growth in the size of organisations has occurred through external growth.

External growth

Growth by acquisition is called **external growth** and occurs through **takeover** or **merger**. A merger is the voluntary coming together of two companies with the agreement of the management of both companies, the result of which is the creation of a new legal identity. A takeover is where one company makes an offer to the shareholders of another. If the management of the threatened company resist, it is called a hostile takeover, but if the price offered to shareholders is high enough, they will accept. Takeover bids can be and have been successfully fought off by the management of the second firm. A holding company is a new company that is formed to acquire assets in other companies. The acquired companies retain their independent identities but are directed by the holding company.

External growth can be seen to have a number of advantages:

1 It is fast, so that productive capacity can be increased very quickly.
2 The acquiring firm has access to an established management team and system.
3 If the shares of the acquiring company have sufficiently high values relative to the acquired firm, there might be no need for additional cash to be raised.
4 The purchase of existing assets could be cheaper than building new productive capacity.

But set against these is the fact that the process might not be an easy one; it is a difficult job to merge two companies smoothly and successfully and there are likely to be many teething problems. Research by PricewaterhouseCoopers found that top executives regarded half of the takeovers in which they had been involved as failures. The main reasons for failure were lack of planning and managerial problems.

Although the definitions of merger and takeover are clear enough, it is often difficult to tell them apart in practice and they are usually put together in official publications under the heading of acquisitions. In order to understand fully the motivation for mergers and takeovers it is important to recognise that there are different types of mergers.

Horizontal mergers

A **horizontal merger** is where a combination between firms at the same stage in a production process takes place, for example between two car manufacturers or between two brewers. The vast majority of mergers that take place are of this type and many of our largest companies have been formed through horizontal merger. Examples include mergers between banks and building societies. The main motives for this type of merger are as follows:

- To benefit from economies of scale. Horizontal mergers allow the merged firms a greater level of specialisation and the benefits of other economies of scale.

- Greater market share. When firms come together there will be a reduction in competition in the market and the resulting firm will automatically have a much larger share of the market.
- Rationalisation of output. If the level of demand for a good is shrinking, merger between the producers could be necessary in order to rationalise output.
- Reaction to competitors. In markets where mergers are taking place, companies may feel that they have to do the same in order to maintain their market position.

A recent example of a horizontal merger is that between American Airlines and US Airways in December 2013, which created the biggest airline in the world.

Vertical mergers

A vertical merger involves firms at different stages of the same production process. It is vertical since it runs along the production process from extraction of raw materials to distribution. An example would be a merger between a car manufacturer and a metal-pressing company. **Vertical integration** can take place 'backwards' towards the beginning of the production process or 'forwards' towards the end of it and it can occur for several reasons:

1 In the case of backwards integration, to control the supplies of raw materials with respect to their quantity and quality. This brings greater security to the acquiring firm.
2 To restrict supplies of the raw materials to competitors.
3 In the case of forwards integration, to control the quality of the outlets for the finished product. Manufacturers finance the majority of advertising and they might well feel that a forwards merger would enable them to ensure that the good was being sold in the most appropriate setting.
4 In both cases, economies of scale are possible if different parts of the production process are brought together.
5 Again, vertical mergers can be carried out as a reaction to the activities of competitors.

The proposed and talked about takeover of Intel by Apple in 2013 is an example of a vertical merger as Apple has been using Intel processors since 2005.

Conglomerate mergers

These mergers are neither vertical nor horizontal but involve a merger between firms involved in producing different goods. The takeover of Boston Dynamics, a manufacturer of robots, by Google in 2013 is an example of a **conglomerate merger**. The main motivation for this type of merger is diversification. It reduces the risk involved in producing for only one market and allows the firm to spread risk further. It can also provide the firm with another option if the original market declines in size. There has been much speculation over Google's motive in taking over Boston Dynamics, its ninth such acquisition in 2013, so there is a clear indication that Google is diversifying into new territory.

As far as the economy is concerned, the main gains of mergers are in increased efficiency resulting from economies of scale and also the increased scope for research and development. A common view is that merger and takeover activity serves the purpose of rationalising business. The weak businesses go and the strong survive. Even when a takeover is carried out for the purpose of asset stripping this will be the case.

---

mini case   The story of a failed merger

In 2012 a merger was proposed and agreed between two large soft drinks producers in the UK, A. G. Barr, which produces Irn-Bru and Orangina, and Britvic, which produces Tango and Robinsons. The merger would produce a new company called Barr Britvic Soft Drinks, 37 per cent owned by shareholders of A. G. Barr and 63 per cent owned by shareholders of Britvic. This is an example of a horizontal merger, both companies producing similar products, and as such benefits would accrue to both companies. It was argued that the merger would:

1 Enhance the market position of each company – A. G. Barr has a strong presence in Scotland and Britvic has a strong pub presence, so they complemented each other.
2 Achieve synergies for both companies – the merger would give rise to £40 million in cost savings through rationalisation of production and the subsequent loss of up to 500 jobs.
3 Increase shareholder value.

Despite these strong arguments, some commentators suggested that the proposed merger was a defensive one, as the soft drinks market in the UK had suffered as a result of the bad weather in the summer of 2012 and Britvic had experienced an embarrassing recall of its Fruit Shoot brand because of problems with the bottle tops, an exercise which cost the company £25 million. Early in 2013 the merger was referred for investigation to the Competition Commission, which cleared it in June 2013. It ruled that the proposed merger would not adversely affect competition in the market or affect prices to the consumer. By the time the Competition Commission had ruled, Britvic had managed to regroup, recruited a new CEO and recovered from the Fruit Shoot recall. Britvic rejected the revised offer from A. G. Barr. The merger was off. The negotiations had cost A. G. Barr £5 million and Britvic £9.6 million.

What has happened to these companies since then? The market for soft drinks did well in 2013, largely due to very hot weather in the UK in the summer. Both companies posted positive sales and profits growth for the second half of 2013. A. G. Barr has managed to expand into England and Wales successfully without the help of Britvic, and has opened new production capacity in Milton Keynes. Britvic has managed to expand into the USA and Europe and had India in its sights for 2014. It has managed to obtain synergies without merger through the proposed closure of two factories in 2014 and the loss of 300–400 jobs.

It seems that the two companies have gained the benefits resulting from merger without having to go ahead with the merger, and this is at least partly due to market conditions.

Growth by merger and takeover

Growth through merger and takeover first appeared in the USA more than 100 years ago and merger activity tends to come in waves (see the discussion later in this chapter). Six periods of heightened merger activity have been identified in the USA:

● The period 1880 to 1905 – this coincided with the proliferation of the joint stock company and the international establishment of stock exchanges. This period was characterised by mergers of a horizontal nature.

- The 1920s – at this time the mergers were largely vertical in nature, as manufacturers took control of both suppliers and distributors.
- The 1960s – mergers in this period were mainly about diversification and the establishment of conglomerates.
- The post-1980 period – this wave of activity took place in a period of recession and was largely about cost-cutting and rationalisation.
- The late 1990s – companies in mature industries attempted to become global operators. The pace of this surge of activity slowed for a period after September 11th 2001, but by 2004 the boom in activity had restarted.
- The 2000s – from 2004 to 2007 the boom continued until the credit crunch in the USA caused a sharp fall in merger activity, including a 36 per cent decline in the first half of 2008. Since then the level of activity has remained fairly constant.

The first two periods of heightened merger activity in the USA had little effect in Europe; however, there were waves of activity in Europe which coincided with the later periods. The first wave of merger activity in Europe came in the 1960s after obstacles to trade were removed by the establishment of the European Economic Community (EEC) in 1957. The second wave of mergers came in the 1980s in the run-up to the establishment of the Single European Market in 1992. Since then the cycles in merger and acquisition activity in the USA have been mirrored in Europe. Since 2008 the level of global mergers and acquisition activities has gradually fallen, and in 2013 the level of mergers and acquisitions was at its lowest for eight years.

Finance for growth

Internal sources

As part of its operation the firm will generate income in the form of **profit**. Part of this profit will be distributed in the form of **dividends** to shareholders, the rest can be used for reinvestment and to finance growth. Although this is seen as a relatively easy and cheap source of finance, it does carry an opportunity cost and therefore should be judged on its rate of return like any other source of finance. Table 11.3 is provided for illustrative purposes and shows that internal funds were the largest single source of finance for UK industry during the 1990s. It also shows that the totals available and the pattern of sources vary a great deal from year to year. (This data is no longer compiled by the Office for National Statistics.)

External sources

As the size and availability of retained earnings will be limited, most firms will also have to seek other sources of finance for expansion. There are many external sources of finance and a typical firm's capital structure will comprise a combination of these. The sources are as follows.

Table 11.3 Sources of funds for industry, 1990, 1994 and 1997 (£ million)

Source	1990	1994	1997
Internal funds	33 838	61 406	56 363
Banks and other short-term borrowing	19 911	−4841	6630
Loans and mortgages	9120	4557	4384
Ordinary shares	1880	8495	19 616
Debentures and preference shares	6367	1008	10 640
Other capital issues	7485	5067	10 526
Other overseas investment	11 233	−1400	25 938
Other	1444	3766	953
Total	91 278	78 056	135 050

Source: Financial Statistics, January 1993, 1996 and 1999. Crown copyright 1999. Reproduced by permission of the Controller of HMSO and of the Office for National Statistics, UK.

Banks

Banks provide short- and medium-term finance to companies in the form of loans or overdrafts. The relative cost of these depends upon how the firm wishes to use the funds. Loans carry a lower rate of interest but the interest is paid on the whole amount, while the interest on overdrafts is paid only on the amount drawn. British banks have been criticised for failing to provide longer-term finance for business, as banks do in other countries.

Capital market

The **capital market** is the place where stocks and shares are traded and is therefore a key provider of long-term finance to firms. The main institution in the capital market is the **Stock Exchange**. The capital market is made up of two parts: the primary part, which involves the buying and selling of new stocks and shares, and the secondary part, which involves the buying and selling of existing stocks and shares. It is therefore the primary part of the market that is the source of finance for firms. The secondary part of the market is also important in this process, however, as individuals and organisations are more likely to buy stocks and shares with the knowledge that there is a ready market on which they can be traded at a later date.

The main institutions that buy stocks and shares are the insurance companies, hedge funds, pension funds, investment trusts, unit trusts and other large financial institutions such as building societies.

A new issue of shares takes place when an existing company needs extra finance or when a company becomes a public limited company.

Types of stocks and shares

1 *Preference shares.* These are shares in a company that carry a fixed dividend. Holders have preference over other shareholders in the payment of dividends and on the liquidation of the firm. Preference shares usually carry no voting rights, so holders have little influence over how the company is run.

2 *Ordinary shares.* Ordinary shares are called the '**equity**' of the company. They do not usually carry a fixed dividend; the company declares a dividend, depending upon its performance in that year. This means that in good years ordinary shareholders

could receive high dividends, while in bad years possibly none at all. Ordinary shares are therefore more risky than preference shares, and in recognition of this they usually carry voting rights, so that holders can exercise some influence over how the company is run.

3   *Debentures.* **Debentures** or loan stock are bonds that are given in exchange for a loan to the company. The company agrees to repay the borrowed amount at some date in the future and to make annual payments of interest in the meantime. Interest on debentures is paid before payment of any dividends and the interest is allowable against tax. A debenture holder is a creditor of the company, a shareholder is an owner of the company.

New issue of shares

A company will go to an issuing house or investment bank, which will advise it on the type and number of shares to issue, the price at which they should be offered and other matters. They will often carry out the issue of shares on behalf of the firm. A new issue of shares is not a big source of finance for growth as it is fairly expensive; retained earnings are more convenient and cheaper. Also the amount of information that is required from companies that issue shares to the general public can act as a disincentive.

It is worth noting that in recent years in the UK the stock market has had two main equity markets, the main market and the Alternative Investment Market (AIM), the former dealing in the shares of large and well-established companies, the latter providing an opportunity for growing smaller companies to raise capital and to have their shares traded in a market without the considerable expense of a full market listing.

Money market

The **money markets** provide short-term finance for companies, often for as brief a period as overnight.

Government and other institutions

The government is a source of finance for firms. Through its regional policy it gives tax allowances, loans, grants and training allowances to firms in certain parts of the country. It has many schemes for helping business, particularly small businesses. This will be covered more fully later in this chapter.

Other sources

Other sources include trade credit and hire purchase (i.e. receiving assets now and paying later). This is only a small source of finance for companies. UK businesses also draw a fairly high proportion of their funding from overseas. This includes finance from many different sources, including individuals, governments, financial institutions overseas and companies.

Firms will typically go for a mixture of different types of finance. The exact combination will depend upon many factors, including their relative costs, their availability and the desired capital structure of the firm. A firm's desired capital structure will largely depend upon the type of market in which it operates. The different types of finance are classified under the two headings of debt and equity. Debt refers to all types of capital on which payments have to be made each year regardless of how the firm has performed;

this would include loans and preference shares. Equity refers to ordinary shares where the payment of a dividend depends upon the performance of the firm. As a source of finance, debt is generally cheaper but it is also more risky since in bad years the firm will have to meet the interest payments. The ratio of debt to equity is called the **gearing** of the company. Debt is not well suited to firms in industries where profits fluctuate and such firms will have lower gearing than those in more stable markets.

Limits to growth

Several factors tend to act as a limit to organisational growth:

- To finance growth, excessive borrowing might have taken place and the firm may have trouble meeting debt repayments; therefore there is increased risk of bankruptcy.
- A serious constraint to growth might be the abilities of management. As organisations grow in size they may experience **diseconomies of scale**, which are mainly to do with managerial problems, including communication and control.
- If the size of the market for the product is stagnant or declining it may be both unnecessary and impossible for the firm to grow.
- Government policies, too, can have an important impact on growth. Every government has policies on competition which seek to limit anti-competitive practices and which normally regulate merger activity.

Merger activity in the United Kingdom

There are two common ways of measuring the level of merger activity – by the number of transactions or by the total value of the transactions. Figure 11.1 shows the level of merger activity in the UK according to the number of companies acquired in the UK by UK companies. It can be seen that there was a sharp rise in merger activity in the mid-1980s and a downturn in 1989. The cyclical pattern continues into the 1990s and 2000s but

Figure 11.1 UK merger activity by number, 1983–2012

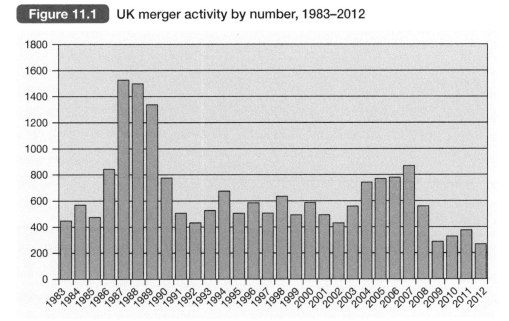

Source: Adapted from Table 8, 'Mergers and acquisitions involving UK companies, Q2 2013', ONS.

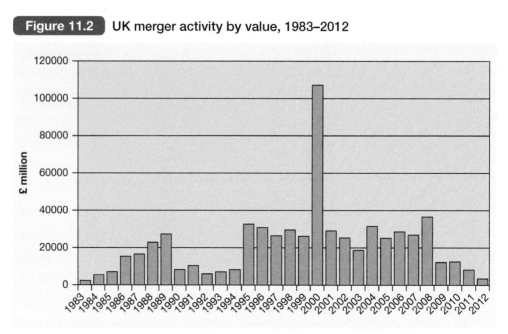

Figure 11.2 UK merger activity by value, 1983–2012

Source: Adapted from Table 8, 'Mergers and acquisitions involving UK companies, Q2 2013', ONS.

the amplitude is reduced. This cyclical pattern is repeated in other countries and in the EU as a whole and it implies that the level of mergers is in some way related to the state of the economy.

The rise in the mid-1980s was due partly to an improvement in the state of the economy and partly to the liberalisation of the financial markets, which made finance for takeover bids more freely available. The fall in 1989 was due partly to the recession and partly to the problems that some companies subsequently experienced by overstretching themselves in the mid-1980s. The subsequent rise in the level of merger activity was due to the restructuring that took place in many diverse industries, such as the financial services sector and the public utilities. Since 2008 – the start of the credit crunch – both the number of transactions and their value have fallen.

Figure 11.2 shows the level of merger activity in the UK according to the value of the transactions, and the same cyclical path can be discerned, although the peaks and troughs do not exactly coincide with the number of transactions. The use of the value of the transactions as a measure of merger activity is problematic in that it will be distorted by any very high-value deals that take place, as in 1995–7 and 2000 when the number of transactions fell but their value rose. The first half of 2007 showed record activity but by the end of the year markets had slowed because of the impact of the global financial crisis.

Global merger activity

The cyclical pattern seen in the UK data is also evident in the EU and the world as a whole (see Table 11.4). There was a decline in merger and acquisitions in the early 2000s followed by a surge in activity in 2004. During the 1990s the boom in merger activity was dominated by the telecommunications sector, while in the 2004–8 recovery the activity was taking place mainly in the financial services sector.

The impact of the credit crunch on merger and acquisition activity can be seen in Table 11.4, with a dramatic fall in 2009. The market recovered somewhat after that but

Table 11.4 Cross-border mergers and acquisitions to and from OECD countries, 1999–2012 ($ billion)

Year	Outwards	Inwards
1999	801	775
2000	1166	1136
2001	606	585
2002	376	410
2003	321	338
2004	422	444
2005	673	635
2006	847	818
2007	1028	1033
2008	1644	1060
2009	912	650
2010	1052	737
2011	1284	916
2012	982*	578*

*Estimated.
Source: Adapted from Figures D.10.1. and D.10.2. from OECD (2010), Measuring Globalisation: OECD Economic Globalisation Indicators 2010, OECD Publishing. http://dx.doi.org/10.1787/9789264084360-en.

fell back again in 2012. Global merger and acquisition activity was at its lowest for eight years in 2013 and in the EU it was at its lowest for three years[5] and there were fewer 'mega-deals' (over $10 million) in 2013. The number of deals globally was 37,257 in 2013 and the total value of those deals was $2.3 trillion.[6] Globally, the biggest market for mergers is the USA, followed by Asia-Pacific, with the EU in third place. General political and economic uncertainty and low growth rates in the EU have contributed to this – the markets are still cautious. Many analysts were predicting a pick-up in merger activity in 2014 based on surveys of companies' expectations.[7]

Small firms

There are serious problems in the analysis of the small-firm sector, including the lack of data over a long period of time and the problem of defining exactly what is a **small firm**. *The Bolton Report*,[8] published in 1971, was the report of a committee set up to look into the role of small firms in the UK economy. It used various definitions for statistical purposes, depending upon the industry being considered, on the grounds that what is small in one industry might be large in another. Table 11.5 shows the size distribution of firms based on their turnover for a selection of industries for 2012.

It is clear from Table 11.5 that the definition of 'big' will vary with the industry. In the *Bolton Report* the definition used for small firms in manufacturing was 'less than 200 employees', while in construction it was 'less than 25 employees'. In some industries turnover limits were chosen while in others a mixture of employment and turnover was used. Although this is confusing and makes comparison between industries and countries difficult, it was accepted that there could not be a single definition that would apply to all sectors. The European Commission in 2005 introduced a new measure based on employment and turnover to improve consistency between member

Table 11.5 Size of companies by turnover across different industries, 2012 (%)

Industry	Turnover size ('000)		
	up to £250	£250–£500	over £500
Agriculture, forestry and fishing	80	11	9
Mining and quarrying and public utilities	53	13	34
Manufacturing	57	13	30
Construction	70	13	17
Wholesaling	47	14	39
Retailing	63	19	18
Financial services and insurance	72	11	17
Business services	71	11	18

Source: Adapted from Table B5.1, *UK Business Activity by Size and Location,* National Statistics, 2012.

states and to facilitate the aid offered to SMEs in the EU. This definition is shown in Table 11.6 and uses employment size and annual turnover *or* annual balance sheet total in its definition.

Table 11.6 The EU SME definition

Enterprise category	Headcount	Annual turnover or	Annual balance sheet total
Micro	0–9	<€2 million	<€2 million
Small	0–49 (includes micro)	<€10 million	<€10 million
Medium	50–249	<€50 million	<€43 million
Large	250 +	Over €50 million	Over €43 million

Source: Implementing the SME definition, 2009, *http://ec.europa.eu/enterprise/policies/sme/files/sme_definition/sme_report_2009_en.pdf*

Applying this definition to Table 11.2, it can be seen that 82.7 per cent of enterprises in the UK are micro businesses, 96.7 per cent are small, 2.9 per cent are medium sized and 0.4 per cent are large. Although there are some national differences (the southern-most countries have relatively more micro businesses than the northern countries), the pattern of size structure is similar in the EU as a whole – 92.1 per cent of all enterprises are micro businesses, 6.6 per cent are small, 1.1 per cent are medium sized and 0.2 per cent are large.[9] Using these definitions it is estimated that 99.8 per cent of all enterprises in the EU-27 were SMEs and that they provided around 86.8 million jobs.

No matter how small firms are defined, they will suffer from similar problems, which are very different from those faced by larger companies.

Trends in the small-firm sector

The percentage share of small establishments in total manufacturing employment in the UK was in decline for the 1930s up to the early 1970s, when its importance increased dramatically.[10] In recent years the percentage has stayed around 40 per cent. Table 11.2 showed that for UK industry small firms are very important in terms of the number of businesses, accounting for almost 97 per cent of total firms. Even though they were less important in terms of employment, they still accounted for 36.6 per cent of total employment. Figure 11.3 shows the share of employment in SMEs by sector; as can be seen, there is a great deal of variation between sectors.

Figure 11.3   Share of employment of SMEs, UK, 2010

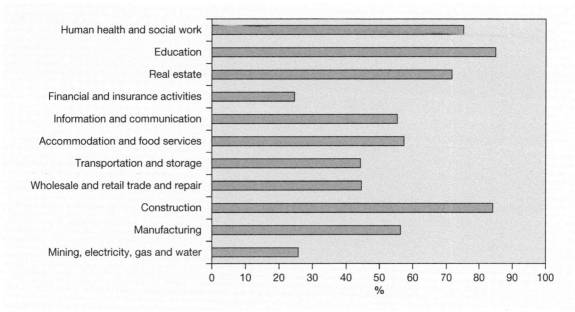

Source: Adapted from Figure 4, 'Business Population Estimates, 2010', Department for Business Innovation and Skills.

mini case   'Olderpreneurs' and small firms

The recent rise in the number of over 50 year olds starting their own businesses in the UK has given rise to the new term 'olderpreneurs'. Table 11.7 shows that there has been a gradual increase in the level of self-employment in the UK over time, with a more rapid increase after 2008, the start of the economic downturn. According to the Office for National Statistics, 85 per cent of the increase in self-employment since 2008 has been in those over the age of 50 years.

Table 11.7 shows the age profile of all self-employed people in 2008, 2011 and 2012 and it can be seen that the overall growth varies by age group. There has been a growth in the 16 to 24 age group and the over 50s. The other two age groups have declined in importance.

Table 11.7 The age profile of the self-employed (shown as a percentage of the total)

Age group	2008	2011	2012
16–24	4	4.1	4.4
25–34	16.2	15.9	15.8
35–49	41.7	39.1	37.8
50 and over	38.1	40.7	42.1

Source: Adapted from Annual Abstract of Statistics (various), *www.ons.gov.uk*

In terms of growth characteristics, there are two time periods:

- Between 2008 and 2011, the growth in self-employment was concentrated in the over 65s, women (who accounted for 80 per cent of the increase) and people working less than 30 hours per week.
- Between 2011 and 2012 the increase was mainly in those aged 50 to 64, men (64 per cent of the total) and people working more than 30 hours per week.

According to PRIME (the Prince's Initiative for Mature Enterprise), the over 50s are more successful – 70 per cent of the businesses started by people over the age of 50 survive for more than five years, compared with 28 per cent for younger age groups. Olderpreneurs' start-ups tend to be smaller and often in the craft sector, catering or services.

Why should olderpreneurs be more successful than other age groups? Possible explanations include:

- capital – many olderpreneurs start business after redundancy or retirement so they have some degree of financial fallback;

- networks – olderpreneurs have had more time to build up networks of clients and helpers;
- experience – learning through mistakes;
- good knowledge of the sector – competitive advantage.

Their number is likely to increase with lower pensions, increased health and higher retirement ages.

Reasons for the growth in the small-firm sector

There has clearly been a resurgence in the importance of the small-firm sector, which appears to have been more pronounced in the United Kingdom than in other countries. Why? Some causal factors are as follows:

1 *The changing pattern of industry.* There has been a change in the industrial structure of the UK away from manufacturing and towards services.Since many services are dominated by small firms, there will be a corresponding change in average firm size. However, this does not provide the full explanation as there has been a growth in the share of small firms even in the manufacturing sector. And it does not explain the international differences since there have been similar changes in industrial structure in other countries.

2 *Changes in consumer spending habits.* A move from mass produced goods to more specialised products puts small firms at an advantage as they can react more quickly to changes in demand and shorter product life cycles.

3 *Flexible specialisation and the growth of subcontracting.* A debate that started in the late 1980s centres round the idea of the **flexible firm**.[11] As a result of the recession of the early 1980s there was a drive by firms to reduce their costs in order to remain competitive. One way of reducing overhead costs was to move to a flexible firm structure whereby the firm's activities are divided into core and peripheral activities. The core activities, which are central to the activities of the firm, would be kept 'in-house' and carried out by full-time permanent workers. The peripheral activities would be carried out by temporary workers or would be subcontracted. The firm has then reduced its overheads and can react to peaks in demand by increasing the amount of temporary labour it uses or increasing the amount of **subcontracting**. This might also have had the effect of increasing the relative importance of the small-firm sector, although, outsourcing does not happen only to small firms.

4 *Reorganisation and job reduction.* There has been an increase in the phenomenon of downsizing by organisations in an attempt to reduce costs. Ninety per cent of large companies have reorganised and cut jobs since 1985.

5 *Government policy.* After the *Bolton Report* there was much greater interest in the role of the small firm in the regeneration of the economy and in the provision of jobs. But most of the initiatives designed to help the small firm came after the start of the resurgence of the small-firm sector in the early 1970s.

6 *The growth in self-employment.* A part of the growth in the small-firm sector has been due to the growth in the number of self-employed. The self-employed accounted for 9.8 per cent of the workforce in 1984 and 14.3 per cent in 2013 (see Table 11.8). This represents a 35 per cent increase in the number of those self-employed over this period, much of it since 2008, the beginning of the economic downturn (see mini case study on 'olderpreneurs').

The level of self-employment is likely to be related to the level of unemployment, so that as unemployment increased after 2008, there was an increase in the level of self-employment. Again, however, it does not provide the full explanation as business births were growing in the late 1960s when unemployment was falling.

7 *Technological change.* Changes in technology, particularly information technology and the miniaturisation of components, have made it possible for small firms to benefit to a similar extent to large firms. This has had the effect of reducing the importance of economies of scale and enabling small firms to compete more effectively with large ones. The use of 3D printers could potentially benefit small firms at the expense of other businesses.

8 *Competitive forces.* As far as the international differences are concerned, the *Bolton Report* found that industry in the UK was biased towards large size in comparison with other countries. So what may have happened as a result of competitive forces is that the balance of industry in the UK has moved towards the norm of other countries.

Table 11.8 Percentage of workforce self-employed, 1984–2013 (UK)

Year	% self-employed
1984	9.8
1985	10.0
1986	10.0
1987	10.9
1988	11.3
1989	12.1
1990	12.3
1991	11.9
1992	11.3
1993	11.2
1994	11.7
1995	11.6
1996	11.6
1997	11.5
1998	10.9
1999	10.8
2000	10.6
2001	11.3
2002	11.2
2003	11.6
2004	11.7
2005	11.6
2006	11.8
2007	12.4
2008	12.9
2009	13.2
2010	13.1
2011	13.8
2012	14.0
2013*	14.3

*June 2013.
Source: Adapted from *Annual Abstract of Statistics* (various), *www.ons.gov.uk*

The role of the small-firm sector

The growing importance of the small-firm sector implies that small firms do have a valuable role in the economy apart from being mere providers of employment. The areas in which the small firm has advantages over large firms are those where there are:

1 *Clearly defined small markets.* It is not worthwhile for large firms to enter such markets since there are no economies of scale and no scope for mass production.
2 *Specialist, quality, non-standardised products.* Again it would not be worth a large firm entering such a market as the benefits of large-scale production cannot be reaped.
3 *Geographically localised markets.* For example, the small corner shop.
4 *Development of new ideas.* It is often argued that the small firm is the 'seedbed' of ideas and that, because of greater motivation and commitment on the part of the owner of the small firm, it is conducive to invention and innovation.

Aid to the small-firm sector

The thinking on small firms has changed over time. Initially they were viewed favourably, but after the Second World War the dominant thinking was that large-scale production could take advantage of large economies of scale and that costs would be lower and production more efficient. It was not until more recently that the interest in the small-firm sector increased again. The main reasons for the renewed interest are seen in the results of empirical studies which have shown that the role of the small firm is greater than previously thought in areas such as innovation, the balance of payments and employment.

The main argument for giving support to the small-firm sector is that it has a valuable role to play in the economy. In the 1980s and 1990s, for example, small firms were seen as a mechanism for reducing the very high levels of unemployment. Between 1983 and 1993 the small-firm sector created 2.5 million jobs. The basic premise for support is that small firms are at a disadvantage with respect to large businesses in areas such as raising capital, research and development and risk bearing. The 2007 EU Observatory Survey of SMEs in Europe found that there were three main problems facing small firms:

● The burden of regulation – reported as acting as a constraint by 36 per cent of SMEs within Europe. It is estimated that large firms spend €1 per employee on regulatory compliance compared with €10 for SMEs. The Small Business Act for Europe (2008) has put in place measures to reduce the regulatory burden for SMEs.
● Access to finance – including cash flow problems resulting from late or non-payment of bills. In the UK all public limited companies are required by law to state in their annual reports the average length of time it takes to pay their bills. The Federation of Small Business in the UK publishes a 'name and shame' list of slow payers.
● Access to new markets – between 1996 and 2010 it has been estimated that 58 per cent of the UK's productivity growth came from exporting firms. Only 13 per cent of European SMEs export outside of the EU single market.

Government policy

Within the UK, national policy for small firms has increasingly become a vital component of governmental attempts to create a competitive economy capable of achieving sustainable economic growth. To this end policy initiatives in recent years have become more focused and have tended to adopt a multi-agency approach, aimed at improving the environment in which small businesses emerge and grow, and at fostering enterprise and innovation. Key developments over the last decade or so have included:

- Business Link – a national network of 'one-stop shops' to provide information and support to small firms – this was disbanded in 2011;
- The Knowledge Transfer Partnerships – these are part-government-funded measures to link UK higher education establishments and businesses;
- the SMART Awards – designed to promote technological development and innovation;
- the Red Tape Challenge – a scheme which aims to identify areas where regulations can be simplified and reduced;
- Greatbusiness – a joint private/public partnership which brings together links on growing, financing and exporting for small business;
- Mentorsme – an online gateway which brings together mentors with small companies needing mentoring;
- Funding for Lending Scheme – a government scheme which provides banks and building societies with £17.6 billion at low rates of interest for lending to businesses and households;
- other state-backed SME lending and equity schemes, including Start-Up Loans, the Enterprise Finance Guarantee, UK Export Finance and Angel Coinvestment Funds.

There have also been a number of legislative and fiscal changes aimed at reducing the burdens on small businesses (e.g. levels of corporation tax). Some of the more recent developments have included the launch of the University for Industry (now a charitable trust), the Business Enterprise Fund (a social enterprise) and the H2020 initiative of the EU. The latter, introduced in 2013, aims to provide a single online portal for all EU financial instruments for SMEs. There have also been attempts to reduce the flow and improve the quality of regulation affecting smaller businesses and an action plan to make the UK the number one location for starting and growing a business.

In November 2013 the UK government announced a major campaign to help small firms. The measures included the initial funding for the Business Bank (£1 billion to dispose of to business starting in 2014), a new Mentoring Challenge Fund with £1 million of funding, a fund of £10 million to the Biotechnology and Biological Sciences Research Council to help synthetic biological start-ups, and a Growth Accelerator Scheme, which provides coaching to small businesses with high growth potential. In addition to these, in January 2014, other measures were announced which included a doubling of the Small Business Rate Relief, the introduction of growth vouchers to help small firms with the cost of hiring and marketing, and the Red Tape Challenge.

 www.greatbusiness.gov.uk

Networking between firms

While competition between firms remains the norm in a market economy, cooperation between businesses can, and does, also sometimes occur.[12] This cooperation can take many forms: for example, subcontracting, networking (both formal and informal) and joint ventures. Such cooperation can be (and is) used by large as well as small and medium-sized enterprises. For large companies it is a way to grow and diversify without risk. For smaller firms it allows them to stay small but at the same time to benefit from some of the advantages of large-scale production such as specialisation.

Subcontracting

There has been an increase in the amount of subcontracting, where firms do not carry out the whole of the production process themselves but subcontract some of their activities to other firms. This represents a rejection of vertical integration and it is related to the notion of the flexible firm mentioned earlier. Subcontracting goes some way to explaining the phenomenal growth rate in 'business services' that occurred in the 1980s. It is increasingly common for businesses to subcontract specialist work in areas such as human resource management to outside consultancies. 'Partnering' between companies and consultancies is becoming more common where the consultancy is retained on a semi-permanent basis to give advice on a whole range of human resource matters, from recruitment to planning for succession. This will obviously boost the small-firm sector. There has also been an increase in 'partnership sourcing' as large firms are developing long-term relationships between themselves and their suppliers. This phenomenon brings benefits to the large firms in the form of reducing stock levels and associated costs and facilitating just-in-time production methods. It also brings benefits to small firms, many of which are the suppliers, in the form of greater security.

Networking

Networking refers to the relationships that exist between organisations and the people within those organisations. These relationships can be of different types, both formal and informal, and there is increasing recognition of the importance of these relationships, especially to small firms (e.g. they may be based on the exchange of goods and services, like the relationship between a firm and its supplier or client). Subcontracting is an example of this kind of network, but there are other links not based on exchange, such as the relationship between a firm and the bank manager or other advisers. There are also informal links between the entrepreneur and family and friends, and between entrepreneurs in different organisations. There might also be cooperative links between firms. This can be seen in the market for executive recruitment where there has been a growth in the links between consultancies, particularly for international work. The creation of the Single European Market and the increased internationalisation of business left the smaller consultancies in a weak position relative to the large international recruitment firms such as Korn Ferry International, which have branches in most European countries.

The smaller consultancies have reacted by forming networks. There are basically two types of network:

1 Where firms are members of a network but where the network has a different name from the individual firms and the firms operate under their own name (i.e. the network has an identity of its own). The members are independent firms that cooperate in carrying out their business. There are 16 such groups in Europe, including EMA Partners International and Amrop.

2 Where firms are part of a network of independent firms but where the network does not have a separate identity and the firms operate under their own names. There are ten such groups in Europe.

web link For information on companies mentioned see *www.kornferry.com, www.ema-partners.com* and *www.amrop.com*

The firm is seen as existing within a spider's web of relationships, as Figure 11.4 shows. It is possible for two firms to be linked in a variety of ways; in one market they may be competitors, in the next co-operators, customers in another and suppliers in another.

Networking has taken on greater significance because of changes that are taking place in the economy, which include the reversal of the trend towards higher **industrial concentration**, the adoption of Japanese methods of production, the decline of 'mass markets' and technological change that requires greater specialisation than previously. All of these changes favour the formation of networks.

The role of strategic alliances between firms has been recognised, especially in the small-firm sector where expansion through other means is often impossible and in the process of internationalisation.

The virtual organisation

The **virtual organisation** is a network-based structure built on partnerships where a small core operating company outsources most of its processes. It is a network of small companies specialising in various aspects of production. The organisation can be very big in trading terms but very small in the numbers of permanent staff. The process is typically mediated by information technology.

Figure 11.4 A typical network

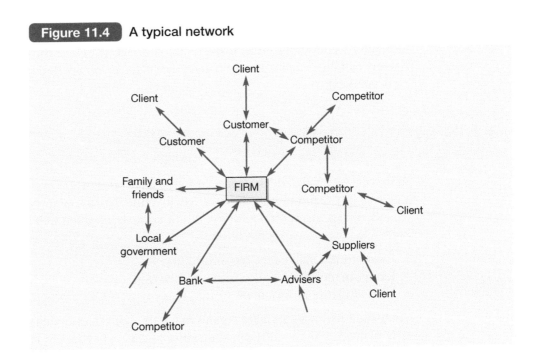

The main benefit of the virtual structure is that it helps organisations to deal with uncertainty. When virtual organisations are managed properly they can simultaneously increase efficiency, flexibility and responsiveness to changes in market conditions. The organisation is reaping the benefits of specialisation without having to develop those specialisms itself. Therefore overhead costs are minimised, as are training costs and support costs. Information technology assumes many of the coordinating and managing roles that managers and committees carry out in large organisations. Information technology enables communication and the sharing of information across geographical boundaries. It is often the case, however, that the creation of a virtual organisation is driven solely by cost considerations rather than strategic considerations, in which case the benefits might not be realised. There will be a loss of control over outsourced activities and it may actually cost more to manage such activities. The organisation can become locked into contracts and specific relationships so that flexibility is reduced. There may be a lack of commitment of key resources (i.e. contractors) to the company and the loss of a contractor will be very serious.

There is some evidence that the incidence of virtual organisations is on the increase, facilitated by developments in information technology. It is a matter of 'wait and see' if this will become the dominant organisational structure in the future.

Joint ventures

As indicated earlier in this chapter, **joint ventures** are a good way for firms to diversify and enter other countries' markets. Joint ventures benefit both parties as each can diversify with the benefit of the experience of the other, and the level of risk is minimised. Again, there are examples in the area of executive recruitment. The International Search Group, for instance, was set up as a joint venture between five companies in France, the UK, Austria, Germany and Italy in order to offer a European service to its customers.

Consortia

In some industries cooperative behaviour has come about for particular reasons. In process plant contracting, for example, the projects are often too large for single firms and so they form consortia in order to bid for the contract. The consortium will include contractors, suppliers and bankers who together will have the expertise and the resources to carry out the project.

Multinationals

At the opposite end of the scale from the very small business are companies which have the capability to produce goods or services in more than one country but where control usually resides in a central location. Multinationals are often well-known household names, as the examples below illustrate:

- UK multinationals – BP, GlaxoSmithKline.
- European multinationals – Nestlé, Volkswagen.
- US multinationals – General Motors, IBM.

These multinationals are huge organisations and their market values often exceed the GNP of many of the countries in which they operate. They are estimated to account for a quarter of the world's output.

The growth in the multinationals is due to relaxation of exchange controls making it easier to move money between countries, and the improvements in communication which make it possible to run a worldwide business from one country.

For information on the companies mentioned on this page see: *www.bp.com, www.gsk.com, www.nestle.com, www.vw.com, www.gm.com* and *www.ibm.com*

Synopsis

This chapter has looked at the size structure of industry in the United Kingdom and Europe as a whole. It examined the motives for and the methods of growth, as well as the sources of finance for such growth. The role of the small firm was considered, including the growth in self-employment. Although many industries are dominated by huge companies, the trend seems to be moving away from growth towards a process of disintegration for a variety of reasons. As a result of this trend there has been an upsurge in the small-firm sector, and an increase in the level of cooperative behaviour between firms.

Summary of key points

- The size structure of firms varies greatly within industries, within a country and between countries.

- Firms can grow internally through organic growth or externally through merger and takeover.

- There are many motivations for growth, including increased market share, the reaping of economies of scale, the diversification of risk.

- Growth can be financed internally through reinvested profits or externally through banks, the capital market and the money market.

- There are limits to organisational growth, such as diseconomies of scale.

- The level of merger activity in the UK and in Europe follows a cyclical pattern and is related to economic conditions.

- The small-firm sector is an important source of output and employment, and this importance has increased over time.

- Many factors have influenced the growth of the small-firm sector, including the changing pattern of industries, changes in demand, technological change, the trend towards increased subcontracting and government policy.

- At the other end of the size spectrum, multinational corporations have a massive impact on world output and employment through their activities.

case study   Gazprom, the Russian giant

Gazprom was created in 1989 as a result of the privatisation of the Russian Ministry of Gas, and the Russian government still owns 50.002 per cent of the company. The company is the biggest extractor of natural gas in the world and it is one of the world's largest companies. Gazprom supplies natural gas to Russia and the rest of the world – in 2012 it accounted for 14 per cent of the world output and 74 per cent of Russian output of natural gas. It owns the largest gas transmission network in the world – 168,000km of pipeline – and exports gas to more than 30 countries. It extracts natural gas from very difficult terrains, most of it coming from the Yamal Peninsula, which lies east of Moscow in North West Siberia, a permanently frozen area.

The sheer size of Gazprom protected it; it has a monopoly in domestic gas production and on gas exports. The price of gas worldwide was high and as a result profits flowed back into Russia. The situation, however, is changing. Gazprom has been badly affected by:

1 Economic downturn in Europe, which has had a negative impact on the demand for gas. Europe is a very important market for Gazprom – 25 per cent of the gas bought in Europe in 2012 came from Gazprom.
2 The exploitation of shale gas (see case study in Chapter 8) through fracking, which has increased the supply of natural gas from other countries and made them more self-sufficient in gas.
3 The price of Gazprom's gas, which compares unfavourably with the price of shale gas.
4 Negative reputational effects – in 2009 Gazprom cut off the supply of gas to Ukraine for two weeks, making people nervous and distrustful. More recently, the arrest of the Arctic 30 has impacted upon Gazprom's reputation.

Gazprom reported that profits were down by 9.5 per cent in 2012, the first time a decline had been reported for ten years, and cited two main reasons for this: declining demand from Europe and higher operating costs. Many business commentators say that Gazprom is too big (e.g. it has subsidiaries in banking, media, agriculture and other industries) and needs to be broken up. This is unlikely to happen.

One problem Gazprom faces is that it has to keep two groups of people happy – on the one hand it has shareholders who are expecting returns on their investment, and on the other it has the government. Russian President Vladimir Putin has made Gazprom a 'national champion', which gives it two objectives – making profits and advancing Russian national interests. These sometimes come into conflict, for example gas is sold inside Russia at lower than the price set outside through the use of subsidies. This advances Russian national interests but at the expense of lower profitability. The controlling interest of the government makes Gazprom susceptible to political meddling, in fact, Putin oversees all major energy deals in Russia and many claim that it is used as a tool of Russian foreign policy. Putin has recently agreed a big reduction in the price of gas for the Ukraine ($268.5 per 1000 cubic metre instead of the previous price of $400). This could be seen as an attempt to deter Ukraine from turning towards Europe and the EU plans for a 'Eurasian Union'.

So what is the future for Gazprom? Increased production of shale gas will push the price of gas downwards and means that other countries do not have to buy from Gazprom. Putin has been negotiating for several years with China, which is the world's biggest user of energy, to supply it with gas. They have not managed to agree on a price so far, but if they did it would reduce the dependence of Gazprom on Europe. A year-long anti-trust investigation by the European Union into some of the activities of Gazprom was due to conclude in early 2014. Gazprom has allegedly blocked supplies of gas in central and eastern Europe and been overcharging its customers by linking the price of gas to oil. Depending upon the outcome of this investigation, Gazprom could face a €10 billion fine. There are also problems with bilateral agreements made with six EU members regarding the construction of gas pipelines; the agreements do not comply with EU rules. Within Russia itself Gazprom is facing increased competition from two other gas producers: Novatek, established in 1994, and Rosneft, established in 1993.

Many argue that the way forward involves the splitting up of the business into parts – the pipeline business from the gas production – but as this case study shows, the situation is a complex one where market forces are not the most important factor.

Case study questions

1 Why does the nature of the product, natural gas, make this an industry that is likely to be dominated by large companies?

2 What impact is fracking (see Chapter 8) likely to have on this market and this company?

Review and discussion questions

1 How might a global financial crisis impact on merger and acquisition behaviour?

2 Can you see any dangers in the creation of super-utilities (large, diversified organisations which supply a range of utilities – gas, electricity and water)?

3 What advantages does networking bring to small firms and the economy as a whole?

4 How has the balance between large and small firms in manufacturing changed in the last ten years? Do you expect these trends to continue?

Assignments

1 You are an information officer at your local business advice centre and you have been given the job of designing and writing a leaflet aimed at the proprietors of small firms, outlining the government aid that is available to small businesses. Your brief is to keep the leaflet short and readable but with maximum information. (Information on government aid will be available at your local library or business advice centre.)

2 As part of 'Business Week' you have been asked to give a short talk on the size structure of UK industry to local sixth formers doing Business Studies A-level. Prepare your talk by choosing two industries, describing and giving reasons for the typical size structure of the firms in those industries.

Notes and references

1 See Vehorn, C. L., Kopf, J. and Carnevale, J., *Global Markets: Four Firm Concentration Ratios,* 2012 available at *www.sbrconferences.com*

2 *Penguin Dictionary of Economics.*

3 See *http://ec.europa.eu/economy_finance/structural_reforms/product/mergers_acquisitions*

4 See OECD, *Dynamic Efficiencies in Merger Analysis,* May 2008.

5 See *European M & A Outlook,* October 2013, available at *www.cmslegal.com*

6 See 'Mergers and Acquisitions – more and larger deals expected', October 2013, Ernst & Young.

7 See last two references and also *www.kpmg.com*

8 *The Bolton Committee Report,* HMSO, 1971.

9 See *Annual Report on European SMEs 2012/2013,* available at *http://epp.eurostat.ec.europa.eu*

10 See Figure 9.4 in the fifth edition of this book.

11 Atkinson, J., 'Flexibility, uncertainty and manpower management', Report no. 89, Institute of Manpower Studies, 1984.

12 Pyke, F., 'Co-operative practices among small and medium-sized establishments', *Work, Employment and Society,* 2 (3), September 1988.

Further reading

Griffiths, A. and Wall, S., *Applied Economics,* 12th edition, Financial Times Press, 2011.

Stanworth, J. and Gray, C., *Bolton 20 Years On: The Small Firm in the 1990s,* Chapman, 1991.

CHAPTER 12
Government, public sector and not-for-profit strategies

LEARNING OUTCOMES

When you have worked through this chapter, you will be able to:

- explain why public sector strategy is different and why it is important;
- outline the two main public sector models and explain the concept of public value;
- analyse the public sector environment;
- analyse the resources of a public sector institution;
- explain how the purpose of a public sector institution can be developed and defined;
- outline the development of strategy in the public sector from the perspectives of context, content and process;
- develop either a plan to implement the selected strategy or an incremental approach for an emergent strategy.

INTRODUCTION

This chapter focuses on the special considerations that apply to strategy in the government, public and not-for-profit sectors. 'Government' means areas like defence and the law, which are the responsibility of the nation state. 'Public' means the provision of health, transport, energy and other services which may be the responsibility of the state or may have been privatised, depending on the political views of the government. 'Not-for-profit' means institutions that work for the common public good but are independent of the state – for example, charities, trusts and similar institutions. In order to avoid unnecessary repetition throughout this chapter, these organisations are simply called 'public' institutions and their strategies are called public strategies to distinguish them from the 'private' strategies of commercial businesses. The differences between the three different types of public sector institutions are discussed where required.

Why does public sector strategy deserve a separate chapter? There are two main reasons. The first is that the public sector in every nation around the world is important. Even for high-income countries such as the USA, where many services are devolved to the private sector, the wealth expended on the public sector is over 34 per cent of gross domestic product.[1] In other words, every country spends considerable sums on its public sector. Public sector strategy therefore matters and deserves to be explored in depth.

The second reason for a separate chapter is that the public sector is more complex and involves factors that do not apply in the private sector.[2] For example, companies like Kelloggs and Cereal Partners compete in the private sector breakfast cereal market. A measure of their success is their ability to deliver profits to shareholders and offer value for money products to customers. But in a public sector example like the local or national police force, there is no question of delivering a 'profit' on the police budget and a 'value for money' policing service needs considerable clarification if it is to have any meaning at all.[3]

If public sector strategy is so different, then it follows that the principles that have been explored for business strategy in the rest of this book may not apply in public sector strategy. Competitive strategies like 'head-on' and 'flanking' attacks against a dominant competitor. These have little meaning where the state runs a monopoly such as its defence or police force.[4] We therefore need to reconsider the elements of business strategy in a public sector context.

An additional difficulty faces the business strategist in redefining its concepts for the public sector. Theories on *public sector administration* have been around for longer than those in business strategy.[5] This means that there is another stream of intellectual thought that needs to be considered in re-examining business strategy. It is not possible in one chapter to explore *all* the many public sector administration theories that have been developed. The approach of this chapter has been to focus only on those that have a direct connection with the rest of this book. However, the chapter contains sufficient references to allow the reader to follow up those areas that deserve greater depth. Interestingly, theories in public sector administration in the past 20 years have been moving closer to private sector concepts – as we shall see when we explore the *new public management* concepts later in the chapter.[6]

To explore strategic management in the public sector, we will follow the basic structure of the book as developed for business strategy. This approach is summarised in Figure 12.1.

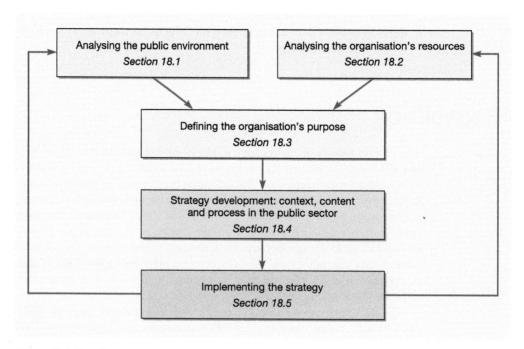

Figure 12.1 Developing strategy in public and not-for-profit sectors

CASE STUDY 12.1

Public sector strategy: how Galileo ended up in serious trouble

In 1999, politicians from European Union finally agreed the development and launch of a new global satellite system called Galileo. By 2012, political decision making and European company rivalries had delayed the project by seven years and tripled the initial cost. This case explores an extraordinary failure in public sector strategy.

Background

Some years ago, the US government launched a global network of satellites aimed to assist navigation everywhere in the world. Essentially, the signals from the satellites allowed virtually anyone on the planet with the right equipment to obtain an accurate fix on a geographical location: the Global Positioning System (GPS). In addition to its civilian use, the GPS is also used by the American military and its NATO allies for military purposes in time of conflict. There is also a Russian system, called GLONASS, that provides similar services.

In 2012, the GPS system was widely used in both military and civilian life: for example, there was a totally new market for car satellite navigation systems ('satnavs') that was entirely dependent on the GPS system. Mobile phone location systems also relied essentially on GPS signals. However, some countries within the European Union were not entirely happy with this arrangement for four reasons:

1 In theory at least, the US Government could switch off the GPS system at any time without consulting anyone.

2 For some European countries, the reliance on American military technology was seen as a serious military weakness. President Chirac of France was reported as saying that Europe risked becoming a 'vassal' of the USA.

3 European countries realised that their national defence companies risked losing key technological know-how and skills in satellite communications if they continued to rely on the US system and technology.

4 Some European nations also identified a world commercial business opportunity to sell satellite receivers and related services. According to some estimates, there would be world market demand for around 3 billion receivers worth around $250 billion by year 2020.

The problem for an individual European country and/or company was the heavy investment cost required to put up an alternative satellite system – around $3.5 billion in the late 1990s. This figure was beyond the resources of most individual European countries.

The Galileo joint venture

In 1999, the 15 countries (now 28) of the European Union agreed to the joint development of a pan-European satellite system to be called *Galileo*. The European Commission – the central administration of the EU – was granted a new frequency from the International Telecommunications Union to use with its

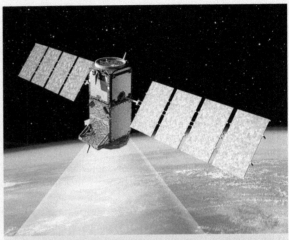

Europe's new Galileo satellite will compete directly against the American GPS system.

proposed Galileo satellite system. Around the same time, each state within the EU agreed its share of the funding and design. Importantly, Galileo would use more sophisticated, new digital technology to deliver its positioning signals. This meant that in addition to a free signal, like the American GPS system, Galileo would also have another service called the Public Regulated Service (PRS): this latter service would *not* be free to the general public. The PRS would be encrypted so that it was available only on subscription from commercial organisations.

Galileo would also contain two other channel services: the first would only be available to Europe's military and defence establishments; the second would be used by its emergency services, such as the police and sea rescue. In summary, Galileo would be more accurate and have a wider range of services than the American GPS system as a result of using digital technology. In addition, the new European co-operative venture would make Europe independent of the American system. The EU Commission was so enthusiastic that it claimed that Galileo would create more than 150,000 jobs and generate an annual income of $10 billion. It would be a 'trump card that will greatly enhance Europe's influence in the world'.

After the final agreement amongst European nations, experimental contracts were then prepared and a complete timetable developed for the European launch. Prototype satellites were planned for launch in 2005 and, depending on the testing, the full Galileo system would become operational late in 2006. As matters then turned out, this timetable proved to be wildly optimistic. All these negotiations were dependent on basic progress with the Galileo system itself. Unfortunately, the Galileo satellite system was about to take a turn for the worse.

Crisis at Galileo

In May 2007, the German transport minister Wolfgang Tiefensee said that Galileo was in 'a deep and profound crisis. We have reached a dead end street.' The roots of the major problems had begun two years earlier. Originally, the EU expected that the private sector would provide most of the Galileo finance amounting to around $4 billion and therefore share most of the risk of failure. It was this principle that secured the approval of some EU governments – particularly the UK – who were dubious about the whole Galileo project: they considered that the private sector rather than the public sector would be taking much of the responsibility.

In addition to covering the risk, the big advantage of private sector funding was that the Galileo project would be open to competitive tendering from rival companies. Initially, two main consortia (a consortium is a group of companies) were bidding for the Galileo contract. The EU thought that their desire to gain the business would keep their bids low and the costs down. Each of the companies forming part of a consortium was a major company in an individual European country in either satellite manufacture or telecommunications. Unfortunately, political considerations within the EU destroyed this approach. The EU's awarding authority could not decide between the two bidders for fear of offending the national governments behind each of the companies. The result was that the two competitive bidders were combined into one single consortium. The combined company now had many of the EU's most powerful companies in the market: the major French and German aerospace company EADS, France's Thales and Alcatel-Lucent, the UK's Inmarsat, Italy's Finmeccanica, Spain's AENA and Hispasat and a German group called TeleOp that was led by Germany's largest telecommunications company Deutsche Telekom. Thus the bidding process to reduce costs had been lost.

Even this decision by the EU's awarding authority also had another major flaw. The authority never made any decision on how to split up the elements of the contract. This meant that, 'If the companies cannot get what they want, they go back to London, Paris or Rome' according to an anonymous person close to the negotiations.

After much further negotiation, the share-out of the contract was decided largely using political rather than industrial logic. For example, the headquarters would be in Toulouse, France, with operations run from London, England. Germany and Italy would operate control centres with a back-up in Spain.

What happened next?

The original plan was that Galileo would be fully operational by 2007. The first experimental Galileo satellite was launched in 2005 with another in 2006. Then Spain 'took the view that it should have as much as Italy and Germany. It was a matter of pride', according to an informed source. There was then another 18 months of negotiations.

Eventually, the EU gave the consortium a deadline of May 2007. The members of the single consortium then demanded new business terms from the EU. These included some guarantees about the profitability of the project for members of the consortium and also some special insurance in the event of a catastrophic failure of a Galileo satellite. The EU was in a weak position to argue since it was negotiating with a monopoly bidder for its business. The original estimated cost of Galileo was around $2 billion. The outcome of the new negotiations was that the EU governments were asked to find at least another $1.5 billion. This was finally agreed by the EU governments and four test satellites were planned for launch in 2011–2012.

In 2011, the consortium returned to the EU and said that the full system would need additional funds of around $2.5 billion. This would allow the launch of another 14 satellites in 2014 to complete the initial system. However, another 12 satellites would be needed to provide full global coverage and back-ups in the period from 2014 onwards.

To summarise, the original cost of Galileo had tripled from $2 billion to an estimated cost of $6 billion. The original completion date of the Galileo system was 2007. This was initially put back to the year 2011. The latest estimated completion date of the basic system at the time of writing this case (in 2011) was 2014 – seven years late.

In spite of this poor record, many European countries remained optimistic about the many potential uses such as mapping crop areas, tracking cargo and freight and assessing coastal erosion. The EU judged that the market for GPS systems had real potential: the market size was around $800 billion with a high annual growth of around 25 per cent. 'It is a fantastic project that has already lost a lot of time it cannot afford,' according to Karel van Miert, a former EU Transport Commissioner. But sceptics remained to be convinced that Galileo would even be finished by 2014.

Case questions

1 What were the main benefits from launching the Galileo satellite system? And what were the European Union's main mistakes? Do you think that the benefits outweighed the problems?

2 To what extent were the political difficulties predictable within the EU? How would you have handled these issues if you were a public sector official at the EU? Would you have changed the strategy? If so, in what way?

3 What, if any, are the lessons that can be learnt about public sector strategy from the Galileo experience?

12.1 ANALYSING THE STRATEGIC ENVIRONMENT IN PUBLIC SECTOR STRATEGY

Definition ▶

In public sector strategy, the analysis of the strategic environment is more complex than in the private sector. The main reason is that public sector strategy involves the wide-ranging and ill-defined subject of the *public interest*: **the public interest concerns both the objectives and the institutions that make and implement public decisions.** This basic concept in public sector strategy has two elements: the 'public' referring to citizens in general and 'interest' referring to the individual[8] wishes of the public.[9] The public interest is quite different from a company operating in a competitive market place. For example, the Galileo case shows that the public interest – as interpreted by national governments and various international agencies on behalf of their citizens – is important and quite different from a company selling its products in the market place. There are four main environmental factors that deserve to be analysed:

1 the extent of the market mechanism in public service;

2 the concept of public value;

3 stakeholder power and complexity;

4 special issues in not-for-profit organisations.

After exploring these factors, this section then concludes by analysing the public sector environment.

12.1.1 The extent of the market mechanism in public service

We can explore this under three main headings:

1 the benefits of the market mechanism in the public sector;

2 the costs of the market mechanism in the public sector;

3 the balance between laissez-faire and dirigiste policies of national governments.

The benefits of the market mechanism in the public sector

In public sector administration theory, governments are assumed to take decisions on behalf of *all* their citizens, rather than a few. For example in the European Union's Galileo satellite investment, the funds were made available to *all* the relevant companies associated with their bids and the general public were not consulted. If the public goods and services must be available to all relevant parties, then public sector theorists have argued that this is most effectively and efficiently achieved through government agencies with centralised decision making:[10] for example, one agency to manage police services. In public administration theory, centralised decision making is regarded as being beneficial.

Taking decisions on behalf of all citizens is quite different from private markets where the 'buyer' can choose whether to buy a product from a 'seller'. The citizen has no such choice in public administration theory and, in market terms, the centralised public bureaucracy is effectively a monopoly. For many economists, a monopoly is unresponsive and inefficient as a service supplier. Centralised decision making is therefore not beneficial. Hence, there is a basic conflict in public service between *public administration* theory and *market economic* theory.[11] For many countries in the past 20 years, the view has shifted towards introducing market forces to reduce the price of public goods. For such countries, public administration theory has therefore moved closer to market economic theory.

The public sector approach accompanying this shift towards market forces has been to break up the state monopoly supplier of such goods into several companies, which then compete against each other on price and service levels in the market place. Competition is likely to reduce the costs of the former monopolistic state enterprise and therefore the prices paid by the customer: in essence, this is the *privatisation* of former state monopolies. Even in countries with a strong socialist tradition like China, there have been moves to privatise former state monopolies like civil air transport. The underpinning principle of privatisation is that market competition – often referred to as the *market mechanism* – is more efficient than monopoly in the management of state resources.

In some countries, this market-based approach has taken an additional form: co-operation between the public interest and private enterprise – called *public private partnerships* – with private finance and management being used to develop and subsequently administer public services. For example, private finance might be raised to develop a new state hospital in the public sector and then a private company appointed for a period of years to manage all the hospital services on behalf of the public. This co-operative approach remains controversial – particularly the allegedly high level of fees paid for the management contract – but is an example of another form of market mechanism in the public sector.

The costs of the market mechanism in the public sector

In addition to market-based benefits in public sector strategy, there are also costs associated with such an approach. There are two main areas: first, there are clear *limits* to how far the market approach can be implemented. Market theory suggests that failed products disappear from markets because they are not meeting demand. In principle, this would therefore suggest that any public sector body that is subject to market pressures and fails to deliver on its public sector objectives should be closed. While this may be possible for a failing school because there may be other schools, it is clearly not possible to allow a large regional hospital with specialist staff and equipment to fail. There is a cost to keeping such organisations open in terms of efficiency and lack of market pressures.

There is a second problem associated with introducing the market mechanism – the *transaction costs* of privatisation. There is a need to set standards, monitor progress, evaluate performance and other activities associated with giving former monopolies the freedom to undertake public services. If this were not done, such organisations might not deliver the full level of service previously provided by the monopoly: the market mechanism is powerful and can potentially distort performance. Setting such standards and monitoring the outcome has two main costs:

1 the public monitoring organisations needed to check on the activities of the newly privatised public sector organisations and ensure that they continue to deliver their public service obligations;

2 the administrative costs at the newly privatised organisations involved in providing data on their performance and related activities.

In theory, the benefit of the market mechanism should outweigh the two costs outlined above. In practice, there is some disagreement over such matters. Importantly in public sector strategy, it is essential to consider carefully the monitoring mechanisms, performance targets and their related costs in the development of strategy. It is also appropriate to build network contacts with those involved in the monitoring process – the public regulators – and discuss proposed strategy change with them.

The balance between laissez-faire and dirigiste policies of national governments

Definition ▶ In public sector policy, **the market mechanism is the means by which the state uses competition between suppliers, market pricing and quasi-market mechanisms to determine the supply and demand of goods that were previously state monopolies.** In both the EU and the USA, there are differing views on the extent to which the state should become involved in markets. In France, Italy and Greece, it has long been the tradition that state-owned companies and state intervention are important elements of the national economy. In the UK, New Zealand and the USA, the opposing view has been taken. The approach adopted is essentially a *political* choice made by those in power. The two approaches – often referred to as *laissez faire* and *dirigiste* – are summarised in Table 12.1. Adam Smith, Karl Marx and many other political commentators have all contributed to the important political debate in this area. Table 12.1 is intended merely to summarise areas that are the most relevant to the development of strategic management.

Table 12.1 Two models of the public sector environment

Laissez faire: free-market model	Dirigiste: centrally directed model
• Low entry barriers • Competition encouraged • Little or no state support for industry • Self-interest leads to wealth creation • Belief in laws of supply and demand • Higher unemployment levels • Profit motive will provide basis for efficient production and high quality	• High entry barriers • National companies supported against international competition • State ownership of some key industries • Profit motive benefits the few at the expense of the many • Failure in market mechanism will particularly affect the poor and can only be corrected by state intervention • Need to correct monopolies controlled by private companies

In practice, the distinctions drawn in Table 12.1 are very crude. Some countries offer a *balance* between strong state-sponsored policies in some areas – for example, education, favoured industries (as in Singapore), investment in roads, power and water – and then couple this with a free-market approach in other areas – for example, privatisation of state monopolies or lower barriers to entry to encourage investment by multinational enterprises (MNEs). (MNEs are the large global companies such as Ford, McDonald's and Unilever.) Each country will have its own approach, so any public sector environmental analysis will have to be conducted on a country-by-country basis.

12.1.2 The concept of public value

Definition ▶ **Public value refers to the benefits to the whole of the nation from owning and controlling certain products and services.** For example, the national defence forces and the police service have a clear benefit to all the citizens of a country. The government, on behalf of the nation, takes the decision of which public goods and services should be under national control and which services should be controlled privately by business. In practice in many countries, there are some grey areas which are neither totally in government control nor totally private; the public value is therefore mixed. Figure 12.2 gives some examples.

Given the concept of public value, there are three important consequences for public sector strategy analysis:

1 Unlike a private sector market for a car or a hotel room, the public service for defence forces or clean air needs to be a binding collective decision for it to be effective. Public sector strategy needs to be enacted and supported by a *legal framework* and laws that bind, govern and distribute the public value. This legal framework needs to be analysed.

2 There is a need to ensure that the public value is genuinely available to all citizens, with everyone having a fair share or an equal opportunity – the concept of *equity*. This is fundamentally different from business strategy. The extent and nature of public equity needs to be analysed in developing public sector strategy.

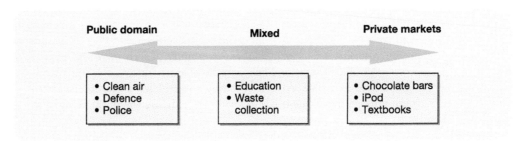

Figure 12.2 Public value is highest in the public domain

3 Occasionally, there is a need to remedy problems in distributing the public value: the market mechanism may fail after privatisation has occurred. Market failure can take many forms: for example, the newly privatised companies may attempt to control the market and keep their prices artificially high. The government may therefore appoint a special independent *public regulator* to oversee the results of privatisation and ensure full and fair distribution of the benefits of the public value arising from the privatisation. This is particularly important where public value is mixed with private wealth – for example, in a privatised telecommunications company. The mechanism for ensuring the fair distribution of public value therefore needs to be analysed.

As an example of the implications of the areas above, we can examine the European Union's handling of the Galileo satellite case. The *legal framework* environment analysis will cover the basic legal articles of association setting up the contracts for Galileo, the membership of its board and their responsibilities. The *equity analysis* will need to examine the way that funds are actually distributed by the Galileo overseeing authority so that its funds are distributed in accordance with the negotiated agreement and without undue influence. In the case of the Galileo contract, a *public regulator* is highly relevant given the strong element of competition involved in the distribution of the European Union's funds and given the way that the funds were then diverted according to various government pressures that bore little relation to the efficient use of resources.

12.1.3 Stakeholder power and complexity

In the public sector, stakeholder power is possessed by those citizens who are able to influence the decisions of the state. In practice, this may be through democratic elections, with a change of government leading to substantial changes in the services provided by the state. But it may be through other forms of state structure that do not rely on democracy. The difficulty here is that all such changes can be short-term and involve quite substantial and unpredictable changes in public sector strategy. Such uncertainty deserves to be analysed in developing public sector strategy.

In addition, there are other ways for citizens to exert their influence – pressure groups, campaigns, even riots and disturbances. For example, during the Galileo contract negotiations described in Case 12.1, press reports of the problems plus the various review meetings of the governing body exerted pressure for considerable change – not always for the better. This is important because it shows how public bodies can be lobbied and pressured in their decision making. A stakeholder power analysis can be undertaken but this may only show that the stakeholder group is more powerful than the politician who is theoretically directing the public service. We return to this matter in Section 12.3 on power and democracy.

12.1.4 Special issues in not-for-profit organisations

Although the definition of not-for-profit organisations is very broad, it will certainly cover charitable, voluntary and other public interest bodies that are not owned by the state. Such organisations are not concerned with the distribution of public value in the sense of delivering this equitably to all citizens. In addition, not-for-profit organisations are quite different from government institutions with regard to their sources of funds. Public sector governmental institutions derive their income from taxes on all citizens. Not-for-profit organisations need to raise their income from a variety of private, voluntary and variable sources. An example of such an institution is the Olympic movement described in the Olympic case linked to this chapter and available free on this book's website. This is not owned by a state, exists to 'contribute to building a peaceful and better world by educating youth through sport', and needs to finance its activities without state support.

On the website

Case study: Olympic Games 2012: five cities bid to host the games.

The main focus of an environmental analysis in such organisations will need to explore two main areas:

1 *The precise role and purpose of such organisations.* The role will define the environment in which the not-for-profit organisation exists and with whom it is engaged. For example, the role of the international Red Cross organisation (and Red Crescent in Muslim countries) is to bring human itarian and disaster relief to those in distress around the world. Its environment is therefore that of other relief agencies, governments and countries needing such relief and the individuals in those countries benefiting from such work. In practice, this needs careful definition to ensure that the environment is adequately described.

2 *The fund-raising mechanism of the organisation.* Virtually every not-for-profit organisation needs financial support to undertake its work. Such organisations may even compete against each other for public support and public funds. For example, the public funds raised around the world in 2005 for the Asian tsunami disaster meant that some other public charities had difficulty in raising sufficient funds for their own activities. This suggests that an environmental analysis needs to examine carefully the current and future sources of funds of the organisation and the implications in terms of related, similar organisations. It also needs to explore the more general mood and public acceptance of the country or region in which the organisation operates, since this will impact on its ability to generate adequate funds.

12.1.5 Analysing the public sector strategy environment

We can summarise the implications of the discussion above by returning to the basic strategic environmental analysis and considering its implications for public sector analysis. This is shown in Table 12.2.

KEY STRATEGIC PRINCIPLES

- In public sector strategy, the analysis of the strategic environment is more complex than in the private sector. The main reason is that public sector strategy involves the wide-ranging and ill-defined subject of the public interest: the public interest concerns both the objectives and the institutions that make and implement public decisions. There are two main public sector models – centrally directed (*dirigiste*) and free-market (*laissez-faire*).
- The market mechanism is the means by which the state uses market pricing and quasi-market mechanisms to determine the supply and demand of goods that were previously state monopolies. In practice, over the past 20 years many states have moved to greater use of the market through privatising state-owned companies. Each individual country will have its own approach to the use of such mechanisms. A public sector environmental analysis will have to be conducted on a country-by-country basis. There are also two costs associated with the market mechanism: first, the cost of being unable to close inefficient services because they provide vital public services; second, the cost of administering the market mechanism to ensure that it serves the agreed public objectives.
- Public value refers to the benefits to the whole of the nation from owning and controlling certain products and services. But such value needs to be considered within the legal framework that binds and governs the value. In addition, public value requires the concept of equity to make sure that the value is distributed to all citizens. In some circumstances, public value needs a regulator to deal with any market imperfections.
- In the public sector, stakeholder power is possessed by those citizens who are able to influence the decisions of the state. Such power may be expressed through democratic elections but these can lead to short-termism in strategic decisions. Power can also be exercised through pressure groups and other forms of interest. Such power needs to be analysed.
- In the not-for-profit sector, an environmental analysis needs to consider the role and purpose of the organisation. It also needs to identify its actual and potential sources of funds. Such organisations cannot rely on public taxes to pay for their activities and need to seek voluntary contributions that will vary with a range of factors.
- The nine stages in environmental analysis used for business strategy can be adapted for use in public sector strategy analysis, though they need to be treated with caution.

Table 12.2 Analysing the public sector strategic environment[12]

Stage	Business strategy techniques	Can they be used in the public sector?
1 Environment basics – an opening evaluation to define and explore basic characteristics of the environment (see Section 10.2)	Estimates of some basic factors surrounding the environment: • Market definition and size • Market growth • Market share	Possibly but they need to be redefined: • Demand for a public service • Political will to supply the public service • The relevant funding and costs of supplying the service
2 Consideration of the degree of turbulence in the environment (see Section 10.3)	General considerations: • Change: fast or slow? • Repetitive or surprising future? • Forecastable or unpredictable? • Complex or simple influences on the organisation?	Yes, but perhaps not so easy to analyse. It will need judgement, especially on the influence of political and pressure groups • Is the environment too turbulent to undertake useful predictions? • What are the opportunities and threats for the organisation?
3 Green strategy	• Government policies • Market opportunities • Customer and industry attitudes	Yes – clear public interest issues plus opportunity for government to influence 'green' market
4 Background factors that influence the competitive environment (see Section 10.4)	PESTEL analysis and scenarios	Yes, definitely • Predict, if possible • Understand interconnections between events
5 Analysis of stages of market growth (see Section 10.5)	Industry life cycle	Possibly but not really clear what this could mean beyond the natural rhythm of country change
6 Factors specific to the industry: what delivers success? (see Section 10.6)	Key factors for success analysis	Yes in the sense that KFS will help identify issues with regard to the priorities needed for successful public sector strategy
7 Factors specific to the competitive balance of power in the industry (see Section 10.7)	Five Forces Analysis	• Possibly for 'customers' and even 'competitors' (many public sector institutions compete for funds) • 'Supplier' analysis is also relevant because governments should be powerful buyers • But difficult to see relevance of 'substitutes' and 'new entrants' in a monopoly
8 Factors specific to co-operation in the industry (see Section 10.8)	Four Links Analysis	• Definitely worth undertaking this analysis – the Galileo example shows its importance • Network analysis will also be useful
9 Factors specific to immediate competitors (see Section 10.9)	Competitor analysis and product portfolio analysis	• Difficult to envisage any significant benefit here
10 Customer analysis (see Section 10.10)	Market and segmentation studies	Customer analysis is useful but needs to be considered in relation to the broader concepts of public value and choice in the public sector

12.2 ANALYSING RESOURCES IN THE PUBLIC AND NOT-FOR-PROFIT SECTORS

The concept of sustainable competitive advantage underpins resource-based analysis in business strategy. However, the public sector has traditionally been regarded as not engaging in competitive activities – for example, the public fire and rescue service is non-competitive. If there is no competition in the public sector, then resource analysis will be quite different from its equivalent in business strategy. The first issue therefore is whether sustainable competitive advantage has any meaning in the public sector. If there is 'competition', then what form does this take?

The second issue with regard to public sector resources is the broader one of the *nature* of such resources beyond competitive issues and compared with business resources. By 'nature' is meant the range of resources available to the public sector strategist and the costs associated with public sector resources. The third issue is to identify the analytical tools for such work.

12.2.1 Does sustainable competitive advantage have any meaning in the public sector?

The Galileo satellite case perhaps implies that the company is unique and does not compete with other institutions. However, governments can divert or withhold funds if a company is underperforming and, in a sense, the Galileo satellite system therefore has had to compete for funds that might have been used for alternative projects within the European Union. The Shetland Islands case later in this chapter deals with the difficult choice between economic development and preserving wildlife – see Case 12.2. But it also explores the need for a public sector organisation to find finance to provide its services such as education, transport and local police. The Council may obtain some extra funds from its new wind farm development, if its plans are successful. Equally, it may also find funds from other sources such as local taxes and central government. But the Shetland Island Council arguably has no competitors. Do most public sector bodies conform to the monopolistic view of government and rarely engage in competition? The answer depends on the type of public administration model adopted by the nation – the *public sector administration* model or the *new public management* model. Resource analysis needs to begin by identifying which model is used by the state.

Definition ▶ For many years, **the *public sector administration model* was that of an organisation that did the bidding of its political masters.**[13] **In this model, a professional civil service enacted government legislation and administered the activities of the state on behalf of the government. The same public sector also contained public sector enterprises, such as electricity or telecommunications, that made the public pay for their monopolistic services.**[14] Competition played a relatively minor role in such a scheme: for example, one regional police force did not normally compete with another to make arrests. However, the annual budget of the police force – perhaps – 'competed' for funds from the government against the budget for other public services like defence and, in this sense, there was a small element of competition. Importantly, in this description of public services, there was little incentive for public employees to reduce their costs and increase their efficiencies because their services were essentially monopolistic.[15] More generally, such a model of public sector decision making did not lend itself to the rigorous economic logic of competitive advantage.

For many national governments around the world over the past 20 years, the situation has changed from the model outlined above, which has been replaced, at least in part, by the *new public management (NPM) model.*[16] **New public management is a model of public sector decision making where the professional civil service operates with more market competition coupled with former state monopolies being divided and competing against each other for business from citizens. However, the nation retains some areas under state control, such as the defence of the nation.** The new model offered a set of ideas about how government can operate based to a much greater extent on the

Definition ▶

efficiencies derived from market competition.[17] There are six core issues in NPM[18] – productivity, marketisation, service orientation, decentralisation, policy and accountability – but from a strategy perspective the key issue is marketisation, so that is the issue explored here. This means that this section is not a full discussion of the many other aspects of NPM, which can be explored through the books listed at the end of this chapter.

NPM is based on two main assumptions.[19] The first is that demand for government services can be separated from the supply of those services. The second is that it is possible to introduce competition into the supply of such services. We can explore these assumptions by examining what has happened in those countries that have sold into the private sector previously nationalised industries. Examples of such state companies sold into the private sector include electricity generation and telecommunications services. After privatisation, demand for such services has not fundamentally changed, so the assumption that supply can be separated from demand has proved correct. Moreover, privatisation has taken place in such a way that the monopolies have been split into several competing companies, thus introducing competition into supply.

From a resource analysis perspective, it follows that competition does exist when a nation has adopted NPM policies. It is not possible to set out all the evidence in this brief review, but many researchers in both public sector administration[20] and strategy development in the public sector[21] support such a conclusion. This means that it is relevant to consider resource-based competitive analysis in the public sector. Such competitive advantages as tangible and intangible resources, core competencies, architecture, reputation, innovative capability and knowledge may all be explored in the public sector. It also follows that a SWOT analysis can be employed to summarise such issues.[22]

Although the above argument has focused largely on government organisations, the same basic principles can be applied in not-for-profit organisations. This is explored more fully in Section 12.2.3.

12.2.2 The special nature of public sector resources

In addition to issues of competitive advantage, public sector resource analysis also needs to explore the special nature of public sector resources in four areas:

1 Sufficient and appropriate resources for purpose
2 Public power as a resource
3 The costs and benefits of public resources
4 Persuasion and education as a public resource.

Sufficient and appropriate resources for purpose – trade-offs and balances

As we have seen, some parts of the public sector are essentially monopolies – for example, defence forces and the fire and rescue service – and therefore do not compete amongst themselves. Nevertheless, such services do need to deliver the service identified by the nation and its politicians and they need to do this at 'reasonable' levels of cost (with 'reasonable' usually being defined by the governing politicians of the country). Nevertheless, many recent government initiatives in many countries have been directed at achieving greater efficiencies, higher levels of service and lower costs with the same service[23] – Pollitt and Bouckaert call these 'trade-offs and balances'.

Definition ▶   In order to undertake such tasks, **public sector resource analysis needs to assess whether sufficient and appropriate resources are available to deliver the purposes set by the state.** The first step in analysing resources is therefore to examine the objectives set by the state – for example, if a public sector ambulance is required to answer an emergency within 15 minutes, appropriate numbers of ambulances and trained medical staff need to be available. Public sector resource analysis then needs to set the service levels and other requirements of the state against the available resources.[24] Such an approach to resource analysis goes beyond the identification of competitive advantage and similar concepts from business strategy.

In analysing the required resources to deliver public sector objectives, one of the main difficulties rests with the words 'sufficient and appropriate'. The reason is that many state institutions will be able to make a case for more resources. To overcome this difficulty, careful exploration of the defined purpose and the tasks to be undertaken, coupled with comparisons from past experience and similar activities in other areas, will provide at least some of the answers. In practice, one of the main deciding factors is likely to be a government policy decision on 'trade-offs and balances' based on the political judgement of the public governing body. The case on the Kings Theatre at the end of this chapter captures many of the dilemmas and policy decisions required: public sector expertise, political pressure for re-election, pressure groups from within the local community. Resource analysis needs to consider these many complex aspects.

Public power as a resource

In strategic management, resource analysis often focuses on economic power, with cash and profitability as the dominant outcome. Even human resources like leadership and knowledge are often assessed by their ability to deliver profits or some form of added value to employees or management. In contrast, public resources have another dimension.

By definition, the nation state has an authority that is lacking to an individual business, however large. The state can be considered as having three distinctive, interactive systems that are not present in business: politics, a market economy and a system of public administration and the law.[25] Each of these is set within the larger context of a civil society of the nation – see Figure 12.3. The citizens of that nation both participate in and form judgements upon the legitimacy of that society and its institutions – not necessarily through a democracy.

From a public strategy perspective, this view of the state implies that citizens give their open or tacit approval to the events and decisions of the state. In this sense, citizens give power to public servants – for example, power to the defence forces to defend the state and support to the police and judiciary to uphold the law. This power can be mobilised at various times and forms a significant part of public sector strategy.[26] For example, the state can decide that it should lay increased emphasis

Definition ▶ on environmental 'green' issues in a way that is beyond that of individual businesses. **Public power is a resource possessed by nation states and consists of the collective decision making that derives from the nation state.** The analysis of such a resource is important in developing public sector strategy.

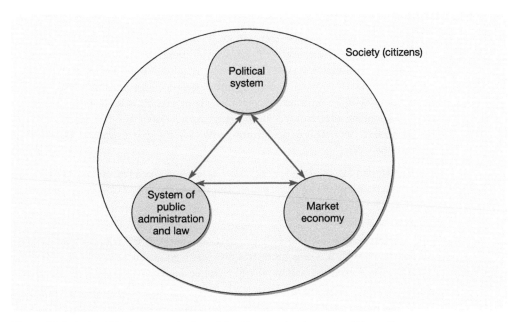

Figure 12.3 A simplified representation of the three main elements of the nation

Source: Pollitt, C and Bouckaert, G (2000) *Public Management Reform*, Oxford University Press. Used by permission of Oxford University Press.

The costs and benefits of public resources

Coupled with the state's exercise of power, there are also costs. Costs arise as the state goes about its business, investing in defence, in legal institutions and other areas of governmental activity.[27] They also include the costs associated with the misuse of power and the unintended side effects of political decisions[28] – for example, the higher costs associated with sorting waste when recycling becomes part of government policy in order to preserve the environment for future generations. Importantly, the state does not have unlimited funds for such activities because of the limitations on raising taxes. **Public resources need to be analysed for their ability to deliver the maximum benefit for the least cost.** 'Benefit' here has a broader social definition than simply delivering shareholder profitability in the private sector – for instance, social benefits associated with improvements in public health. This means that the task of the public sector manager has some similarities to that in the private sector but has a far wider brief and consequences. In practice in the public sector, this may require a strategic choice between making cost resource savings and improving performance through resource investment. It has been suggested that this can be resolved if there is some spare capacity in the governmental system or the possibility of employing new technology to improve efficiency.[29] Other resource-based solutions have included privatisation, as explored earlier, and setting public sector service quality and service standards in order to make comparisons across a part of the public sector – comparisons of health treatment in various parts of a country, perhaps.

Definition ▶ (margin)

Persuasion and education as a public resource

Unlike individual businesses, the state has the opportunity to help individuals and groups improve their own lives by persuasion and education.[30] For example, the state can set up a public education programme to show citizens how to prevent fires. This may be just as useful and productive as the fire fighting service itself. This role for the state implies a public sector resource that is not readily available to individual businesses and needs to be considered in any resource-based analysis of public sector activity. **Public sector resource analysis therefore needs to consider whether persuasion and education are possible resources of the state and, if so, how and where they might be employed.**

Definition ▶ (margin)

12.2.3   Some special characteristics of resources in the not-for-profit sector

Unlike the public sector, the resources of the not-for-profit sector will require funds that do not come from public taxes: there is a need to raise funds from private sources. The majority of such institutions need to rely on public donations and commercial business support of one kind or another. Inevitably, there is likely to be some competition to obtain those funds, even if this might seem somewhat distasteful to those engaged in such activity. Fund-raising expertise for some of these institutions has become a major area of resource that requires careful analysis – covering such resource areas as networks of contacts, branding and reputation, and organisational capability in energising the supporters of the organisation, many of whom may be volunteers.

Describing the resources in this way also identifies another aspect of resource analysis that is particularly important in the not-for-profit sector: *human resources*. Typically, there are three relevant resources here:[31]

1 *Voluntary help in raising funds and delivering the service.* Such helpers can be highly dedicated and provide a real strength to an organisation. But they can also be fickle in the sense that they are volunteers and are unpaid.

2 *Specialist technical knowledge in delivering the service.* The purpose of some types of not-for-profit organisations is to deliver highly specialised expertise – for example, the highly respected organisation Médecins sans Frontières provides high quality medical relief for refugees. Such specialist levels of expertise require careful resource analysis.

3 *Leadership and governance.* Each institution is unique but benefits over time from leaders who have the imagination and the ability to carry their workers, supporters and outside institutions with them as they develop and deliver their services. Arguably, this resource is even more important than in the public sector, because there is no acceptance and tradition of the public bureaucracy that is usually available to government institutions.

12.2.4   Analysing resources in the public sector

To summarise, the analysis of public sector resources will need to consider the main areas for business strategy: tangible, intangible and organisational resources; core competencies; architecture, reputation and innovative capability; and knowledge. In addition, the areas covered in more depth in this section need to be explored – public power, costs and benefits, persuasion and education – as possible resources available in the public sector. In not-for-profit organisations, this needs to be supplemented by an analysis of fund-raising and human resources.

The outcome of the resource analysis will identify the public organisation's strongest abilities and most effective actions and policies. From an administrative viewpoint, it will also set out the resources that it employs on a regular basis to perform well.[32] This latter point is important because the public sector is often involved in delivering an efficient administration with its routine tasks and legal frameworks that go beyond much of private sector activity.

One final aspect of public sector resource analysis also deserves to be emphasised – the necessary and appropriate resources to deliver the purpose of the organisation.[33] We explore purpose in the next section.

KEY STRATEGIC PRINCIPLES

- Public sector resource analysis needs to begin by examining which of the two public sector models – public sector administration or new public management – is adopted by the state. The *public sector administration* model consists of a professional civil service bureaucracy that enacts government legislation and administers the activities of the state on behalf of the government alongside state monopolies that supply services to the citizens. The *new public management* model is a model of public sector decision-making where the professional civil service operates with more market competition while former state monopolies are divided and compete against each other for business from citizens. However, the nation retains some areas under state control, such as the defence of the nation.

- The former does not support competitive advantage while the latter is underpinned by concepts of market competition in what was formerly the monopolistic state sector. Resource-based analysis in the public sector for the second approach will include similar concepts to those in business strategy – tangible, intangible and organisational resources, etc.

- There are four additional considerations that apply in analysing resources in the public sector: appropriate and sufficient resources for purpose; public power as a resource; the costs and benefits of public resources; and persuasion and education as a public resource.

- Public sector resource analysis needs to assess whether sufficient and appropriate resources are available to deliver the purpose and objectives set by the state. This means that resource analysis needs to identify public purpose and then assess resource requirements against this.

- Public power is a resource possessed by nation states and consists of the collective decision making that derives from the nation state. The analysis of such a resource is important in developing public sector strategy.

- With regard to costs and benefits of public resources, the task of the public sector manager is often that of obtaining the maximum benefit for the least cost. 'Benefit' here has a broader social definition than simply delivering shareholder profitability in the private sector. Such a balance needs to be considered in resource analysis in the public sector.

- Public sector resource analysis also needs to consider whether persuasion and education are possible resources of the state and, if so, how and where they might be employed.

- In not-for-profit organisations, there is a need to examine the fund-raising resource of the organisation. In addition, there is a specific need to examine human resources of such organisations in three areas: voluntary help, specialist technical knowledge and leadership and governance.

- The outcome of the resource analysis will identify the public organisation's strongest abilities and most effective actions and policies. From an administrative viewpoint, it will also set out the resources that it employs on a regular basis to perform well.

CASE STUDY 12.2
Windfarm or wildlife? A public interest dilemma for green strategy

Green strategy has forced a difficult choice in Shetland between a major windfarm to generate carbon free electricity and a threat to the wild, natural habitat of the Shetland Islands. This case explores the issues.

Early beginnings

Like the rest of the UK, the Shetland Islands Council is expected to support alternative sources of renewable energy. The islands are located nearly 200 miles (320 km) north of the Scottish mainland and have some of the highest and most reliable wind speeds in the world. This makes them attractive for land-based windfarms.

Back in 2003, both the local Shetland Islands Council (SIC) and Scotland's largest producer of electricity, Scottish and Southern Energy (SSE), independently decided that a new wind-farm complex should be explored for Shetland. Subsequently, the SIC handed over its interest in the project to another body, a charitable trust called the Shetland Charitable Trust (SCT). These two groups, the SSE and the SCT, then came together in a new company called Viking Energy.

As background, the Shetland Charitable Trust possesses around £180 million ($270 million) of funds donated by the oil industry for the inconvenience to Shetland from having a large oil terminal located at Shetland's Sullom Voe. The interest from this trust fund is used in Shetland for arts festivals, subsidised transport and other community schemes. The SCT is nominally independent of the SIC, but local Shetland councillors had the largest share of votes on both bodies at the time of writing this case.

Viking Energy

Set up in 2005, Viking Energy is 50 per cent owned by SSE, 45 per cent owned by SCT with the remaining 5 per cent owned by some local islanders who had previously invested in a small Shetland windfarm. The planning laws in the UK require that schemes of this nature prepare an Environmental Impact Assessment, which was initially done in 2006–0707. This was then followed by a period of consultation with the local communities in Shetland starting in 2007. A revised environmental impact assessment was then completed in 2009 and a formal planning application was then made. By that time, the objections from some (but not all) islanders to the scheme had been running for two years.

Viking Energy's proposal

After various surveys, SSE determined that a major new wind farm on central Shetland would provide a substantial renewable power source. However, the amount of power generated would be best served if it could be sent to the Scottish mainland. This meant that the construction of a 200-mile undersea cable was a crucial element of the proposal. In turn, this meant that a smaller scale windfarm for Shetland alone was not part of the proposal.

To generate and transmit renewable energy to the Scottish grid, Viking Energy proposed to construct 127 wind turbines, each 476 feet (145 metres) high. The site would be around 11 miles by 7 miles (18 km by 11 km) located on the northern part of the main island of the Shetland Isles. There would then be a cable running down the island and out to sea at the southern end. The development cost was estimated to be £685 million ($1.2 billion) for the windfarm plus another £500 million ($800 million) for the connecting cable to the mainland. The scheme would create only around 42 direct jobs but would generate an income of around £23 million ($38 million) per year for the SCT.

In addition, the proposal included habitat and heritage management schemes. However, it also involved the construction of over 60 miles of roads to service the windmills, cables to carry the power and a significant service infrastructure. The proposal was to build this across the largely untouched heather moorland, peat and bogland of central northern Shetland where birds, wild animals and people roamed freely up to that time. Viking Energy estimated that the carbon payback time would be around one year. But this figure was disputed by the objectors who produced figures claiming to show that it might be as much as 48 years.

At the time of writing this case, it was not clear how this £1.2 billion ($2 billion) project would be funded. It was assumed that SSE would be able to find their share of the total costs. However, the Trust has assets of only around £180 million. Nevertheless, it was estimated by Viking Energy that for various reasons the Trust would only need to find £30–60 million ($45–90 million). It was known that various banks, including the European Investment Bank, were willing to lend additional sums, but nothing had been agreed. Importantly, the high initial investment in this project was dictated by the large scale of the project and the related need to fund the cost of the cable to the mainland.

Objections to the proposals

Through contacts made using the local newspaper, the *Shetland Times*, and through local community groups, an organisation was set up called Sustainable Shetland. Its website is located at www.sustainableshetland.org/ and it has nearly 800 members. The organisation did not object to windfarm development in principle but did object to the size, impact and consequences of Viking Energy's proposals. Specifically, it complained to the UK Advertising Standards Authority (ASA) that one of Viking

Formal public consultation and approvals

In accordance with normal UK planning procedures, Viking Energy presented its assessment first for local consultation across Shetland and then as a formal planning application for comments by the SIC. The main elements of the Viking Energy proposal can be viewed at **http://www.vikingenergy.co.uk/project-facts-figures.asp**. Various consultation and briefing meetings were held across Shetland in the years 2007–2009. As a result of these consultations, the windfarm was reduced in size from 150 to 127 turbines with the final application being sent to SIC in September 2010. The council must be consulted on the plans, but the final approval rests with the Scottish Government in Edinburgh. In December 2010, the Council approved the revised development.

Readers may find it odd that the company, Viking Energy, submitting plans to the Council is part-owned by a charitable trust whose members also sit on the Council. In other words, it would appear that the Council was being asked to support plans for a scheme of which it was a part-owner. Some members of the Council with an immediate interest withdrew from the planning meeting, but objectors to the scheme insisted that the relationship was still too close. Subsequently, this relationship has been the subject of a separate investigation by an independent lawyer for the Charities Commission which governs all trust activities in Scotland. The conclusion was that the relationship needed to be changed. But this does not seem to have persuaded the Council in the short term to reconsider its approval of the Viking Energy scheme.

In 2013, Viking Energy's scheme proposals were approved by the Scottish Government. The Government had to consider the following questions: Is the public interest best served by a major contribution to reducing the nation's carbon footprint with cheap renewable energy? Or is it better served by preserving the wildlife and natural habitat that would undoubtedly be disturbed by such a large-scale development? The Government chose to agree with Viking Energy.

But that was not the end of the matter. The development was then challenged legally in the Scottish High Court by the Sustainable Shetland organisation. At the time of updating this case, the legal decision was still pending.

© Copyright Richard Lynch 2015. All rights reserved. Case written by Richard Lynch from published information only.[34]

In 2012, this was just one of the five windmills generating electricity on Shetland. But all this was about to change if the new proposals were approved by the Scottish Government.

Energy's leaflets was seriously misleading. The leaflet had been distributed to all households in Shetland. The ASA upheld three of the five objections and told Viking Energy that the leaflet could not be repeated in its current form. The ASA said, 'We told Viking Energy to amend their ad so that it did not claim that 50 per cent of profits would stay with the Shetland community; that it did not claim that a total of £25M to £30M would be injected into the Shetland economy every year; that it did not claim that upwards of £18M profits on average would go to Shetland Charitable Trust, and that it did not suggest the carbon payback time of the development was likely to be less than three years.' (The full adjudication is available at **http://www.asa.org.uk/ASA-action/Adjudications/2009/11/Viking-Energy-Partnership/TF_ADJ_47582.aspx**.)

More generally, the views of the majority of Shetland Islanders were unclear. A *Shetland Times*-commissioned poll in 2010 showed that one-third of islanders were in favour, one-third against and one-third undecided. Sustainable Shetland responded by pointing out that there were far more objections to the final plans submitted by Viking Energy than favourable comments: 2,735 versus 1,144 people. All these comments were considered by the Shetland Island Council when considering the public interest and approval procedure.

Case questions

1. Where does the public interest rest in this case? Wildlife or windfarm? What criteria are needed to arrive at a decision?

2. Viking Energy's campaign was better funded than the objectors' response: is it inevitable that public sector strategy should be decided by this unequal debate?

3. In determining public green strategy, does it matter that the deciding local authority had an business interest in the application?

12.3 EXPLORING THE PURPOSE OF PUBLIC AND NOT-FOR-PROFIT ORGANISATIONS

Public sector organisations face a difficulty that does not apply to business organisations. They are directed, at least in part, by politicians who need to be re-elected – unlike business leaders. This means that the purpose of a public sector body may change significantly after an election. It also means that long-term strategic direction can be difficult to sustain in the public sector. For example, it is possible that the leaders of the SIC – see Case 12.2 – will be defeated at the next election due to the unpopularity of their policies. What would then happen to any decision to press ahead with the Viking Energy windfarm development? The long-term direction of a significant part of Shetland Islands' strategy might be fundamentally altered.

In not-for-profit organisations, the reliance on voluntary, often unpaid assistance also means that such help is relatively unpredictable: it can even be withdrawn without warning for a variety of reasons. Moreover, unlike business organisations, many public sector bodies do not have shareholders expecting dividends and capital gains from their investments. Particularly in the not-for-profit sector, the objectives may well involve – perfectly justifiably – objectives that are more imprecise than shareholder value added. Such objectives may be difficult to measure and measurement may even be inappropriate: for example, the many voluntary groups that help the sick and dying deserve to be more than just a series of statistics. So how do public organisations develop their purpose? We examine this under three headings:

1 Stakeholders and the will of the people

2 Exploring and restating the purpose

3 Dilemmas and conflicts.

12.3.1 Stakeholders and the will of the people

In developing the purpose of public sector organisations, 'the key to success for public and non-profit organisations (and for communities) is the satisfaction of key stakeholders'.[35] The starting point in exploring the purpose has to be the opinions, views and judgements of the stakeholders. We explore and emphasis the need to analyse the influence of *stakeholder power*. The reader is therefore referred back to the earlier material on this important topic.

In addition to stakeholder theory, the public sector also relies on citizens expressing their opinions to politicians, arguably – though not necessarily – through their votes in public elections. This applies particularly to government organisations but can also apply to some not-for-profit bodies. Such a choice has its antecedents in the underlying principles to ascertain the will of the people developed by such scholars as Rousseau[36] and John Stuart Mill.[37] However, as pointed out by Nobel Laureate Amartya Sen,[38] similar thinking can be traced back to leaders in other non-Western countries including India and Japan, and some Muslim thinkers. He argues that 'democracy is best seen as the opportunity of participatory reasoning and public decision making – as government by discussion'. On this definition, democracy goes beyond voting in national elections every few years.

From a public sector strategy development perspective, there is a problem because some strategic decisions are complex and rely on expert knowledge. Sometimes it is difficult for the public to be fully informed about such matters, even if they participate in the 'participatory reasoning' of Sen above.[39] The relationship between informed public choice and its public sector consequences is therefore underpinned by an unavoidable tension. Namely, there is the need for the public debate and decision making to be mature and insightful while at the same time allowing citizens – even the ignorant – to express their opinion and even vote.[40] Britain's former prime minister Winston Churchill's observation that 'democracy is the worst form of government except for all the others' expresses the difficulty neatly.

In forming public sector strategy, there are times when ignoring the will of the people can invite problems. Hence, it is essential to attempt to understand the public perspective in developing purpose in public sector strategy. However, there are many ways to engage and represent the people around the world.[41] Churchill's comment on the weakness of democracy can be extended to the need for a range of methods to ascertain the will of the people in deciding the purpose of public sector strategy.

12.3.2 Exploring and restating the purpose

The starting point in defining the purpose of the strategy must lie with the basic mandate of the public sector organisation – What precisely is the organisation meant to do? Who is it meant to serve? There needs to be an identifiable social or political need that the organisation seeks to fill. This should be clarified, if necessary, by revisiting the formal charter or other legal, constitutional device that was agreed at the outset. This will lead to the mission of the organisation that, ideally, needs to be stated in a paragraph. An exploration of the strategic context in which the organisation is operating at a particular time will then suggest its purpose. For example, the mission of the European Union's Galileo satellite system to deliver a completely new and modern world navigation system, has led the company to re-examine its purpose, its timing and its delivery in the context of the changing interests of different national governments and companies.

For many public and not-for-profit organisations, the mission may also need to remind the stakeholders of the *inspiration* that originally led to the foundation of the organisation – in the case of volunteer organisations in particular, this may be what will drive them forward.[42] Such a purpose sometimes requires restating in strategy development.

12.3.3 Dilemmas and conflicts

One of the problems in public sector purpose is that many statements of purpose have to consider objectives that may conflict with each other.[43] For example, the European Union's Galileo satellite project has needed to find further funds to support the delays in developing the system while at the same time some, but not all, national governments have been highly critical of the way that the project has been managed. More generally, we can usefully identify two dilemmas that regularly impact on public sector strategy development:

1 *Steering versus rowing.*[44] Some commentators have argued that, in the setting of purpose in government strategy, government would work better if it concentrated on *steering* – setting policy, providing suitable funding to relevant public bodies and evaluating performance – rather than *rowing* – delivering the services. We do not need to resolve this matter here but simply recognise that this conflicting view of the role of government will impact directly on the ability to define strategic purpose.

2 *Improving public sector performance versus cost saving.* Commentators have varied in the emphasis they lay on these two different areas.[45] Performance improvements take as their starting point the need to adapt to the changing needs of society, new cultures and technologies. Cost saving begins by emphasising the need for the state to do less, cut back on public services and let market demand decide what is really needed. Again, we do not need to resolve this conflict here but recognise that such conflicts need to be identified and explored in the context of purpose.

In practice, these and other conflicts will vary with the strategic context of the time and the beliefs of the stakeholders. They need to be recognised and discussed. If they remain unresolved then it will be difficult for the purpose to be defined with sufficient clarity for strategy to be developed.

KEY STRATEGIC PRINCIPLES

- When developing the purpose of public sector organisations, the key to success for public and non-profit organisations is the satisfaction of main stakeholders. It is essential to conduct a stakeholder power analysis and seek the views of leading stakeholders.

- In addition to stakeholder theory, the development of public sector purpose also needs to reflect the general will of the people. Public opinion therefore needs to be identified and explored. It is sometimes difficult for citizens to develop an informed choice on complex issues, but such difficulties need to be recognised and resolved.

- The starting point in defining the purpose of strategy in the public sector must lie with the basic mandate of the public sector organisation, its role and its reason for its existence. This will lead to the mission of the organisation and a definition of its purpose in the context of the issues that it faces at that time.

- Many public sector organisations receive conflicting objectives. These need to be resolved if purpose is to be successfully defined and strategy developed.

12.4 CONTEXT, CONTENT AND PROCESS IN PUBLIC SECTOR STRATEGY

Having defined and clarified purpose, we are now in a position to develop strategies to deliver that purpose. It is possible to employ prescriptive models such as the options-and-choice approach.[46] The outcome, with some variations, is similar to that explored in the earlier chapters and is outlined briefly under the 'content' section below. However, given our focus on public sector strategy and the need to avoid repetition of areas covered previously, this section concentrates on the *differences* from business strategy. We examine this under three familiar strategy headings: context, content and process.

12.4.1 Strategic context

From the environmental and resource analyses, we established the chief differences in strategic context between public and business strategies:

- the change over the past 20 years from a public administration model of public sector strategy to a market-driven model in many countries;

- the dilemmas and contradictions that often exist between different policy directives in the public sector;

- the short-term and shifting nature of the political environment;

- the difficulty of raising funds and the reliance on specialist and voluntary human resources in parts of the not-for-profit sector.

Resource pressures to reduce numbers, privatisation of state monopolies and cost reduction policies all contribute to strategic context in the public sector. Shifting public attitudes on political, moral and social issues may determine the not-for-profit context. Such issues also need to be coupled with more radical changes in world environments when analysing strategic context in the public sector. For example, global warming, poverty and diseases, war and conflict, the increasing power of the internet and the ethical issues arising from biological advances all provide challenges in the public sector that may be important. Each public sector organisation will have its own list of factors against which to develop its strategy. The point here is that strategic context is arguably *broader* in the public sector than in business because of the wider role of government and not-for-profit institutions. The danger is that strategic context becomes over-complex. It can be focused by at least three methods:

1 *Developing some priorities with regard to strategic purpose* – identifying, possibly through group meetings, what will have a substantial impact on purpose and strategy.

2 *Using scenarios to develop some possible outcomes* for the leading strategic context issues. This will help to examine the consequences of particular situations.

3 *Keeping the strategic context analysis simple.* Complex and elaborate procedures are more likely to confuse than produce workable strategies.

12.4.2 Strategic content

Just as in business strategy, public sector content development can employ prescriptive strategy concepts of options-and-choice approaches.[47] In developing such options, Bryson recommends developing those that are both 'practical alternatives and dreams' for achieving the strategic purpose of the organisation.[48] He suggests that a useful procedure is to identify the barriers to achieving those outcomes and then ways of overcoming the barriers. Finally, he recommends that the chosen options are developed into specific proposals. Such an approach is not greatly different from business strategy, though the word 'dreams' might not appear in the latter.

In developing the strategic options, the question will arise as to whether the business strategy options can be employed. The options fell into two distinct areas – those associated with the strategic *environment* – such as Porter's generic strategies – and those associated with strategic *resources* – such as cost reduction and the resource-based options. Can public sector strategy use these concepts?

Dealing first with environment-based options, Porter is probably the dominant strategist in this area. It is unlikely that business strategy environment options can be used in public sector strategy. To quote Professor Ewen Ferlie of London University: 'With its strong focus on markets, profitability and competitiveness, [Porter's] models are difficult to apply literally, as prices, markets and profits all remain underdeveloped in the public sector.'[49] Nevertheless, Ferlie concludes that Porter's approach does have some merit where market-based concepts have been introduced into the public sector: 'Porterian models may prove especially useful for public sector regulators and purchasers, guiding them in their market development tasks.'[50] Such approaches may therefore be more appropriate in *new public management* treatments of public sector strategy. In addition, strategy in the not-for-profit sector may benefit from options that identify the possibility of competition in the environment for funds and people.

Resource-based strategic options offer the opportunity to focus on those competitive resources that allow some public sector bodies to offer superior public service to others.[51] To quote Ferlie again: 'Resource-based models can be applied to public sector organisations, as their profile of intangible assets is surely closely correlated with their performance in such important managerial tasks as the management of strategic change.'[52] Hence, options based on public sector resource analysis are worth pursuing, including cost reductions where relevant.

We explore emergent approaches to options development in the next section.

12.4.3 Strategic process

Because of the uncertainties involved in the public sector – regime change at the political level and unforeseen cataclysmic events at the general level – some public sector strategists favour the *controlled chaos* or *logical incrementalism* of J B Quinn.[53] This consists of a series of small decisions within the overall purpose of the organisation, with the outcome of each step determining the next steps – in other words, an emergent process for strategy development. Nevertheless, the extended strategic options process called the *Oval Mapping Process,* developed by Professor Colin Eden of Strathclyde University along with Professor Bryson and others,[54] would seem to derive much of its basis from learning-based approaches.

An alternative to logical incrementalism that has found favour with some public sector strategists[55] is the approach recommended by Lindblom. He wrote a theoretical paper – it quoted no empirical evidence – some 50 years ago called 'The Science of Muddling Through' that is still quoted with approval today.[56] Essentially, Lindblom argued that it is impossible in public sector strategy to analyse fully all the options that are available: there are just too many factors involved, from political ideas through economic pressures to social trends. He set out an alternative strategic process that was more realistic and concentrated particularly on small-scale, incremental decisions. It differs from logical incrementalism in that Lindblom made no reference to using the outcome of one stage to decide the next. 'Muddling through' is more basic in that regard. Bryson argues that Lindblom's approach can have real merit in some circumstances: it reduces risk, breaks a project into small do-able steps, eases implementation, quickly makes real change, provides immediate reward and preserves gains.[57]

Pollitt and Bouckaert take a similar approach and favour small steps over major change in many situations in the public sector:

> To launch, sustain and implement a comprehensive strategy for reform requires certain conditions and these are seldom satisfied in the real world of public management reform . . . Thus talk of 'strategy' is usually an idealization, or post hoc rationalization of a set of processes which tend to be partial, reactive and of unstable priority.[58]

This all argues in favour of the realism of a small-scale, incremental process in public sector strategy development.

Comment

The strategic context of public sector strategy is relatively uncertain for a variety of reasons and it is also complex. There is little to be gained by speculating about whether it is *more* complex than business strategy. The essential point is that public sector strategy development has a number of dimensions that make it difficult to manage. This all suggests that radical change in public sector strategy needs to be treated with some caution – it can be done, but it requires a very clear vision, strong leadership and substantial resources which may need specialist training.[59] Incrementalism in public sector strategy may be the better option in many cases.

KEY STRATEGIC PRINCIPLES

- For a variety of reasons, the strategic context of public sector strategy is broader than its counterpart in business strategy. The danger is that it becomes more complex and difficult to handle. There are three main mechanisms to simplify the process: priorities, scenarios and simplicity.

- Strategic content in public sector strategy can follow the options-and-choice route commonly used in some business strategy. However, options associated with the strategic environment need to be treated with considerable caution because the market mechanism is still lacking in much of the public sector. Nevertheless, options derived from resource-based analysis can be employed.

- With regard to strategic process, the uncertainties of the public sector favour the use of 'logical incrementalism' as a process. An alternative is the 'muddling through' approach which reduces public sector strategy to a series of small decisions.

- Importantly, a number of strategists argue that major strategic decisions in public sector strategy usually require substantial commitment in terms of resources and leadership. Such an approach is not so easy in practice.

12.5 IMPLEMENTATION IN PUBLIC SECTOR STRATEGY[60]

As with business strategy, effective implementation of proposed strategies is essential in the public sector. Such activity needs to be carefully planned and is best undertaken quickly and smoothly. Beyond this, the form of implementation depends upon the scale of changes planned:

- *Major changes in strategic direction.* These need a strong group of supporters and implementers, a clear agreement on the change that is required, an understanding of the main elements of that change and adequate resources to carry out the task.

- *Incremental changes in strategic direction.* These represent the better option when some of those affected hold reservations about – even objections to – the proposed strategic change. It may be possible to undertake pilot projects, use learning-based approaches, circulate the results of first initiatives so others can analyse the consequences and so that adjustments can be made.

Beyond these basic matters, strategic implementation in the public sector needs to develop specific, testable plans in a number of specific areas:

- *Explanation and understanding of the value added.* If successful strategies add value, as has been argued throughout this text, then it follows that those implementing the strategy must clearly understand this added value, its purpose and the strategies by which it will be achieved. An education and explanation phase is therefore desirable. Agreement by those involved may also be necessary in order to overcome objections to such a strategy.

- *Fixing difficulties.* In most implementation procedures, problems will arise. It is important that such difficulties are recognised as they occur. This means building monitoring mechanisms and milestones into the process.

- *Summative evaluations.* It is desirable to find out if the purpose of the strategy has been achieved. This needs to be built into the implementation process. Bryson draws a useful distinction between two aspects of such a process: *outputs*, which are the actions produced by the strategies, and *outcomes*, which are the larger ramifications of such changes – especially the symbolic changes that occur.[61] He suggests that such an evaluation can be difficult and lengthy, but it is important to establish whether things are 'better' as a result of a new strategy. However, such an approach has also been used recently to justify an army of managers who do little beyond evaluating the results of strategic change – an obvious recipe for over-bureaucratic management.[62]

- *New organisations and culture.* It may be necessary to reorganise existing public sector areas and possibly to recruit or redefine management responsibilities. It may even be necessary to develop a new organisational culture to ensure long-lasting changes. These areas need to form part of the overall plan at the outset, but it should be recognised that they may take years to implement. Some recent public sector strategies in the UK have under-estimated the difficulties here.[63] In both the public and business sectors, people need to be given time to learn, adjust and adapt to new situations.

- *Recognise the need for flexibility.* There are very few public sector strategies that have a single, clear outcome. Many strategies will be challenged and others will need to adapt as events – including political changes – occur in the surrounding strategic context. Implementation therefore has to be alert to such issues and respond as they occur.

In the public sector, budget allocations for a period of time can often be a crucial factor in strategy implementation – 'no money, no strategy'. The difficulty is that such budgets are subject to political pressures and are often short-term, incremental and reactive. There are no simple ways to overcome this problem, but it is desirable if the strategic planning stage comes *before* budget setting. In addition, it may be important to recognise the importance of individual leaders in developing the strategy – agreement and ownership of a strategy are important factors in strategy development and are not confined simply to the 'implementation phase'. In this sense, this whole section on implementation needs to be re-evaluated as being part of a broader, ongoing strategy development process, rather than an add-on process after the strategy has been decided.

Comment

Finally, it is important to make the point that public servants involved in the development of strategy have an important responsibility with regard to strategy development. To quote Robert Reich:

> The core responsibility of those who deal in public policy – elected officials, administrators, policy analysts – is not simply to discover as objectively as possible what people want for themselves and then to determine and implement the best means to satisfying these wants. It is also to provide the public with alternative visions of what is desirable and possible, to stimulate deliberation about them, provoke a re-examination of premises and values, and thus to broaden the range of potential responses and deepen society's understanding of itself.[64]

KEY STRATEGIC PRINCIPLES

- Strategy implementation in the public sector needs to be carefully planned and is best undertaken quickly and smoothly.

- The form of implementation depends on the scale of what is proposed. Major changes need substantial support. Smaller changes are probably best treated incrementally.

- In implementing public sector strategy, it is important to identify the value added and then explain this to those involved in its implementation. It is also necessary to have a mechanism that can fix the inevitable difficulties that will arise as new strategies are implemented.

- It may be appropriate to have a summative evaluation of the strategy after it has been implemented to find out whether the planned improvements have been achieved. However, such an approach can be lengthy and time-consuming. It can also be over-bureaucratic.

- A new organisational structure and culture may be necessary for some new strategies. This will take time that needs to be built into the process from the beginning. Such processes should not be under-estimated and may require years to complete. There is also a need to build some degree of flexibility into the implementation process as circumstances change.

- The budget process can be crucial for new strategies and should ideally be undertaken after the strategy has been agreed. Importantly, this is only a part of a broader implementation process that needs to include the agreement of key decision makers. Arguably, implementation needs to be re-evaluated as being part of a broader, ongoing strategy development process, rather than an add-on process after the strategy has been decided.

CASE STUDY 12.3

'Should we close the Kings Theatre?'
A tough strategic decision for Portsmouth City Council

Portsmouth city councillors had a difficult strategic decision to make in July 2003: should they withdraw the city's financial support for the Kings Theatre, Portsmouth, UK?

The theatre had only been relaunched in 2001, but its subsidiary commercial operating company went bankrupt in early 2003 with over £200,000 debts. Closure would cause immense local anger and negate the 'Two Theatres' strategy of the city. But keeping the theatre open would be fraught with many financial problems and major risks. This case explores the strategic options available to the city.

Background

City councils are not required to make profits. They have a broader responsibility to their electorate - to provide a range of services from education and social services to the arts and sporting activities. They operate within limits defined by the national government on the services that *must* be provided locally - like education and social welfare - and services over which the council has some *choice* - like selecting the level of support for local libraries or local sport. This case explores this

Portsmouth's Kings Theatre became a major focus for political pressure with the threat of total closure

typical mix of strategic decisions in one particularly acute case – the possible closure of a well-loved local theatre and its sale to a national brewery chain as a public house.

With over 170,000 people and an annual budget of around £200 million, it might be thought that Portsmouth was well placed to provide live theatre for its citizens. The difficulty comes in balancing the various demands on the council's limited budget. The decisions are more difficult when activities have been under-funded in the past and when local pride and passion are involved. Local councillors are politicians and, understandably, want to be re-elected. The city is a major tourist venue as well as offering employment in a range of local companies. But

Portsmouth's theatres were a victim of its past – it had four live theatres in 1950 that were packed every week. By the late 1990s, there were only two remaining major theatres – the Kings Theatre and the New Theatre Royal – plus a small Arts Theatre for experimental plays that was to be relocated to save money in mid-2003. The reasons for this decline were not hard to find – television, mass car ownership, the demand for nightclubs and more intimate entertainment.

It was against this background that the city council drafted its 'Two Theatres in Portsmouth' strategy in 1999 – see Exhibit 12.1. The concept was one theatre for major popular musicals, entertainment and drama – the Kings Theatre, with around 1,500 seats – and another theatre for smaller commercial productions such as small-scale experimental drama and concerts – the New Theatre Royal, with around 500 seats.

As Exhibit 12.1 also shows, the city's strategy across its two main venues was particularly difficult because both its major theatres were old and unmodernised. Portsmouth is unique in the UK as the only city with two beautiful old theatres designed by the great theatrical architect, Frank Matcham – there were only 23 Matcham theatres left in the whole of the UK in 2003. But the two unmodernised theatres were also an immense financial burden on the city, which the central government had done nothing to alleviate.

Competition from other theatres in the region

The nearby cities of Southampton and Chichester both had thriving theatres – see Exhibit 12.2. The Mayflower Theatre in Southampton and the Festival Theatre in Chichester had the benefit of substantial monies being spent on them in the 1980s. As a result, the rival theatres were already able to operate

---

EXHIBIT 12.1

Kings Theatre – the 'Two Theatres in Portsmouth' strategy

Kings Theatre

- 1,500 seats, to be used for major touring companies plus local amateur companies needing a large venue.
- Grade II* listed early twentieth-century beautiful building – never been modernised – poor car parking, away from city centre.
- Was relaunched by city council in 2001 as a non-profit theatre trust.
- Trust set up a limited company in 2001 with new manager/proprietor appointed – bankrupt with over £200,000 debts by early 2003 – company then liquidated.
- Needs minimum £7.5 million capital spend to modernise – possibly as much as £13 million to bring to the standard of competitors such as Mayflower Theatre, Southampton.

New Theatre Royal

- 500 seats, to be used for smaller touring companies, local drama education projects, Portsmouth University drama and music venue.
- Grade II* listed early twentieth-century beautiful building – never been modernised – partly burnt down so cannot take large scenery; city centre location, good parking.
- Needs minimum £5 million capital spend to modernise and create flexible performance space.

EXHIBIT 12.2

Kings Theatre, Portsmouth – the competitors

Mayflower Theatre, Southampton

- 1,800 seats, regular audience developed over years.
- Fully modernised theatre – compare to Kings Theatre, which is still using scenery handling built nearly 100 years ago.
- Takes top London musicals – King's Theatre will *never* compete here.
- City centre location, plenty of parking – compared with Kings Theatre, which is located away from Portsmouth town centre with poor parking for cars.

Festival Theatre, Chichester plus adjacent small experimental theatre

- 1,600 seats, strong local audience built over years.
- Modernised theatre, runs own productions – some transfer to London.
- Located on own site with good parking – just outside city centre.

Plus Portsmouth Guildhall Concert Hall and Portsmouth night clubs, comedy clubs plus other major venues in other local towns – e.g. Fareham, Havant.

Financing the Portsmouth two theatres strategy

The [Kings] theatre could be solvent and operated successfully with continued subsidy at the present level.

(Sam Shrouder, theatre consultant, after studying the Kings bankruptcy in April 2003)

Portsmouth city council took over the Kings Theatre in 2001. It gave an urgent capital injection of £300,000 and an annual subsidy of £135,000. It also decided to relaunch the theatre through a non-profit company and with a new director, David Rixon. He was given some freedom to test local customer demand during the period 2001–2003. The council always accepted that the first few years of the Kings Theatre would be experimental. However, no one bargained for the theatre actually going bankrupt in March 2003, with Mr Rixon resigning through ill-health.

How provincial theatres make profits

To understand the bankruptcy and judge its relevance to the long-term impact on the Kings Theatre, it is necessary to understand how provincial theatres make profits in the UK. Precise figures are not available, but it is likely that the Kings had an annual turnover of around £550,000. It was not open every week – probably around 30 weeks of the year. Some weeks there would be a full week of activity, perhaps with a local amateur theatrical company or with a touring opera or drama company. Other weeks, there might be just one or two nights with a well-known comedian or singer. It was the responsibility of the theatre's managing director – in this case, Rixon – to negotiate commercial terms with each touring company or individual artist. Typically in a modern theatre, the touring company would take 70 per cent or more of the revenue from that week – see Figure 12.4.

More than 200,000 seats were sold for 350 performances at the Kings Theatre during its 18 months of operation from late 2001 to early 2003. This was seen as satisfactory over this period. But the crucial matter to impact on the targets was the

more attractive, popular programmes. This meant that their seat prices were higher than the Kings Theatre – typically a yield of £12–14 per head compared to around £6–10 per head at the Kings. The competitors had developed loyal audiences over many years from a wide geographical area and would provide formidable competition to any refurbished Kings Theatre, Portsmouth.

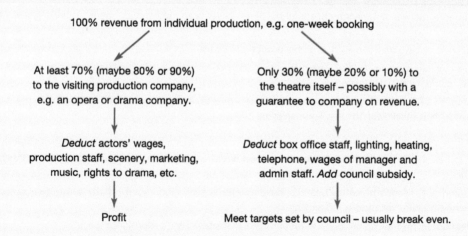

Figure 12.4 How local council-owned theatres achieve financial targets

bankruptcy of the theatre in March 2003. What precisely happened during the 18 months of operation that led to this situation was unclear. It is probable that some financial guarantees were given to touring companies that were too generous. In addition, there was probably some mis-management of costs, especially during the Christmas season in 2002–2003 which normally made a profit.

Strategic options for the future

There were three major options:

1 To provide new funds and new management to keep the theatre operating.

2 To sell the theatre to a national pub chain and convert it to public house entertainment venture.

3 To simply close down the venue and sell the land.

Option 1 Preserve the theatre

Many local people wanted to preserve the theatre. Unquestionably, there would be tremendous sadness among some members of the local and national theatre community if the Kings Theatre were to close as a theatre venue. 'Over my dead body' was how one well-known theatre expert expressed his views on the possible closure. Funds had been raised and excitement generated about the theatre's upcoming centenary in 2006. The city councillors were therefore under considerable voter pressure to choose this option.

'No political party is going to want to be seen as the one that closed the Kings' was how one observer summed up the local political pressure.

A city with cultural ambitions like ours must be seen to do something with its theatres. That is the challenge.
(Former council leader, Frank Worley, April 2003)

Hence, Portsmouth city councillors were faced with a strong local lobby that wanted to see the theatre preserved. This pressure was particularly acute because the local council was a hung council – each of the three main political parties had approximately equal representation – leaving decision making by one political party open to easy attack by the other two.

Option 2 Convert the theatre to a pub

Back in 1999 a UK national pub chain company – J D Wetherspoon – had expressed interest in purchasing the Kings Theatre as a public house entertainment venture. It said that it would preserve the fabric, spend funds to restore the interior and honour the grade II* listed status of the building. Importantly, the company had developed a proven tradition of preserving the fabric of historic buildings that it had acquired. But there would no longer be any live theatre for the general public.

The influential local newspaper, *The News*, had come out in favour of such a pub sale. The Arts Council of England was also in favour of this option. This was important because its views

could influence the award of substantial capital grants and it could support local arts activity.

Option 3 Close down the venue and sell the land

This was a real option because it was not clear that options 1 and 2 were commercially viable. The funds generated from the sale could be used to help the other Portsmouth theatre, the New Theatre Royal, that was also under threat.

Expert recommendation of the leading council official

After careful consideration, the city council's leisure officer – David Knight – recommended to the council that the Kings Theatre should be closed and sold to the highest bidder. However, if possible, it should be preserved as a theatre and not just pulled down. He argued that the council's limited funds would be better deployed in developing the New Theatre Royal and such a policy was much more likely to find favour with the Arts Council.

Strategic choice by the elected city councillors

In spite of this expert recommendation, the council was not obliged to accept it. The council needed to make its decision about the future of the Kings Theatre at a full council meeting on 22 July 2003.

Case questions

1 What are the key strategy issues here? Political pressure and local choice? Customer demand? Theatre run with innovative flair on a tight budget? You may wish to use the strategy concepts of context, content and process to structure your answer.

2 What are the sustainable competitive advantages of the Kings Theatre? Are they strong or weak? You should use well-established resource-based strategy concepts – like reputation and core competencies – to develop your answer.

3 What would you recommend to the city council? Which strategic option would you choose? Why?

4 Having chosen an option, what is the strategic process that should then be adopted to implement that option? You may wish to identify the key players with whom the city council will need to bargain and what game plan will be required.

CRITICAL REFLECTION

Public sector strategy: increased service or lower costs?

One of the underpinning themes throughout public sector strategy in recent years is where to focus the effort. Some argue that it is important for the public sector to increase the quality of the service that it offers to citizens. Others argue that the public sector has become too large and it would be better to make cutbacks, even if this reduces the services offered to the public. Such a conflict needs to be resolved if strategy is to be developed, so an answer is needed. Where do you stand on this issue? What is your view?

SUMMARY

- In public sector strategy, the analysis of the strategic environment is more complex than in the private sector. The main reason is that public sector strategy involves the wide-ranging and ill-defined subject of the public interest: the public interest concerns both the objectives and the institutions that make and implement public decisions. There are two main public sector models – centrally directed (*dirigiste*) and free-market (*laissez-faire*). The market mechanism is the means by which the state uses market pricing and quasi-market mechanisms to determine the supply and demand of goods that were previously state monopolies. In practice over the past 20 years, many states have moved to greater use of the market through privatising state-owned companies. Each individual country will have its own approach to the use of such mechanisms. A public sector environmental analysis will have to be conducted on a country-by-country basis. There are also two costs associated with the market mechanism: first, the cost of being unable to close inefficient services because they provide vital public services; second, the cost of administering the market mechanism to ensure that it serves the agreed public objectives.

- Public value refers to the benefits to the whole of the nation from owning and controlling certain products and services. However, such value needs to be considered within the legal framework that binds and governs the value. In addition, public value requires the concept of equity to make sure that the value is distributed to all citizens. In some circumstances, public value needs a regulator to deal with any market imperfections.

- In the public sector, stakeholder power is possessed by those citizens who are able to influence the decisions of the state. Such power may be expressed through democratic elections but these can lead to short-termism in strategic decisions. Power can also be exercised through pressure groups and other forms of interest. Such power needs to be analysed.

- In the not-for-profit sector, an environmental analysis needs to consider the role and purpose of the organisation and also its actual and potential sources of funds. Such organisations cannot rely on public taxes to pay for their activities and need to seek voluntary contributions that will vary with a range of factors.

- The nine stages in environmental analysis used for business strategy can be adapted for use in public sector strategy analysis. But they need to be treated with caution.

- Public sector resource analysis needs to begin by examining which of the two public sector models – public sector administration or new public management – is adopted by the state. The public sector administration model consists of a professional civil service bureaucracy that enacts government legislation and administers the activities of the state on behalf of the government coupled with state monopolies that supply services to the citizens. The new public management model is a model of public sector decision making where the professional civil service operates with more market competition, while former state monopolies are divided and compete against each other for business from citizens. However, the state retains some areas under state control, such as the defence of the nation.

- The former does not support competitive advantage while the latter is underpinned by concepts of market competition in what was formerly the monopolistic state sector. Resource-based analysis in the public sector for the second approach will include similar concepts to those in business strategy – tangible, intangible and organisational resources, etc.

- There are four additional considerations that apply in analysing resources in the public sector: appropriate and sufficient resources for purpose; public power as a resource; the costs and benefits of public resources; and persuasion and education as a public resource. Public sector resource analysis needs to assess whether sufficient and appropriate resources are available to deliver the purpose and objectives set by the state. This means that resource analysis needs to identify public purpose and then assess resource requirements against this.

- Public power is a resource possessed by nation states and consists of the collective decision making that derives from the nation state. The analysis of such a resource is important in developing public sector strategy. With regard to costs and benefits of public resources, the task of the public sector manager is often that of obtaining the maximum benefit for the least cost. 'Benefit' here has a broader social definition than simply delivering shareholder profitability in the private sector. Such a balance needs to be considered in resource analysis in the public sector. Public sector resource analysis also needs to consider whether persuasion and education are possible resources of the state and, if so, how and where they might be employed.

- In not-for-profit organisations, there is a need to examine the fund-raising resource of the organisation. In addition, there is a specific need to examine the human resources of such organisations in three areas: voluntary help, specialist technical knowledge and the leadership and governance.

- The outcome of the resource analysis will identify the public organisation's strongest abilities and most effective actions and policies. From an administrative viewpoint, it will also set out the resources that it employs on a regular basis to perform well.

- When developing the purpose of public sector organisations, the key to success for public and non-profit organisations is the satisfaction of main stakeholders. It is essential to conduct a stakeholder power analysis and seek the views of leading stakeholders. In addition to stakeholder theory, the development of public sector purpose also needs to reflect the general will of the people. Public opinion therefore needs to be identified and explored. It is sometimes difficult for citizens to develop an informed choice on complex issues but such difficulties need to be recognised and resolved.

- The starting point in defining the purpose of strategy in the public sector must lie with the basic mandate of the public sector organisation, its role and its reason for its existence. This will lead to the mission of the organisation and a definition of its purpose in the context of the issues that it faces at that time. Many public sector organisations receive conflicting objectives. They need to be resolved if purpose is to be successfully defined and strategy developed.

- For a variety of reasons, the strategic context of public sector strategy is broader than its counterpart in business strategy. The danger is that it becomes more complex and difficult to handle. There are three main mechanisms to simplify the process: priorities, scenarios and simplicity.

- Strategic content in public sector strategy can follow the options-and-choice route commonly used in some business strategy. However, options associated with the strategic environment need to be treated with considerable caution because the market mechanism is still lacking in much of the public sector. Nevertheless, options derived from resource-based analysis can be employed.

- With regard to strategic process, the uncertainties of the public sector favour the use of 'logical incrementalism' as a process. An alternative is the 'muddling through' approach which reduces public sector strategy to a series of small decisions. Importantly, a number of strategists argue that major strategic decisions in public sector strategy usually require substantial commitment in terms of resources and leadership. Such an approach is not so easy in practice.

- Strategy implementation in the public sector needs to be carefully planned and is best undertaken quickly and smoothly. The form of implementation depends on the scale of what is proposed. Major changes need substantial support. Smaller changes are probably best treated incrementally.

- In implementing public sector strategy, it is important to identify the value added and then explain this to those involved in its implementation. It is also necessary to have a mechanism that can fix the inevitable difficulties that will arise as new strategies are implemented.

- It may be appropriate to have a summative evaluation of the strategy after it has been implemented to find out whether the planned improvements have been achieved. However, such an approach can be lengthy and time-consuming. It can also be over-bureaucratic.

- A new organisational structure and culture may be necessary for some new strategies. This will take time that needs to be built into the process from the beginning. Such processes should not be under-estimated and may require years to complete. There is also a need to build some degree of flexibility into the implementation process as circumstances change.

- The budget process can be crucial for new strategies and should ideally be undertaken after the strategy has been agreed. Importantly, this is only a part of a broader implementation process that needs to include the agreement of key decision-makers. Arguably, implementation needs to be re-evaluated as being part of a broader, ongoing strategy development process, rather than an add-on process after the strategy has been decided.

QUESTIONS

1 Take your own country and analyse the extent to which it employs *laissez-faire* or *dirigiste* policies in the public sector. How does this compare with other countries?

2 What public sector strategy would you expect the following organisations to have?

   (a) A public library based in a small town.

   (b) A voluntary group providing volunteers to visit the elderly and house-bound.

   (c) A prosperous town with 100,000 inhabitants and a range of industrial activities from manufacturing to leisure.

   (d) The police force associated with a region of a country.

3 'The need to improve service quality has been and remains a major pre-occupation for many public sector organisations and those who fund their activities.' (G Johnson and K Scholes (2001) *Exploring Public Sector Strategy*, p 250) Take an organisation with which you are familiar and consider this comment: is the comment correct for your chosen organisation? How has it been tackled? How should it be approached?

4 If you were asked to make the European Union's Galileo satellite project more responsive to public pressures, what would you do? In answering this question, you should take into account the existing structure of the institution.

5 Winston S Churchill commented: '*Democracy is the worst form of government except for all the others*' (see Section 12.3). Is this correct? What are the implications for public sector strategy?

6 Undertake a stakeholder power analysis for a public sector organisation of your choice: it could be a voluntary organisation like a student society or club. What are the implications of your analysis for the development of strategy in that organisation?

7 Why is it difficult to apply Porter's market-based concepts in public sector strategy? Do they have any relevance at all in a city-based fire and rescue service?

8 The chief executive of a not-for-profit charity serving those who are terminally ill has become worried by declining levels of income, believing the organisation has lost out to others that have a stronger public presence, and has turned to you for advice. What would you recommend?

9 '*To launch, sustain and implement a comprehensive strategy for reform requires certain conditions and these are seldom satisfied in the real world of public management reform.*' This is the view of Pollitt and Bouckaert – see Section 12.4. Are they being too gloomy about the prospects for radical reform of public sector strategy? Does this mean that major reform in the public sector is almost certainly doomed to failure?

ACKNOWLEDGEMENTS

This chapter breaks new ground in strategy textbooks. The author is therefore particularly grateful to three people who have commented on earlier drafts of this chapter: Dr Paul Baines of Cranfield University, Dr Paul Hughes of Loughborough University and Marc Coleman, former Economics Editor of the *Irish Times*. Any remaining errors and omissions remain solely the responsibility of the author.

FURTHER READING

Bryson, J M (1998) *Strategic Planning for Public and Nonprofit Organizations*, Jossey Bass, San Francisco, CA is one of the leading texts in this area and has strong, practical advice. There is also a more recent special issue that has some useful insights: Kochan, T, Guillen, M F, Hunter, L W and O'Mahoney, S (2009) 'Public Policy and Management Research: Finding the Common Ground', *Academy of Management Journal*, Vol 52, No 6, pp 1088 onwards.

Two books on public administration are Lane, J-E (2000) *The Public Sector: Concepts, Models and Approaches*, 3rd edn, Sage, London and Frederickson, H G and Smith, K B (2003) *The Public Administration Theory Primer*, Westview, Oxford. Both provide useful summaries of the basics of theories that follow a completely different academic tradition from strategic management.

A text with substantial cross-country empirical comparisons and interesting comment is Pollitt, C and Bouckaert, G (2000) *Public Management Reform: A Comparative Analysis*, Oxford University Press, Oxford, which is well written and thought-provoking.

Three recommended texts on strategic management in the public sector are: Joyce, P (1999) *Strategic Management for the Public Services*, Open University Press, Buckingham; Bovaird, T and Loffler, E (eds) (2003) *Public Management and Governance* Routledge, London; Johnson, G and Scholes, K (eds) (2001) *Exploring Public Sector Strategy*, Pearson Education, Harlow.

NOTES AND REFERENCES

1 Ferlie, E (2002) 'Quasi strategy: strategic management in the contemporary public sector', in Pettigrew, A, Thomas, H and Whittington, R (eds) *Handbook of Strategy and Management*, Sage, London.

2 Lane, J-E (2000) *The Public Sector: Concepts, Models and Approaches*, 3rd edn, Sage, London.

3 Frederickson, H G and Smith, K B (2003) *The Public Administration Theory Primer*, Westview, Oxford.

4 Lane, J-E (2000) Op. cit.

5 Lane, J-E (2000) Op. cit.; Frederickson, H G and Smith, K B (2003) Op. cit. and many other public strategy texts.

6 See many reviews. For example: Hood, C (1987) 'British administrative trends and the public choice revolution', in Lane, J-E (1987) (ed) *Bureaucracy and Public Choice*, Sage, London; Joyce, P (1999) *Strategic Management for the Public Services*, Open University Press, Buckingham; Pollitt, C (1990) *The New Managerialism and the Public Services: The Anglo-American Experience*, Basil Blackwell, Oxford; Pollitt, C (1993) *Managerialism in the Public Services*, 2nd edn, Blackwell, Oxford; Boyne, G A (2002) 'Public and private management: what's the difference?', *Journal of Management Studies*, Vol 39, No 1, pp 97–122.

7 The Galileo case was written by the author from numerous sources: The European Union has an extensive website devoted to the basic details of the project at http://europa.eu.int/comm/dgs/energy_transport/galileo/index_en.htm. *Financial Times*: 18 September 2003, p 24; 24 January 2005, p 20; 18 April 2005, p 28; 12 October 2006, p 9; 14 October 2006, p 6; 5 February 2007, p 6; 4 May 2007, p 7; 10 May 2007, p 13; 3 October 2007, p 26. *BBC News* from website: 6 March 2008 'Galileo demo sat to be despatched'; 5 January 2009 'Galileo, Europe's much delayed and costly satellite navigation project, takes a major step forward'; 26 October 2010 'Spaceopal named as Galileo European satnav operator'.

8 Some readers will detect a contradiction here but that is beyond the scope of this strategy text. You can explore it in: Lane, J-E (2000) Op. cit.

9 Lane, J-E (2000) Op. cit., p 6.

10 Frederickson, H G and Smith, K B (2003) Op. cit., p 193.

11 Back in the 1950s, Charles Tiebout attempted to resolve this problem by arguing that a theoretical competitive market could be created in a nation. It would need citizens to be mobile and different levels of public service to be offered in different parts of their country. If such citizens were able to shop around between local government areas for their preferred package of services and pay the taxes related to the choice that best suited their preferences, then such mobility would deliver 'the local public goods counterpart to the private market's shopping trip'. In essence, he was proposing a theoretical market in public services. Tiebold's hypothesis was that it was more efficient to have alternative government agencies competing rather than a centralised bureaucracy. For a fuller treatment, see Frederickson, H G and Smith, K B (2003) Op. cit., pp 193–194.

12 Bryson, J M (1998) *Strategic Planning for Public and Nonprofit Organizations*, Jossey Bass, San Francisco, CA.

13 Frederickson, H G and Smith, K B (2003) Op. cit., p 113; Lane, J-E (2000) Op. cit., p 2.

14 Lane, J-E (2000) Op. cit., p 305.

15 Lane, J-E (2000) Op. cit., p 304.

16 Pollitt, C and Bouckaert, G (2000) *Public Management Reform: A Comparative Analysis*, Oxford University Press, Oxford.

17 Frederickson, H G and Smith, K B (2003) Op. cit. has a comparison of the two systems on p 113.

18 Kettl, D (2000) *The Global Public Management Revolution: A Report on the Transformation of Governance*, Brookings Institute, Washington, D.C.

19 Lane, J-E (2000) Op. cit., p 307.

20 See extensive reviews in Lane, J-E (2000) Op. cit. and Pollitt and Bouckaert (2000) Op. cit.

21 See for example, Ferlie, E (2002) 'Quasi strategy: strategic management in the contemporary public sector', in Pettigrew, A, Thomas, H and Whittington, R (eds) *Handbook of Strategy and Management*, Sage, London; Bryson, J M (1998) Op. cit.; Bovaird, T (2003) 'Strategic management in public sector organizations', in Bovaird, T and Loffler, E (eds) *Public Management and Governance*, Routledge, London.

22 Bryson, J M (1998) Op. cit. uses SWOT extensively with many examples in both the public and non-profit sectors in his text.

23 Pollitt, C and Bouckaert, G (2000) Op. cit., Ch 7.

24 Bryson, J M (1998) Op. cit., Ch 5.

25 Pollitt, C and Bouckaert, G (2000) Op. cit., p 173.

26 See, for example, Hood, C (1983) *The Tools of Government*, Macmillan, London; Heymann, P (1987) *The Politics of Public Management*, Yale University Press, CT; Moore, M (1995) *Creating Public Value: Strategic Management in Government*, Harvard University Press, Cambridge, MA.

27 Lane, J-E (2000) Op. cit.

28 See for example, Bardach, E and Kagan, R (1982) *Going by the Book: The Problem of Regulatory Unreasonableness*, Temple University Press, PA; Wolf, C (1988) *Markets or Governments*, MIT Press, Cambridge, MA.

29 Pollit, C and Bouckaert, G (2000) Op. cit., p 170.

30 Osborne, D and Gaebler, T (1992) *Reinventing Government: How the Entrepreneurial Spirit is Transforming the Public Sector*, Plume, N Y; Alford, J (1998) 'Corporate Management', in Shafritz, J, *International Encyclopedia of Public Policy and Administration*, Vol 1, Westview Press, Boulder, CO.

31 Readers may care to note that this area remains somewhat under-researched. The author has therefore developed these comments from personal observation with the usual words of caution that derive from such an approach – partial, incomplete and a biased sample.

32 Bryson, J M (1998) Op. cit., p 30.

33 Bryson, J M (1998) Op. cit., Ch 5.

34 Sources for the Viking Energy case: in addition to the website sources quoted in the case, Professor Lynch made a 10-day visit to Shetland in August 2010. He interviewed seven local residents, some of whom were in favour of the proposal and some not. He also sourced further material particularly from the *Shetland Times* news stories which are available online.

35 Bryson, J M (1998) Op. cit., p 27.

36 Cranston, M (1968) (Trans and ed) *Jean-Jacques Rousseau – The Social Contract*, Penguin, Harmondsworth.

37 Mill, J S (1962) *Utilitarianism* – Edited with an Introduction by Mary Warnock, Collins/Fontana, London.

38 Sen, A (2005) 'The diverse ancestry of democracy', *Financial Times*, 13 June, p 19.

39 Lynch, R (2004) 'When majority opinion conflicts with expert judgment – the case of the Kings Theatre', *British Academy of Management Conference Paper*, St Andrews.

40 Lynch, R (2004) Ibid.

41 Wolf, M (2005) 'A more efficient Union will be less democratic', *Financial Times*, 15 June, p 19. This has an informed, if complex, discussion on such issues in the European Union. According to this argument, 'democracy' is more than just voting for European politicians every few years.

42 Bryson, J M (1998) Op. cit., p 27.

43 Pollit, C and Bouckaert, G (2000) Op. cit. Ch 7 has a long and interesting list of such conflicts and dilemmas which they discuss in detail.

44 Osborne, D and Gaebler, T (1992) *Re-inventing Government*, Addison Wesley, Reading, MA.

45 Bryson, J M (1998) Op. cit., p 159.

46 Bryson, J M (1998) Op. cit. Ch 7 provides a long and useful description in this area.

47 Bryson, J M (1998) Op. cit., p 33.

48 Bryson, J M (1998) Op. cit., p 33.

49 Ferlie, E (2002) Op. cit., p 289.

50 Ferlie, E (2002) Op. cit., p 289.

51 Bryson, J M (1998) Op. cit., Ch 5.

52 Ferlie, E (2002) Op. cit., p 289.

53 See, for example, Bryson, J M (1998) Op. cit., Ch 7.

54 Outlined in some depth with extensive references in Bryson, J M (1998) Op. cit.; Bryson, J M, Ackermann, F, Eden, C, Finn, C B (1995) 'Using the "*oval mapping process*" to identify strategic issues and formulate effective strategies', in *Strategic Planning for Public and Nonprofit Organizations*, Jossey Bass, San Francisco, CA, pp 257–275.

55 See, for example, Bryson, J M (1998) Op. cit., p 147 and Pollit, C and Bouckaert, G (2000) Op. cit., pp 183–187.

56 Lindblom, C (1959) 'The science of muddling through,' *Public Administration Review*, Vol 19, No 2, pp 79–88.

57 Bryson, J M (1998) Op. cit., p 147.

58 Pollitt, C and Bouckaert, G (2000) Op. cit., p 185.

59 Several research studies have shown that while the Margaret Thatcher privatisation reforms of the 1980s may have been presented as radical change, in practice, they were much more gradual and incremental, with the final outcomes being unknown at the start of the process. Quoted and referenced in Pollit, C and Bouckaert, G (2000) Op. cit.

60 This section of the chapter has benefited particularly from Ch 9 of Bryson, J M (1998) Op. cit.

61 Bryson, J M (1998) Op. cit., p 167.

62 One inevitable consequence of the introduction of the market mechanism into the public sector is the pressure for public servants to be accountable. This can 'distort priorities, consume time and effort in form-filling and produce changes locally that make no sense' – *Financial Times* Editorial, 31 January 2005, p 18. But, as the *FT* goes on to argue, there is good evidence that they have their uses and what is the alternative?

63 As one example, see Timmings, N (2005) 'Flagship hospital hit by barrage of changes', *Financial Times*, 31 January 2005, p 8.

64 Reich, R (1988) (ed) *The Power of Public Ideas*, Ballinger, Cambridge, MA. Quoted in: Alford, J (2001) 'The implications of "publicness" for strategic management theory', Ch 1 of Johnson, G and Scholes, K (eds) *Exploring Public Sector Strategy*, Pearson Education, Harlow. More generally, Ch 18 of *Strategic Management,* 7th edn, has benefited from Alford's introductory chapter to this edited book. It has also gained from the contributions of the other authors and the editors of this text.

65 Sources for the Kings Theatre case: The author has known the theatres of Portsmouth all his life. He declares an interest in the Kings Theatre, having made a small donation to its renovation fund in 2002. Other sources: *The News*, Portsmouth: 17 April 2003, p 5; 24 April 2003, pp 6, 8–9; 25 April 2003, p 22; 28 April 2003, p 5; 30 April 2003, p 6; 9 May 2003, p 11; 26 June 2003, p 6; 27 June 2003, p 10; 1 July 2003, p 6; 3 July 2003, p 5; 7 July 2003, p 5; 10 July 2003, pp 8 and 9; 10 July 2003, p 6; 11 September 2003, p 22; 21 February 2004, p 7. Interviews as outlined in the acknowledgements at the end of the case.

Globalisation, challenges and changes

Ian Brooks, Jamie Weatherston and Graham Wilkinson

Learning outcomes

On completion of this chapter you should be able to:

- understand the impact of globalisation;
- understand the move towards greater dynamism, complexity and uncertainty (turbulence) in the international business environment of most firms;
- speculate about the future prospects for organisations, individuals, governments and groups in society as a result of environmental turbulence;
- outline the nature of chaotic and turbulent environments and the implications of these for long-term planning and flexible working;
- reflect on the differences between predictable and unpredictable change and the implications of this for organisations;
- understand the characteristics of the advantages and drawbacks of flexible working;
- discuss the influences that the changing international business environment and, in particular, the trend towards flexible working, have upon individuals and groups in the social community;
- explore environmental scenarios;
- discuss the future role of government and understand the environmental forces acting on public sector organisations.

Key concepts

- dynamism, complexity, uncertainty and turbulence
- predictable and unpredictable change
- chaos theory
- futurology
- long-term planning
- environmental scenarios and planning
- flexible working
- demographic time bomb
- social inclusion and exclusion
- interventionist and *laissez-faire* government.

Minicase 13.1	Dealing with unexpected changes

Twice in the last decade events have shown how vulnerable an advanced society can be. On both occasions fuel prices in the UK had risen substantially above the general price index due to government tax policies and global price increases. Businesses, in particular farmers and hauliers, for whom fuel costs are especially important, protested against continuing rises by picketing fuel refineries. The normal flow of tankers to petrol stations was affected. In some areas many stations ran dry as consumers fearful of long-term shortages filled up. The sudden rise in demand for fuel made the supply situation worse. Supermarkets reported 'panic' buying of foods. The government was suspicious that the oil companies were not doing all they could to get tankers out, in the hope that the government might cave in and reduce taxes, something it pledged not to do. Oil company executives were summoned to Number 10 and the Cabinet's emergency committee met regularly. Troops were on standby to move fuel supplies. After about a week the protestors gave up their picketing and normality resumed. The Home Secretary was quoted as saying, 'as a consequence of these protests, essential services, the basic fabric of our society and national life, were brought to the brink'.

Such is the extent of the integration of critical resources and concerns about vulnerability that the UK government created the Centre for the Protection of National Infrastructure. The Centre advises on the security of essential services such as food, water, energy and other services that if compromised would lead to severe economic or social consequences. The threats, they say, are largely from terrorist groups or espionage by foreign powers. Terrorism is not just about bombs and bullets; electronic or chemical attacks are capable of causing massive disruption and harm.

Questions

1 Identify the ways in which businesses and consumers may be affected by industrial action or terrorist attacks.
2 How might governments deal with this increased vulnerability to global events?

13.1 Introduction

Chapter will, in significant measure, depart from the format of the bulk of this text. It is more exploratory in nature, focusing to some extent on the future. It is hoped that you will develop your imagination and differentiate between the more certain and the speculative aspects of the future world. We look at both reasonably predictable changes, such as the aging of many societies, as well as more speculative change. The pace of change is also discussed. However, whether predictable or not, the greatest challenge is actually coping with change. The chapter explores various responses to macro-environmental change, such as flexible working. It examines the impact of change on organisations, groups, individuals and government.

We are constantly reminded that the pace of change is speeding up and, by other commentators, that 'we' are moving in unpredictable directions. Of course if we fully accept the 'unpredictable thesis' then there would be little point in attempting to plan for change and we would just have to accept whatever came our way! Futurology is the name often given to the art of imagining or at least reflecting upon likely future scenarios for change. Ironically, futurology is probably one of the oldest arts we have – people have attempted to predict the future, no doubt, since the origins of our species, with varying degrees of success. Some cultures adopt a broadly accepting position regarding the future, suggesting that, for example, it is God's will, while others have a greater tendency to believe that mankind can forge its own future. We will not enter that particular debate here. Instead, we will explore some of the previous ideas and reflect on more current visions of our future. These visions for change in the business environment may have a profound impact on organisational activity and our social and work lives.

13.2 Globalisation

Globalisation can be referred to as a phenomenon, a process, a state or a concept. It has evolved partly due to the trend for increasing international trade across national boundaries and the conduct of business activities in more than one country – and because of the changes in the various aspects of the international business environment discussed throughout this book. Put simply, it is a process that refers to the growth of inter-dependencies between national markets and industries on a worldwide scale. This growing interdependence between national economies has resulted in a trend towards global markets, global production and global competition. There are many theories and models that try to explain the process of globalisation; we will look at some of them.

Many commentators take the view that globalisation probably started some way back in the nineteenth century. From this perspective, it is possible to identify four phases of globalisation. The first phase, which peaked in about 1880, was mainly due to improvements in transportation and automation that enabled reliable long-distance trade. Telegraph and telephone communication in the late 1800s facilitated information transfer, which many firms found to be especially useful in managing their supply chains.

Phase two reached its height in the first decades of the twentieth century, when territories under the control of European colonial powers were seen as sites to establish multinational subsidiaries. This period also saw some overseas expansion by American corporations into profitable European markets. This phase is perceived to have ended with the economic crash in 1929, which caused a global depression and a move to inward-looking polices by many governments.

The third phase was based on the lowering of tariff barriers and the resultant increase in international trade after the end of World War II. As individuals, particularly in the richer economies, became wealthier and the austerity of the war years faded, there was massively increased demand for consumer goods. As the largest and least war-damaged economy post 1945, it was, perhaps, inevitable that the USA would become the most dominant power in terms of globalisation.

The fourth (and final) phase of the process has depended largely on two of the changes discussed in this book. These are, first, changes in technology, such as the widespread availability of the personal computer (PC) linked to the internet/world wide web, the increasing use of mobile communications and the development of robotics both for tracking components and finished goods and in the automation of production. Bear in mind, also, that these factors have not only affected manufacturing industry; the service sector, for example banking and tourism, have also benefited from these changes. Distance is no longer an issue – the world has shrunk to a manageable size. The second factor is the change in political attitudes and economic policies that have allowed companies (and consumers) to take advantage of these technological advances. It is apparent that there has been much convergence of global economic thinking, with many more countries moving towards an acceptance of liberal, free-market ideas. Social trends changed, too, as consumers apparently became less concerned with products' national identities. *Table 13.1* shows these phases.

Figure 13.1 shows some factors in the macro-environment that have had an impact on globalisation.

Theodore Levitt (1983) was one of the first academics to write about globalisation. In 1983 he said that technology is the driving force behind the globalisation of markets and, thus, a 'converging commonality' in countries around the planet. He suggested that:

- communications (e.g. TV);
- transport;
- travel;
- products; and
- processes;

| Table 13.1 | Four phases of globalisation |
| | |

Phase of globalisation	Period	Trigger	Characteristics
First phase	1830–1890	Rail and ocean transport	Automated manufacturing; cross-border trading of commodities
Second phase	1900–1930	Electricity and steel production	Emergence of European and American manufacturing and extracting industries
Third phase	1948–1970s	GATT, end of World War II rebuilding	Efforts to reduce trade barriers. Rise of Japanese multinationals, triad nations and branded products
Fourth phase	1980–Current	ICT, automation, consultancy, privatisation	FDI fuelling growth in LDCs, technology and transport innovations, global media and branding

were all leading to an 'irrevocable homogenisation' of demand. Levitt's key assumption or hypothesis was that local tastes and preferences will vanish if the product is cheap enough. The implication of this is that:

- identical products will be sold in all markets; and
- industries will be dominated by global corporations benefiting from huge economies of scale.

An alternative view is put forward by writers such as Douglas and Wind (1987) and Ohmae (1989) who suggest that some products are 'global', others are not. They point out that there are many barriers to standardisation and that companies cannot ignore local consumer needs. Indeed, companies can gain considerable benefits by making minor changes to suit different national markets. That is not to say companies should ignore the attractions of standardisation. If companies can standardise, even to a small extent, then they will be able to avoid duplication of effort in, for example, research and development and provide the same products in markets where this is acceptable. The emphasis is, perhaps, best summed up by Kenichi Ohmae's famous phrase 'Think globally, act locally'. In essence, this can be seen to mean that companies should regard the globe as one market, but should make changes to their products and services when necessary, to better serve each local market.

It is clear that some markets are in line with Levitt's 'converging commonality' e.g. designer clothing where consumers are more than happy to buy the latest exclusive design. A second example would be CDs, which are produced to identical technical specifications the world over. Other markets are, however, locally differentiated. This can be seen in the variation in menus that McDonald's, for instance, offer around the world, even while the core image and branding of the company remain constant. While it is possible to recognise both of these viewpoints, one thing is clear: customer needs are becoming more complex and so are markets.

George Yip's (2003) model provides further insight into the forces driving globalisation. It helps us to understand the pressure that industries are under to globalise: see *Figure 13.2*.

Yip also says that an understanding of the global forces assists a company to identify the critical success factors in a global industry and market.

Market drivers:

- similar customer needs and tastes;
- the existence of global customers;
- transferable marketing between different countries.

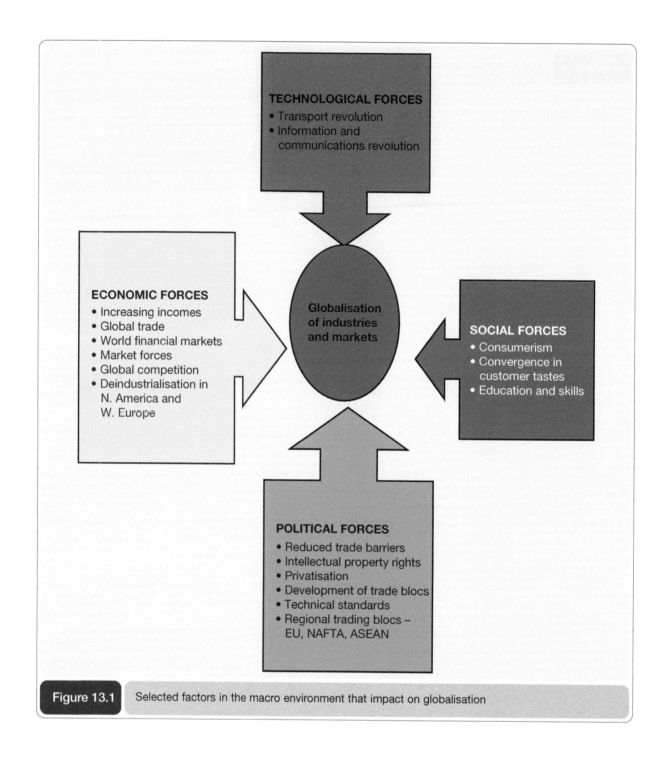

Figure 13.1   Selected factors in the macro environment that impact on globalisation

Competitive drivers:

- competitors' global strategies;
- country interdependence.

Cost drivers:

- scale economies and scope including product development costs – experience curve;
- favourable logistics;
- country-specific differences.

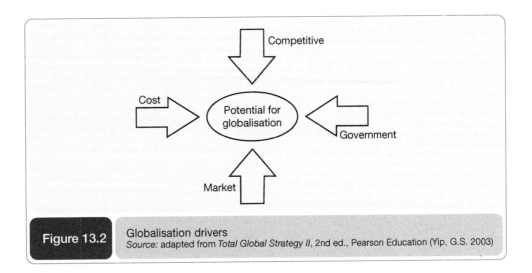

Figure 13.2	Globalisation drivers
	Source: adapted from *Total Global Strategy II*, 2nd ed., Pearson Education (Yip, G.S. 2003)

Government drivers are numerous and include:

- trade policies; tariff barriers; subsidies to local companies; ownership restrictions;
- local content requirements; controls over technology transfer; intellectual property regimes; currency and capital flows;
- marketing regulations; host government concerns; technical standards.

Overall, then, it can be seen that there is a great deal of evidence that globalisation has been on the rise, increasingly rapidly as the twentieth century came to an end and the twenty-first began. Even the turbulence and the problems of the 2008 credit crunch have not stopped the process. It may have slowed some international expansion by companies, indeed, that is certainly the case, but there is little evidence of any reversal of the trends of the previous three decades. On the contrary, policy-makers around the world have called for a global response to a global problem, acknowledging the inter-connected nature of the global economy (and global societies). As we have shown throughout this book, it is possible to use the PESTLE C model to look at these forces driving globalisation (and some of the obstacles too).

At a political level the formation of world institutions such as WTO, UN, the World Bank, OECD and IMF have been necessary to facilitate globalisation. We can also see global legal entities such as the International Court of Justice based in The Hague, as well as countries becoming more willing to share criminal intelligence to fight against global crime. The increase in the number of global standards including patent protection and electrical standards also break down barriers to international trade.

At an industry level the emergence of worldwide markets, including new businesses based on internet trading, is a good indicator. Global production, global competition and global brands, e.g. McDonald's, Coca-Cola, Toyota and Adidas, are now commonplace across all the continents, not just the richer parts of the world. There has also been an increase in cross-border mergers and acquisitions throughout the 1990s and beyond until the economic downturn of 2008 has (temporarily, perhaps) slowed the process. Even so, this activity has resulted in even more global corporations, some (such as India's Tata) based in developing economies. World financial markets have developed to support all this activity.

Technological change, often based on developments in information technology and the fall in the cost of computer processing (widely accepted to have fallen at around 30 percent per year for 20 years), have been vital in pushing globalisation. IT developments allow companies to produce new goods and reduce production costs through advances in CAD and robotics. Now even the smallest SME (e.g. a musician in a bedroom) can reach a global market. This in turn alters industry structure and markets.

The increase in information flows between geographically remote locations has been made easier by high-speed global telecommunications. Satellites and submarine fibre-optic cables enable high-speed data transfer vital to support global business. Satellites are vital for mobile communication and tracking goods in the supply chain. Innovation has provided access to information through search engines that provide information for huge numbers of people and provides for more rapid research and development. Some countries are clearly further advanced in this process than others. For example, South Korea, which has almost 100 percent internet access and some of the fastest broadband networks in the world, could be in a position to take more advantage of the changes than countries with less fully developed systems.

We can illustrate how communication has speeded up over the centuries:

- in 1492 it took five months for the King of Spain to hear that the voyage of Christopher Columbus to the Americas had been a success;
- in 1865 two weeks passed before news of the assassination of Abraham Lincoln in Washington, DC reached Europe;
- in 2001 it took two seconds for the world to *witness* the collapse of the twin towers of the World Trade Center in New York City.

Social and cultural developments, such as the increased amount of travel by citizens of many nations with low-cost flights and fewer restrictions, have increased awareness, interaction and the desire to experience foreign cultures; Levitt's idea of converging lifestyles may be getting closer. And to this can be added the increase in personal connectivity, e.g. MySpace and Facebook give the impression of a globalising world.

Ecological awareness is also developing a global reach with international treaties. For example, the Kyoto Protocol agreed in 1992 and ratified by the majority of the world's national governments (but not the USA) indicated a growing international agreement to recognise and combat the threat to humanity from increasing economic activity. This, and the meeting at Copenhagen in December 2009 to discuss and decide upon a replacement for Kyoto, have been criticised by environmental campaigners as being insufficient to tackle the problems that exist. Nevertheless, the very existence of such agreements and conferences indicates an increasing recognition of the problems and a desire, however limited in some cases, for action – internationally agreed and co-ordinated action – to tackle those problems.

In short, it can be seen that there are both costs and benefits, and advantages and disadvantages, in the process of globalisation. That is why the topic is one that arouses much passion and much debate. Supporters of globalisation see it as being of benefit to all, if not now, then at some point in the future. Opponents worry about the inequalities they perceive as being inherent in the process (the rich get richer, the poor get exploited) and nationalists are concerned about what they see as the diminishing power of the nation state. These issues are discussed in a little more detail in the next section.

13.3 The consequences of globalisation

As can be seen from *Tables 9.2* and *9.3*, there are many contentious issues involved and much debate about the consequences of globalisation. Much has been written about the consequences of globalisation – both good and bad. *Table 9.2* outlines some advantages of globalisation for businesses, customers and countries; *Table 9.3* some disadvantages.

Let us begin this part of the discussion by concentrating on one of the main worries expressed by many governments (and individuals) around the world, the view that globalisation can threaten a country's national sovereignty and capacity for independent action in a number of ways. These may include such issues as:

- the size and scale of multinational companies, which gives them significant influence over policy making of governments;

| Table 13.2 | Advantages of globalisation for businesses, customers and countries |

To business	To customers	To countries
Access to mass markets – increased sales	Lower prices	Improved standards of living in both developed and developing countries
Economies of scale and reduced costs	Wider choice	Increased democracy – fall of communism
Access to resources	Improved quality	
Access to finance and tax savings		

| Table 13.3 | Disadvantages of globalisation for businesses, customers and countries |

To business	To customers	To countries
Increased competition	Standardisation	Exploitation
More demanding consumers		Loss of national culture and identity
Increasing volatility		Uneven benefits
		Environmental factors

- increased international competition may necessarily mean that some countries miss out;
- the increasing number and variety of international laws and standards may be difficult for some countries to keep up with;
- governance issues are coming to the fore, which may cause problems for some countries with less developed legal frameworks.

A second area of concern for government is that companies may take advantage of changes to move their activities to cheaper locations, an activity known as offshoring. However, it must be remembered that offshoring can also create employment. Offshoring is typically defined as the establishment of a business or part of a business overseas. We can see it in the relocation of manufacturing from more developed economies to those that are less developed, or in the transfer of call centres from the UK to India or from the USA to Puerto Rico. Offshoring will inevitably involve the loss of employment in the country that the business leaves. As costs increase in one country then companies can move their operations to cheaper and cheaper locations as they chase lower costs. The result is that new jobs could be only temporary.

The effect on the workers, who in many less developed nations may be poor, needs to be taken into account. A number of multinational companies have been accused of offering very poor rates of pay and forcing employees to work in sweatshop conditions. Some have also been accused of employing child labour, which means that these children could be missing out on education. There is pressure on global companies such as Gap, Next, Nike and Matalan to enforce rigid standards throughout their supply chains.

It is not all bad news. Conditions do seem to improve in many countries over time. In Vietnam it has been estimated that wages have increased five-fold in recent years. Developing

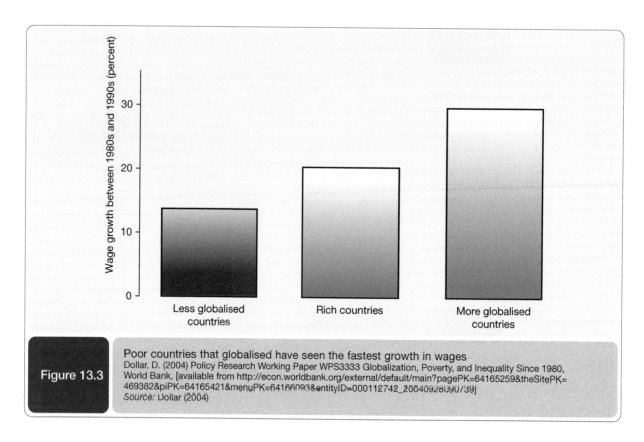

Figure 13.3

Poor countries that globalised have seen the fastest growth in wages
Dollar, D. (2004) Policy Research Working Paper WPS3333 Globalization, Poverty, and Inequality Since 1980, World Bank, [available from http://econ.worldbank.org/external/default/main?pagePK=64165259&theSitePK=469382&piPK=64165421&menuPK=64166093&entityID=000112742_20040928090739]
Source: Dollar (2004)

countries such as India, China, Vietnam and Bangladesh have all benefited from global production. The World Bank (Dollar, 2004) found that wages have generally been rising faster in globalising developing countries than in rich ones, and faster in rich ones than in non-globalising developing countries: see *Figure 13.3*. The point is that the fastest wage growth is occurring in developing countries that are actively increasing their integration with the global economy.

The impact on the environment is rather more difficult to accurately quantify. Growth brought about by increased economic activity does have a negative impact: see section 6.3.1 '*Externalities*'. Pollution is some countries is reaching critical levels; at certain times of the day it may be dangerous for some people to leave their homes. China's economy has grown at a spectacular rate over the last 15 years. Rising energy needs led to the building of the Three Gorges Dam, used to produce hydro-electric power. While this is a spectacular achievement, it has been at the expense of flooded agricultural lands, flooded cities, the displacement of millions of people and the loss of vital habitat for wildlife. Increased carbon emissions could in the medium to long term have a catastrophic impact on the planet, which we are already starting to see now.

The impact on national cultures will vary from country to country. Writers warn of the 'McDonaldisation' of society and Western companies and brands gaining a dominant position. There is even a chance that familiar national foods could be replaced by their global counterparts and even languages may be affected by the global use of English.

13.4 Changes in the international business environment

Here we identify, by way of a summary or stock-take, a number of dynamic environmental issues that have been raised in this book. These critical environmental trends include:

- globalisation in manufacturing and service provision;

- large-scale geographical changes in the distribution of manufacturing (e.g. vast increase in parts of South East Asia and stable, even declining, outputs in much of North America and Europe);
- some economies specialising in manufacturing while others specialise in service industry and consumption;
- global recession and vastly differential national economic growth rates creating rapidly shifting patterns of global wealth and income distribution;
- growth in the power and influence of economic and political unions, such as the EU, and countries, such as the BRIC economies – Brazil, Russia, India and China;
- the spread of nuclear weapons capability;
- religious fundamentalism;
- the threat of international terrorism;
- changing emphasis from multilateralism (e.g. power lying with the UN) to unilateralism (e.g. power with the USA or others);
- increasing debate on the future role of government;
- failed states;
- the prevalence of long-term unemployment and under-employment;
- the continuing integration of Europe and of other regional blocs;
- atmospheric, water, space, land and noise pollution, resource depletion and water shortages;
- global warming;
- increasing availability of information and ease of communication;
- technological advances, including ICT, biotechnology, genetics, robotics, virtual worlds;
- the demographic transition typified by declining fertility rates and increasing life expectancy leading to an ageing population in most countries – the so-called 'demographic time bomb' – with serious long-term implications for caring for the old, levels of taxation and government and individual indebtedness;
- dynamic national and international cultures, mass migration and cultural interaction, tolerance and intolerance; and
- changing attitudes towards the family, health, crime and society.

This list provides ample food for thought. Many of the issues raised have crucial implications for all governments and organisations, groups and individuals. Collectively, these environmental forces are fundamentally influencing, and being influenced by, patterns of economic growth, employment and investment.

13.5 The nature of the international business environment

This book identifies dynamism and complexity as two key factors in the business environment of many organisations. These are the prime characteristics of a turbulent environment (see *Minicases 13.1* and 13.6). However, Johnson *et al.* (2008) argue that organisations need to understand the *nature* of their environments before they audit the individual environmental factors. Such an analysis might be expected to help an organisation decide upon the sorts of systems which are required to monitor and respond to environmental change.

New technologies and increased globalisation of many markets encourage environmental turbulence, such that organisational planning cannot be seen as a continuous 'rolling out' of previous plans. Merely from scanning a quality daily newspaper, it is possible to catalogue a range of increasingly 'commonplace' surprises which threaten today's organisations, such as major global accidents, terrorism, kidnappings, hostile company takeovers, sabotage via product tampering, investigative journalism, equipment breakdowns, political upheaval and pressure group activity.

If environmental factors are less predictable, then planning needs to be seen as a more flexible, adaptive and responsive process. It is these two key areas, that is, the planning process and the need for organisational flexibility, which are given considerable attention in the next section. However, during this discussion we should be aware of the impact an organisation can have on its environment and the operation of the market by way of its strategic, tactical and operational actions. If dynamism and complexity are key factors in analysing the nature of an organisation's business environment it seems reasonable to ask whether there are any academic models which may be of assistance to us. Miles (1980) devised a useful series of questions for evaluating the nature of an organisation's environment. The suggested process involves mapping an organisation's environment using a series of continuums, for example, from simple to complex and static to dynamic.

There is a growing field of literature on crisis, chaos and shock event management. Underlying analysis of such 'shock events' in the business sphere, however, is the developing body of knowledge about the concept of chaos. Gleick (1987), in a seminal work, offered some fascinating insights into the discoveries about the behaviour of things in the natural world. These included the graphically termed 'butterfly effect' in global weather forecasting: the notion that a butterfly stirring its wings today in one part of the world might transform weather systems next month in another far-off area. He also said that these ideas have begun to 'change the way business executives make decisions about insurance, the way astronomers look at the solar system, the way political theorists talk about the stresses leading to armed conflict'.

A number of largely American researchers have looked for such chaotic patterns in the movements of the stock market, in an attempt to predict its behaviour. However, this work has been criticised because:

- any small errors made at the start of the process would be likely to result in huge forecasting errors over time;
- huge amounts of data are required to model chaotic systems and these were unavailable in most markets; and
- the ability to spot chaotic patterns is small given the large number of variables which influence the markets – particularly if we think that new factors are now affecting performance.

Writers such as Stacey (2007) have looked at the business impact of chaos theory. He notes the tendency in many business cycles towards the sort of 'non-linear feedback loops' observable in the natural world. Although the value of chaos theory may be questioned, it is possible that the mathematical models designed to explore non-linearity will generate useful analytical tools for managers in the future.

13.5.1 Implications for individuals and groups

When environmental change demands organisational change, as it almost continuously does, then we as individuals have to respond. It is becoming increasingly uncommon for people to work within a stable environment and undertake similar tasks and responsibilities for any length of time. Individuals are required to change at least as rapidly as the business environment if they are to remain effective. They need to continually develop their capabilities in order to function effectively within changing organisations. As the now clichéd saying goes: 'standing still is not an option'. We have to develop new skills and behaviours and, perhaps more importantly, new attitudes and ways of thinking, as the environment demands flexibility and the capacity and willingness to seek personal development opportunities.

Moves towards greater flexible working and the growth of the flexible firm are of direct relevance to individuals in the workplace. It is individuals who are being made 'flexible' and it is they who will, or will not, cope with the changes in working patterns outlined above. In developing economies, many people who work in factories are on short-term contracts and/or fear for their jobs as costs increase or demand drops. In developed economies, many people in higher-paid jobs now have what has been called a 'portfolio career'. This is multi-faceted and may include holding a number of 'loose' employment contracts, with a number of employers. For example, a management consultant might work on a few short-term projects with a number of organisations, undertake to write a management textbook for a publishing company and work for a university business school as a part-time lecturer.

Most individuals (particularly in the richer countries of the world) have been accustomed to regular 9 to 5, permanent, pensioned employment, so that new developments present personal challenges in balancing work and life patterns. Changes in employment and career patterns have important and far-reaching consequences for pension provision and some welfare payments. With an ageing population, government fears the rising burden of pension and welfare demands upon the public purse. The picture is more pronounced in some Western countries. By 2030, people over 65 in Germany, the world's third-largest economy, will account for almost half the adult population, compared with one-fifth now. Unless the country's fertility rate recovers over the same period, its population of under-35s will shrink about twice as fast as the older population will grow. The total population, now 82 million, will decline to 72 million while the number of working age will fall by a quarter, from 40 million to 30 million. The pattern is similar in Japan, Italy, France, Spain, Portugal, the Netherlands and Sweden. Curiously, perhaps, China faces a similar concern due to its long-standing 'one-child' policy.

Increasing numbers of middle-aged and older people are having to adjust to changing employment patterns. The OECD has calculated that only just over a third of UK citizens aged over 55 years are in paid work. The equivalent figure for France is 27 percent while for Italy it was just 15 percent. Redundancy, early retirement opportunities and the lack of employment prospects for those over 55, together with youth unemployment and increasing numbers in higher education, ensure that the vast bulk of the workforce in Western Europe is between 25 and 55 years old. Many people's working life is restricted to just 30 years, which seems at odds with the much reported increases in life expectancy and the demographic time bomb most countries are facing. *Minicase 9.2* explores these quite contrasting demographic trends.

Increasingly governments and commentators are suggesting that people (especially in European countries with aging populations) will in fact have to consider working into their 70s in order to continue to enjoy an acceptable standard of living. This may be taking us back a generation or two. In the 1960s in the UK, for example, the majority of young adults started work aged 15 or 16 and were expected to retire at 65 (male) or 60 (female) – a working life of up to 50 years (albeit one which started at an earlier age than is likely to be the case in the future). For some people changes in this regard have been unwelcome and have led to a reduction in their standard of living. Many have had to adjust their work-life expectations. Increasingly, the lack of adequate pension provision for vast numbers of now young and middle-aged people suggests that early retirement, or indeed retirement at all, may not be an option in the near future. Whereas retirement has not been an option for many in developing countries, increasingly, especially in the USA and even Europe, more are opting to work post-retirement age (and age discrimination legislation is supporting this trend).

Previously predictable life-cycle patterns have, in the last two decades, changed considerably. The Sigmoid Curve, see *Figure 13.4,* is an analytical model for depicting a person's working life cycle. It is often suggested that people start life falteringly, then make steady and consistent progress before peaking and enjoying a 'decline' during retirement. However, the timeframe for the Sigmoid Curve, rather like many product life cycles, is now being squeezed. This means people need to develop new options for a second or even third career during their working lives. Evidence suggests that an increasing number of people (especially in developed economies) switch careers at least once during their working life and undertake a seemingly different occupation (e.g. from executive to management lecturer). *Figure 13.4* shows this secondary curve superimposed on the Sigmoid Curve, indicating that many people can sustain personal growth by developing a second career.

| Minicase 13.2 | A parting of the ways |

Demographic forces are pulling America and Europe apart. If the trend continues America's strong position in the world may grow further. The population in the USA is rising faster than many had expected. The fertility rate in the USA remains buoyant while in Europe it is low and decreasing. Even America's immigration rate is higher than in Europe and immigrants are reproducing faster than native-born Americans. The population of Europe is ageing rapidly; in the USA its median age is far more stable. It is estimated that the median age of Americans in the year 2050 might be 37–40 (very close to the current state at about 35) while in Europe it could easily be over 50 (currently it is about 39). This represents a stunning difference largely accounted for by the ageing of Europe's population. To move within just 40 years to a difference in median age of about 15 years represents a major parting of the ways with far-reaching cultural, social, economic and political implications. If the trend continues, America's population will overtake that of Europe (excluding Russia) well before 2050. Unlike Europe, America's older people, their 'seniors', will remain a more stable proportion of the total population than in Europe.

The fertility rates in most of Europe are below replacement level which is about 2.1 children per woman. In some countries, for example Germany, it is only 1.3, meaning that natural population change in Europe is rapidly downwards (the population of Germany and Italy, for example, is in decline). Inward migration does reduce such falls to an extent. Immigrant populations usually have higher fertility rates. For example, in the USA the non-Hispanic whites' fertility rate is 1.8 (below replacement levels) while for the black population it is 2.1 and 3.0 for the Hispanic population. In many areas in the south of the USA (e.g. Los Angeles and Houston) Latino groups account for well over half of the under-14-year-olds. Whereas traditionally America's cultural ties with Europe have been strong, things might change. The majority of immigrants come from Latin America or South and East Asia and this might, in time, pull America's attention away from Europe.

Questions

1 Discuss the likely implications of these changes on richer economies (e.g. Europe, the USA, Japan and Australasia) for organisations, individuals and governments.
2 Discuss the likely implications of these changes on the poorer economies of Asia, Africa and Latin America for organisations, individuals and governments.

This discussion has highlighted a trend in society towards greater life and employment uncertainty. For many people flexible working improves choice and freedom while for others it constrains or sidelines them. Unfortunately, as individuals we are powerless to change societal trends or governmental policy. Globalisation and technological change conspire to transform our social and working worlds. What we can do is exercise some control

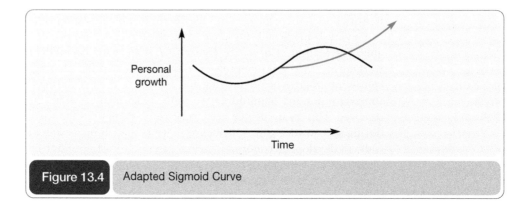

| Figure 13.4 | Adapted Sigmoid Curve

over our own patterns of living. The paradox is that fragmentation and flexible working can offer new freedoms for those able to take advantage of them.

One further aspect of this needs to be discussed: the impact on groups of people as distinct from individuals. Over a generation ago, Pawley (1974) considered that Western society was withdrawing from 'the whole system of values and obligations that has historically been the basis of public, community and family life'. He was of the opinion that technological developments such as televisions in children's bedrooms, computers, games consoles and MP3 players which he termed 'socially atomising appliances', were fuelling a retreat into 'private lives of an unprecedented completeness'. During the 1980s the then UK Prime Minister Margaret Thatcher famously denied that there was such a thing as society, as distinct from groups of individuals. Pawley's assessment has, perhaps, proved to be particularly pertinent, especially in Western countries in the twenty-first century.

Concern has been expressed about the degree to which young people feel 'disconnected' from the political and social system and about the generally acknowledged scale and growth of an underclass of permanently or long-term unemployed, poorly educated, living on benefits and surviving at the fringes of society. Many other, particularly young, people have been attracted by single-issue campaigning on such matters as animal rights and environmental protection. The mainstream political parties have struggled in many democracies to energise people and motivate them even to vote. Election turnout in the European parliament elections held across the EU every four years, has progressively fallen in the last two decades to below 50 percent. However, this is not always the case, as demonstrated by the enthusiastic participation of many in the 2008 USA presidential election that brought Barack Obama to power.

13.5.2 Implications for organisations

Whatever their objectives and legal status, organisations have, almost without exception, changed over the last decade. Very many have restructured internally, realigned their business processes to improve customer service, made focused strategic changes to their management control systems, developed their staff, improved their technological positioning to achieve competitive advantage and adjusted their product market portfolio. Most of these changes reflect a conscious response to turbulence in the business environment, including recession, and a deliberate effort to influence that environment. Many organisations have undergone fundamental change because the environment has itself transformed. The global forces for change really are profound.

A number of researchers, among them some notable management 'gurus', have attempted to predict the ways in which organisations will change in the next decade and beyond. Such predictions are often based on current trends and collective expectations together with a pinch of 'educated' guesswork. To a large extent it is the changing nature of the international business environment that will dictate the nature of these changes and, in turn, the way organisations respond to change will alter the nature of the environment for all. The next section will first look at the implications of the changing business environment for long-term planning and will then explore one particular organisational response to environmental turbulence, that is the growth of flexible working, touching on its different forms in different countries.

Operational plans have always been distinguished from strategic plans on the basis of the time period they cover and the scope and detail they contain. Strategic plans have tended to imply a planning horizon of about five years and to cover the organisation as a whole. To be able to plan over this sort of period implies a reasonable level of certainty about the environment in which the organisation operates. However, turbulence in the environment leads to an increasing lack of stability and predictability which, in turn, makes long-term strategic planning hazardous. This has led many writers on strategy to question whether organisations should adopt long-term, centralised approaches to planning. Mintzberg (2000) believes that incremental and emergent approaches to the process of strategy formulation should increasingly be considered by organisations. Increased environmental turbulence also suggests that systems of planning which devolve responsibility to individual business units are likely to make organisations more adaptable and responsive to environmental change.

Stacey (2007) questions many of the underlying assumptions used by firms in the process of long-term planning. He points out that many of these assumptions are based upon a range of quantitatively based analytical techniques. These techniques contribute to an underlying assumption, on the part of some theorists and many managers, that there is a 'best way' to plan. However, as noted above, long-term organisational planning is becoming less and less reliable or valid in today's turbulent environments.

Perhaps we should not over-react; after all, Mintzberg (2000) reminded us that each succeeding generation tends to perceive its present situation as more turbulent than its predecessors. He suggests the key factor is whether organisations can learn to think strategically and avoid inappropriately formal processes of planning. He reminds us that:

> changes that appear turbulent to organisations that rely heavily on planning may appear normal to, even welcomed by, those that prefer more of a visionary or learning approach. Put more boldly, if you have no vision but only formal plans then every unpredicted change in the environment makes you feel that the sky is falling.

Mintzberg also suggests that the perceptual filters may operate differently in different countries. However, turbulence demands an organisational response. One such 'reaction' has been for organisations to attempt to develop far greater flexibility; hence the growth of the concepts of the 'flexible firm' and of 'flexible working', discussed in section 9.6 *'Flexible working'*.

13.5.3 Implications for governments

This section explores some of the implications for government of environmental change before looking at the ongoing debate concerning the role of government. Government at local, national, regional and global levels is a powerful environmental force which influences the business environment of all organisations. However, there is a range of environmental phenomena which are themselves of major concern to governments at various levels. Many of these are listed in the introductory section of this chapter. We will look at just two of these changes and briefly assess the consequences for governments; these are international competitiveness and technological change.

International competitiveness

As we have seen, progress towards the globalisation of production and trade has been rapid in recent decades. It has been hastened by the successes of the GATT, replaced in 1994 by the WTO, by market and political union between countries, and by many genuine attempts on the part of world leaders to reduce 'distance' between nations and communities. Moreover the growth of reasonably unfettered capitalism has made the world a very different place today than it was just a couple of decades ago. *Figure 13.5* shows the estimated GDP of the top ten economies in 2050. Note the enormous growth of China and India, significant growth in Brazil and Mexico, and the *relative* decline in most Western economies such as the USA. The recession from 2008 to date will only serve to hasten the change in world order.

Despite the volatility in economic growth, the last two decades have witnessed large increases in global income and in levels of international trade in both goods and services. Many protective barriers have been removed or reduced, such that competition between nations and companies is, by and large, more fierce than in previous decades. It is now important for companies and governments to consider the level of national and regional competitiveness. Undoubtedly, some countries enjoy political, social, technological and economic advantages which encourage multinational, transnational or global companies to invest in them. A number of organisations and researchers have attempted to calculate

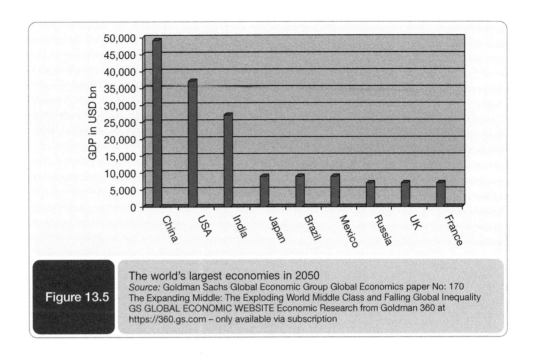

Figure 13.5	The world's largest economies in 2050
	Source: Goldman Sachs Global Economic Group Global Economics paper No: 170 The Expanding Middle: The Exploding World Middle Class and Falling Global Inequality GS GLOBAL ECONOMIC WEBSITE Economic Research from Goldman 360 at https://360.gs.com – only available via subscription

national competitiveness and produce 'league tables'. They consider such things as average wage rates, workforce skills and capabilities, income and corporation tax rates and the degree of political stability. The World Economic Forum Global Competitiveness Index (GCI) ranking for 2006–2007 and, for comparison purposes, 2001–2002, are shown in *Table 13.4*.

Many individuals, groups and organisations in most countries argue that government should play a major part in attempting to maintain or improve their national competitiveness. By so doing they may facilitate the achievement of comfortable economic growth rates, better and secure employment opportunities and improvements in standards of living. Although most governments actively pursue policies which they believe will enhance the competitiveness of their country and its organisations, there is considerable disagreement

Table 13.4	World Economic Forum GCI ranking		

	Top 10 rankings 2001–2002		Top 10 rankings 2006–2007
1	Finland	1	Switzerland
2	USA	2	Finland
3	Canada	3	Sweden
4	Singapore	4	Denmark
5	Australia	5	Singapore
6	Norway	6	USA
7	Taiwan	7	Japan
8	Netherlands	8	Germany
9	Sweden	9	Netherlands
10	New Zealand	10	UK

on how best to achieve this aim. Some argue for a heavily 'interventionist' policy in which government plays a major role, for example by:

- directly investing in industry;
- providing training;
- building state-of-the-art infrastructure;
- facilitating international trade.

Conversely, other arguments favour a more *laissez-faire* approach, such as was traditionally the case in the USA or Hong Kong. Broadly, government's role in this scenario is to 'free' private enterprise from many 'constraints', such as high social costs and taxes, and to allow it to compete in free markets. In this scenario government does not significantly intervene, for example to subsidise public transport or to invest directly in industry.

Both broad schools of thought can claim successes. The USA, for example, flourished by adopting a predominantly *laissez-faire* approach, while Singapore has experienced rapid economic growth, in part, it is argued, by active government interventionist policies. Whatever one's views, it is clear that national and/or regional competitiveness is increasingly becoming an important determinant of the material well-being of a population. Consequently, government has an obligation to its citizens to ensure they share in global successes.

Technological change

Technological change has a significant influence over economic growth. Goverment, therefore, has a role to play in the development of conditions suitable for technological advances to be made and transformed into economic wealth-creating opportunities. The approach governments adopt will largely depend on their ideological stance, as indicated above. One government may, for example, invest a significant element of revenue collected from taxation into research which might lead to economic wealth-creating opportunities largely for private industry. Another may prefer to allow market mechanisms to dictate research and development spending levels within industry. Clearly, the role of government, although crucial, varies considerably across the world. It is reported, for example, that in Hong Kong multinational organisations have for decades been invited to invest, irrespective of the technological benefits they might bring to the province. However, the government of Singapore has been somewhat more vigilant and active in encouraging companies which bring transferable technological advances to their country.

Although there is often government involvement, private sector organisations are the major sources and users of new technologies. The extent of their involvement varies from industry to industry. One notable example is discussed in *Minicase 13.3.* which illustrates the impact of technological developments in the petroleum industry.

In addition to creating the 'right' conditions for technological development and diffusion, government also has a regulatory role to perform. This role may involve prohibiting, or otherwise regulating, potentially unethical research and technological development. Many countries are currently debating issues concerning the advances in genetic engineering which have been made in recent years. There are important and far-reaching ethical consequences of many technological advances. Although self-regulation, by researchers and professional bodies for example, is important, many people expect governments to adopt an ideological and regulatory stance in this regard.

13.6 Flexible working

Given the dynamic nature of the business environment outlined throughout this book, it is clear that there has been, and will continue to be, a major impact on all the actors discussed,

---

| Minicase 13.3 | Making the earth move – seismic shifts in the petroleum sector |

Companies in the oil exploration business look for oil. One way of finding it uses a relatively new technique of three-dimensional seismology. This uses sound waves to map underlying layers of rock to create a picture of what it is like deep underground. Seismology helps explorers to find deposits that previous exploration methods would not have discovered. It therefore improves the success rate for drilling oil wells, which is an expensive business, especially if the bores turn out to be either dry or don't produce enough oil to make them worthwhile. Shell, Amoco and Exxon among others all use three-dimensional seismology to cut the costs of exploration that have to be recovered in prices per barrel. Other effects of the technology of the industry are:

- The formation of new companies that assist in collecting data from three-dimensional seismology surveys and also companies that support them.
- Sophisticated computing systems are needed to analyse data and specialist software, and hardware companies have evolved to fill this niche. *Earth Vision* is one such system.
- The fast pace of technology development and investment costs catalysed consolidation among companies providing seismic surveys – the numbers of companies declined.
- Mergers among big oil exploration companies brought about a more concentrated industry. Mergers were a way for big firms to maintain their relative standing in the industry. The big seven firms of the 1960s reduced to four, e.g. Exxon Mobil combined as did BP and Amoco.

Source: based on Voola (2006)

Questions

1 How has the use of technology changed in the oil/ petroleum industry in the last 30 years?
2 What are the costs and benefits to society of the widespread use of these techniques to discover ever more remote sources of oil?

---

that is governments, organisations, groups and individuals. We need to look at one of the most common responses to these pressures in the environment, the move towards greater flexibility in working practices.

There are a number of highly contentious issues associated with flexible working. For example, government policy may favour a reduction in the legal restrictions on the hiring and dismissal of workers, which would most certainly increase flexibility. However, this could have significant, often harmful, consequences for many groups and individuals. This is a key issue for many developing and advanced economies. Many countries have a legally enforceable minimum wage, but the consequences may be higher unemployment levels among low-skilled, particularly young, people. In many countries governments are considering age-discrimination legislation, in particular to prevent discrimination in the employment of older people. Although it is recognised that government has a role to play, the impact of often unintentional consequences of government intervention, can be damaging. Getting it 'right' is rarely straightforward.

It is evident that this real or perceived need for flexibility is increasingly influencing employment conditions. Within organisations, people are both the most vital and the most costly resource. Traditionally, however, people have often been seen, rightly or wrongly, as being prone to inflexibility and inertia. As a consequence many organisations have sought to achieve greater flexibility in employment conditions in recent decades. Both employers and employees lead the trend, with governments often regulating, sometimes supporting, developments via legislation. That said, 'flexibility' often means different things to individuals as opposed to businesses. It is also true to say that the concept has an ethnocentric quality so that the very concept of flexible working and the flexible firm is more familiar in, say, the

UK than in France, whereas the term is far less in common usage in China or India than in Western countries. Nevertheless, globalisation has a tendency to ensure that methods of coping with turbulence are replicated across national boundaries and cultures. For example, despite the cultural resistance to flexible working in France, many forms of such working, outlined below, are increasingly practised. The same may well be true of practices in the developing world in the coming decades.

In the richer Western economies, the old 'industrialised' scenario of reliable employment, which allowed families shared times for shopping, travel and leisure, together with patterns of work and retirement within the nuclear family, is metamorphosing into what some have called a 'post-industrial' age. Alvin Toffler (1985), a well-known writer about the future shape of work and of organisations, termed such a society a 'super-industrial' age or a 'third wave'. More and more countries are now moving into this new phase of development. Toffler suggests that this new wave follows on logically from the 'first wave' – the Agricultural Revolution and the 'second wave' – the Industrial Revolution. Others have referred to it as post-Fordism – that is, following Henry Ford's mass-production era. In this evolutionary phase certain types of work are in decline as other types of work are emerging. However, it is at least arguable that newly industrialising economies in the developing world are still in the process of entering the second wave as they industrialise, usually on the basis of mass-production techniques.

It is clear that as new waves occur it can cause us to think again about our underlying assumptions about the nature of work. Key characteristics of this new age are expectations on the part of employers that workers will be very flexible (examined in some detail below) and be able to adapt products and services, almost at will, to meet the particular needs of individual customers. The enhanced capabilities of many organisations to customise products and services have been strongly influenced by developments in, for example, microprocessor technology and management techniques. Computers enable us to process and communicate data and information extremely rapidly. Advances in telecommunications technology have delivered significant improvements in the quality of data about life and work throughout the globe. These technologies have been harnessed by organisations which wish to operate in a range of countries.

As long ago as 1995, Bridges identified some rather ruthless 'new rules' which are still evolving but apply to many parts of the global economy today. The rules are divided into three key points:

- everyone's employment is dependent on the organisation's performance and, as a result, employees need to continuously prove their worth to the organisation and to behave more like an external supplier than a traditional employee;
- workers should, therefore, plan for career-long self-development by taking primary responsibility for their development, their pension and by renegotiating their compensation arrangements with each organisation when, and if, the organisation needs to change; and
- wise companies will need to work closely with these new-style workers to maximise the benefits for both parties and to bring a range of projects to satisfactory completion.

13.6.1 Forms of flexible of working

Having looked at some of the assumptions which underlie recent trends we can now examine the different forms of flexible working which may be found. All of these are driven by external forces. First, we can identify various types of 'numerical' flexibility, which generally affect employees' hours of work. These include long-standing practices such as:

- overtime;
- home working;
- shift work;
- part-time work;

- flexi-time;
- teleworking;
- annual hours contracts;
- zero hours contracts;
- the use of temporary staff;
- job-sharing.

A few of these require some further explanation.

Some companies offer employees work as and when required by the employer, these 'zero-hours' contracts enable the organisation to adjust staff levels in line with customer demand. Employees on these types of contract are likely to be less than satisfied with this arrangement as it introduces considerable uncertainty into their working lives. Another market-driven change is apparent in the electricity generating business. One company encourages some employees to engage in 'winter/summer stagger', where they work longer hours in the winter to accommodate increased demand. Hence people are employed on an annual hours basis. There has also been an increasing number of people employed as temporary and agency labour over the last few decades in many developed economies.

The hours employees in different countries work vary considerably, although increasingly legislation has been put in place to restrict excessively long hours working in most developed and many developing economies. Throughout the twentieth century many developed economies established firstly a 48-hour working week, as the norm, reducing to a 40-hour week. This 'rule of thumb' remains today. In 1995 the People's Republic of China adopted the 40-hour week as its recommended 'normal' working week. Most developing economies in Asia have now adopted a 40- to 48-hour working week. The European Union Working Time Directive of 1993 established a maximum working week as 48 hours, with the added intention of restraining the use of overtime above this limit. There are of course many exceptions to these practices. In both Pakistan and Thailand, for example, it is suggested that over 40 percent of employees work in excess of 48 hours a week. Hours worked impacts on individual and family life directly and is particularly significant in considerations of work–life balance. This is true of all employees but particularly significant to many women who also find that they are 'required' to assume a major role in the provision of unpaid work in the home. Female participation in paid work has increased significantly, especially since the 1980s, in most countries with the lowest participation rates being in the Middle East, North Africa and South Asia.

Home working is not new, although the scale of this activity is increasing. However, teleworking goes a step further by connecting home-based employees by the use of computer modems to the organisation and/or other teleworkers. The availability of communications technology has also led to the 'virtual office' where laptop computers, the internet and mobile phones enable people to work in any location. Linked with this is the practice of 'hotdesking' where employees 'touch base' at the office and use whatever workspace is available, picking up messages on email. 'Telecottaging', where a local venue acts as a central point for teleworkers, may be one way of solving the problem of isolation. From an ecological perspective an increase in teleworking, which is particularly commonplace among management consultants, computing and sales personnel, may help reduce rush hour traffic and air pollution.

A second form of flexibility, referred to as 'distancing', is where employees are replaced by subcontractors and employment contracts are replaced by contracts for service. Again this has been commonplace in many industries, such as construction and manufacturing, for many decades. However, the process is increasingly popular in other types of activity, including service industries, and in the public sector.

A third form of flexible working is broadly termed 'functional flexibility'. Although in many organisations strict lines of demarcation exist between jobs, these are seen as offering little flexibility and often prove obstacles to effective teamwork and subsequent productivity gains. Hence multi-skilling, where individuals are trained to undertake a broader array of tasks, is becoming more commonplace.

A fourth form of flexibility, pay flexibility, is increasingly commonplace. This may involve the harmonisation of terms and conditions, including the removal of artificial barriers between white-collar and blue-collar workers, such as differences in pension, sick pay and holiday entitlements.

Many flexible working practices find their ultimate focus in the concept of a virtual business or virtual enterprise. Amazon.com was an early example of a virtual business, competing with traditional high-street booksellers without such a physical presence, relying purely on electronic, internet interaction with its customers. Clearly, however, there is also a physical location, for the various warehouses store the items and a physical distribution system is used to deliver to the consumer. Despite some early doubts about the viability of such a business model, Amazon has survived, prospered and expanded its activity to include CDs/DVDs and an ever-wider range of consumer goods. Of course, it still operates without a shop presence. Other businesses rely even more heavily on the virtual world, as consumers move from buying physical products that need to be delivered to their homes to simply downloading items over the internet. Apple's iTunes uses just such a system – although Apple does still retain a high-street presence in many cities to sell the devices onto which music, games, photos and so on are downloaded.

Finally, there are a number of related concepts including career breaks, paternity and maternity leave, secondments, domestic leave for careers, childcare assistance and school holiday leave. Many of these measures may be considered as 'family-friendly' and are intended to help motivate and retain staff.

Minicase 13.4 explores the two-tier 'flexibility' found in Spain.

About 17 percent of the workforce in the EU works part-time, growth in this respect being most notable in Germany, while rates have always been well above average in the UK (refer to *Figure 13.6*).

Minicase 13.4	Spanish two-tier flexibility

There is strong evidence to suggest that flexible work practices are on the increase, although less agreement concerning whether this is part of a strategically planned reaction to changing environmental circumstances, including employee needs/wants, a result of short-term economic expedience or the outcome of a shifting balance between capital (employers) and labour (employees). Recent studies into flexible working in Europe suggest that, although there is an overall trend towards greater use of flexible working patterns, there is considerable variation in practice between countries, sectors and sizes of organisation.

In very broad terms there are two tiers of employees or workers in Spain. About two-thirds of workers have very secure permanent contracts while the rest simply do not. Unemployment in Spain is among the highest in Europe (around 20 percent in 2010) and increased significantly throughout the recession in 2008 onwards. The vast bulk of those losing their job were employees on short-term, non-permanent employment arrangements. Employers have been wary of employing new staff on permanent contracts or of training or developing these people. They provide flexibility in the system – a source of labour that can be turned on or off at short notice. Meanwhile those on secure contracts continue to be shielded from the harsh economic environment. They are usually highly unionised and continue to enjoy pay rises despite the recession. But, for how long?

Questions

1 Is a unionised system of working sustainable in rapidly changing global circumstances where competitive forces for change are significant?
2 What benefits could flexible working bring to employers and employees?

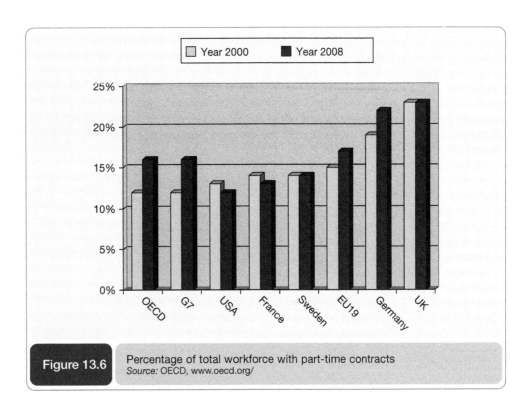

Figure 13.6 Percentage of total workforce with part-time contracts
Source: OECD, www.oecd.org/

Non-permanent employment has increased as has subcontracting. *Figure 13.7* highlights the vast differences in this regard within the EU with Spain (see *Minicase 13.4*) having almost a third of its workforce on temporary contracts. The majority of part-time workers are female. Around 50 percent of women employees in the UK work part-time; the EU average is just 30 percent.

The UK has the most flexible workforce in the EU with over 10 million people (almost 40 percent of all employees) either:

- part-time workers;
- temporary workers;

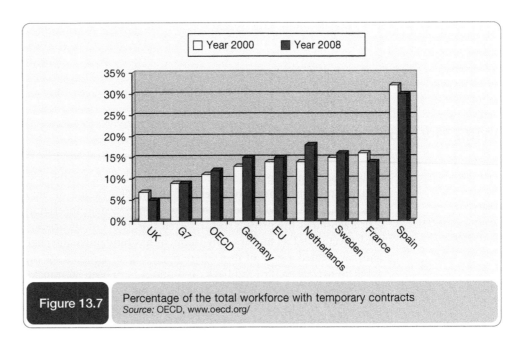

Figure 13.7 Percentage of the total workforce with temporary contracts
Source: OECD, www.oecd.org/

- self-employed;
- on a government training scheme;
- unpaid family workers.

This represents an increase of almost 2 million in a decade. Over 80 per cent of all medium-sized and large organisations in the United Kingdom employ some temporary staff. The BBC, for example, now offers the majority of new recruits only short or fixed-term contracts, as do many universities. In the UK there has also been an increase in the number of men working flexibly, from 23 per cent in 1994 to about one-third today, while the proportion of women in this category remained stable and high at 50 per cent. Over a million employees work school term-time only while about 200,000 people job-share. These family-friendly measures attempt to motivate employees and help parents balance work and family demands. They also facilitate the retention of competent and well-trained staff.

Changes in the international environment, which may have encouraged the moves towards flexible working, ensure that the flexible firm and flexible working will become an increasing reality. Summarised here, they include:

- increased national competition;
- globalisation and consequent competitive pressures;
- uncertainty created by market volatility and, in part, from recessionary periods;
- government intervention to support and extend employees' and/ or employers' rights;
- technological change, particularly in information technology and communications, which facilitates some forms of flexible working;
- investment in new plant requiring new and ever-changing skills;
- greater awareness of the need to pursue active policies and practices to ensure environmental sustainability (and to reduce the traffic congestion on many roads and in most cities!);
- a move from Fordism to post-Fordism, from mass production to flexible specialisation;
- continued emphasis on costs and budgets and financial stringency in the public sector;
- political influence, particularly in the public sector;
- reductions in trade union power;
- increasing numbers of women and other employee groups 'demanding' alternative employment conditions; and
- a change in attitudes to work and life, to levels of organisational loyalty (both ways) and responsibility for personal and career development.

In summary, it has been noted that as the business environment becomes more turbulent many organisations have sought ways of managing change. This has encouraged them to seek increased short-term operational flexibility and more adaptive approaches to long-term planning.

13.7 The public sector

Both the scale of the public sector and the rate of change within its environment make it a valuable but often neglected field of study. The theme of environmental change or dynamism, together with ever-increasing complexity and uncertainty, prevails in the public sector as well as the private sector. Given this, it is not surprising that the nature of the public sector and its business environment has fundamentally changed in recent decades. This has created a state of flux where many organisations have changed ownership from public to private sector (and back) and others have been so transformed as to be virtually unrecognisable. There is little doubt that the complex range of political, social and economic objectives of governments over the last two decades has created enormous pressures for change within publicly owned organisations, creating a state of near-permanent tension between different interest groups. *Minicase 13.5* illustrates how these forces impact on a public sector organisation in the UK.

Public sector organisations often conduct government business, are largely funded from the public purse via taxation and are usually accountable to government at some level. As a result it is the duty of government to ensure that proper care is taken when allocating resources. Hence, government at local, national and international levels has an all-encompassing and powerful influence over public sector bodies.

The environmental changes are themselves part of a global transformation in the nature of public sector organisations. In most countries the public sector is a major employer and service provider. Governments wishing to cut back on their spending face substantial difficulties. An ageing population continues to put increased demands upon healthcare, state pension and welfare systems, necessitating increased government expenditure. What is more, as the population ages there will be fewer people working and potentially fewer taxpayers.

13.7.1 The changing scope of the public sector

It can be argued that the existence of the public sector is due to the failure of the free-market system to provide all the services required by the general public and by government. However,

---

Minicase 13.5 — Change in a National Health Service hospital

An objective expressed in the hospital's plan is to 'produce a multi-skilled workforce', more specifically, 'to introduce teams of generic hotel service assistants at ward level so as to improve flexibility and responsiveness to patient needs by combining the role of porters, domestics and catering staff'.

At the hospital all domestics, unqualified nurses and ward clerks are to be based at ward level, a relocation which is involving severing many existing formal and informal relationships. Most of the 260 personnel are being trained in patient care, cleaning and portering skills in order to develop multi-skilled competencies. Staff will then undertake a wider array of tasks and be required to embrace flexibility and teamwork. There may be reduced role certainty. They will need to manage the interface with clinical and other staff groups on the ward. All existing formal status and pay differentials between the hitherto separate groups will be removed. Some staff will be required to change their shift pattern and the total hours they work within any one week.

It is argued that successful implementation will help to 'provide good value for money' and 'make cost savings'. It will ensure, for the time being at least, competitiveness with external commercial players. The single grade and pay spine will reduce status differentials and simplify the highly complex bonus schemes that had evolved. From an operational point of view it will bring benefits of flexibility and simplify work scheduling. It will serve to even out the workload for staff and improve efficiency by avoiding waiting-for-action time and duplication of effort. Managers believe it will improve worker motivation as people will feel part of a team. They will, it is believed, take a pride in their work at ward level.

In conclusion, the philosophy underpinning the care assistant concept is a familiar one. A multi-skilled, flexible workforce is thought to facilitate operational planning and enhance both the efficiency and effectiveness of service provision. The assumption is that employees benefit from the resultant job enrichment and co-operative teamwork, cost savings are there for the making, via enhanced efficiency, and patient care is improved.

Questions

1 What are the benefits and drawbacks to the *employer* of these changes?
2 What are the benefits and drawbacks to the *employee* of these changes?

both the scope and scale of the public sector in any country are in part the result of prevailing political ideologies, or those that prevailed in the past. A multitude of other factors also influence both the level of government involvement in the economy and the scale of public expenditure. However, there is no indisputable law of economics which argues that the public sector should, for example, operate the wide range of services found in most developed countries. Neither is there, at any time, a 'correct' or indisputable level of government expenditure.

There are a certain, strictly limited, number of services which most politicians, academics and the general public agree should be delivered by the government or at least be under its tight scrutiny. Relatively uncontroversial examples include the judiciary, the police and the armed services. However, there are a large and growing number of activities which are the subject of considerable public debate in many countries regarding the most appropriate form of ownership and operation.

Throughout the nineteenth and twentieth centuries, the trend towards a mixed economy, where economic activity is shared via both public and private ownership, proceeded apace in the developed industrialised world with the introduction and growth of government-owned services. The scope of government activity in most countries grew to include responsibility for education, health, law and order, defence and more. Additionally, many industrial organisations were nationalised, meaning that they were not owned by private shareholders but by government on behalf of the nation, e.g. the coal-mining, steel, gas, railways, electricity and water supply businesses.

There has been a major reversal of this trend since the 1980s. In the last two decades of the twentieth century there was a tendency in many countries, both developed and developing, for governments to move away from direct provision of goods and services towards a focus on regulating more and producing less. The range of mechanisms which governments have employed includes:

- privatisation;
- deregulation;
- contracting-out public sector services;
- establishing non-governmental-organisations (NGOs – often paid for by government) in order to perform a service;
- quality charters, league tables and published performance targets;
- tougher and more independent inspectorates; and
- private/public sector financial partnerships.

Many politicians, businesspeople and academics still believe that private markets are capable of providing some services that are (or were) more usually regarded as 'public goods'. They would argue that in many circumstances the market is a sound and appropriate mechanism for the allocation of scarce resources. As such the marketplace, via the price system, allocates goods and services to individuals and organisations. These include healthcare (supported by private insurance) and education (backed with meanstested student loans and private schools). Although the market economy is far from faultless, the alternatives are not necessarily guaranteed to be more efficient or effective in servicing the needs of society or individuals.

Others argue that the marketplace would lead to a multi-tiered system and a restriction of access to high-quality services for a significant section of the community. Additionally, objectors to the idea of a pure market economy argue that competition in the provision of many public services, such as healthcare, is morally unacceptable and practically unworkable.

Although the move to more market-friendly policies was pursued vigorously in many countries, the global recession of 2008 onwards has caused a rethink by policy-makers in many quarters. This is based on the belief that deregulation has gone too far, particularly in respect of the banking sector, which has seen a number of nationalisations and other public involvement, especially in the UK and USA.

The political forces outlined above are themselves driven by powerful economic, social and technological changes within the global arena. Wider environmental changes inform political agendas and mould ideologies. However, the mechanism of influence between the wider environment and political activity is two-way as government decisions profoundly influence those environmental forces. For example, whereas changing social needs create dynamism to which government and public organisations have to respond, those same social changes are, in part, the result of government policy and behaviour. The relative poverty of some groups has contributed to many social problems such as urban deprivation, long-term unemployment, crime, drug abuse and social exclusion and unrest. As a result government and public sector organisations are faced with a social environment which is, in part, a consequence of their previous activity.

13.8 Future trends?

Let us start this look forward by looking backwards. By going back 30 years, approximately one generation, well within the lifetime of a majority of the European and North American populations and close to the mean age of global population, we can see the changes that have occurred. (Mean age in Western Europe is about 40 years of age.) Thirty years ago the majority of current industry and public sector senior leaders at national level, had already left school. Thirty years ago the world wide web did not exist. How many times in the last week have you used the internet to facilitate your learning, your social life and your work or commercial well-being? The answer to that question for all leaders of the top 20 countries in the world, the G20, when they were at university is a resounding 'none'. In fact it is unlikely that any would have recognised the word 'internet' when they were first at university. As well as the world wide web, there were no PCs – or at least anything we would recognise today as a PC. As well as this now taken-for-granted form of communication, there were no mobile phones or, of course, PDAs, iPods, laptops, smart phones or email. Communications have been revolutionised in recent decades and greater change is yet to impact the fundamentals of our working and social lives.

Politically, the world has changed equally as dramatically. Thirty years ago, highly authoritarian Communist governments ruled Eastern Europe, Russia and its 'empire', and many other countries. The threat of world war between the Western powers and the Communist bloc was very real. China was isolated and economically backward, India remained in a perilous economic state and the European Union had only just begun to expand. Globalisation, as we know it today, was in an embryonic state and the WTO did not exist. There was no global 'war on terror'; most terror organisations were nationalist groups 'fighting' within one country.

Environmentally, there was concern about the destruction of the rain forests and the potential exhaustion of natural resources. However, concern about the existence or impact of global warming was in its infancy; in fact the fear of a new ice age was frequently discussed. Genetic engineering was a fringe activity, HIV/AIDS was unknown and world population was around 2.3 billion lower than today, i.e. about two-thirds its current size.

Looking back at these points we can see just how much and how quickly the world has changed. The question then becomes: what of looking forward 30 years?

Perhaps the most significant factor regarding these dramatic changes is that most were not predicted. Had someone 30 years ago outlined the nature of the fundamental advances or changes in communication technologies or of global politics that have actually occurred, they would have been considered (at best) a dreamer. The history books are littered with examples of poor forecasting or predictions. We need only go back to late 2007 to note that the bulk of governments, economists and commentators around the world completely failed to predict the extremely devastating and deep economic crisis which the world plunged into just months later. On a lighter note, many commentators have got it wrong regarding the

| Minicase 13.6 | The pace of change |

Over the ten years to 2010 world population has grown by about 750 million. That growth figure alone represents more than double the total population of the world at the time of the Romans or ancient Greeks (when it was about 300 million). It was not until about 1750 that world population actually reached a total of 750 million. So, in just ten years we have added to world population what previously had taken many millennia to produce and support. In many ways this might be considered a great achievement of the modern world but it has its negative consequences. About 80 per cent of that increase is accounted for by growth in the developing world, where living standards are far lower than in the developed world. In the same time period the concentration of greenhouse gases has increased. Chlorine concentrations acting with other chemicals in the atmosphere have opened a hole in the ozone layer above the Antarctic, a hole which is now three times the size of the USA. Deforestation of tropical forests (never, realistically, to be reversed) proceeds at about 2 percent a year. Over half of all mangrove forests have been lost. Fish stocks have collapsed in many of our oceans, in some cases to irretrievable levels. Oil consumption and that of most finite mineral resources have increased by about 50 percent in the decade. Known reserves have fallen. More oil (and many other minerals) has been consumed in the lifetime of today's baby boomers (about 60-year-olds) than in the history of the world up to the time of their birth. A lot more!

Questions

1 To what extent are these trends predictable and how might they continue?
2 Could currently unknown factors radically alter future trends?

likely popularity of new technologies. Lord Kelvin, an eminent scientist of his day, said, in 1895 that 'heavier-than-air flying machines are impossible' and 'there is nothing new to be discovered in physics …'. A journalist wrote in 1939 in the USA that 'TV will never be a serious competitor for radio because people must sit and keep their eyes glued on a screen …'. *Minicase 13.6* demonstrates some of the changes to key social and ecological global concerns over a ten-year period by way of illustration.

It *is* remarkably difficult to hypothesise or predict discontinuous change. For example, it *might* be considered reasonable to assume that there will be an increase in the number of so-called 'failed states'. Some countries around the world are struggling with democracy and often violent extremist groups challenge for power. But what would a discontinuous global political change actually look like? A world of total peace and harmony perhaps, or one which saw a major nuclear-armed, Islamic mega-state challenge the existing global order? Perhaps it might be China assuming political and economic dominance in all aspects of global activity. Are these scenarios fanciful? Perhaps. Nevertheless, it is interesting to consider what one influential organisation predicts when looking at the global economy. Goldman Sachs have a view that the continuing growth in developing economies will result in a very different global distribution of wealth (and power and influence) by the middle of this century. As was seen in *Figure 13.5*, their idea of what the world will be like in 2050 shows it to be a very different place, with the US economy, currently the world's largest being overtaken by China – and with India not that far behind.

There are some trends which are already in place and which are to a large extent predictable. One such change is the aging of population in developed economies. How governments, organisations, groups and each of us as individuals cope with those changes, however, remains uncertain. For example, the global demographic situation is shifting with a rapidly ageing population in most of Europe, and to an extent in much of the developed and developing world, as life expectancy increases and birth rates contract. Will we see increasing retirement ages, major skill and talent shortages, ever-increasing taxation to pay for extra pension payments and healthcare provision? The answer is quite likely to be yes. Again socially, are we experiencing the early decades of the increasing dominance of women in society? Women achieve better than men in education, are released in many societies from many of the 'burdens' society previously placed upon them and, by all accounts, are increasingly ambitious. Women conduct around 70 percent of online banking in the USA, while two-thirds of wealth is owned by over-60-year-olds; the majority of this age group are women. By 2050 women may control around 60 percent of the total wealth in the UK. Will the top boardrooms and parliaments be female-dominated in 30 years times as they are male dominated today? And, then there is technology. What will technological changes in the next 30 years mean for industry, commerce and the public sector? Can we realistically predict that?

13.9 Conclusion

Our approach has been to focus on many of the environmental (PESTLE C) factors outlined in this text and on the increasing dynamism and uncertainty in the global business environment. In doing this we have commented upon some of the major changes that surround both the concept and impact of globalisation. We have also explored the implications of all this for organisations, groups, individuals and governments.

We have attempted to identify issues that may be important for organisations in the future, but have made few predictions, other than commenting on the unpredictable nature of many of the changes that have occurred and will continue to occur. We have used much factual data throughout this chapter – and the rest of the book. However, in a rapidly changing environment, there is a tendency for such data to become obsolete very quickly. This will, undoubtedly, mean that when you read this book there will be some information which no longer holds true. This will make it necessary for you to undertake your own research to update the figures as the world around you changes.

For this reason we recognise that the most lasting impact of the book will be your understanding of the processes and models used to examine the business environment. We have placed strong emphasis on ways of evaluating and understanding the business environment. For example, we have stressed the importance of examining problems from different perspectives. This includes a consideration of the individual, the group and the organisation at various different geo-political scales from local to global. The reason for this is simple: it seems to us that an analysis of the international business environment cannot confine itself to examining environmental factors in any one of these ways, as each influences all the others.

Summary of main points

This chapter has focused upon the nature of change in the business environment and organisational, individual, group and government responses to environmental dynamism. The main points are:

- The international business environment is increasingly complex, dynamic, uncertain (turbulent) and even chaotic for many organisations, individuals, groups and governments.

- Major economic, political, technological and social changes have transformed the business environment in the last decade, necessitating organisational change and increased flexibility.

- There may be a trend towards high-profile 'shock events' and non-linear chaotic patterns in many areas of the natural world (to some extent such patterns are also observable in the business world) which suggests that organisations might do well to make contingency plans.
- The nature of the international business environment calls into question the validity of organisational approaches to long-term planning and suggests the need for processes which build in flexibility and adaptability.
- There has been a rapid increase in previously considered 'non-standard' temporal and contractual patterns of work such as part-time work, teleworking, contracting-out, self-employment and temporary work as a means of enabling organisations to adapt to change.
- People of different generations have very different expectations and behaviours; culture is changing.
- Turbulent environments demand government attention.
- The future role of government is likely to remain a fiercely debated issue for some time.
- Global problems, such as climate change, demand global solutions.

Discussion questions

1 What are the implications of increased turbulence and chaos in the business environment for the ways in which organisations plan for the future?

2 Discuss the opposing ideological positions concerning the role of government in encouraging national competitiveness and technological development.

3 Assess the implications for individual workers of the increased use of flexible working practices by organisations.

4 Contrast your parents' work–life experiences with those of your grandparents. How do you expect your work–life experiences will differ from those of your parents?

5 Outline the ways in which the increasingly interconnected 'global' environment represents both a threat and an opportunity for business.

Further reading/sources of information

BBC (http://news.bbc.co.uk/) The BBC website provides up-to-date information on business topics, economics, politics, technology and much more from around the world.

European Union (EU) http://ec.europa.eu/index_en.htm Home page of the EC with access to the Directorate General for Competition of the EU.

Friends of the Earth (www.foe.co.uk) The website of one of the main green pressure groups, frequently updated with current issues. You may also want to look at **www.greenbiz.com/** which looks at the business end of the debate. **Innovation www.innovation.gov.uk/rd scoreboard** UK government site giving details on R&D.

Legal information can be found at **www.statutelaw.gov.uk/,** the UK statute law database which enables you to view UK laws and trace how they have changed over time. You can also consult **www.law.cornell.edu/world/** and **www.jus.uio.no/lm/index.html,** two excellent sources of material on international law and trade law by country.

OECD, *The* **www.oecd.org/** The OECD website covers the main industrialised countries. It provides a wide range of economic statistics and forecasts on these economies. It is good for most aspects of country data. Follow links to science and technology for information on effects on economic development.

Daniels, J.D., Radebaugh L.H. and Sullivan, D.P (2009) *International Business – Environments and Operations,* 12th edn. Upper Saddle River, NJ: Prentice Hall. This American textbook contains much useful information on both the international business environment and businesses' operations.

Dicken, P. (2007) *Global Shift; Mapping the Changing Contours of the Global Economy,* 5th edn. London: Sage A useful survey of how the global economy has changed in the last 30 years.

Johnson, G., Scholes, K. and Whittington R. (2008) *Exploring Corporate Strategy,* 8th edn. Harlow: FT Prentice Hall.

Sloman, J. and Wride, A. (2009) *Economics,* 7th edn. Harlow: Prentice Hall. A good introduction to economics. Wide range of short cases but a book that covers a lot more than just the internal macro economy.

Stiglitz, J. (2002) *Globalization and its Discontents.* London: Allen Lane. This book, written by a former chief economist at the World Bank, gives a devastating critique of the effects of many of the Bretton Woods institutions' policies in both economic and political terms.

Todaro, M.P. and Smith, S.C. (2009) *Economic Development,* 10th edn. Harlow: Addison-Wesley. A long-established book surveying global issues with an emphasis on a developing world perspective. Some sections are rather heavy on economic theory for non-economists, but there is still much of value and interest to be found.

Vignali, C. (2001) McDonald's: 'Think Global, Act Local' – the Marketing Mix, *British Food Journal,* 103 (2), 97–111.

This article focuses on the marketing mix of McDonald's and highlights how the company combines internationalisation and globalisation elements according to various fast-food markets. It illustrates the effect of McDonald's on the global environment and how it adapts to local communities.

Newspapers

Newspapers are a good source of information on many topics. Three of the more important UK papers may found on the following sites:

Financial Times	**www.ft.com**
The Guardian	**www.guardian.co.uk**
The Telegraph	**www.telegraph.co.uk**

References

Dollar, D. (2004) Policy Research Working Paper WP3333 Globalization, Poverty, and Inequality Since 1980, World Bank, available from **http://econ.worldbank.org/external/ default/main?pagePK=64165259&thesitePK=469382&piPK=64165421&menuPK=6416 6093&entityID=000112742_20040928096739**

Gleick, J. (1987) *Chaos: Making a New Science,* New York: Viking Penguin.

Johnson, G., Scholes, K. and Whittington, R. (2008) *Exploring Corporate Strategy.* 8th edn. Harlow: Prentice Hall.

Levitt, T. (1983) The Globalization of Markets. *Harvard Business Review,* May–June, 92–102.

Miles, R.E. (1980) *Macro Organisational Behaviour.* Sutt Foresman & Co.

Mintzberg, H. (2000) *The Rise and Fall of Strategic Planning.* Harlow: FT Prentice Hall.

Ohmae, K. (1989) Managing in a Borderless World. *Harvard Business Review,* 67(3), 152–161.

Pawley, M. (1974) *The Private Future.* London: Pan.

Stacey, R.D. (2007) *Strategic Management and Organisational Dynamics,* 5th edn. Harlow: FT Prentice Hall.

Toffler, A. (1985) *The Adaptive Corporation.* London: Pan.

Voda, J.J. (2006) Technological Change and Industry Structure: A Case Study of the Petroleum Industry. *Economics* of *Innovation and New Technology,* 15(3), 271–288.

Yip, G.S. (2003) *Total Global Strategy II: Updated for the Internet and Service Era,* 2nd edn. Upper Saddle River, NJ: Prentice Hall, NJ.

14 The global context of business

Chris Britton

Businesses of all sizes operate in international markets – products are sold across borders; the resources used in production can come from anywhere in the world; communication is instantaneous; and financial markets are inextricably linked, as the events of 2013/14 demonstrate. Individual businesses operate across borders in a variety of ways – they can do this directly, through the formation of strategic alliances, or through merger and takeover. It is clear then that businesses need to be aware of the global context of their markets.

Learning outcomes

Having read this chapter you should be able to:

- understand the difference between globalisation and internationalisation
- outline the main elements of globalisation
- illustrate the role of the multinational enterprise
- introduce the implications of globalisation for business

Key terms

Capital market flows
Consortium
Cross-subsidisation
Customs union
Emerging economies
Foreign direct investment (FDI)
Franchising

Free trade area
Globalisation
Hyperglobalisation
International trade
Internationalisation
Joint venture
Licensing

Multinational enterprises (MNEs)
Regional trade agreements (RTAs)
Regionalism
Strategic alliance
Transfer pricing
Transformationalism

Introduction

Businesses operate in a global context: even if they do not trade directly with other countries, they might be affected by a domestic shortage of skilled labour or may be subject to developments on the global financial markets. There is a difference between globalisation and internationalisation in the business literature but both result in increased exposure to global forces. This means that businesses need an understanding of the process of globalisation. The nature of globalisation is changing; it used to mean the westernisation of the developing world, but the newly emerging economies such as Brazil, China and India are redefining processes and institutions. In 1980 the share of the developing countries in world exports was 34 per cent; by 2011 it was 47 per cent and share of world imports had gone up from 29 per cent to 42 per cent in the same period. Globalisation is here to stay and the World Bank forecasts that the share of global gross domestic product (GDP) for developing countries will rise from 29 per cent (2010) to 39 per cent (2030).

Globalisation versus internationalisation

These terms are often used interchangeably but they refer to different processes. Although there is not a single accepted definition of **globalisation**, it is a term used to describe the process of integration on a worldwide scale of markets and production. The world is moving away from a system of national markets isolated from each other by trade barriers, distance or culture. Advances in technology and mass communications have made it possible for people in one part of the world to watch happenings in far-off places on television or via the internet. So, for globalisation, national boundaries are not important economically; free trade and movement of labour and other resources result in the breakdown of these boundaries and one big global marketplace. **Internationalisation**, meanwhile, refers to the increased links between nation states with respect to trade and the movement of resources. The relevant thing here is that the nation state is still important; it is participating and cooperating with other nation states to a common end.

Regionalism and regional trade agreements are also important in this process, the European Union (EU) being an example. The main difference is that with internationalisation, the nation state remains important whereas the process of globalisation breaks down the barriers between nation states. An extreme view of this process is called **hyperglobalisation**, where the world market is seen as a borderless global marketplace consisting of powerless nation states and powerful multinational corporations.[1] The more generally accepted view is called **transformationalism**, which sees the process of globalisation as bringing about changes both in the power of countries and companies and in national characteristics and culture.[2] Any differences do not disappear but are maintained, albeit in changed forms. The population in India might drink Coca-Cola and listen to western music, but this does not mean that they hold the same views and values as the west. Similarly, even within the EU national differences remain important (especially in times of crisis).

Although these definitions are important theoretically, they are difficult to apply in practice, so here the term globalisation is used to mean the process of integration of markets, however that happens. Until recently globalisation meant the westernisation (or Americanisation) of markets, but the world has started to change. Companies from **emerging economies** have started to compete with the older **multinational enterprises (MNEs)** and the nature of the MNE is being redefined. Globalisation has taken place because of closer economic ties between countries and because of developments in mass communications, transportation, electronics and the greater mobility of labour. A heated debate has taken place over the past decade between the pro- and the anti-globalisation lobbies.

The arguments put forward by the proponents of globalisation stem from the benefits brought about by increased **international trade** and specialisation. They argue that all countries open to international trade have benefited – only those that are closed to international trade (some African countries, for example) have become poorer. In the case of China, the opening up to world trade in 1978 has led to increases in GDP per capita, up from $1460 per head in 1980 to $6188 per head in 2013. The pro-globalisation arguments can be summarised as follows:

- Increased globalisation leads to greater specialisation so that all countries involved benefit from the increased international trade.
- Countries that are open to international trade have experienced much faster growth than countries that are not.
- Barriers to trade encourage industries to be inefficient and uncompetitive.
- It is not just the large multinationals that benefit from globalisation – small and medium-sized companies are also engaged in global production and marketing.

The arguments against globalisation are just as strong. It is claimed that the benefits of higher world output and growth brought about through globalisation have not been shared equally by all countries. The main beneficiaries have been the large multinationals rather than individual countries or people. It is suggested that the international organisations that promote free trade should pay more attention to the issues of equity, human rights and the natural environment rather than focusing simply on trade. It is also argued that increased globalisation leads to economic instability. The anti-globalisation arguments can be summarised thus:

- The benefits of globalisation have not been shared equitably throughout the world.
- Globalisation undermines the power of nation states – it empowers the large multinationals at the expense of governments, many multinationals being financially bigger than nation states.
- The large organisations that promote free trade (such as the WTO and the IMF) are not democratically elected and their decisions are not made in the public eye.
- The policies of these organisations are aimed at trade only – human rights and environmental concerns are often ignored.

The main international organisations concerned with globalisation are the World Trade Organisation (WTO), the International Monetary Fund (IMF), the World Bank and the Organisation for Economic Co-operation and Development (OECD). In addition to these there is the United Nations Conference on Trade and Development (UNCTAD), which is a permanent intergovernmental body of the United Nations that aims to maximise investment to the developing nations and to help them in their integration into the world economy.

There are several key elements of economic globalisation: international trade, **foreign direct investment (FDI)** and capital market flows. The OECD categorises members into three bands – high-income countries, which includes the EU, North America and Australasia; middle-income countries, which includes East Asia and the Pacific Rim; and low-income countries, which includes South Asia and Africa.

International trade

The share of international trade in goods as a percentage of GDP increased between 1990 and 2011 for all income groups and particularly for the low-income group (see Table 14.1). The same is true for services. Thus there is evidence of increased globalisation. Note that there are differences within each group – in the low-income group, for example, although the share has increased overall, there are countries that have experienced negative growth (Botswana and Togo for instance, both of which are open to international trade). Although the share of developing countries has increased over time, world markets are still dominated by the developed world, especially in high-value, high-tech products. It is also true that increased trade does not automatically lead to increased development, as in parts of sub-Saharan Africa where the products sold are basic primary products.

Table 14.1 Elements of economic globalisation

	Trade in goods as a % of GDP		Gross private capital flows as a % of GDP*		Gross FDI as a % of GDP	
	1990	*2011*	*1990*	*2005*	*1990*	*2011*
Low income	23.6	58.1	2.4	6.7	0.4	3.8
Middle income	32.5	53.0	6.6	13.3	0.9	2.7
High income	32.3	53.0	11.0	37.2	1.0	2.7

*Not available after 2005.
Source: Adapted from Table 6.1, *World Development Indicators*, 2013, and the Little Data Book 2013, both World Bank.

Capital market flows

This refers to the flows of money from private savers wishing to include foreign assets in their portfolios. This also increased in all income bands between 1990 and 2005 (Table 14.1) – later figures are not available. The overall figures hide a greater volatility than in international trade or foreign direct investment and the fact that the flows have been largely restricted to emerging economies in East Asia. **Capital market flows** occur because investors want to diversify their portfolios to include foreign assets; it is therefore aimed at bringing about short-term capital gains. Unlike FDI, there is no long-term involvement on the part of the investor.

Foreign direct investment

This refers to the establishment of production facilities in overseas countries and therefore represents a more direct involvement in the local economy (than capital market flows) and a longer-term relationship. Between 1990 and 2000, the value of FDI worldwide more than doubled; since then FDI has moved in line with world economic conditions (see case study on FDI at the end of the chapter). FDI represents the largest form of private capital inflow into the developing countries. Each of the three elements of economic globalisation has a different effect and carries different consequences for countries. Capital market flows are much more volatile and therefore carry higher risk – these flows introduce the possibility of 'boom and bust' for countries where capital market flows are important. The financial crisis in the emerging countries in 2013–14 had a lot to do with these capital flows. Openness to trade and FDI are less volatile and it is these that are favoured by the international organisations such as the World Bank and the WTO. It is also true that the benefits of globalisation have not been shared equally between those taking part – the developed nations have reaped more benefit than the poorer nations.

The role of multinational enterprises

Substantial amounts of foreign trade and hence movements of currency result from the activities of very large multinational companies or enterprises. Multinational enterprises/companies (MNEs/MNCs), strictly defined, are enterprises operating in a number of countries and having production or service facilities outside the country of their origin. These multinationals usually have their headquarters in a developed country, but this is beginning to change. At one time globalisation meant that businesses were expanding from developed to developing economies. The world is a different place now – business flows in the opposite direction and often between developing countries. One indication of this is the number of companies from the emerging nations that appear in the Global 500 list of the world's biggest companies. In 1980, 23 (5 per cent) came from emerging countries; in 2010, the number had gone up to 85 (17 per cent) and of these 54 were Chinese, including Lenovo, a Chinese computer manufacturer which bought IBM's personal computer business in 2005.

Multinationals can diversify their operations across different countries and many are well-known household names (see Table 14.2). The footloose nature of such companies brings with it certain benefits.

T able 14.2 The world's ten largest non-financial MNEs, ranked by foreign assets, 2012

Rank	Company	Home economy	Transnationality index %*
1	General Electric	United States	23
2	Royal Dutch Shell plc	UK/Netherlands	77
3	BP	United Kingdom	84
4	Toyota Motor Corporation	Japan	55
5	Total SA	France	79
6	Exxon Mobil Corporation	United States	65
7	Vodafone Group plc	United Kingdom	90
8	GDF Suez	France	59
9	Chevron Corporation	United States	60
10	Volkswagen Group	Germany	58

Note: *Measured as the average of three ratios: foreign assets to total assets, foreign sales to total sales, and foreign employment to total employment.
Source: Adapted from Annex Table 28, *World Investment Report,* UNCTAD, 2013.

1 MNEs can locate their activities in the countries that are best suited for them. For example, production planning can be carried out in the parent country, and the production itself can be carried out in one of the newly industrialised countries where labour is relatively cheap and marketing can be done in the parent country where such activities are well developed. The relocation of production may go some way to explaining the decline in the manufacturing sector in the developed nations.

2 An MNE can cross-subsidise its operations. Profits from one market can be used to support operations in another one. The **cross-subsidisation** could take the form of price cutting, increasing productive capacity or heavy advertising.

3 The risk involved in production is spread not just over different markets but also over different countries.

4 MNEs can avoid tax by negotiating special tax arrangements in one of their host countries (tax holidays) or through careful use of **transfer pricing**. Transfer prices are the prices at which internal transactions take place. These can be altered so that high profits can be shown in countries where the tax rate is lower. The principle in place is that the transfer price should represent what an 'arm's length' customer would pay or an 'arm's length' supplier would charge. In 2019, Shell India was sold to its parent company for the price of Rs 8,000 crore but the Indian tax department valued the sale as Rs 80,000 crore. The Indian government is trying to tax the difference of Rs 72,000 crore (see mini case study on transfer pricing).

5 MNEs can take advantage of subsidies and tax exemptions offered by governments to encourage start-ups in their country.

The very size of MNEs gives rise to concern as their operations can have a substantial impact upon the economy. For example, the activities of MNEs will affect the labour markets of host countries and the balance of payments. If a subsidiary is started in one country there will be an inflow of capital to that country. Once it is up and running, however, there will be outflows of dividends and profits that will affect the invisible balance. Also, there will be flows of goods within the company, and therefore between countries, in the form of semi-finished goods and raw materials. These movements will affect the exchange rate as well as the balance of payments and it is likely that the effects will be greater for developing countries than for developed countries.

mini case   Transfer pricing

Although transfer pricing has always been a feature of the operation of multinationals, it became a huge public issue in 2013 and very unpopular. A survey by the Institute of Business Ethics in the UK found that tax avoidance had replaced remuneration as the issue that most concerned them about corporate behaviour.[3] In times of austerity, cutbacks in government spending and falls in real wages, anything that reduces the tax liability of large companies is seen as bad. There were many reports of the small amount of tax paid by multinationals such as Google, Starbucks and Amazon in countries where they do large amounts of business. In 2011, in the UK Amazon had sales of £3.35 billion but reported a tax expense of £1.8 million, while Google paid the UK government £6 million on a turnover of £395 million. Neither of these is illegal, both companies were operating within the law – it is tax avoidance, not tax evasion. This is an issue that affects all countries, rich and poor alike – according to Christian Aid, poor countries lose an estimated $160 billion per year from tax avoidance by multinational companies.

The problem with multinationals is that they can use tax loopholes such as transfer pricing to pay tax in the country where the tax rate is lower and as tax rates are largely under the control of individual countries, there is little that one country can do alone. There are international controls over transfer pricing which have been in place for some time. The European Commission, for instance, has had a Joint Transfer Pricing Forum since 2002, and the OECD issued guidelines in 1979 which were updated in 2010.[4]

The greater public awareness and the outcry the issue has created has increased the calls for more controls, both nationally and internationally. In 2013 the Global Alliance for Tax Justice was formed, made up of tax campaigners from many different countries, with the aim of increasing the pressure on international organisations. There is agreement in the OECD and the EU that multinational companies must reveal more information about their activities on a country-by-country basis, which would make action possible. Also, there are moves towards greater transparency; some tax havens (countries where tax rates are low) have agreed to start sharing information about bank accounts.

As well as government action on tax laws and increased transparency at national and international levels, there has been the 'naming and shaming' of the companies avoiding tax. This may have several effects on a company. First, the information could encourage customers to boycott the company – there have been such campaigns against Amazon and Google. Second, there will be reputational effects on the companies involved, and this could damage their claims to act with corporate responsibility. Third, as in the case of Starbucks in the UK, it could result in the payment of tax to the government. There has been direct action against these companies around the world, including sit-down protests and occupations which have sometimes caused stores to close. Social media has increased the velocity of these protests. It is difficult to assess the impact of naming and shaming – information on the extent of any boycott or its financial impact is impossible to come by. What is true is that with continued austerity there will be continued public pressure on governments and international organisations and that the campaign will continue.

There is also the possibility of exploitation of less developed countries, and it is debatable whether such footloose industries form a viable basis for economic development. Added to this, MNEs take their decisions in terms of their overall operations rather than with any consideration of their effects on the host economy. There is therefore a loss of economic sovereignty for national governments.

The main problem with multinationals is the lack of control that can be exerted by national governments. As the mini case study shows, there are increased calls from around the world for more transparency, monitoring and control of their activities. In 2011 the OECD updated its *Guidelines for Multinational Enterprises,* which are not legally binding but are promoted by OECD member governments. These seek to provide a balanced framework for international investment that clarifies both the rights and responsibilities of the business community. The publication contains guidelines on business ethics, employment relations, information disclosure and taxation, among other things. Against all this is the fact that without the presence of MNEs, output in host countries would be lower, and there is evidence that on labour market issues the multinationals do not perform badly.

Transnationality

The transnationality index gives a measure of an MNE's involvement abroad by looking at three ratios – foreign assets/total assets, foreign sales/total sales and foreign employment/total employment. As such it captures the importance of foreign activities in its overall activities. In Table 14.2 Vodafone Group plc has the highest index – this is because in all three ratios it has a high proportion of foreign involvement. Since 1990 the average index of transnationality for the top 100 MNEs has increased from 51 per cent to 54.4 per cent.

These multinationals are huge organisations and their market values often exceed the gross national product (GNP) of many of the countries in which they operate. There are more than 60,000 MNEs around the world and they are estimated to account for a quarter of the world's output. The growth in MNEs is due to relaxation of exchange controls, making it easier to move money between countries, and the improvements in communication, which make it possible to run a worldwide business from one country. The importance of multinationals varies from country to country, as Table 14.3 shows.

T able 14.3 Share of foreign affiliates in manufacturing production and employment, 2010

Country	% share of foreign affiliates in manufacturing production	% share of foreign affiliates in manufacturing employment
Ireland	83	48
Hungary	63	46
Czech Republic	59	41
Great Britain	40	31
Netherlands	41	30
Luxembourg	34	25
Germany	27	16
Finland	24	19
Italy	18	11

Source: Adapted from OECD (2013), Foreign affiliates, in OECD Science, Technology and Industry Scoreboard 2013: Innovation for Growth, OECD Publishing. http://dx.doi.org/10.1787/sti_scoreboard-2013-64-en.

As we can see, foreign affiliates are very important for some countries and not so important for others; in the case of Italy the level of foreign presence is low. For all of the countries, foreign affiliates have a bigger impact on production than employment.

Globalisation and business

Businesses of all sizes need to have an awareness of their international context. As noted above, even if they are not directly involved in international trade, firms will be affected by international forces that lie largely outside their control. Globalisation has meant that the financial crisis of 2008, for instance, affected virtually the whole world. Some of the issues facing businesses are discussed below in brief; many of them are discussed later in the book in more detail.

Markets

Globalisation means that firms are faced with bigger markets for their products. Many of these markets are covered by **regional trade agreements (RTAs),** which are group-ings of countries set up to facilitate world trade. All such agreements have to be notified to the World Trade Organisation and they can take a variety of forms. The most basic relationship and the most common is a **free trade area**, where trade barriers between members are abolished but where each member maintains its own national barriers with non-members. An example of this is the North American Free Trade Agreement

(NAFTA). Agreements can also take the form of a **customs union** or common market, where members abolish trade barriers among themselves and adopt a common external tariff which is applied to non-members, as in the EU. All of these agreements increase the size of the marketplace for producers in the member countries and the enlargement of these agreements (the EU, for example) means that markets are increasing all the time.

In addition to these trade agreements, the opening up of the emerging economies (e.g. China and India) to international trade, their high growth rates and the corresponding increase in per capita income mean that there has been a huge increase in the demand for goods and services. The population in India is 1237 million, income per head has doubled since 2000 and GDP growth rate was 9.3 per cent between 2010 and 2011. The Chinese population stood at 1351 million in 2012, income per head has doubled since 2000 and the growth rate in 2012 was 7.8 per cent. Many believe that China's high growth rate has been fuelled by exports, but recent research shows that demand is more consumption driven than previously thought. It also shows that consumer demand has changed in favour of products that have a higher imported content. This is good news for the rest of the world.

Labour markets

It has been estimated that the global integration of emerging markets has doubled the supply of labour for the global production of goods. The OECD estimates that the percentage of the world population living outside their country of birth doubled between 1985 and 2010. About half of this is between the developed countries, the other half from developing to developed countries. The impact of migration is considered in more detail in the international case study at the end of Part Two ('Contexts').

International labour mobility can be used by businesses for hard-to-fill vacancies. Typically these are at the low-skill, high-risk and low-paid end of the spectrum and at the high-skill, high-paid end. Legal labour migration can be permanent (where migrants settle permanently) or temporary (where migrants eventually return home). The regulations pertaining to these will differ. In addition to international labour migration there are three other alternatives: outsourcing (for example, the location of US call centres in India involves the movement of jobs rather than people); cross-border commuting (for example, the commuting of Poles into western Europe); or the use of internet trade (where the work could take place anywhere).

For businesses wishing to recruit internationally, there are practical problems including locating the necessary people and dealing with the rules and regulations involved in employing migrants, such as work permits and visas. These requirements will vary from one country to another.

Other resources

As well as labour, businesses have to source and purchase other resources such as raw materials and energy. Natural resources are differentially distributed around the world and therefore they require international trade to take place if firms are to acquire these inputs. The market for energy, for example, is a global market, with attendant concerns about the environmental impact of the methods used for its generation.

mini case   Currency crisis in emerging markets

Since the start of the global financial crisis in 2008, the emerging economies have done well out of international capital flows. Low interest rates in the developed nations (designed to stimulate the economies) made international capital look for higher rates of return and the emerging economies with their high growth rates were the recipients. It is estimated that $4 trillion has flowed into the emerging economies since 2008. This is speculative money looking for high rates of return. The tapering of quantitative easing (QE) in the USA in 2014 has made it a more attractive place to invest and there are worries that the emerging economies may face a sudden stop to these capital flows.

How did this happen? Since 2008 there have been four rounds of quantitative easing in the USA where the Federal Reserve Bank pledged to buy up bank debt, Treasury bonds and longer-term bonds. This has the effect of increasing liquidity in the economy – like 'printing money' – in the hope that this will stimulate economic growth. It also has the effect of reducing the rate of interest, which is good for borrowers and business but bad for savers and investors. Speculators want to maximise their rate of return and if the rate of interest in the USA (and other developed nations) is too low, they look to other places to put their money. The emerging nations, including India, Turkey and South Africa, had high growth rates and were the recipients of these speculative flows.

With improvements in the state of the US economy, a tapering of QE was signalled by the Federal Reserve Bank in May 2013 and announced formally in December. The tapering off of the purchase of bonds will continue at a measured rate until the end of 2014 and the expectation is that it will have finished by spring 2015. This announcement had a significant effect on the emerging countries – there were dramatic falls in their exchange rates (the Turkish lira lost 10 per cent of its value between December 2013 and

January 2014 and smaller falls have occurred in South Africa, Argentina, Brazil, India and Chile). Five countries have been identified as 'fragile' as they have large balance-of-payments deficits that need financing – these are Turkey, India, South Africa, Brazil and Indonesia. Hours before the December announcement, the Turkish central bank increased the benchmark interest rate from 4.5 per cent to 10 per cent. In South Africa the rate of interest went up to 5.5 per cent and in India it was 8 per cent. These interest rate rises attempt to stop the flow of international capital away from the country and to prop up their currencies, but of course have undesirable effects on other economic variables. It reduces the level of demand in the economy; it causes inflation through the higher price of imports; it means that the countries cannot service their external debts so there may be political repercussions; it affects their ability to finance their large balance-of-payments deficits. In 2001, in similar circumstances, Argentina defaulted on its external debts and the repercussions of that are still being felt.

It is not clear where this will end; the measures introduced in Turkey to support its currency have not worked and the pressure is still on all of these countries. Of course, this crisis is not only about US monetary policy, there are factors specific to each country, such as a major corruption scandal in Turkey and political unrest in the Ukraine. But many argue that the Federal Reserve is, in effect, the banker to the whole world and should consider other economies and not just the American one when deciding on policy.

This mini case shows how interrelated global markets are and how quickly measures announced in one part of the world can affect others. By the same argument, the repercussions of tapering of QE in the USA will find its way back to the USA. Globalisation is contagious.

Financial markets

Businesses need to raise capital to be able to produce, trade and invest. Although much of this takes place domestically, banks operate internationally and so businesses are exposed to global forces. Never has this been seen more vividly than in the events of recent years.

Globalisation and the small and medium-sized firm

There are problems for small and medium-sized enterprises (SMEs) wishing to trade internationally. They will not have the same access to resources, finance or markets as the large multinationals or even the large national companies which could either trade directly or expand internationally through mergers and takeovers. SMEs, however, have a number of options, which are outlined briefly below.

- A **strategic alliance** is a collaborative agreement between firms to achieve a common aim, in this context a presence in other markets. These agreements can take many forms.
- **Franchising** is an arrangement where one party (the franchiser) sells the rights to another party (the franchisee) to market its product or service. There are different types of franchise relationship and this is a possibility for international expansion. It is an attractive option for companies seeking international expansion without having to undertake substantial direct investments.
- **Licensing** is where a company (the licensor) authorises a company in another country (the licensee) to use its intellectual property in return for certain considerations, usually royalties. Licensors are usually multinationals located in developed countries.
- A **joint venture** is usually a jointly owned and independently incorporated business venture involving two or more organisations. This is a popular method of expanding abroad as each party can diversify, with the benefit of the experience of the others involved in the venture and a reduction in the level of risk. Where a large number of members are involved in such an arrangement, this is called a **consortium**.

Synopsis

This chapter has looked at the global context of business. No business is immune from international forces, no matter what it is producing or how small its markets are. The whole concept of globalisation has been discussed, along with the claimed costs and benefits. The elements of globalisation have been outlined together with the impact of globalisation on businesses.

Summary of key points

- There is a difference between globalisation and internationalisation that centres on the role of national boundaries.

- There are costs and benefits associated with the process of globalisation.

- There are three main elements of globalisation – international trade, capital market flows and foreign direct investment.

- Multinational enterprises are very important in the process of globalisation.

- With the arrival of the emerging economies in the global marketplace, some changes in the nature and the process of globalisation are evident.

- Globalisation affects all firms in one way or another – either through markets, access to resources or finance.

- There are several different possibilities for small and medium-sized businesses wishing to expand internationally.

case study   FDI flows

Foreign direct investment is an important element in the process of globalisation and economic integration as it creates long-term links between economies. Unlike capital market flows, it carries a long-term interest in an economy and it is a source of investment funds, it promotes sharing of ideas between countries and can be an important tool in development. Inward flows are all direct investment in a country by non-residents; outflows represent direct investment by residents in other countries. FDI can take the form of the opening of new factories or subsidiaries, or mergers and acquisitions, and as would be expected multinational enterprises are very active in the process. FDI flows since 2000 have been mixed and volatile. There have been record flows of FDI and great variability in the performance of countries and groupings of countries. Tables 14.4 and 14.5 show changes in inflows and outflows between 2001 and 2012 for selected groupings of countries.

Most of the groupings are well known but the one that might be less so is the 'Next 11' or N11.[5] This term was coined by Jim O'Neill of Goldman Sachs

Table 14.4 Change in FDI inflows for selected groupings of countries 2001–12 (%)

	2001–2	2003–4	2005–7	2008–12
G8	−26	+31	+73	−40
EU27	−18	−30	+71	−53
Developed	−26	+9	+112	−45
Developing	−25	+44	+76	+5
Emerging	−30	+57	+88	+48
N11				−25

Source: adapted from *unctadstat.unctad.org*

Table 14.5 Change in FDI outflows for selected groupings of countries 2001–12 (%)

	2001–2	2003–4	2005–7	2008–12
G8	–18	+79	+220	–27
EU27	–39	+27	+108	–66
Developed	–28	+53	+154	–43
Developing	–49	+110	+136	+24
Emerging	–60	+127	+164	+60
N11				+110

Source: adapted from *unctadstat.unctad.org*

International Bank and it includes 11 countries that have good prospects for growth and openness to trade. Many commentators argue that the N11, along with the BRIC countries, are the ones that will push forward the global engine of growth. In 2012 it was forecast that the BRIC economies would be larger than the USA by 2015 and the G7 by 2032 and the N11 would be larger than the USA and twice the size of the EU by 2050.

These tables show great variability between the groupings and within each grouping there is even greater variability. The reasons put forward for the dramatic decline in total FDI flows in the early 2000s were the sluggishness of the global economy, some uncertainty over monetary policy in some countries and, most significantly, increasing international political instability and insecurity. The reasons put forward for the recovery in FDI flows between 2003 and 2008 were the relative decline in the value of the US dollar and large-value mergers and acquisitions during the period. The fall in flows from 2008 onwards was due to the global financial crisis, which has been well documented elsewhere in this book.

What is most interesting about Table 14.4 is the differences in performance between the groupings. In the period 2003–4, FDI inflows fell for the EU while there was growth for all other groupings. The main reasons for this were the continuing effects of the recession and the expansion of the EU that occurred in 2004. The rapid growth in the 2005–7 period was universal, even if the growth was variable. In the last time period, 2008–12, the only groupings where flows increased were for the developing and emerging countries. The fall in inflows for the N11 countries was mainly due to political factors in individual countries – Egypt experienced a big reduction due to the repercussions of the 'Arab Spring', Turkey experienced a fall mainly due to corruption allegations against the government. By 2012 both FDI inflows and outflows for many countries and groupings

had started to recover. The OECD compiles the FDI Regulatory Restrictiveness Index each year, which measures the restrictions to FDI according to four factors: limitations on foreign equity, screening mechanisms, restrictions of foreign employment and operational restrictions. The index can take any value between 0 – completely open – and 1 – completely closed. There does not seem to be very much correlation between the level of FDI flows and the FDI index. The three biggest recipients of FDI inflows in 2012 were (FDI index shown in brackets) USA (0.09), China (0.4) and Belgium (0.04). The biggest source of FDI outflows were USA, Japan (0.3) and the UK (0.06). The OECD calculates that the FDI index is higher in the service sector and that manufacturing is the most open sector for FDI.

As a growing number of countries have emerged from the financial crisis, the global landscape is changing. After 2008, the highly indebted developed nations were in trouble and the emerging economies showed the most resilience and growth potential. But this was before the currency crisis of 2013–14 (see mini case study). At the time of writing it is unclear how this will end, but it does seem that the well-known developed economies may be resuming their position in the global economy. The USA, Canada and Japan are returning to slow growth, while in the EU the position is mixed and still uncertain. But the USA did not fall off a 'fiscal cliff',[6] the Japanese tsunami did not return Japan to low growth, and the EU did not break up, even though there are still problems in these countries. As the case study shows, things change very quickly in such an interrelated world.

Case study questions

1 Why are FDI flows cyclical in nature?

2 How might a country make itself more attractive to inward FDI?

Review and discussion questions

1 What role does the advancement of ICT have in the process of globalisation?

2 What are the arguments for and against foreign ownership of strategic industries such as energy?

3 How are multinationals changing?

4 For a business considering expansion into another country, what methods of expansion are available? What are the advantages and disadvantages of each?

5 What has been the impact of the financial crisis in 2008 on the process of globalisation?

Assignments

1 You work in a local office of a multinational enterprise and your line manager has been invited to take part in a discussion arranged by the local newspaper on the pros and cons of globalisation. You have been asked to provide a briefing paper outlining the arguments for your line manager.

2 You have been asked to give a presentation on regional trade agreements to students of business at a local college. Research which regional trade agreements your country is a member of and what effects membership has on labour mobility. Prepare PowerPoint slides together with notes to accompany each slide.

Notes and references

1 See Gray, J., *False Dawn: The Delusions of Global Capitalism,* Granta Books, 1998.

2 See Held, D., McGrew, A., Goldblatt, D. and Perraton, J., *Global Transformations: Politics, Economics and Culture,* Polity Press, 1999.

3 http://*www.ibe.org.uk/userfiles/pressreleases/attitudes2013.pdf*

4 Transfer Pricing Guidelines for MNE and Tax Administrations, OECD, 2010.

5 N11: Bangladesh, Egypt, Indonesia, Iran, South Korea, Mexico, Nigeria, Pakistan, the Philippines, Turkey and Vietnam.

   Emerging economies: (UNCTAD) Argentina, Brazil, Chile, Mexico, Peru, China, South Korea, Malaysia, Singapore and Thailand.

   There is some overlap between these two groupings.

6 In 2013 the USA faced a 'fiscal cliff' where attempts by President Obama to increase the debt ceiling to deal with the huge public sector budget deficit were rejected by the Republican House of Representatives. A stalemate ensued and public buildings were closed and public employees sent home. Eventually the crisis was averted when the House of Representatives agreed a compromise. The roots of the fiscal cliff go right back to 2001.

Further reading

Daniels, J. D., Radebaugh, L. and Sullivan, D., *International Business: Environments and Operations,* 13th edition, Prentice Hall, 2010.

Griffiths, A. and Wall, S., *Applied Economics,* 12th edition, Financial Times/Prentice Hall, 2011.

Worthington, I., Britton, C. and Rees, A., *Business Economics: Blending Theory and Practice,* 2nd edition, Financial Times/Prentice Hall, 2005.

International business in action

The global car industry and the changing business environment

All businesses are affected by external factors, many of which lie outside their direct control. While some of these influences concern developments within an organisation's operational environment (e.g. loss of a supplier), others relate to changes of a more general or contextual kind, which can affect a wide variety of businesses, sometimes in different ways (e.g. fluctuations in the exchange rate). As the opening chapter of this book has illustrated, these general/contextual variables include political, economic, socio-cultural, technological, legal and ethical influences that can occur at all spatial levels from the local to the global. For organisations operating in the international/global marketplace, developments at both the micro- and macroenvironmental levels can represent a significant challenge (or opportunity) and can have a substantial influence on the strategic decision-making process.

To illustrate how organisations can be affected by some of the broader contextual changes discussed in Part Two, we examine the car industry, which comprises many well-known international brands, including Ford, Toyota, General Motors, Chrysler, Honda, Renault, PSA Peugeot Citroën, Fiat, Nissan, BMW and Volkswagen. As the mini case in Chapter 1 demonstrates, even some of the world's largest and most powerful businesses in this industry have faced variable trading conditions over recent years because of developments in their external environment and many have been forced to respond in a variety of ways.

What have been some of the major challenges and how have they affected the key players?

Rises in oil and other commodity prices

A combination of increased demand (e.g. because of growth in China and India) and tight supply has meant that oil and other commodity prices (e.g. steel) have risen quite substantially and this has affected production costs in the industry. As these price rises also affect consumers, sales of vehicles in some countries have tended to decline and many customers are switching to more economical/fuel-efficient models as petrol prices increase.

Economic downturn

The falling sales of vehicles being experienced in some parts of the world have not been helped by a general downturn in many economies as a result of the impact of the global financial crisis. As many countries have gone into recession, consumers have tended to defer spending on larger, more expensive items such as cars. This has affected both the market for new vehicles and the second-hand market in many parts of the world.

Emerging markets

While many economies are facing difficult circumstances, growth in some countries (e.g. China, India, Brazil, Russia) has created an opportunity for car producers to exploit new and expanding markets. By the same token, this growth is encouraging newer companies to come into the marketplace and to increase the possibility of future competition in the traditional areas of the international car market (e.g. Europe and the USA).

Environmental issues

The growing threat of climate change has led to the environmental impact of cars and other vehicles becoming a prime concern for both governments (see below) and consumers. As far as the latter are concerned, there has been a slight shift in consumer taste away from high-polluting, gas-guzzling models (e.g. SUVs, 4×4s, pick-ups) towards more fuel-efficient vehicles that have a smaller environmental impact. Rising oil prices have reinforced this trend towards smaller cars. There has also been increased investment in electric vehicles and hybrids.

Legislative/policy developments

Concerns over cars' contribution to climate change have resulted in governmental and intergovernmental negotiations over future legislation and/or targets regarding vehicle CO_2 emissions. In the EU, for example, member states have set obligatory targets for vehicle emissions for the period up to 2020. Discussions on future emissions standards have also taken place in the United States.

Currency fluctuations

For firms involved in international trade, exchange rate fluctuations/volatility can sometimes be problematical. Such fluctuations in the values of the dollar, yen and euro in recent years have had a direct impact on the major car producers in the USA, Japan and Europe, making prices sometimes more and sometimes less competitive. As oil is also priced in dollars, a fluctuation in the dollar exchange rate has also impacted on the industry.

How should the major players respond/ how have the major players responded?

As the analysis above illustrates, the international car industry has faced significant changes in the external environment over recent years. While some of these changes have generated opportunities for the major players, many have been particularly challenging and have caused vehicle manufacturers to look at both the supply side (e.g. costs) and the demand side (e.g. market development) of their businesses. Some of the key questions being faced by the major brands are:

- How can costs be reduced (e.g. should the workforce be reduced)?
- What product mix should be offered to the consumers (e.g. should some of the less fuel-efficient models be phased out)?
- What markets should be targeted (e.g. should the focus shift towards the emerging markets)?

- How should the new markets be accessed (e.g. are cross-national collaborations a better solution than direct manufacturing)?
- Where should production take place (e.g. can costs be reduced and/or new markets be exploited more effectively by manufacturing cars in the emerging countries)?
- How can the new, emerging competitors be challenged (e.g. should new models be developed)?
- How can legislative requirements be met (e.g. how and where should the industry lobby against tougher emission standards)?
- Where should future investment take place (e.g. if the UK withdraws from the EU following a planned referendum, should production facilities be relocated to mainland Europe)?

For the major international players in the car industry, these are some of the important strategic issues they are facing and a number of key trends have emerged. For example, many car producers are looking towards Asia as a suitable place for manufacture and/or joint venture, with India and China potentially becoming global hubs for small car production, thanks to lower costs and the skills of the workforce. Added to this, the big players are being forced towards global product development (with future models likely to be based on a common platform and sold on a global basis) and/or some form of integration (e.g. Chrysler's merger with Fiat and the decision by Daimler, Renault and Nissan to work together in certain areas, particularly technology sharing). Political uncertainties (e.g. the UK's relationship with the EU) are also likely to delay future investment decisions.

CHAPTER 15

Stakeholders, governance and ethics

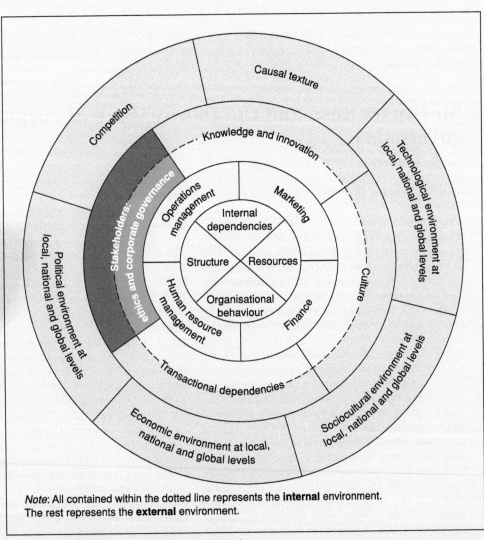

Note: All contained within the dotted line represents the **internal** environment.
The rest represents the **external** environment.

Figure 15.1 Business environment model

Chapter objectives

This chapter provides an overview of stakeholders, **corporate governance**, **ethics** and **corporate social responsibility**. These activities and the role they play in good management of organisations is summarised.

Therefore, when you have read this chapter and worked through the associated activities you should be able to achieve the objectives specified below.

1 **Identify and analyse an organisation's stakeholders.**

2 **Explain and summarise good corporate governance and the key roles involved.**

3 **Discuss ethics and corporate responsibility in relation to a business and its stakeholders.**

This case study examines Marks & Spencer and their decision to combine the roles of chairman and chief executive by appointing Stuart Rose to both positions. This goes against current thinking, which is that good corporate governance is best achieved by separating these two roles.

Sir Stuart Rose and the thorny issue of corporate governance

by Tom Braithwaite and Elizabeth Rigby

Sir Stuart Rose has often said he wanted to remain as Marks & Spencer's chief executive until early 2009. In private though, the man responsible for turning round the retail chain's fortunes harboured ambitions towards the chairmanship. Two potential obstacles stood in his path: the UK's Combined Code on corporate governance and Lord Burns, who was only hired as chairman less than two years ago.

Yesterday, both concerns were swept aside as Sir Stuart's wish was granted, with his elevation to the post of executive chairman from June this year. Lord Burns, whose relationship with his chief executive has always been somewhat strained, according to company insiders, will step down, leaving Sir Stuart the task of running the business and the board. 'We want to develop the team,' says Sir Stuart, who along with his board has failed to single out a successor from his executive team over the past couple of years. 'Keeping me and bringing on new people is the best solution. It gives breathing space for me to step back and gives more elbow room around the boardroom.' But the changes have made some shareholders furious. Legal & General Investment Management, which rarely speaks out on corporate governance issues, says it believes strongly in the separation of the chairman and chief executive. 'We believe today's announcement from M&S is unwelcome.' Investors, analysts

and other M&S watchers are all mystified about why the company has decided to embark on this route, which is unusual at best and extremely controversial at worst.

Lord Burns says he and Sir Stuart looked at a range of alternatives over the past few months, running from Sir Stuart stepping up to the chairmanship to carrying on in the role as chief executive for a set period beyond 2009. 'He didn't want to carry on as chief executive indefinitely. He wanted a process that signalled an end point at which he would step down and through which we would develop people,' says Lord Burns. 'There was a fear that he might leave in 2009,' he adds. 'The alternative [then] was to begin the process of recruiting someone else immediately. This was going to cause a great deal of uncertainty at this point in the company's development and we thought this was not an attractive option. We wanted to find a way of keeping Stuart Rose in the business.' That the only option of keeping Sir Stuart in the business is to go against the spirit of the Combined Code is a source of concern among shareholders, wary of the concentration of power.

They are also irritated that the company has not managed its succession better, given Sir Stuart's clear statements that he would stay at M&S until 2009. Sir Stuart has been talking about beefing-up his 'bench strength' of executives for some time, but has been unable to translate that potential into a concrete successor. M&S

↓ ENTRY CASE STUDY 12.1

watchers say this is due in part to the previous management's failure to nurture the next generation of talent. But it also indicates that those with the skills needed to run a business such as M&S are in very short supply.

M&S insiders admit that while the new arrangement is unorthodox, it at least keeps Sir Stuart at the helm during a difficult period. The retailer has not escaped the effects of a worsening British consumer downturn, with trading figures falling to their lowest level in more than two years during Christmas 2007. Meanwhile, the shares are languishing at 375p, having fallen another 3p yesterday. This is half the 750p level hit last summer, when the Sir Stuart Rose revival was in full swing. It is not a legacy that Sir Stuart will wish to leave.

One insider argued that a strong board of non-executives, led by Sir David Michels – who could replace Sir Stuart as chairman, when he steps down in 2011 – would be 'no-one's patsies'. The insider also said that the precise end date to Sir Stuart's tenure provided a safeguard. 'He is not Vladimir Putin.' Sir David admits that while 'no-one likes flouting a rule, sometimes you have to do something a little skew-whiff in the short-term'. 'It is not simply to find the right successor to Stuart Rose,' Sir David adds. 'We believe it is what this company needs in this environment for the next three years. Stuart is the single best person to lead the company.'

Sir Stuart, meanwhile, wants to offer evidence that he is moving ahead with a wider management shake-up as he encourages his would-be successors. Ian Dyson, the finance director, Kate Bostock, head of the clothing operations, and Steven Esom of the food division are all now on the board. Sir Stuart has also added a raft of 30- and 40-something-year-olds to his executive committee, including Clem Constantine, a former Arcadia man, and Steve Rowe, who is replacing outgoing Guy Farrant as director of retail.

Source: from 'Sir Stuart Rose and the thorny issue of corporate governance', *The Financial Times*, 11 March 2008 (Braithwaite, T. and Rigby, E.).

Introduction

This chapter examines stakeholders, corporate governance, ethics and corporate social responsibility. Stakeholders are individuals with an interest in an organisation and are able to influence an organisation to act in their best interests. Ethics and corporate social responsibility are concerned with the standards of conduct that an organisation sets itself in dealing with all relevant associated stakeholders.

Stakeholders and the organisation

Stakeholders are any individuals or a collection of individuals with an **interest** in an organisation. Some stakeholders will be internal to an organisation and others will be external. Internal stakeholders include employees, managers, directors, trade unions and shareholders. External stakeholders include suppliers, customers, competitors, financiers, government and the general public. Various categories of stakeholder will affect or be affected by the organisation in diverse ways, hence stakeholders have different interests or stakes in the organisation. This is shown in Table 15.1.

Stakeholders are also able to influence an organisation to act in their best interests. However, the interests of different stakeholder groups will vary and may even conflict with each other. For example, employees may seek high wages and above-inflation pay rises, while customers would prefer lower prices and lower costs, which are not possible if labour costs are high. The interests

Table 15.1 Stakeholders' power and interest

Internal stakeholders	Stakeholder interests are:	Stakeholder power arises from:
Employees Managers Directors	• security of employment • wage levels • fringe benefits • responsibility • promotion prospects • working conditions	• job grade or title • position in organisational hierarchy • personal reputation • departmental reputation
Trade unions	• number of union members in the organisation • same as its members (see list in box above)	• number of union members • nature of bargaining (local or national)
Shareholders	• profit levels • size of dividend payments • capital growth in share price	• number of shares held
External stakeholders	**Stakeholder interests are:**	**Stakeholder power arises from:**
Suppliers	• size and value of contracts • speed of invoice payment	• location and availability of other suppliers
Customers	• quality of goods and services available • prices and payment terms	• location of other suppliers • quality of goods and services offered by other suppliers • prices and payment terms offered by other suppliers
Competition	• quality of goods and services available • prices and payment terms	• behaviour of other competitors
Financiers	• how promptly repayment of large and short-term loans occurs	• offering better deal (improved quality or better prices and payment terms)
Government	• payment of corporation tax • implementation of legislation (e.g. competition and employment legislation)	• enforcing the legislation via the legal system if necessary

of stakeholders in an organisation and the ways in which **power** is exercised by stakeholders are shown in Table 15.1.

An organisation's stakeholders will be important for an assortment of reasons and to varying degrees; therefore, different stakeholders will respond to the organisation and its behaviour in different ways. Stakeholders whose interests and expectations are met will tend to remain with the organisation. Unsatisfied stakeholders will leave or remain and use their sources of power in an attempt to persuade the organisation to meet their expectations or interests.

Stakeholders who experience a high level of satisfaction with an organisation will tend to demonstrate loyalty and choose to retain their position as stakeholders. For example, employees who feel that their well-paid jobs are secure and offer future prospects are likely to remain with that employer. In contrast, stakeholders who are disappointed with the organisation and its behaviour are more likely to relinquish their stake. The likelihood of an unhappy stakeholder withdrawing their stake in an organisation is increased if better opportunities and potentially greater satisfaction appear to be available by acquiring a similar stake in a different organisation. For example, shareholders in a company who feel that they are not gaining a good enough return on their investment may decide to sell their shares and invest the money in a company that will give a better level of return.

Alternatively, stakeholders who are unhappy with the organisation may decide to remain and attempt to change things. Unsatisfied shareholders may decide to try to influence changes to the organisation's leadership and strategies, with the aim of benefiting in the long run. To achieve this they will have to be able to exert the necessary amount of influence on planning and decision making within the organisation. This requires a suitable combination of authority, determination and ability. It is usually large institutional investors that stand the best chance of being successful with this type of approach, as they have greater power than smaller investors.

Check your understanding

Do you understand the different ways in which stakeholders in an organisation could behave?

Check your understanding by explaining how the following stakeholder might behave:

- a first-year undergraduate student who is very unhappy on their business studies course;
- a teenager who is always happy with the clothes she buys from New Look;
- a finance director who believes the managing director is making poor strategic decisions for the company.

Analysing stakeholders

The analysis of stakeholders involves identifying who they are and considering their power and interest with regard to the organisation. Stakeholders can be identified by brainstorming and are shown on a stakeholder diagram – *see* Figure 5.2. Once identified, the relative power and interest of the stakeholders can be mapped on to a power and interest matrix – *see* Figure 5.3.[1] Additionally, this analysis can be extended to consider the reaction, behaviour and position of stakeholders if a particular strategy or plan were to be implemented by the organisation.

Stakeholders with high power and high interest (category D)

Stakeholders with high power and high interest are key players in the organisation and are often involved in managing the organisation and its future. If

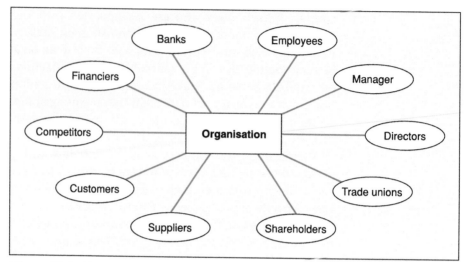

Figure 15.2 Stakeholder diagram

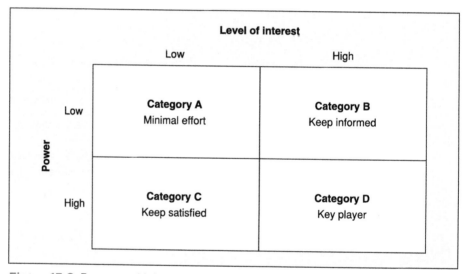

Figure 15.3 Power and interest matrix

Source: Johnson, G and Scholes, K (1999) *Exploring corporate Strategy*, 5th edition, Prentice Hall Europe. Reprinted with permission.

key players are not directly involved in managing the organisation, it is vital that they are given serious consideration in the development of long-term plans and the future direction of the organisation, as they have the power to block proposed plans and implement their own alternative agenda.

Stakeholders with high power and low interest (category C)

Stakeholders with high power and low interest are those who must be kept satisfied, for example institutional shareholders. Institutional shareholders will often remain compliant while they receive acceptable returns on their investment and are pleased with the organisation's management and activities. However, the ability of category C stakeholders to reposition themselves on the power and interest matrix into category D and become stakeholders with a continuing high degree of power and an increase in their level of interest should not be underestimated. This occurs when category C stakeholders are not kept satisfied and feel that their interests are not being best served. Hence stakeholders with high power and low interest will increase their level of interest to make sure that their interests are met. The shift in position of unsatisfied category C stakeholders may impede an organisation's plans and prevent the expectations of key players or category D stakeholders from being met as expected.

Therefore, a canny organisation will ensure that the expectations of category C stakeholders are well met and the necessary adjustments made to meet changing expectations arising as the current issues facing the organisation change. This helps ensure that category C stakeholders do not feel that their interests are being marginalised at the expense of the interests of key players, category D stakeholders. Hence the repositioning of category C stakeholders should not be an unexpected occurrence if they are managed appropriately. This requires a good working relationship and open channels of communication to be developed between category C stakeholders, the organisation and key players or category D stakeholders.

Stakeholders with low power and high interest (category B)

The stakeholders in category B are those with low power and high interest, who are able to exert relatively little power in influencing the organisation and its actions. However, these stakeholders have a high level of interest in the organisation and will voice their concerns if that interest is not being considered in a suitable manner. If category B stakeholders voice their concerns loudly enough and in the right way, e.g. via lobbying or petitions, they may be able to influence one of the powerful group of stakeholders in either category C or D and affect their behaviour. Therefore, organisations need to keep category B stakeholders informed of the organisation's activities and decisions and in doing so convince them that their interests are being taken into account and considered seriously.

Stakeholders with low power and low interest (category A)

Stakeholders with low power and low interest are those in whom the organisation need invest only minimal effort. However, category A stakeholders should not be ignored as they may acquire a stake in the organisation by becoming, for example, a customer, supplier or competitor, which will mean an increased level of interest and/or power.

The Automobile Association and its stakeholders

It should be recognised that the position of stakeholders on the power and interest matrix is dynamic and will vary over time according to the current issues that the stakeholders are considering. The situation in which the Automobile Association (AA) found itself during April 1999 provides a good example of an organisation with groups of stakeholders who line up in a certain way due to a particular issue, in this case demutualisation.

The AA was founded in 1905 and by 1999 held around half the motor breakdown market, a market that was experiencing significant change. These changes included the acquisition of Green Flag by Cendant, the entry of the insurance company Direct Line into the market, and the RAC's expected trade sale or flotation. Therefore, in April 1999 the AA considered its options with regard to retaining its mutual status or demutualising. It was rumoured that Ford had informally approached the AA with a takeover offer that would end the latter's mutual status. Other interested bidders were thought to include Centrica and a number of venture capitalists. The then Director-General of the AA, John Maxwell, initiated a strategic review to allow the AA to assess its options. The options available included demutualisation, a joint venture with a suitable partner or takeover by another company. The merchant bank Schroders was advising the AA.

In 1999 the AA had annual sales of around £600 million from its businesses, which included roadside service, publications and driving schools, and its value was estimated to be between £1 billion and £1.5 billion. Pursuit of the demutualisation option and stock market flotation would give each full member of the AA a moderate windfall of £200–250. In 1999 the AA had 9.5 million members, of which 4.3 million were full-paying members who would receive the windfall payouts. However, excluded from the demutualisation windfall were the 1.7 million associate members, including the families of full-paying members who benefit from the association's service. Also excluded were the 3.5 million members who were drivers of fleet cars with AA cover and drivers who received their AA membership as part of a package when purchasing a car.

The AA and stakeholders with high power and high interest (category D)

The key players were the Director-General of the AA and his immediate management team carrying out the strategic review, as well as the full members of the AA – *see* Figure 5.4. John Maxwell and his management team were key players with high power and high interest, as their planning and decision making would determine their future with the AA, the future of the AA, the future of those who worked for the AA, and the future of AA members. The full members would collectively decide whether the AA was to demutualise. They

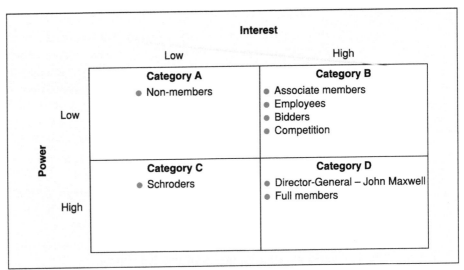

Figure 15.4 Power and interest matrix for the Automobile Association (AA)

might have chosen to support any demutualisation recommendations made by John Maxwell and his team, or to reject them in favour of a bidder, such as Ford, buying the AA. The full members, for example, might have decided this if they were to lose confidence in John Maxwell and his management team and their ability to carry out the demutualisation successfully. Alternatively, full members might have taken the following view, expressed by one of their number in the press in April 1999:

> I got my membership when I bought a much-loved but temperamental MG Midget. If the AA does choose to demutualise, I would hope they would pay a differential for members who have been with the AA longer. I might vote in favour of the move if they were going to pay me a £300 windfall but the down-side could be that if they become a corporate commercial entity, the cost of its services could soar.[2]

The AA and stakeholders with high power and low interest (category C)

The merchant bank Schroders was a category C stakeholder, as it had relatively little interest in whether the AA finally decided to demutualise. However, while in the position of corporate adviser to the AA, it was relatively powerful as it was able to advise and potentially influence John Maxwell and his management team.

The AA and stakeholders with low power and high interest (category B)

The category B stakeholders, those with high interest and low power in the demutualisation issue, included associate members and employees. The associate members clearly had a high interest in whether or not the AA decided to demutualise. The primary concerns for associate members were the effect of demutualisation on the services they received and the cost of associate membership. However, as non-voting members, associates had no direct power to influence the outcome of any ballot on demutualisation. Equally, employees had a high interest in the future of the AA and would be concerned as to the effects of demutualisation. Potential effects of demutualisation could have included the AA becoming more competitive and this being achieved via cost cutting and job losses. However, employees had no direct role in the ballot and would ultimately have to accept its outcome.

The **stakeholder matrix** suggests that category B stakeholders, high interest and low power, have to be kept informed, which is true of stakeholder groups such as associate members and employees. In April 1999, the AA kept its members and employees informed by issuing the following statement to the media and via answerphones in its own offices:

> The AA has always kept an open mind about its structure as it pursues its prime purpose: to serve the best interests of its members. No decisions have been made in this respect.

However, also with high interest and low power were other stakeholders like potential bidders such as Ford and competitors like Direct Line and Green Flag. These were external stakeholders with a great deal of interest in what the AA would eventually decide to do, as their business and the marketplace in which they operated would be directly influenced by that decision. Any organisation should be aware that any information it releases with the intention of keeping stakeholders such as employees and associate members informed will be in the public arena and therefore available to stakeholders such as competitors and potential bidders.

The AA and stakeholders with low power and low interest (category A)

The category A stakeholders are those with low power and low interest. For the AA, non-members fell into this category. They were unable to receive breakdown services from the organisation and had no influence over its demutualisation decision. However, it should be recognised that stakeholders' power and influence can alter over time. The opportunity of a £200–250 windfall might have encouraged some non-members to become members and move to category D, high interest and high power. This was perfectly possible, as the AA made it clear that it was not closing its doors to new members, nor was it expecting to distinguish between long-term and short-term full members:

> The AA has no intention of bringing the shutters down on membership. Everyone is as free to join the AA as they were before.[3]

> There is no distinction made among full members.[4]

If the number of new full members joining had been very large and there was no differentiation between new and longer-term members, the value of the windfall paid to full members could have decreased. This could have pushed longer-term full members to seek to lobby or influence John Maxwell and his management team to distinguish between long- and short-term members.

Stakeholder alliances and coalitions

When analysing stakeholders, two points should be noted. First, people and organisations may belong to more than one category of stakeholder. Second, stakeholders and organisations may depend on one another, with the nature of the dependency varying according to the amount of power and/or interest the stakeholder has in the organisation. For example, if the Director-General of the AA favoured demutualisation, he would have depended on the full-time members voting in large enough numbers for the demutualisation proposals. However, he would have needed to recognise that full members might have been subject to influence by associate members, who may have been related to full members, e.g. husband and wife. Similarly, some employees (category B) were also full members of the AA and how they were treated and informed as employees might have influenced their voting behaviour as full members. The employees might have felt that cost cutting and job losses were likely to result from demutualisation. Hence they might have lobbied and sought to influence the voting full members to vote against a change in the AA's structure or to vote for a takeover rather than demutualisation if they thought their best interests would be served in this way. Equally, if associate members were concerned about the service they received and its cost, they might have sought to influence full voting members, which would perhaps have been easy if the full voting members were family members. In addition, associate members and employees might have sought to influence John Maxwell and his management team directly, via letter-writing campaigns and petitions.

Therefore, the arguments in favour of demutualisation had to focus on the benefits for full members (cash windfall and service levels at least maintained, preferably improved in some way), associate members (service levels at least maintained, preferably improved in some way), and employees, particularly those who were also full members (issues of job security and future operation of the AA for employees were crucial).

The members of the AA were balloted in August 1999 on the proposed sale of the AA to Centrica. The result of the ballot was announced in mid-September 1999 and showed 67 per cent of eligible members voted and 96 per cent of them voted in favour of the sale. The sale to Centrica was completed in July 2000 for £1.1 billion.

Check your understanding

Do you understand the nature of stakeholders' power and interest?

Check your understanding by answering the following questions.

(a) A production operative has more power than a senior manager. True or false?
(b) A corporate investor is more powerful than an individual investor. True or false?
(c) The government is usually a stakeholder with low power and low interest in an organisation. True or false?
(d) The interest of a small individual customer is not high. True or false?

Corporate governance

Corporate governance refers to the influence of stakeholders and their exercising of power to control the strategic direction of the organisation. The stakeholders who have the biggest and most important role to play in corporate governance are the key stakeholders, namely the managing director, other directors and senior staff in the organisation. Their role in corporate governance is important as they are able to influence the development and implementation of strategy.

Therefore, corporate governance includes regular monitoring and evaluation of strategy that has been implemented and approval of strategy yet to be implemented. This allows the organisation to adjust and moderate its strategy to ensure the interests of all stakeholders are appropriately met and that one group of stakeholders does not benefit at the expense of another group of stakeholders. For example, good corporate governance would stop directors receiving excessive pay rises at the expense of high prices for customers. The example of directors of utility companies receiving high pay rises, while steeply increasing the price for essentials, such as gas, electricity and water, illustrate poor corporate governance. Equally, at the time of writing, October 2008, the collapse or near collapse of banks, including retail banks around the world, due to their over-ambitious borrowings, must surely call into question the quality of corporate governance at many of these institutions.

Conduct and control

Directors and senior staff are responsible for developing and implementing strategy, meaning they act as agents for other stakeholders. Hence there is a separation of the control of the organisation by the directors and the interests of other stakeholders. Good corporate governance will help ensure that directors do not abuse their power and control to gain benefits at the expense of other stakeholders. In large companies ownership and control are separated, with executive directors managing the business and non-executive directors monitoring management decisions and activity, but having no day-to-day management responsibility for the organisation's operations.

Non-executive directors

The non-executive director will normally hold a senior management job or role in an organisation that has no links to the organisation in which they hold a non-executive directorship. Hence they have no interest whatsoever in the organisation but will have significant senior experience to comment on the decisions and activities of the organisation in their role as a non-executive director.

The appointment of non-executive directors is seen as a way of ensuring that the conduct of the organisation is beyond reproach. It should be noted that organisations appoint their own non-executive directors to undertake the monitoring role. In March 2008 HSBC instituted a boardroom shake-up, which saw three long-serving non-executive directors step down, partly as they had been in office for a long period of time and were no longer considered independent by shareholders. Two new non-executive directors from the software group Oracle and Infosys, an Indian IT services company, replaced them.[5] However, if non-executive directors are of sufficient calibre in their own field and hold tenure for a fixed period time, for example three years, then other stakeholders should be able to have confidence in their independence and good judgement.

The chairman and managing director

Today corporate governance often sees the executive roles of chairman and managing director separated, whereas in the past the chairman and managing director were often the same person. The chairman, the most senior person in the organisation, often focuses on the organisation's relationship with powerful external stakeholders such as financiers, governments and shareholders.

In contrast the managing director, the most senior manager in the organisation, will be responsible for running the organisation and ensuring its operations are efficient and effective. This means a critical part of the managing director's role are the relationships with internal stakeholders, such as other directors, managers, staff and trade unions, and the transactional relationships with external stakeholders, such as suppliers, that effect the running of the organisation. An organisation which chooses not to follow this accepted approach to corporate governance is Marks & Spencer, as illustrated when it appointed Stuart Rose as executive chairman while he continued to hold his chief executive role.

Small companies that cannot afford to separate the roles of chairman and managing director may choose to undertake corporate governance by monitoring decisions and activities via a series of committees which each have responsibility for specific areas of the organisation, e.g. pay and remuneration.

Corporate governance and information

Important to good corporate governance is how senior staff exercise their power in making information available for inspection by other stakeholders. However, this can be fraught with difficulty due to the limitations of the information. On occasions the full picture may not be given and some commercially sensitive information will not be made available outside the organisation, nor will it be fully circulated within the organisation. For example, the annual report and accounts made available to shareholders and the public is limited to what the organisation chooses to tell its shareholders, although it is audited to say it is a true and fair representation of the business at that point in time. In contrast, the main board will have access to very full information, and it is important that this is used correctly when making decisions and informing other stakeholders. The role of the non-executive director is key in ensuring full disclosure of relevant issues. This is why the independence and good character of non-executive directors are important.

In the UK there have been several commissions on standards and corporate governance that have produced reports; for example, the Cadbury, Greenbury and Hampel reports. In the US, corrupt corporate behaviour resulted in the Sarbanes-Oxley Act (2002). This Act makes it essential for all companies operating in the US, including overseas companies, to keep an audit trail of all decisions taken by the company. This has involved companies in setting up new, expensive and time-consuming procedures for documenting decisions.

 Check your understanding

Do you understand the different roles involved in good corporate governance?

Check your understanding by summarising the role of each of the following members of senior management in corporate governance.

(a) The chairman.
(b) The managing director.
(c) The non-executive director.

Ethics and corporate social responsibility

Ethics and **corporate social responsibility** are standards of conduct that an organisation sets itself in dealing with both the internal and external environments and all associated stakeholders – *see* Table 5.2. Ethics are the basic standards by which organisations conduct business and include honesty, health and safety, and corrupt practice. In contrast, corporate social responsibility covers a wider range of issues, which will vary from organisation to organisation, but could include climate change, global poverty, charitable and political donations. For example, was it right that Bernie Ecclestone, chairman of

Table 15.2 Ethical and corporate social responsibility issues

Ethical issues	Corporate social responsibility issues
• Honesty in dealing with workforce, suppliers and customers • Health and safety of workforce • Doing business in countries with tyrannical regimes • Corrupt practice, espionage and bribery	• Climate change and sustainability in business • Global poverty • Charitable and political donations • Provision of education and healthcare for workforce and their families

Formula One motor racing made a political donation of cash to the Labour Party around the same time that the Labour government in power exempted Formula One from a ban on tobacco advertising and sponsorship? This should illustrate that in reality both ethics and corporate social responsibility are interrelated and most organisations accept that ethics and corporate social responsibility influence how they conduct business.

Organisations need to accept that ethics that are present in society need to be conformed to and may be legally enforceable, for example health and safety legislation. The behaviour of an organisation can also include being responsible with regard to other issues that are not legally enforceable, for example being carbon neutral. An organisation may choose to serve its own interests by behaving professionally and ethically with respect to its stakeholders, such as its workers, suppliers and customers. This is done in the belief that such stakeholders value ethical and professional behaviour and will be loyal to and remain with the organisation (*see* earlier section of this chapter). This approach means the organisation exercises good judgement in regard to its behaviour and hence decreases the likelihood of inappropriate behaviour and the resulting bad publicity.

Any organisation needs to consider how far beyond the legal minimum it wishes to go with regard to ethical and responsible behaviour. An organisation may choose to have a number of policies that it implements, covering a range of issues, for example environmental sustainability, work–life balance, dealing with suppliers. In contrast, it may choose to have no such policies and leave the management of these issues with the individual mangers who make decisions on behalf of the organisation. Underpinning the decisions taken regarding ethical and responsible behaviour will be the consideration of cost. The cost of developing any ethical policy will be evaluated against the advantages of implementing it and the disadvantages of not implementing it. The organisation may also want to consider if it has a responsibility beyond the legal minimum towards stakeholders who may benefit from the implementation of corporate social responsibility policies. For example, a company may choose to pay staff more than a minimum amount and provide education for the children of staff, particularly if the company is operating in a developing country where education may not be easily available and free. Companies may also take the view that it will benefit if its workforce enjoys good health, and provide health clinics or private medical insurance as appropriate.

Occasionally companies may undertake or find themselves caught up in allegations of bribery and corruption. In July 2008 an employee of the German company Siemens was found guilty on 49 counts of breach of trust; he was fined and given a two-year suspended sentence. He stated he was acting on the orders of more senior staff and indeed several other witnesses at his trial implied senior managers knew the extent of the bribery taking place. Siemens is alleged to have bribed corporate customers all over the world in a bid to win contracts. The allegation is that this was done by channelling up to €1.3 billion via a series of false companies and slush funds.[6,7] Equally, it is also possible for a company to find itself linked to allegations of bribery, which are unknown to it. This happened to Tesco in Turkey: an entrepreneur who sold Tesco land with commercial planning consents in place was accused of bribery in relation to the planning consents he gained for the land before selling to Tesco.[8]

Whistle-blowing

Whistle-blowing is the release of confidential corporate information to an external third party. The third party may be the media, although a conversation with a colleague, friend or family member, in which corporate information and concerns are revealed, can be whistle-blowing. This applies even if the third party, e.g. a friend, was unaware that confidential information was being revealed to them. In the United Kingdom, the Public Interest Disclosure Act 1998 (PIDA) allows for the whistle-blower to loose the protection of the law if it comes to light that they voiced their concerns with a third party before raising their concerns via the organisation's formal internal procedures and are dismissed. Therefore, whistle-blowing is not an action to be undertaken lightly. Whistle-blowers often suffer personal damage, such as losing their job and finding it difficult to find alternative employment, especially in the same industry, which in turn leads to stressful financial and emotional hardship, which will be felt by the whole family of the whistle-blower.

This raises the question, 'why whistle-blow?' The simple answer is to prevent a tragedy. There are examples of tragedies, such as the Piper-Alpha oil-rig disaster in the North Sea, the *Herald of Free Enterprise* ferry disaster at Zeebrugge and the Clapham railway crash outside London. In such tragedies employees raised concerns before the tragedy occurred and had these concerns been acted upon the tragedy in question might have been avoided. Hence such tragedies are predictable and occur due to the failure to listen to and act on the concerns of employees, along with poor practice, control and checks. In some instances employee concerns may have been unreported due to the authoritarian nature of management.

In 1987 the Townsend Thoresen ferry the *Herald of Free Enterprise* capsized 100 yards from the shore as it left Zeebrugge harbour in Belgium due to its bow doors being left open. This resulted in the death of 193 people.

On five occasions prior to the capsizing of the *Herald of Free Enterprise*, staff had raised their concern about ships leaving port with their bow doors open, but they were not acted upon. The suggestion was made that lights should be fitted to the bridge to indicate whether or not the bow doors were closed. This suggestion was described as 'sensible' and likely to have prevented the disaster by the final report.[9] The fitting of lights would have allowed the captain and staff on the bridge taking the ship to sea to know if the bow doors were closed. The concerns had been reported, but not been conveyed to the top management, as they were lost in middle management.

Is whistle-blowing justified?

As discussed earlier in this section, the consequences of whistle-blowing and getting it wrong can be harmful for both the whistle-blower and the organisation. Hence there have been some attempts to draw up conditions and criteria, which if met make whistle-blowing justifiable. De George[10] is one such author and he argues that there are six such conditions, and that whistle-blowing is justifiable if the overall effects are likely to be positive. De George argues that that the first three conditions (*see* Table 15.3) make whistle-blowing allowable, but not obligatory. However, if conditions 4 and 5 can also be met, then the whistle-blowing becomes a far more compelling option. Hence, without these conditions being met it is very difficult to justify whistle-blowing and it is likely the result will be harmful for both whistle-blower and organisation.

DeGeorge also argues that the whistle-blower, in meeting these criteria, should avoid confrontation and look for effective ways to resolve the issues. The whistle-blower should also be sure their claims are justifiable, and seeking the support of professional colleagues can be helpful here, as can support from management if possible. Before whistle-blowing and probably resigning,

Table 15.3 De George's conditions for whistle-blowing

1 Product possesses the potential to do serious harm to members of the public.
2 Concerned employee should report all the facts to their immediate superiors.
3 If the immediate superiors fail to act effectively, then more senior managers, including directors, should be approached and all available internal channels should be exhausted.
4 The whistle-blower should have documentary evidence that will convince the impartial external observer that the product posses a serious danger.
5 The whistle-blower must believe appropriate changes will be implemented as a result of their whistle-blowing and prevent serious harm.
6 The whistle-blower must be acting in good faith, without malice or vindictiveness.

Source: Fisher, C. and Lovell, A. (2003) Business Ethics and Value, FT/Prentice Hall.

make sure all the formal internal procedures have been exhausted. The act of whistle-blowing should be one of last resort.[11]

Summary

This chapter examined stakeholders and their role in corporate governance, ethics and corporate social responsibility. The following summary covers all aspects of this chapter.

1   Stakeholders are individuals or groups who have an interest in an organisation. Different stakeholders have varying levels of power and interest in an organisation.

2   Stakeholders whose interests are satisfied by an organisation will remain with it. In contrast, those stakeholders who are dissatisfied will seek to leave the organisation or they may chose to remain and try to change things.

3   Stakeholder relative power and interest can be mapped on to a power and interest matrix. Additionally, this analysis can be extended to consider the reaction, behaviour and position of stakeholders if a particular strategy or plan were to be implemented.

4   Category D stakeholders, those with high power and high interest, are key players, such as the managing director. Category C stakeholders are those with high power and low interest, an example being a corporate shareholder in a company. Individual customers and employees often fall into category B, having low power and high interest. Those stakeholders in which the organisation has minimal interest are category A, low power and low interest.

5   Different categories of stakeholders may not always act individually – they may form coalitions with another category of stakeholders. For example, individual employees (usually category B) may band together and try to influence category C stakeholders who have high power, unlike themselves.

6   Corporate governance refers to the influence of stakeholders and their exercising of power to control the strategic direction of the organisation. The key stakeholders who have the biggest and most important role to play in corporate governance are the managing director, other directors and senior staff in the organisation. In good corporate governance the roles of chairman and managing director are normally separated.

7   Corporate governance includes regular monitoring and evaluation of strategy that has been implemented and approval of strategy yet to be implemented. This allows the organisation to adjust and moderate its strategy to ensure the interests of all stakeholders are appropriately met and that one group of stakeholders does not benefit at the expense of another group of stakeholders.

8 Ethics are the basic standards by which organisations conduct business and include honesty, health and safety, and corrupt practice. In contrast, corporate social responsibility covers a wider range of issues, which will vary from organisation to organisation, but could include climate change, global poverty, and charitable and political donations.

9 Therefore, ethics and corporate social responsibility are standards of conduct that an organisation sets itself in dealing with both the internal and external environments. Hence in reality both ethics and corporate responsibility are interrelated and most organisations accept that ethics and corporate social responsibility influence how they conduct business.

10 Whistle-blowing is the release of confidential corporate information to an external third party. The consequences of whistle-blowing and getting it wrong can be harmful for both the whistle-blower and the organisation. Hence there have been some attempts to draw up conditions and criteria which, if met, make whistle-blowing justifiable. De George is one such author and he argues that there are six such conditions (*see* Table 15.3) and that whistle-blowing is justifiable if the overall effects are likely to be positive.

Chapter objectives and the exit case study

While reading this chapter and engaging in the activities, you should have learned how to apply theory and models and analyse situations. This means you should be able to meet the chapter objectives outlined at the beginning of the chapter. The table below shows which chapter objectives can be tested by the different questions.

Chapter objective	Check you have achieved this by
1 Identify and analyse an organisation's stakeholders.	answering case study questions 1 and 2.

No help for charities in Iceland plight

by Jim Pickard and Tom Braithwaite

Scores of charities came away empty-handed on Friday after seeking emergency compensation from the Treasury for the potential loss of millions of pounds left on deposit in failed Icelandic banks. In the latest twist to this week's Icelandic saga, the National Council for Voluntary Organisations suggested that charities could lose up to £120m deposited in Iceland's banks. But after talks with government on Friday, the NCVO was blunt about the help offered: 'None,' said a representative. That figure takes the total of public sector cash in Icelandic banks up to nearly £1bn, including at least £800m from councils, £40m from Transport for London, £30m from the Metropolitan Police and £2m from NHS foundation trusts.

The nationalisation of three Icelandic banks this week – Glitnir, Landsbanki and Kaupthing – has prompted wider fears about the safety of an estimated £6bn of retail deposits from 300,000 British citizens and an unknown quantity of business savings. As UK Treasury officials flew into Iceland on Friday to discuss a solution to the crisis – talks begin on Saturday – Gordon Brown pledged to do 'everything in our power to get this money returned'.

The UK government was talking to Icelandic authorities and taking legal action to secure investments at risk, the prime minister said.

On Wednesday, the UK put Kaupthing Singer & Friedlander into administration, prompting the nationalisation of parent company Kaupthing in Iceland. It also froze an estimated £4bn of Landsbanki assets in the UK using anti-terror laws, to the fury of Icelandic authorities. That action was questioned by Shami Chakrabarti, director of pressure group Liberty, who said: 'This may not be an abuse of "terror laws" but it certainly demonstrates the way that very broad security measures are sneaked into such legislation for creative use later on.'

Mr Brown authorised the move after failing to receive assurances that UK citizens would receive compensation from Icelandic authorities. As political leaders in Reykjavik and London stepped up their war of words, some drew comparisons with the 'Cod Wars' of the 1970s. On Friday 10 Downing Street complained that the Icelanders had withheld information and indicated preferential treatment for domestic creditors. But the rhetoric was toned down a notch, with Mr Brown hailing 'strong bilateral relations' between the two countries and his spokesman predicting 'cooperative' talks.

The NCVO has identified seven charities with £30m at risk but estimates the total investment of UK charities at risk to be more than £120m. Among those hit was Cats Protection, with £11.2m of deposits in Kaupthing Singer & Friedlander. Separately, the National Housing Federation is seeking to establish how many housing associations have been hit.

Councils were forced to defend themselves against accusations of naivety after leaving their money in Icelandic banks – despite warnings of financial instability. They said the banks had reasonable credit ratings when they made the deposits. Landsbanki, in particular, had huge numbers of British depositors who invested £4.6bn through its 'Icesave' internet bank, which had customers across Europe.

It is hoped most of the money can be recovered from the sale of the bank's assets. If not, Treasury officials had hoped to secure £2.2bn from Iceland's depositor compensation scheme – up to £16,000 per account – though this is now the subject of wrangling between the two countries. Of the remainder, £1.4bn could come from the UK's Financial Services Compensation Scheme – which covers up to £50,000 per account – with the rest from

the government. But with insufficient money in the FSCS, public cash could be needed to cover the gap until Landsbanki's assets are sold.

Icesave house purchasers face completion problems. Savers hoping to buy a home with their Icesave savings may find themselves unable to complete the deal, with consequences for property chains, Alice Ross reports.

David Pedrick, 31, an accountant, and his wife Hayley, 28, are in the process of buying their first house but the money they need to pay the deposit is in an Icesave account. The couple, currently renting in Surbiton, Surrey, said they had decided to buy as house prices have fallen so much they can now buy a larger place in their price range. The house they are looking to buy, also in Surbiton, is at an agreed price of £243,500. The couple have £24,000 saved for their 10 per cent deposit. Some £6,000 is with NatWest but a further £18,000 is now locked away in Icesave. 'You almost take it as a personal offence as you're only two weeks away from buying your first house,' said Mr Pedrick. They are hoping to exchange contracts within three weeks, which is likely to mean they will not have the cash to pay the deposit. 'If we don't have the money, we're considering personal loans or we might even start phoning friends and family,' said Mr Pedrick.

But Ray Boulger, senior technical manager at John Charcol, warned that with no clarity on how long Icesave customers have to wait, this could mean hefty loan repayments. Mr and Mrs Pedrick are safe as they have not exchanged contracts yet. But for those who have, the consequences could be serious. Lawyers warn that people who cannot complete on a property transaction could be sued.

Source: from 'No help for charities in Iceland plight, *The Financial Times*, 10 October 2008 (Pickard, J. and Braithwaite, T.).

Exit case study questions

1 Identify the stakeholders in Icesave and comment on the likelihood of the different stakeholders getting their money back.

2 What lessons are to be learned from the Icesave experience with regard to investing money as a large organisation and as an individual?

Short-answer questions

1   Define a stakeholder.

2   Define a key player.

3   Identify a stakeholder in an organisation and their source of interest.

4   Identify a stakeholder in an organisation and their source of power.

5   Briefly summarise the expected behaviour of satisfied stakeholders in an organisation.

6   Briefly summarise the expected behaviour of unsatisfied stakeholders in an organisation.

7   What should organisations seek to do with stakeholders who have high power and low interest?

8   What should organisations seek to do with stakeholders who have low power and high interest?

9   What should organisations seek to do with stakeholders who have low power and low interest?

10   Define corporate governance.

11   Explain the differing roles of chairman, managing director and non-executive director.

12   Explain the difference between ethics and corporate social responsibility.

13   How are ethics and corporate social responsibility linked?

14   Summarise the role of ethics and corporate social responsibility in managing stakeholders.

15   Define whistle-blowing.

16   List the six conditions that make whistle-blowing justifiable.

17   Explain how the whistle-blower could ensure they have met the criteria listed in response to question 16.

Chapter objectives and assignment questions

While reading this chapter and engaging in the activities, you should have learned how to apply theory and models and analyse situations. This means you should be able to meet the chapter objectives outlined at the beginning of the chapter. The table below shows which chapter objectives can be tested by the different questions.

Chapter objective	Check you have achieved this by
1 Identify and analyse an organisation's stakeholders.	answering assignment question 1.
2 Explain and summarise good corporate governance and the key roles involved.	answering assignment question 2.
3 Discuss ethics and corporate responsibility in relation to a business and its stakeholders.	answering assignment question 3.

Assignment questions

1 Choose and research an organisation. Identify all its stakeholders and plot them on a power and interest matrix. Comment on how and why you think the power and interest of the stakeholders will change in the next 12 months and the next five years. How does this analysis help you understand the organisation's environment?

2 Choose any two organisations and discuss the similarities and differences in their approaches to corporate governance.

3 Identify two organisations, one with sound ethical behaviour and corporate social responsibility and one with a poor record on ethics and corporate social responsibility. Compare and contrast these two organisations and their behaviour.

WEBLINKS available at www.pearsoned.co.uk/capon

- The website below looks at the National Grid and its stakeholders:
  http://www.nationalgrid.com/uk/social&environment/stakeholders.asp
- The website below is for the UK Shareholders Association – shareholders are important stakeholders in organisations:
  http://www.uksa.org.uk/
- The two websites listed below are for Monsanto, a company that produces genetically modified crops. Ethical issues concerning genetically modified food are often debated:
  http://www.monsanto.com/monsanto/
  http://www.monsanto.co.uk/
- This is the CIPD webpage for whistle-blowing:
  http://www.cipd.co.uk/subjects/empreltns/whistleblw/whistle.htm
- This is the Health and Safety Executive webpage for whistle-blowing:
  http://www.hse.gov.uk/workers/whistleblowing.htm
- This is a government page on whistle-blowing:
  http://www.direct.gov.uk/en/employment/resolvingworkplacedisputes/index.htm

FURTHER READING

The following chapters all look at aspects of the material covered in this chapter.

- Fisher, C and Lovell, A (2008) *Business Ethics and Values*, 3rd edn, Chapters 6 and 9, Harlow: Financial Times Prentice Hall.

- Johnson, G, Scholes, K and Whittington, R (2008) *Exploring Corporate Strategy*, 8th edn, Chapter 4, Harlow: Financial Times Prentice Hall.

- Lynch, R (2006) *Corporate Strategy*, 4th edn, Chapter 10, Harlow: Financial Times Prentice Hall.

- Martin, J (2005) *Organisational Behaviour*, 3rd edn, Chapter 12, London: Thomson Learning.

- Palmer, A and Hartley, B (2006) *The Business Environment*, 5th edn, Chapter 9, Maidenhead: McGraw-Hill.

- Torrington, D, Hall, L and Taylor, S (2008) *Human Resource Management*, 7th edn, Chapter 30, Harlow: Financial Times Prentice Hall.

- Worthington, I and Britton, C (2006) *The Business Environment*, 5th edn, Chapter 17, Harlow: Financial Times Prentice Hall.

REFERENCES

1 Johnson, G, Scholes, K and Whittington, R (2008) *Exploring Corporate Strategy*, 8th edn, Harlow: Financial Times Prentice Hall.
2 Jagger, S (1999) 'AA ponders its road to the future', *Daily Telegraph*, 24 April.
3 Ibid.
4 Ibid.
5 Larsen, P T and Burgess, K (2008) 'Board shake-up after criticisms over corporate governance', *Financial Times*, 4 March.
6 Schafer, D (2008) 'Siemens enters crunch week in long running bribery scandal', *Financial Times*, 28 July.
7 Schafer, D (2008) 'Former Siemens executive found guilty over bribery schemes role', *Financial Times*, 29 July.
8 Barker, A T and Braithwaite, T (2008) 'Tesco pulled into bribery case over Turkish site', *Financial Times*, 15 August.
9 http://www.maib.gov.uk/publications/investigation_reports/herald_of_free_enterprise.cfm
10 De George, R T (1999) *Business Ethics*, 5th edn, Englewood Cliffs, NJ: Prentice Hall.
11 Ibid.